T0192628

# Practical LPIC-3 300

## Prepare for the Highest Level Professional Linux Certification

Antonio Vazquez

Apress®

*Practical LPIC-3 300*

Antonio Vazquez
Mostoles, Spain

ISBN-13 (pbk): 978-1-4842-4472-2 ISBN-13 (electronic): 978-1-4842-4473-9
https://doi.org/10.1007/978-1-4842-4473-9

Managing Director, Apress LLC: Welmoed Spahr
Acquisitions Editor: Louise Corrigan
Development Editor: James Markham
Coordinating Editor: Nancy Chen

Cover designed by eStudioCalamar

Distributed to the book trade worldwide by Springer Science+Business Media New York, 233 Spring Street, 6th Floor, New York, NY 10013. Phone 1-800-SPRINGER, fax (201) 348-4505, e-mail orders-ny@springer-sbm.com, or visit www.springeronline.com. Apress Media, LLC is a California LLC and the sole member (owner) is Springer Science + Business Media Finance Inc (SSBM Finance Inc). SSBM Finance Inc is a **Delaware** corporation.

For information on translations, please e-mail rights@apress.com, or visit http://www.apress.com/rights-permissions.

Apress titles may be purchased in bulk for academic, corporate, or promotional use. eBook versions and licenses are also available for most titles. For more information, reference our Print and eBook Bulk Sales web page at http://www.apress.com/bulk-sales.

Any source code or other supplementary material referenced by the author in this book is available to readers on GitHub via the book's product page, located at www.apress.com/9781484244722. For more detailed information, please visit http://www.apress.com/source-code.

Printed on acid-free paper

*This book is dedicated to my family, especially to my daughter and my wife.*

# Table of Contents

# About the Author

**Antonio Vazquez** is an IT professional who has been working with Linux for more than a decade. He studied computer engineering at Universidad Nacional de Educación a Distancia (UNED) in Spain, and he currently holds many IT certifications from the main vendors in the industry. At present, he works for a public institution and is in charge of almost 1,000 Linux servers spread across the country, providing web services, FTP services, file services, virtualization, and more. He is also the author of *Learn CentOS Linux Network Services* (Apress, 2016).

# About the Technical Reviewer

**Thiago Magalhães** is a Linux Infrastructure Analyst with more than ten years of experience in the IT industry. He also works in a DevOps role with hands-on experience in supporting, automating, and optimizing mission-critical deployments.

A Linux lover at heart, he focuses on security, high availability, containers, and cloud. He administrates and maintains Linux services including DNS, OpenLDAP, Samba, Mail, HTTPS, Apache Tomcat, Squid, DHCP, SMTP, SFTP, IMAP, NIS, and NFS.

At present, he works for a private multinational mass media company, responsible for the ongoing maintenance, growth, and development of large-scale servers running primarily on Linux.

In his spare time, he loves cooking for his friends and watching movies with his family.

# Acknowledgments

I'd like to show my gratitude to the people at Apress, specially the team I worked with: Louise, Nancy, and James. It's been a pleasure working with you again. I would also like to thank all those working at LPI for their great job, as well to everyone involved in the open source community.

# Introduction

When I started studying for the LPIC-3 certification a few years ago, I noticed how few resources were available. In addition, some of the resources were also quite dated and thus they were not very useful. The aim of this book is to help fill that gap.

The LPI certification program is platform independent, but as it is obviously impossible to check every single topic in every Linux distribution, I decided to use CentOS Linux as the main operating system throughout the book. The choice of this distribution is due to the fact that RedHat and its derivatives like CentOS are currently one of the main Linux distributions. Of course, most of the topics learned in the book can be equally applied to other major Linux distributions such as SUSE, Ubuntu, and so on.

The topics covered in this book are those official for the LPIC-3 300 exam at the time of writing, as well as those topics planned to be included in the new revision of the exam.

If you have any suggestions, opinions, questions, or criticisms about this book you can contact me via LinkedIn at `https://www.linkedin.com/in/antoniojosevazquez/`. Note, however, that I cannot promise to answer everyone.

# PART I

# OpenLDAP

# CHAPTER 1

# Starting with OpenLDAP

This chapter doesn't cover the topics you are supposed to be familiar with to apply for the LPIC-3 300 exam. Instead, it shows you how to perform a simple OpenLDAP installation that will be the base in the upcoming sections to study more advanced topics.

If you are already familiar with OpenLDAP, feel free to skip this chapter and move on to the following chapters; if you're not, though, this chapter will show you how easy it is to deploy an OpenLDAP server in CentOS 7.

## The LDAP Protocol

The Lightweight Directory Access Protocol (LDAP) is an open protocol for accessing distributed directory services over a network connection. It is closely related with the X.500 Directory Access Protocol (DAP). It follows some of the same rules, such as these:

- An entry consists of a set of attributes.

- Every attribute has a name and one or more values. The attributes are defined in the schema.

- Each entry will have a full path associated with it, the *distinguished name* (DN). Sometimes we can see the term *relative distinguished name* (RDN), too, which describes the partial path to an object relative to its parent. For instance, a DN could be cn=Antonio, ou=users,dc=linuxaholics,dc=com, the parent could be ou=users, dc=linuxaholics,dc=com, and the RDN relative to its parent would be cn=Antonio.

LDAP was designed to be a lightweight alternative to access directory services over Transmission Control Protocol/Internet Protocol (TCP/IP).

© Antonio Vazquez 2019
A. Vazquez, *Practical LPIC-3 300*, https://doi.org/10.1007/978-1-4842-4473-9_1

The client connects to the server, also called the Directory System Agent (DSA), in one of three possible ways:

- Over the LDAP protocol using TCP port 389 by default.

- Over the LDAPS protocol using TCP port 636 by default.

- Using Unix Inter Process Communication (ldapi).

The server offers the client access to the Global Catalog on port 3268 or port 3269. These are the operations that the client can request:

- Bind

- SearchCompare

- Add

- Delete

- Modify

- Modify DN/RDNRename

- Abandon

- Unbind

- Extended

# The OpenLDAP Project

OpenLDAP is a free, open source implementation of the LDAP protocol. It is included with most major Linux distributions, but it is a multiplatform software, and there are versions for Windows, Mac OS X, Solaris, and other operating systems.

OpenLDAP has three main components:

- slapd, which is the stand-alone LDAP server itself.

- Libraries that implement the LDAP protocol.

- Client software.

In turn, when we talk about the stand-alone server (slapd), we must differentiate between a front end, which handles the network connections, and a back end, which deals with data storage. In OpenLDAP the front end is the **slapd** binary, which will be running in the background as a service. For the back end, however, there are many options available. We'll cover some of the most common.

We could divide the different back ends into three main groups: data storage back ends, proxy back ends, and dynamic back ends. In the first group we have **back-bdb**, the first transactional back end for OpenLDAP, built on Berkeley Database (Berkeley DB). This back end has been recently replaced by **back-hdb**, a variant of back-bdb that is hierarchical and supports subtree renames. Another example of a storage back end is back-ldif, which uses plain LDAP Data Interchange Format (LDIF) files as storage. The second group, the proxy back ends, consists basically of gateways to other data storage systems. For cxample, we could use **back-ldap** to proxy requests to another LDAP server. Finally, the third group doesn't store any data or redirect requests to other systems. Instead it generates data on the fly.

In addition to the front end/back end structure just outlined, OpenLDAP can use overlays, binary modules placed between the front end and the back end. Thus they can execute different actions regarding the request received by the front end or the information given by the back end. For instance, it can log access to the directory, replicate information, and so on. We'll see some examples of overlays throughout the book.

# Installing an OpenLDAP Server

First, we have to install the packages openldap, openldap-servers, and openldap-clients.

```
[root@alpha ~]# yum install -y openldap-servers openldap-clients
```

We make sure that the slapd service is configured to boot automatically, and we start the service.

```
[root@alpha ~]# systemctl enable slapd
ln -s '/usr/lib/systemd/system/slapd.service' '/etc/systemd/system/
multiuser.target.wants/slapd.service'
[root@alpha ~]# systemctl start slapd
```

That's it; now we have to fine-tune the installation according to our preferences and needs.

# Customizing the Installation

Once the server is installed, we have to generate a password for the admin user. In this example, we use a simple password: pass.

```
[root@alpha ~]# slappasswd
New password:
Re-enter new password:
{SSHA}I/h5CtsNIfOOFS71TuKMNUOoPgyKxCVg
```

Formerly, there was a file named /etc/openldap/slapd.d/slapd.conf in which the configuration of the OpenLDAP server was kept. Now, however, the configuration is kept in the LDAP database itself. Nevertheless, the relevant files we need to modify are still in /etc/openldap/slapd.d:

```
[root@alpha ~]# ls /etc/openldap/slapd.d/
cn=config   cn=config.ldif
```

We can either modify these files directly or use the **ldapmodify** command. For a beginner, it is probably easier to edit the files, but as the recommended way to edit OpenLDAP is by using ldapmodify, this is what we'll do. We'll see in much more detail how to use ldapmodify in the upcoming sections; for now, just to initiate a working OpenLDAP installation, we'll review the necessary steps briefly.

# Modifying Objects

As we already saw, OpenLDAP actually stores its information in back ends. One of the most used back ends has always been the Berkeley DB back ends, such as **bdb**, or the more recent **hdb**. In fact, the latter is the default back end used when we install the OpenLDAP binaries. The information stored in the hdb back end can be found in the /etc/openldap/slapd.d/cn=config/olcDatabase={2}hdb.ldif file.

These are the contents of the /etc/openldap/slapd.d/cn=config/olcDatabase={2}hdb.ldif file after a fresh installation:

```
# AUTO-GENERATED FILE - DO NOT EDIT!! Use ldapmodify.
# CRC32 373d43d6
dn: olcDatabase={2}hdb
```

```
objectClass: olcDatabaseConfig
objectClass: olcHdbConfig
olcDatabase: {2}hdb
olcDbDirectory: /var/lib/ldap
olcSuffix: dc=my-domain,dc=com
olcRootDN: cn=Manager,dc=my-domain,dc=com
olcDbIndex: objectClass eq,pres
olcDbIndex: ou,cn,mail,surname,givenname eq,pres,sub
structuralObjectClass: olcHdbConfig
entryUUID: b8596292-eb3d-1034-860a-e7b4503cc451
creatorsName: cn=config
createTimestamp: 20150909125458Z
entryCSN: 20150909125458.235214Z#000000#000#000000
modifiersName: cn=config
modifyTimestamp: 20150909125458Z
```

.

.

.

When working with LDAP servers we'll often have to work with LDIF files. LDIF is a text format designed to retrieve information from an LDAP server, as well as for updating it. In an LDIF file, we first identify the element we want to add, change, or otherwise work with. To uniquely identify an element, we use the distinguished name attribute (dn), which was created precisely for that purpose. The first line of our LDIF file could be something like this:

```
dn: olcDatabase={2}hdb,cn=config
```

Next, we specify if we want to add an attribute, modify it, and so on:

```
changeType: modifydn
```

If we want to modify an entry, we also need to clarify whether we'll be replacing an attribute, deleting it, or otherwise changing it:

```
replace: olcSuffix
```

Finally, we type the new value of the modified attribute.

```
olcSuffix: dc=linuxaholics,dc=com
```

We'll see many LDIF examples throughout the book, but for now let's get back to the /etc/openldap/slapd.d/cn=config/olcDatabase={2}hdb.ldif file. We have to modify (at least) these two entries:

```
olcSuffix: dc=my-domain,dc=com
olcRootDN: cn=Manager,dc=my-domain,dc=com
```

We also have to add a new entry to store the admin's password (olcRootPW), where we'll store the password we just created with the **slappasswd** command.

To make all these changes with **ldapmodify** we need to prepare an LDIF file.

---

**Note**    Throughout this chapter, we'll be using a lot of LDIF files. To keep things simple, we'll create the /root/ldap folder and we'll save our LDIF files there, unless explicitly stated otherwise.

---

Our first LDIF file, config.ldif, located at /root/ldap, should have content such as this:

```
dn: olcDatabase={2}hdb,cn=config
changeType: modify
replace: olcSuffix
olcSuffix: dc=linuxaholics,dc=com
-
replace: olcRootDN
olcRootDN: cn=admin,dc=linuxaholics,dc=com
```

The first line identifies the main entry in the LDAP that we are going to change. Just a moment ago we saw the parameter olcSuffix inside the /etc/openldap/slapd.d/cn=config/olcDatabase={2}hdb.ldif file. In this file the dn attribute was dn: olcDatabase={2}hdb, and as the file was inside the config folder, the full dn attribute will be dn: olcDatabase={2}hdb,cn=config.

Another, and perhaps a better way to identify the data we require to create the LDIF file, could be to use the **ldapsearch** command.

```
[root@alpha ~]# ldapsearch -Y EXTERNAL -H ldapi:/// -b cn=config
olcDatabase=\*
SASL/EXTERNAL authentication started
SASL username: gidNumber=0+uidNumber=0,cn=peercred,cn=external,cn=auth
SASL SSF: 0
# extended LDIF
#
# LDAPv3
# base <cn=config> with scope subtree
# filter: olcDatabase=*
# requesting: ALL
#

# {-1}frontend, config
dn: olcDatabase={-1}frontend,cn=config
objectClass: olcDatabaseConfig
objectClass: olcFrontendConfig
olcDatabase: frontend

# {0}config, config
dn: olcDatabase={0}config,cn=config
objectClass: olcDatabaseConfig
olcDatabase: {0}config
olcAccess: {0}to * by dn.base="gidNumber=0+uidNumber=0,cn=peercred,
cn=external,cn=auth" manage by * none

# {1}monitor, config
dn: olcDatabase={1}monitor,cn=config
objectClass: olcDatabaseConfig
olcDatabase: {1}monitor
olcAccess: {0}to * by dn.base="gidNumber=0+uidNumber=0,cn=peercred,
cn=external,cn=auth" read by dn.base="cn=Manager,dc=my-domain,dc=com"
read by * none

# {2}hdb, config
dn: olcDatabase={2}hdb,cn=config
objectClass: olcDatabaseConfig
```

```
objectClass: olcHdbConfig
olcDatabase: {2}hdb
olcDbDirectory: /var/lib/ldap
olcSuffix: dc=my-domain,dc=com
olcRootDN: cn=Manager,dc=my-domain,dc=com
olcDbIndex: objectClass eq,pres
olcDbIndex: ou,cn,mail,surname,givenname eq,pres,sub

# search result
search: 2
result: 0 Success

# numResponses: 5
# numEntries: 4
```

We return to the LDIF file we created and saved previously, config.ldif, and we execute **ldapmodify**.

```
[root@alpha ldap]# ldapmodify -Y EXTERNAL -H ldapi:/// -f config.ldif
SASL/EXTERNAL authentication started
SASL username: gidNumber=0+uidNumber=0,cn=peercred,cn=external,cn=auth
SASL SSF: 0
modifying entry "olcDatabase={2}hdb,cn=config"
```

Now we create another LDIF file(config2.ldif) to add the olcRootPW attribute.

```
dn: olcDatabase={2}hdb,cn=config
changeType: modify
add: olcRootPW
olcRootPW: {SSHA}I/h5CtsNIfOOFS71TuKMNUOoPgyKxCVg
```

We then execute **ldapmodify** to apply the changes.

```
[root@alpha ldap]# ldapmodify -Y EXTERNAL -H ldapi:/// -f config2.ldif
SASL/EXTERNAL authentication started
SASL username: gidNumber=0+uidNumber=0,cn=peercred,cn=external,cn=auth
SASL SSF: 0
modifying entry "olcDatabase={2}hdb,cn=config"
```

To check the changes, we can use **ldapsearch** again.

```
[root@alpha ldap]# ldapsearch -Y EXTERNAL -H ldapi:/// -b cn=config
olcDatabase=\*
SASL/EXTERNAL authentication started
SASL username: gidNumber=0+uidNumber=0,cn=peercred,cn=external,cn=auth
SASL SSF: 0
# extended LDIF
#
# LDAPv3
# base <cn=config> with scope subtree
# filter: olcDatabase=*
# requesting: ALL
#

# {-1}frontend, config
dn: olcDatabase={-1}frontend,cn=config
objectClass: olcDatabaseConfig
objectClass: olcFrontendConfig
olcDatabase: frontend

# {0}config, config
dn: olcDatabase={0}config,cn=config
objectClass: olcDatabaseConfig
olcDatabase: {0}config
olcAccess: {0}to * by dn.base="gidNumber=0+uidNumber=0,cn=peercred,
cn=external,cn=auth" manage by * none

# {1}monitor, config
dn: olcDatabase={1}monitor,cn=config
objectClass: olcDatabaseConfig
olcDatabase: {1}monitor
olcAccess: {0}to * by dn.base="gidNumber=0+uidNumber=0,cn=peercred,
cn=external,cn=auth" read by dn.base="cn=admin,dc=linuxaholics,dc=com"
read by * none
```

11

```
# {2}hdb, config
dn: olcDatabase={2}hdb,cn=config
objectClass: olcDatabaseConfig
objectClass: olcHdbConfig
olcDatabase: {2}hdb
olcDbDirectory: /var/lib/ldap
olcDbIndex: objectClass eq,pres
olcDbIndex: ou,cn,mail,surname,givenname eq,pres,sub
olcSuffix: dc=linuxaholics,dc=com
olcRootDN: cn=admin,dc=linuxaholics,dc=com
olcRootPW: {SSHA}I/h5CtsNIfOOFS71TuKMNUOOPgyKxCVg

# search result
search: 2
result: 0 Success

# numResponses: 5
# numEntries: 4
```

We also have to allow access to the LDAP database to the admin user we specified earlier (cn=admin,dc=linuxaholics,dc=com). If we take a look at the olcDatabase={1} monitor.ldif file, we'll see the following line:

```
olcAccess: {0}to *  by dn.base="gidNumber=0+uidNumber=0,cn=peercred,
cn=external,cn=auth" read  by dn.base="cn=manager,dc=my-domain,dc=com"
read  by * none
```

Again, we could obtain the same information by using **ldapsearch**.

```
[root@alpha ldap]# ldapsearch -Y EXTERNAL -H ldapi:/// -b cn=config
olcAccess=\*
SASL/EXTERNAL authentication started
SASL username: gidNumber=0+uidNumber=0,cn=peercred,cn=external,cn=auth
SASL SSF: 0
# extended LDIF
#
# LDAPv3
# base <cn=config> with scope subtree
```

```
# filter: olcAccess=*
# requesting: ALL
#

# {0}config, config
dn: olcDatabase={0}config,cn=config
objectClass: olcDatabaseConfig
olcDatabase: {0}config
olcAccess: {0}to * by dn.base="gidNumber=0+uidNumber=0,cn=peercred,
cn=external,cn=auth" manage by * none

# {1}monitor, config
dn: olcDatabase={1}monitor,cn=config
objectClass: olcDatabaseConfig
olcDatabase: {1}monitor
olcAccess: {0}to * by dn.base="gidNumber=0+uidNumber=0,cn=peercred,
cn=external,cn=auth" read by dn.base="cn=Manager,dc=my-domain,dc=com"
read by * none

# search result
search: 2
result: 0 Success

# numResponses: 3
# numEntries: 2
```

We'll have to use **ldapmodify** again to change the entry, and the new LDIF file that will be named config3.ldif should be something like this:

```
dn: olcDatabase={1}monitor,cn=config
changeType: modify
replace: olcAccess
olcAccess: {0} to * by dn.base="gidNumber=0+uidNumber=0,cn=peercred,
cn=external,cn=auth" read by dn.base="cn=admin,dc=linuxaholics,dc=com"
read by * none
```

Once again, we execute **ldapmodify** by passing the new LDIF file as a parameter.

```
[root@alpha ldap]# ldapmodify -Y EXTERNAL -H ldapi:/// -f config3.ldif
SASL/EXTERNAL authentication started
SASL username: gidNumber=0+uidNumber=0,cn=peercred,cn=external,cn=auth
SASL SSF: 0
modifying entry "olcDatabase={1}monitor,cn=config"
```

Now we check with **ldapsearch** whether the value for the attribute was actually changed.

```
[root@alpha ldap]# ldapsearch -Y EXTERNAL -H ldapi:/// -b cn=config
olcAccess=\*
SASL/EXTERNAL authentication started
SASL username: gidNumber=0+uidNumber=0,cn=peercred,cn=external,cn=auth
SASL SSF: 0
# extended LDIF
#
# LDAPv3
# base <cn=config> with scope subtree
# filter: olcAccess=*
# requesting: ALL
#

# {0}config, config
dn: olcDatabase={0}config,cn=config
objectClass: olcDatabaseConfig
olcDatabase: {0}config
olcAccess: {0}to * by dn.base="gidNumber=0+uidNumber=0,cn=peercred,
cn=external,cn=auth" manage by * none

# {1}monitor, config
dn: olcDatabase={1}monitor,cn=config
objectClass: olcDatabaseConfig
olcDatabase: {1}monitor
olcAccess: {0}to * by dn.base="gidNumber=0+uidNumber=0,cn=peercred,
cn=external,cn=auth" read by dn.base="cn=admin,dc=linuxaholics,dc=com"
read by * none
```

```
# search result
search: 2
result: 0 Success

# numResponses: 3
# numEntries: 2
```

As we can see, the value was changed according to what we specified in the LDIF file. Another useful tool we can use to check the configuration is the **slaptest** command.

```
[root@alpha ldap]# slaptest -u
config file testing succeeded
```

If there were some error in the configuration, we'd get the corresponding information message.

```
[root@alpha ldap]# slaptest -u
58fe677c ldif_read_file: checksum error on "/etc/openldap/slapd.d/
cn=config/olcDatabase={2}hdb/olcOverlay={0}accesslog.ldif"
58fe677c UNKNOWN attributeDescription "STRUCTURALOBJECTCLASSS" inserted.
config file testing succeeded
```

# Adding Objects

Now we have to manually create an entry for dc=linuxaholics,dc=com in our LDAP server. The easiest way to do this is to create an LDIF file for this entry and pass it to the **ldapadd** command.

We therefore create a file at the usual location, /root/ldap/, named linuxaholics.ldif with the following content:

```
dn: dc=linuxaholics,dc=com
objectClass: dcObject
objectClass: organization
dc: linuxaholics
o: linuxaholics
```

We specify a series of attributes such as distinguished name (dn), domain component (dc), and organization (o). We also define the new entry as an object of the types dcObject and organization.

15

Depending on the type of object we are creating, there are a series of attributes that can be optional or mandatory. We can check this by consulting the schema. For example, if we want to know what attributes must be defined when adding an object of the organization type, we can check this on the schema. We should go to /etc/openldap/schema, which contains all the files that define the openldap schema. If we are not sure about where a certain object is defined, we can use the grep command. As far as our example is concerned, the object organization is defined in the core.schema file, in which we will find an entry like this:

```
objectclass ( 2.5.6.4 NAME 'organization'
DESC 'RFC2256: an organization'
SUP top STRUCTURAL
MUST o
MAY ( userPassword $ searchGuide $ seeAlso $ businessCategory $
x121Address $ registeredAddress $ destinationIndicator $
preferredDeliveryMethod $ telexNumber $ teletexTerminalIdentifier $
telephoneNumber $ internationaliSDNNumber $
facsimileTelephoneNumber $ street $ postOfficeBox $ postalCode $
postalAddress $ physicalDeliveryOfficeName $ st $ l $ description ) )
```

As we can see, in this case the only mandatory attribute is o.

Now we execute **ldapadd** and pass it the linuxaholics.ldif file as a parameter. We specify the name of the file (-f), the admin user (-D), and the password we defined for that admin user (-w).

```
[root@alpha ldap]# ldapadd -f linuxaholics.ldif -D
cn=admin,dc=linuxaholics,dc=com -w pass
adding new entry "dc=linuxaholics,dc=com"
```

We can check whether the entry was created successfully using the **ldapsearch** command.

```
[root@alpha ldap]# ldapsearch -x -b dc=linuxaholics,dc=com
# extended LDIF
#
# LDAPv3
# base <dc=linuxaholics,dc=com> with scope subtree
```

```
# filter: (objectclass=*)
# requesting: ALL
#

# linuxaholics.com
dn: dc=linuxaholics,dc=com
objectClass: dcObject
objectClass: organization
dc: linuxaholics
o: linuxaholics

# search result
search: 2
result: 0 Success

# numResponses: 2
# numEntries: 1
```

We just saw how to add the object dc=linuxaholics,dc=com to our LDAP server. Now we'll see how to add organizational units (OUs), groups, and users.

## Adding an Organizational Unit

Maybe we'd like to have an organizational unit (OU) called users in which to store every LDAP user. To do so, we will create a new LDIF file named users.ldif, with the following content:

```
dn: ou=users,dc=linuxaholics,dc=com
objectClass: organizationalUnit
ou: users
```

We execute **ldapadd** again to create the OU.

```
[root@alpha ldap]# ldapadd -f users.ldif -D cn=admin,dc=linuxaholics,
dc=com -w pass
adding new entry "ou=users,dc=linuxaholics,dc=com"
```

## Adding a User

We can now include a user inside the OU. The procedure is quite similar to what we have seen so far. First, we create a file named `tux.ldif`, with the following content:

```
dn: cn=Tux,ou=users,dc=linuxaholics,dc=com
cn: Tux
sn: Tuxon
objectClass: inetOrgPerson
userPassword: linuxrules
uid: Tux
```

Then we execute **ldapadd** again.

```
[root@alpha ldap]# ldapadd -f tux.ldif -x -D cn=admin,dc=linuxaholics,
dc=com -w pass
adding new entry "cn=Tux,ou=users,dc=linuxaholics,dc=com"
```

We might receive this error:

```
ldap_add: Invalid syntax (21)
additional info: objectClass: value #0 invalid per syntax
```

This message means that the object `inetOrgPerson` isn't loaded in the core schema, so we'll have to include it. In the `/etc/openldap/schema` folder, there are many LDIF files to extend the schema when we need it. We can see there is an `inetorgperson.ldif` file, which contains the schema definition for the `inetOrgPerson` object.

The schema itself is contained in the LDAP database, so we can add new definitions to it with the **ldapadd** command. As we're going to modify the configuration itself, instead of the data, we'll authenticate ourselves as the external root user (`-Y EXTERNAL`), who has full access.

```
[root@alpha ldap]# ldapadd -Y EXTERNAL -H ldapi:// -f /etc/openldap/schema/
inetorgperson.ldif
SASL/EXTERNAL authentication started
SASL username: gidNumber=0+uidNumber=0,cn=peercred,cn=external,cn=auth
SASL SSF: 0
adding new entry "cn=inetorgperson,cn=schema,cn=config"
ldap_add: Other (e.g., implementation specific) error (80)
additional info: olcObjectClasses: AttributeType not found: "audio"
```

As we can see, we get an error, because the attribute type audio isn't defined. We therefore have to include this definition in the schema, too.

If we perform a search of the string "audio" in the files located in the /etc/openldap/ schema/ folder, we'll see that the attribute audio is defined in the cosine.ldif file. We therefore extend the schema with this LDIF file first.

```
[root@alpha ldap]# ldapadd -Y EXTERNAL -H ldapi:// -f /etc/openldap/schema/
cosine.ldif
SASL/EXTERNAL authentication started
SASL username: gidNumber=0+uidNumber=0,cn=peercred,cn=external,cn=auth
SASL SSF: 0
adding new entry "cn=cosine,cn=schema,cn=config"
```

Now we do the same thing with the inetorgperson.ldif file.

```
[root@alpha ldap]# ldapadd -Y EXTERNAL -H ldapi:// -f /etc/openldap/schema/
inetorgperson.ldif
SASL/EXTERNAL authentication started
SASL username: gidNumber=0+uidNumber=0,cn=peercred,cn=external,cn=auth
SASL SSF: 0
adding new entry "cn=inetorgperson,cn=schema,cn=config"
```

Finally, we add the user with the tux.ldif file we created before.

```
[root@alpha ldap]# ldapadd -f tux.ldif -x -D
cn=admin,dc=linuxaholics,dc=com -w pass
adding new entry "cn=Tux,ou=users,dc=linuxaholics,dc=com"
```

If at some point we need to take a look at the currently used schema, we can use the **slapcat** command like this:

```
[root@alpha ldap]# slapcat -b "cn=schema,cn=config"
dn: cn=config
objectClass: olcGlobal
cn: config
olcArgsFile: /var/run/openldap/slapd.args
olcPidFile: /var/run/openldap/slapd.pid
olcTLSCACertificatePath: /etc/openldap/certs
olcTLSCertificateFile: "OpenLDAP Server"
```

```
olcTLSCertificateKeyFile: /etc/openldap/certs/password
structuralObjectClass: olcGlobal
entryUUID: bb38e2c0-4f85-1034-8587-e9dda2aed256
creatorsName: cn=config
createTimestamp: 20150223085725Z
entryCSN: 20150223085725.426340Z#000000#000#000000
modifiersName: cn=config
modifyTimestamp: 20150223085725Z
```

.
.
.

## Adding a Group

To add a group, we repeat the same process. First we create the groups.ldif file with the following content:

```
dn: cn=scientists, ou=users, dc=linuxaholics, dc=com
cn: scientists
objectClass: groupOfNames
member: cn=Tux, ou=users, dc=linuxaholics, dc=com
```

We add the group with **ldapadd**.

```
[root@alpha ldap]# ldapadd -f groups.ldif -x -D
cn=admin,dc=linuxaholics,dc=com -w pass
adding new entry "cn=scientists,ou=users,dc=linuxaholics,dc=com"
```

## Editing Objects

Besides adding new entries to our LDAP server, we can change the existing entries. To achieve this, we create a new LDIF file and use the **ldapmodify** tool.

Just a moment ago we added the user Tux, and we can check this entry with **ldapsearch**.

```
[root@alpha ldap]# ldapsearch -x -b "dc=linuxaholics,dc=com" "(cn=Tux)"
# extended LDIF
#
```

```
# LDAPv3
# base <dc=linuxaholics,dc=com> with scope subtree
# filter: (cn=Tux)
# requesting: ALL
#

# Tux, users, linuxaholics.com
dn: cn=Tux,ou=users,dc=linuxaholics,dc=com
cn: Tux
sn: Tuxon
objectClass: inetOrgPerson
userPassword:: bGludXhydWxlcw==
uid: Tux

# search result
search: 2
result: 0 Success

# numResponses: 2
# numEntries: 1
```

Let's suppose we want to change the sn attribute from Tuxon to Penguin. We'll have to prepare an LDIF file like this:

```
dn: cn=Tux,ou=users,dc=linuxaholics,dc=com
changeType: modify
replace: sn
sn: Penguin
```

Now, we're ready to launch the **ldapmodify** command.

```
[root@alpha ldap]# ldapmodify -x -D "cn=admin,dc=linuxaholics,dc=com" -W -f
tux_edit.ldif
Enter LDAP Password:
modifying entry "cn=Tux,ou=users,dc=linuxaholics,dc=com"
```

If we check the entry again, we'll see that it has been changed.

```
[root@alpha ldap]# ldapsearch -x -b "dc=linuxaholics,dc=com" "(cn=Tux)"
# extended LDIF
#
# LDAPv3
# base <dc=linuxaholics,dc=com> with scope subtree
# filter: (cn=Tux)
# requesting: ALL
#

# Tux, users, linuxaholics.com
dn: cn=Tux,ou=users,dc=linuxaholics,dc=com
cn: Tux
sn: Penguin
objectClass: inetOrgPerson
userPassword:: bGludXhydWxlcw==
uid: Tux

# search result
search: 2
result: 0 Success

# numResponses: 2
# numEntries: 1
```

So far we have seen how to add or change attributes, but sometimes we might need to delete attributes. Let's look at an example. If we want to delete the sn attribute of the Tux user, first we create the corresponding LDIF file:

```
dn: cn=Tux,ou=users,dc=linuxaholics,dc=com
changeType: modify
delete: sn
```

We then execute **ldapmodify**.

```
[root@alpha ldap]# ldapmodify -x -D cn="admin,dc=linuxaholics,dc=com" -W -f
tux_delete.ldif
Enter LDAP Password:
modifying entry "cn=Tux,ou=users,dc=linuxaholics,dc=com"
```

# Deleting Objects

Apart from adding or editing, we can also delete objects from the LDAP server. The procedure is even easier, as we don't need to create any LDIF file. We just execute **ldapdel** with the cn we want to delete. Let's suppose we had previously added the user John Doe.

```
dn: cn=john,ou=users,dc=linuxaholics,dc=com
cn: John
sn: Doe
objectClass: inetOrgPerson
userPassword: nobody
uid: john
```

```
[root@alpha ldap]# ldapadd -f john.ldif -x -D cn=admin,dc=linuxaholics,
dc=com -w pass
adding new entry "cn=john,ou=users,dc=linuxaholics,dc=com"
```

We can now delete this entry with the **ldapdelete** command. We only need to pass the object we want to delete as a parameter.

```
[root@alpha ldap]# ldapdelete "cn=john,ou=users,dc=linuxaholics,dc=com"
-D  cn=admin,dc=linuxaholics,dc=com -w pass
```

If we search the LDAP tree, we can see that the user john no longer exists.

```
[root@alpha ldap]# ldapsearch -x -b "dc=linuxaholics,dc=com" "(cn=john)"
# extended LDIF
#
# LDAPv3
# base <dc=linuxaholics,dc=com> with scope subtree
# filter: (cn=john)
# requesting: ALL
#

# search result
search: 2
result: 0 Success

# numResponses: 1
```

# Logging Access

Being able to log every access to our OpenLDAP server is very important for auditing and troubleshooting purposes. To log accesses to the LDAP server we can use the **accesslog** overlay. To use it we need to load the corresponding module. As this is the first module we are loading, we need to create a new entry olcModuleList and specify the path to the module, in this case /usr/lib64/openldap/accesslog.la.

The corresponding LDIF file (/root/ldap/module1.ldif) would be this one:

```
dn: cn=module{0},cn=config
objectClass: olcModuleList
cn: module{0}
olcModuleLoad: /usr/lib64/openldap/accesslog.la
```

```
[root@alpha ldap]# ldapadd -Y EXTERNAL -H ldapi:// -f module1.ldif
SASL/EXTERNAL authentication started
SASL username: gidNumber=0+uidNumber=0,cn=peercred,cn=external,cn=auth
SASL SSF: 0
adding new entry "cn=module{0},cn=config"
```

The accesslog overlay logs all information in another database, so we'll need to create it. First, we prepare the folder where the new database will be placed.

```
[root@alpha ldap]# mkdir /var/lib/ldap/accesslog
```

We then make the ldap user and group the owners of the new folder.

```
[root@alpha ldap]# chown ldap.ldap /var/lib/ldap/accesslog/
```

Next, we prepare an LDIF file to create the new database itself.

```
dn: olcDatabase={3}hdb,cn=config
objectClass: olcDatabaseConfig
objectClass: olcHdbConfig
olcDatabase: {3}hdb
olcDbDirectory: /var/lib/ldap/accesslog
olcSuffix: cn=accesslog
olcRootDN: cn=admin,dc=linuxaholics,dc=com
olcDbIndex: default eq
```

After executing **ldapadd** with the new LDIF file, the database will be created.

```
[root@alpha ldap]# ldapadd -Y EXTERNAL -H ldapi:// -f bdlog.ldif
SASL/EXTERNAL authentication started
SASL username: gidNumber=0+uidNumber=0,cn=peercred,cn=external,cn=auth
SASL SSF: 0
adding new entry "olcDatabase={3}hdb,cn=config"
```

We also need to define in the main database what actions should be logged and where, so we create another LDIF file.

```
dn: olcOverlay=accesslog,olcDatabase={2}hdb,cn=config
objectClass: olcOverlayConfig
objectClass: olcAccessLogConfig
olcOverlay: accesslog
olcAccessLogDB: cn=accesslog
olcAccessLogOps: writes
olcAccessLogSuccess: TRUE
```

We then apply the changes by executing **ldapadd**.

```
[root@alpha ldap]# ldapadd -Y EXTERNAL -H ldapi:// -f accesslog.ldif
SASL/EXTERNAL authentication started
SASL username: gidNumber=0+uidNumber=0,cn=peercred,cn=external,cn=auth
SASL SSF: 0
adding new entry "olcOverlay=accesslog,olcDatabase={2}hdb,cn=config"
```

From now on every write access will be logged. In the section "Deleting Objects" earlier in this chapter we created and deleted the user john. If we repeat this action again the result will be logged.

```
[root@alpha ldap]# ldapadd -f john.ldif -x -D "cn=admin,dc=linuxaholics,
dc=com" -w pass
adding new entry "cn=john,ou=users,dc=linuxaholics,dc=com"
[root@localhost ldap]# ldapdelete "cn=john,ou=users,dc=linuxaholics,dc=com"
-D "cn=admin,dc=linuxaholics,dc=com" -w pass
```

We can check the results with a simple LDAP query.

```
[root@alpha ldap]# ldapsearch -x -b cn=accesslog
# extended LDIF
#
# LDAPv3
# base <cn=accesslog> with scope subtree
# filter: (objectclass=*)
# requesting: ALL
#

# accesslog
dn: cn=accesslog
objectClass: auditContainer
cn: accesslog

# 20170226013503.000001Z, accesslog
dn: reqStart=20170226013503.000001Z,cn=accesslog
objectClass: auditAdd
reqStart: 20170226013503.000001Z
reqEnd: 20170226013503.000002Z
reqType: add
reqSession: 1042
reqAuthzID: cn=admin,dc=linuxaholics,dc=com
reqDN: cn=john,ou=users,dc=linuxaholics,dc=com
reqResult: 0
reqMod: cn:+ john
reqMod: sn:+ Doe
reqMod: objectClass:+ inetOrgPerson
reqMod: userPassword:+ nobody
reqMod: uid:+ john
reqMod: structuralObjectClass:+ inetOrgPerson
reqMod: entryUUID:+ 8a4aca80-900f-1036-97df-1dfeeaf5a24b
reqMod: creatorsName:+ cn=admin,dc=linuxaholics,dc=com
reqMod: createTimestamp:+ 20170226013503Z
reqMod: entryCSN:+ 20170226013503.644189Z#000000#000#000000
```

```
reqMod: modifiersName:+ cn=admin,dc=linuxaholics,dc=com
reqMod: modifyTimestamp:+ 20170226013503Z
reqEntryUUID: 8a4aca80-900f-1036-97df-1dfeeaf5a24b

# 20170226013619.000001Z, accesslog
dn: reqStart=20170226013619.000001Z,cn=accesslog
objectClass: auditDelete
reqStart: 20170226013619.000001Z
reqEnd: 20170226013619.000002Z
reqType: delete
reqSession: 1044
reqAuthzID: cn=admin,dc=linuxaholics,dc=com
reqDN: cn=john,ou=users,dc=linuxaholics,dc=com
reqResult: 0
reqEntryUUID: 8a4aca80-900f-1036-97df-1dfeeaf5a24b

# search result
search: 2
result: 0 Success

# numResponses: 4
# numEntries: 3
```

# Logging to rsyslog

By default, **slapd** sends information to the local4 facility. In a fresh CentOS 7 installation **rsyslog** doesn't log information sent to the local4 facility to any file, so we'll have to add this line to the /etc/rsyslog.conf file:

```
# Log OpenLDAP messages
local4.*                        /var/log/ldap.log
```

We restart the **rsyslog** and **slapd** service and we check that the new log file has been updated with information.

```
[root@alpha ~]# systemctl restart rsyslog
[root@alpha ~]# systemctl restart slapd
```

```
[root@alpha ~]# cat /var/log/ldap.log
.
.
.
Apr 22 00:16:32 alpha slapd[5223]: @(#) $OpenLDAP: slapd 2.4.40 (Nov  6
2016 01:21:28) $
        mockbuild@worker1.bsys.centos.org:/builddir/build/BUILD/
openldap-2.4.40/openldap-2.4.40/servers/slapd
Apr 22 00:16:32 alpha slapd[5225]: hdb_db_open: warning - no DB_CONFIG file
found in directory /var/lib/ldap: (2).
Expect poor performance for suffix "dc=linuxaholics,dc=com".
Apr 22 00:16:32 alpha slapd[5225]: hdb_db_open: warning - no DB_CONFIG file
found in directory /var/lib/ldap/accesslog: (2).
Expect poor performance for suffix "cn=accesslog".
Apr 22 00:16:32 alpha slapd[5225]: slapd starting
```

# Berkeley Database

We already saw in this chapter that the most often used back end with OpenLDAP is Berkeley DB. This database stores the actual information and metadata in a series of files, located by default in /var/lib/ldap.

```
[root@alpha ldap]# ls /var/lib/ldap/
accesslog  cn.bdb    __db.002  dn2id.bdb      log.0000000001  ou.bdb
alock      __db.001  __db.003  id2entry.bdb   objectClass.bdb  sn.bdb
```

We can see a series of files with the .bdb extension, which are the database files, as well as one or more transaction files (log.0000000001). According to the official OpenLDAP manual, these files should be periodically backed up for recovery purposes. To do that we can take one of two approaches:

1. Back up the entire database and also back up periodically the transaction log files.

2. Generate an LDIF file with **slapcat**.

If we choose the first option, we can make a hot backup with the **db_hotbackup** command.

```
[root@alpha ldap]# db_hotbackup -h /var/lib/ldap/ -b ./bdb_backup/
[root@alpha ldap]# ls bdb_backup/
alock    dn2id.bdb       log.0000000001    ou.bdb
cn.bdb   id2entry.bdb    objectClass.bdb   sn.bdb
```

This way we copied the database files, as well as the transaction log, to a new location. From there, they can be restored if we need to do so. The restoration would be performed with the **db_recover** tool.

```
[root@alpha ldap]# db_recover -v -h /var/lib/ldap/
BDB2526 Finding last valid log LSN: file: 1 offset 3571
BDB1514 Recovery starting from [1][2997]
BDB1518 Recovery complete at Thu Jun 15 10:33:38 2017
BDB1519 Maximum transaction ID 80000002 recovery checkpoint [1][3746]
[root@alpha ldap]#
```

If we decide to use the second option, we should generate an LDIF file that would be used later to restore the data.

```
[root@alpha ldap]# slapcat -b "dc=linuxaholics,dc=com" > myOpenLDAP.ldif
```

In this case, though, if the database files get corrupted, we might need to perform a fresh installation and insert the data from the LDIF file later, once the OpenLDAP server is operational again.

Another utility we haven't seen so far that can be also very useful is db_verify, used to verify database files.

```
[root@alpha ldap]# db_verify -h /var/lib/ldap/ /var/lib/ldap/dn2id.bdb
BDB5105 Verification of /var/lib/ldap/dn2id.bdb succeeded.
[root@alpha ldap]#
```

# Tools

There are several useful tools that we can use to query and manage our LDAP server. Some of them have already been used in this chapter, and others will be used in the upcoming chapters.

# Server Tools

These tools are included with the OpenLDAP server binaries and work directly over the slapd database. They should be used with caution because they could easily lead to database corruption. This could happen, for instance, if the admin tries to update the database content with a tool like slapadd and at the same time someone else tries to do the same with ldapadd. For that reason, it is recommended that the slapd service is stopped when using server tools. In test environments like the one we are working with, however, it is acceptable to execute the server tools without stopping the service, as there will be no other people accessing the LDAP database at the same time.

## Slapcat

Similar to **ldapsearch**, **slapcat** shows us information about the LDAP server.

## Slapadd

This tool is used to add objects at the server level, without the need for a network connection.

## Slapindex

This utility creates index files according to the index directive used in the configuration.

## Slappasswd

This tool generates a password that can be used as a value of the `userPassword` attribute. We used this tool in this chapter to generate a password for the LDAP admin.

## Slapacl

This command can be used to check the behavior of access control lists (ACLs). We'll see an example in Chapter 2 when talking about access control.

## Slaptest

This tool checks the configuration of the OpenLDAP.

# Client Tools

Client tools don't work by directly accessing the database files as server tools do; they do use library calls instead. The libraries should take care of the concurrent access to the LDAP server, so they do not have the same risk of accidentally leaving the LDAP database in an inconsistent state as the server tools do.

## Ldapsearch

As the name implies, this tool is used to perform searches. We have already seen a few examples of the use of this command.

## Ldapwhoami

We can use this command to check the effective user we are validating as. This is especially useful when mapping users, as we'll see in the forthcoming chapters.

## Ldapadd

This command is used to add new objects to our LDAP server. It is really a link to **ldapmodify**.

## Ldapdelete

This tool is used to delete entries in the LDAP.

## Ldapmodify

This command can be used to modify LDAP entries and add new ones.

## Ldapmodrn

This utility renames LDAP entries.

# Summary

This first chapter introduced the basic concepts of LDAP and laid the foundation for the later study of more advanced topics. We installed an OpenLDAP server and we customized it according to our needs by adding users and groups.

We have seen how to log LDAP-related information to OpenLDAP itself as well as to rsyslog. We also introduced several useful command-line utilities.

# CHAPTER 2

# Securing the Directory

In this chapter, we'll see how to secure our OpenLDAP server. We'll encrypt the communication between client and server with Transport Layer Security (TLS). Configuration of the firewall to permit access and use of different authentication methods is also addressed.

This chapter covers the following concepts:

- Securing the directory with Secure Sockets Layer (SSL) and TLS.

- Firewall considerations.

- Unauthenticated access methods.

- User/password authentication methods.

- Maintanence of Simple Authentication and Security Layer (SASL) user database.

- Client/server certificates.

We will also be introduced to the following terms and utilities: SSL/TLS, Security Strength Factors (SSF), SASL, proxy authorization, StartTLS, and iptables.

## Securing LDAP Connections with TLS

By default, when using LDAP connections, all information is sent in plain text. There's no need to insist again on the importance of ciphering all traffic transmitted between the client and the server. To achieve this goal, we can use the SSL or TLS protocols.

SSL and its successor TLS were designed to allow for secure communications on the Internet. They provide privacy by encrypting transmitted data through the use of symmetric cryptography. They can also authenticate the server, the client, or both using public key cryptography. Finally, these protocols provide integrity through the use of a message integrity check transmitted with each message.

33

© Antonio Vazquez 2019
A. Vazquez, *Practical LPIC-3 300*, https://doi.org/10.1007/978-1-4842-4473-9_2

Both SSL and TLS can be used to secure communications. However, as the SSL protocol has many known vulnerabilities, it is advisable to use its succesor, the TLS protocol.

LDAP, and many other protocols such as Hypertext Transfer Protocol (HTTP) or Simple Mail Transfer Protocol (SMTP), can communicate in a secure way (by using TLS), as well as in an insecure way, so server and client need to agree on whether to establish a secure connection or not. The typical way to achieve this is by using different port numbers for secure and insecure connections, but it is also possible to use the same port number for both. In this case, when the client wants to set up a TLS connection it sends a STARTTLS request.

**STARTTLS** is an extension to plain text protocols that allows for the encryption of the communication using the same port number as the standard, nonencrypted version of the protocol. For that purpose, many protocols such as SMTP, FTP, and LDAP use the command STARTTLS.

TLS relies on the use of X.509 certificates to carry the server identity, so we'll need a server certificate. In addition, depending on how we configure our system, we might need a client certificate. We'll see some examples of this later in this book.

We are all familiar with certificates used by well-known e-commerce sites, these certificates are signed by a trusted certification authority (CA). In our case, however, we are going to create our own CA and we'll sign our own certificates to use them with LDAP. To do this, we begin by installing the openssl package, unless it is already installed.

```
[root@alpha ~]# yum install openssl
```

# Preparing the Environment

It is very important that every computer involved is able to resolve server names accordingly. In our example, the server name is alpha.linuxaholics.com and the associated IP address is 192.168.1.229. If we use a Domain Name System (DNS) server in our infrastructure we should add the corresponding A and PTR records. However, if we're working in a lab environment without a DNS server, we could simply edit the /etc/hosts file for every computer involved in the process. To edit the file, we could use one of the many editors available in Linux, such as vi, vim, nano, and so on. The content of the file should be similar to this:

```
[root@alpha ~]# cat /etc/hosts
127.0.0.1  localhost localhost.localdomain localhost4 localhost4.localdomain4
::1        localhost localhost.localdomain localhost6 localhost6.localdomain6
192.168.1.229     alpha.linuxaholics.com
```

If the hostname or the IP of the server differs, we should edit the file accordingly. The hostname can be easily set with the **hostnamectl** command like this:

```
[root@alpha ~]# hostnamectl set-hostname alpha.linuxaholics.com
```

# Creating a CA and a Server Certificate

After installing the openssl package, we should have a predefined tree structure under /etc/pki/CA.

```
[root@alpha ~]# cd /etc/pki/CA/
[root@alpha CA]# ls -l
drwxr-xr-x.  2 root root 4096 abr 11  2018 certs
drwxr-xr-x.  2 root root    6 abr 11  2018 crl
drwxr-xr-x.  2 root root   45 abr 11  2018 newcerts
drwx------.  2 root root 4096 abr 11  2018 private
```

To track the issued certificates we create an index.txt and serial files. When creating the serial file, we should pay attention to the leading zeros.

```
[root@alpha CA]# touch index.txt
[root@alpha CA]# echo 0001 > serial
```

Now we create the key for the CA. We'll set a password for that key, otherwise we'll get an error:

```
[root@alpha CA]# openssl genrsa -aes256 -out /etc/pki/CA/private/ca.key.pem
Generating RSA private key, 1024 bit long modulus
........................++++++
..........................++++++
e is 65537 (0x10001)
```

```
Enter pass phrase for /etc/pki/CA/private/ca.key.pem:
Verifying - Enter pass phrase for /etc/pki/CA/private/ca.key.pem:
```

Once we have the key file, we create the CA certificate itself.

```
[root@alpha CA]# openssl req -new -x509 -days 3650 -key /etc/pki/CA/
private/ca.key.pem -extensions v3_ca -out /etc/pki/CA/certs/ca.cert.pem
Enter pass phrase for /etc/pki/CA/private/ca.key.pem:
You are about to be asked to enter information that will be incorporated
into your     certificate request.
What you are about to enter is what is called a Distinguished Name or a DN.
There are quite a few fields but you can leave some blank
For some fields there will be a default value,
If you enter '.', the field will be left blank.
-----
Country Name (2 letter code) [XX]:ES
State or Province Name (full name) []:Madrid
Locality Name (eg, city) [Default City]:Madrid
Organization Name (eg, company) [Default Company Ltd]:linuxaholics
Organizational Unit Name (eg, section) []:
Common Name (eg, your name or your server's hostname) []:alpha.
linuxaholics.com
Email Address []:
```

Now we are ready to generate the key and certificate files to use with openldap. It is very important that the Common name matches the server's hostname.

```
[root@alpha CA]# openssl genrsa -out /etc/pki/CA/private/alpha.
linuxaholics.com.key
Generating RSA private key, 1024 bit long modulus
.........................++++++
..++++++
e is 65537 (0x10001)
```

```
[root@alpha CA]# openssl req -new -key /etc/pki/CA/private/alpha.
linuxaholics.com.key -out /etc/pki/CA/certs/alpha.linuxaholics.com.csr
You are about to be asked to enter information that will be incorporated
into your certificate request.
```

What you are about to enter is what is called a Distinguished Name or a DN.
There are quite a few fields but you can leave some blank
For some fields there will be a default value,
If you enter '.', the field will be left blank.
-----
Country Name (2 letter code) [XX]:ES
State or Province Name (full name) []:Madrid
Locality Name (eg, city) [Default City]:Madrid
Organization Name (eg, company) [Default Company Ltd]:linuxaholics
Organizational Unit Name (eg, section) []:
Common Name (eg, your name or your server's hostname) []:alpha.
linuxaholics.com
Email Address []:

Please enter the following 'extra' attributes
to be sent with your certificate request
A challenge password []:
An optional company name []:

We already have the certificate, but now we have to sign it with our CA.

```
[root@alpha CA]# openssl ca -keyfile /etc/pki/CA/private/ca.key.pem -cert
/etc/pki/CA/certs/ca.cert.pem -in /etc/pki/CA/certs/alpha.linuxaholics.com.
csr -out /etc/pki/CA/certs/alpha.linuxaholics.com.crt
Using configuration from /etc/pki/tls/openssl.cnf
Enter pass phrase for /etc/pki/CA/private/ca.key.pem:
Check that the request matches the signature
Signature ok
Certificate Details:
Serial Number: 1 (0x1)
Validity
Not Before: Sep 11 02:49:08 2015 GMT
Not After : Sep 10 02:49:08 2016 GMT
Subject:
countryName            = ES
stateOrProvinceName    = Madrid
organizationName       = linuxaholics
```

```
commonName                    = alpha.linuxaholics.com
X509v3 extensions:
X509v3 Basic Constraints:
CA:FALSE
Netscape Comment:
OpenSSL Generated Certificate
X509v3 Subject Key Identifier:
DD:35:3F:30:9E:54:DD:CA:05:62:A7:AD:82:DE:3B:DE:75:09:39:68
X509v3 Authority Key Identifier:
keyid:08:8D:D2:5F:9E:3E:F0:80:38:37:BF:06:E1:93:2D:1D:D3:F8:EE:1E

Certificate is to be certified until Sep 10 02:49:08 2016 GMT (365 days)
Sign the certificate? [y/n]:y

1 out of 1 certificate requests certified, commit? [y/n]y
Write out database with 1 new entries
Data Base Updated
```

We can see now that the index.txt file has been updated.

```
[root@alpha CA]# cat index.txt
V       160910024908Z           01      unknown /C=ES/ST=Madrid/
O=linuxaholics/CN=alpha.linuxaholics.com
```

We can also verify the issued certificate against our CA.

```
[root@alpha CA]# openssl verify -CAfile /etc/pki/CA/certs/ca.cert.pem
/etc/pki/CA/certs/alpha.linuxaholics.com.crt
/etc/pki/CA/certs/alpha.linuxaholics.com.crt: OK
```

After signing the certificate, we copy both the certificate and the key file to /etc/openldap/certs/. We also copy the CA certificate to /etc/openldap/cacerts/, and we'll have to create this folder if it doesn't exist yet. Later we'll need to modify the openldap configuration accordingly.

```
[root@alpha CA]# mkdir /etc/openldap/cacerts/
[root@alpha CA]# cp certs/ca.cert.pem /etc/openldap/cacerts/
[root@alpha CA]# cp certs/alpha.linuxaholics.com.crt /etc/openldap/certs/
[root@alpha CA]# cp private/alpha.linuxaholics.com.key /etc/openldap/certs/
```

# Securing the LDAP Protocol

In the OpenLDAP version included in CentOS 7 there are already default values for the TLS-related attributes. We can see these values with **slapcat**:

```
[root@alpha CA]# slapcat -b "cn=schema,cn=config"
dn: cn=config
objectClass: olcGlobal
cn: config
olcArgsFile: /var/run/openldap/slapd.args
olcPidFile: /var/run/openldap/slapd.pid
olcTLSCACertificatePath: /etc/openldap/certs
olcTLSCertificateFile: "OpenLDAP Server"
olcTLSCertificateKeyFile: /etc/openldap/certs/password
structuralObjectClass: olcGlobal
entryUUID: b85880a2-eb3d-1034-8604-e7b4503cc451
creatorsName: cn=config
createTimestamp: 20150909125458Z
entryCSN: 20150909125458.229137Z#000000#000#000000
modifiersName: cn=config
modifyTimestamp: 20150909125458Z
.
.
.
```

We need to modify the values of the olcTLSCACertificatePath, olcTLSCertificateFile, and olcTLSCertificateKeyFile attributes, and we also need to add the olcTLSCACertificateFile attribute. We therefore create this LDIF file:

```
dn: cn=config
changeType: modify
replace: olcTLSCertificateFile
olcTLSCertificateFile: /etc/openldap/certs/alpha.linuxaholics.com.crt
-
replace: olcTLSCertificateKeyFile
olcTLSCertificateKeyFile: /etc/openldap/certs/alpha.linuxaholics.com.key
-
```

```
add: olcTLSCACertificateFile
olcTLSCACertificateFile: /etc/openldap/cacerts/ca.cert.pem
-
replace: olcTLSCACertificatePath
olcTLSCACertificatePath: /etc/openldap/cacerts
```

We also run the **ldapmodify** command by passing the LDIF file as a parameter.

```
[root@alpha ldap]# ldapmodify -Y EXTERNAL -H ldapi:// -f tls.ldif
SASL/EXTERNAL authentication started
SASL username: gidNumber=0+uidNumber=0,cn=peercred,cn=external,cn=auth
SASL SSF: 0
modifying entry "cn=config"
```

Now we edit the /etc/sysconfig/slapd file to add ldaps:/// to the SLAPD_URLS parameter.

```
SLAPD_URLS="ldapi:/// ldap:/// ldaps:///"
```

We then restart the service.

```
[root@alpha ldap]# systemctl restart slapd
```

If we query the LDAP again, we'll see that the entries have actually been changed.

```
[root@alpha ldap]# slapcat -b "cn=schema,cn=config" | less
dn: cn=config
objectClass: olcGlobal
cn: config
olcArgsFile: /var/run/openldap/slapd.args
olcPidFile: /var/run/openldap/slapd.pid
structuralObjectClass: olcGlobal
entryUUID: 42310ede-8e3f-1036-840d-f3757e79c279
creatorsName: cn=config
createTimestamp: 20170223181136Z
olcTLSCertificateFile: /etc/openldap/certs/alpha.linuxaholics.com.crt
olcTLSCertificateKeyFile: /etc/openldap/certs/alpha.linuxaholics.com.key
```

```
olcTLSCACertificateFile: /etc/openldap/cacerts/ca.cert.pem
olcTLSCACertificatePath: /etc/openldap/cacerts
.
.
.
```

We can check whether the TLS connection is working by executing the **ldapsearch** command with the -ZZ parameter.

When we establish a client connection to the LDAP server, ldapsearch assumes we are using the parameters specified in the /etc/openldap/ldap.conf file. By default, this is the original content of that file:

```
#
# LDAP Defaults
#

# See ldap.conf(5) for details
# This file should be world readable but not world writable.

#BASE    dc=example,dc=com
#URI     ldap://ldap.example.com ldap://ldap-master.example.com:666

#SIZELIMIT      12
#TIMELIMIT      15
#DEREF          never

TLS_CACERTDIR   /etc/openldap/certs

# Turning this off breaks GSSAPI used with krb5 when rdns = false
SASL_NOCANON    on
```

We can specify several options in this file, as we can see in the man page. These are some of the more common ones:

- URI: As the name implies, this option specifies the URI of the LDAP server to connect to.

- BASE: When defined, all searches will be performed using this default base DN.

- TIMEOUT: Once this time threshold is exceeded without response the query is aborted.

- PORT: This specifies the port to which to connect.

- TLS_CACERTDIR: This is the path that contains the certificates.

- TLS_REQCERT: This option specifies how to deal with certificates depending on the value assigned:

  - never: The client will never request a server certificate.

  - allow: The client requests a server certificate, but if no valid certificate is provided, the session proceeds normally.

  - try: The client requests a certificate. If a bad certificate is provided, the session is terminated immediately.

  - demand|hard: These options are equivalent to try. This is the default setting.

These options, however, can be overriden when executing ldapsearch with the appropriate parameters.

In our case we'll have to change the value of the TLS_CACERTDIR parameter to /etc/openldap/cacerts.

```
#
# LDAP Defaults
#

# See ldap.conf(5) for details

# This file should be world readable but not world writable.

#BASE    dc=example,dc=com
#URI     ldap://ldap.example.com ldap://ldap-master.example.com:666

#SIZELIMIT      12
#TIMELIMIT      15
#DEREF          never

TLS_CACERTDIR   /etc/openldap/cacerts

# Turning this off breaks GSSAPI used with krb5 when rdns = false
SASL_NOCANON    on
```

After making the change, we launch the **ldapsearch** command with the -ZZ option. This way we're indicating that we want to use StartTLS to encrypt the connection. We also specify the base search with -s, we use simple authentication (we'll see more details about authentication later), and we search only the Tux user we created in Chapter 1.

```
[root@alpha ~]# ldapsearch -x -ZZ -b "dc=linuxaholics,dc=com" "(cn=Tux)"
```

However, we might get this error:

```
ldap_start_tls: Connect error (-11)
additional info: TLS error -8172:Peer's certificate issuer has been marked
as not trusted by the user.
```

This happens because openssl expects the CA certificate file name to be a numeric hash. This hash can be obtained like this:

```
[root@alpha ~]# openssl x509 -in /etc/openldap/cacerts/ca.cert.pem -hash
a9ff5841
-----BEGIN CERTIFICATE-----
MIICqjCCAhOgAwIBAgIJAM2tTmaqRXg/MA0GCSqGSIb3DQEBCwUAMG4xCzAJBgNV
BAYTAkVTMQ8wDQYDVQQIDAZNYWRyaWQxDzANBgNVBAcMBk1hZHJpZDEVMBMGA1UE
CgwMbGludXhhaG9saWNzMSYwJAYDVQQDDB1DZW50b3M3LUxQSTMubGludXhhaG9s
aWNzLmNvbTAeFw0xNTA5MTEwMTI3MzBaFw0yNTA5MDgwMTI3MzBaMG4xCzAJBgNV
.
.
.
```

Then we create a symbolic link with the hash we just obtained (plus the string .0).

```
[root@alpha ~]# ln -s /etc/openldap/cacerts/ca.cert.pem /etc/openldap/
cacerts/a9ff5841.0
```

An alternative way to create the symbolic links needed would be to execute the **cacertdir_rehash** command.

```
[root@alpha ~]# cacertdir_rehash /etc/openldap/cacerts/

[root@alpha ~]# ls /etc/openldap/cacerts/
2ba50568.0  ca.cert.pem                ldap.linuxaholics.com.key
a9ff5841.0  ldap.linuxaholics.com.crt
```

Now we can execute `ldapsearch -ZZ`.

```
[root@alpha ~]# ldapsearch -x -ZZ -b "dc=linuxaholics,dc=com" "(cn=Tux)"
# extended LDIF
#
# LDAPv3
# base <dc=linuxaholics,dc=com> with scope subtree
# filter: (cn=Tux)
# requesting: ALL
#

# Tux, users, linuxaholics.com
dn: cn=Tux,ou=users,dc=linuxaholics,dc=com
cn: Tux
objectClass: inetOrgPerson
userPassword:: bGludXhydWxlcw==
uid: Tux
sn: Penguin

# search result
search: 3
result: 0 Success

# numResponses: 2
# numEntries: 1
```

If we still have problems connecting with the LDAP server with the `-ZZ` parameter we need to make sure that the client's hostname matches the subject defined in the CA certificate. If we are not sure about this, we can check the subject with the **openssl** command:

```
[root@alpha cacerts]# openssl x509 -subject -in ca.cert.pem -text
subject= /C=ES/ST=Madrid/L=Madrid/O=linuxaholics/CN=alpha.linuxaholics.com
Certificate:
    Data:
        Version: 3 (0x2)
    .
    .
    .
```

We can check the hostname with **hostnamectl**:

```
[root@alpha cacerts]# hostnamectl status
   Static hostname: alpha.linuxaholics.com
 .

 .

 .
```

As we can see, in this case the hostname matches the one we defined in the CA certificate file. If that weren't the case, we'd need to change it accordingly.

```
[root@alpha cacerts]# hostnamectl set-hostname alpha.linuxaholics.com
[root@alpha cacerts]# hostnamectl status
   Static hostname: alpha.linuxaholics.com
 .

 .

 .
```

# Firewall Considerations

To allow external clients to connect to our OpenLDAP server, we need to allow that traffic in the firewall. If we have followed the instructions in this book thus far, our server listens for connections to the TCP ports 389 (LDAP) and 636 (LDAPS). So far, we've connected to our LDAP server from the localhost, but if we try to connect from a different computer we'll need to allow that traffic in the firewall, otherwise we won't be able to connect.

```
[root@bravo ~]# ldapsearch -x -H ldap://alpha.linuxaholics.com -b
dc=linuxaholics,dc=com
ldap_sasl_bind(SIMPLE): Can't contact LDAP server (-1)
```

In this case, after checking that name resolution is working properly, we should check whether the LDAP port on the server can be accessed from the client computer.

```
[root@bravo ~]# nmap -p 389 alpha.linuxaholics.com

Starting Nmap 6.40 ( http://nmap.org ) at 2017-01-20 12:46 EST
 .

 .

 .
```

```
PORT     STATE     SERVICE
389/tcp filtered ldap
.

.

.
```

As we can see, the port is filtered so we need to allow that traffic in the OpenLDAP server's firewall. The easiest way to allow those incoming connections in the firewall would be like this:

```
[root@alpha ~]# firewall-cmd --add-service=ldap
success
[root@alpha ~]# firewall-cmd --add-service=ldaps
success
```

These changes will be effective immediately, but to make them permanent we need to launch the same two commands with the --permanent parameter.

```
[root@alpha ~]# firewall-cmd --permanent --add-service=ldap
success
[root@alpha ~]# firewall-cmd --permanent --add-service=ldaps
success
```

Now we'll be able to connect from the client computer.

```
[root@bravo ~]# ldapsearch -x -H ldap://alpha.linuxaholics.com -b
dc=linuxaholics,dc=com
# extended LDIF
#
# LDAPv3
# base <dc=linuxaholics,dc=com> with scope subtree
# filter: (objectclass=*)
# requesting: ALL
#
```

```
# linuxaholics.com
dn: dc=linuxaholics,dc=com
objectClass: dcObject
.

.

.
```

We have already established an LDAP connection from another computer. However, if we want to connect securely through the use of LDAPS we still have some additional work to do. Right now, the firewall allows incoming connections to the 636 TCP port, but the client computer doesn't trust the certificate used by the server.

```
[root@bravo ~]# ldapsearch -x -ZZ -H ldap://alpha.linuxaholics.com -b
dc=linuxaholics,dc=com
ldap_start_tls: Connect error (-11)
        additional info: TLS error -8172:Peer's certificate issuer has been
        marked as not trusted by the user.
```

As we saw previously, the system will search for the CA certificates in the folder specified in the TLS_CACERTDIR parameter, which is defined in the /etc/openldap/ldap. conf file in the client computer.

```
[root@bravo ~]# cat /etc/openldap/ldap.conf
#
# LDAP Defaults
#

# See ldap.conf(5) for details
# This file should be world readable but not world writable.

#BASE   dc=example,dc=com
#URI    ldap://ldap.example.com ldap://ldap-master.example.com:666

#SIZELIMIT    12
#TIMELIMIT    15
#DEREF        never

TLS_CACERTDIR      /etc/openldap/certs

# Turning this off breaks GSSAPI used with krb5 when rdns = false
SASL_NOCANON on
```

In a previous section, when we were securing the LDAP connection in the LDAP server, we created the /etc/openldap/cacerts to keep the CA certificates. To be consistent we'll do the same thing in the client computer. Later we'll modify the /etc/openldap/ldap.conf file like this:

```
[root@bravo ~]# cat /etc/openldap/ldap.conf
.

.

.

TLS_CACERTDIR        /etc/openldap/cacerts
.

.

.
```

We copy the CA certificate from the server to the client and we execute **cacertdir_rehash**.

```
[root@bravo ~]# mkdir /etc/openldap/cacerts
[root@bravo ~]# scp root@alpha.linuxaholics.com:/etc/openldap/cacerts/
ca.cert.pem /etc/openldap/cacerts
The authenticity of host 'alpha.linuxaholics.com (192.168.1.229)' can't be
established.
ECDSA key fingerprint is 6f:fb:50:b6:52:1d:7c:a3:5a:78:97:df:e3:d3:d2:02.
Are you sure you want to continue connecting (yes/no)? yes
Warning: Permanently added 'alpha.linuxaholics.com,192.168.1.229' (ECDSA)
to the list of known hosts.
root@alpha.linuxaholics.com's password:
ca.cert.pem                                     100% 1318     1.3KB/s   00:00
[root@bravo ~]# cacertdir_rehash /etc/openldap/cacerts/
```

Now we're ready to establish a secure connection through LDAPS.

```
[root@bravo ~]# ldapsearch -x -ZZ -H ldap://alpha.linuxaholics.com -b
dc=linuxaholics,dc=com "(cn=Tux)"
# extended LDIF
#
# LDAPv3
# base <dc=linuxaholics,dc=com> with scope subtree
```

```
# filter: (cn=Tux)
# requesting: ALL
#

# Tux, users, linuxaholics.com
dn: cn=Tux,ou=users,dc=linuxaholics,dc=com
cn: Tux
objectClass: inetOrgPerson
userPassword:: bGludXhydWxlcw==
uid: Tux
sn: Penguin

# search result
search: 3
result: 0 Success

# numResponses: 2
# numEntries: 1
```

In this case any client will be able to connect to our OpenLDAP server, but maybe we just want to allow access to those computers in a certain network, denying access to the rest. We can accomplish that with a rich rule, but before that we have to remove the LDAP and LDAPS service.

```
[root@alpha ~]# firewall-cmd --remove-service=ldap
success
[root@alpha ~]# firewall-cmd --remove-service=ldaps
success
```

Now we add the service again, so that it is allowed only for the local network computers.

```
[root@alpha ~]# firewall-cmd --add-rich-rule='rule family="ipv4" source
address="192.168.1.0/24" service name="ldap" accept'
success
[root@alpha ~]# firewall-cmd --add-rich-rule='rule family="ipv4" source
address="192.168.1.0/24" service name="ldaps" accept'
success
```

The use of **firewall-cmd** is the preferred way to interact with the local firewall in CentOS 7. However, as the LPIC-3 300 objectives specifically mention **iptables** we'll see the equivalent commands that we'd need to execute by using **iptables** instead of **firewall-cmd**.

We'd allow incoming traffic like this:

```
[root@alpha ~]# iptables -I INPUT -p tcp --dport 389 -j ACCEPT
[root@alpha ~]# iptables -I INPUT -p tcp --dport 636 -j ACCEPT
```

To make the changes permanent with iptables we could create a backup of the firewall configuration with **iptables-save**.

```
[root@alpha ~]# iptables-save > iptables.bk
```

To restore the backed up configuration, we'd use **iptables-restore**.

```
[root@alpha ~]# iptables-restore iptables.bk
```

Even though it is not exactly a firewall, we can also use TCP wrappers to limit access to the OpenLDAP server. TCP wrappers allow us to explicitly permit or deny access to certain services based on IP addresses. To work, the service binary file, **slapd** in this case, must have been linked to the libwrap library. We can check this with **ldd**.

```
[root@alpha ~]# ldd /usr/sbin/slapd | grep wrap
        libwrap.so.0 => /lib64/libwrap.so.0 (0x00007fc00afed000)
```

We're ready now to use TCP wrappers to protect the LDAP service. The configuration is very easy, as there are only two files involved: /etc/hosts.allow and /etc/hosts.deny. The first file is checked first, and as soon as line matches a certain connection no further rules are applied.

As a proof of concept, we'll only allow the computer 192.168.1.230 to access our LDAP server. The syntax of the /etc/hosts.allow file is very simple: We specify in a single line the service, the host or hosts affected, and optionally whether we want to grant (by default) or deny access. We'll edit the file with our favorite editor (vim, nano, etc.). The content should be similar to this:

```
[root@alpha ~]# cat /etc/hosts.allow
.
.
.
```

```
slapd: 192.168.1.230
slapd: ALL: DENY
```

In the first line we allow access to the 192.168.1.230 computer and in the second line we deny access to every computer. This way the only computer able to access will be the one with the IP address 192.168.1.230. If we had changed the order of the lines no one would have access to our LDAP, because as soon as a line matches a connection, the following lines are ignored.

We coud also have combined both lines in a single line:

```
slapd: ALL except 192.168.1.230: DENY
```

If we prefer to stick to the use of the local firewall instead of TCP wrappers, we only need to delete the lines we just added to the /etc/hosts.allow file.

# Access Control

As long as the directory gets populated with more and more data, we need to control the access to different parts of the directory. In Chapter 1 we already saw a brief example when we gave access to the admin user.

The general syntax to configure access control is as follows:

```
olcAccess: to <what> [ by <who> [<accesslevel>] [<control>]]+.
```

For example:

```
olcAccess    to * by * read
```

We already used olcAccess to give permissions to the admin user (cn=admin, dc=linuxaholics,dc=com) in Chapter 1. Now we'll see another example. First we create another user:

```
[root@alpha ldap]# cat dummy.ldif
dn: cn=dummy,dc=linuxaholics,dc=com
cn: dummy
sn: dummy
objectClass: inetOrgPerson
userPassword: dummy
uid: dummy
```

```
[root@alpha ldap]# ldapadd -f dummy.ldif -D cn=admin,dc=linuxaholics,
dc=com -w pass
adding new entry "cn=dummy,dc=linuxaholics,dc=com"
```

We can now search for users in ou=users,dc=linuxaholics,dc=com by authenticating as the user dummy.

```
[root@alpha ldap]# ldapsearch -x -D "cn=dummy,dc=linuxaholics,dc=com" -b
"ou=users,dc=linuxaholics,dc=com" -w dummy
.
.
.
# users, linuxaholics.com
dn: ou=users,dc=linuxaholics,dc=com
objectClass: organizationalUnit
ou: users

# Tux, users, linuxaholics.com
dn: cn=Tux,ou=users,dc=linuxaholics,dc=com
cn: Tux
objectClass: inetOrgPerson
userPassword:: bGludXhydWxlcw==
uid: Tux
sn: Penguin
.
.
.
```

This is possible because by default any user can perform a query like this, but we're going to change this behavior by including an olcAccess parameter in the OpenLDAP configuration. To do it we create an appropriate LDIF file.

```
dn: olcDatabase={2}hdb,cn=config
changeType: modify
add: olcAccess
olcAccess: {0} to dn.children="dc=linuxaholics,dc=com" by self write by
dn.base="gidNumber=0+uidNumber=0,cn=peercred,cn=external,cn=auth" manage by
dn.base="cn=admin,dc=linuxaholics,dc=com" read by dn.base="cn=dummy,
dc=linuxaholics,dc=com" none by * search
```

We apply the changes with ldapmodify.

```
[root@alpha ldap]# ldapmodify -Y EXTERNAL -H ldapi:/// -f acceso2.ldif
SASL/EXTERNAL authentication started
SASL username: gidNumber=0+uidNumber=0,cn=peercred,cn=external,cn=auth
SASL SSF: 0
modifying entry "olcDatabase={2}hdb,cn=config"
```

From now on if we try to search for users in "ou=users,dc=linuxaholics,dc=com" as the user named "dummy" this is what we'll get:

```
[root@alpha ldap]# ldapsearch -x -D "cn=dummy,dc=linuxaholics,dc=com" -b
"ou=users,dc=linuxaholics,dc=com" -w dummy
# extended LDIF
#
# LDAPv3
# base <ou=users,dc=linuxaholics,dc=com> with scope subtree
# filter: (objectclass=*)
# requesting: ALL
#

# search result
search: 2
result: 32 No such object

# numResponses: 1
```

However, the admin user can perform this query successfully.

```
[root@alpha ldap]# ldapsearch -x -D "cn=admin,dc=linuxaholics,dc=com" -b
"ou=users,dc=linuxaholics,dc=com" -w pass
.
.
.
# users, linuxaholics.com
dn: ou=users,dc=linuxaholics,dc=com
objectClass: organizationalUnit
```

```
ou: users
```

.

.

.

We'll give access back to the dummy user by modifying the olcAccess attribute we just added. We create another LDIF file and execute ldapmodify again.

```
[root@alpha ldap]# cat acceso3.ldif
dn: olcDatabase={2}hdb,cn=config
changeType: modify
replace: olcAccess
olcAccess: {0}to dn.children="dc=linuxaholics,dc=com" by self write by
dn.base="gidNumber=0+uidNumber=0,cn=peercred,cn=external,cn=auth" manage by
dn.base="cn=admin,dc=linuxaholics,dc=com" read by dn.base="cn=dummy,
dc=linuxaholics,dc=com" read by * search

[root@alpha ldap]# ldapadd -Y EXTERNAL -H ldapi:/// -f acceso3.ldif
SASL/EXTERNAL authentication started
SASL username: gidNumber=0+uidNumber=0,cn=peercred,cn=external,cn=auth
SASL SSF: 0
modifying entry "olcDatabase={2}hdb,cn=config"
```

The user dummy will be able to perform the query again.

```
[root@alpha ldap]# ldapsearch -x -D "cn=dummy,dc=linuxaholics,dc=com" -b
"ou=users,dc=linuxaholics,dc=com" -w dummy
```

.

.

.

```
# Tux, users, linuxaholics.com
dn: cn=Tux,ou=users,dc=linuxaholics,dc=com
cn: Tux
objectClass: inetOrgPerson
userPassword:: bGludXhhholicXhlcw==
```

```
uid: Tux
sn: Penguin
```
.

.

.

Writing access control lists (ACLs) can be tricky sometimes, but fortunately we can use the **slapacl** command to check the effective permissions when LDAP users try to access a certain object in the directory.

```
[root@alpha ldap]# slapacl -v -D "cn=dummy,dc=linuxaholics,dc=com" -b
"ou=users,dc=linuxaholics,dc=com"
58f6e058 hdb_db_open: warning - no DB_CONFIG file found in directory
/var/lib/ldap: (2).
Expect poor performance for suffix "dc=linuxaholics,dc=com".
58f6e058 hdb_db_open: warning - no DB_CONFIG file found in directory
/var/lib/ldap/accesslog: (2).
Expect poor performance for suffix "cn=accesslog".
authcDN: "cn=dummy,dc=linuxaholics,dc=com"
entry: read(=rscxd)
children: read(=rscxd)
objectClass=organizationalUnit: read(=rscxd)
ou=users: read(=rscxd)
structuralObjectClass=organizationalUnit: read(=rscxd)
entryUUID=8a8ff1a8-b6bd-1036-9538-698365415334: read(=rscxd)
creatorsName=cn=admin,dc=linuxaholics,dc=com: read(=rscxd)
createTimestamp=20170416065620Z: read(=rscxd)
entryCSN=20170416065620.713885Z#000000#000#000000: read(=rscxd)
modifiersName=cn=admin,dc=linuxaholics,dc=com: read(=rscxd)
modifyTimestamp=20170416065620Z: read(=rscxd)
```

If we had launched the **slapacl** utility before granting access back to the dummy user, this is what we would have seen.

```
[root@alpha ldap]# slapacl -v -D "cn=dummy,dc=linuxaholics,dc=com" -b
"ou=users,dc=linuxaholics,dc=com"
58f6e1bc hdb_db_open: warning - no DB_CONFIG file found in directory
/var/lib/ldap: (2).
```

```
Expect poor performance for suffix "dc=linuxaholics,dc=com".
58f6e1bc hdb_db_open: warning - no DB_CONFIG file found in directory
/var/lib/ldap/accesslog: (2).
Expect poor performance for suffix "cn=accesslog".
authcDN: "cn=dummy,dc=linuxaholics,dc=com"
entry: none(=0)
children: none(=0)
objectClass=organizationalUnit: none(=0)
ou=users: none(=0)
structuralObjectClass=organizationalUnit: none(=0)
entryUUID=8a8ff1a8-b6bd-1036-9538-698365415334: none(=0)
creatorsName=cn=admin,dc=linuxaholics,dc=com: none(=0)
createTimestamp=20170416065620Z: none(=0)
entryCSN=20170416065620.713885Z#000000#000#000000: none(=0)
modifiersName=cn=admin,dc=linuxaholics,dc=com: none(=0)
modifyTimestamp=20170416065620Z: none(=0)
```

# Authentication Methods

Usually when we access any server we have to authenticate first; that is, we provide a valid username/password combination. Nevertheless, some services allow us to access unauthenticated. To authenticate the clients, OpenLDAP can use different approaches. It can use the **bind** operation to authenticate, which in turn can use two different methods: simple and SASL.

## Simple Bind Authentication

The simple method provides three authentication mechanisms:

- Anonymous
- Unauthenticated
- User/password

Let's review each one in detail.

# Anonymous Access

In this case of an anonymous authentication mechanism, the user and the password we provide are both empty strings. Here's an example:

```
[root@alpha ldap]# ldapsearch -x -b "cn=Tux,ou=users,dc=linuxaholics,
dc=com" -D "" -w ""
# extended LDIF
#
# LDAPv3
# base <cn=Tux,ou=users,dc=linuxaholics,dc=com> with scope subtree
# filter: (objectclass=*)
# requesting: ALL
#

# search result
search: 2
result: 0 Success

# numResponses: 1
```

We got a 0 result (Success), as there is indeed a `"cn=Tux,ou=users,dc=linuxaholics,` `dc=com"` in our LDAP. If we search for an element that does not exist, the result will be pretty different.

```
[root@alpha ldap]# ldapsearch -x -b "cn=Gecko,ou=users,dc=linuxaholics,
dc=com" -D "" -w ""
# extended LDIF
#
# LDAPv3
# base <cn=Gecko,ou=users,dc=linuxaholics,dc=com> with scope subtree
# filter: (objectclass=*)
# requesting: ALL
#

# search result
search: 2
result: 32 No such object
matchedDN: ou=users,dc=linuxaholics,dc=com

# numResponses: 1
```

This time we got a 32 result (No such object), a self-explanatory message.

As we have seen so far, by accessing anonymously we can search for any entry in our LDAP, but we cannot read the attributes associated to each user, group, and so on. This behavior is normal, as the permission for the everybody user is search. We can check it like this:

```
[root@alpha ldap]# ldapsearch -Y EXTERNAL -H ldapi:/// -b "cn=config"
.

.

.

olcAccess: {0} to dn.children="dc=linuxaholics,dc=com" by self write by dn.base=
 "gidNumber=0+uidNumber=0,cn=peercred,cn=external,cn=auth" manage by dn.base=
 "cn=admin,dc=linuxaholics,dc=com" read by dn.base="cn=dummy,dc=linuxaholics,
 dc=com" none by * search
.

.

.

```

We have seen that OpenLDAP by default allows anonymous access, but of course we can disable this characteristic by adding this parameter to the configuration.

```
olcDisallows: bind_anon
```

To change this parameter, we use this LDIF file:

```
[root@alpha ldap]# cat unauth.ldif
dn: cn=config
changetype: modify
add: olcDisallows
olcDisallows: bind_anon
```

We also execute **ldapmodify**.

```
[root@alpha ldap]# ldapmodify -Y EXTERNAL -H ldapi:/// -f unauth.ldif
SASL/EXTERNAL authentication started
SASL username: gidNumber=0+uidNumber=0,cn=peercred,cn=external,cn=auth
```

```
SASL SSF: 0
modifying entry "cn=config"
```

From now on, if we try to access anonymously, we get the following error:

```
[root@alpha ldap]# ldapsearch -x -b "dc=linuxaholics,dc=com" -D "" -w ""
ldap_bind: Inappropriate authentication (48)
        additional info: anonymous bind disallowed
```

If we want to undo this change, we'll need to use **ldapmodify** again with the following LDIF file:

```
dn: cn=config
changetype: modify
delete: olcDisallows
```

```
[root@alpha ldap]# ldapmodify -Y EXTERNAL -H ldapi:/// -f reauth.ldif
SASL/EXTERNAL authentication started
SASL username: gidNumber=0+uidNumber=0,cn=peercred,cn=external,cn=auth
SASL SSF: 0
modifying entry "cn=config"
```

We will then be able to access anonymously again.

## Unauthenticated Access

As opposed to the first mechanism, with the unauthenticated authentication mechanism, we specify a user, but we provide an empty string as the password. This mechanism is disabled by default as we can see in the following example:

```
[root@alpha ldap]# ldapsearch -v -x -b "ou=users,dc=linuxaholics,dc=com" -D "cn=admin,dc=linuxaholics,dc=com" -w ""
ldap_initialize( <DEFAULT> )
ldap_bind: Server is unwilling to perform (53)
        additional info: unauthenticated bind (DN with no password)
        disallowed
```

If we want to enable unauthenticated access, we need to add a new parameter to the configuration with **ldapmodify** and a proper LDIF file.

```
dn: cn=config
changeType: modify
add: olcAllows
olcAllows: bind_anon_dn
```

```
[root@alpha ldap]# ldapmodify -Y EXTERNAL -H ldapi:/// -f unauthen.ldif
SASL/EXTERNAL authentication started
SASL username: gidNumber=0+uidNumber=0,cn=peercred,cn=external,cn=auth
SASL SSF: 0
modifying entry "cn=config"
```

If we repeat the query now, we'll see that we can query the LDAP server with an empty password.

```
[root@alpha ldap]# ldapsearch -x -b "ou=users,dc=linuxaholics,dc=com" -D
"cn=admin,dc=linuxaholics,dc=com" -w ""
# extended LDIF
#
# LDAPv3
# base <ou=users,dc=linuxaholics,dc=com> with scope subtree
# filter: (objectclass=*)
# requesting: ALL
#

# search result
search: 2
result: 0 Success

# numResponses: 1
```

However, as it is a good idea to keep unauthenticated access disabled, we'll revert the change by deleting the parameter olcAllows we just added.

```
dn: cn=config
changeType: modify
delete: olcAllows
```

```
[root@alpha ldap]# ldapmodify -Y EXTERNAL -H ldapi:/// -f dis_unauthen.ldif
SASL/EXTERNAL authentication started
SASL username: gidNumber=0+uidNumber=0,cn=peercred,cn=external,cn=auth
SASL SSF: 0
modifying entry "cn=config"
```

## Access with User/Password

Finally, a username/password authentication mechanism uses credentials consisting of a name (in the form of an LDAP DN) and a password. We have already used this type of authentication several times in the book.

```
[root@alpha ldap]# ldapsearch -v -x -b "dc=linuxaholics,dc=com" -D
"cn=admin,dc=linuxaholics,dc=com" -w "pass"
```

# SASL

In turn, the SASL method is a framework that allows the use of several authentication mechanisms: GSSAPI for Kerberos, PLAIN, EXTERNAL, and so on.

In previous sections we have already used SASL with the EXTERNAL authentication mechanism. This is an example:

```
[root@alpha ldap]# ldapsearch -Y EXTERNAL -H ldapi:/// -b cn=config
olcDatabase=\*
SASL/EXTERNAL authentication started
SASL username: gidNumber=0+uidNumber=0,cn=peercred,cn=external,cn=auth
SASL SSF: 0
.
.
.
```

We launched **ldapsearch**, without the -x flag, so that SASL instead of simple bind is used. Next, we specify the SASL mechanism to use (EXTERNAL in this case). The EXTERNAL mechanism uses authentication services offered by lower network services. When used with the ldapi:/// transport it can report the User Identifier (UID) and Group Identifier (GID) of the client process.

The libraries needed for the SASL framework to work are provided by the `cyrus-sasl` package, which is installed as a dependency when installing OpenLDAP. We have already used SASL when executing utilities like **ldapsearch**. SASL can be used with EXTERNAL mechanisms, Kerberos, and so on, but it can also use secrets stored in the directory itself or in its own database.

## Sasldb

One of the SASL mechanisms is sasldb, which is one of the key concepts included in the LPIC-300 objectives. Curiously, this doesn't seem to be the preferred way to authenticate users currently. In fact, if we take a look at the man page of the SLAS service (saslauthd), this is what we'll see:

```
sasldb     (All platforms)
```

```
Authenticate against the SASL authentication database.  Note
that this is probably not what you want to use, and is even
disabled at compile-time by default.  If you want to use
sasldb with the SASL library, you probably want to use the
pwcheck_method of "auxprop" along with the sasldb auxprop
plugin instead.
```

Anyway, because sasldb is included in the certification objectives, we'll go over how we can configure it. First of all, check whether the sasldb plug-in is ready.

```
[root@alpha ~]# pluginviewer -a

Installed and properly configured auxprop mechanisms are:
sasldb
List of auxprop plugins follows
Plugin "sasldb" ,         API version: 8

        supports store: yes
```

Because SASL can be used by different applications, we can create a customized configuration file in the `/usr/lib64/sasl2` folder for every service that uses SASL. The name of the file must be that of the service with the `conf` extension, so in our case we'll create a `slapd.conf` file with this content:

```
[root@alpha ldap]# cat /usr/lib64/sasl2/slapd.conf
pwcheck_method: auxprop
sasldb_path: /etc/sasldb2
```

> **Note**    Somehow, there seems to be some bug when using the auxprop plug-in. Occasionally it seems not to be able to get a list of the supported SASL mechanisms. In this case you'd probably need to either add or remove and add this line to the configuration file:
>
> ```
> [root@alpha ldap]# cat /usr/lib64/sasl2/slapd.conf
> .
> .
> .
>
> mech_list: PLAIN LOGIN EXTERNAL CRAM-MD5 DIGEST-MD5 GSSAPI
> .
> .
> .
> ```

In addition, we need to include the olcSaslAuxprops in the LDAP configuration, so that we can authenticate against the local SASL database.

```
[root@alpha ldap]# cat sasldb.ldif
dn: cn=config
changetype: modify
replace: olcSaslAuxprops
olcSaslAuxprops: sasldb
[root@alpha ldap]# ldapmodify -Y EXTERNAL -H ldapi:/// -f sasldb.ldif
SASL/EXTERNAL authentication started
SASL username: gidNumber=0+uidNumber=0,cn=peercred,cn=external,cn=auth
SASL SSF: 0
modifying entry "cn=config"
```

We create users in the SASL user database through the use of the **saslpasswd2** command.

```
[root@alpha ldap]# saslpasswd2 -c Tux
Password:
Again (for verification):
```

We can also list the existing users with the **sasldblistusers** command.

```
[root@alpha ldap]# sasldblistusers2
Tux@alpha.linuxaholics.com: userPassword
```

When using SASL, we must also specify the mechanism used. By default, DIGEST-MD5 is used, so we must be sure that our OpenLDAP server supports it. We can check this point with the following command:

```
[root@alpha ldap]# ldapsearch -Y EXTERNAL -H ldapi:/// -b "" -s base -LLL
supportedSASLMechanisms
SASL/EXTERNAL authentication started
SASL username: gidNumber=0+uidNumber=0,cn=peercred,cn=external,cn=auth
SASL SSF: 0
dn:
supportedSASLMechanisms: EXTERNAL
supportedSASLMechanisms: PLAIN
supportedSASLMechanisms: LOGIN
```

In this case our OpenLDAP server does not support DIGEST-MD5, so we need to install the corresponding package.

```
[root@alpha ldap]# yum install -y cyrus-sasl-md5
```

After restarting the LDAP service, we'll see that our server now supports DIGEST-MD5.

```
[root@alpha ldap]# systemctl restart slapd
[root@alpha ldap]# ldapsearch -Y EXTERNAL -H ldapi:/// -b "" -s base -LLL
supportedSASLMechanisms
SASL/EXTERNAL authentication started
SASL username: gidNumber=0+uidNumber=0,cn=peercred,cn=external,cn=auth
SASL SSF: 0
```

```
dn:
supportedSASLMechanisms: DIGEST-MD5
supportedSASLMechanisms: EXTERNAL
supportedSASLMechanisms: CRAM-MD5
supportedSASLMechanisms: LOGIN
supportedSASLMechanisms: PLAIN
```

From now on we should be able to use simple bind authentication as well as SASL authentication. To check it, we'll execute a query as the Tux user we defined initially in LDAP, with the associated password linuxrules:

```
[root@alpha ldap]# ldapsearch -x -D "cn=Tux,ou=users,dc=linuxaholics,
dc=com" -b "ou=users,dc=linuxaholics,dc=com" "(cn=Tux)" -w linuxrules
# extended LDIF
#
# LDAPv3
# base <ou=users,dc=linuxaholics,dc=com> with scope subtree
# filter: (cn=Tux)
# requesting: ALL
#

# Tux, users, linuxaholics.com
dn: cn=Tux,ou=users,dc=linuxaholics,dc=com
cn: Tux
objectClass: inetOrgPerson
userPassword:: bGludXhydWxlcw==
uid: Tux
sn: Penguin

# search result
search: 2
result: 0 Success

# numResponses: 2
# numEntries: 1
```

Now we launch the query as the Tux user we created in the SASL local database with password Tux.

```
[root@alpha ldap]# ldapsearch -U Tux -b "ou=users,dc=linuxaholics,dc=com"
-w Tux
SASL/DIGEST-MD5 authentication started
SASL username: Tux
SASL SSF: 128
SASL data security layer installed.
# extended LDIF
#
# LDAPv3
# base <ou=users,dc=linuxaholics,dc=com> with scope subtree
# filter: (objectclass=*)
# requesting: ALL
#

# search result
search: 4
result: 0 Success

# numResponses: 1
```

We're not able to see anything, but we see that the authentication was successful. We couldn't read the data because currently we don't have access permissions to it. Remember from a previous section the user everybody (*) only has search permissions. For didactic purposes and because we are working in a lab environment, we'll change this setting to allow those users below the ou=users,dc=linuxaholics,dc=com branch to read data, although this might not be the best solution in a production environment. We create the corresponding LDIF file and apply it.

```
[root@alpha ldap]# cat acceso4.ldif
dn: olcDatabase={2}hdb,cn=config
changeType: modify
replace: olcAccess
olcAccess: {0}to dn.children="dc=linuxaholics,dc=com" by self write by
dn.base="gidNumber=0+uidNumber=0,cn=peercred,cn=external,cn=auth" manage
by dn.base="cn=admin,dc=linuxaholics,dc=com" read by dn.base="cn=dummy,
```

```
dc=linuxaholics,dc=com" read by dn.children="ou=users,dc=linuxaholics,
dc=com" read by * search

[root@alpha ldap]# ldapmodify -Y EXTERNAL -H ldapi:/// -f acceso4.ldif
SASL/EXTERNAL authentication started
SASL username: gidNumber=0+uidNumber=0,cn=peercred,cn=external,cn=auth
SASL SSF: 0
modifying entry "olcDatabase={2}hdb,cn=config"
```

If we repeat the query now, we'll be able to read the data.

```
[root@alpha ldap]# ldapsearch -U Tux -b "ou=users,dc=linuxaholics,dc=com"
-w Tux
SASL/DIGEST-MD5 authentication started
SASL username: Tux
SASL SSF: 128
SASL data security layer installed.
# extended LDIF
#
# LDAPv3
# base <ou=users,dc=linuxaholics,dc=com> with scope subtree
# filter: (objectclass=*)
# requesting: ALL
#
.
.
.
# Tux, users, linuxaholics.com
dn: cn=Tux,ou=users,dc=linuxaholics,dc=com
cn: Tux
objectClass: inetOrgPerson
userPassword:: bGludXhydWxlcw==
uid: Tux
sn: Penguin
.
.
.
```

When a user authenticates through the use of SASL, the OpenLDAP server will receive the following pieces of information from the client:

- Username.

- Realm (this is optional).

- SASL mechanism.

- Authentication information.

This information will be compacted in a string like this:

```
uid=Tux,cn=digest-md5,cn=auth
```

Of course, right now we don't have any DN in our LDAP that matches this DN, so we'll need to convert the given string into something like this:

```
uid=Tux,ou=users,dc=linuxaholics,dc=com
```

Because we already created the ou=users,dc=linuxaholics,dc=com branch in our LDAP server.

## Mapping UID Identities

To map the original string SASL generates into the new one, we'll have to include a string replacement rule. This can be done with the **olcAuthzRegexp** directive.

We include this new directive the usual way, by creating an LDIF file and executing **ldapadd**. However, let's look at an easy example. Previously, we created a local database user named Tux. If we use the **ldapwhoami** command, we can see the effective user ID to which it maps.

```
[root@alpha ldap]# ldapwhoami -U Tux -w Tux
SASL/DIGEST-MD5 authentication started
SASL username: Tux
SASL SSF: 128
SASL data security layer installed.
dn:uid=tux,cn=digest-md5,cn=auth
```

Now we'll create the following LDIF file and apply the changes to the server.

```
[root@alpha ldap]# cat mapexample.ldif
dn: cn=config
changetype: modify
add: olcAuthzRegexp
olcAuthzRegexp: "uid=tux,cn=digest-md5,cn=auth" "uid=Tux,ou=users,
dc=linuxaholics,dc=com"

[root@alpha ldap]# ldapmodify -Y EXTERNAL -H ldapi:/// -f mapexample.ldif
SASL/EXTERNAL authentication started
SASL username: gidNumber=0+uidNumber=0,cn=peercred,cn=external,cn=auth
SASL SSF: 0
modifying entry "cn=config"
```

After executing **ldapwhoami** again, we see that the mapping is working as expected.

```
[root@alpha ldap]# ldapwhoami -U Tux -w Tux
SASL/DIGEST-MD5 authentication started
SASL username: Tux
SASL SSF: 128
SASL data security layer installed.
dn:uid=tux,ou=users,dc=linuxaholics,dc=com
```

It only works for the user Tux, though. If we add another user to the local user database it won't be mapped. To solve this problem, we need to create a generic rule that maps every local user. We can do it by using regular expressions. How to write regular expresions is a subject beyond the scope of this book, and there are already many good books and tutorials available. We'll just replace the mapping here without discussing the many details of the regular expression used.

```
[root@bravo ldap]# cat regexp.ldif
dn: cn=config
changeType: modify
replace: olcAuthzRegexp
olcAuthzRegexp: "^uid=([^,]+).*,cn=auth$" "uid=$1,ou=users,dc=linuxaholics,
dc=com"
```

```
[root@bravo ldap]# ldapmodify -Y EXTERNAL -H ldapi:/// -f regexp.ldif
SASL/EXTERNAL authentication started
SASL username: gidNumber=0+uidNumber=0,cn=peercred,cn=external,cn=auth
SASL SSF: 0
modifying entry "cn=config"
```

From now on we can use commands like **ldapsearch** using SASL authentication.

## Using LDAP as a Back End

So far, we have used SASL with a local database. As we mentioned before, this is not the preferred way to implement SASL, so this time we'll take a different approach.

As we won't be using the local database, we need to edit the olcSaslAuxprops parameter in our LDAP configuration.

```
[root@alpha ldap]# cat sasl_ldap.ldif
dn: cn=config
changetype: modify
replace: olcSaslAuxprops
olcSaslAuxprops: slapd
[root@alpha ldap]# ldapmodify -Y EXTERNAL -H ldapi:/// -f sasl_ldap.ldif
SASL/EXTERNAL authentication started
SASL username: gidNumber=0+uidNumber=0,cn=peercred,cn=external,cn=auth
SASL SSF: 0
modifying entry "cn=config"
```

When using the LDAP server itself to store the SASL users, we need the users to have a UID defined and the password in clear text. We'll create a new user taking this into consideration.

```
[root@alpha ldap]# cat antonio.ldif
dn: uid=Antonio,ou=users,dc=linuxaholics,dc=com
cn: Antonio
sn: Vazquez
objectClass: inetOrgPerson
userPassword: antonio
uid: Antonio
```

```
[root@alpha ldap]# ldapadd -x -D "cn=admin,dc=linuxaholics,dc=com" -w
pass  -f antonio.ldif
adding new entry "uid=Antonio,ou=users,dc=linuxaholics,dc=com"
```

After restarting the service, we are ready to use SASL authentication against the LDAP server. To check it we can execute the **ldapwhoami** command.

```
[root@alpha ldap]# systemctl restart slapd
[root@alpha ldap]# ldapwhoami -U Antonio -w antonio
SASL/DIGEST MD5 authentication started
SASL username: Antonio
SASL SSF: 128
SASL data security layer installed.
dn:uid=antonio,ou=users,dc=linuxaholics,dc=com
```

Alternatively, we can perform a typical search with **ldapsearch**.

```
[root@alpha ldap]# ldapsearch -H ldap://alpha.linuxaholics.com -U Antonio
-w antonio -b "ou=users,dc=linuxaholics,dc=com"
SASL/DIGEST-MD5 authentication started
SASL username: Antonio
SASL SSF: 128
SASL data security layer installed.
# extended LDIF
#
.
.
.

# users, linuxaholics.com
dn: ou=users,dc=linuxaholics,dc=com
objectClass: organizationalUnit
ou: users
.
.
.
```

## saslauthd

SASL can use different mechanisms to authenticate a user, the default being DIGEST-MD5. We'll check the currently supported mechanisms, and if DIGEST-MD5 isn't supported we'll install the necessary packages.

```
[root@alpha ~]# ldapsearch -x -H ldapi:/// -b "" -s base -LLL
supportedSASLMechanisms
dn:
supportedSASLMechanisms: EXTERNAL
supportedSASLMechanisms: LOGIN
supportedSASLMechanisms: PLAIN

[root@alpha ~]# yum install cyrus-sasl-md5
[root@alpha ~]# systemctl restart slapd

[root@alpha ~]# ldapsearch -x -H ldapi:/// -b "" -s base -LLL
supportedSASLMechanisms
dn:
supportedSASLMechanisms: DIGEST-MD5
supportedSASLMechanisms: EXTERNAL
supportedSASLMechanisms: CRAM-MD5
supportedSASLMechanisms: LOGIN
supportedSASLMechanisms: PLAIN
```

As we said before, for SASL authentication to work we rely on the saslauthd service, which in turn is configured in the /etc/sysconfig/saslauthd file. If we take a look at it, this is what we'll see:

```
[root@alpha ~]# cat /etc/sysconfig/saslauthd
.
.
.
# Mechanism to use when checking passwords.  Run "saslauthd -v" to get a list
# of which mechanism your installation was compiled with the ablity to use.
MECH=pam
.
.
.
```

We need to indicate the right mechanism to use, and we can see the available mechanisms by executing **saslauthd -v**.

```
[root@alpha ~]# saslauthd -v
saslauthd 2.1.26
authentication mechanisms: getpwent kerberos5 pam rimap shadow ldap
httpform
```

So, in our case we'll have to change the value of the MECH parameter to ldap.

```
MECH=ldap
```

To keep configuring SASL authentication we can take a quick look at the help file in the /usr/share/doc/cyrus-sasl folder.

This is part of the information we can see in it:

- 
- 
- 

```
2. START SASLAUTHD WITH LDAP
----------------------------

Create /usr/local/etc/saslauthd.conf and add the following (modify to fit your
environment):
ldap_servers: ldap://10.1.1.15/ ldap://10.1.1.25/
ldap_bind_dn: cn=operator,ou=Profile,o=foo.com
ldap_password: secret

Do not specify ldap_bind_*/ldap_password if you want to bind anonymously to
your ldap server(s).
```

- 
- 
- 

Even though the document says to create a configuration file at /usr/local/etc/saslauthd.conf, the right location should be at /etc/saslauthd.conf. We can check this in the man page of the **saslauthd** command.

```
[root@alpha ~]# man saslauthd
•

•

•

FILES
    /run/saslauthd/mux  The default communications socket.

    /etc/saslauthd.conf
                    The default configuration file for ldap support.
•

•

•
```

We'll create a configuration file with the following lines:

```
[root@alpha ~]# cat /etc/saslauthd.conf
ldap_servers: ldap://127.0.0.1
ldap_bind_dn: cn=Tux,ou=users,dc=linuxaholics,dc=com
ldap_password: linuxrules
```

We indicate the address of our LDAP server as well as the LDAP account used to perform the queries and the password associated with this account. Once we're done with all the changes, we restart the LDAP and the saslauthd services.

We can check that SASL authentication is working with the **testsaslauthd** command.

```
[root@alpha ~]# testsaslauthd -u Tux -p linuxrules -f /run/saslauthd/mux
0: NO "authentication failed"
```

We can see that the authorization failed, so we'll include an additional parameter to indicate the base search.

```
[root@alpha ~]# cat /etc/saslauthd.conf
ldap_servers: ldap://127.0.0.1
ldap_search_base: ou=users,dc=linuxaholics,dc=com
ldap_bind_dn: cn=Tux,ou=users,dc=linuxaholics,dc=com
ldap_password: linuxrules
```

After restarting the **saslauthd** service, if we repeat the test, this time the result will be successful.

```
[root@alpha ~]# testsaslauthd -u Tux -p linuxrules -f /run/saslauthd/mux
0: OK "Success."
```

# SASL Proxy Authorization

SASL has a nice feature known as **proxy authorization**, which allows an authenticated user to request that they act on behalf of another user. This is useful in many cases. For instance, if a group of users need to have the same access rights to a certain resource, we could grant access to a single account and allow every user needing these access rights to act on behalf of that account. This can be achieved by using SASL proxy authorization.

Let's suppose we have defined the user cn=WebApp,ou=apps,dc=linuxaholics,dc= com in our LDAP server for the Web application. If we haven't created it yet, we can do it now.

```
[root@alpha ldap]# cat apps.ldif
dn: ou=apps,dc=linuxaholics,dc=com
objectClass: organizationalUnit
ou: apps
[root@alpha ldap]# ldapadd -H ldap://alpha.linuxaholics.com -f apps.ldif -D
cn=admin,dc=linuxaholics,dc=com -w pass
adding new entry "ou=apps,dc=linuxaholics,dc=com"

[root@alpha ldap]# cat Webapp.ldif
dn: cn=WebApp,ou=apps,dc=linuxaholics,dc=com
cn: WebApp
sn: User for WebApp
objectClass: inetOrgPerson
userPassword: WebApp
uid: WebApp

[root@alpha ldap]# ldapadd -H ldap://alpha.linuxaholics.com -f Webapp.ldif -D
cn=admin,dc=linuxaholics,dc=com -w pass
adding new entry "cn=WebApp,ou=apps,dc=linuxaholics,dc=com"
```

Now we'll suppose that user webmaster has read permission over ou=apps,
dc=linuxaholics,dc=com but the rest of the users don't. We can create the webmaster
user the same way we did before when we created the user Antonio.

```
[root@alpha ldap]# cat webmaster.ldif
dn: uid=webmaster,ou=users,dc=linuxaholics,dc=com
cn: webmaster
sn: Web Master
objectClass: inetOrgPerson
userPassword: webmaster
uid: webmaster

[root@alpha ldap]# ldapadd -H ldap://alpha.linuxaholics.com -x -D "cn=admin,
dc=linuxaholics,dc=com" -w pass  -f webmaster.ldif
adding new entry "uid=webmaster,ou=users,dc=linuxaholics,dc=com"
```

We also have to add a new olcAccess directive to grant read access to the ou=apps,
dc=linuxaholics,dc=com branch only to the webmaster user.

```
[root@alpha ldap]# cat acceso7.ldif
dn: olcDatabase={2}hdb,cn=config
changeType: modify
add: olcAccess
olcAccess: {0}to dn.children="ou=apps,dc=linuxaholics,dc=com" by self write
by dn.base="gidNumber=0+uidNumber=0,cn=peercred,cn=external,cn=auth" manage
by dn.base="cn=admin,dc=linuxaholics,dc=com" read by dn="uid=webmaster,
ou=users,dc=linuxaholics,dc=com" read by * search

[root@alpha ldap]# ldapmodify -Y EXTERNAL -H ldapi:/// -f acceso7.ldif
SASL/EXTERNAL authentication started
SASL username: gidNumber=0+uidNumber=0,cn=peercred,cn=external,cn=auth
SASL SSF: 0
modifying entry "olcDatabase={2}hdb,cn=config"
```

By default, the processing of proxy authorization rules is disabled, so we need to
change this default behavior by adding the olcAuthzPolicy parameter to the global
configuration.

```
[root@alpha ldap]# cat preproxy.ldif
dn: cn=config
changetype: modify
add: olcAuthzPolicy
olcAuthzPolicy: both
[root@alpha ldap]# ldapmodify -Y EXTERNAL -H ldapi:/// -f preproxy.ldif
SASL/EXTERNAL authentication started
SASL username: gidNumber=0+uidNumber=0,cn=peercred,cn=external,cn=auth
SASL SSF: 0
modifying entry "cn=config"
```

Now we'll modify the Web App user definition to include the saslAuthzFrom
parameter.

```
[root@alpha ldap]# cat modwebmaster.ldif
dn: uid=webmaster,ou=users,dc=linuxaholics,dc=com
changetype: modify
add: saslAuthzFrom
saslAuthzFrom: dn:uid=Antonio,ou=users,dc=linuxaholics,dc=com

[root@alpha ldap]# ldapmodify -x -D cn=admin,dc=linuxaholics,dc=com -w pass
-f modwebmaster.ldif
modifying entry "uid=webmaster,ou=users,dc=linuxaholics,dc=com"
```

Initially, we see that the webmaster user has read access to ou=apps,dc=linuxaholics,
dc=com.

```
[root@alpha ldap]# ldapsearch -U webmaster -w webmaster -b "ou=apps,
dc=linuxaholics,dc=Com" "(uid=webApp)"
SASL/DIGEST-MD5 authentication started
SASL username: webmaster
SASL SSF: 128
SASL data security layer installed.
.
.
.
```

```
# WebApp, apps, linuxaholics.com
dn: uid=WebApp,ou=apps,dc=linuxaholics,dc=com
cn: WebApp
sn: User for WebApp
objectClass: inetOrgPerson
userPassword:: V2ViQXBw
uid: WebApp

# search result
search: 4
result: 0 Success

# numResponses: 2
# numEntries: 1
```

Antonio, though, has no read access to that branch.

```
[root@alpha ldap]# ldapsearch -U Antonio -w antonio -b "ou=apps,
dc=linuxaholics,dc=com" "(uid=webApp)"
SASL/DIGEST-MD5 authentication started
SASL username: Antonio
SASL SSF: 128
SASL data security layer installed.
# extended LDIF
#
# LDAPv3
# base <ou=apps,dc=linuxaholics,dc=Com> with scope subtree
# filter: (uid=webApp)
# requesting: ALL
#

# search result
search: 4
result: 0 Success

# numResponses: 1
```

However, we can use SASL proxy authorization when executing **ldapsearch**.

```
[root@alpha ldap]# ldapsearch -U Antonio -w antonio -b "ou=apps,
dc=linuxaholics,dc=com" "(uid=webApp)" -X u:webmaster
SASL/DIGEST-MD5 authentication started
SASL username: u:webmaster
SASL SSF: 128
SASL data security layer installed.
.

.

.

# WebApp, apps, linuxaholics.com
dn: uid=WebApp,ou=apps,dc=linuxaholics,dc=com
cn: WebApp
sn: User for WebApp
objectClass: inetOrgPerson
userPassword:: V2ViQXBw
uid: WebApp

# search result
search: 4
result: 0 Success

# numResponses: 2
# numEntries: 1
```

We can see that this way Antonio was able to read the data without needing to type any additional passwords.

# Client Certificate

We've already seen in this same chapter how to use a server certificate to secure connections to the LDAP server. To add an additional layer of security we can also use client certificates.

We'll create a new certificate for our client computer (bravo.linuxaholics.com). The procedure is quite similar to what we did when creating the server certificate.

We already created our own CA, so we don't need to repeat this process. We'll start by generating the key for the new client certificate.

```
[root@alpha CA]# openssl genrsa -out /etc/pki/CA/private/bravo.
linuxaholics.com.key
Generating RSA private key, 2048 bit long modulus
..........................................+++
.................+++
e is 65537 (0x10001)
```

Next, we create the certificate request.

```
[root@alpha CA]# openssl req -new -key /etc/pki/CA/private/bravo.
linuxaholics.com.key -out /etc/pki/CA/certs/bravo.linuxaholics.com.csr
You are about to be asked to enter information that will be incorporated
into your certificate request.
What you are about to enter is what is called a Distinguished Name or a DN.
There are quite a few fields but you can leave some blank
For some fields there will be a default value,
If you enter '.', the field will be left blank.
-----
Country Name (2 letter code) [XX]:ES
State or Province Name (full name) []:Madrid
Locality Name (eg, city) [Default City]:Madrid
Organization Name (eg, company) [Default Company Ltd]:linuxaholics
Organizational Unit Name (eg, section) []:
Common Name (eg, your name or your server's hostname) []:bravo.linuxaholics.com
Email Address []:

Please enter the following 'extra' attributes
to be sent with your certificate request
A challenge password []:
An optional company name []:
```

We sign the request with our CA to obtain the actual certificate file.

```
[root@alpha CA]# openssl ca -keyfile /etc/pki/CA/private/ca.key.pem -cert
/etc/pki/CA/certs/ca.cert.pem -in /etc/pki/CA/certs/bravo.linuxaholics.com.
csr -out /etc/pki/CA/certs/bravo.linuxaholics.com.crt
Using configuration from /etc/pki/tls/openssl.cnf
Enter pass phrase for /etc/pki/CA/private/ca.key.pem:
Check that the request matches the signature
Signature ok
Certificate Details:
        Serial Number: 2 (0x2)
        Validity
            Not Before: Jan 24 12:22:09 2018 GMT
            Not After : Jan 24 12:22:09 2019 GMT
        Subject:
            countryName               = ES
            stateOrProvinceName       = Madrid
            organizationName          = linuxaholics
            commonName                = bravo.linuxaholics.com
        X509v3 extensions:
            X509v3 Basic Constraints:
                CA:FALSE
            Netscape Comment:
                OpenSSL Generated Certificate
            X509v3 Subject Key Identifier:
                31:DD:BA:DF:34:3F:C2:EC:3A:1E:0E:38:38:BF:0F:3A:88:5A:93:B0
            X509v3 Authority Key Identifier:
                keyid:86:89:9E:9C:4F:A9:34:6A:38:CB:EE:EF:78:2A:4F:BD:CD:
                8F:59:07

Certificate is to be certified until Jan 24 12:22:09 2019 GMT (365 days)
Sign the certificate? [y/n]:y

1 out of 1 certificate requests certified, commit? [y/n]y
Write out database with 1 new entries
Data Base Updated
```

Now we just need to transfer the client certificate file, as well as the CA certificate file, to the client computer.

```
[root@bravo ~]# mkdir /etc/keys
[root@bravo ~]# mkdir /etc/CAcertificates
[root@bravo ~]# mkdir /etc/certificates
[root@bravo ~]# cd /etc/certificates/
[root@bravo certificates]# scp root@alpha.linuxaholics.com:/etc/pki/CA/
certs/bravo.linuxaholics.com.crt .
root@alpha.linuxaholics.com's password:
bravo.linuxaholics.com.crt                    100% 3012     2.9KB/s   00:00
[root@bravo certificates]# scp root@alpha.linuxaholics.com:/etc/pki/CA/
certs/ca.cert.pem ../CAcertificates
root@alpha.linuxaholics.com's password:
ca.cert.pem                                   100%  875     0.9KB/s   00:00
[root@bravo certificates]# scp root@alpha.linuxaholics.com:/etc/pki/CA/
private/bravo.linuxaholics.com.key ../keys/
root@alpha.linuxaholics.com's password:
bravo.linuxaholics.com.key                    100% 1679     1.6KB/s   00:00
```

We'll start by trying to establish a secure connection from the bravo client computer to the LDAP server.

```
[root@bravo ~]# ldapsearch -H ldaps://alpha.linuxaholics.com -U Antonio -w
antonio -b "ou=users,dc=linuxaholics,dc=com"
ldap_sasl_interactive_bind_s: Unknown authentication method (-6)
    additional info: SASL(-4): no mechanism available: No worthy mechs
    found
```

As we're trying to use SASL, we get an error because we haven't installed the needed libraries in the client computer. We'll install the cyrus-sasl and cyrus-sasl-md5 packages.

```
[root@bravo ~]# yum install -y cyrus-sasl cyrus-sasl-md5
```

We then repeat the query again, and it will work as expected.

```
[root@bravo ~]# ldapsearch -H ldaps://alpha.linuxaholics.com -U Antonio -w
antonio -b "ou=users,dc=linuxaholics,dc=com"
SASL/DIGEST-MD5 authentication started
SASL username: Antonio
SASL SSF: 128
SASL data security layer installed.
.
.
.
# users, linuxaholics.com
dn: ou=users,dc=linuxaholics,dc=com
objectClass: organizationalUnit
ou: users
.
.
.
```

For the OpenLDAP server to request a valid client certificate, we need to include the olcTLSVerifyClient parameter. This parameter can take different values:

- never: The server will not request any client certificate.

- allow: The client certificate is requested, but the session proceeds normally even if no certificate or a bad certificate is provided.

- try: The client certificate is provided. If no certificate is provided, the session proceeds normally, but if a bad certificate is provided the session is terminated immediately.

- demand | hard: These two keywords are equivalent. The server requests a valid client certificate. If a valid client certificate is not provided, the session is terminated.

```
[root@alpha ldap]# cat certclient.ldif
dn: cn=config
changetype: modify
add: olcTLSVerifyClient
```

```
olcTLSVerifyClient: demand

[root@alpha ldap]# ldapmodify -Y EXTERNAL -H ldapi:/// -f certclient.ldif
SASL/EXTERNAL authentication started
SASL username: gidNumber=0+uidNumber=0,cn=peercred,cn=external,cn=auth
SASL SSF: 0
modifying entry "cn=config"
```

If we try to connect again from the bravo computer, we'll get this error.

```
[root@bravo ~]# ldapsearch -H ldaps://alpha.linuxaholics.com -U Antonio -w
antonio -b "ou=users,dc=linuxaholics,dc=com"
ldap_sasl_interactive_bind_s: Can't contact LDAP server (-1)
    additional info: TLS error -12271:SSL peer cannot verify your
    certificate.
```

The **ldapsearch** command executed in bravo couldn't present a valid certificate, so according to the new server configuration, the connection was rejected.

In the /etc/openldap/ldapconf file we can add many parameters to tune the behavior of **ldapsearch** and other LDAP client utilities. We need to add the TLS_CERT parameter, which specifies the file that contains the client certificate, and the TLS_KEY, which indicates where the key file is located. We should also specify the CA certificate location with the TLS_CACERTDIR parameter.

We have seen previously that many OpenLDAP client utilities like **ldapsearch** use the /etc/openldap/ldap.conf file as a configuration file from which to get the default values for many different parameters, such as the LDAP server name or address and the base search. This file is global; that is, it applies for every user executing the client utilities. There are also two more files with the same syntax that can be found in the user's home directory and apply only to that user. These two files are ldaprc and .ldaprc.

For the client certificate to be correctly verified by the server, the two parameters we talked about earlier, TLS_CERT and TLS_KEY, must be specified in the .ldaprc file. If they are included in the /etc/openldap/ldap.conf file they will be ignored.

```
[root@bravo ~]# cat .ldaprc
TLS_CERT        /etc/certificates/bravo.linuxaholics.com.crt
TLS_KEY         /etc/keys/bravo.linuxaholics.com.key
```

Now we can establish the secure connection again.

```
[root@bravo ~]# ldapsearch -H ldaps://alpha.linuxaholics.com -U Antonio -w
antonio -b "ou=users,dc=linuxaholics,dc=com" "(cn=Tux)"
SASL/DIGEST-MD5 authentication started
SASL username: Duke
SASL SSF: 128
SASL data security layer installed.
# extended LDIF
#
# LDAPv3
# base <ou=users,dc=linuxaholics,dc=com> with scope subtree
# filter: (cn=Tux)
# requesting: ALL
#

# Tux, users, linuxaholics.com
dn: cn=Tux,ou=users,dc=linuxaholics,dc=com
cn: Tux
objectClass: inetOrgPerson
userPassword:: bGludXhydWxlcw==
uid: Tux
sn: Penguin

# search result
search: 4
result: 0 Success

# numResponses: 2
# numEntries: 1
```

After checking that the server verifies correctly the client's certificate, we'll revert the change so that this behavior doesn't interfere with the next examples in the book.

```
[root@alpha ldap]# cat nocertclient.ldif
dn: cn=config
changetype: modify
replace: olcTLSVerifyClient
olcTLSVerifyClient: never
```

```
[root@alpha ldap]# ldapmodify -Y EXTERNAL -H ldapi:/// -f nocertclient.ldif
SASL/EXTERNAL authentication started
SASL username: gidNumber=0+uidNumber=0,cn=peercred,cn=external,cn=auth
SASL SSF: 0
modifying entry "cn=config"
```

# Security Strength Factor

The Security Strength Factor (SSF) indicates how strong the security is. If the value is 0 the connection is not secure. If the value is 1 only the integrity is checked. Finally, if the value is greater than 1 the connection is considered secure and in addition to integrity, encryption and authorization are supported. The exact value indicates the key length. By this point we have seen many examples of this in this book.

# Debugging and Troubleshooting

The proper setup of SASL is not trivial and it is very easy to make mistakes that prevent the service from working in the expected way. In these cases, it can be useful to execute slapd with debugging options.

First, we stop the slapd service.

```
[root@alpha ~]# systemctl stop slapd
```

To execute slapd with debugging options we need to use the -d parameter. Simply by passing the ? value we get a list of the values that correspond with the different debug options.

```
[root@alpha ~]# slapd -d ?
Installed log subsystems:

        Any                             (-1, 0xffffffff)
        Trace                           (1, 0x1)
        Packets                         (2, 0x2)
        Args                            (4, 0x4)
        Conns                           (8, 0x8)
        BER                             (16, 0x10)
```

| | |
|---|---|
| Filter | (32, 0x20) |
| Config | (64, 0x40) |
| ACL | (128, 0x80) |
| Stats | (256, 0x100) |
| Stats2 | (512, 0x200) |
| Shell | (1024, 0x400) |
| Parse | (2048, 0x800) |
| Sync | (16384, 0x4000) |
| None | (32768, 0x8000) |

The numeric values can be combined, so we can, for instance, select Conns, BER, and Filter at the same time:

```
[root@alpha ~]# slapd -u ldap -g ldap -d 184 -h ldap:///
58d2bd68 @(#) $OpenLDAP: slapd 2.4.39 (Jun  9 2014 23:23:12) $
        mockbuild@worker1.bsys.centos.org:/builddir/build/BUILD/
        openldap-2.4.39/openldap-2.4.39/servers/slapd
58d2bd68 => test_filter
58d2bd68     PRESENT
58d2bd68 => access_allowed: search access to "cn=config" "objectClass"
requested
58d2bd68 <= root access granted
.
.
.
```

We can see a lot of information on the console, and to test the server we can perform a query from another console:

```
[root@alpha ldap]# ldapsearch -LLL -U Tux -v '(uid=Tux)' uid
```

In the first console we'll see a lot of information:

```
58c37d06 slap_listener_activate(7):
58c37d06 >>> slap_listener(ldapi:///)
58c37d06 connection_get(20): got connid=1000
58c37d06 connection_read(20): checking for input on id=1000
ber_get_next
```

```
ber_get_next: tag 0x30 len 24 contents:
58c37d06 op tag 0x60, time 1489206534
ber_get_next
58c37d06 conn=1000 op=0 do_bind
ber_scanf fmt ({imt) ber:
ber_scanf fmt ({m) ber:
ber_scanf fmt (}}) ber:
58c37d06 >>> dnPrettyNormal: <>
58c37d06 <<< dnPrettyNormal: <>, <>
58c37d06 do_bind: dn () SASL mech DIGEST-MD5
58c37d06 SASL [conn=1000] Debug: DIGEST-MD5 server step 1
58c37d06 send_ldap_sasl: err=14 len=195
58c37d06 send_ldap_response: msgid=1 tag=97 err=14
ber_flush2: 242 bytes to sd 20
58c37d06 <== slap_sasl_bind: rc=14
58c37d09 connection_get(20): got connid=1000
58c37d09 connection_read(20): checking for input on id=1000
ber_get_next
ber_get_next: tag 0x30 len 320 contents:
58c37d09 op tag 0x60, time 1489206537
ber_get_next
58c37d09 conn=1000 op=1 do_bind
ber_scanf fmt ({imt) ber:
ber_scanf fmt ({m) ber:
ber_scanf fmt (m) ber:
ber_scanf fmt (}}) ber:
58c37d09 >>> dnPrettyNormal: <>
58c37d09 <<< dnPrettyNormal: <>, <>
58c37d09 do_bind: dn () SASL mech DIGEST-MD5
58c37d09 SASL [conn=1000] Debug: DIGEST-MD5 server step 2
58c37d09 slap_sasl_getdn: u:id converted to uid=Tux,cn=DIGEST-MD5,cn=auth
58c37d09 >>> dnNormalize: <uid=Tux,cn=DIGEST-MD5,cn=auth>
58c37d09 <<< dnNormalize: <uid=tux,cn=digest-md5,cn=auth>
58c37d09 ==>slap_sasl2dn: converting SASL name uid=tux,cn=digest-
md5,cn=auth to a DN
```

```
58c37d09 ==> rewrite_context_apply [depth=1] string='uid=tux,cn=digest-md5,
cn=auth'
58c37d09 ==> rewrite_rule_apply rule='^uid=([^,]+).*,cn=auth$'
string='uid=tux,cn=digest-md5,cn=auth' [1 pass(es)]
58c37d09 ==> rewrite_context_apply [depth=1] res={0,'uid=tux,ou=users,
dc=linuxaholics,dc=com'}
58c37d09 slap_parseURI: parsing uid=tux,ou=users,dc=linuxaholics,dc=com
ldap_url_parse_ext(uid=tux,ou=users,dc=linuxaholics,dc=com)
58c37d09 >>> dnNormalize: <uid=tux,ou=users,dc=linuxaholics,dc=com>
58c37d09 <<< dnNormalize: <uid=tux,ou=users,dc=linuxaholics,dc=com>
58c37d09 <==slap_sasl2dn: Converted SASL name to uid=tux,ou=users,
dc=linuxaholics,dc=com
58c37d09 slap_sasl_getdn: dn:id converted to uid=tux,ou=users,
dc=linuxaholics,dc=com
58c37d09 => hdb_search
58c37d09 bdb_dn2entry("uid=tux,ou=users,dc=linuxaholics,dc=com")
58c37d09 => hdb_dn2id("dc=linuxaholics,dc=com")
58c37d09 <= hdb_dn2id: got id=0x1
58c37d09 => hdb_dn2id("ou=users,dc=linuxaholics,dc=com")
58c37d09 <= hdb_dn2id: got id=0x2
58c37d09 => hdb_dn2id("uid=tux,ou=users,dc=linuxaholics,dc=com")
58c37d09 <= hdb_dn2id: get failed: BDB0073 DB_NOTFOUND: No matching key/
data pair found (-30988)
58c37d09 entry_decode: ""
58c37d09 <= entry_decode()
58c37d09 send_ldap_result: conn=1000 op=1 p=3
58c37d09 SASL [conn=1000] Failure: unable to canonify user and get auxprops
58c37d09 SASL [conn=1000] Debug: DIGEST-MD5 common mech dispose
58c37d09 send_ldap_result: conn=1000 op=1 p=3
58c37d09 send_ldap_response: msgid=2 tag=97 err=80
ber_flush2: 81 bytes to sd 20
58c37d09 <== slap_sasl_bind: rc=80
58c37d09 connection_get(20): got connid=1000
58c37d09 connection_read(20): checking for input on id=1000
ber_get_next
```

```
ber_get_next: tag 0x30 len 5 contents:
58c37d09 op tag 0x42, time 1489206537
ber_get_next
58c37d09 ber_get_next on fd 20 failed errno=0 (Success)
58c37d09 conn=1000 op=2 do_unbind
58c37d09 connection_close: conn=1000 sd=20
```

Most of the client utilities we have used so far include the -d option for debugging. For instance, when using **ldapsearch** we might get this error:

```
[root@bravo ~]# ldapsearch -x -ZZ -b "dc=linuxaholics,dc=com" "(cn=Tux)" -D
cn=admin,dc=linuxaholics,dc=com -w pass
ldap_start_tls: Connect error (-11)
        additional info: TLS error -8157:Certificate extension not found.
```

Unfortunately, the error message is not very helpful, but if we include the debugging option, we'll find out what the real problem is:

```
[root@bravo ~]# ldapsearch -d 8 -x -ZZ -b "dc=linuxaholics,dc=com"
"(cn=Tux)" -D cn=admin,dc=linuxaholics,dc=com -w pass
TLS: hostname (bravo) does not match common name in certificate (bravo.
linuxaholics.com).
TLS: can't connect: TLS error -8157:Certificate extension not found..
ldap_start_tls: Connect error (-11)
        additional info: TLS error -8157:Certificate extension not found.
```

Let's see another example:

```
[root@foxtrot ldap]# ldapsearch -x -ZZ -b "dc=linuxaholics,dc=com"
ldap_start_tls: Connect error (-11)
        additional info: TLS error -5938:Encountered end of file
```

In this case the system says that it encountered the end of file. Assuming the file itself is correct, we can try to get some more information by manually launching slapd, as we saw in an earlier example. Looking at the server console we'll see the following lines:

```
TLS: error: the certificate '/etc/openldap/certs/foxtrot.linuxaholics.com.
crt' could not be found in the database - error -12274:Peer only supports
SSL version 2, which is locally disabled..
TLS: certificate '/etc/openldap/certs/foxtrot.linuxaholics.com.crt'
successfully loaded from PEM file.
TLS: no unlocked certificate for certificate 'CN=foxtrot.linuxaholics.com,
O=linuxaholics,ST=Madrid,C=ES'.
TLS: certificate [CN=foxtrot.linuxaholics.com,O=linuxaholics,ST=Madrid,
C=ES] is not valid - error -8181:Peer's Certificate has expired..
TLS: error: unable to find and verify server's cert and key for certificate
CN=foxtrot.linuxaholics.com,O=linuxaholics,ST=Madrid,C=ES
TLS: error: could not initialize moznss security context - error
-8157:Certificate extension not found.
```

As we see, the problem is that the certificate has expired.

# Summary

In this chapter we've seen how to secure connections to the LDAP server through the use of TLS. We also set up the firewall to allow access only to the clients that we want to allow to connect. We also learned how to control access to different branches of the LDAP tree with the olcAccess parameter. We studied different types of authentication and introduced SASL proxy authentication. Finally we learned how to include an additional layer of secutiry by using client certificates and practiced some useful debugging techniques.

## CHAPTER 3

# LDAP Integration with PAM and NSS

By default, Linux systems use local users for authentication. Those users are listed in the /etc/passwd file. This can become a nuisance when there are many Linux systems in the network, as every user needs a local account in each and every one of them. A first approach to the use of a centralized repository for authentication was Network Information Services (NIS) developed initially by Sun. Now, this has been largely replaced by LDAP.

In this chapter we'll cover the following concepts:

- Configure Linux Pluggable Authentication Modules (PAM) to use LDAP for authentication.

- Configure Name Service Switch (NSS) to retrieve information from LDAP.

- Configure PAM modules in various Unix environments.

We will also be introduced to the following terms and utilities: PAM, NSS, /etc/pam.d/, and /etc/nsswitch.conf.

## PAM

When a user tries to access a computer through SSH, FTP, or another protocol, the system will decide whether to grant or deny access. During this process, it will execute many libraries and check many parameters depending on the local configuration. In Linux this process is managed by the PAM. PAM is made up of a series of libraries, as well as a series of text files that specify many possible options.

© Antonio Vazquez 2019
A. Vazquez, *Practical LPIC-3 300*, https://doi.org/10.1007/978-1-4842-4473-9_3

# Authenticating Users with LDAP

Traditionally, Linux users authenticate themselves by using local accounts locally stored on /etc/passwd. Now we'll see how to authenticate users with LDAP.

First of all, in the server we'll have to allow incoming traffic to port LDAP (389) and LDAPS (636).

```
[root@alpha~]# firewall —cmd ——permanent ——add—service=ldap
success
[root@alpha~]# firewall —cmd ——permanent ——add—service=ldaps
success
[root@alpha~]# firewall —cmd ——reload
success
```

In the client we need to install a series of packages to allow LDAP authentication.

```
[root@bravo~]# yum install openldap—clients nss—pam—ldap
```

Next, we can use the **system-config-authentication** command (Figure 3-1). If this command is not installed, we'll have to install the authconfig-gtk package with **yum**. If we need to install any additional library, we'll install it as well.

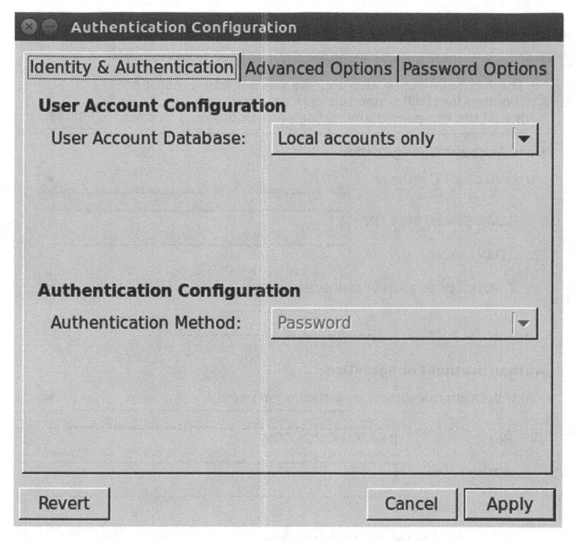

***Figure 3-1.*** *System-config-authentication*

Click User Account Database and select LDAP. Notice that the dialog box changes (Figure 3-2).

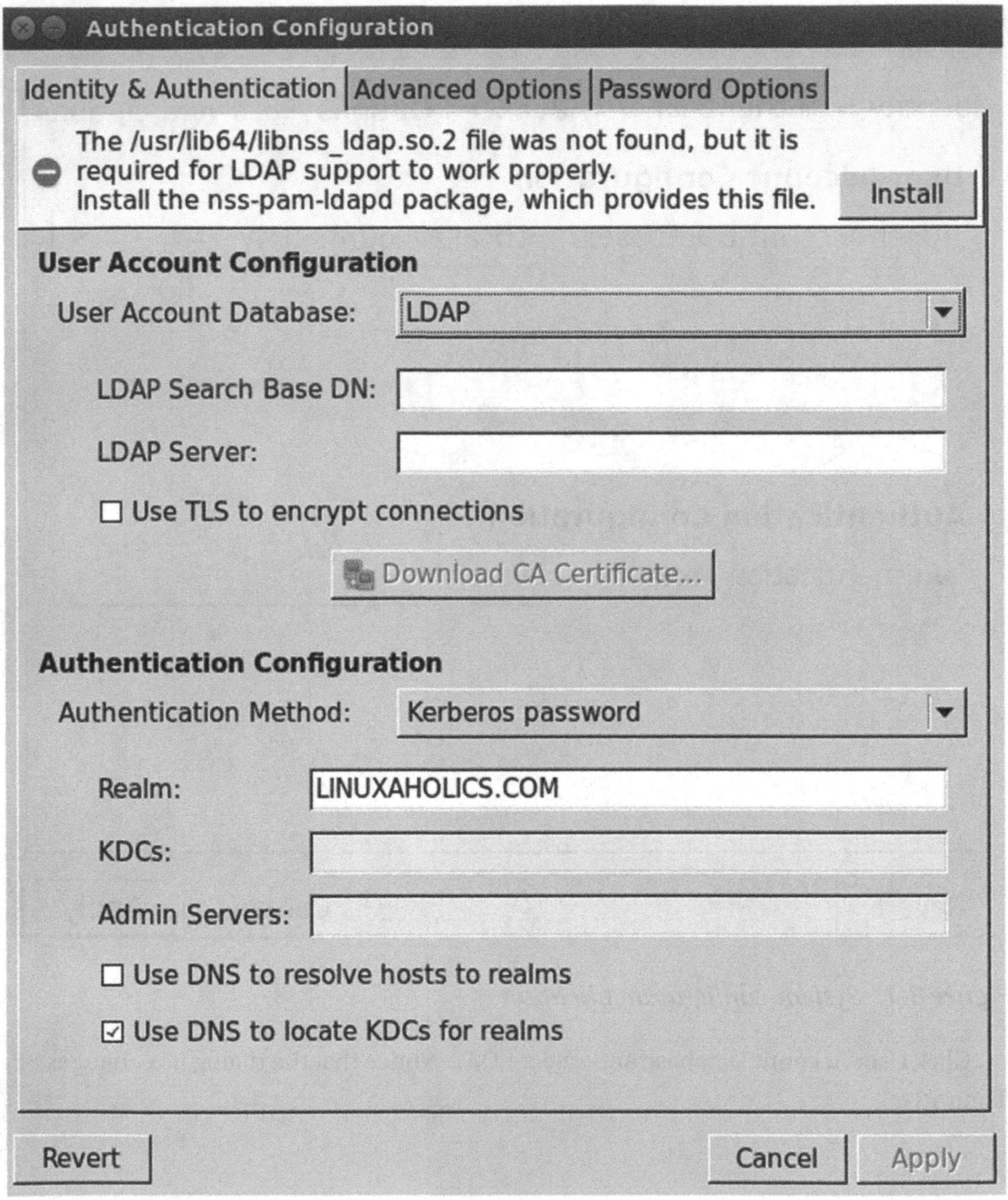

*Figure 3-2.*  *LDAP settings in system-config-authentication*

At the top of the new window we might get a warning message if there is some required library missing. If that's the case, we'll install it and execute system-config-authentication again.

If we take a look at the different fields, we'll see two main sections: User Account Configuration and Authentication Configuration. Under User Account Configuration we have the settings User Account Database (in which we previously selected LDAP), LDAP Search Base DN, and LDAP Server.

The term User Account Database is self-explanatory and it refers to the location of the user accounts, which is in this case the LDAP database. The LDAP Server field will have to be filled with the name or address of our LDAP server. Finally, we need to indicate the search base in which the user accounts have been created. If we have followed the instructions from the previous chapters, this will be `ou=users,dc=linuxaholics,dc=com`.

In the Authentication Configuration section we see that the default value is Kerberos; that is, the user accounts will be located in the LDAP server, but the authentication will be performed by a Kerberos server, not by the LDAP server itself. In a forthcoming chapter we'll talk more about Kerberos and we'll configure Kerberos authentication, but at this point we'll change the Authentication Configuration value to LDAP password so that the LDAP server will perform the authentication, too. After completing all the fields, the dialog box will look like the one shown in Figure 3-3.

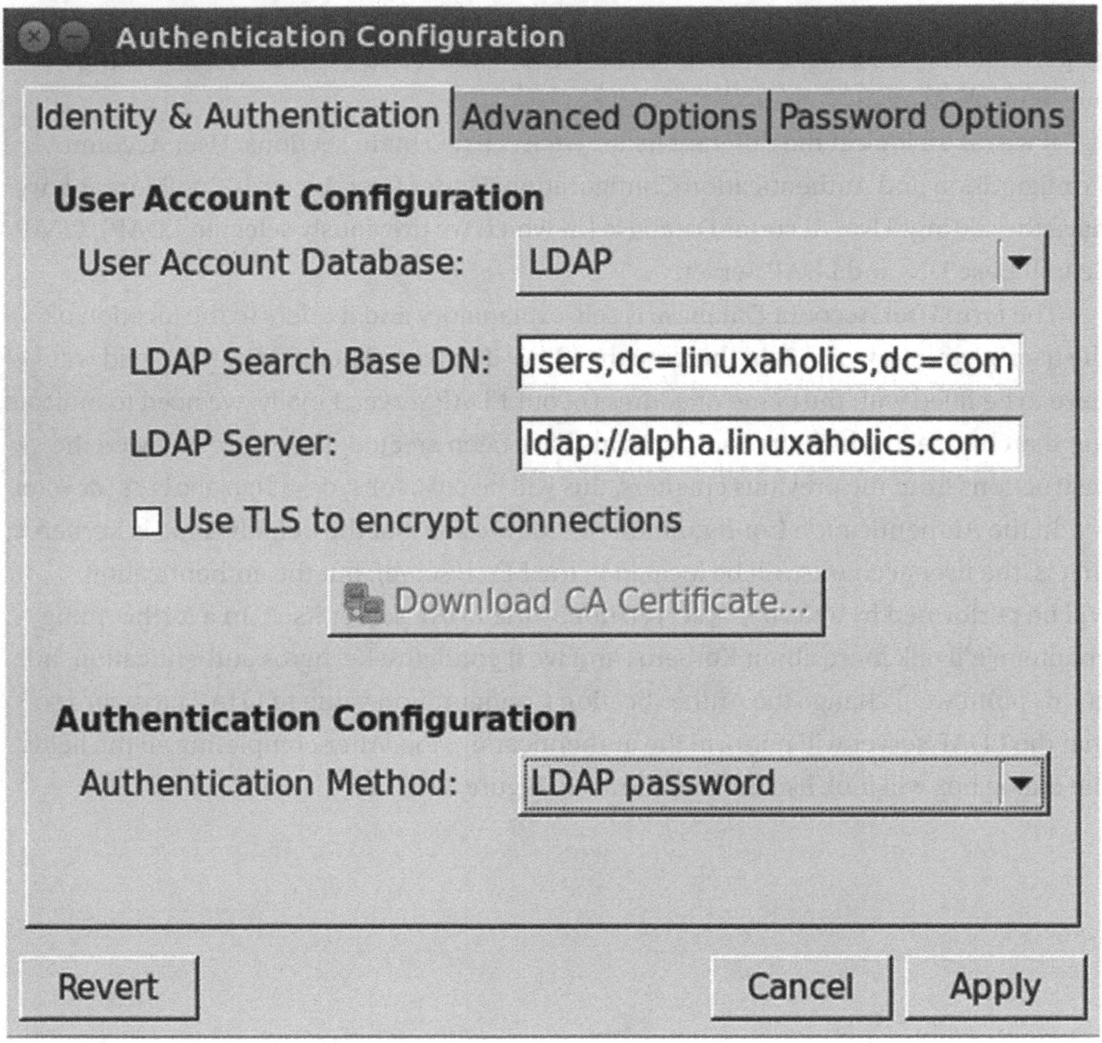

*Figure 3-3.* *Configuring LDAP authentication*

As we can see, by default the system requires us to use a secure connection, so we need to either activate TLS or use LDAPS instead of LDAP to be able to authenticate with LDAP. In our case we select the Use TLS check box and click Download CA Certificate. Now we type the URL from which the server certificate can be downloaded (Figure 3-4).

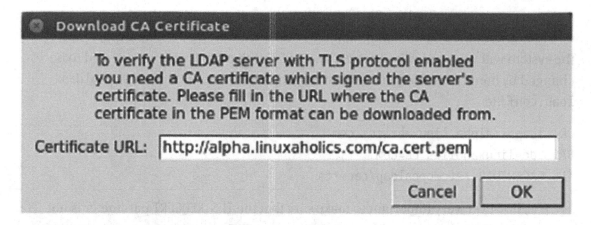

*Figure 3-4. Downloading the certificate*

When we created the certificate on the server, we placed it in /etc/openldap/ cacerts. To make it available for download we can copy it to a web site, FTP site, and so on We're not going into much detail about how to configure a web server so we'll only explain how to perform a default installation.

First, we install the Apache server (httpd package).

```
[root@alpha~]# yum install —y httpd
```

Then we start the service and we enable it.

```
[root@alpha~]# systemctl start httpd
[root@alpha~]# systemctl enable httpd
Created symlink from /etc/systemd/system/multi—user.target.wants/
httpd.service to /usr/lib/systemd/system/httpd.service
```

The default DocumentRoot after a fresh installation is the /var/www/html/ folder, so we copy our CA certificate file there.

```
[root@alpha~]# cp /etc/pki/CA/certs/ca.cert.pem /var/www/html/
```

We allow access to the HTTP port in the firewall.

```
[root@alpha~]# firewall—cmd ——permanent ——add—service=http
success
[root@alpha~]# firewall—cmd ——add—service=http
success
```

Now we can download the file to the client. Once the certificate has been downloaded, in the system-config-authentication window, we can click Apply. Then the system will automatically change a series of files that otherwise would need to be changed by hand. For example, it will add the following lines to the /etc/openldap/ldap.conf file:

```
URI ldap://alpha.linuxaholics.com
BASE dc=linuxaholics,dc=com
TLS CACERTDIR /etc/openldap/cacerts
```

It is, however, very important to make sure that the TLS REQCERT parameter is not set to never. If this is the case, ldapsearch won't use TLS when communicating with the server.

If we don't have a graphical environment available to execute system-config-authconfig we can get the same result with the **authconfig** command.

```
[root@bravo~]# authconfig ——enableldap ——enableldapauth
——ldapserver=alpha.linuxaholics.com ——ldapbasedn="dc=linuxaholics,dc=com"
——enableldaptls ——update
```

In this case, however, we'll need to download the CA certificate file by hand, for instance, by using **wget** or **curl**.

```
[root@bravo cacerts]# wget http://alpha.linuxaholics.com/ca.cert.pem
--2017-12-21 06:34:19--  http://alpha.linuxaholics.com/ca.cert.pem
Resolving alpha.linuxaholics.com (alpha.linuxaholics.com)... 192.168.1.229
Connecting to alpha.linuxaholics.com (alpha.linuxaholics.com)|192.168.1.229|:
80... connected.
HTTP request sent, awaiting response... 200 OK
Length: 1318 (1,3K)
Saving to: 'ca.cert.pem.1'

100%[=====================================>] 1.318        --.-K/s    in 0s

2017-12-21 06:34:19 (168 MB/s) - 'ca.cert.pem' saved [1318/1318]
```

As we mentioned earlier, we need to generate a soft link with the file hash as the name. We can do it with **cacertdir_rehash**.

```
root@bravo cacerts]# cacertdir_rehash .
[root@bravo cacerts]# ls -l
total 4
lrwxrwxrwx. 1 root root  11 sep 24 00:17 06c388c4.0 -> ca.cert.pem
-rw-r--r--. 1 root root 989 sep 10 10:40 ca.cert.pem
```

To be able to authenticate as an LDAP user, when we create the user we need to include a series of fields, such as the shell, UID, GID, and so on. These are attributes included in the posixAccount and shadowAccount objects. For this reason, we need to extend the schema first.

```
[root@alpha ~]# ldapadd -Y EXTERNAL -H ldapi:/// -f /etc/openldap/schema/
nis.ldif
SASL/EXTERNAL authentication started
SASL username: gidNumber=0+uidNumber=0,cn=peercred,cn=external,cn=auth
SASL SSF: 0
adding new entry "cn=nis,cn=schema,cn=config"
```

After extending the schema we can prepare the LDIF file for the new user.

```
[root@alpha ldap]# cat Gecko.ldif
dn: uid=Gecko,ou=users,dc=linuxaholics,dc=com
uid: Gecko
cn: Gecko
objectClass: account
objectClass: posixAccount
objectClass: top
objectClass: shadowAccount
userPassword: suse
shadowLastChange: 10000
shadowMax: 99999
shadowWarning: 7
loginShell: /bin/bash
uidNumber: 1500
gidNumber: 500
homeDirectory: /home/Gecko
```

We must take into account that in recent versions of OpenLDAP the uidNumber value must be above 1000. Otherwise the user insertion will be rejected. Likewise, there seem to be some problems when passwords are specified in clear text, so we'll generate a hash for it.

```
[root@alpha ldap]# slappasswd
New password:
Re-enter new password:
{SSHA}u4Ajfy93GpnHmheW7o+vqPoBmWrD97os
```

We substitute the corresponding line in the LDIF file just created.

.

.

.

```
userPassword: {SSHA}u4Ajfy93GpnHmheW7o+vqPoBmWrD97os
```

.

.

.

After this change, we are ready to add the new user.

```
[root@alpha ldap]# ldapadd -f Gecko.ldif -x -D
cn=admin,dc=linuxaholics,dc=com -w pass
adding new entry "uid=Gecko,ou=users,dc=linuxaholics,dc=com"
```

To simplify the process of authentication we should also install **sssd** on the client.

---

**Note**    In the LPIC-202 exam objectives, **sssd** is covered specifically in the exam topics. However in the LPIC-300 exam objectives it is not. Of course, this implies that when applying for the exam, the reader could be expected to know how to configure authentication without using sssd. We have decided to use sssd because it is the preferred way to authenticate. A bit later in this chapter we'll see how to authenticate from different Unix machines without using sssd so that the reader has a clear picture about the authentication process.

---

```
[root@bravo ~]# yum -y install sssd
```

The **sssd** service manages access to remote directories and authentication mechanisms in a centralized manner. Its main configuration file is /etc/sssd/sssd.conf, but after a fresh installation this file does not exist. We can create it by hand after taking a look at the sssd man page or we can copy the example file at /usr/share/doc/sssd-common-1.15.2/sssd-example.conf and customize it according to our needs.

```
[root@bravo ~]# cp /usr/share/doc/sssd-common-1.15.2/sssd-example.conf
/etc/sssd/sssd.conf
```

The file must also be owned by the root user and be accessible only by the owner.

```
[root@bravo ~]# ls -l /etc/sssd/sssd.conf
-rw-------. 1 root root 1909 dic 21 08:29 /etc/sssd/sssd.conf
[root@bravo ~]# chmod 600 /etc/sssd/sssd.conf
```

This is the original content of the configuration file.

```
[root@bravo ~]# cat /etc/sssd/sssd.conf
[sssd]
config_file_version = 2
services = nss, pam
# SSSD will not start if you do not configure any domains.
# Add new domain configurations as [domain/<NAME>] sections, and
# then add the list of domains (in the order you want them to be
# queried) to the "domains" attribute below and uncomment it.
; domains = LDAP

[nss]

[pam]

# Example LDAP domain
; [domain/LDAP]
; id_provider = ldap
; auth_provider = ldap
.
.
.
```

If we start the **sssd** service now, we'll get an error because the config file is not correct. We'll need to edit it by hand to create a domain entry. From that moment on, we should be able to edit the file using tools like **authconfig**.

Sometimes, though, the configuration file is not updated properly, and we'll have to edit it by hand. In the end, either way, the content of the file will look something like this:

```
[root@bravo ~]# cat /etc/sssd/sssd.conf
[domain/default]

autofs_provider = ldap
cache_credentials = True
ldap_search_base = ou=users,dc=linuxaholics,dc=com
id_provider = ldap
auth_provider = ldap
chpass_provider = ldap
ldap_uri = ldap://alpha.linuxaholics.com/
ldap_id_use_start_tls = True
ldap_tls_cacertdir = /etc/openldap/cacerts
[sssd]
config_file_version = 2
services = nss, pam, autofs
# SSSD will not start if you do not configure any domains.
# Add new domain configurations as [domain/<NAME>] sections, and
# then add the list of domains (in the order you want them to be
# queried) to the "domains" attribute below and uncomment it.
# domains = LDAP

domains = default
[nss]

[pam]

[autofs]
```

After configuring **sssd** we restart the service.

```
[root@bravo ~]# systemctl restart sssd
```

We must also give read access to the everybody user (*). We have already seen many examples of adding access rights in previous sections.

```
[root@alpha ldap]# cat acceso8.ldif
dn: olcDatabase={2}hdb,cn=config
changeType: modify
replace: olcAccess
olcAccess: {0}to dn.children="dc=linuxaholics,dc=com" by self write by
dn.base="gidNumber=0+uidNumber=0,cn=peercred,cn=external,cn=auth" manage by
dn.base="cn=admin,dc=linuxaholics,dc=com" read by dn.base="cn=dummy,
dc=linuxaholics,dc=com" read by dn.children="ou=users,dc=linuxaholics,
dc=com" read by dn.children="cn=digest-md5,cn=auth" read by * read
[root@alpha ldap]# ldapmodify -Y EXTERNAL -H ldapi:/// -f acceso8.ldif
SASL/EXTERNAL authentication started
SASL username: gidNumber=0+uidNumber=0,cn=peercred,cn=external,cn=auth
SASL SSF: 0
modifying entry "olcDatabase={2}hdb,cn=config"
```

We check that the everybody (*) user now has read access to ou=users, dc=linuxaholics,dc=com.

```
[root@alpha ldap]# ldapsearch -Y EXTERNAL -H ldapi:/// -b cn=config | grep
-A4 olcAccess
SASL/EXTERNAL authentication started
SASL username: gidNumber=0+uidNumber=0,cn=peercred,cn=external,cn=auth
SASL SSF: 0
.
.
.
olcAccess: {0}to dn.children="dc=linuxaholics,dc=com" by self write by
dn.base="gidNumber=0+uidNumber=0,cn=peercred,cn=external,cn=auth" manage by
dn.base="cn=admin,dc=linuxaholics,dc=com" read by dn.base="cn=dummy,
dc=linuxaholics,dc=com" read by dn.children="ou=users,dc=linuxaholics,
dc=com" read by dn.children="cn=digest-md5,cn=auth" read by * read
```

Now we'll be able to authenticate with an LDAP user.

```
[root@bravo ~]# ssh Gecko@bravo.linuxaholics.com
Gecko@bravo.linuxaholics.com's password:
Could not chdir to home directory /home/Gecko: No such file or directory
/usr/bin/id: cannot find name for group ID 500
-bash-4.2$
```

# Troubleshooting LDAP Authentication

If we experience any problem when authenticating against an LDAP server there are many things we should do. The first thing would be checking whether the slapd service is running in the server or not.

```
[root@alpha ~]# systemctl status slapd
● slapd.service - OpenLDAP Server Daemon
   Loaded: loaded (/usr/lib/systemd/system/slapd.service; enabled; vendor
   preset: disabled)
   Active: active (running) since vie 2017-04-21 06:47:38 CEST; 3min 54s ago
     Docs: man:slapd
           man:slapd-config
           man:slapd-hdb
           man:slapd-mdb
           file:///usr/share/doc/openldap-servers/guide.html
  Process: 2786 ExecStart=/usr/sbin/slapd -u ldap -h ${SLAPD_URLS} $SLAPD_
  OPTIONS (code=exited, status=0/SUCCESS)
  Process: 2735 ExecStartPre=/usr/libexec/openldap/check-config.sh
  (code=exited, status=0/SUCCESS)
 Main PID: 2788 (slapd)
   CGroup: /system.slice/slapd.service
           └─2788 /usr/sbin/slapd -u ldap -h ldapi:/// ldap:/// ldaps:///

abr 21 06:47:57 alpha.linuxaholics.com slapd[2788]: conn=1000 op=9 SEARCH
RES...
```

```
abr 21 06:48:31 alpha.linuxaholics.com slapd[2788]: conn=1002 fd=27 ACCEPT
fr...
```

.

.

.

We should also make sure that the firewall permits traffic to the LDAP and LDAPS ports in the OpenLDAP server.

```
[root@alpha ~]# firewall-cmd --get-default-zone
public
[root@alpha ~]# firewall-cmd --zone=public --list-services
dhcpv6-client http ldap ldaps ssh
```

We can also execute **ldapsearch** from the client.

```
[root@bravo ~]# ldapsearch -x -ZZ -b dc=linuxaholics,dc=com "(uid=Gecko)"
```

.

.

.

```
# Gecko, users, linuxaholics.com
dn: uid=Gecko,ou=users,dc=linuxaholics,dc=com
uid: Gecko
cn: Gecko
objectClass: account
objectClass: posixAccount
objectClass: top
objectClass: shadowAccount
userPassword:: e1NTSEF9MjIramJlYOVOZOhmTjZCRzROTFdlWHh1KzlFUE41TVAg
```

.

.

.

We can also obtain some important information by taking a look at the /var/log/ messages file, as well as the sssd log files, located in the /var/log/sssd/ folder.

To obtain more information from the log files we can stop the sssd service and start it manually, adding a parameter to increase the debug information.

```
[root@alpha ~]# sssd -d10 -f
```

This is an example of what we could see in the /var/log/sssd/sssd_default.log file.

.

.

.

```
(Fri Aug  7 01:00:23 2015) [sssd[be[default]]] [sdap_sys_connect_done]
(4): Executing START TLS
(Fri Aug  7 01:00:23 2015) [sssd[be[default]]] [sdap_connect_done]
(3): START TLS result: Success(0), (null)
(Fri Aug  7 01:00:23 2015) [sssd[be[default]]] [sdap_get_generic_step]
(6): calling ldap_search_ext with [(objectclass=*)][].
(Fri Aug  7 01:00:23 2015) [sssd[be[default]]] [sdap_get_generic_step]
(7): Requesting attrs: [*]
(Fri Aug  7 01:00:23 2015) [sssd[be[default]]] [sdap_get_generic_step]
(7): Requesting attrs: [altServer]
(Fri Aug  7 01:00:23 2015) [sssd[be[default]]] [sdap_get_generic_step]
(7): Requesting attrs: [namingContexts]
(Fri Aug  7 01:00:23 2015) [sssd[be[default]]] [sdap_get_generic_step]
(7): Requesting attrs: [supportedControl]
(Fri Aug  7 01:00:23 2015) [sssd[be[default]]] [sdap_get_generic_step]
(7): Requesting attrs: [supportedExtension]
(Fri Aug  7 01:00:23 2015) [sssd[be[default]]] [sdap_get_generic_step]
(7): Requesting attrs: [supportedFeatures]
(Fri Aug  7 01:00:23 2015) [sssd[be[default]]] [sdap_get_generic_step]
(7): Requesting attrs: [supportedLDAPVersion]
(Fri Aug  7 01:00:23 2015) [sssd[be[default]]] [sdap_get_generic_step]
(7): Requesting attrs: [supportedSASLMechanisms]
(Fri Aug  7 01:00:23 2015) [sssd[be[default]]] [sdap_get_generic_step]
(7): Requesting attrs: [defaultNamingContext]
(Fri Aug  7 01:00:23 2015) [sssd[be[default]]] [sdap_get_generic_step]
(7): Requesting attrs: [lastUSN]
(Fri Aug  7 01:00:23 2015) [sssd[be[default]]] [sdap_get_generic_step]
(7): Requesting attrs: [highestCommittedUSN]
(Fri Aug  7 01:00:23 2015) [sssd[be[default]]] [sdap_process_result]
(4): ldap_result gave -1, something bad happend!
```

```
(Fri Aug  7 01:00:23 2015) [sssd[be[default]]] [fo_set_port_status]
(4): Marking port 389 of server '192.168.10.24' as 'not working'
(Fri Aug  7 01:00:23 2015) [sssd[be[default]]] [fo_resolve_service_send]
(4): Trying to resolve service 'LDAP'
(Fri Aug  7 01:00:23 2015) [sssd[be[default]]] [get_server_status]
(7): Status of server '192.168.10.24' is 'name resolved'
(Fri Aug  7 01:00:23 2015) [sssd[be[default]]] [get_port_status]
(7): Port status of port 389 for server '192.168.10.24' is 'not working'
(Fri Aug  7 01:00:23 2015) [sssd[be[default]]] [fo_resolve_service_send]
(1): No available servers for service 'LDAP'
(Fri Aug  7 01:00:23 2015) [sssd[be[default]]] [sdap_id_op_connect_done]
(1): Failed to connect, going offline (5 [Input/output error])
.
.
.
```

We can also get some debug information by adding (-d 1) to the **ldapsearch** command.

```
[root@bravo ~]# ldapsearch -H ldap://alpha.linuxaholics.com -d 1 -x -ZZ -b
dc=linuxaholics,dc=com "(cn=Tux)"
ldap_create
ldap_extended_operation_s
ldap_extended_operation
ldap_send_initial_request
ldap_new_connection 1 1 0
ldap_int_open_connection
ldap_connect_to_host: TCP alpha.linuxaholics.com:389
ldap_new_socket: 3
ldap_prepare_socket: 3
ldap_connect_to_host: Trying 192.168.1.229:389
ldap_pvt_connect: fd: 3 tm: -1 async: 0
ldap_open_defconn: successful
ldap_send_server_request
ber_scanf fmt ({it) ber:
ber_scanf fmt ({) ber:
```

```
ber_flush2: 31 bytes to sd 3
ldap_result ld 0x977b0e0 msgid 1
wait4msg ld 0x977b0e0 msgid 1 (infinite timeout)
wait4msg continue ld 0x977b0e0 msgid 1 all 1
** ld 0x977b0e0 Connections:
* host: alpha.linuxaholics.com  port: 389  (default)
  refcnt: 2  status: Connected
  last used: Fri Aug  7 01:50:11 2015
.

.

.
```

# Configure NSS to Retrieve Information from LDAP

NSS is an interface provided in Unix-like systems that allows us to configure several authentication mechanisms and name resolution. Most Linux administrators become familiar with NSS and its configuration file /etc/nsswitch.conf when setting up name resolution.

In the /etc/nsswitch.conf file we can see the following lines:

```
#
# /etc/nsswitch.conf
#
# An example Name Service Switch config file. This file should be
# sorted with the most-used services at the beginning.
#
.

.

.
hosts:       files dns
```

According to the hosts line, when the computer needs to resolve the name of a host computer it will look it up in the /etc/hosts file, and only if it can't find the name there it will query the DNS server. This behavior could be changed by editing the file. For example, if we change the hosts line deleting the word files, the computer will always query the DNS server, ignoring the contents of the /etc/hosts file.

We can do many more things to fine tune the way NSS works. If we look again at the /etc/nsswitch.conf file, we'll also see the following lines:

```
passwd:     files
shadow:     files
```

These two lines determine the way to authenticate the users. By default, every Linux system will authenticate any incoming user by querying the /etc/passwd and /etc/shadow files to check whether a valid username and password have been provided.

When we installed sssd in a previous section, the installation process changed the /etc/nsswitch.conf file to include the following:

```
passwd:     files sss ldap
shadow:     files sss ldap
group:      files sss ldap
```

As we can see, the sss word was added, so from that point, if a user tries to authenticate and its username and password combination is not found in the /etc/passwd and /etc/shadow files, the system will query the sssd service.

In turn, sssd will check different services to decide whether the user is granted or denied access. This behavior depends on what is configured in the /etc/sssd/sssd.conf file.

```
[root@bravo ~]# cat /etc/sssd/sssd.conf
[domain/default]

autofs_provider = ldap
cache_credentials = True
ldap_search_base = ou=users,dc=linuxaholics,dc=com
id_provider = ldap
auth_provider = ldap
chpass_provider = ldap
ldap_uri = ldap://alpha.linuxaholics.com/
ldap_id_use_start_tls = True
ldap_tls_cacertdir = /etc/openldap/cacerts
[sssd]
config_file_version = 2
services = nss, pam, autofs
```

```
# SSSD will not start if you do not configure any domains.
# Add new domain configurations as [domain/<NAME>] sections, and
# then add the list of domains (in the order you want them to be
# queried) to the "domains" attribute below and uncomment it.
# domains = LDAP

domains = default
[nss]

[pam]

[autofs]
```

This file is usually autogenerated by the **authconfig** command or any of the graphical front ends like **system-config-auth**. The content is generated based on a series of configuration files like /etc/openldap/ldap.conf or /etc/sysconfig/authconfig.

In this example we see that sssd will try to authenticate the user by default against an LDAP server.

```
id_provider = ldap
auth_provider = ldap
chpass_provider = ldap
```

It will try to contact the LDAP server alpha.linuxaholics.com.

```
ldap_uri = ldap://alpha.linuxaholics.com/
```

It will use a secure connection.

```
ldap_id_use_start_tls = True
ldap_tls_cacertdir = /etc/openldap/cacerts
```

# Configure PAM Modules in Various UNIX Environments

Previously we have seen how to correctly set up the PAM modules to authenticate users against an LDAP server in CentOS Linux. The procedure in other Linux and Unix systems is very similar, as we'll see in the following examples.

# Authenticating from a FreeBSD Box

In a freshly installed FreeBSD box, we'll need to install the OpenLDAP client.

```
root@charlie:~ # cd /usr/ports/
root@charlie:/usr/ports # cd net/openldap24-client/
root@charlie:/usr/ports/net/openldap24-client # make install
===> Building/installing dialog4ports as it is required for the config dialog
===>  Cleaning for dialog4ports-0.1.5_2
===>  License BSD2CLAUSE accepted by the user
===>   dialog4ports-0.1.5_2 depends on file: /usr/local/sbin/pkg - found
=> dialog4ports-0.1.5.tar.gz doesn't seem to exist in /usr/ports/distfiles/.
=> Attempting to fetch http://m1cro.me/dialog4ports/dialog4ports-0.1.5.tar.gz
.
.
.
```

We select the With GSSAPI support option (Figure 3-5).

***Figure 3-5.***  *Installing OpenLDAP client with GSSAPI support in FreeBSD*

We also need to install two additional ports for LDAP authentication to work on FreeBSD: security/pam_ldap and net/nss_ldap.

```
root@charlie:/usr/ports/security/pam_ldap # make install
.
.
.
Installing pam_ldap-1.8.6_3...
===============================================================================
Copy /usr/local/etc/ldap.conf.dist to /usr/local/etc/ldap.conf, then edit
/usr/local/etc/ldap.conf in order to use this module. Add a line similar to
the following to /etc/pam.conf on 4.X, or create an /etc/pam.d/ldap on 5.X
and higher with a line similar to the following:

login    auth    sufficient        /usr/local/lib/pam_ldap.so
root@charlie:/usr/ports/net/nss_ldap # make install
.
.
.
Installing nss_ldap-1.265_12...
===============================================================================
The nss_ldap module expects to find its configuration files at the
following paths:

LDAP configuration:     /usr/local/etc/nss_ldap.conf
LDAP secret (optional): /usr/local/etc/nss_ldap.secret
```

During the installation we'll see a window asking about default configuration parameters (Figure 3-6).

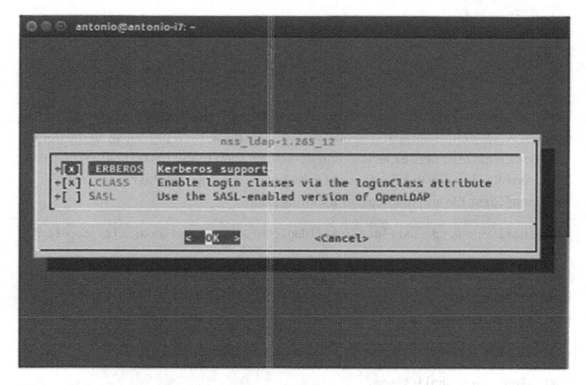

***Figure 3-6.*** *Configuring the nss_ldap module in FreeBSD*

Our FreeBSD computer is ready to authenticate against our OpenLDAP server. We only need to configure the client, but before doing so we'll make sure that we can execute LDAP queries as the Gecko user.

```
root@charlie:~ # ldapsearch -H ldap://alpha.linuxaholics.com -x -D
"uid=Gecko,ou=users,dc=linuxaholics,dc=com" -w suse -b "ou=users,
dc=linuxaholics,dc=com"
.
.
.
# Gecko, users, linuxaholics.com
dn: uid=Gecko,ou=users,dc=linuxaholics,dc=com
uid: Gecko
cn: Gecko
objectClass: account
objectClass: posixAccount
objectClass: top
```

```
objectClass: shadowAccount
.
.
.
```

If the query doesn't return the right result, we should check again the firewall settings, ACLs, permissions, and so on. We have seen these steps previously in the book.

The OpenLDAP client expects to find its configuration in the /usr/local/etc/ ldap.conf file. Initially this file does not exist, but we can copy the /usr/local/etc/ ldap.conf.dist file and rename it as a starting point.

```
root@charlie:~ # cp /usr/local/etc/ldap.conf.dist /usr/local/etc/ldap.conf
```

Most of the file contents are commented, but these two parameters are not:

```
host 127.0.0.1
base dc=padl,dc=com
```

Obviously, we need to change these values accordingly.

```
host alpha.linuxaholics.com
base ou=users,dc=linuxaholics,dc=com
```

We must also edit the /usr/local/etc/nss_ldap.conf file, which has the same default values for the **host** and **base** parameters

```
root@:~ # cat /usr/local/etc/nss_ldap.conf
# @(#)$Id: ldap.conf,v 2.49 2009/04/25 01:53:15 lukeh Exp $
#
# This is the configuration file for the LDAP nameservice
# switch library and the LDAP PAM module.
.
.
.
# network or connect timeouts (see bind_timelimit).
host alpha.linuxaholics.com
```

```
# The distinguished name of the search base.
base ou=users,dc=linuxaholics,dc=com
.

.

.
```

In addition, we need to tell NSS to use LDAP when searching for valid users. The original content of the /etc/nsswitch.conf file is this:

```
#
# nsswitch.conf(5) - name service switch configuration file
# $FreeBSD: releng/11.0/etc/nsswitch.conf 301711 2016-06-09 01:28:44Z markj
$
#
group: compat
group_compat: nis
hosts: files dns
netgroup: compat
networks: files
passwd: compat
passwd_compat: nis
shells: files
services: compat
services_compat: nis
protocols: files
rpc: files
```

We must change the passwd and group parameters into files ldap. So that the new file looks something like this:

```
#
# nsswitch.conf(5) - name service switch configuration file
# $FreeBSD: releng/11.0/etc/nsswitch.conf 301711 2016-06-09 01:28:44Z markj $
#
group: files ldap
group_compat: nis
hosts: files dns
```

```
netgroup: compat
networks: files
passwd: files ldap
passwd_compat: nis
shells: files
services: compat
services_compat: nis
protocols: files
rpc: files
```

Now the FreeBSD computer is able to use LDAP authentication to work. We can check it with the **getent** command.

```
root@:~ # getent passwd Gecko
Gecko:*:1500:500:Gecko:/home/Gecko:/bin/bash
```

We see that Gecko's shell is /bin/bash. However, in FreeBSD **bash** is in a different location, at /usr/local/bin/bash, and it is not installed by default. Consequently, Gecko won't be able to log in to the system. To solve this problem, we need to install the bash shell and create a symbolic link.

```
root@:~ # cd /usr/ports/shells/bash
root@:/usr/ports/shells/bash # make install
.
.
.
root@:/usr/ports/shells/bash # ln -s /usr/local/bin/bash /bin/bash
```

In addition to the initial setup, we need to tell PAM to use LDAP. The configuration files for PAM are located in the /etc/pam.d folder. We'll edit the /etc/pam.d/sshd file to include the following line:

```
auth            sufficient      /usr/local/lib/pam_ldap.so  no_warn
```

Now Gecko will be able to log in to our FreeBSD box through SSH.

```
antonio@alpha:~$ ssh Gecko@192.168.1.228
Password:
FreeBSD 11.0-RELEASE-p1 (GENERIC) #0 r306420: Thu Sep 29 01:43:23 UTC 2016
```

```
Welcome to FreeBSD!
.
.
.
[Gecko@ /]$
```

# Authenticating from a Solaris Box

First of all, we'll use **ldapsearch** to check the connection with the OpenLDAP server. We have seen many examples of the use of this command, but the syntax in Solaris is slightly different. The -H parameter is not supported and we must always specify a filter, such as objectClass=*.

```
root@delta:~# ldapsearch -b "ou=users,dc=linuxaholics,dc=com" -D "cn=admin,
dc=linuxaholics,dc=com" -w pass  -h alpha.linuxaholics.com "(objectClass=*)"
version: 1
dn: ou=users,dc=linuxaholics,dc=com
objectClass: organizationalUnit
ou: users

dn: cn=Tux,ou=users,dc=linuxaholics,dc=com
cn: Tux
objectClass: inetOrgPerson
userPassword: linuxrules
uid: Tux
sn: Penguin
.
.
.
```

As the connection is working fine, we can proceed. We can get a list of the existing network services with the **svcs** command. We can see that the client LDAP service is disabled by default, so we'll enable it with **svcadm**.

```
root@delta:~# svcs \*ldap\*
STATE          STIME    FMRI
disabled       22:28:51 svc:/network/ldap/client:default
disabled       22:28:55 svc:/network/ldap/server:openldap_24
```

```
root@delta:~# svcadm enable svc:/network/ldap/client:default

root@delta:~# svcs \*ldap\*
STATE          STIME    FMRI
disabled       22:28:55 svc:/network/ldap/server:openldap_24
offline        23:50:56 svc:/network/ldap/client:default
```

Now we must configure the LDAP client with the **ldapclient** utility.

```
root@delta:~# ldapclient manual -a authenticationMethod=simple -a default
SearchBase=ou=users,dc=linuxaholics,dc=com -a defaultServerList=alpha.
linuxaholics.com -a credentialLevel=proxy -a proxyDN=cn=Tux,ou=users,
dc=linuxaholics,dc=com -a proxyPassword=linuxrules -a domainname=
linuxaholics.com -a attributeMap=group:gidnumber=gidNumber -a attribute
Map=passwd:gidnumber=gidNumber -a attributeMap=passwd:uidnumber=uidNumber
-a attributeMap=passwd:homedirectory=homeDirectory -a attributeMap=passwd:
loginshell=loginShell -a attributeMap=shadow:userpassword=userPassword -a
objectClassMap=group:posixGroup=posixgroup -a objectClassMap=passwd:
posixAccount=posixaccount -a objectClassMap=shadow:shadowAccount=
posixaccount -a serviceSearchDescriptor=passwd:ou=users,dc=linuxaholics,
dc=com
System successfully configured
```

These commands will change the contents of the /etc/nsswitch.conf file to include the value ldap.

```
root@delta:~# cat /etc/nsswitch.conf
.
.
.
passwd: files ldap
group:  files ldap
.
.
.
```

Once the system is configured, we can get a list of the LDAP users.

```
root@delta:~# ldaplist
dn: cn=Tux,ou=users,dc=linuxaholics,dc=com

dn: cn=scientists,ou=users,dc=linuxaholics,dc=com

dn: uid=Antonio,ou=users,dc=linuxaholics,dc=com

dn: uid=webmaster,ou=users,dc=linuxaholics,dc=com

dn: uid=Gecko,ou=users,dc=linuxaholics,dc=com
```

We're almost done, but we still need to edit the /etc/pam.d/login file to include the line auth required pam_ldap.so.1 and comment out the line auth required pam_unix_auth.so.1.

```
root@delta:~# cat /etc/pam.d/login
#
# Copyright (c) 2012, Oracle and/or its affiliates. All rights reserved.
#
# PAM configuration
#
# login service (explicit because of pam_dial_auth)
#
auth definitive         pam_user_policy.so.1
auth requisite          pam_authtok_get.so.1
auth required           pam_dhkeys.so.1
#auth required          pam_unix_auth.so.1
auth required           pam_unix_cred.so.1
auth required           pam_dial_auth.so.1
auth required           pam_ldap.so.1
```

We can use the **getent** utility to check whether our Solaris box recognizes Gecko as a valid user.

```
root@delta:~# getent passwd Gecko
Gecko:x:1500:500::/home/Gecko:/bin/bash
```

From now on, we can log on to the physical console of the Solaris computer (Figure 3-7) .

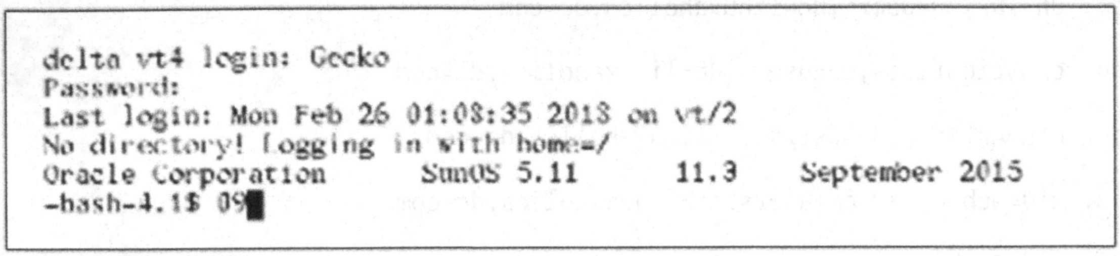

```
delta vt4 login: Gecko
Password:
Last login: Mon Feb 26 01:08:35 2018 on vt/2
No directory! Logging in with home=/
Oracle Corporation        SunOS 5.11        11.3        September 2015
-bash-4.1$ 09
```

***Figure 3-7.*** *Logging in to Solaris with an LDAP user*

# Summary

In this chapter we learned how to use our OpenLDAP server to authenticate users from different Linux and Unix computers. We studied the basics of PAM and NSS and how to configure both client and server to have a centralized authentication server. We also practiced some troubleshooting tips that will be very helpful in the rest of the book.

## CHAPTER 4

# Integrating LDAP with Active Directory and Kerberos

In today's heterogeneous networks, the use of different operating systems in the same network is increasingly common. In such environments integrating the different systems can be a real challenge. Fortunately, there are many solutions available that allow different systems to work effectively in a cooperative manner.

In this chapter we'll cover the following concepts:

- Kerberos integration with LDAP.

- Cross-platform authentication.

- Single sign-on concepts.

- Integration between OpenLDAP and Active Directory.

We will explore the following terms and utilities: Kerberos, Active Directory, single sign-on, and DNS.

## Kerberos

Kerberos is a computer network authentication protocol that provides a secure authentication mechanism. It works by using tickets. The client authenticates to the authentication server (AS), which forwards the request to a key distribution center (KDC), usually located on the same machine. The KDC, in turn, issues a ticket-granting-ticket (TGT), as shown in Figure 4-1.

© Antonio Vazquez 2019

A. Vazquez, *Practical LPIC-3 300*, https://doi.org/10.1007/978-1-4842-4473-9_4

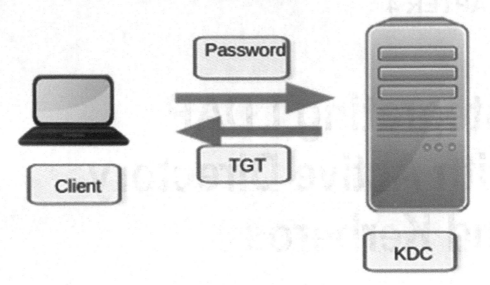

**Figure 4-1.** *Kerberos authentication: Getting a TGT*

When the client needs to access a service in a different node (or *principal* in Kerberos jargon), it sends the TGT and the ID of the requested service to the ticket-granting server (TGS), which is usually the KDC, too. The KDC then sends a ticket-granting service to the client, which can be used to access the service (Figure 4-2).

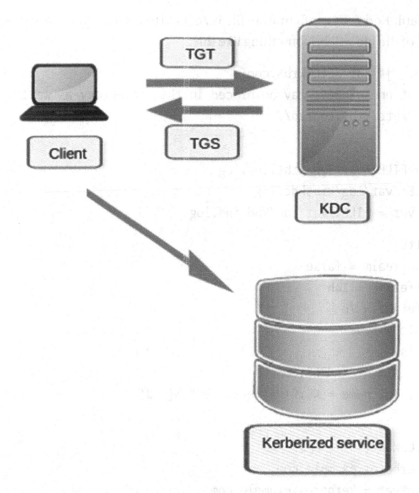

*Figure 4-2.* *Kerberos authentication: Using a TGS to access a service*

# Installing Kerberos on CentOS

The installation of a Kerberos server in CentOS is very easy. We only need to install the krb5-server package, but we will also install the client utilities contained in the krb5-workstation package.

```
[root@alpha ~]# yum install -y krb5-server
.
.
.
[root@alpha ~]# yum install -y krb5-workstation
```

The default Kerberos configuration file is /etc/krb5.conf. After a fresh installation, the content of the file will be something like this:

```
[root@alpha ~]# cat /etc/krb5.conf
# Configuration snippets may be placed in this directory as well
includedir /etc/krb5.conf.d/

[logging]
 default = FILE:/var/log/krb5libs.log
 kdc = FILE:/var/log/krb5kdc.log
 admin_server = FILE:/var/log/kadmind.log

[libdefaults]
 dns_lookup_realm = false
 ticket_lifetime = 24h
 renew_lifetime = 7d
 forwardable = true
 rdns = false
# default_realm = EXAMPLE.COM
 default_ccache_name = KEYRING:persistent:%{uid}

[realms]
# EXAMPLE.COM = {
#  kdc = kerberos.example.com
#  admin_server = kerberos.example.com
# }

[domain_realm]
# .example.com = EXAMPLE.COM
# example.com = EXAMPLE.COM
```

The config file for the KDC is /var/kerberos/krb5kdc/kdc.conf. This is the default content after a fresh installation:

```
[root@alpha ~]# cat /var/kerberos/krb5kdc/kdc.conf
[kdcdefaults]
 kdc_ports = 88
 kdc_tcp_ports = 88
```

```
[realms]
 EXAMPLE.COM = {
  #master_key_type = aes256-cts
  acl_file = /var/kerberos/krb5kdc/kadm5.acl
  dict_file = /usr/share/dict/words
  admin_keytab = /var/kerberos/krb5kdc/kadm5.keytab
  supported_enctypes = aes256-cts:normal aes128-cts:normal des3-hmac-sha1:
  normal arcfour-hmac:normal camellia256-cts:normal camellia128-cts:normal
  des-hmac-sha1:normal des-cbc-md5:normal des-cbc-crc:normal
 }
```

# Configuring the EXAMPLE.COM Realm

An easy proof of concept to check that Kerberos authentication is working is to use the
EXAMPLE.COM realm, which is preconfigured in the config files. We only need to make
some minor adjustments to get it to work. We need to specify a default realm, as well as
the location of the KDC and admin servers, so we'll edit the following lines:

```
.
.
.
 default_realm = EXAMPLE.COM
.
.
.
[realms]
 EXAMPLE.COM = {
  kdc = alpha.linuxaholics.com
  admin_server = alpha.linuxaholics.com
 }

[domain_realm]
 .example.com = EXAMPLE.COM
 example.com = EXAMPLE.COM
```

Therefore the new config file will be something like this:

```
[root@alpha ~]# cat /etc/krb5.conf
# Configuration snippets may be placed in this directory as well
includedir /etc/krb5.conf.d/

[logging]
 default = FILE:/var/log/krb5libs.log
 kdc = FILE:/var/log/krb5kdc.log
 admin_server = FILE:/var/log/kadmind.log

[libdefaults]
 dns_lookup_realm = false
 ticket_lifetime = 24h
 renew_lifetime = 7d
 forwardable = true
 rdns = false
 default_realm = EXAMPLE.COM
 default_ccache_name = KEYRING:persistent:%{uid}

[realms]
 EXAMPLE.COM = {
  kdc = alpha.linuxaholics.com
  admin_server = alpha.linuxaholics.com
 }

[domain_realm]
 .example.com = EXAMPLE.COM
 example.com = EXAMPLE.COM
```

To initialize Kerberos, we use the **kdb5_util** command.

```
[root@alpha ~]# kdb5_util create -s
Loading random data
Initializing database '/var/kerberos/krb5kdc/principal' for realm
'EXAMPLE.COM',
master key name 'K/M@EXAMPLE.COM'
You will be prompted for the database Master Password.
It is important that you NOT FORGET this password.
```

```
Enter KDC database master key:
Re-enter KDC database master key to verify:
[root@alpha ~]#
```

Now we start and enable the services associated with Kerberos.

```
[root@alpha ~]# systemctl start krb5kdc
[root@alpha ~]# systemctl enable krb5kdc
Created symlink from /etc/systemd/system/multi-user.target.wants/krb5kdc.
service to /usr/lib/systemd/system/krb5kdc.service.
[root@alpha ~]# systemctl start kadmin
[root@alpha ~]# systemctl enable kadmin
Created symlink from /etc/systemd/system/multi-user.target.wants/kadmin.
service to /usr/lib/systemd/system/kadmin.service.
```

Of course, we need to open the corresponding port in the firewall.

```
[root@alpha ~]# firewall-cmd --add-service=kerberos
success
[root@alpha ~]# firewall-cmd --permanent --add-service=kerberos
success
```

We administer kerberos with **kadmin.local**.

```
[root@alpha ~]# kadmin.local
Authenticating as principal root/admin@EXAMPLE.COM with password.
kadmin.local:
```

In Kerberos, each record belonging to a user, host, service, and so on, is called a *principal*. We can list the principals defined in a Kerberos system with the **listprincs** command.

```
kadmin.local:  listprincs
K/M@EXAMPLE.COM
kadmin/admin@EXAMPLE.COM
kadmin/alpha.linuxaholics.com@EXAMPLE.COM
kadmin/changepw@EXAMPLE.COM
kiprop/alpha.linuxaholics.com@EXAMPLE.COM
krbtgt/EXAMPLE.COM@EXAMPLE.COM
```

We can add new principals with **addprinc**. Later, when we authenticate our users with Kerberos, we'll need to have a principal for any LDAP user that we want to authenticate.

```
Authenticating as principal root/admin@EXAMPLE.COM with password.
kadmin.local:  addprinc Gecko
WARNING: no policy specified for Gecko@EXAMPLE.COM; defaulting to no policy
Enter password for principal "Gecko@EXAMPLE.COM":
Re-enter password for principal "Gecko@EXAMPLE.COM":
Principal "Gecko@EXAMPLE.COM" created.
```

# Kerberos Authentication

In Chapter 3 we saw how to authenticate with LDAP passwords. Now that we have set up a Kerberos server, we'll authenticate with Kerberos instead.

Previously we used in the client computer the graphical utility **system-config-auth**, but now we'll use the n-curses equivalent, **authconfig-tui**. In the Authentication section we clear Use LDAP Authentication and select Use Kerberos instead (Figure 4-3).

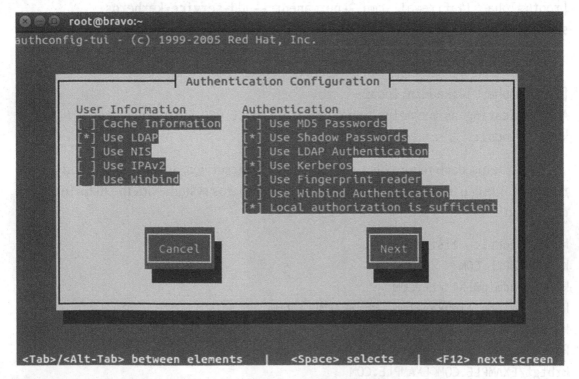

***Figure 4-3.*** *authconfig-tui authentication configuration*

Click Next and check the LDAP settings (Figure 4-4), then click Next again.

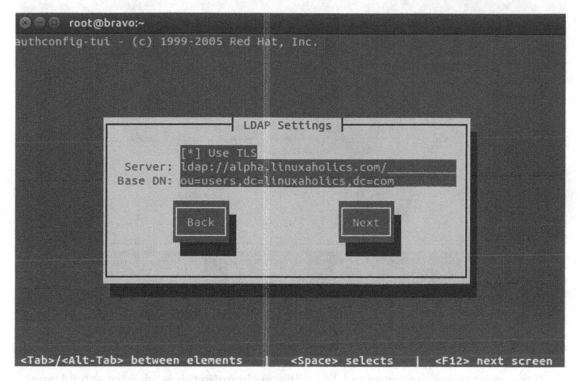

*Figure 4-4.* *authconfig-tui LDAP settings*

On the last screen we are presented with the Kerberos settings (Figure 4-5). We specify the Realm, as well as the KDC and the admin server. We could configure a DNS server as part of the Kerberos infrastructure, but we'll do it later. For now, we'll leave cleared the two check boxes related to DNS.

131

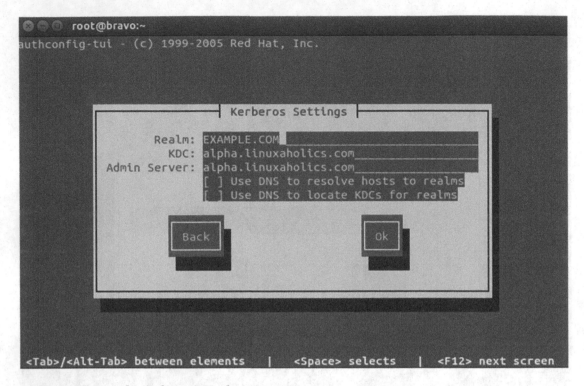

**Figure 4-5.** *authconfig-tui Kerberos settings*

If we prefer to use the command-line utility **authconfig** this is what we should type:

```
[root@bravo ~]# authconfig --enableldap --enablekrb5 --ldapserver=alpha.
linuxaholics.com --ldapbasedn="ou=users,dc=linuxaholics,dc=com"
--enableldaptls --krb5adminserver="alpha.linuxaholics.com" --krb5kdc=
"alpha.linuxaholics.com" --krb5realm="EXAMPLE.COM" –update
```

By default, sssd stores authentication information in a cache. When we change the authentication method, as we have just done, we should disable this cache.

To check whether caching is enabled or not we can use the **authconfig** command with the --test option.

```
[root@bravo ~]# authconfig --test
caching is disabled
.
.
.
```

```
pam_sss is enabled by default
 credential caching in SSSD is enabled
 SSSD use instead of legacy services if possible is enabled
.

.

.
```

To disable caching, we launch the following command:

```
[root@bravo ~]# authconfig --disablecachecreds --update
```

If we check the current configuration again, we'll see that now caching is disabled.

```
[root@bravo ~]# authconfig --test | grep caching
caching is disabled
 credential caching in SSSD is disabled
```

To check Kerberos authentication, we can try to log in from any other computer.

```
[root@hotel ~]# ssh Gecko@bravo.linuxaholics.com
Gecko@bravo.linuxaholics.com's password:
Last login: Thu Dec 21 13:44:05 2017 from bravo.linuxaholics.com
Could not chdir to home directory /home/Gecko: No such file or directory
/usr/bin/id: cannot find name for group ID 500
-bash-4.2$
```

If we have the krb5-workstation package installed, we can list the ticket assigned to the Gecko user.

```
-bash-4.2$ kinit
Password for Gecko@EXAMPLE.COM:
-bash-4.2$ klist
Ticket cache: KEYRING:persistent:1500:krb_ccache_4hIBstN
Default principal: Gecko@EXAMPLE.COM

Valid starting     Expires            Service principal
21/04/17 17:35:02  22/04/17 17:35:02  krbtgt/EXAMPLE.COM@EXAMPLE.COM
-bash-4.2$
```

# Configuring a Customized Realm

On the other hand, we might want to use a customized Kerberos realm. If this is the case, we'll have to create it with the **kdb5_util** command:

```
[root@alpha ~]# kdb5_util create -s -r LINUXAHOLICS.COM -d /var/kerberos/
krb5kdc/linuxaholics
Loading random data
Initializing database '/var/kerberos/krb5kdc/linuxaholics' for realm
'LINUXAHOLICS.COM',
master key name 'K/M@LINUXAHOLICS.COM'
You will be prompted for the database Master Password.
It is important that you NOT FORGET this password.
Enter KDC database master key:
Re-enter KDC database master key to verify:
```

We have to specify the location of the realm database with -d, as well as the name of the realm with -r.

We also need to edit the Kerberos configuration files to include the new realm, so we open the /etc/krb5.conf file and add a new realm under EXAMPLE.COM.

```
    .
    .
    .
[realms]
 EXAMPLE.COM = {
  kdc = alpha.linuxaholics.com
  admin_server = alpha.linuxaholics.com
 }
 LINUXAHOLICS.COM = {
  kdc = alpha.linuxaholics.com
  admin_server = alpha.linuxaholics.com
  database_name = /var/kerberos/krb5kdc/linuxaholics
 }
    .
    .
    .
```

If we take a look at the man page of the krb5.conf file, we'll see that there are lots of parameters we can include in the file. One of these parameters is database_name, which determines the location of the realm database. The default value for this parameter is /var/kerberos/krb5kdc/principal, which is also the location of the database of the EXAMPLE.COM realm. We therefore didn't need to include this parameter implicitly when we used the EXAMPLE.COM realm. Nevertheless, now we are using a new realm, LINUXAHOLICS. COM, located in a different path, and we must include this parameter in the definition.

We also add the following lines to the domain_realm section:

```
linuxaholics.com = LINUXAHOLICS.COM
.linuxaholics.com = LINUXAHOLICS.COM
```

We make the new realm the default.

```
default_realm = LINUXAHOLICS.COM
```

Finally, the file will look something like this:

```
# Configuration snippets may be placed in this directory as well
includedir /etc/krb5.conf.d/

[logging]
 default = FILE:/var/log/krb5libs.log
 kdc = FILE:/var/log/krb5kdc.log
 admin_server = FILE:/var/log/kadmind.log

[libdefaults]
 dns_lookup_realm = false
 ticket_lifetime = 24h
 renew_lifetime = 7d
 forwardable = true
 rdns = false
 default_realm = LINUXAHOLICS.COM
 default_ccache_name = KEYRING:persistent:%{uid}

[realms]
 EXAMPLE.COM = {
  kdc = alpha.linuxaholics.com
  admin_server = alpha.linuxaholics.com
 }
```

```
 LINUXAHOLICS.COM = {
  kdc = alpha.linuxaholics.com
  admin_server = alpha.linuxaholics.com
  database_name = /var/kerberos/krb5kdc/linuxaholics
 }

[domain_realm]
 .example.com = EXAMPLE.COM
 example.com = EXAMPLE.COM
 linuxaholics.com = LINUXAHOLICS.COM
 .linuxaholics.com = LINUXAHOLICS.COM
```

We'll also need to edit the /var/kerberos/krb5kdc/kdc.conf file to include the new realm.

```
[kdcdefaults]
 kdc_ports = 88
 kdc_tcp_ports = 88

[realms]
 EXAMPLE.COM = {
  #master_key_type = aes256-cts
  acl_file = /var/kerberos/krb5kdc/kadm5.acl
  dict_file = /usr/share/dict/words
  admin_keytab = /var/kerberos/krb5kdc/kadm5.keytab
  supported_enctypes = aes256-cts:normal aes128-cts:normal des3-hmac-sha1:
  normal arcfour-hmac:normal camellia256-cts:normal camellia128-cts:normal
  des-hmac-sha1:normal des-cbc-md5:normal des-cbc-crc:normal
 }
 LINUXAHOLICS.COM = {
  #master_key_type = aes256-cts
  acl_file = /var/kerberos/krb5kdc/kadm5l.acl
  dict_file = /usr/share/dict/words
  admin_keytab = /var/kerberos/krb5kdc/kadm5l.keytab
  supported_enctypes = aes256-cts:normal aes128-cts:normal des3-hmac-sha1:
  normal arcfour-hmac:normal camellia256-cts:normal camellia128-cts:normal
  des-hmac-sha1:normal des-cbc-md5:normal des-cbc-crc:normal
 }
```

We restart the krb5kdc and kadmin services as we did previously. After that we're ready to manage Kerberos with the **kadmin.local** command.

```
[root@alpha ~]# kadmin.local
Authenticating as principal root/admin@LINUXAHOLICS.COM with password.
kadmin.local:
```

As we changed the default realm in the /etc/krb5.conf file, we don't need to specify which realm we're connecting to. Otherwise we'd need to use the -d and -r parameters, as in the following example:

```
[root@alpha ~]# kadmin.local -r LINUXAHOLICS.COM -d /var/kerberos/krb5kdc/
linuxaholics
Authenticating as principal root/admin@LINUXAHOLICS.COM with password.
kadmin.local:
```

We can list the principals.

```
kadmin.local:  listprincs
K/M@LINUXAHOLICS.COM
kadmin/admin@LINUXAHOLICS.COM
kadmin/alpha.linuxaholics.com@LINUXAHOLICS.COM
kadmin/changepw@LINUXAHOLICS.COM
kiprop/alpha.linuxaholics.com@LINUXAHOLICS.COM
krbtgt/LINUXAHOLICS.COM@LINUXAHOLICS.COM
```

We can also add new ones.

```
kadmin.local:  addprinc Gecko
WARNING: no policy specified for Gecko@LINUXAHOLICS.COM; defaulting to no
policy
Enter password for principal "Gecko@LINUXAHOLICS.COM":
Re-enter password for principal "Gecko@LINUXAHOLICS.COM":
Principal "Gecko@LINUXAHOLICS.COM" created.
kadmin.local:  listprincs
Gecko@LINUXAHOLICS.COM
K/M@LINUXAHOLICS.COM
kadmin/admin@LINUXAHOLICS.COM
kadmin/alpha.linuxaholics.com@LINUXAHOLICS.COM
kadmin/changepw@LINUXAHOLICS.COM
```

```
kiprop/alpha.linuxaholics.com@LINUXAHOLICS.COM
krbtgt/LINUXAHOLICS.COM@LINUXAHOLICS.COM
kadmin.local:
```

We configure our client computer so that it connects to the LINUXAHOLICS.COM realm instead of the EXAMPLE.COM realm (Figure 4-6).

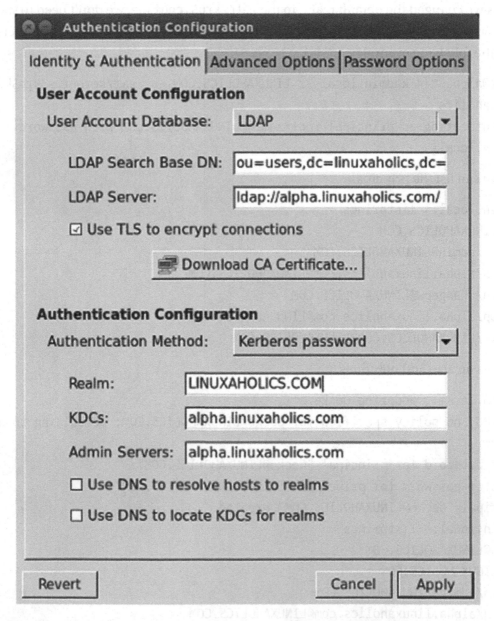

***Figure 4-6.*** *system-config-authentication: Configuring Kerberos authentication*

We can also check that we can log in correctly.

```
[root@hotel ~]# ssh Gecko@bravo.linuxaholics.com
Gecko@192.168.1.230's password:
Last login: Thu Dec 21 14:34:23 2017 from antonio.home
Could not chdir to home directory /home/Gecko: No such file or directory
/usr/bin/id: cannot find name for group ID 500
-bash-4.2$
```

## DNS and Kerberos

When using the EXAMPLE.COM realm in our previous configuration, we decided to manually configure the address of the KDC and admin servers. However, in more extensive deployments it is more convenient to use DNS instead.

To use DNS to discover Kerberos services, DNS must support the use of SRV record types, as specified in RFC-2782. This could be a sample SRV record:

```
_kerberos._udp.LINUXAHOLICS.COM.          IN SRV  10 0 88
alpha.linuxaholics.com.
```

The format of an SRV record is as follows:

- The name of the service preceded by an underscore sign.

- The protocol (TCP or UDP) preceded by an underscore sign.

- The realm followed by a trailing dot.

- The record class, which is always IN.

- The record type, in this case SRV.

- The priority; the lower this value is, the more priority the server will be given.

- The weight; this value is used for load balancing when the priority is equal.

- The port number on which the service listens.

- The fully qualified domain name (FQDN) of the host.

The _kerberos._udp.LINUXAHOLICS.COM. record is used for contacting the KDC by UDP. We could also add a _kerberos._tcp.LINUXAHOLICS.COM. entry if we wanted the client to use TCP when contacting the Kerberos server, but usually this is not necessary. The next entry, _kerberos-master._udp.LINUXAHOLICS.COM, is used to locate the main KDC server. As in our case we only have one KDC server, this record will point to that server.

Next we have the _kerberos-adm._tcp.LINUXAHOLICS.COM. record. The kerberos-adm service listens on TCP port 749 and is used by the **kadmin** program. Finally, the _kpasswd_udp.LINUXAHOLICS.COM, the **kpasswd** service will listen for incoming connections on UDP/TCP port 464 of our Kerberos server. This service is in charge of managing user password changes, so if we want users to be able to change their passwords, we'll need to open this port in the firewall, too.

Setting up a DNS server is beyond the scope of this book, but a simplified zone file could be similar to this:

```
;
;Data file for linuxaholics.com
;
$TTL 3H
linuxaholics.com.    IN SOA  alpha.linuxaholics.com. root.linuxaholics.com (
                2018032001      ; serial
                1D      ; refresh
                1H      ; retry
                1W      ; expire
                3H )    ; minimum
        IN NS alpha.linuxaholics.com.

alpha                           IN A   192.168.1.229
bravo                           IN A   192.168.1.230
_kerberos._udp.LINUXAHOLICS.COM.        IN SRV  10 0 88  alpha.linuxaholics.com.
_kerberos-master._udp.LINUXAHOLICS.COM. IN SRV  0  0 88  alpha.linuxaholics.com.
_kerberos-adm._tcp.LINUXAHOLICS.COM.    IN SRV  0  0 749 alpha.linuxaholics.com.
_kpasswd._udp.LINUXAHOLICS.COM.         IN SRV  0  0 464 alpha.linuxaholics.com.
```

Of course, we need to edit the DNS settings in our client accordingly. We can check that the DNS server can be reached and queried by using the **dig** utility.

```
[root@bravo ~]# dig @192.168.1.229 -t SRV _kerberos._udp.LINUXAHOLICS.COM.
.
.
.
;; ANSWER SECTION:
_kerberos._udp.LINUXAHOLICS.COM. 10800 IN SRV   10 0 88 alpha.linuxaholics.
com.
.
.
.
```

If the query fails, we should make sure that the firewall as well as the DNS server itself are accepting external connections.

Once we're done configuring the DNS infrastructure, we again edit the authentication settings. As we've seen previously, we can do it with **system-config-authentication**, **authconfig-tui**, or **authconfig**. This time we'll select the Use DNS ... options (Figure 4-7).

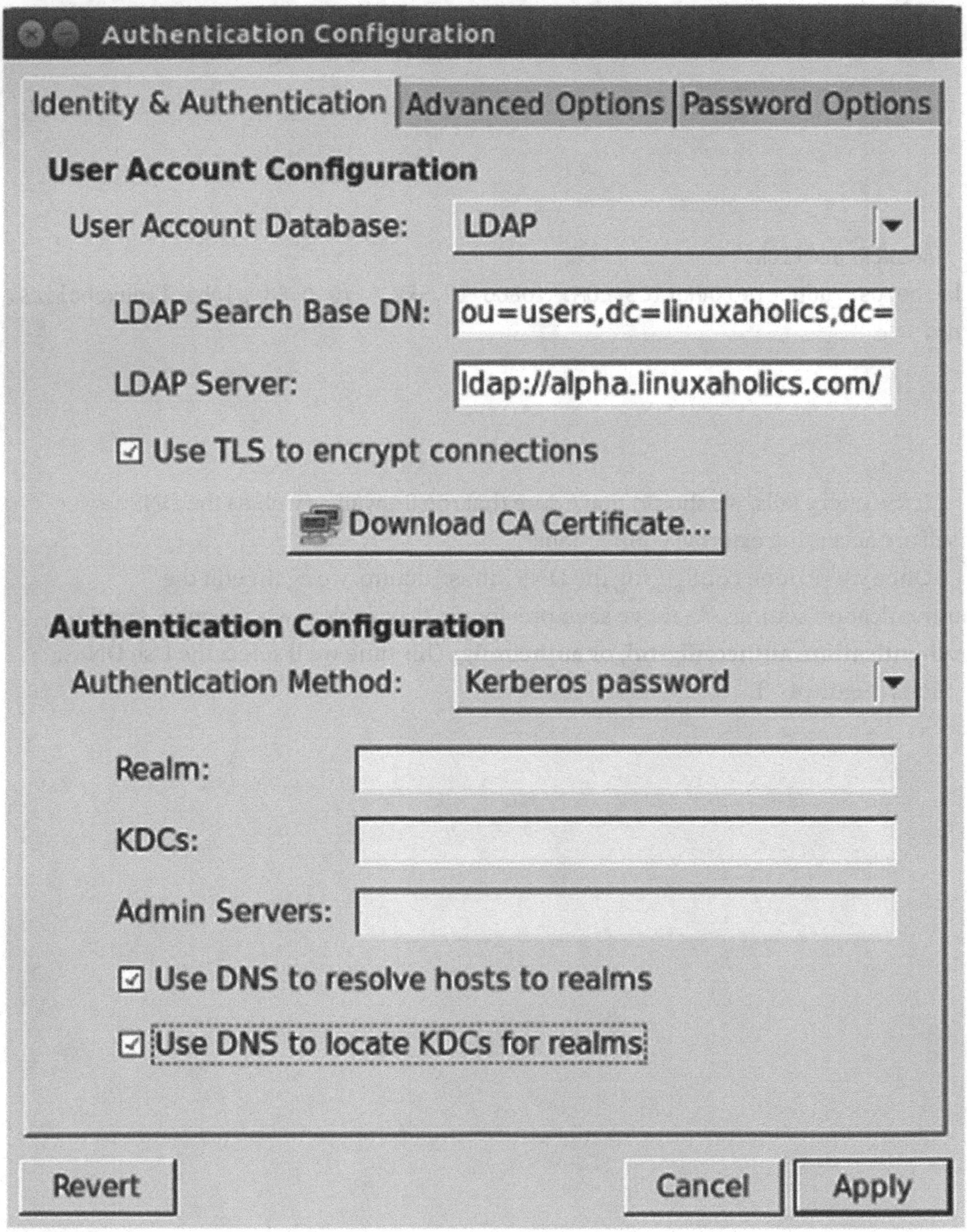

*Figure 4-7.*  *system-config-authentication: Using DNS to locate Kerberos services*

After restarting the DNS server, we try to connect again.

```
[root@hotel named]# ssh Gecko@bravo.linuxaholics.com
Gecko@bravo.linuxaholics.com's password:
Last login: Tue Mar 13 14:52:34 2018 from hotel.linuxaholics.com
Could not chdir to home directory /home/Gecko: No such file or directory
id: cannot find name for group ID 500
-bash-4.2$
```

## Troubleshooting Kerberos Authentication

When troubleshooting Kerberos authentication, the first thing we should do is to take a look at the log files. According to the settings in the /etc/krb5.conf file, the log file for the KDC is /var/log/krb5kdc.log.

If the authentication works as expected, we should see a line similar to this one:

```
Apr 21 19:23:35 alpha.linuxaholics.com krb5kdc[4456](info): AS_REQ
(8 etypes {18 17 20 19 16 23 25 26}) 192.168.1.230: ISSUE: authtime
1492795415, etypes {rep=18 tkt=18 ses=18}, Gecko@LINUXAHOLICS.COM for
krbtgt/LINUXAHOLICS.COM@LINUXAHOLICS.COM
```

However, if, for instance, the principal or user has not been created yet, we'll see a message similar to this one:

```
Apr 21 19:20:34 alpha.linuxaholics.com krb5kdc[4456](info): AS_REQ
(8 etypes {18 17 20 19 16 23 25 26}) 192.168.1.230: CLIENT_NOT_FOUND:
Gecko@LINUXAHOLICS for krbtgt/LINUXAHOLICS@LINUXAHOLICS.COM, Client not
found in Kerberos database
```

Of course, we need to check that the appropriate firewall ports are open, and that name resolution is working as expected.

## Cross-Platform Authentication

Until now we have authenticated users working from Linux machines, but in today's heterogeneous networks it is much more convenient to be able to authenticate users independent of the platform used. In Chapter 3, we saw how to authenticate against a Linux OpenLDAP server from a Solaris box and a FreeBSD box. Now we'll see how to authenticate from a Windows workstation.

# Authenticating from Windows

To authenticate against an OpenLDAP server from a Windows workstation, we could use pGina, an open source project that allows Windows workstations to authenticate against an OpenLDAP server.

We can download pGina from its official web site at `http://pgina.org/`. The installation process is very easy, as is usually the case with Windows executables. After clicking `pGinaSetup-3.1.8.0.exe` we'll see the image shown in Figure 4-8.

***Figure 4-8.*** *Installing pGina*

After clicking Next and accepting the software license, we choose the destination folder and proceed with the actual installation. It is possible that we need to install some software dependencies, so if that's the case we'll install them as well.

Once the installation is complete, we can configure pGina by clicking its icon (Figure 4-9).

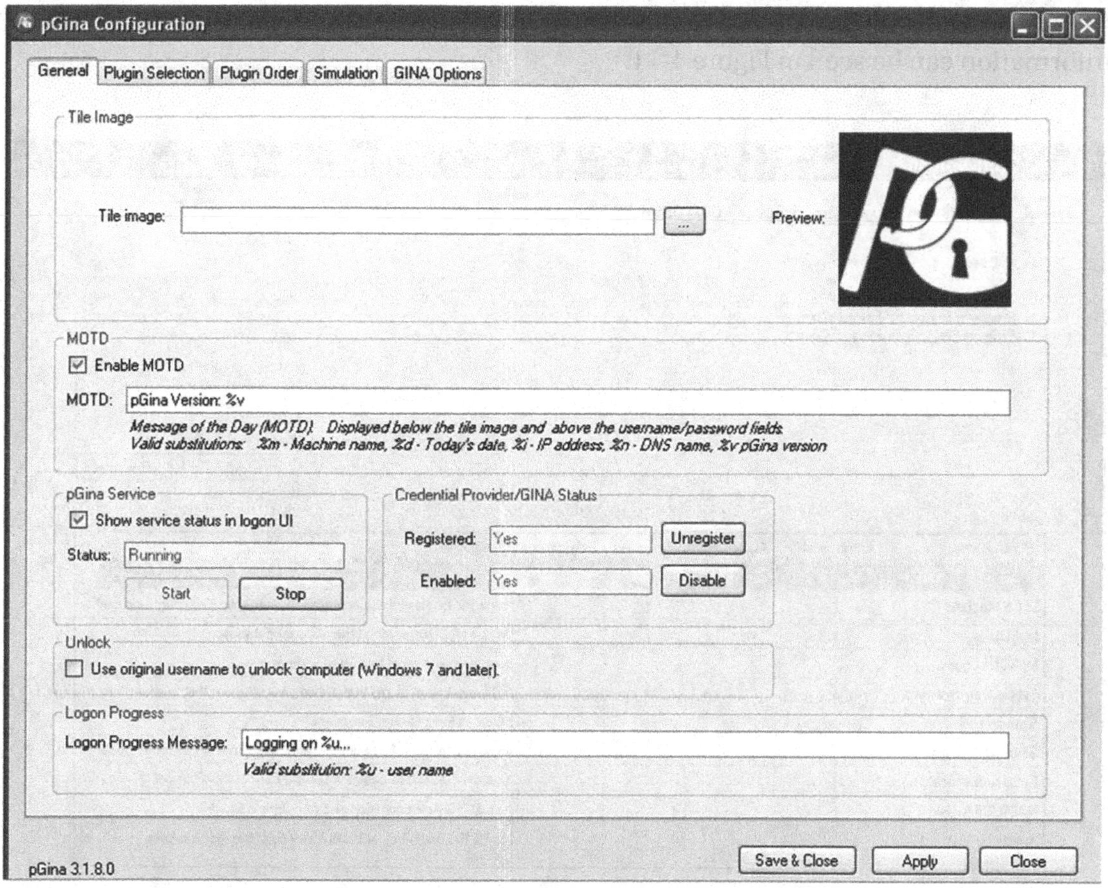

***Figure 4-9.*** *Configuring pGina*

On the Plugin Selection tab, we select the LDAP Authentication and LDAP Authorization check boxes (Figure 4-10) and click Configure. In the new window that open, we'll type in the necessary data to connect to the LDAP server, such as the server name, the port, the LDAP user that will perform the searches, and so on. All this information can be seen in Figure 4-11.

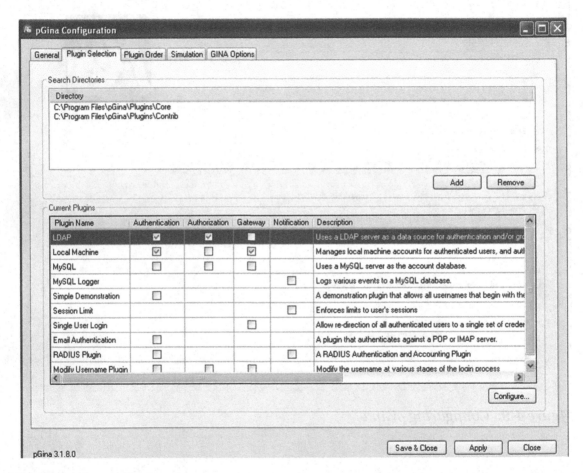

***Figure 4-10.*** *Selecting LDAP Authentication and Authorization in pGina*

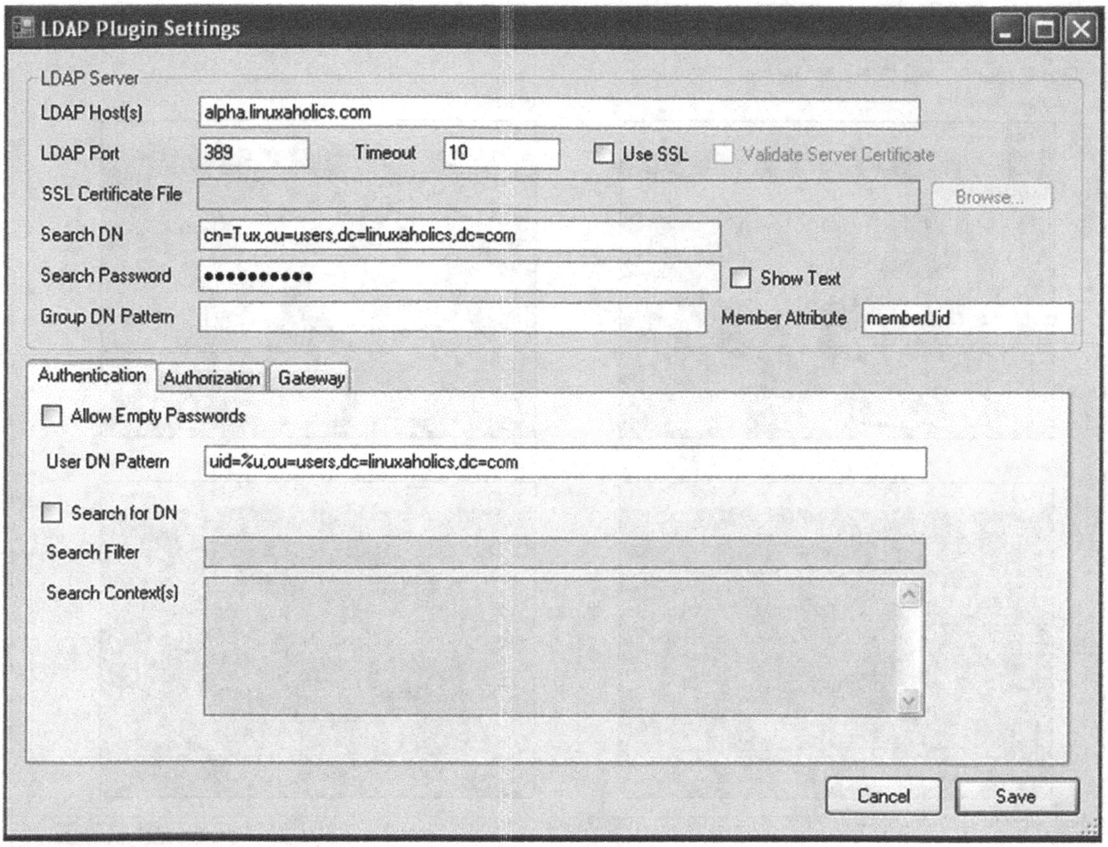

***Figure 4-11.*** *LDAP connection settings*

In this example we connect as the user cn=Tux, ou=users,dc=linuxaholics,dc=com and we'll authenticate users in ou=users,dc=linuxaholics,dc=com. It is important that the user we choose in the Search DN field has enough permissions to read that branch of the LDAP tree.

Next on the Plugin Order tab, we make sure that LDAP is selected before Local machine when authenticating users (Figure 4-12).

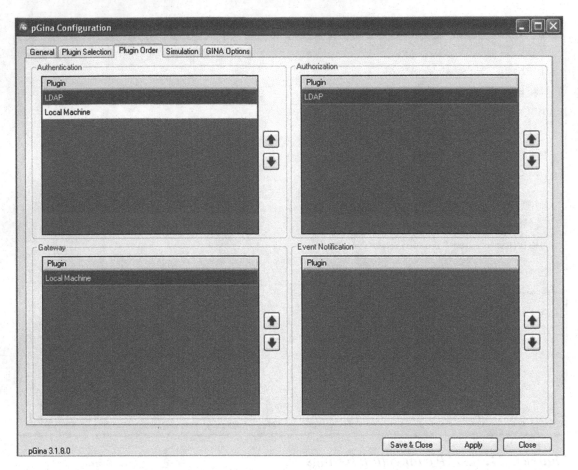

***Figure 4-12.*** *Setting the plugin order*

To check whether the LDAP users can authenticate successfully we can click the
Simulation tab and enter the credentials of a valid LDAP user (Figure 4-13).

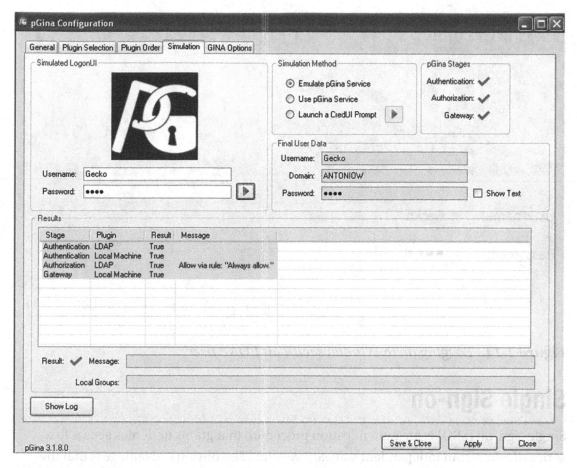

***Figure 4-13.*** *Simulating LDAP authentication*

In our case the simulation was successful. We are ready to log into the Windows workstation with an LDAP user (Figure 4-14).

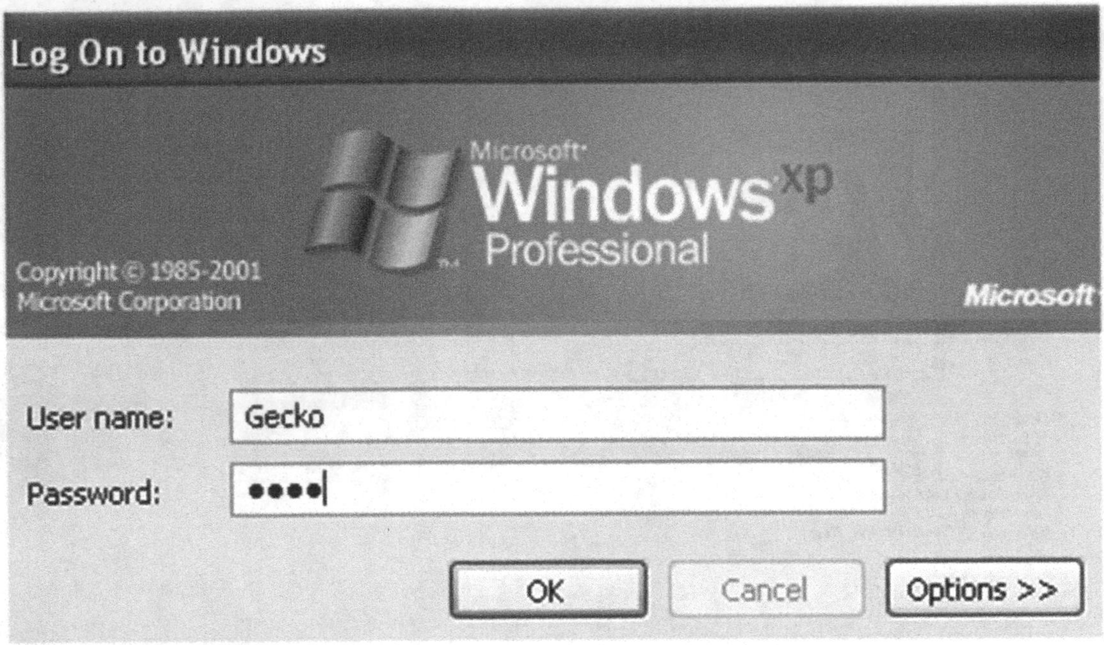

*Figure 4-14.*   *Logging on to Windows with an LDAP user*

# Single Sign-on

Single sign-on (SSO) is an authentication procedure that grants or denies access to a series of related but independent software systems. The obvious advantage is that the users don't need to authenticate against each and every software system they connect to; instead they authenticate against a common centralized authentication server.

One of the most used SSO implementations is based on the use of Kerberos. After being granted a TGT, the user will be able to access any Kerberized application without needing to reauthenticate.

# Integrating OpenLDAP and Active Directory

In the first chapter of this book we saw that OpenLDAP is a free implementation of the LDAP protocol. There are, however, many other implementations, both free and commercial. One of these is Microsoft Active Directory

# Active Directory

With Windows NT, many of us became familiar with a new concept, the *domain*. A domain could be defined as a group of users, computers, and other network resources that are centrally managed. This was a great leap forward compared to *workgroups*. In a workgroup, the computers could be interconnected, but any user who needed to access a certain computer was required to have a local account on that computer. This made the management of the network increasingly difficult as the network grew. This is not the case when working in a domain. Indeed, when users log into a domain they authenticate against a server called the *domain controller,* which keeps a registry of every network resource in the domain. Once the authentication is successful, the users can access all the network resources they have access to.

In Windows NT every domain controller kept a local copy of every network resource in the domain. This copy was replicated to every domain controller, but there could only be a single domain controller with write access to the domain registry. This domain controller was called the primary domain controller (PDC). The other domain controllers had read-only copies and they were called backup domain controllers (BDCs). When a client needed to read data from a domain controller, it could contact either the PDC or the BDC, but every time that a change was to be performed the PDC had to be contacted.

Obviously, this type of infrastructure could end up overloading the existing PDC, so a better approach was needed. With this goal in mind, Microsoft began to work on their own LDAP server implementation called Active Directory, which was officially launched with Windows 2000. Since then Active Directory has undergone many changes and improvements.

# Delegating Authentication to Active Directory

Being both LDAP servers, OpenLDAP and Active Directory share many similarities, as well as differences, which makes it possible for them to integrate in a common infrastructure reasonably well. One of the first things we might want to do is delegate authentication from OpenLDAP to Active Directory

The installation of an Active Directory domain controller is well beyond the scope of this book, but there are a plethora of tutorials and videos on the Internet that explain how to do this. From now on we'll assume we have a Windows 2012 domain controller with the following characteristics:

- Name: echo.linuxaholics.com

- IP Address: 192.168.1.128

- Domain: linuxaholics.com

We'll also need to check that the Windows Firewall allows access to the LDAP ports. Once we have finished configuring our Active Directory domain we can try and access it from our CentOS box by using the Active Directory administrator credentials:

```
[root@alpha ~]# ldapsearch -x -h 192.168.1.128 -D "Administrador@
linuxaholics.com" -w Passw0rd -b "cn=users,dc=linuxaholics,dc=com"
# extended LDIF
#
# LDAPv3
# base <cn=users,dc=linuxaholics,dc=com> with scope subtree
# filter: (objectclass=*)
# requesting: ALL
#

# Users, linuxaholics.com
dn: CN=Users,DC=linuxaholics,DC=com
objectClass: top
objectClass: container
cn: Users
description: Default container for upgraded user accounts
distinguishedName: CN=Users,DC=linuxaholics,DC=com
instanceType: 4
whenCreated: 20170615140039.0Z
.
.
.
```

When we first introduced SASL (Chapter 2), we used the **sasldb** plug-in, but we can also use the **saslauthd** service itself. With that in mind, we'll create an /etc/saslauthd. conf file, so that **saslauthd** knows where to get the information it needs to authenticate users. In the file we'll tell **saslauthd** to query the Active Directory server. Previously we'll have created an SASL user in Active Directory that we'll use to authenticate and query the server.

The /etc/saslauthd.conf file will be something like this:

```
[root@alpha ~]# cat /etc/saslauthd.conf
ldap_servers: ldap://192.168.1.128
ldap_search_base: cn=users,dc=linuxaholics,dc=com
ldap_filter: sAMAccountName=%U
ldap_bind_dn: CN=sasl,CN=Users,DC=linuxaholics,DC=com
ldap_password: PasswOrd
```

The parameters are almost self-explanatory. We define the server we are connecting to (ldap://192.168.1.128), as well as the search base (cn=Users,dc=linuxaholics, dc=com). We also specify the user we'll use to query the Active Directory LDAP tree (cn=sasl,cn=Users,dc=linuxaholics,dc=com) and the associated password (PasswOrd).

After restarting the saslauthd service we can test that the authentication against Active Directory is working by using **testsaslauthd**.

```
[root@alpha ~]# testsaslauthd -u "bill@linuxaholics.com" -p PasswOrd -f
/run/saslauthd/mux
0: OK "Success.
```

As we can see, the authentication worked as expected. On the other hand, if we specify the wrong password, the authentication will obviously fail.

```
[root@alpha ~]# testsaslauthd -u "bill@linuxaholics.com" -p not_the_good_
password -f /run/saslauthd/mux
0: NO "authentication failed"
```

We now create a local user named Bill to map the user that already exists in our Active Directory domain controller. We'll need a new LDIF file that we'll call bill.ldif, and we'll store it in the /root/ldap folder as in previous examples. The content of the LDIF file will be something like this:

```
dn: uid=Bill,ou=users,dc=linuxaholics,dc=com
objectClass: inetOrgPerson
objectClass: organizationalPerson
objectClass: person
```

```
objectClass: top
uid: Bill
cn: Bill Windows
sn: Windows
userPassword: {SASL}Bill@linuxaholics.com
```

We are already familiar with the creation of LDAP users, so this shouldn't be a problem. The only thing we might not know of is the following line:

```
userPassword: {SASL}Bill@linuxaholics.com
```

In this line we are telling OpenLDAP that it should query **saslauthd** for the password of the user named Bill.

We load the LDIF file in our OpenLDAP with **ldapadd.**

```
[root@alpha ldap]# ldapadd -f bill.ldif -x -D
cn=admin,dc=linuxaholics,dc=com -w pass
adding new entry "uid=Bill,ou=users,dc=linuxaholics,dc=com"
```

Now we are ready to execute **ldapsearch** and see if the authentication delegation is working as expected.

```
[root@alpha ldap]# ldapsearch -H ldap://alpha.linuxaholics.com -x -D
"uid=Bill,ou=users,dc=linuxaholics,dc=com" -w PasswOrd -b "ou=users,
dc=linuxaholics,dc=com" "uid=Bill"
# extended LDIF
#
# LDAPv3
# base <ou=users,dc=linuxaholics,dc=com> with scope subtree
# filter: uid=Bill
# requesting: ALL
#

# Bill, users, linuxaholics.com
dn: uid=Bill,ou=users,dc=linuxaholics,dc=com
objectClass: inetOrgPerson
objectClass: organizationalPerson
objectClass: person
objectClass: top
```

```
uid: Bill
cn: Bill Windows
sn: Windows
userPassword:: e1NBUOx9QmlsbEBsaW51eGFob2xpcY3MuY29t

# search result
search: 2
result: 0 Success

# numResponses: 2
# numEntries: 1
[root@alpha ldap]#
```

As we can see, everything worked as expected and the OpenLDAP server was able to delegate authentication to Active Directory.

# Summary

In this chapter we took a step forward to keep integrating different systems. We studied the concept of SSO and implemented Kerberos, used in many SSO solutions. We also saw how to authenticate against an OpenLDAP server from a Windows computer and how to delegate authentication in OpenLDAP to an Active Directory server.

# CHAPTER 5

# OpenLDAP Replication

Authenticating every user against a common central repository such as LDAP has many advantages, but it also presents some pitfalls. In this case the LDAP server would be a single point of failure, and it could also become a bottleneck in certain situations. For that reason, it is advisable for performance, as well as for fault tolerance reasons, to have two or more OpenLDAP servers.

Obviously, the information in every OpenLDAP server must be consistent, so we need to configure some replication procedure among them.

In this chapter we'll cover the following concepts:

- Replication concepts.

- Configuring OpenLDAP replication.

- Understanding replica hubs.

- LDAP referrals.

- LDAP sync replication.

We will also introduce the following terms and utilities: master/slave server, multimaster replication, consumer, replica hub, one-shot mode, referral, syncrepl, pull-based/push-based synchronization, refreshOnly and refreshAndPersist, and replog.

## Replication Concepts

So far we have used a single LDAP server. This is an acceptable solution for a lab environment, but if we're working in a production environment, we need some degree of fault tolerance, so we'll have to add (at least) another LDAP server to our infrastructure.

Obviously, the information stored in LDAP will have to be the same in both servers, so we need to replicate the changes we make in one server to the other(s).

© Antonio Vazquez 2019
A. Vazquez, *Practical LPIC-3 300*, https://doi.org/10.1007/978-1-4842-4473-9_5

In previous releases of OpenLDAP the terms *master* and *slave* were used. The updates were made in the master server, which in turn updated the slave servers. This model was quite rigid, with the roles perfectly defined. In recent versions, however, OpenLDAP suppports a great variety of replication topologies and the former terms have been replaced by *provider* and *consumer.* A provider propagates the directory updates to one or more consumers. The same server can act as a consumer and a provider simultaneously.

The replication can be done in several ways. There are several replication models that can be used with OpenLDAP, and we will see them throughout the book. At present, the recommended way to replicate the information between OpenLDAP servers is by using the LDAP Sync Replication engine, **syncrepl** for short.

Syncrepl is a consumer-side replication engine that enables the consumer/slave LDAP server to keep a copy of a Directory Information Tree (DIT) fragment. It executes as a thread of the **slapd** service and maintains the consumer replica by connecting to the provider/master to perform the initial load and polling periodically to update the content changes.

Syncrepl uses the LDAP Content Synchronization protocol (LDAP Sync), which supports pull-based as well as push-based replication. In *pull-based replication* the consumer polls the provider for updates; on the other hand, in *push-based replication* the provider itself sends the updates to the consumer. LDAP Sync supports these replication modes by defining two synchronization operations: refreshOnly and refreshAndPersist.

When the consumer polls the provider and uses a refreshOnly operation, it uses an LDAP Search request and updates its own information with the result of the search. When the search operation finishes, the provider sends a SearchResultDone control message.

On the other hand, when using a refreshAndPersist operation, the consumer also starts by sending a LDAP Search request to the provider. In this case, though, after returning the result of the search, the operation remains persistent in the provider, so that any subsequent updates in the provider are sent to the consumer.

In addition to these provider–consumer models of replication, we could also have a multimaster replication in which data are replicated to multiple servers.

# Preparation

For the replication to work, the two (or more) servers need to have the same time and date and be able to resolve each other's name. The preferred way to resolve names in a network is by using a DNS infrastructure with one or more name servers, but we could also use local hosts files.

Once we check that the name resolution is working properly, we need to install an OpenLDAP server in the new replica machine. Then, we need to add the admin user, with the same password we used in the first OpenLDAP server, and we'll grant this user the appropriate permissions. We also create an entry for our domain, `linuxaholics.com`, As well as the users OU, which is the LDAP branch that we'll replicate later. All of this has already been done in the first OpenLDAP server (Chapter 1), so it shouldn't be a problem at this point.

Although it is not absolutely necessary for the replication to work, it is always a good idea to set up secure access for the new server as we did previously in the first OpenLDAP server (Chapter 2). We already created a CA in the `alpha.linuxaholics.com` computer, so we'll create a new key and certificate request for the replica server.

```
[root@alpha CA]# openssl genrsa -out /etc/pki/CA/private/foxtrot.
linuxaholics.com.key
Generating RSA private key, 1024 bit long modulus
.++++++
...........................++++++
e is 65537 (0x10001)
[root@alpha CA]# openssl req -new -key /etc/pki/CA/private/foxtrot.
linuxaholics.com.key -out /etc/pki/CA/certs/foxtrot.linuxaholics.com.csr
You are about to be asked to enter information that will be incorporated
into your certificate request.
What you are about to enter is what is called a Distinguished Name or a DN.
There are quite a few fields but you can leave some blank
For some fields there will be a default value,
If you enter '.', the field will be left blank.
-----
Country Name (2 letter code) [XX]:ES
State or Province Name (full name) []:Madrid
Locality Name (eg, city) [Default City]:Madrid
```

```
Organization Name (eg, company) [Default Company Ltd]:linuxaholics
Organizational Unit Name (eg, section) []:
Common Name (eg, your name or your server's hostname) []:foxtrot.
linuxaholics.com
Email Address []:

Please enter the following 'extra' attributes
to be sent with your certificate request
A challenge password []:
An optional company name []:
```

We sign the csr file and get the new certificate.

```
[root@alpha CA]# openssl ca -keyfile /etc/pki/CA/private/ca.key.pem -cert
/etc/pki/CA/certs/ca.cert.pem -in /etc/pki/CA/certs/foxtrot.linuxaholics.
com.csr -out /etc/pki/CA/certs/foxtrot.linuxaholics.com.crt
Using configuration from /etc/pki/tls/openssl.cnf
Enter pass phrase for /etc/pki/CA/private/ca.key.pem:
Check that the request matches the signature
Signature ok
Certificate Details:
        Serial Number: 4 (0x4)
        Validity
            Not Before: Apr 23 15:19:57 2018 GMT
            Not After : Apr 23 15:19:57 2019 GMT
        Subject:
            countryName               = ES
            stateOrProvinceName       = Madrid
            organizationName          = linuxaholics
            commonName                = foxtrot.linuxaholics.com
        X509v3 extensions:
        X509v3 Basic Constraints:
            CA:FALSE
        Netscape Comment:
            OpenSSL Generated Certificate
        X509v3 Subject Key Identifier:
            30:07:35:74:73:46:F5:D9:41:99:11:91:15:41:43:5B:72:DB:65:12
```

```
     X509v3 Authority Key Identifier:
          keyid:86:89:9E:9C:4F:A9:34:6A:38:CB:EE:EF:78:2A:4F:BD:CD:
          8F:59:07
```

Certificate is to be certified until Apr 23 15:19:57 2019 GMT (365 days)
Sign the certificate? [y/n]:y

1 out of 1 certificate requests certified, commit? [y/n]y
Write out database with 1 new entries
Data Base Updated

Once the server certificate is signed, we copy both the certificate and the key files to the foxtrot.linuxaholics.com server. We also copy the CA certificate file. If the destination folders still don't exist on the foxtrot.linuxaholics.com machine, we'll create them beforehand.

```
[root@alpha CA]# scp /etc/pki/CA/certs/ca.cert.pem foxtrot.linuxaholics.
com:/etc/openldap/cacerts/
The authenticity of host 'foxtrot.linuxaholics.com (192.168.44.14)' can't
be established.
ECDSA key fingerprint is cb:a9:3e:66:46:24:95:ec:f5:09:19:85:a2:9d:3c:5f.
Are you sure you want to continue connecting (yes/no)? yes
Warning: Permanently added 'foxtrot.linuxaholics.com' (ECDSA) to the list
of known hosts.
root@foxtrot.linuxaholics.com's password:
ca.cert.pem                                   100%  875     0.9KB/s   00:00

[root@alpha CA]# scp /etc/pki/CA/certs/foxtrot.linuxaholics.com.crt
foxtrot.linuxaholics.com:/etc/openldap/certs/
root@foxtrot.linuxaholics.com's password:
foxtrot.linuxaholics.com.crt                  100%  3018    3.0KB/s   00:00

[root@alpha CA]# scp /etc/pki/CA/private/foxtrot.linuxaholics.com.key
foxtrot.linuxaholics.com:/etc/openldap/certs/
root@foxtrot.linuxaholics.com's password:
foxtrot.linuxaholics.com.key                  100%  887     0.9KB/s   00:00
```

We also create the corresponding hashes.

```
[root@foxtrot ldap]# cacertdir_rehash /etc/openldap/cacerts/
[root@foxtrot ldap]# cacertdir_rehash /etc/openldap/certs/
```

As we did for the original server, we need to change the TLS default settings in the foxtrot server. We create an LDIF file.

```
dn: cn=config
changeType: modify
replace: olcTLSCertificateFile
olcTLSCertificateFile: /etc/openldap/certs/foxtrot.linuxaholics.com.crt
-
replace: olcTLSCertificateKeyFile
olcTLSCertificateKeyFile: /etc/openldap/certs/foxtrot.linuxaholics.com.key
-
add: olcTLSCACertificateFile
olcTLSCACertificateFile: /etc/openldap/cacerts/ca.cert.pem
-
replace: olcTLSCACertificatePath
olcTLSCACertificatePath: /etc/openldap/cacerts
```

We then execute **ldapmodify**.

```
[root@foxtrot ldap]# ldapmodify -Y EXTERNAL -H ldapi:/// -f tls.ldif
SASL/EXTERNAL authentication started
SASL username: gidNumber=0+uidNumber=0,cn=peercred,cn=external,cn=auth
SASL SSF: 0
modifying entry "cn=config"
```

We also need to edit the /etc/sysconfig/slapd file to include ldaps:/// in the SLAPD_URLS parameter. It is also a good idea to edit the /etc/openldap/ldap.conf file according to our needs.

Finally, we restart the service and check that OpenLDAP accepts secure connections.

```
[root@foxtrot ldap]# ldapsearch -x -ZZ -H ldap://alpha.linuxaholics.com -b
"dc=linuxaholics,dc=com"
```

If we get the following error:

```
ldap_start_tls: Connect error (-11)
additional info: TLS error -8172:Peer's certificate issuer has been marked
as not trusted by the user.
```

we'll have to check the contents of the /etc/openldap/ldap.conf file, specifically the TLS_CACERTDIR entrance, which indicates the location of the CA certificate file. In our example, the right value for TLS_CACERTDIR would be /etc/openldap/cacerts.

Once the configuration file is checked, the secure connection with **ldapsearch** should work fine.

```
[root@foxtrot ldap]# ldapsearch -x -ZZ -H ldap://alpha.linuxaholics.com -b
"dc=linuxaholics,dc=com"
# extended LDIF
#
# LDAPv3
# base <dc=linuxaholics,dc=com> with scope subtree
# filter: o=linuxaholics
# requesting: ALL
#

# linuxaholics.com
dn: dc=linuxaholics,dc=com
objectClass: dcObject
objectClass: organization
dc: linuxaholics
o: linuxaholics

# search result
search: 3
result: 0 Success

# numResponses: 2
# numEntries: 1
```

As both the original and the replica server will need to communicate with each other, we allow traffic to ports LDAP and LDAPS in the firewall.

```
[root@foxtrot ldap]# firewall-cmd --add-service=ldap
success
[root@foxtrot ldap]# firewall-cmd --permanent --add-service=ldap
success
[root@foxtrot ldap]# firewall-cmd --add-service=ldaps
success
[root@foxtrot ldap]# firewall-cmd --permanent --add-service=ldaps
success
```

# Setting Up the Replication

To replicate the contents via syncrpl we first need to load the syncprov module into the OpenLDAP server. As usual, we do this with the help of an LDIF file. We need to do this on every server that takes part in the replication process, in our case alpha and foxtrot.

```
[root@foxtrot ldap]# cat modulesync.ldif
dn: cn=module{0},cn=config
objectClass: olcModuleList
cn: module{0}
olcModuleLoad: /usr/lib64/openldap/syncprov.la

[root@foxtrot ldap]# ldapadd -Y EXTERNAL -H ldapi:/// -f modulesync.ldif
SASL/EXTERNAL authentication started
SASL username: gidNumber=0+uidNumber=0,cn=peercred,cn=external,cn=auth
SASL SSF: 0
adding new entry "cn=module{0},cn=config"
```

On the alpha.linuxaholics.com server we already added a module to log OpenLDAP events (Chapter 1), so we'll need to edit the dn and cn parameters accordingly.

```
[root@alpha ldap]# cat modulesync.ldif
dn: cn=module{1},cn=config
objectClass: olcModuleList
```

```
cn: module{1}
olcModuleLoad: /usr/lib64/openldap/syncprov.la

[root@alpha ldap]# ldapadd -Y EXTERNAL -H ldapi:/// -f modulesync.ldif
SASL/EXTERNAL authentication started
SASL username: gidNumber=0+uidNumber=0,cn=peercred,cn=external,cn=auth
SASL SSF: 0
adding new entry "cn=module{1},cn=config"
```

We should then restart the OpenLDAP server.

Once the syncprov.la module is loaded we need to add an overlay definition in the LDAP server.

```
[root@alpha ldap]# cat overlay.ldif
dn: olcOverlay={0}syncprov,olcDatabase={2}hdb,cn=config
objectClass: olcSyncProvConfig
olcOverlay: syncprov

[root@alpha ldap]# ldapadd -Y EXTERNAl -H ldapi:/// -f overlay.ldif
SASL/EXTERNAL authentication started
SASL username: gidNumber=0+uidNumber=0,cn=peercred,cn=external,cn=auth
SASL SSF: 0
adding new entry "olcOverlay={0}syncprov,olcDatabase={2}hdb,cn=config"
```

When defining the overlay, we need to add a few parameters for the Syncrepl replication to work properly:

- olcSpCheckpoint <ops> <minutes>: Every <ops> operations or after <minutes> minutes a new checkpoint is performed.

- olcSpSessionlog <ops>: Sets the maximum number of session log entries the log can record.

```
[root@alpha ldap]# cat modify_overlay.ldif
dn: olcOverlay={0}syncprov,olcDatabase={2}hdb,cn=config
changeType: modify
add: olcSpCheckpoint
olcSpCheckpoint: 100 10
-
```

```
add: olcSpSessionlog
olcSpSessionlog: 100

[root@alpha ldap]# ldapmodify -Y EXTERNAL -H ldapi:/// -f modify_overlay.
ldif
SASL/EXTERNAL authentication started
SASL username: gidNumber=0+uidNumber=0,cn=peercred,cn=external,cn=auth
SASL SSF: 0
modifying entry "olcOverlay={0}syncprov,olcDatabase={2}hdb,cn=config"
```

We also need to define a user for the synchronization. First, we create a new OU called system in the original server.

```
[root@alpha ldap]# cat system.ldif
dn: ou=system,dc=linuxaholics,dc=com
objectClass: organizationalUnit
ou: system

[root@alpha ldap]# ldapadd -D cn=admin,dc=linuxaholics,dc=com -f system.
ldif -w pass
adding new entry "ou=system,dc=linuxaholics,dc=com"
```

We then create the user.

```
[root@alpha ldap]# cat replicator.ldif
dn: uid=syncrepl,ou=system,dc=linuxaholics,dc=com
objectClass: account
objectClass: simpleSecurityObject
uid: syncrepl
userPassword: replicant

[root@alpha ldap]# ldapadd -D cn=admin,dc=linuxaholics,dc=com -w pass -f
replicator.ldif
adding new entry "uid=syncrepl,ou=system,dc=linuxaholics,dc=com"
```

From the consumer server, we check that we can actually access the information located in ou=users,dc=linuxaholics,dc=com by using the credentials of the **syncrepl** user.

```
[root@foxtrot ldap]# ldapsearch -x -H ldap://alpha.linuxaholics.com -b
ou=users,dc=linuxaholics,dc=com -D uid=syncrepl,ou=system,dc=linuxaholics,
dc=com -w replicant
# extended LDIF
#
# LDAPv3
# base <ou=users,dc=linuxaholics,dc=com> with scope subtree
# filter: (objectclass=*)
# requesting: ALL
#

# users, linuxaholics.com
dn: ou=users,dc=linuxaholics,dc=com
objectClass: organizationalUnit
ou: users
.
.
.
```

As we can see, the user has read permissions to the LDAP branch. Another way to check it is by looking at the ACLs defined in the LDAP server.

```
[root@alpha ldap]# ldapsearch -Y EXTERNAL -H ldapi:/// -b cn=config | grep
-B3 -A3  -i access
SASL/EXTERNAL authentication started
SASL username: gidNumber=0+uidNumber=0,cn=peercred,cn=external,cn=auth
SASL SSF: 0
dn: cn=module{0},cn=config
objectClass: olcModuleList
cn: module{0}
olcModuleLoad: {0}/usr/lib64/openldap/accesslog.la
.
.
.
olcDatabase: {2}hdb
olcDbDirectory: /var/lib/ldap
olcSuffix: dc=linuxaholics,dc=com
```

```
olcAccess: {0}to dn.children="dc=linuxaholics,dc=com" by self write by
dn.base
 ="gidNumber=0+uidNumber=0,cn=peercred,cn=external,cn=auth" manage by
 dn.base=
 "cn=admin,dc=linuxaholics,dc=com" read by dn.children="ou=users,dc=linuxah
 olics,dc=com" read by * read
```

In this case, the **syncrepl** user has not been explicitly given read permissions; however, as everybody (*) has read access, we could access it without problems. If this wasn't the case we should give them access explicitly, as we saw in more detail in Chapter 2.

The line we should add should be something like this:

```
by dn.base="uid=syncrepl,ou=system,dc=linuxaholics,dc=com" read
```

In the consumer we need to add the olcSyncrepl attribute to the configuration.

```
[root@foxtrot ldap]# cat replica_client.ldif
dn: olcDatabase={2}hdb,cn=config
changeType: modify
add: olcSyncrepl
olcSyncrepl: rid=2 provider="ldap://alpha.linuxaholics.com" searchbase=
"ou=users,dc=linuxaholics,dc=com" scope="sub" type="refreshAndPersist"
retry="120 +" bindmethod="simple" binddn="uid=syncrepl,ou=system,dc=linuxah
olics,dc=com" credentials="replicant"

[root@foxtrot ldap]# ldapmodify -Y EXTERNAL -H ldapi:/// -f replica_client.
ldif
SASL/EXTERNAL authentication started
SASL username: gidNumber=0+uidNumber=0,cn=peercred,cn=external,cn=auth
SASL SSF: 0
modifying entry "olcDatabase={2}hdb,cn=config"
```

Besides all the changes we have made so far, we need to declare a couple of indexes in the provider that will be used during the replication.

```
[root@alpha ldap]# cat indexes.ldif
dn: olcDatabase={2}hdb,cn=config
changeType: modify
```

```
add: olcDbIndex
olcDbIndex: entryUUID eq
olcDbIndex: entryCSN eq

[root@alpha ldap]# ldapmodify -Y EXTERNAL -H ldapi:/// -f indexes.ldif
SASL/EXTERNAL authentication started
SASL username: gidNumber=0+uidNumber=0,cn=peercred,cn=external,cn=auth
SASL SSF: 0
modifying entry "olcDatabase={2}hdb,cn=config"
```

After adding the indexes in LDAP we need to stop the **slapd** service and execute **slapindex** to actually create those indexes. If we're using the default location for the database files, we can launch it without parameters; otherwise we'll need to specify its location. We can check the man page for more details.

```
[root@alpha ldap]# slapindex
```

After executing **slapindex** we check that the database file still has the right ownership and permissions for the ldap user.

```
[root@alpha ldap]# ls -l /var/lib/ldap/
total 10620
drwxr-xr-x. 2 ldap ldap     4096 May  2 12:09 accesslog
-rw-r--r--. 1 ldap ldap     4096 May  2 12:42 alock
-rw-------. 1 ldap ldap     8192 Mar 26 18:54 cn.bdb
-rw-------  1 ldap ldap   262144 May  2 12:42 __db.001
-rw-------  1 ldap ldap    32768 May  2 12:42 __db.002
-rw-------  1 ldap ldap   231624 May  2 12:42 __db.003
-rw-------. 1 ldap ldap     8192 Apr 30 15:54 dn2id.bdb
-rw-------  1 ldap ldap     8192 May  2 10:36 entryCSN.bdb
-rw-------  1 ldap ldap     8192 May  2 10:36 entryUUID.bdb
-rw-------. 1 ldap ldap    32768 Apr 30 15:54 id2entry.bdb
-rw-------. 1 ldap ldap 10485760 May  2 12:42 log.0000000001
-rw-------. 1 ldap ldap     8192 Apr 30 15:54 objectClass.bdb
-rw-------. 1 ldap ldap     8192 Apr 30 15:54 ou.bdb
-rw-------. 1 ldap ldap     8192 Mar 26 18:54 sn.bdb
```

If the ownership had been changed to root we should change it back to ldap.

We also need the schema in both the provider and the consumer server to be the same, so we'll have to extend the schema in the consumer server as we had done previously in the provider.

```
[root@foxtrot ldap]# ldapadd -Y EXTERNAL -H ldapi:/// -f /etc/openldap/
schema/cosine.ldif
SASL/EXTERNAL authentication started
SASL username: gidNumber=0+uidNumber=0,cn=peercred,cn=external,cn=auth
SASL SSF: 0
adding new entry "cn=cosine,cn=schema,cn=config"

[root@foxtrot ldap]# ldapadd -Y EXTERNAL -H ldapi:/// -f /etc/openldap/
schema/inetorgperson.ldif
SASL/EXTERNAL authentication started
SASL username: gidNumber=0+uidNumber=0,cn=peercred,cn=external,cn=auth
SASL SSF: 0
adding new entry "cn=inetorgperson,cn=schema,cn=config"

[root@foxtrot ldap]# ldapadd -Y EXTERNAL -H ldapi:/// -f /etc/openldap/
schema/nis.ldif
SASL/EXTERNAL authentication started
SASL username: gidNumber=0+uidNumber=0,cn=peercred,cn=external,cn=auth
SASL SSF: 0
adding new entry "cn=nis,cn=schema,cn=config"
```

Once we're done, we restart the **slapd** service and check whether the information has been replicated from the provider.

```
[root@foxtrot ldap]# ldapsearch -x -H ldap://foxtrot.linuxaholics.com -b
ou=users,dc=linuxaholics,dc=com -D cn=admin,dc=linuxaholics,dc=com -w admin
# extended LDIF
#
# LDAPv3
# base <ou=users,dc=linuxaholics,dc=com> with scope subtree
# filter: (objectclass=*)
# requesting: ALL
#
```

```
# users, linuxaholics.com
dn: ou=users,dc=linuxaholics,dc=com
objectClass: organizationalUnit
ou: users

.

.

.

# Tux, users, linuxaholics.com
dn: cn=Tux,ou=users,dc=linuxaholics,dc=com
cn: Tux
objectClass: inetOrgPerson
userPassword:: bGludXhydWxlcw==
uid: Tux
sn: Penguin

.

.

.
```

As we can see, the information in the consumer is now the same as in the provider. If the replication is not working, we should take a look at the journal in the consumer server. We'll see more details in the "Troubleshooting" section later in this chapter.

---

**Note**   In older versions of OpenLDAP another replication technology was used, the **slurpd** service. This was a stand-alone service running along with **slapd** in the master server. The way it worked was quite simple: The **slapd** service maintained a replication log, or replog for short, in which it kept track of all the updates performed in the master server. **Slurpd** analyzed this log file and pushed all the updates to the slave(s) server(s). **Slurpd** could monitor the replog file regularly to search for and replicate the updates as soon as possible, but it could also scan the replog file just once and remain silent until explicitly instructed to do it again. This was called a **one-shot** mode. This replication technology was soon deprecated in favor of **syncrepl** because it was too rigid and prone to errors. In fact, in the most recent OpenLDAP versions it has been completely removed.

---

# Replication Topologies

In the practical example we've seen before we had a provider (`alpha`), as well as a consumer (`foxtrot`). This is a typical example of a master/slave replication (Figure 5-1).

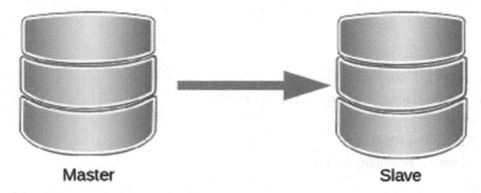

Master                                          Slave

*Figure 5-1.*  *Master/slave or provider/consumer replication topology*

We could also use the `foxtrot` server as a *replica hub*. That is, we could propagate updates from the provider to it. We could then use it as a provider for other consumers. This topology is also known as *hub and spoke* (Figure 5-2).

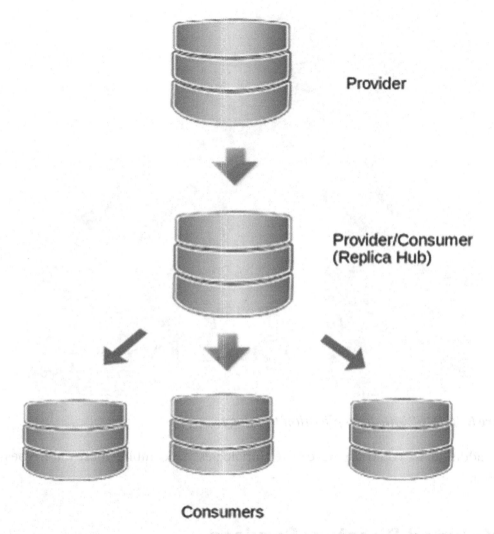

**Figure 5-2.** *Replica hub topology*

Another option would be to use a multimaster replication topology. In this case we have two or more master servers. The changes can be made on any of these servers and they are replicated to the remaining servers (Figure 5-3).

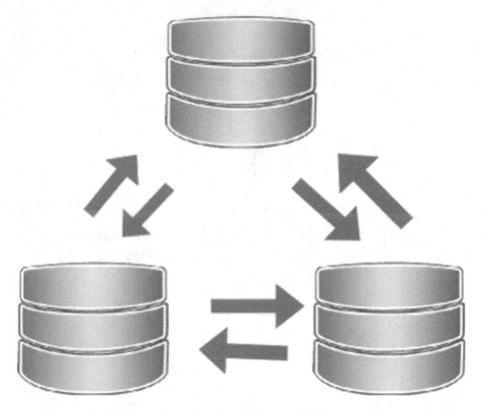

**Figure 5-3.** *Multimaster replication topology*

In addition, we could also have mixed topologies that combine these main types together.

# Distributed Directory Services

For a small site, it is perfectly acceptable to run one or two LDAP servers that hold an entire LDAP tree. However, as the size of the LDAP tree increases, it is desirable to have an LDAP server refer to other directory services for a certain part of the LDAP tree. For instance, in a previous section we created a replica of the ou=users,dc=linuxaholics, dc=com LDAP branch on the foxtrot server. If we connect to this server we can search for objects in ou=users,dc=linuxaholics,dc=com. If we try to search for other branches, though, we'll get an error.

```
ldap_add: Server is unwilling to perform (53)
        additional info: shadow context; no update referral
```

To make sure that the information is consistent in our servers we should add a **referral** to the configuration of the foxtrot server.

```
[root@foxtrot ~]# cat referral.ldif
dn: cn=config
changeType: modify
add: olcReferral
olcReferral: ldap://alpha.linuxaholics.com

[root@foxtrot ~]# ldapmodify -Y EXTERNAL -H ldapi:/// -f referral.ldif
SASL/EXTERNAL authentication started
SASL username: gidNumber=0+uidNumber=0,cn=peercred,cn=external,cn=auth
SASL SSF: 0
modifying entry "cn=config"
```

Now, if we try to access any branch that is not in this server, we'll be returned the URL of the LDAP server that has a copy of the data.

```
referrals:                ldap://alpha.linuxaholics.com/ou=customers,
                          dc=linuxaholics,dc=com
```

Both servers, alpha and foxtrot, have a copy of the ou=users,dc=linuxaholics, dc=com branch, but it is also possible that we have another LDAP branch located on a different server. To illustrate this, we'll install a new server called golf.linuxaholics. com. We have seen many times how to install an OpenLDAP server (Chapter 1). After the server is installed, we'll create a new OU.

```
[root@golf ldap]# cat customers.ldif
dn: ou=customers,dc=linuxaholics,dc=com
objectClass: organizationalUnit
ou: customers

[root@golf ldap]# ldapadd -x -D cn=admin,dc=linuxaholics,dc=com -w pass -f
customers.ldif
adding new entry "ou=customers,dc=linuxaholics,dc=com"
```

We also add a new user to the OU we just created.

```
[root@golf ldap]# cat jdoe.ldif
dn: cn=jdoe,ou=customers,dc=linuxaholics,dc=com
cn: Jane
sn: Doe
objectClass: inetOrgPerson
userPassword: Jane
uid: jdoe

[root@golf ldap]# ldapadd -x -D cn=admin,dc=linuxaholics,dc=com -w pass -f
jdoe.ldif
adding new entry "cn=jdoe,ou=customers,dc=linuxaholics,dc=com"
```

If we launch **ldapsearch** against the golf server we'll get the expected result.

```
[root@golf ldap]# ldapsearch -H ldap://golf.linuxaholics.com -x -D
cn=admin,dc=linuxaholics,dc=com -w pass -b "ou=customers,dc=linuxaholics,
dc=com"
.
.
.

# customers, linuxaholics.com
dn: ou=customers,dc=linuxaholics,dc=com
objectClass: organizationalUnit
ou: customers

# jdoe, customers, linuxaholics.com
dn: cn=jdoe,ou=customers,dc=linuxaholics,dc=com
.
.
.
```

In the alpha server, however, we need to tell the server where the ou=customers, dc=linuxaholics,dc=com branch is located. We do this by using a **referral**.

```
[root@alpha ldap]# cat customers.ldif
dn: ou=customers,dc=linuxaholics,dc=com
objectClass: referral
```

```
objectClass: extensibleObject
ou: customers
ref: ldap://golf.linuxaholics.com/ou=customers,dc=linuxaholics,dc=com

[root@alpha ldap]# ldapadd -H ldap://alpha.linuxaholics.com -x -D
cn=admin,dc=linuxaholics,dc=com -w pass -f customers.ldif
adding new entry "ou=customers,dc=linuxaholics,dc=com"
```

From now on, if we execute an LDAP search in alpha for the customers OU, we'll be given the URL of the server where the actual data are stored.

```
[root@alpha ldap]# ldapsearch -H ldap://alpha.linuxaholics.com -x -D
cn=admin,dc=linuxaholics,dc=com -w pass -b "ou=customers,dc=linuxaholics,
dc=com"
.
.
.
result: 10 Referral
matchedDN: ou=customers,dc=linuxaholics,dc=com
ref: ldap://golf.linuxaholics.com/ou=customers,dc=linuxaholics,dc=com??sub
.
.
.
```

Some LDAP utilities are able to recover the actual information by connecting to the URL specified in the referral and show it to the user. This is known as *referral chasing*. The command line utility **ldapsearch** doesn't seem to support this feature, but as a proof of concept we could code our own utility in Python.

We'll need the python-ldap library installed, which is located in the python-ldap package in CentOS. We'll start by listing the users of the type **inetOrgPerson** in a certain LDAP branch. Later we'll chase the referral.

```
#!/usr/bin/python

import sys
import ldap

def usage():
    print "Usage: %s <server> <base> <user> <password>" % sys.argv[0]
```

```
def main():
     server = "ldap://" + sys.argv[1]
     base = sys.argv[2]
     user = sys.argv[3]
     password = sys.argv[4]
     filter = "(objectClass=inetOrgPerson)"
     print "Connecting to %s on %s" % (base, server)
     try:
           ldapclient = ldap.initialize(server)
           ldapclient.simple_bind(user, password)
           print "User connected: %s" % ldapclient.whoami_s()
           result = ldapclient.search_s(base=base, scope=ldap.SCOPE_
           SUBTREE, filterstr=filter)
           for line in result:
                 print line[0]
           ldapclient.unbind_s()
     except Exception, e:
           print str(e)
if __name__ == '__main__':
     if len(sys.argv)<5:
           usage()
           sys.exit(1)
     main()
```

The code is quite simple to understand and almost self-explanatory. We provide a series of parameters in the command line, such as the LDAP server, the base search, the user to connect, the password, and so on. Later we initialize and establish a simple bind connection. We show the effective user, we perform the search, and print the result onto the screen. Finally, we disconnect from the server.

Of course, we check that the utility actually works by listing the users in ou=users, dc=linuxaholics,dc=com.

```
[root@alpha tools]# ./LDAPclient.py alpha.linuxaholics.com
ou=users,dc=linuxaholics,dc=com cn=admin,dc=linuxaholics,dc=com pass
Connecting to ou=users,dc=linuxaholics,dc=com on ldap://127.0.0.1
User connected: dn:cn=admin,dc=linuxaholics,dc=com
```

```
cn=Tux,ou=users,dc=linuxaholics,dc=com
uid=Antonio,ou=users,dc=linuxaholics,dc=com
uid=webmaster,ou=users,dc=linuxaholics,dc=com
```

If we try to list the users in ou=customers,dc=linuxaholics,dc=com on the alpha server we should be able to chase the referral and get the needed information.

```
[root@alpha tools]# ./LDAPclient.py alpha.linuxaholics.com ou=customers,
dc=linuxaholics,dc=com cn=admin,dc=linuxaholics,dc=com pass
Connecting to ou=customers,dc=linuxaholics,dc=com on ldap://alpha.
linuxaholics.com
User connected: dn:cn=admin,dc=linuxaholics,dc=com
cn=jdoe,ou=customers,dc=linuxaholics,dc=com
```

If for some reason, the **slapd** service in golf.linuxaholics.com is stopped, or it is unreachable, the client will throw an exception and show the referral.

```
[root@alpha tools]# ./LDAPclient.py alpha.linuxaholics.com ou=customers,
dc=linuxaholics,dc=com cn=admin,dc=linuxaholics,dc=com pass
Connecting to ou=customers,dc=linuxaholics,dc=com on ldap://alpha.
linuxaholics.com
User connected: dn:cn=admin,dc=linuxaholics,dc=com
{'info': 'Referral:\nldap://golf.linuxaholics.com/ou=customers,dc=linuxahol
ics,dc=com??sub', 'matched': 'ou=customers,dc=linuxaholics,dc=com', 'desc':
'Referral'}
```

We have seen that by combining LDAP replication and the use of referrals we can have a distributed LDAP tree.

# Troubleshooting

If the servers are not replicating, we can take a look at the journal in the consumer server to look for error messages.

.

.

.

```
May 02 11:29:11 foxtrot.linuxaholics.com slapd[8184]: syncrepl_message_to_
entry: rid=002 mods check (objectClass: value #0 invalid per syntax)
May 02 11:29:11 foxtrot.linuxaholics.com slapd[8184]: do_syncrepl: rid=002
rc 21 retrying
.
.
.
```

In this case we see the message "invalid per syntax," which means that the consumer server needs to extend its schema, so that it can replicate all the LDAP objects. It is mandatory that both servers, provider and consumer, have the same schema.

Sometimes, however, we don't see anything unusual in the journal. In these cases, it is useful to launch slapd manually, as we saw in Chapter 2. This way we can see a lot of useful information in the console.

```
.
.
.
5ae98121 olcSyncrepl: value #0: Error: incomplete syncrepl retry list.
.
.
.
```

In this example, there was an error in the definition of the olcSyncrepl object.

# Summary

In this chapter we have seen the concepts associated with OpenLDAP replication, master/slave and provider/consumer, as well as the different replication infrastructures that can be implemented. We also set up an OpenLDAP server that successfully updated its data via syncrpl replication. Finally, we implemented an example of a distributed directory and studied a couple of troubleshooting tips.

# CHAPTER 6

# OpenLDAP Server Performance Tuning

We already have a working OpenLDAP infrastructure; however, if we don't tune any of the default parameters in our OpenLDAP installation we might end up experiencing performance issues. We'll have to measure how well our server performs and make the necessary adjustments to optimize performance.

In this chapter we'll cover the following concepts:

- MeasuringOpenLDAP performance.

- Tuning software configuration to increase performance.

- Understanding indexes.

We will also learn about the following terms and utilities: indcx and `DB_CONFIG`.

## Measure OpenLDAP Performance

To measure the performance of a certain service, many applications, free as well as propietary, have been developed through the years so that we can test web server performance, database server performance, and so on.

However, as far as OpenLDAP is concerned, there aren't many choices, but fortunately we can try some open source tools or create our own. In the previous chapter we created a simple LDAP client in Python. We'll make some minor changes to this client to measure the performance of our OpenLDAP server.

© Antonio Vazquez 2019
A. Vazquez, *Practical LPIC-3 300*, https://doi.org/10.1007/978-1-4842-4473-9_6

We can use Python profiling libraries to measure the performance of our LDAP client, and consequently of our OpenLDAP server. We'll begin by getting a baseline performance report by executing our `LDAPclient.py` script this way:

```
[root@alpha tools]# python -m cProfile ./LDAPclient.py alpha.linuxaholics.com
ou=users,dc=linuxaholics,dc=com cn=admin,dc=linuxaholics,dc=com pass
```

After executing the Python script we'll see the expected results and a long list of information about the time the different operations took to accomplish.

```
Connecting to ou=users,dc=linuxaholics,dc=com on ldap://alpha.linuxaholics.com
User connected: dn:cn=admin,dc=linuxaholics,dc=com
cn=Tux,ou=users,dc=linuxaholics,dc=com
uid=Antonio,ou=users,dc=linuxaholics,dc=com
uid=webmaster,ou=users,dc=linuxaholics,dc=com
        887 function calls (886 primitive calls) in 0.058 seconds

  Ordered by: standard name

  ncalls tottime percall cumtime percall filename:lineno(function)
       1   0.000   0.000   0.000   0.000 <string>:1(<module>)
       1   0.000   0.000   0.058   0.058 LDAPclient.py:3(<module>)
       1   0.000   0.000   0.050   0.050 LDAPclient.py:9(main)
       2   0.000   0.000   0.000   0.000 UserDict.py:4(__init__)
       6   0.000   0.000   0.000   0.000 __init__.py:106(RequestControlTuples)
       2   0.000   0.000   0.000   0.000 __init__.py:12(<module>)
  .
  .
  .
```

We could also redirect the profile information to a file, which is probably much more convenient, with the `-o` parameter.

```
[root@alpha tools]# python -m cProfile -o 180515ProfilingInformation.txt
./LDAPclient.py alpha.linuxaholics.com ou=users,dc=linuxaholics,dc=com
cn=admin,dc=linuxaholics,dc=com pass
```

In this case, though, the data in the file are in binary format. They can be read from Python with the `pstats` module, but cannot be properly processed by command-line utilities like **grep**, **cut**, and so on. To ease the handling of the file, we won't use the -o parameter; instead, we'll use standard redirection to send the output to a file.

```
[root@alpha tools]# python -m cProfile ./LDAPclient.py alpha.linuxaholics.
com ou=users,dc=linuxaholics,dc=com cn=admin,dc=linuxaholics,dc=com pass >
180515ProfilingInformation.txt2
```

To add a significant number of users we'll code a simple tool that generates an LDIF file with the specified number of users.

```
[root@alpha tools]# cat genLDAPusers.py
#!/usr/bin/python

import datetime
import sys
import datetime

def usage():
        print "Usage: %s number_of_users" % sys.argv[0]

def main():
        if len(sys.argv)<2:
                usage()
                sys.exit(1)
        nusers = int(sys.argv[1])
        print "Generating LDIF file for %d users..." % nusers
        fd = open("users.ldif", "w")
        for i in range(1, nusers+1):
                print "Generating user %d..." % i
                ahora = datetime.datetime.now()
                nombre = "dummy" + str(ahora.year) + str(ahora.month) +
                str(ahora.day) + str(ahora.hour) + str(ahora.minute) +
                str(ahora.second) + str(ahora.microsecond)
                linea = "dn: cn=%s,ou=users,dc=linuxaholics,dc=com" % nombre
                fd.write(linea)
                fd.write('\n')
                linea2 = "cn: %s" % nombre
                fd.write(linea2)
                fd.write('\n')
```

```
                fd.write('sn: dummys\n')
                fd.write('objectClass: inetOrgPerson\n')
                linea4 = "userPassword: %s" % ahora.microsecond
                fd.write(linea4)
                fd.write('\n')
                linea5 = "uid: %s" % nombre
                fd.write(linea5)
                fd.write('\n')
            fd.write('\n')
        fd.close()
if __name__ == '__main__':
        main()
[root@alpha tools]# ./genLDAPusers.py 30000
```

The tool will create a users.ldif file with 30,000 users, which can be used with
**ldapadd** to populate the LDAP tree.

```
[root@alpha tools]# ldapadd -x -D cn=admin,dc=linuxaholics,dc=com -w pass
-f users.ldif
.
.
.
adding new entry "cn=dummy2018523172520542946,ou=users,dc=linuxaholics,
dc=com"

adding new entry "cn=dummy2018523172520542952,ou=users,dc=linuxaholics,
dc=com"

adding new entry "cn=dummy2018523172520542958,ou=users,dc=linuxaholics,
dc=com"

adding new entry "cn=dummy2018523172520542965,ou=users,dc=linuxaholics,
dc=com"
.
.
.
```

We can launch our tool **LDAPclient** and see how long it takes to get the desired results.

```
[root@alpha tools]# python -m cProfile ./LDAPclient.py alpha.linuxaholics.
com ou=users,dc=linuxaholics,dc=com cn=admin,dc=linuxaholics,dc=com pass >
180524ProfilingInformation.txt
```

By looking at the output file we can see the time consumed by the search.

```
[root@alpha tools]# grep -i ldap 180524ProfilingInformation.txt | grep
search
        1   0.000     0.000     0.000     0.000 ldapobject.py:490(search_ext)
        1   0.000     0.000     0.456     0.456 ldapobject.py:544(search_ext_s)
        1   0.000     0.000     0.456     0.456 ldapobject.py:551(search_s)
```

# Indexes

In our previous search, performed with LDAPclient.py, we used the filter
objectClass=inetOrgPerson, which is hard-coded in the source code.

```
def main():
.

.

.

        filter = "(objectClass=inetOrgPerson)"

.

.

.
```

At this moment this attribute (objectClass) is indexed in our OpenLDAP server. We can check this point.

```
[root@alpha tools]# slapcat -b cn=config
.

.

.

dn: olcDatabase={2}hdb,cn=config
objectClass: olcDatabaseConfig
```

```
objectClass: olcHdbConfig
olcDatabase: {2}hdb
olcDbDirectory: /var/lib/ldap
olcDbIndex: objectClass eq,pres
olcDbIndex: ou,cn,mail,surname,givenname eq,pres,sub
olcDbIndex: entryUUID eq
olcDbIndex: entryCSN eq
structuralObjectClass: olcHdbConfig
entryUUID: 4231623a-8e3f-1036-8413-f3757e79c279
creatorsName: cn=config
createTimestamp: 20170223181136Z
olcSuffix: dc=linuxaholics,dc=com
```

.

.

.

When performing a search in the database, if there are no usable indexes we need to scan for the entire database. This can be very time consuming for a large database.

The use of indexes greatly improves the performance of the search. An index is a data structure that improves the speed of a search operation. The drawback is that in order to do it, it needs additional storage and write operations to keep the index structure. To illustrate this point, we'll edit the Python program we have been using so far to change the defined filter for a new one that uses an attribute that is not indexed. The userPassword attribute is not indexed, so it is a perfect candidate for the test.

We'll change the following line in the LDAPClient.py program:

```
filter = "(objectClass=inetOrgPerson)"
```

For this one:

```
filter = "(userPassword=337850)"
```

In this example, we used the value 337850 for the userPassword attribute, because this value is associated with a single user. That value was assigned when creating the LDIF file and it will be different every time we create an LDIF file with the genLDAPusers. py program. The reader should therefore use a value that is assigned to one of the users they generated with genLDAPusers.py.

We'll profile our modified Python script to get a performance baseline.

```
[root@alpha tools]# python -m cProfile ./LDAPclient.py alpha.linuxaholics.
com ou=users,dc=linuxaholics,dc=com cn=admin,dc=linuxaholics,dc=com pass >
180524ProfilingInformationNOINDEX.txt
```

```
[root@alpha tools]# grep -i ldap 180524ProfilingInformationNOINDEX.txt |
grep search
        1    0.000    0.000    0.000    0.000 ldapobject.py:490(search_ext)
        1    0.000    0.000    0.233    0.233 ldapobject.py:544(search_ext_s)
        1    0.000    0.000    0.233    0.233 ldapobject.py:551(search_s)
```

Now we'll index this attribute. We create the corresponding LDIF file.

```
dn: olcDatabase={2}hdb,cn=config
changeType: modify
add: olcDbIndex
olcDbIndex: userPassword eq
```

We then load it in OpenLDAP with **ldapadd**.

```
[root@alpha ldap]# ldapadd -Y EXTERNAL -H ldapi:/// -f index_userPassword.ldif
SASL/EXTERNAL authentication started
SASL username: gidNumber=0+uidNumber=0,cn=peercred,cn=external,cn=auth
SASL SSF: 0
modifying entry "olcDatabase={2}hdb,cn=config"
```

After including the index definition in the server, we should execute **slapindex**. This is the command that actually creates the index. Before executing it, we need to stop the **slapd** service.

```
[root@alpha ~]# systemctl stop slapd
```

If the OpenLDAP database is in the default location /var/lib/ldap, we can launch the command without any parameters; otherwise we should specify the location of the database folder with -F. We can also use the b parameter and specify a suffix to determine the database for which we want to create the index.

```
[root@alpha ~]# slapindex -b "dc=linuxaholics,dc=com"
5b07fad0 hdb_db_open: warning - no DB_CONFIG file found in directory
/var/lib/ldap: (2).
Expect poor performance for suffix "dc=linuxaholics,dc=com".
```

After executing **slapindex** we'll see that a new file has been created in the database folder.

```
[root@alpha ldap]# ls -l /var/lib/ldap/
.
.
.
-rw-------. 1 ldap ldap     8192 abr 17 13:02 userPassword.bdb
.
.
.
```

---

**Note**   It is very important that the newly created index file is owned by the LDAP user and group. If it's not, the service won't start and we'll need to change the owner manually.

---

Next time we execute a query that uses that index, it won't be necessary to scan the whole database. The index file will be used instead. We start the service and repeat the search query to prove this point.

```
[root@alpha ~]# systemctl start slapd
[root@alpha tools]# python -m cProfile ./LDAPclient.py alpha.linuxaholics.
com ou=users,dc=linuxaholics,dc=com cn=admin,dc=linuxaholics,dc=com pass >
180524ProfilingInformationINDEX.txt
```

```
[root@alpha tools]# grep -i ldap 180524ProfilingInformationINDEX.txt | grep
search
        1    0.000    0.000    0.000    0.000 ldapobject.py:490(search_ext)
        1    0.000    0.000    0.083    0.083 ldapobject.py:544(search_ext_s)
        1    0.000    0.000    0.083    0.083 ldapobject.py:551(search_s)
```

It's clear that this time the search was much more efficient.

# DB_CONFIG

After a fresh installation of OpenLDAP if we take a look at the system log (the systemd-journal in CentOS 7), we can see the following message:

```
Sep 24 00:13:22 foxtrot.linuxaholics.com slapd[21412]: hdb_db_open:
warning - no DB_CONFIG file found in directory /var/lib/ldap: (2).
                Expect poor performance for suffix "dc=linuxaholics,dc=com".
```

We already mentioned briefly that OpenLDAP stores data in a storage back end. The storage back end can be changed by the admin, but by default it is the Berkeley HDB. There are many options we can use to fine tune the behavior of this back end, and this can be done by modifying the DB_CONFIG file.

By default, there is no DB_CONFIG file in the OpenLDAP installation directory, but there is a sample DB_CONFIG file in /usr/share/openldap-servers/DB_CONFIG.example.

```
[root@centos7-lpi3 ~]# cat /usr/share/openldap-servers/DB_CONFIG.example
# $OpenLDAP$
# Example DB_CONFIG file for use with slapd(8) BDB/HDB databases.
#
# See the Oracle Berkeley DB documentation
#    <http://www.oracle.com/technology/documentation/berkeley-db/db/ref/env/
      db_config.html>
# for detailed description of DB_CONFIG syntax and semantics.
#
# Hints can also be found in the OpenLDAP Software FAQ
#         <http://www.openldap.org/faq/index.cgi?file=2>
# in particular:
#    <http://www.openldap.org/faq/index.cgi?file=1075>

# Note: most DB_CONFIG settings will take effect only upon rebuilding
# the DB environment.

# one 0.25 GB cache
set_cachesize 0 268435456 1

# Data Directory
#set_data_dir db
```

```
# Transaction Log settings
set_lg_regionmax 262144
set_lg_bsize 2097152
#set_lg_dir logs
```

We can copy it to /var/lib/ldap.

```
[root@alpha ~]# cp /usr/share/openldap-servers/DB_CONFIG.example /var/lib/
ldap/DB_CONFIG
```

There are several options that can be modified to customize the behavior of the HDB back end according to our needs. These are some of the most important:

- set_cachesize <gbytes> <bytes> <ncache>: As the name implies, this option sets the cache size in memory. We can specify the size in gigabytes or bytes. We can also specify the number of cache segments to use.

- set_data_dir: This option is self-explanatory. If defined, it specifies the location of the data files. It is usually commented, as by default the data directory will be the same directory the DB_CONFIG file is located in. It should only be specified if that's not the case.

- set_lg_regionmax: It sets the maximum size in bytes in the memory cache for database file name caching.

- set_lg_bsize: It sets the size in memory cache for log information. When this value is exceeded the information is written to disk.

- set_lg_dir: It specifies the log directory.

For example, if we want to keep the logs in the logs folder inside /var/lib/ldap we should edit the DB_CONFIG file we just created from the sample file. We comment out the following line:

```
set_lg_dir logs
```

Of course, we create the folder.

```
[root@alpha ~]# mkdir /var/lib/ldap/logs
```

We also assign ownership of the folder to the LDAP user and group.

```
[root@alpha ~]# chown ldap:ldap /var/lib/ldap/logs
```

After restarting the **slapd** service, we'll see that the database transaction logs are kept in that location.

# Summary

In the previous chapters we learned how to install an OpenLDAP server, secure communication with the clients, integrate LDAP authentication with PAM, and more. In this final chapter about OpenLDAP we focused on the performance, and the different factors that can have affect it. We have seen how indexes can dramatically improve the overall performance of an OpenLDAP server.

# PART II

# Samba

# CHAPTER 7

# Starting with Samba

As we did when we studied OpenLDAP in the previous section, we're going to start with a brief introduction to Samba. Samba is an open source implementation of the Server Message Block (SMB) protocol, later renamed the Common Internet File System protocol. This protocol was originally developed by Microsoft to provide file access over the network.

## Installing Samba

Obviously, the first thing we need to do is install the software.

```
[root@hotel ~]# yum install samba
```

The main configuration file is /etc/samba/smb.conf. At first it might look complicated, but despite its length it is really well documented. It is always a good exercise to take a look at this file and the comments on it. For now, though, we'll start with something simple.

## Creating a Share

Let's suppose we want to share a folder among several Windows clients. The first step is to create the folder on the server:

```
[root@hotel ~]# mkdir /shared_docs
```

If we have **SELinux** enabled, which is usually a good idea, we also have to relabel the folder we just created so that it can be shared with Samba.

```
[root@hotel ~]# ls -lZd /shared_docs/
drwxr-xr-x. root root unconfined_u:object_r:default_t:s0 /shared_docs2/
[root@hotel ~]# chcon -t samba_share_t /shared_docs/
[root@hotel ~]# ls -lZd /shared_docs/
drwxr-xr-x. root root unconfined_u:object_r:samba_share_t:s0 /shared_docs/
```

© Antonio Vazquez 2019
A. Vazquez, *Practical LPIC-3 300*, https://doi.org/10.1007/978-1-4842-4473-9_7

Now we can use the folder as a Samba share. However, if we want the changes to survive an SELinux relabel, we should execute this command instead:

```
[root@hotel ~]# semanage fcontext -a -t samba_share_t "/shared_docs(/.*)?"
```

Depending on the exact version of CentOS 7 we are working on, we can have an /etc/samba/smb.conf.sample file with many configuration examples or we can have those same examples commented in the /etc/samba/smb.conf file itself. In any case, we can see some examples of commented network shares like this one:

```
# A publicly accessible directory that is read only, except for users in the
# "staff" group (which have write permissions):
;       [public]
;       comment = Public Stuff
;       path = /home/samba
;       public = yes
;       writable = yes
;       printable = no
;       write list = +staff
```

We see the name of the share ([public]), a comment, and the path it points to. We can also see a series of parameters that define many characteristics of the share. In this case the public share is (would be) writable, can be browsed by anyone (public), and the users in the staff group can write to it. The printable parameter means that spool files can be written in this location; this is only useful when defining Samba printers.

Now that we know a bit more about Samba shares, we're going to create a new one. We'll name our shared resource Docs, with the comment Public documents, and the path will be that of the folder we just created (/shared_docs). Initially we'll make the resource readable but not writable. The lines we'll have to add to the file are these:

```
[Docs]
comment = Public documents
path = /shared_docs
public = yes
writable = no
```

We can check whether the syntax of the file is correct with the **testparm** command.

```
[root@hotel ~]# testparm
Load smb config files from /etc/samba/smb.conf
rlimit_max: increasing rlimit_max (1024) to minimum Windows limit (16384)
Processing section "[homes]"
Processing section "[printers]"
Processing section "[Docs]"
Loaded services file OK.
Server role: ROLE_STANDALONE

Press enter to see a dump of your service definitions

# Global parameters
[global]
        workgroup = MYGROUP
        server string = Samba Server Version %v
        security = USER
        log file = /var/log/samba/log.%m
        max log size = 50
        idmap config * : backend = tdb
        cups options = raw

[homes]
        comment = Home Directories
        read only = No
        browseable = No

[printers]
        comment = All Printers
        path = /var/spool/samba
        printable = Yes
        print ok = Yes
        browseable = No

[Docs]
        comment = Public documents
        path = /shared_docs
        guest ok = Yes
```

In the output we see that the file seems to be correct, and the new share we just created was successfully recognized. We restart the Samba service to apply the changes.

```
[root@hotel ~]# systemctl restart smb
```

We also enable the service so that it starts automatically.

```
[root@hotel ~]# systemctl enable smb
Created symlink from /etc/systemd/system/multi-user.target.wants/smb.
service to /usr/lib/systemd/system/smb.service.
```

# Accessing the Share

To access the server from our Windows clients we'll have to allow the associated traffic in the firewall.

```
[root@hotel ~]# firewall-cmd --add-service=samba
success
[root@hotel ~]# firewall-cmd --permanent --add-service=samba
success
```

We create a simple text file and place it in the shared folder.

```
[root@hotel ~]# cat > /shared_docs/example.txt << EOF
> This is an example file
> EOF
```

If we try to connect from any other Linux station with the Samba client, we'll be able to see and download the file we just created. If the **smbclient** tool is currently not installed we'll have to install the corresponding package; in CentOS 7 this package is samba-client. As the shared resource was declared as public, any user and password we use when connecting will do.

```
[root@alpha ~]# smbclient //hotel.linuxaholics.com/Docs -U guest
WARNING: The "syslog" option is deprecated
Enter SAMBA\guest's password:
Anonymous login successful
Domain=[MYGROUP] OS=[Windows 6.1] Server=[Samba 4.2.3]
smb: \>
```

However, depending on the exact versions of Samba, the default configuration values might differ, and we could get this error when trying to access anonymously, even though we specified that the share should be accessible (guest ok = Yes).

```
[root@alpha ~]# smbclient //hotel.linuxaholics.com/Docs -U guest
Enter SAMBA\guest's password:
session setup failed: NT_STATUS_LOGON_FAILURE
```

Besides the guest ok parameter we included in the share definition, there are also a few more options regarding guest access that should be considered. One of them is map to guest. This parameter can take four different values that will make the server behave differently regarding guest access. We haven't included this parameter in our smb.conf file, but it has a default value. To check this default value, we execute testparm with the -v option.

```
[root@hotel ~]# testparm -sv | grep "map to guest"
.
.
.
        map to guest = Never
```

As we can see, the default value in this case is Never. We'll see in more detail the different values associated with this parameter in Chapter 13, when we talk about user mapping. For now, we'll say that this default value implies that any request with an invalid username/password combination will be rejected, thus effectively denying guest access. We'll edit the /etc/samba/smb.conf file and add this line in the global section:

```
        map to guest = Bad User
```

This value means that every access with an invalid password will be mapped to the guest user.

After restarting the SMB service we'll be able to access the share anonymously.

```
[root@alpha ~]# smbclient //hotel.linuxaholics.com/Docs -U guest
Enter SAMBA\guest's password:
Try "help" to get a list of possible commands.
```

```
smb: \> ls
  .                                   D        0   Sun Jan 31 19:28:30 2016
  ..                                  D        0   Sun Jan 31 19:14:59 2016
  test.txt                            N       30   Sun Jan 31 19:23:46 2016
  example.txt                         N       24   Sun Jan 31 19:28:30 2016

              7022592 blocks of size 1024. 6102416 blocks available
smb: \> get example.txt
getting file \example.txt of size 24 as example.txt (5,9 KiloBytes/sec)
(average 5,9 KiloBytes/sec)
smb: \> exit
[root@alpha ~]# cat example.txt
This is an example file
```

We have logged in anonymously with a guest account, but we could also have used Samba user accounts. We can create these Samba accounts with the **smbpasswd** command, as long as they already exist in Linux; otherwise we should create them first with **useradd**.

```
[root@hotel ~]# useradd -m Antonio
[root@hotel ~]# smbpasswd -a Antonio
New SMB password:
Retype new SMB password:
Added user Antonio.
```

We can also access the Samba server as the user we just created.

```
[root@alpha ~]# smbclient //hotel.linuxaholics.com/Docs -U Antonio
Enter Antonio's password:
Domain=[MYGROUP] OS=[Unix] Server=[Samba 4.1.1]
smb: \>
```

In the examples we have seen so far, the clients were Linux machines, but of course we can connect from a Windows machine by going to Start → Run and typing \\hotel.linuxaholics.com\Docs (Figure 7-1).

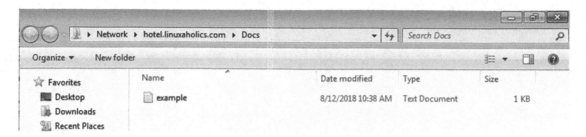

***Figure 7-1.*** *Accessing a Samba share from a Windows computer*

Now we have our Samba server ready.

# Summary

In this brief chapter we performed a simple installation of a Samba server, laying the foundation for the more advanced topics we'll see in the upcoming chapters. We installed the needed binaries and we created our first share. We opened the necessary ports on the firewall and accessed our just created share from Linux as well as from Windows.

# CHAPTER 8

# Samba Concepts and Architecture, Configuring Samba, and Internationalization

In Chapter 7, installed our first Samba server and saw very briefly how to create a new share. In this chapter we'll move on to the following more advanced topics:

- Understanding the roles of the Samba daemons and components.

- Identifying key TCP/UDP ports used with SMB/CIFS.

- Knowledge of Samba3 and Samba4 differences.

- Understanding the major features of SMB protocol versions 1.0, 2.0, 2.1, and 3.0.

- Knowledge of Samba server configuration file structure.

- Knowledge of Samba server registry-based configuration.

- Knowledge of Samba variables and configuration parameters.

- Troubleshooting and debuggin configuration problems with Samba.

- Understanding internationalization character codes and code pages.

We will also encounter the following terms and utilities: /etc/services, Samba services (**smbd**, **nmbd**, **winbindd**), smb.conf, smb.conf parameters, smb.conf variables, **testparm**, secrets.tdb, **samba-regedit**, Microsoft regedit, character codes, code pages, dos charset, display charset, and unix charset.

© Antonio Vazquez 2019
A. Vazquez, *Practical LPIC-3 300*, https://doi.org/10.1007/978-1-4842-4473-9_8

# Samba Services and Components

Samba is composed of many services:

- The **smbd** service is responsible for providing file sharing and printing services to clients using the SMB/CIFS protocol.

- The **nmbd** service provides name services based on NetBIOS.

- Finally, the **winbindd** service is used when we need to get information from Windows servers in a way that can be understood by Linux. This service is not included in a standard Samba server installation, and if we need it we'll have to install the `samba-winbindd` package with **yum**.

To fully understand what Samba is, we need to be familiar with Windows networking. Microsoft developed the SMB protocol, later renamed CIFS, as a way to share resources in a network. Through the years this protocol has undergone many changes. Initially, it was developed at IBM with the goal of turning the DOS application programming interface (API) local file access into a networked file system. Later, Microsoft added many changes to the protocol and merged it with the LAN Manager protocol. Microsoft continued adding features to the protocol when it was released with Windows for Workgroups. SMB was originally designed to run on top of the NetBIOS API, but since Windows 2000 it runs by default on top of TCP.

This first version of the protocol (SMB 1.0) was very "noisy" and thus it made an inefficient use of network resources. Microsoft therefore worked hard to make a new version of the protocol (SMB 2.0) less noisy. This new version appeared with Windows Vista by the end of 2006. Besides the improvement in performance, SMB 2.0 also included support for symbolic links, as well as the caching of file properties and better scalability, increasing the number of users, shares, and open files per server.

A minor upgrade of the protocol, SMB 2.1, was introduced by Microsoft with Windows Server 2008 R2. It included some minor performance improvements. With the release of Windows 8 and Windows 2016, however, a major overhaul of the protocol (SMB 3.0) took place, adding new functionalities and improving overall performance. It also added several security features.

According to the role a computer plays in the network, we can divide them into different groups. The simplest classification would be to divide the computers between servers and clients. Of course, the servers are those that provide shared resources to the rest of the computers.

There are also many other things to take into account, however. For instance, a network could consist of two or three independent computers, which use the same network; each one of them manages its own local users, though. In this case we have a *workgroup*. On the other hand, if we have more computers, perhaps tens, hundreds, or even more, it would become a nightmare to manage the users locally in each computer. It would be far more efficient to have a server where all the user accounts are stored; this server is called the domain server. In this case we have a *domain* instead of a workgroup.

Considering the fact that we might be working in a workgroup or a domain, we have different names for our Samba servers depending on their role in the network. If we're working in a workgroup the Samba server will be a stand-alone server. On the other hand, if a Samba server is added to a domain, then the Samba server will be a domain member server. This server will be able to get the user list from the domain by querying the domain controllers, but it won't keep a local copy of the domain users. Finally, we could decide to make our Samba an Active Directory domain controller.

# Ports Used

The **smbd** service by default listens on ports TCP 445 and 139. On the other hand, the **nmbd** service listens on ports UDP 137 and 138.

```
[root@hotel ~]# ss -l -t -n -p | grep smbd
LISTEN   0   50                    *:445         *:*      users:(("smbd",2726,35))
LISTEN   0   50                    *:139         *:*      users:(("smbd",2726,36))
LISTEN   0   50                  :::445        :::*      users:(("smbd",2726,33))
LISTEN   0   50                  :::139        :::*      users:(("smbd",2726,34))
[root@hotel ~]# ss -l -u -n -p | grep nmbd
UNCONN   0   0     192.168.56.255:137         *:*      users:(("nmbd",3471,14))
UNCONN   0   0     192.168.56.128:137         *:*      users:(("nmbd",3471,13))
UNCONN   0   0                  *:137         *:*      users:(("nmbd",3471,11))
UNCONN   0   0     192.168.56.255:138         *:*      users:(("nmbd",3471,16))
UNCONN   0   0     192.168.56.128:138         *:*      users:(("nmbd",3471,15))
UNCONN   0   0                  *:138         *:*      users:(("nmbd",3471,12))
```

On port UDP 137 the NetBIOS Name Service listens. This service is in charge of name resolution. We can query this service with the **nmblookup** command.

```
[root@hotel ~]# nmblookup hotel
192.168.56.128 hotel<00>
[root@hotel ~]# nmblookup zulu
name_query failed to find name zulu
```

The NetBIOS Datagram listens on port UDP 138, and the NetBIOS Session Service listens on port TCP 139. Finally port TCP 445 is used by the SMB service.

# Samba 3 and Samba 4

Samba has been evolving since the very moment of its creation back in 1992, including more and more features. A big leap took place in 2012 when Samba 4 was released.

With Samba 3 we could emulate a Windows NT BDC. In addition, we could create a member server (a server that is part of the domain but does not store a copy of the domain users database), or a stand-alone server (a server that is not part of a domain and uses only local users). It was not possible at all, however, to emulate an Active Directory domain controller.

All this changed when Samba 4 was launched. This new release could emulate perfectly the way an Active Directory domain controller works. To do that, it combines several components:

- An LDAP server.

- A Kerberos server.

- A dynamic DNS server.

- Remote procedure calls (RPCs).

# Server Configuration

When we first talked about Samba in Chapter 7, we saw that Samba stores its configuration in a text file, /etc/samba/smb.conf in a default CentOS 7 installation. Since Samba 3.2, though, we also have the possibility to use a registry-based configuration.

# Registry-Based Configuration

The Samba configuration can be stored in the registry key HKLM\Software\Samba\ smbconf. Registry configuration can be activated in three levels:

- Registry shares: Share definitions are loaded from the registry, in addition to those defined in smb.conf. These shares are not loaded at startup but on demand when accessed. These registry shares are activated by setting the value registry shares = yes in the global section of the smb.conf file.

- Registry only config: If we set the value config backend = registry in the global section of the config file, the rest of the text-based configuration is completely ignored and configuration will be loaded from the registry instead. Registry shares are enabled.

- Mixed text and registry config: In this case, by adding the option include = registry in the global section of the configuration file, global configuration options are read from registry with the same semantics as an include file. Those options found in the configuration file before the include parameter will be overridden by options in the registry, which in turn will be overridden as well by options from the configuration file found after the include = registry line. Registry shares are automatically activated.

We'll look at a simple example. We begin by adding the following line to the global section of the /etc/samba/smb.conf file:

```
registry shares = Yes
```

The usual way to access and edit the Samba registry is with the **net** command. We can view the content of the HKLM\Software\Samba\smbconf registry key, which, of course, is initially empty.

```
[root@hotel ~]# net registry enumerate 'HKLM\Software\Samba\smbconf'
[root@hotel ~]#
```

Another way to view and edit the registry is through the use of the samba-regedit command. This is an ncurses-based tool that works pretty much like the native Microsoft regedit tool (Figure 8-1).

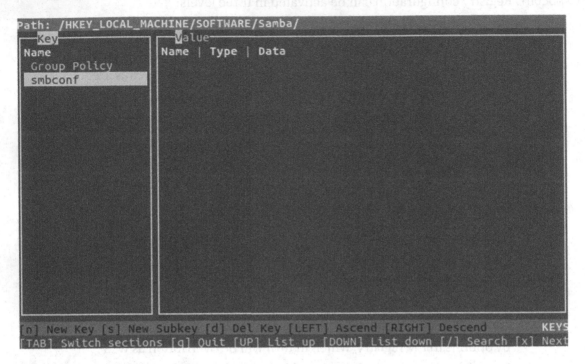

*Figure 8-1.* *Samba-regedit*

Finally, we could even execute Microsoft regedit from a Windows machine and connect to a remote registry (Figure 8-2). We'll need to provide the credentials of a Samba user, and, depending on the permissions the user is granted, we'll see some registry values or not.

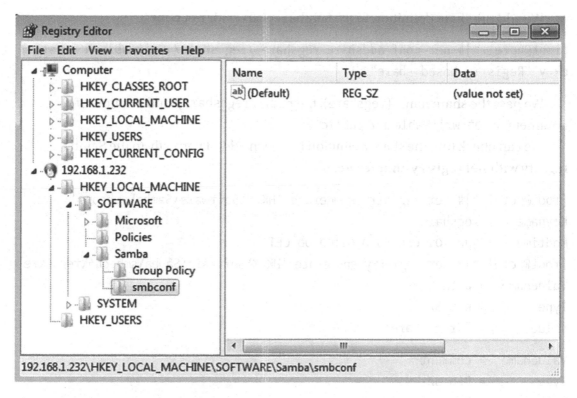

***Figure 8-2.*** *Regedit*

In our case we'll use the net subcommands to manage the registry entries. Let's suppose we want to add a new share. We'll begin by creating the share on the server.

```
[root@hotel ~]# mkdir /reg_share
```

We'll change the SELinux context.

```
[root@hotel ~]# chcon -t samba_share_t /reg_share/
```

We also have to make sure that the folder has the right context when the system reboots.

```
[root@hotel ~]# semanage fcontext -a -t samba_share_t "/reg_share(/.*)?/"
```

We create a sample file inside the share.

```
[root@hotel ~]# echo "123" > /reg_share/file_shared_through_registry.txt
```

We add the share definition to the Samba registry with **net conf**.

```
[root@hotel ~]# net conf addshare regshare /reg_share/ writeable=N guest_
ok=y "Registry based share"
```

We pass the share name (regshare), the path (/reg_share), and a couple of
parameters: not writeable and public.

We can check that the share definition has been added correctly to the Samba
registry with **net registry enumerate**.

```
[root@hotel ~]# net registry enumerate 'HKLM\Software\Samba\smbconf'
Keyname    = regshare
Modtime    = jue, 01 ene 1970 01:00:00 CET
[root@hotel ~]# net registry enumerate 'HKLM\Software\Samba\smbconf\regshare'
Valuename  = path
Type       = REG_SZ
Value      = "/reg_share/"

Valuename  = comment
Type       = REG_SZ
Value      = "Registry based share"

Valuename  = guest ok
Type       = REG_SZ
Value      = "yes"

Valuename  = read only
Type       = REG_SZ
Value      = "yes"
```

We see that the command added several values of the type REG_SZ. This type is a
string terminated by a null character. There are many other types, like REG_MULTISZ,
which is a sequence of strings terminated by null. Besides these two commonly used
types, there are many others that can be studied in the official documentation from
Microsoft.

We can also list the shares and the whole configuration included in the Samba
registry with **net conf**.

```
[root@hotel ~]# net conf listshares
regshare
[root@hotel ~]# net conf list
[regshare]
        path = /reg_share/
        comment = Registry based share
        guest ok = yes
        read only = yes
```

To check that the share is accessible from the network we'll try to connect from a different computer.

```
[root@alpha ~]# smbclient //192.168.1.232/regshare -U Antonio%antonio
Domain=[MYGROUP] OS=[Unix] Server=[Samba 4.1.1]
smb: \> ls
  .                                 D        0  Tue Aug 21 01:30:01 2018
  ..                                D        0  Tue Aug 21 01:10:06 2018
  file_shared_through_registry.txt  N        4  Tue Aug 21 01:30:01 2018

              54864 blocks of size 131072. 41048 blocks available
smb: \>
```

We could access the share the same way as if it had been defined in the configuration file.

# Server Configuration File Structure

We have already seen in Chapter 7 that the main configuration file for the Samba service is /etc/samba/smb.conf. We even have modified this file to create a new resource. Now we'll see in more detail the different sections of this file.

The file is divided into two main sections: global and shares. Depending on the exact version of CentOS 7 used, we can have a sample file /etc/samba/smb.conf.sample with many comments and examples, or we can have all those examples in the /etc/samba/smb.conf file itself. Anyway, in the first lines of the file we can see a couple of references to official documentation and a few notes about SELinux and the way to properly configure it for Samba to work properly. Right after these notes the global section begins.

The global section defines a series of parameters that apply to the server as a whole. Usually we can see a description of the parameter as well as its current value. For example:

```
.
.
.
#======================= Global Settings ====================================

[global]

# ---------------------- Network-Related Options ------------------------
#
# workgroup = the Windows NT domain name or workgroup name, for example,
  MYGROUP.
#
# server string = the equivalent of the Windows NT Description field.
#
.
.
.
#

        workgroup = MYGROUP
        server string = Samba Server Version %v

.
.
.
```

After the global section we can see the shares section, in which are defined a series of shared resources such as home directories, printers, or folders.

# Samba Variables and Configuration Parameters

We'll now look at some of the most important variables and parameters we'll find in /etc/samba/smb.conf. For instance, at this point we have the following parameters:

```
        workgroup = MYGROUP
        server string = Samba Server Version %v
;       netbios name = MYSERVER
```

We can see these parameters if we execute the **testparm** command.

```
[root@hotel ~]# testparm
Load smb config files from /etc/samba/smb.conf
rlimit_max: increasing rlimit_max (1024) to minimum Windows limit (16384)
Processing section "[homes]"
Processing section "[printers]"
Processing section "[Docs]"
Loaded services file OK.
Server role: ROLE_STANDALONE
Press enter to see a dump of your service definitions

[global]
        workgroup = MYGROUP
        server string = Samba Server Version %v
        log file = /var/log/samba/log.%m
        max log size = 50
        idmap config * : backend = tdb
        cups options = raw

.
.
.
```

When used without parameters, **testparm** shows the values of the parameters specified in smb.conf. If we want to see all the values assigned to each and every Samba parameter, we need to use the verbose (-v) option.

```
[root@hotel ~]# testparm -v
Load smb config files from /etc/samba/smb.conf
rlimit_max: increasing rlimit_max (1024) to minimum Windows limit (16384)
Processing section "[homes]"
Processing section "[printers]"
Processing section "[print$]"
Processing section "[Docs]"
Loaded services file OK.
Server role: ROLE_STANDALONE
```

```
Press enter to see a dump of your service definitions

# Global parameters
[global]
        abort shutdown script =
        add group script =
        add machine script =
        addport command =
        addprinter command =
        add share command =
        add user script =
        add user to group script =
        afs token lifetime = 604800
        afs username map =
        aio max threads = 100
```

.

.

.

As the command output will be very long, if we just want to check the value of a certain parameter, we might want to use **grep**.

```
[root@hotel ~]# testparm -v | grep "preferred master"
Load smb config files from /etc/samba/smb.conf
rlimit_max: increasing rlimit_max (1024) to minimum Windows limit (16384)
Processing section "[homes]"
Processing section "[printers]"
Processing section "[print$]"
Processing section "[Docs]"
Loaded services file OK.
Server role: ROLE_STANDALONE

Press enter to see a dump of your service definitions

        preferred master = Auto
```

We are going to change the values of the parameters we've seen previously.

```
workgroup = MY_SAMBA_GROUP
server string = My Samba Server %v
netbios name = HOTEL
```

After restarting the SMB service, if we execute **testparm** again we'll see the output has changed.

```
[root@hotel ~]# testparm
Load smb config files from /etc/samba/smb.conf
rlimit_max: increasing rlimit_max (1024) to minimum Windows limit (16384
Processing section "[printers]"
Processing section "[Docs]"
Loaded services file OK.
Server role: ROLE_STANDALONE
Press enter to see a dump of your service definitions

[global]
        workgroup = MY_SAMBA_GROUP
        netbios name = HOTEL
        server string = My Samba Server %v
        log file = /var/log/samba/log.%m
        max log size = 50
        idmap config * : backend = tdb
        cups options = raw
.
.
.
```

Another interesting parameter is "log file".

```
# log files split per-machine:
log file = /var/log/samba/log.%m
# maximum size of 50KB per log file, then rotate:
max log size = 50
```

The default configuration states that the log file will be placed in the /var/log/ samba/ folder and it will be named log.machine_name. The maximum size of every log file will be 50 KB, before they begin to rotate. We can keep these values for now.

Next we get to the security parameter. We should use one value or another depending on the role of our Samba server in the network (see Chapter 9 to learn more about the Samba server roles). For a stand-alone server, such as the one we have right now, the security parameter should be set to user. There are two more possible values (shared and server), but they are deprecated and should be avoided according to the official Samba documentation.

The passdb backend parameter specifies where the user information shoud be stored: either in a local database (tdbsam) or in LDAP (ldapsam).

```
security = user
passdb backend = tdbsam
```

In the current configuration we use a local database to store Samba users. We used the **smbpasswd** command to create the user Antonio, but there is a more complete tool to manage user accounts in Samba, the **pdbedit** command. For instance, if we want to create a new Samba user, we create the user in Linux and then execute pdbedit -a:

```
[root@hotel ~]# useradd -m -c "Antonio Vazquez" avazquez
[root@hotel ~]# pdbedit -a avazquez
new password:
retype new password:
Unix username:        avazquez
NT username:
Account Flags:        [U          ]
User SID:             S-1-5-21-892619289-2955383375-3350856941-1002
Primary Group SID:    S-1-5-21-892619289-2955383375-3350856941-513
Full Name:
Home Directory:       \\hotel\avazquez
HomeDir Drive:
Logon Script:
Profile Path:         \\hotel\avazquez\profile
Domain:               HOTEL
Account desc:
Workstations:
```

```
Munged dial:
Logon time:            0
Logoff time:           mié, 06 feb 2036 16:06:39 CET
Kickoff time:          mié, 06 feb 2036 16:06:39 CET
Password last set:     dom, 12 ago 2018 15:35:47 CEST
Password can change:   dom, 12 ago 2018 15:35:47 CEST
Password must change:  never
Last bad password    : 0
Bad password count   : 0
Logon hours          : FFFFFFFFFFFFFFFFFFFFFFFFFFFFFFFFFFFFFFFFFF
```

The information will be stored in the file passdb.tdb, located in /var/lib/samba/private. In this same location we can also find the secrets.tdb file, which stores internal settings such as the machine and domain SID, passwords used with LDAP, and so on.

If at any time we want to list existing users, we do it by passing the -L parameter to **pdbedit**.

```
[root@hotel ~]# pdbedit -L
Antonio:1001:
avazquez:1000:Antonio Vazquez
```

When the number of users is not very high, this is acceptable, but if we have several hundreds of users we should use an LDAP server to store the users, and use the ldapsam back end instead of tdbsam. This is clearly not the case, as we only have a couple of users, but for didactic purposes we're going to use LDAP anyway. First of all, we should make sure that the Samba server can communicate with the LDAP server.

```
[root@hotel ~]# ldapsearch -H ldap://alpha.linuxaholics.com -x -D cn=admin,
dc=linuxaholics,dc=com -w pass -b "ou=users,dc=linuxaholics,dc=com"
# extended LDIF
#
# LDAPv3
# base <ou=users,dc=linuxaholics,dc=com> with scope subtree
# filter: (objectclass=*)
# requesting: ALL
#
```

```
# users, linuxaholics.com
dn: ou=users,dc=linuxaholics,dc=com
objectClass: organizationalUnit
ou: users
.

.

.
```

We see that we successfully queried the LDAP server, but we also need to check whether we can establish a secure connection.

```
[root@hotel ~]# ldapsearch -ZZ -H ldap://alpha.linuxaholics.com -x -D
cn=admin,dc=linuxaholics,dc=com -w pass -b "ou=users,dc=linuxaholics,dc=com"
ldap_start_tls: Connect error (-11)
        additional info: error:14090086:SSL routines:ssl3_get_server_
        certificate:certificate verify failed (self signed certificate in
        certificate chain)
```

If we get an error as in this example, we'll need to check the TLS settings. In Chapter 2, we created a CA, and now we'll need to create a certificate for our Samba server hotel.linuxaholics.com. We already had to do the same thing when preparing the OpenLDAP replication. In that case we created a certificate for the foxtrot.linuxaholics.com server and copied both the server certificate and the CA certificate to the destination. We edited the /etc/openldap/ldap.conf file and checked that the secure connections worked fine. To review more details, take a look back at Chapter 5.

We next create the new server certificate.

```
[root@alpha CA]# openssl genrsa -out /etc/pki/CA/private/hotel.
linuxaholics.com.key
Generating RSA private key, 2048 bit long modulus
.............................................................................+++
........................+++
e is 65537 (0x10001)
[root@alpha CA]# openssl req -new -key /etc/pki/CA/private/hotel.
linuxaholics.com.key -out /etc/pki/CA/certs/hotel.linuxaholics.com.csr
.

.

.
```

```
Country Name (2 letter code) [XX]:ES
State or Province Name (full name) []:Madrid
Locality Name (eg, city) [Default City]:Madrid
Organization Name (eg, company) [Default Company Ltd]:linuxaholics
Organizational Unit Name (eg, section) []:
Common Name (eg, your name or your server's hostname) []:hotel.
linuxaholics.com
.
.
.
```

We sign the csr file to obtain the certificate.

```
[root@alpha CA]# openssl ca -keyfile /etc/pki/CA/private/ca.key.pem -cert
/etc/pki/CA/certs/ca.cert.pem -in /etc/pki/CA/certs/hotel.linuxaholics.com.
csr -out /etc/pki/CA/certs/hotel.linuxaholics.com.crt
.
.
.
Sign the certificate? [y/n]:y
.
.
.
```

We then copy the certificates to the Samba server and create the corresponding directories if they don't exist.

```
[root@hotel ~]# mkdir /etc/openldap/cacerts

[root@alpha CA]# scp /etc/pki/CA/certs/ca.cert.pem hotel.linuxaholics.com:/
etc/openldap/cacerts/
.
.
.
ca.cert.pem                                    100% 1318    1.3KB/s   00:00
[root@alpha CA]# scp /etc/pki/CA/certs/hotel.linuxaholics.com.crt hotel.
linuxaholics.com:/etc/openldap/certs/
```

```
root@hotel.linuxaholics.com's password:
hotel.linuxaholics.com.crt                    100% 4464      4.4KB/s   00:00
```

From this point on we can query the LDAP server through a secure connection.

```
[root@hotel ~]# ldapsearch -ZZ -H ldap://alpha.linuxaholics.com -x -D
cn=admin,dc=linuxaholics,dc=com -w pass -b "ou=users,dc=linuxaholics,
dc=com"
.

.

.

dn: ou=users,dc=linuxaholics,dc=com
objectClass: organizationalUnit
ou: users
```

After checking that everything is working, we change the back end in /etc/samba/ smb.conf.

```
security = user
passdb backend = ldapsam:"ldap://alpha.linuxaholics.com"
```

We still need to add a series of parameters to /etc/samba/smb.conf, though. In fact, if we now try to restart the SMB service, we will get this error:

```
[root@hotel ~]# systemctl restart smb
Job for smb.service failed. See 'systemctl status smb.service' and
'journalctl -xn' for details.
```

```
[root@hotel ~]# systemctl status smb
smb.service - Samba SMB Daemon
   Loaded: loaded (/usr/lib/systemd/system/smb.service; enabled)
   Active: failed (Result: exit-code) since Tue 2018-06-12 23:54:08 EDT;
           23s ago
  Process: 23273 ExecStart=/usr/sbin/smbd $SMBDOPTIONS (code=exited,
           status=1/FAILURE)
 Main PID: 23273 (code=exited, status=1/FAILURE)
   Status: "Starting process..."
```

```
Jun 12 23:54:08 hotel.linuxaholics.com systemd[1]: Starting Samba SMB
Daemon...
Jun 12 23:54:08 hotel.linuxaholics.com smbd[23273]: [2018/06/12
23:54:08.326106,  0] ../source3/passdb/secrets.c:366(fetch_ldap_pw)
Jun 12 23:54:08 hotel.linuxaholics.com smbd[23273]: fetch_ldap_pw: neither
ldap secret retrieved!
Jun 12 23:54:08 hotel.linuxaholics.com smbd[23273]: [2018/06/12
23:54:08.326196,  0] ../source3/passdb/pdb_ldap.c:6427(pdb_init_ldapsam_
common)
Jun 12 23:54:08 hotel.linuxaholics.com smbd[23273]: pdb_init_ldapsam_
common: Failed to retrieve LDAP password from secrets.tdb
Jun 12 23:54:08 hotel.linuxaholics.com smbd[23273]: [2018/06/12
23:54:08.326222,  0] ../source3/passdb/pdb_interface.c:178(make_pdb_method_
name)
Jun 12 23:54:08 hotel.linuxaholics.com smbd[23273]: pdb backend ldapsam did
not correctly init (error was NT_STATUS_NO_MEMORY)
Jun 12 23:54:08 hotel.linuxaholics.com systemd[1]: smb.service: main
process exited, code=exited, status=1/FAILURE
Jun 12 23:54:08 hotel.linuxaholics.com systemd[1]: Failed to start Samba
SMB Daemon.
Jun 12 23:54:08 hotel.linuxaholics.com systemd[1]: Unit smb.service entered
failed state.
```

If you have followed the OpenLDAP chapters you will already have a working OpenLDAP server installed; if not, we'll have to install it now. In any case, after having a working LDAP we need to store the LDAP password in the secrets.tdb file. Otherwise we'll keep getting the same error message, Failed to retrieve LDAP password from secrets.tdb.

We store the LDAP password in secrets.tdb by ussing the **smbpasswd** command. If we access the help page, we'll see the following:

```
[root@hotel ~]# smbpasswd -h
.
.
.
```

```
options:
  -L                    local mode (must be first option)
  .
  .
  .

extra options when run by root or in local mode:
  .
  .

  .

  -W                    use stdin ldap admin password
  -w PASSWORD           ldap admin password
  .

  .

  .
```

In addition to storing the password, we need to specify the admin DN in smb.conf. In fact, if we try to execute smbpasswd -L -w admin_password before doing it, we'll get this message:

```
[root@hotel ~]# smbpasswd -L -w admin
ERROR: 'ldap admin dn' not defined! Please check your smb.conf
```

So we get back to the /etc/samba/smb.conf and add the new parameter.

```
security = user
passdb backend = ldapsam:"ldap://alpha.linuxaholics.com"
ldap admin dn = cn=admin,dc=linuxaholics,dc=com
```

Now we can store the password in secrets.tdb.

```
[root@hotel ~]# smbpasswd -L -w admin
Setting stored password for "cn=admin,dc=linuxaholics,dc=com" in secrets.tdb
```

We're almost there, but there is still something to fix before the SMB service starts correctly. If we start it now, we'll get the following errors:

```
[root@hotel ~]# systemctl restart smb
Job for smb.service failed. See 'systemctl status smb.service' and
'journalctl -xe' for details.
```

```
[root@hotel ~]# systemctl -l status smb
● smb.service - Samba SMB Daemon
   Loaded: loaded (/usr/lib/systemd/system/smb.service; enabled; vendor
   preset: disabled)
   Active: failed (Result: exit-code) since dom 2018-08-12 17:16:22 CEST;
   42s ago
  Process: 11764 ExecStart=/usr/sbin/smbd --foreground --no-process-group
  $SMBDOPTIONS (code=exited, status=1/FAILURE)
 Main PID: 11764 (code=exited, status=1/FAILURE)

ago 12 17:16:21 hotel.linuxaholics.com smbd[11764]: [2018/08/12
17:16:21.229607,  0] ../source3/lib/smbldap.c:622(smbldap_start_tls)
ago 12 17:16:21 hotel.linuxaholics.com smbd[11764]:   Failed to issue the
StartTLS instruction: Connect error
ago 12 17:16:22 hotel.linuxaholics.com smbd[11764]: [2018/08/12
17:16:22.231893,  0] ../source3/passdb/pdb_ldap.c:6643(pdb_ldapsam_init_
common)
ago 12 17:16:22 hotel.linuxaholics.com smbd[11764]:   pdb_init_ldapsam:
WARNING: Could not get domain info, nor add one to the domain. We cannot
work reliably without it.
ago 12 17:16:22 hotel.linuxaholics.com smbd[11764]: [2018/08/12
17:16:22.232506,  0] ../source3/passdb/pdb_interface.c:180(make_pdb_method_
name)
ago 12 17:16:22 hotel.linuxaholics.com smbd[11764]:   pdb backend
ldapsam:"ldap://alpha.linuxaholics.com" did not correctly init (error was
NT_STATUS_CANT_ACCESS_DOMAIN_INFO)
ago 12 17:16:22 hotel.linuxaholics.com systemd[1]: smb.service: main
process exited, code=exited, status=1/FAILURE
ago 12 17:16:22 hotel.linuxaholics.com systemd[1]: Failed to start Samba
SMB Daemon.
ago 12 17:16:22 hotel.linuxaholics.com systemd[1]: Unit smb.service entered
failed state.
ago 12 17:16:22 hotel.linuxaholics.com systemd[1]: smb.service failed.
```

For OpenLDAP to be able to store Samba accounts we must expand the schema. We already saw how to do this when we studied OpenLDAP in the first chapters of this book. The LDIF file necessary to extend the schema is located in the /usr/share/doc/ samba-4.1.1/LDAP folder.

```
[root@hotel ~]# ls /usr/share/doc/samba-4.7.1/LDAP/samba.ldif
/usr/share/doc/samba-4.7.1/LDAP/samba.ldif
```

We therefore need to copy the samba.ldif file from the Samba server to the OpenLDAP server.

```
[root@hotel ~]# scp /usr/share/doc/samba-4.7.1/LDAP/samba.ldif alpha.
linuxaholics.com:/root
root@alpha.linuxaholics.com's password:
samba.ldif                                      100%   15KB 168.1KB/s   00:00
```

We also extend the schema.

```
[root@alpha ~]# ldapadd -Y EXTERNAL -H ldapi:/// -f samba.ldif
SASL/EXTERNAL authentication started
SASL username: gidNumber=0+uidNumber=0,cn=peercred,cn=external,cn=auth
SASL SSF: 0
adding new entry "cn=samba,cn=schema,cn=config"
```

The man page of the smb.conf file says that, in addition to ldap admin dn, we must include a series of parameters for OpenLDAP and Samba to integrate properly. This is the configuration example included:

```
 An example configuration can be the following:

                encrypt passwords = true
                passdb backend = ldapsam

                ldapsam:trusted=yes
                ldapsam:editposix=yes

                ldap admin dn = cn=admin,dc=samba,dc=org
                ldap delete dn = yes
                ldap group suffix = ou=groups
                ldap idmap suffix = ou=idmap
```

```
ldap machine suffix = ou=computers
ldap user suffix = ou=users
ldap suffix = dc=samba,dc=org

idmap backend = ldap:"ldap://localhost"

idmap uid = 5000-50000
idmap gid = 5000-50000
```

Obviously, we need to adapt this example to our existing infrastructure. In our case, the lines we'd need to include in the /etc/samba/smb.conf file would be these:

```
security = user
passdb backend = ldapsam:"ldap://alpha.linuxaholics.com"
ldap admin dn = cn=admin,dc=linuxaholics,dc=com

ldapsam:trusted = yes
ldapsam:editposix = yes
ldap delete dn = yes
ldap group suffix = ou=users
ldap idmap suffix = ou=users
ldap machine suffix = ou=users
ldap user suffix = ou=users
ldap suffix = dc=linuxaholics,dc=com

idmap backend = ldap:"ldap://alpha.linuxaholics.com"

idmap uid = 5000-50000
idmap gid = 5000-50000
```

Now we can successfully start the service.

```
[root@hotel ~]# systemctl restart smb
[root@hotel ~]# systemctl status smb
● smb.service - Samba SMB Daemon
   Loaded: loaded (/usr/lib/systemd/system/smb.service; enabled; vendor
   preset: disabled)
   Active: active (running) since dom 2018-08-12 19:09:10 CEST; 1min 33s ago
 Main PID: 11899 (smbd)
   Status: "smbd: ready to serve connections..."
```

```
    CGroup: /system.slice/smb.service
            ├─11899 /usr/sbin/smbd --foreground --no-process-group
            ├─11901 /usr/sbin/smbd --foreground --no-process-group
            ├─11902 /usr/sbin/smbd --foreground --no-process-group
            └─11903 /usr/sbin/smbd --foreground --no-process-group
```

```
ago 12 19:08:25 hotel.linuxaholics.com systemd[1]: Starting Samba SMB
Daemon...
ago 12 19:09:10 hotel.linuxaholics.com smbd[11899]: [2018/08/12
19:09:10.191982,  0] ../lib/util/become_daemon.c:124(daemon_ready)
ago 12 19:09:10 hotel.linuxaholics.com smbd[11899]:   STATUS=daemon 'smbd'
finished starting up and ready to serve connections
ago 12 19:09:10 hotel.linuxaholics.com systemd[1]: Started Samba SMB Daemon.
```

In fact, after restarting the service we can check that a new entry has been created in our OpenLDAP server.

```
[root@hotel ~]# ldapsearch -ZZ -H ldap://alpha.linuxaholics.com -x -D
cn=admin,dc=linuxaholics,dc=com -w pass -b "dc=linuxaholics,dc=com"
.

.

.

# HOTEL, linuxaholics.com
dn: sambaDomainName=HOTEL,dc=linuxaholics,dc=com
sambaDomainName: HOTEL
sambaSID: S-1-5-21-892619289-2955383375-3350856941
sambaAlgorithmicRidBase: 1000
objectClass: sambaDomain
sambaNextUserRid: 1000
sambaMinPwdLength: 5
sambaPwdHistoryLength: 0
sambaLogonToChgPwd: 0
sambaMaxPwdAge: -1
sambaMinPwdAge: 0
sambaLockoutDuration: 30
sambaLockoutObservationWindow: 30
sambaLockoutThreshold: 0
```

```
sambaForceLogoff: -1
sambaRefuseMachinePwdChange: 0
.
.
.
```

However, if we try to authenticate as the LDAP user Tux created in Chapter 1, we still get an error.

```
[root@alpha ~]# smbclient //hotel.linuxaholics.com/Docs -U Tux
Enter SAMBA\Tux's password:
session setup failed: NT_STATUS_LOGON_FAILURE
```

We'll see now some useful tricks to troubleshoot Samba problems. The Samba service can be executed with the -d (debugging) parameter, which will give us more information about what's going on. The -d parameter expects an integer value between 0 and 10, and the higher the value, the more information we get.

We therefore stop the SMB service and we start it interactively (-i) and with the most detailed level of debugging (-d 10).

```
[root@hotel ~]# systemctl stop smb
[root@hotel ~]# smbd -i -d 10
.
.
.
```

We'll get lots of information in the console. If we open another console or SSH connection to the server and we launch the **smbclient** command trying to connect as the Tux user we'll see an enormous amount of data. To extract the information we need, we'll search for the NT_STATUS_LOGON_FAILURE string, and we'll see this line:

```
NT error packet at ../source3/smbd/sesssetup.c(263) cmd=115 (SMBsesssetupX)
NT_STATUS_LOGON_FAILURE
```

To find out why the logon attempt, failed go back a few lines and we'll see this:

```
.
.
.
```

```
smbldap_search_ext: base => [dc=linuxaholics,dc=com], filter =>
[(&(uid=Tux)(objectclass=sambaSamAccount))], scope => [2]
ldapsam_getsampwnam: Unable to locate user [Tux] count=0
pop_sec_ctx (0, 0) - sec_ctx_stack_ndx = 1
check_sam_security: Couldn't find user 'Tux' in passdb.
check_ntlm_password: sam authentication for user [Tux] FAILED with error
NT_STATUS_NO_SUCH_USER
check_ntlm_password:  Authentication for user [Tux] -> [Tux] FAILED with
error NT_STATUS_NO_SUCH_USER
Checking NTLMSSP password for MYGROUP\Tux failed: NT_STATUS_NO_SUCH_USER
../auth/ntlmssp/ntlmssp_server.c:454: Checking NTLMSSP password for
MYGROUP\Tux failed: NT_STATUS_NO_SUCH_USER
SPNEGO login failed: NT_STATUS_NO_SUCH_USER
```

.

.

.

It looks like the Samba server didn't find the Tux user because it searches for a user of the objectclass sambaSamAccount, and the Tux user belongs only to the inetOrgPerson objectclass. To fix this, we'll modify the Tux user and add a sambaSID. We can get the local SID by executing **net getlocalsid** on the Samba server. For troubleshooting purposes, though, we'll assign a dummy value to this parameter, and fix it later.

```
[root@alpha ldap]# cat TuxSamba.ldif
dn: cn=Tux,ou=users,dc=linuxaholics,dc=com
changeType: modify
add: objectClass
objectClass: sambaSamAccount
-
add: sambaSID
sambaSID: S-1-0-0-1234567

[root@alpha ldap]# ldapmodify -H ldap://alpha.linuxaholics.com -f TuxSamba.
ldif -x -D cn=admin,dc=linuxaholics,dc=com -w pass
modifying entry "cn=Tux,ou=users,dc=linuxaholics,dc=com"
```

If we try again to authenticate as the Tux user after restarting OpenLDAP, we'll keep getting an error, but in the debugging info we'll see that some things have changed. Now the LDAP query performed by Samba actually locates the Tux user.

```
smbldap_search_ext: base => [dc=linuxaholics,dc=com], filter =>
[(&(uid=Tux)(objectclass=sambaSamAccount))], scope => [2]
init_sam_from_ldap: Entry found for user: Tux
```

Unfortunately, a few lines later we'll see that Samba tries to find a Unix account for the Tux user, which doesn't exist.

```
Finding user Tux
Trying _Get_Pwnam(), username as lowercase is tux
Trying _Get_Pwnam(), username as given is Tux
Trying _Get_Pwnam(), username as uppercase is TUX
Checking combinations of 0 uppercase letters in tux
Get_Pwnam_internals didn't find user [Tux]!
init_sam_from_ldap: Failed to find Unix account for Tux
```

We can solve this by creating a local Tux account.

```
[root@hotel ~]# useradd -m Tux -u 5000
```

Now if we try to establish a Samba connection with the Tux user this is what we'll see in the debug messages:

```
.
.
.
Finding user Tux
Trying _Get_Pwnam(), username as lowercase is tux
Trying _Get_Pwnam(), username as given is Tux
Get_Pwnam_internals did find user [Tux]!
gid_to_sid: winbind failed to find a sid for gid 1001
push_sec_ctx(0, 0) : sec_ctx_stack_ndx = 3
push_conn_ctx(0) : conn_ctx_stack_ndx = 2
setting sec ctx (0, 0) - sec_ctx_stack_ndx = 3
```

```
Security token: (NULL)
UNIX token of user 0
.
.
.
```

We see that the Tux user was found. However, there seems to be another problem, as the system cannot locate the appropriate password.

```
.
.
ntlm_password_check: NO NT password stored for user Tux.
ntlm_password_check: Lanman passwords NOT PERMITTED for user Tux
ntlm_password_check: LM password check failed for user, no NT password Tux
.
.
check_ntlm_password: sam authentication for user [Tux] FAILED with error
NT_STATUS_WRONG_PASSWORD
check_ntlm_password:  Authentication for user [Tux] -> [Tux] FAILED with
error NT_STATUS_WRONG_PASSWORD
Checking NTLMSSP password for MYGROUP\Tux failed: NT_STATUS_WRONG_PASSWORD
../auth/ntlmssp/ntlmssp_server.c:454: Checking NTLMSSP password for
MYGROUP\Tux failed: NT_STATUS_WRONG_PASSWORD
SPNEGO login failed: NT_STATUS_WRONG_PASSWORD
.
.
.
```

Samba will look for the NT password associated with the user in its internal files in the /var/lib/samba/private folder. We can add a new password with the **smbpasswd** command.

```
[root@hotel ~]# smbpasswd Tux
New SMB password:
Retype new SMB password:
```

If we repeat the test, we'll see that we no longer receive the error message related with the Samba password. Unfortunately, though, we still get an NT_STATUS_ UNSUCCESSFUL, as the SID we assigned initially to the Tux user is not correct.

.

.

.

```
Finding user Tux
Trying _Get_Pwnam(), username as lowercase is tux
Trying _Get_Pwnam(), username as given is Tux
Get_Pwnam_internals did find user [Tux]!
The primary group domain sid(S-1-5-21-892619289-2955383375-3350856941-513)
does not match the domain sid(S-1-0-0) for Tux(S-1-0-0-1234567)
pop_sec_ctx (0, 0) - sec_ctx_stack_ndx = 1
check_sam_security: make_server_info_sam() failed with 'NT_STATUS_
UNSUCCESSFUL'
check_ntlm_password: sam authentication for user [Tux] FAILED with error
NT_STATUS_UNSUCCESSFUL
check_ntlm_password:  Authentication for user [Tux] -> [Tux] FAILED with
error NT_STATUS_UNSUCCESSFUL
Checking NTLMSSP password for MYGROUP\Tux failed: NT_STATUS_UNSUCCESSFUL
../auth/ntlmssp/ntlmssp_server.c:454: Checking NTLMSSP password for
MYGROUP\Tux failed: NT_STATUS_UNSUCCESSFUL
SPNEGO login failed: NT_STATUS_UNSUCCESSFUL
```

.

.

.

Luckily, we can correct this by creating a new LDIF file with the correct SID as seen in the error message.

```
[root@alpha ldap]# cat TuxSambaEdit.ldif
dn: cn=Tux,ou=users,dc=linuxaholics,dc=com
changeType: modify
replace: sambaSID
sambaSID: S-1-5-21-892619289-2955383375-3350856941-1234567
```

```
[root@alpha ldap]# ldapmodify -x -H ldap://alpha.linuxaholics.com -D
cn=admin,dc=linuxaholics,dc=com -w pass -f TuxSambaEdit.ldif
modifying entry "cn=Tux,ou=users,dc=linuxaholics,dc=com"
```

We could also have queried the local SID with the **net getlocalsid** command.

```
[root@hotel ~]# net getlocalsid
SID for domain HOTEL is: S-1-5-21-892619289-2955383375-3350856941
```

Finally, after restarting the slapd service, we can connect as the Tux user.

```
[root@alpha ~]# smbclient //hotel.linuxaholics.com/Docs -U Tux
Enter Tux's password:
Domain=[MYGROUP] OS=[Unix] Server=[Samba 4.1.1]
smb: \> ls
  .                               D        0  Wed Feb 28 00:55:59 2018
  ..                              D        0  Fri Jun  8 05:29:48 2018
  example.txt                     N       24  Wed Feb 28 00:55:59 2018

                35836 blocks of size 524288. 33823 blocks available
smb: \>
```

## Securing the Connections

When using an LDAP server as a back end, the Samba server needs to communicate with the LDAP server. This communication can be encrypted or unencrypted. This behavior can be determined by a series of configuration parameters. If we don't want the communication to be secured, we should make sure that these two parameters apply to our Samba configuration file:

```
        ldap ssl = Off
        tls enabled = No
```

---

**Note**   Depending on the exact version of the Samba software installed, the corresponding default values for a certain parameter might differ. We can see the default values that apply to our installation with the command `testparm -sv`.

---

After adding these two lines to our /etc/samba/smb.conf file and restarting Samba, we can execute tcpdump in our OpenLDAP server to monitor the connections.

```
[root@alpha ~]# tcpdump -w output_guest.pcap -vvv -X "port 389 or port 636"
tcpdump: listening on enp0s3, link-type EN10MB (Ethernet), capture size
262144 bytes
```

We list the shares in the Samba server from any client.

```
[root@bravo ~]# smbclient -L //192.168.1.232 -U Guest%anonymous
```

To return the information, the Samba server will need to communicate with the OpenLDAP server. We can see the connections established by opening the tcpdump file we generated before in Wireshark or any other network monitoring tool (Figure 8-3).

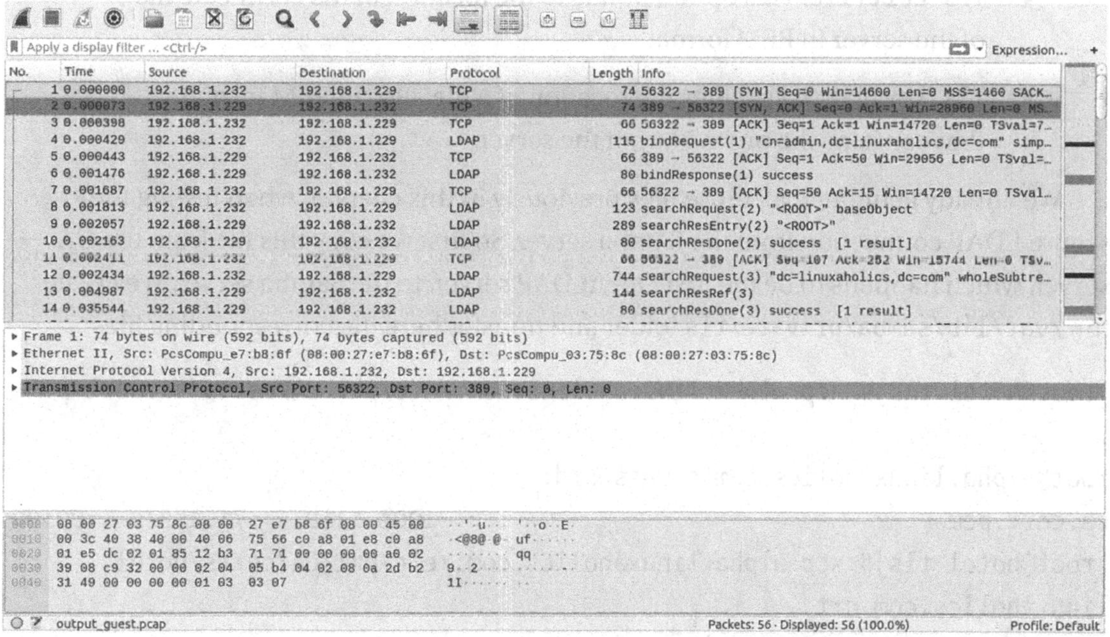

**Figure 8-3.** *Unencrypted communication between the Samba and the OpenLDAP server*

233

We can see that all the communication is unencrypted, without any trace of using SSL or TLS. In turn, if we want the traffic between the Samba and the OpenLDAP server to be ciphered, we need to again change a series of parameters. First, we change the value of the two parameters we added previously:

```
ldap ssl = start tls
        tls enabled = Yes
```

In addition to these parameters, we also need to add some more TLS-related parameters:

- Tls cafile: This option will be set to the location of a file in Privacy-Enhaced Mail (PEM) format that contains the certificates of the root CA.

- Tls certfile: This option points to the location of the certificate file of the server in PEM format.

- Tls keyfile: It specifies the location of a file, also in PEM format, that contains the private key of the server.

We already generated all those files previously in this chapter, when testing the secure LDAP connection from the Samba server. So first we copy this file from the CA server, which happens to be the first OpenLDAP server, to the Samba server. We create the /var/lib/samba/private/tls folder and transfer here the corresponding files.

```
[root@hotel tls]# scp alpha.linuxaholics.com:/etc/pki/CA/certs/ca.cert.pem
.
root@alpha.linuxaholics.com's password:
ca.cert.pem                              100% 1318    71.1KB/s   00:00
[root@hotel tls]# scp alpha.linuxaholics.com:/etc/pki/CA/certs/hotel.
linuxaholics.com.crt .
root@alpha.linuxaholics.com's password:
hotel.linuxaholics.com.crt               100% 4464    4.8MB/s   00:00
[root@hotel tls]# scp alpha.linuxaholics.com:/etc/pki/CA/private/hotel.
linuxaholics.com.key .
root@alpha.linuxaholics.com's password:
hotel.linuxaholics.com.key               100% 1675    2.2MB/s   00:00
```

If we examine each file with the **file** command, we'll see that the server certificate file is not in PEM format.

```
[root@hotel tls]# file *
ca.cert.pem:             PEM certificate
hotel.linuxaholics.com.crt: ASCII text
hotel.linuxaholics.com.key: PEM RSA private key
```

However, if we open the certificate file with a simple text editor like vi, we'll see some text about the validity of the certificate, issuer, and so on, and closer to the bottom a line that starts with ----BEGIN and its followed by some coded text and terminated by an ----END line. We only need to copy everything between the BEGIN and the END lines, both included as well, to a new file. If we execute the file again, the new file will be recognized as a PEM format file.

```
[root@hotel tls]# file *
ca.cert.pem:             PEM certificate
hotel.linuxaholics.com.crt: ASCII text
hotel.linuxaholics.com.key: PEM RSA private key
hotel.linuxaholics.com.pem: PEM certificate
```

As we already have all the files in the right format, we can include the new options in the Samba configuration file:

```
    tls cafile = /var/lib/samba/private/tls/ca.cert.pem
    tls certfile = /var/lib/samba/private/tls/hotel.linuxaholics.com.pem
    tls keyfile = /var/lib/samba/private/tls/hotel.linuxaholics.com.key
```

After restarting Samba, we can repeat the test we performed before and execute tcpdump in the OpenLDAP server to monitor the connections. As soon as a client connects to the Samba server, we can open the file in Wireshark. The result in this case will be very different (Figure 8-4).

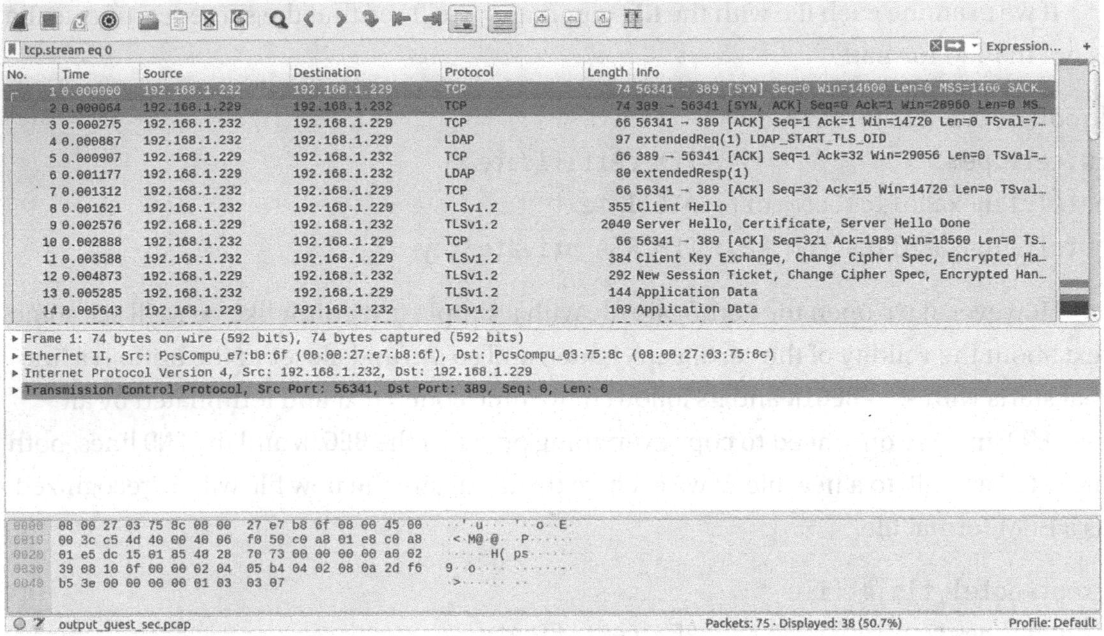

**Figure 8-4.** *Encrypted communication between Samba and OpenLDAP*

Just a simple look reveals that the communication uses TLS to encrypt the data. In addition to the TLS options we used in this section, there are many others that we haven't mentioned. For instance, `tls priority` determines the subset of protocols to be supported. This is very useful, as some protocols are no longer considered secure. Another interesting option is `tls verify peer`, which controls how strictly the client certificate will be checked. The option `tls dh params file` can be set to a file with Diffie-Hellman (DH) parameters, which will be used in DH ciphers.

If we want to revert the changes so that we use the local database again instead of LDAP, we shoud change this line.

```
passdb backend = ldapsam:"ldap://hotel.linuxaholics.com"
```

We then restore the original value of the parameter, before we made the changes.

```
passdb backend = tdbsam
```

We will also comment (or delete) the LDAP-specific parameters we added to the configuration file.

```
#ldap admin dn = cn=admin,dc=linuxaholics,dc=com

#ldapsam:trusted = yes
#ldapsam:editposix = yes
#ldap delete dn = yes
#ldap group suffix = ou=users
#ldap idmap suffix = ou=users
#ldap machine suffix = ou=users
#ldap user suffix = ou=users
#ldap suffix = dc=linuxaholics,dc=com

#idmap backend = ldap:"ldap://alpha.linuxaholics.com"

#idmap uid = 5000-50000
#idmap gid = 5000-50000
```

# Troubleshooting and Debugging Configuration Problems

One of the most useful commands to troubleshoot Samba configuration problems is **testparm**.

Another useful way to find out why Samba isn't working is to manually launch the service with the debug option.

```
[root@bravo ~]# smbd -i -d 1
smbd version 4.1.1 started.
Copyright Andrew Tridgell and the Samba Team 1992-2013
pdb_init_ldapsam: WARNING: Could not get domain info, nor add one to the
domain. We cannot work reliably without it.
pdb backend ldapsam did not correctly init (error was NT_STATUS_CANT_
ACCESS_DOMAIN_INFO)
```

In the previous section we saw many examples of troubleshooting, so we won't review that again here.

# Character Codes and Code Pages

As we know, computers communicate using numbers—0s and 1s—as opposed to humans, who prefer to communicate using languages. When we type some text in a text file, then, that text is translated into a series of numbers. The relation between any given number (or code) and the corresponding character is what we call *character code*. When grouping a series of characters and their associated character codes we get a code page. Probably the best known code page is American Standard Code for Information Interchange (ASCII). Sometimes code pages are called character sets or charsets for short.

Until now the de facto standard charset for computers has been ASCII. That is perfect for the English language, but it lacks support for other characters present in other languages. For that reason, several additional charsets were created to fully support languages like Spanish, French, German, and so on.

At any moment we can check the charset used by Samba with the **testparm** command.

```
[root@hotel ~]# testparm -vs | grep charset
Load smb config files from /etc/samba/smb.conf
rlimit_max: increasing rlimit_max (1024) to minimum Windows limit (16384)
Processing section "[homes]"
Processing section "[printers]"
Processing section "[print$]"
Processing section "[Docs]"
Loaded services file OK.
Server role: ROLE_STANDALONE

        dos charset = CP850
        unix charset = UTF-8
```

As we can see, there are two parameters associated with charset:

- dos charset: This is the charset Samba uses when talking to DOS clients. If the configured value is not available, Samba will fall back to ASCII.

- unix charset. This is the charset used by the operating system. In modern versions this is usually UTF-8, which covers all characters in all languages.

In modern clients, however, the charset is negotiated, so there is no need to specify the same charset in both server and client. We can access our Samba server from a Windows client and create two text files named english.txt and español.txt. To do that, first we make the Docs share writable by editing /etc/samba/smb.conf.

```
[Docs]
comment = Public documents
path = /shared_docs
public = yes
writable = yes
```

In addition we'll have to give write permissions at the OS level.

```
[root@hotel ~]# chmod a+w /shared_docs/
```

From now on we can create files with any user connected. We open the Run dialog box and enter the address of our Samba server (Figure 8-5). We then enter a valid username/password combination (Figure 8-6). We can now create the english.txt and español.txt files (Figure 8-7).

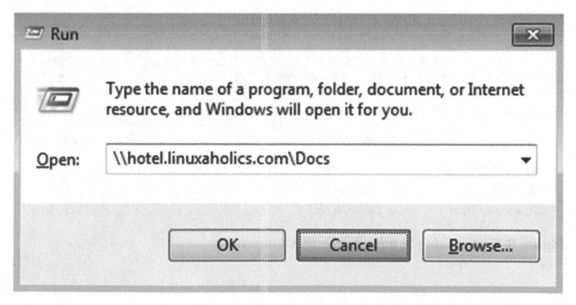

*Figure 8-5.* *Windows Run dialog box*

**Figure 8-6.** *Entering the username and password*

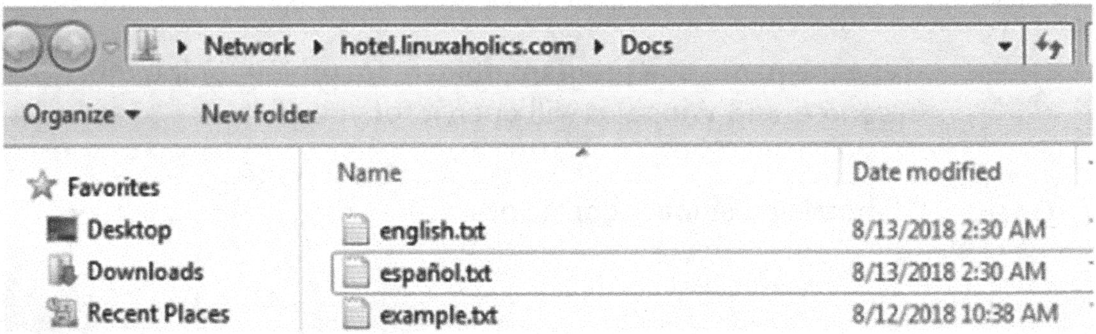

**Figure 8-7.** *Accessing Samba from a Windows client*

The client and the server automatically negotiate the charset and we can read perfectly both file names, even though one of them has a special character. The content of both files can be read correctly, too (Figure 8-8 and Figure 8-9).

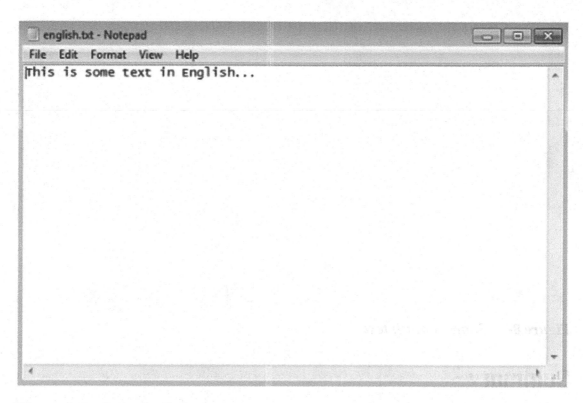

*Figure 8-8.*  *Some English text*

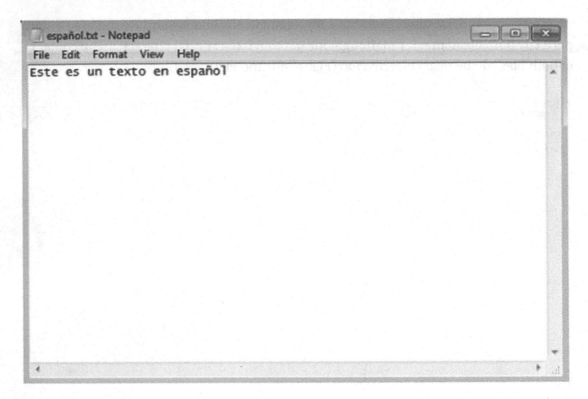

*Figure 8-9.*  *Some Spanish text*

# Summary

After the first contact with Samba in the previous chapter, we moved forward into more advanced topics. We saw the different services that are part of the Samba suite and the ports used to communicate. We also took a look at the characteristics and the differences between Samba 3 and Samba 4.

In addition to editing the configuration file, we also created a share by editing the Samba registry. We dug deeper into the configuration file and changed the workgroup name as well as the NetBIOS name. We also changed the passdb back end to ldapsam, making the necessary adjustments in both the LDAP server and the Samba server. We configured both secure and unsecure conenctions.

We saw how different languages have different code sets associated with them and what it implies when working with Samba. Finally, we also learned some troubleshooting tips.

# CHAPTER 9

# Regular Samba Maintenance and Troubleshooting

We are already familiar with many of the characteristics of a Samba server, and we already saw some troubleshooting examples. In this chapter we'll see more troubleshooting tips as well as some maintenance recommendations. We'll cover the following concepts:

- Monitoring and interacting with running Samba daemons.

- Performing regular backups of Samba configuration and state data.

- Configuring Samba logging.

- Backing up TDB files.

- Restoring TDB files.

- Identifying TDB file corruption.

- Editing and listing TDB file content.

We will also introduce the following terms and utilities: **smbcontrol**, **smbstatus**, **tdbbackup**, /var/log/samba/, log level, debuglevel, **smbpasswd**, **pdbedit**, secrets. tdb, **tdbbackup**, **tdbdump**, **tdbrestore**, and **tdbtool**.

## Monitoring Samba Services

The Samba suite provides a series of tools to monitor Samba services. We'll review some of the most used in the following sections.

243

© Antonio Vazquez 2019
A. Vazquez, *Practical LPIC-3 300*, https://doi.org/10.1007/978-1-4842-4473-9_9

# Smbcontrol

One of the utilities to monitor Samba is **smbcontrol**. The help screen of this command will show us a summary of its use, and we'll see a few examples here, too.

It is quite easy to use. We specify the destination—that is, the service we want to monitor—which can be any of the following: smbd, nmbd, or winbindd. Then we pass the message type and the optional parameters associated.

For example, we can check the current log level of the **smbd** service like this:

```
[root@hotel ~]# smbcontrol smbd debuglevel
PID 12339: all:0 tdb:0 printdrivers:0 lanman:0 smb:0 rpc_parse:0 rpc_srv:0
rpc_cli:0 passdb:0 sam:0 auth:0 winbind:0 vfs:0 idmap:0 quota:0 acls:0
locking:0 msdfs:0 dmapi:0 registry:0 scavenger:0 dns:0 ldb:0 tevent:0
auth_audit:0 auth_json_audit:0 kerberos:0 drs_repl:0
```

We can also change this log level.

```
[root@hotel ~]# smbcontrol smbd debug 3
[root@hotel ~]# smbcontrol smbd debuglevel
PID 12339: all:3 tdb:3 printdrivers:3 lanman:3 smb:3 rpc_parse:3 rpc_srv:3
rpc_cli:3 passdb:3 sam:3 auth:3 winbind:3 vfs:3 idmap:3 quota:3 acls:3
locking:3 msdfs:3 dmapi:3 registry:3 scavenger:3 dns:3 ldb:3 tevent:3
auth_audit:3 auth_json_audit:3 kerberos:3 drs_repl:3
```

We can simply ping the services.

```
[root@hotel ~]# smbcontrol smbd ping
PONG from pid 12339
[root@hotel ~]# smbcontrol nmbd ping
PONG from pid 19469
[root@hotel ~]# smbcontrol winbindd ping
Can't find pid for destination 'winbindd'
```

In this case we see that the services smbd and nmbd are active, but winbindd is not. We can also reload the configuration

```
[root@hotel ~]# smbcontrol smbd reload-config
```

## smbstatus

Another useful monitoring tool is **smbstatus**. Executed without arguments, it shows statistics about the shared resources.

```
[root@hotel ldap]# smbstatus

Samba version 4.1.1
PID       Username       Group         Machine
-------------------------------------------------------------------
25179     Tux            Tux           192.168.1.100 (ipv4:192.168.1.100:34273)

Service        pid     machine         Connected at
------------------------------------------------------------
Docs           25179   192.168.1.100   Wed Jun 13 13:50:23 2018

No locked files
```

In this case, the user named Tux connected from a workstation with IP 192.168.1.100 to the Docs shared, and there are no locked files.

# Backing Up Samba Configuration and State Data

A convenient tool to back up Samba TDB files is **tdbbackup**, included in the `tdb-tools` package. After it is installed, it can be used to back up TDB files, as well as to check the integrity of those files. For instance, if we want to backup the `passdb.tdb` file, we'll execute **tdbbackup** like this:

```
[root@hotel ~]# ls /var/lib/samba/private/
msg.sock  passdb.tdb  secrets.tdb
[root@hotel ~]# tdbbackup /var/lib/samba/private/passdb.tdb
[root@hotel ~]# ls /var/lib/samba/private/
msg.sock  passdb.tdb  passdb.tdb.bak  secrets.tdb
```

So far we've backed up the `passdb.tdb` file, but there are many other files used by Samba that we'll need to back up, too. We are already familiar with the `secrets.tdb` file where we stored the admin password when we integrated Samba and LDAP (Chapter 8). Apart from these two files located in `/var/lib/samba/private`, though, there are many others files we'll have to back up. Most of the Samba files are located in /var/lib/samba. This is the full list:

```
[root@hotel ~]# find / -iname *.tdb
/var/lib/samba/lock/names.tdb
/var/lib/samba/lock/smbXsrv_version_global.tdb
/var/lib/samba/lock/smbXsrv_session_global.tdb
/var/lib/samba/lock/smbXsrv_tcon_global.tdb
/var/lib/samba/lock/brlock.tdb
/var/lib/samba/lock/locking.tdb
/var/lib/samba/lock/leases.tdb
/var/lib/samba/lock/serverid.tdb
/var/lib/samba/lock/gencache_notrans.tdb
/var/lib/samba/lock/mutex.tdb
/var/lib/samba/lock/smbXsrv_open_global.tdb
/var/lib/samba/lock/printer_list.tdb
/var/lib/samba/lock/smbXsrv_client_global.tdb
/var/lib/samba/lock/smbd_cleanupd.tdb
/var/lib/samba/private/secrets.tdb
/var/lib/samba/private/passdb.tdb
/var/lib/samba/smbprofile.tdb
/var/lib/samba/registry.tdb
/var/lib/samba/share_info.tdb
/var/lib/samba/gencache.tdb
/var/lib/samba/group_mapping.tdb
/var/lib/samba/account_policy.tdb
/var/lib/samba/printing/printers.tdb
/var/lib/samba/login_cache.tdb
```

To accomplish a full backup of the Samba server, we'll have to back up each and every one of these files.

```
[root@hotel ~]# tdbbackup /var/lib/samba/*.tdb
[root@hotel ~]# tdbbackup /var/lib/samba/lock/*.tdb
[root@hotel ~]# tdbbackup /var/lib/samba/printing/*.tdb
[root@hotel ~]# tdbbackup /var/lib/samba/private/*.tdb
```

We might get an error when backing up some files.

```
[root@hotel ~]# tdbbackup /var/lib/samba/*.tdb
tdb_mutex_open_ok[/var/lib/samba/smbprofile.tdb]: Can use mutexes only with
MUTEX_LOCKING or NOLOCK
Failed to open /var/lib/samba/smbprofile.tdb
```

If this is the case, we can use **tdbbackup** with the -l parameter, so that it opens the file without locking it.

```
[root@hotel ~]# tdbbackup -l /var/lib/samba/*.tdb
```

The resulting .bak files could be then moved to a different location or media.

```
[root@hotel ~]# mkdir -p /samba_bk/180912/
[root@hotel ~]# mv /var/lib/samba/*.bak /samba_bk/180912/
[root@hotel ~]# mv /var/lib/samba/private/*.bak /samba_bk/180912/
[root@hotel ~]# mv /var/lib/samba/printing/*.bak /samba_bk/180912/
[root@hotel ~]# mv /var/lib/samba/lock/*.bak /samba_bk/180912/
[root@hotel ~]# ls /samba_bk/180912/
account_policy.tdb.bak     mutex.tdb.bak          share_info.tdb.bak
brlock.tdb.bak             names.tdb.bak          smbd_cleanupd.tdb.bak
gencache_notrans.tdb.bak   passdb.tdb.bak         smbprofile.tdb.bak
gencache.tdb.bak           printer_list.tdb.bak   smbXsrv_client_global.tdb.bak
group_mapping.tdb.bak      printers.tdb.bak       smbXsrv_open_global.tdb.bak
leases.tdb.bak             registry.tdb.bak       smbXsrv_session_global.tdb.bak
locking.tdb.bak            secrets.tdb.bak        smbXsrv_tcon_global.tdb.bak
login_cache.tdb.bak        serverid.tdb.bak       smbXsrv_version_global.tdb.bak
```

# Restoring Samba Configuration

Let's assume we have a working Samba stand-alone server, using tdbsam as a back end (Chapter 8). We have created a backup of the passdb.tdb file as we saw in the previous section. If the passdb.tdb file gets corrupted or is accidentally deleted, we won't be able to access the Samba shares anymore. We'll simulate such a scenario by deleting the file. After restarting the SMB service a new passbd.tdb file will be created, but the user information will be gone.

Before deleting the `passdb.tdb` file we check that Samba is working correctly.

```
[root@alpha ~]# smbclient //hotel.linuxaholics.com/Docs -U Antonio
Enter SAMBA\Antonio's password:
Try "help" to get a list of possible commands.
smb: \> ls
  .                                   D        0  Mon Aug 13 02:29:30 2018
  ..                                  DR       0  Mon Aug 13 09:27:15 2018
  example.txt                         N       24  Sun Aug 12 10:38:49 2018
  english.txt                         A       33  Mon Aug 13 02:30:18 2018
  español.txt                         A       29  Mon Aug 13 02:30:39 2018

          7022592 blocks of size 1024. 5585616 blocks available
smb: \> exit
[root@alpha ~]#
```

Now, in the Samba server we delete the file. We restart the server and we check that the file has been re-created.

```
[root@hotel ~]# ls /var/lib/samba/private/
msg.sock  passdb.tdb  secrets.tdb
[root@hotel ~]# rm /var/lib/samba/private/passdb.tdb
rm: remove regular file '/var/lib/samba/private/passdb.tdb'? y
[root@hotel ~]# systemctl restart smb
[root@hotel ~]# ls /var/lib/samba/private/
msg.sock  passdb.tdb  secrets.tdb
```

Of course, the original information will be gone and we won't be able to log in again with the former users.

```
[root@alpha ~]# smbclient //hotel.linuxaholics.com/Docs -U Antonio
Enter SAMBA\Antonio's password:
session setup failed: NT_STATUS_LOGON_FAILURE
```

However, as we have been cautious enough to perform a backup, we can easily restore the original file. To accomplish this, we can use the **tdbrestore** command. This is the syntax of the command:

```
[root@hotel ~]# tdbrestore
Usage: tdbrestore dbname < tdbdump_output
```

To restore the file, we need to dump the contents of the backup with the **tdbdump** command.

```
[root@hotel ~]# cd /var/lib/samba/private/
[root@hotel private]# cp /samba_bk/180912/passdb.tdb.bak .
[root@hotel private]# tdbdump passdb.tdb.bak > dumpfile
```

Once we have dumped the contents of the backup file, we can then restore it. We delete the dummy passdb.tdb file that was re-created when restarting the SMB service and we execute the **tdbrestore** command.

```
[root@hotel private]# rm passdb.tdb
rm: remove regular file 'passdb.tdb'? y
[root@hotel private]# tdbrestore passdb.tdb < dumpfile
[root@hotel private]# ls
dumpfile  msg.sock  passdb.tdb  passdb.tdb.bak  secrets.tdb
```

If we restart the SMB service again we'll be able to access the Samba shares again as any of the existent users.

```
[root@alpha ~]# smbclient //hotel.linuxaholics.com/Docs -U Antonio
Enter SAMBA\Antonio's password:
Try "help" to get a list of possible commands.
smb: \>
```

# Configure Samba Logging

We've seen previously (Chapter 8) that the /etc/samba/smb.conf file has logging enabled by default.

```
log file = /var/log/samba/log.%m
max logsize = 50
```

The two lines are self-explanatory, but there are more options related to logging that we can use. For instance, we can increase the logging level by using the debuglevel or log level parameters (which are equivalent). In addition, the newest versions of Samba make it possible to assign different log levels to multiple debug classes such as smb, passdb, winbind, and so on. We could edit the /etc/samba/smb.conf file to increase the log level like this:

.

.

.

```
    # log files split per-machine:
    log file = /var/log/samba/log.%m
  log level = 4 passdb:5
    # maximum size of 50KB per log file, then rotate:
    max log size = 50
```

.

.

.

In addition to sending log information to a file, Samba also sends log information to syslog. We can specify the threshold to send messages to syslog with the syslog option. For example, if we include the line syslog = 0 only error messages will be logged. With syslog = 1 the warning messages will be logged, too; with syslog = 2 the notice messages will be included as well; and so on.

# Back Up TDB Files

We've already seen how to back up tdb files (see the section "Backing Up Samba Configuration and State Data" earlier in this chapter).

# Identify TDB File Corruption

If our Samba server becomes corrupted and we have been cautious enough to create a backup, the restoration process should be pretty simple.

Let's emulate file corruption in /var/lib/samba/private/passdb.tdb by using the **dd** command.

```
[root@hotel private]# dd if=/dev/zero of=passdb.tdb bs=1k count=10
10+0 records in
10+0 records out
10240 bytes (10 kB) copied, 0,00118678 s, 8,6 MB/s
```

Now if we execute **tdbbackup** with the -v option, it will detect file corruption and will also try to restore a backup copy if there is one in the same folder. Otherwise it will say that it can't locate the passdb.tdb.bak file.

```
[root@hotel private]# tdbbackup -v passdb.tdb
restoring passdb.tdb
```

If we execute **tdbbackup** again it will successfully check the integrity of the file.

```
[root@hotel private]# tdbbackup -v passdb.tdb
passdb.tdb : 7 records
```

# Restore TDB Files

In previous sections we've seen how to restore TDB files using **tdbrestore** and **tdbbackup**.

# Edit and List TDB File Content

Another useful tool to manage TDB files is **tdbtool**. This utility can be used to create and manipulate the contents of TDB files. For instance, we can see the contents of a TDB file with the dump parameter.

```
[root@hotel private]# tdbtool passdb.tdb dump

key 13 bytes
RID_000003e8
data 8 bytes
[000] 61 6E 74 6F 6E 69 6F 00                          antonio
key 13 bytes
RID_000003eb
data 9 bytes
[000] 61 76 61 7A 71 75 65 7A  00                      avazquez

key 14 bytes
USER_avazquez
```

```
data 202 bytes
[000] 00 00 00 00 7F A9 54 7C  7F A9 54 7C 00 00 00 00   ......T| ..T|...
[010] 5F 38 70 5B 00 00 00 00  7F A9 54 7C 09 00 00 00   _8p[... ..T|...
[020] 61 76 61 7A 71 75 65 7A  00 06 00 00 00 48 4F 54   avazquez .....HOT
[030] 45 4C 00 01 00 00 00 00  10 00 00 00 41 6E 74 6F   EL..... ....Anto
[040] 6E 69 6F 20 56 61 7A 71  75 65 7A 00 00 00 00 00   nio Vazq uez....
[050] 00 00 00 00 00 00 00 00  00 00 00 00 01 00 00 00   ....... .......
[060] 00 01 00 00 00 00 01 00  00 00 00 01 00 00 00 00   ....... .......
[070] EB 03 00 00 01 02 00 00  00 00 00 00 10 00 00 00   ....... .......
[080] 04 47 B5 99 97 38 5B 0F  DD 4D 83 DA B8 BF ED B7   .G...8[. .M......
[090] 00 00 00 00 10 00 00 00  A8 00 15 00 00 00 20 00   ....... ......
[0A0] 00 00 FF FF FF FF FF FF  FF FF FF FF FF FF FF FF   ....... ........
[0B0] FF FF FF FF FF FF FF 00  00 00 00 00 00 00 00 00   ....... .......
[0C0] 00 00 00 00 00 00 EC 04  00 00                     ........ .

key 13 bytes
USER_antonio
data 186 bytes
[000] 00 00 00 00 7F A9 54 7C  7F A9 54 7C 00 00 00 00   ......T| ..T|...
[010] AA F4 6F 5B 00 00 00 00  7F A9 54 7C 08 00 00 00   ..o[... ..T|...
[020] 41 6E 74 6F 6E 69 6F 00  06 00 00 00 48 4F 54 45   Antonio ....HOTE
[030] 4C 00 01 00 00 00 00 01  00 00 00 00 00 00 00 00   L....... .......
[040] 00 00 00 00 00 00 00 00  00 00 00 00 01 00 00 00   ....... .......
[050] 00 01 00 00 00 00 01 00  00 00 00 01 00 00 00 00   ....... .......
[060] E8 03 00 00 01 02 00 00  00 00 00 00 10 00 00 00   ....... .......
[070] 04 47 B5 99 97 38 5B 0F  DD 4D 83 DA B8 BF ED B7   .G...8[. .M......
[080] 00 00 00 00 10 00 00 00  A8 00 15 00 00 00 20 00   ....... ......
[090] 00 00 FF FF FF FF FF FF  FF FF FF FF FF FF FF FF   ....... ........
[0A0] FF FF FF FF FF FF FF 00  00 00 00 00 00 00 00 00   ....... .......
[0B0] 00 00 00 00 00 00 EC 04  00 00                     ........ .

key 19 bytes
INFO/minor_version
data 4 bytes
[000] 00 00 00 00                                        ...
```

```
key 9 bytes
NEXT_RID
data 4 bytes
[000] EC 03 00 00                                    ...

key 13 bytes
INFO/version
data 4 bytes
[000] 04 00 00 00
```

We can also get some information about the database.

```
[root@hotel private]# tdbtool passdb.tdb info
Size of file/data: 8192/511
Header offset/logical size: 0/8192
Number of records: 7
Incompatible hash: no
Active/supported feature flags: 0x00000000/0x00000001
Robust mutexes locking: no
Smallest/average/largest keys: 9/13/19
Smallest/average/largest data: 4/59/202
Smallest/average/largest padding: 7/23/60
Number of dead records: 0
Smallest/average/largest dead records: 0/0/0
Number of free records: 1
Smallest/average/largest free records: 6632/6632/6632
Number of hash chains: 131
Smallest/average/largest hash chains: 0/0/1
Number of uncoalesced records: 0
Smallest/average/largest uncoalesced runs: 0/0/0
Percentage keys/data/padding/free/dead/rechdrs&tailers/hashes:
1/5/2/81/0/3/6
```

It is possible to check the integrity of the database, too.

```
[root@hotel private]# tdbtool passdb.tdb check
Database integrity is OK and has 7 records.
```

We can also delete the contents of the database. This action cannot be reverted unless we have a backup, so we must be sure that this is actually what we want to do.

```
[root@hotel temp]# tdbtool passdb.tdb erase
```

This command can also be executed in interactive mode, and here we see an example.

```
[root@hotel temp]# tdbtool
tdb> help
database not open

tdbtool:
  create      dbname    : create a database
  open        dbname    : open an existing database
  transaction_start     : start a transaction
  transaction_commit    : commit a transaction
  transaction_cancel    : cancel a transaction
  erase                 : erase the database
  dump                  : dump the database as strings
  keys                  : dump the database keys as strings
  hexkeys               : dump the database keys as hex values
  info                  : print summary info about the database
  insert    key  data   : insert a record
  move      key  file   : move a record to a destination tdb
  store     key  data   : store a record (replace)
  show      key         : show a record by key
  delete    key         : delete a record by key
  list                  : print the database hash table and freelist
  free                  : print the database freelist
  check                 : check the integrity of an opened database
  repack                : repack the database
  speed                 : perform speed tests on the database
  ! command             : execute system command
  1 | first             : print the first record
```

```
n | next              : print the next record
q | quit              : terminate
\n                    : repeat 'next' command

tdb>
```

# Summary

This chapter focused on monitoring and troubleshooting Samba. Previously we had already seen some basic concepts, but in this chapter we took a step forward. We used **smbcontrol** and **smbstatus** to monitor and control the Samba processes. We also learned how to back up, restore, and check TDB files used with the tdbsam back end.

# CHAPTER 10

# File Services in Samba

Samba, as well as Windows servers, are often used as file servers. We'll see here in more detail how to effectively share files in our network. In this chapter we'll cover the following concepts:

- Creating and configuring file sharing.

- Planning file service migration.

- Limiting access to IPC$.

- Creating scripts for user and group handling.

- Samba share access configuration parameters.

We will also learn about the following terms and utilities: `smb.conf`, `[homes]`, **smbcquotas**, `browseable`, writable, `valid users`, write list, read list, read only and guest ok, IPC$, and **mount**.

## Create and Configure File Sharing

We've already seen in Chapter 7 how to set up a shared folder in Samba. However, we only saw a very simple example. In this section we'll browse through the many options available to create and customize shares.

In the Samba configuration file (`/etc/samba/smb.conf`) toward the bottom there is a Share definitions section. Here, we create and configure the shares. Right after a fresh install there are some predefined shares that we can use as a template when creating our own shares. The first of these shares is `[homes]`.

- 
- 
- 

© Antonio Vazquez 2019
A. Vazquez, *Practical LPIC-3 300*, https://doi.org/10.1007/978-1-4842-4473-9_10

```
[homes]
        comment = Home Directories
        valid users = %S, %D%w%S
        browseable = No
        read only = No
        inherit acls = Yes
```

.

.

.

The [homes] share grants access to every user to his or her home directory. For instance, if the user avazquez access the Samba server from his Windows computer, he'll see the screen shown in Figure 10-1.

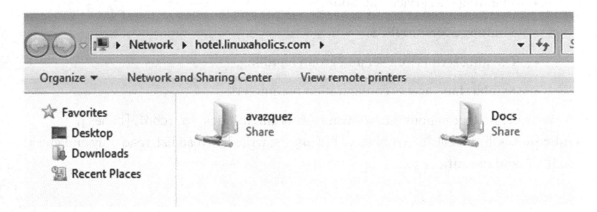

***Figure 10-1.*** *Browsing our Samba server*

The comment parameter is self-explanatory. It is the comment that appears in the Details view when browsing the share from a Windows workstation (Figure 10-2).

***Figure 10-2.*** *Shares and comments*

The valid users parameter tells Samba who is allowed to access this share; here we can specify usernames or groups. If this parameter is not set, then everybody can access the share. In the [homes] share the line valid users = %S, %D%w%S means that every user can access his or her own home directory. There is a similar parameter called invalid users that works exactly the opposite way: It states which users are not allowed to access the share.

The browseable parameter specifies whether the folder is visible to everybody or not. In the case of the [homes] share this parameter has been set to no, as no one will see other users' home directories.

In turn, the read only parameter is set to no, which means that we can write to the Samba share. Of course, this only means that Samba allows the user to write, but for the write to be successfully executed, the user will also need permissions at the file system level. This parameter is an inverted synonym for writeable/writable, thus read only = no is equivalent to writeable = yes.

Finally, we have the inherit acls parameter, the meaning of which is also self-explanatory. We'll see more details about ACLs in the next chapter.

Let's take a look now at the share we created.

```
[Docs]
comment = Public documents
path = /shared_docs
public = yes
writable = yes
```

We didn't specify the value of the browseable parameter, but it takes the default value of yes. In this case, then, the share is browseable, as we can see in Figure 10-1. If we change the value of the browseable parameter to no and we restart the SMB service, we'll see that we don't see it anymore (Figure 10-3).

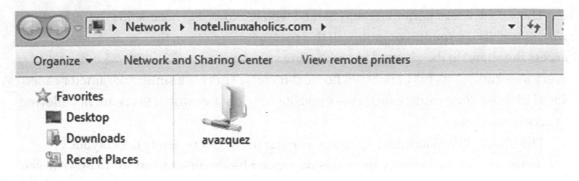

***Figure 10-3.*** *Where is our share?*

However, we can access it directly by specifying its name, as long as we have the appropriate permissions.

```
[root@alpha ~]# smbclient //hotel.linuxaholics.com/Docs -U avazquez
Enter SAMBA\avazquez's password:
Try "help" to get a list of possible commands.
smb: \> ls
  .                                 D        0  Mon Aug 13 02:29:30 2018
  ..                                DR       0  Mon Aug 13 09:27:15 2018
  example.txt                       N       24  Sun Aug 12 10:38:49 2018
  english.txt                       A       33  Mon Aug 13 02:30:18 2018
  español.txt                       A       29  Mon Aug 13 02:30:39 2018

          7022592 blocks of size 1024. 5585828 blocks available
smb: \>
```

Another way to access a Samba share is by actually mounting the share in the file system. We can do this with the **mount** command. First we create the mount point.

```
[root@alpha ~]# mkdir /mnt/samba_hotel
```

Then we mount the share by specifying the file system type, in this case cifs, the Samba server and share location, and the mount point.

```
[root@alpha ~]# mount -t cifs //hotel.linuxaholics.com/Docs /mnt/samba_
hotel/
```

It is possible, though, that we see this error when trying to mount the Samba share:

```
mount: wrong fs type, bad option, bad superblock on //hotel.linuxaholics.
com/Docs,
        missing codepage or helper program, or other error
        (for several filesystems (e.g. nfs, cifs) you might
        need a /sbin/mount.<type> helper program)

        In some cases useful info is found in syslog - try
        dmesg | tail or so.
```

When executing a mount with the -t cifs option the system actually executes the **mount.cifs** command, and if it's not installed we get an error. To install mount.cifs we must install the cifs-utils package.

```
[root@alpha ~]# yum -y install cifs-utils
```

Now we can mount the Samba share.

```
[root@alpha ~]# mount -t cifs //hotel.linuxaholics.com/Docs /mnt/samba_
hotel/
Password for root@//hotel.linuxaholics.com/Docs:
```

By default, it tries to connect to the Samba server using the currently logged user as the username, in this case root. We can specify a different user with the -o username option.

```
[root@alpha ~]# mount -t cifs -o username=Antonio //hotel.linuxaholics.com/
Docs /mnt/samba_hotel/
Password for Antonio@//hotel.linuxaholics.com/Docs:   *******
```

The Samba share is now mounted.

```
[root@alpha ~]# df -h
Filesystem                      Size  Used Avail Use% Mounted on
//hotel.linuxaholics.com/Docs   6,7G  1,5G  5,3G  22% /mnt/samba_hotel
```

# Quotas

The Samba suite includes also a tool named **smbcquotas**, which can be used to manage quotas in a Samba share. For this to work, the file system the share resides on must be mounted with quota support. If that's the case we can list the quotas with the -L parameter.

```
[root@alpha ~]# smbcquotas //hotel.linuxaholics.com/Info -U Antonio -L
Enter SAMBA\Antonio's password:
NT_STATUS_NOT_SUPPORTED cli_list_user_quota
```

Unfortunately, modern versions of the Samba suite have a bug that prevents this tool from working normally. The details can be found at https://bugzilla.samba. org/show_bug.cgi?id=13553. Fortunately, there are already software patches that can be applied to solve this bug. It is also possible to use an older version of the program to check how it works.

If we have an older Samba installation on a server, we can list the existing quotas in a share like this:

```
linux-server:~ # smbcquotas -V
Version 3.6.3-0.39.1-3012-SUSE-CODE11-x86_64
linux-server:~ # smbcquotas -L -v //127.0.0.1/infoquota
Enter root's password:
Quotas for User: LINUX-SERVER\root
Used Space:        5798912
Soft Limit:      NO LIMIT
Hard Limit:      NO LIMIT
```

We can configure a quota for the root user like this:

```
linux-server:~ # smbcquotas -S UQLIM:root:10000000/20000000 //127.0.0.1/
infoquota
Enter root's password:
LINUX-ISCSI-SERVER\root    :        5798912/      9999360/      19999744
```

If we list the existing quotas again, we'll see that the new soft and hard limits have been applied.

```
linux-server:~ # smbcquotas -v -L //127.0.0.1/infoquota
Enter root's password:
Quotas for User: LINUX-SERVER\root
Used Space:          5798912
Soft Limit:          9999360
Hard Limit:         19999744
```

# File Services Migration

Samba services can be migrated from one server to another. Depending on the operating system of the servers, there are several possible scenarios:

- Migrate from a Windows server to a Linux Samba server.

- Migrate from a Linux Samba server to another Linux Samba server.

## Migrate from a Linux Samba Server to Another Linux Samba Server

If we need to migrate our Samba server to a newer Linux server, we'll need to perform several actions:

- Install Samba binaries.

- Copy the Samba configuration (/etc/samba/smb.conf file).

- Migrate the Samba users to the new server.

- Migrate the Samba groups to the new server.

- Create the shares in the new server.

- Migrate the actual data to the new server, retaining the correcct permissions.

Let's now examine each step in detail.

# Install Samba Binaries

This was described in Chapter 7.

## Copy the Samba Configuration

The Samba configuration is defined in the /etc/samba/smb.conf file. This file is pretty long and can be difficult to read due to the many comments. To get a cleaner and more concise version of the file content, we can use **sed**.

```
[root@hotel ~]# sed /^#/d /etc/samba/smb.conf | sed /^\;/d | sed /^$/d |
sed /\w*#/d
[global]
      workgroup = MY_SAMBA_GROUP
      server string = My Samba Server %v
      netbios name = HOTEL
      security = user
      passdb backend = tdbsam
      printing = cups
      printcap name = cups
      load printers = yes
      cups options = raw
[homes]
      comment = Home Directories
      valid users = %S, %D%w%S
      browseable = No
      read only = No
      inherit acls = Yes
[printers]
      comment = All Printers
      path = /var/tmp
      printable = Yes
      create mask = 0600
      browseable = No
```

```
[print$]
     comment = Printer Drivers
     path = /var/lib/samba/drivers
     write list = @printadmin root
     force group = @printadmin
     create mask = 0664
     directory mask = 0775
[Docs]
comment = Public documents
path = /shared_docs
public = yes
writable = yes
browseable = no
```

Now we can simply copy the /etc/samba/smb.conf file to the new server.

```
[root@hotel ~]# scp /etc/samba/smb.conf india.linuxaholics.com:/etc/samba
```

## Migrate the Samba Users to the New Server

We need to migrate the user accounts from the old server as well. We start by getting a list of the Samba users.

```
[root@hotel ~]# pdbedit -L
Antonio:1000:
avazquez:1001:Antonio Vazquez
```

Right now our Samba server only has one user. To make things a bit more realistic, we'll add a couple of users before migrating these users to the new server.

```
[root@hotel ~]# useradd -m -c "Rosalia" Rosalia
[root@hotel ~]# useradd -m -c "Isabel" Isabel
[root@hotel ~]# pdbedit -a Rosalia
new password:
retype new password:
Unix username:        Rosalia
NT username:
Account Flags:        [U          ]
```

```
User SID:              S-1-5-21-3190637888-612994590-2392495275-1002
Primary Group SID:     S-1-5-21-3190637888-612994590-2392495275-513
Full Name:
Home Directory:        \\hotel\rosalia
HomeDir Drive:
Logon Script:
Profile Path:          \\hotel\rosalia\profile
Domain:                HOTEL
Account desc:
Workstations:
Munged dial:
Logon time:            0
Logoff time:           Wed, 06 Feb 2036 10:06:39 EST
Kickoff time:          Wed, 06 Feb 2036 10:06:39 EST
Password last set:     Fri, 15 Jun 2018 18:16:22 EDT
Password can change:   Fri, 15 Jun 2018 18:16:22 EDT
Password must change:  never
Last bad password    : 0
Bad password count   : 0
Logon hours          : FFFFFFFFFFFFFFFFFFFFFFFFFFFFFFFFFFFFFFFFFF
[root@hotel ~]#
[root@hotel ~]# pdbedit -a Isabel
new password:
retype new password:
Unix username:         Isabel
NT username:
Account Flags:         [U          ]
User SID:              S-1-5-21-3190637888-612994590-2392495275-1003
Primary Group SID:     S-1-5-21-3190637888-612994590-2392495275-513
Full Name:
Home Directory:        \\hotel\isabel
HomeDir Drive:
Logon Script:
Profile Path:          \\hotel\isabel\profile
Domain:                HOTEL
```

```
Account desc:
Workstations:
Munged dial:
Logon time:            0
Logoff time:           Wed, 06 Feb 2036 10:06:39 EST
Kickoff time:          Wed, 06 Feb 2036 10:06:39 EST
Password last set:     Fri, 15 Jun 2018 18:16:47 EDT
Password can change:   Fri, 15 Jun 2018 18:16:47 EDT
Password must change: never
Last bad password    : 0
Bad password count   : 0
Logon hours          : FFFFFFFFFFFFFFFFFFFFFFFFFFFFFFFFFFFFFFFFFFFFFFFF
[root@hotel ~]#
```

We'll get the list of the Samba users, and we'll redirect it to a file.

```
[root@hotel ~]# pdbedit -L
Antonio:1000:
Rosalia:1003:Rosalia
avazquez:1001:Antonio Vazquez
Isabel:1004:Isabel

[root@hotel ~]# pdbedit -L > samba_hotel_users.txt
```

Then we copy the file to the destination server.

```
[root@hotel ~]# scp samba_hotel_users.txt india.linuxaholics.com:/root
root@india.linuxaholics.com's password:
samba_hotel_users.txt
```

In this case we only have four users, so we could create them manually. However, when there are hundreds or thousands of users, it is definitely better to use a script. The script could be written in almost any language: Bash Script, Perl, Python, and so on. In this book we use the following Python script:

```
#!/usr/bin/python

import subprocess
import sys
```

```python
def usage():
        print "Usage: %s USERS_FILE" % sys.argv[0]
        sys.exit(1)

if len(sys.argv)<2:
        usage()

FILENAME = sys.argv[1]
try:
        fd = open(FILENAME, "r")
        lines = fd.readlines()
        fd.close()
except Exception, e:
        print str(e)
        sys.exit(2)

for line in lines:
        try:
                print "Creating Linux user %s" % line.split(":")[0]
                cmd = "useradd -m -c '" + line.split(":")[2].strip() + "' "
                + line.split(":")[0]
                output = subprocess.check_output(cmd, shell=True)
                print output
                print "Creating Samba user %s" % line.split(":")[0]
                cmd = "smbpasswd -a -n " +  line.split(":")[0]
                output = subprocess.check_output(cmd, shell=True)
                print output

        except Exception,e:
                print str(e)
```

We execute it by passing the file with the Samba users as the first parameter.

```
[root@india ~]# ./mig_samba_users.py samba_hotel_users.txt
Creating Linux user Antonio

Creating Samba user Antonio
Added user Antonio.

Creating Linux user avazquez
```

```
Creating Samba user avazquez
Added user avazquez.

Creating Linux user Rosalia

Creating Samba user Rosalia
Added user Rosalia.

Creating Linux user Isabel

Creating Samba user Isabel
Added user Isabel.
```

## Migrate the Samba Groups

Analogously, we also need to migrate the groups. In our case, however, there are no Samba groups defined, so we don't need to migrate them.

```
[root@india ~]# net rpc info -S hotel.linuxaholics.com -U avazquez
Enter avazquez's password:
Domain Name: MY_SAMBA_GROUP
Domain SID: S-1-5-21-892619289-2955383375-3350856941
Sequence number: 1534196585
Num users: 4
Num domain groups: 0
Num local groups: 0
```

If we had Samba groups defined, we'd need to get the list of groups and members and create a script to migrate those groups to the new server.

## Create the Shares in the New Server

The next step in our migration plan would be to migrate the shares. We can list remotely the shares of a server with the **net rpc share list** command.

```
[root@india ~]# net rpc share list -S hotel.linuxaholics.com -U avazquez
Enter avazquez's password:
print$
IPC$
avazquez
```

Unfortunately, there is a major disadvantage when using this command, as it will only list the shares that are browsable for the user executing the command (avazquez in our case). That is the reason why in the output the Docs share is omitted, as we had changed its local property browseable to no.

If before executing the **net rpc share list** command, we edit the Samba configuration file in hotel.linuxaholics.com to make the share browsable again, it will be included in the output.

```
[root@india ~]# net rpc share list -S hotel.linuxaholics.com -U avazquez
Enter avazquez's password:
print$
Docs
IPC$
avazquez
```

We also see a share named avazquez, which in truth is the [homes] share as the user avazquez sees it.

Theoretically, we could migrate the shares with the **net rpc share migrate all** command.

```
[root@india ~]# net rpc share migrate all -S hotel.linuxaholics.com -U avazquez
```

However, this command is a bit tricky and prone to errors. To circumvent this, we'll use our own script.

By executing **testparm** we get some information about the Samba configuration, as well as the shares defined.

```
[root@hotel ~]# testparm
Load smb config files from /etc/samba/smb.conf
rlimit_max: increasing rlimit_max (1024) to minimum Windows limit (16384)
Processing section "[homes]"
Processing section "[printers]"
Processing section "[print$]"
Processing section "[Docs]"
Loaded services file OK.
Server role: ROLE_STANDALONE
```

Press enter to see a dump of your service definitions

```
# Global parameters
[global]
        printcap name = cups
        security = USER
        server string = My Samba Server %v
        workgroup = MY_SAMBA_GROUP
        idmap config * : backend = tdb
        cups options = raw

[homes]
        browseable = No
        comment = Home Directories
        inherit acls = Yes
        read only = No
        valid users = %S %D%w%S

[printers]
        browseable = No
        comment = All Printers
        create mask = 0600
        path = /var/tmp
        printable = Yes

[print$]
        comment = Printer Drivers
        create mask = 0664
        directory mask = 0775
        force group = @printadmin
        path = /var/lib/samba/drivers
        write list = @printadmin root

[Docs]
        comment = Public documents
        guest ok = Yes
        path = /shared_docs
        read only = No
```

To process this information more easily, we redirect the command to a text file.

```
[root@hotel ~]# testparm > output_testparm
```

If we look at the file, we'll see some global configuration parameters, the default home and printer share definitions, and the Docs share we created earlier. Depending on the exact version of CentOS 7 we are working on, we might have a print$ share definition, too.

```
[root@hotel ~]# cat output_testparm
# Global parameters
[global]
        printcap name = cups
        security = USER
        server string = My Samba Server %v
        workgroup = MY_SAMBA_GROUP
        idmap config * : backend = tdb
        cups options = raw

[homes]
        browseable = No
        comment = Home Directories
        inherit acls = Yes
        read only = No
        valid users = %S %D%w%S

[printers]
        browseable = No
        comment = All Printers
        create mask = 0600
        path = /var/tmp
        printable = Yes

[print$]
        comment = Printer Drivers
        create mask = 0664
        directory mask = 0775
        force group = @printadmin
        path = /var/lib/samba/drivers
        write list = @printadmin root
```

```
[Docs]
      comment = Public documents
      guest ok = Yes
      path = /shared_docs
      read only = No
```

Similar to what happened when creating the users on the destination server, as we only have one shared resource (apart from the defaults), it would be really easy to create it manually. Nevertheless, there might be situations in which we need to create hundreds of shared resources, so we'll learn how to create them in the new server via a Python script.

```python
#!/usr/bin/python

import sys
import subprocess

def usage():
      print "Usage: %s SHARES_FILE" % sys.argv[0]
      sys.exit(1)

if len(sys.argv)<2:
      usage()

FILENAME = sys.argv[1]
try:
      fd = open(FILENAME, "r")
      lines = fd.readlines()
      fd.close()
      f2 = open("folders_migrated.txt","w")
except Exception, e:
      print str(e)
      sys.exit(1)

flag = False

for line in lines:
      try:
            if flag:
```

```
                if "path" in line:
                        indice = line.find("=")
                        cmd = "mkdir -p %s" % line[indice+1:]
                        try:
                                output = subprocess.check_output(cmd,
                                shell=True)
                                f2.write(line[indice+1:])
                                print "Created %s folder\n" % line[indice+1:]
                         except Exception, e:
                                print str(e)
                        finally:
                                flag = True
        else:

                if line[0]=='[':
                        if "[global]" in line:
                                pass
                        elif "[homes]" in line:
                                pass
                        elif "[printers]" in line:
                                pass
                        elif "[print$]" in line:
                                pass
                        else:
                                flag = True

    except Exception,e:
            pass
f2.close()
```

We copy this Python program to the india server and execute it by passing the output of the **testparm** command as a parameter.

```
[root@india ~]# ./mig_shares.py output_testparm
Created  /shared_docs
```

We see that the program created the /shared_docs folder. It also created a file with the list of the folders created and migrated.

```
[root@india ~]# cat folders_migrated.txt
 /shared_docs
```

## Migrate the Data

The last step in the migration will be to copy the actual data. To retain the permissions we could use the **rsync** command, which should be installed on both servers. We can also take advantage of the folders_migrated.txt file to sync the contents of every share in the original as well as in the new Samba server.

```
[root@india ~]# for i in $(cat folders_migrated.txt) ; do rsync -av
root@hotel.linuxaholics.com:$i $i ; done ;
root@hotel.linuxaholics.com's password:
receiving incremental file list
shared_docs/
shared_docs/english.txt
shared_docs/español.txt
shared_docs/example.txt

sent 85 bytes  received 387 bytes  134.86 bytes/sec
total size is 86  speedup is 0.18
```

Now we have successfully replicated the original Samba server hotel.linuxaholics. com on the new Samba server india.linuxaholics.com. As we previously copied the smb.conf file, the configuration should be exactly the same on both servers. The only thing the admin will have to do now is assign temporary passwords to the Samba users so that they can connect for the first time to the new server and reset their passwords. This can be easily accomplished with the use of scripts.

## Migrating from Windows to Samba

Samba 3 and later versions allow the migration of an NT4 domain to a Samba server. During this process several actions need to be performed:

- Migrate accounts.

- Migrate groups.

- Migrate shares.

- Migrate directories and files.

The way to effectively migrate from a Windows server to a Samba server will depend on many factors. It is thus necessary to adapt the general guidelines we'll see here to whatever the environment is. In the next sections we'll review the four steps of a migration in detail.

## Migrate Accounts

We can get a list of the Windows users with the **net user** command. We'll redirect the output to a file to process it later in the Samba server (Figure 10-4).

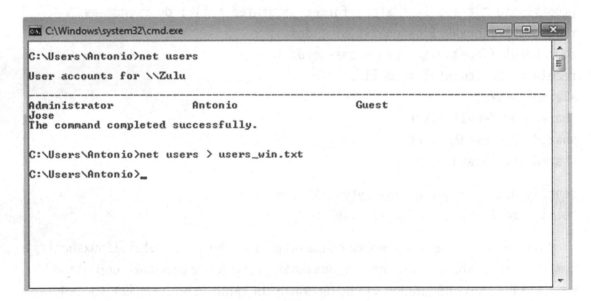

***Figure 10-4.***  *Getting the Windows users*

We can copy the resulting file to the Samba server using any protocol or method: CIFS, HTTP, rsync, a USB device, and so on. Whatever method we choose, we can now process the file with this Python script:

```
#!/usr/bin/python

import sys
import subprocess
```

```python
def usage():
        print "Usage: %s FILE" % sys.argv[0]

if len(sys.argv)<2:
        usage()
        sys.exit(1)

FILE = sys.argv[1]

try:
        fd = open(FILE, "r")
        lines = fd.readlines()
        fd.close()
except Exception,e:
        print str(e)
        sys.exit(2)

top = '---------'
bottom = 'The command completed successfully'
flag = 0
users = []

for line in lines:
        if (flag==1):
                if bottom in line:
                        flag = 0
                else:
                        users.append(line.split())
        else:
                if top in line:
                        flag = 1

for user in users:
        for element in user:
                try:
                        print "Creating Linux user %s" % element
                        cmd = "useradd -m " + element
                        output = subprocess.check_output(cmd, shell=True)
```

277

```
                    print output
                    print "Creating Samba user %s" % element
                    cmd = "smbpasswd -a -n " + element
                    output = subprocess.check_output(cmd, shell=True)
                    print output

        except Exception ,e:
                    print(str(e))
                    sys.exit(3)
```

After this script is executed, the Linux as well as the corresponding Samba users will be created.

```
[root@india ~]# ./get_windows_users.py users_w2k8.txt
Creating Linux user Administrator

Creating Samba user Administrator

Creating Linux user Antonio

Creating Samba user Antonio

Creating Linux user Jose

Creating Samba user Jose

Creating Linux user Guest

Creating Samba user Guest
```

# Migrate Groups

Similar to what we did with the Windows users, we can get a list of the local groups by executing **net localgroup** (Figure 10-5).

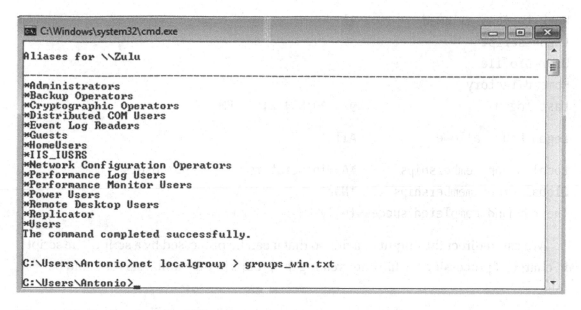

**Figure 10-5.** *Getting the Windows groups*

These are all the groups defined in the Windows server, but we only need to migrate those groups associated with users. We'll get a list of the groups of which our users are members. This information can be obtained with the **net user username** command. In our example there are only four users—Administrator, Antonio, Jose, and Guest—so the command should be **net user Administrator**. The output will be something like this:

```
User name                   Administrator
Full Name
Comment
User's comment
Country code                000 (System Default)
Account active              Yes
Account expires             Never

Password last set           9/5/2018 1:31:23 AM
Password expires            Never
Password changeable         9/5/2018 1:31:23 AM
Password required           No
User may change password    Yes
```

```
Workstations allowed          All
Logon script
User profile
Home directory
Last logon                    9/5/2018 4:24:32 PM

Logon hours allowed           All

Local Group Memberships       *Administrators       *HomeUsers
Global Group memberships      *None
The command completed successfully.
```

We can redirect the output to a file, so that it can be processed by a script. The script in charge of processing the file and creating the groups in the Samba server could be this:

```python
#!/usr/bin/python

import sys
import subprocess

def usage():
        print "Usage: %s FILE" % sys.argv[0]

if len(sys.argv)<2:
        usage()
        sys.exit(1)

FILE = sys.argv[1]

try:
        fd = open(FILE, "r")
        lines = fd.readlines()
        fd.close()
except Exception,e:
        print str(e)
        sys.exit(2)

flag = 0
groups = []
```

```
for line in lines:
    if (line.find("User name")>-1):
        USER = line[9:].strip()
        flag = 1
    if (flag==1):
        if (line.find("Local Group Memberships")>-1):
            while (line.find("*")>-1):
                line2 = line[line.find("*")+1:]
                group = line2[:line2.find(" ")]
                groups.append(group)
                line = line2[line2.find(" "):]
                line = line2
                try:
                        print "Creating group %s if it does not
                        exists" % group
                        cmd = "groupadd " + group
                        output = subprocess.check_output(cmd,
                        shell=True)
                        print output
                except Exception, e:
                        print(str(e))
            lista = ""
            for grupo in groups:
                lista = lista + grupo + ","
            lista = lista[0:len(lista)-1]
            try:
                    print "Adding user %s to the groups" % USER
                    cmd = "usermod -G " + lista + " " + USER
                    output = subprocess.check_output(cmd, shell=True)
                    print output
            except Exception, e:
                    print(str(e))

            flag = 0
            groups = []
```

By passing the file we had created previously redirecting the output of the net user command, the Python script will create the groups and add the users to these groups.

```
[root@india ~]# ./mig_groups.py Administrator.txt
Creating group Administrators if it does not exists

Creating group HomeUsers if it does not exists

Adding user Administrator to the groups
```

If we want to, we can check whether the users were associated with the appropriate groups.

```
[root@india ~]# id Administrator
uid=1007(Administrator) gid=1008(Administrator) groups=1008(Administrator),
1009(Administrators),1010(HomeUsers)
```

## Migrate Shares

Right after migrating users and groups, we need to migrate the shares. We can list the shares on a Windows computer with the **net share** command (Figure 10-6).

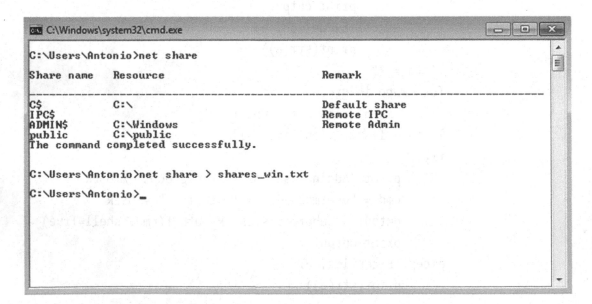

***Figure 10-6.*** *Getting a list of shared resources*

In this example we can see the default administrative shares, as well as the `public` share. As usual, we redirect the output to a file and we'll process that file with a Python program to create the corresponding shares. The program could be something like this:

```python
#!/usr/bin/python

import sys
import subprocess

def usage():
        print "Usage: %s FILE" % sys.argv[0]

if len(sys.argv)<2:
        usage()
        sys.exit(1)

FILE = sys.argv[1]
OUTPUT_FILE = "add_to_smb.conf"

try:
        fd = open(FILE, "r")
        lines = fd.readlines()
        fd.close()
except Exception,e:
        print str(e)
        sys.exit(2)

top = '---------'
bottom = 'The command completed successfully'
flag = 0
users = []

fd2 = open(OUTPUT_FILE, "w")

for line in lines:
        if (flag==1):
                if bottom in line:
                        flag = 0
                else:
```

```
                    if line.find("$")<0:
                        share_name = line[:line.find(" ")]
                        linea = "[" + share_name +']\n'
                        try:
                                fd2.write(linea)
                                ruta = "/samba/" + share_name
                                cmd = "mkdir -p " + ruta
                                print "Creating %s" % share_name
                                output = subprocess.check_output(cmd,
                                shell=True)
                                print output
                                fd2.write('\t')
                                fd2.write('path = ')
                                fd2.write(ruta)
                                fd2.write('\n')
                                fd2.write('\tread only = Yes\n')
                                fd2.write('\tguest ok = No\n')
                        except Exception, e:
                                print str(e)

        else:
                if top in line:
                        flag = 1
fd2.close()
```

The program creates the Windows shares, ignoring the administrative shares, inside the samba folder. It also generates a text file named add_to_smb.conf with the share definitions to add to our /etc/smb/samba.conf file.

The execution is very simple.

```
[root@india ~]# ./mig_winshares.py shares_win.txt
Creating public
```

In our example this is the text file created:

```
[root@india ~]# cat add_to_smb.conf
[public]
      path = /samba/public
      read only = Yes
      guest ok = No
```

This is the share definition that should be added to the Samba configuration file. The share is declared initially as read only and won't be accessed anonymously for security reasons. Later we'll need to apply the right access permissions.

## Migrate Directories and Files

Once users, groups, and shares have been migrated, it is time to migrate the data; that is, the files and directories inside of every share. A useful tool to migrate the data is **smbget**, which allows us to perform recursive downloads on a Windows/Samba share.
It works pretty much like **wget**. In our case we'd move on to the /samba/public folder and execute **smbget** with the proper parameters.

```
[root@india public]# pwd
/samba/public
[root@india public]# smbget -R -u Antonio -p antonio smb://192.168.1.200/
public
```

Unfortunately, the compiled smbget binary included in CentOS seems to have a bug and we might get the following error:

```
You don't have enough permissions to access smb://192.168.1.200/
public/201801_data.txt
You don't have enough permissions to access smb://192.168.1.200/
public/201802_data.txt
```

If we get some debug information with the -d parameter this is what we'll see:

```
.
.
.
NTLMSSP_NEGOTIATE_128
NTLMSSP_NEGOTIATE_KEY_EXCH
```

```
SPNEGO login failed: NT_STATUS_LOGON_TYPE_NOT_GRANTED
```
.

.

.

Obviously, there seems to be some problem with the negotiation process. However, this bug seems to have been fixed in newer versions of the Samba tools. When we study Samba 4 and Active Directory we'll download, compile, and install a more recent Samba version (see Chapter 17 for details).

If we launch the newer **smbget** version we'll be able to recursively download the files.

```
[root@india public]# /root/soft/samba-4.7.11/bin/smbget -R --user Antonio
smb://192.168.1.200/public
Password for [Antonio] connecting to //public/192.168.56.200:
Using workgroup LINUXAHOLICS, user Antonio
smb://192.168.1.200/public/201801_data.txt
smb://192.168.1.200/public/201802_data.txt
Downloaded 15b in 10 seconds
```

We already have the shares defined in the Samba server and the contents copied. Now we only need to adjust the permissions and assign new passwords to the users in Samba. To get the original rights associated with the shared files in Windows we can use **smbcacls**.

```
[root@hotel public]# smbcacls //192.168.1.200/public 201801_data.txt -U
antonio%antonio
REVISION:1
CONTROL:SR|DI|DP
OWNER: ZULU\Antonio
GROUP:S-1-5-21-852636792-403353388-521036446-512
ACL:NT AUTHORITY\SYSTEM:ALLOWED/I/FULL
ACL:ZULU\Antonio:ALLOWED/I/FULL
ACL:BUILTIN\Administradores:ALLOWED/I/FULL
ACL:Todos:ALLOWED/I/READ
```

With this information we could write another program or script to apply the right access permissions to each share.

# Limit Access to IPC$

IPC$ is a special share used by Windows (and Samba) for inter-process communication with Remote Procedure Call (RPC). The client connecting can perform a series of actions on the server, like listing users, listing shares, and so on. Nevertheless IPC$ can also be used by hackers to create an anonymous connection and get information about the server. To minimize this risk, we can add an [IPC$] entry to the /etc/samba/smb.conf file and add the following access list.

```
[IPC$]
hosts allow = 192.168.1.0/24 127.0.0.1
hosts deny = 0.0.0.0/0
```

# Scripts for User and Group Handling of File Shares

We have seen so far that for a user to successfully connect to a Samba share, that user must exist in Samba as in the operating system itself. When we studied file services migration earlier in this chapter, we used scripts that dealt with the creation of the corresponding Linux users before adding those same users in the local Samba database. In fact, when using the **tdbsam** back end, if we try to add a Samba user who doesn't exist in Linux, we get the following error:

```
[root@hotel ~]# smbpasswd -a Ivan
New SMB password:
Retype new SMB password:
Failed to add entry for user Ivan.
```

However, if we use the **ldapsam** back end (see Chapter 8), we could have a Samba user without the corresponding Linux user. In this situation we could instruct the **samba** service to automatically create the Linux user as soon as he or she connects to a Samba share. This can be done with the add user script global parameter, which by default has no value.

```
[root@hotel ~]# testparm -v | grep "add user script"
Load smb config files from /etc/samba/smb.conf
rlimit_max: increasing rlimit_max (1024) to minimum Windows limit (16384)
Processing section "[homes]"
```

```
Processing section "[printers]"
Processing section "[Docs]"
Loaded services file OK.
Server role: ROLE_STANDALONE
Press enter to see a dump of your service definitions

        add user script =
```

We can easily point it to the full path of a script that will be executed by root in the situation described earlier. For example:

```
add user script = /usr/local/samba/bin/add_user %u
```

The same thing applies to the creation of groups, but in this case the parameter is add group script. An example would be this:

```
add group script = /usr/sbin/groupadd %g
```

# Samba Share Access Configuration Parameters

We can use many parameters to control user access to the shares defined. For instance, when we created the Docs share we used the guest ok parameter. This meant that the share was public for every user in the network, at least from a share access point of view. Similarly, the writable parameter states that users can have write access to the share; of course, the user would also need the appropriate permissions at the file system level. To make things simpler, we'll assume that the permissions at the file system level are relaxed enough not to interfere with the share permissions and that SELinux is either permissive or disabled.

Instead of the guest ok parameter we could have used its equivalent, public, which has the same effect. We could also allow or deny access with the directives hosts allow or hosts deny. For instance, if we want to deny access to the [Docs] Samba share to a specific host, we could add this line to the share definition:

```
hosts deny = 192.168.1.229
```

After restarting the SMB service, if we try to access the share from that host, we'll get the following error.

```
[root@alpha ~]# smbclient //hotel.linuxaholics.com/Docs -U Antonio
Enter SAMBA\Antonio's password:
tree connect failed: NT_STATUS_ACCESS_DENIED
```

However, we'll be able to access the share from other hosts.

```
[root@india ~]# smbclient //hotel.linuxaholics.com/Docs -U Antonio
Enter MYGROUP\Antonio's password:
Try "help" to get a list of possible commands.
smb: \> ls
  .                                   D        0  Mon Aug 13 02:29:30 2018
  ..                                  DR       0  Mon Aug 13 09:27:15 2018
  example.txt                         N       24  Sun Aug 12 10:38:49 2018
  english.txt                         A       33  Mon Aug 13 02:30:18 2018
  español.txt                         A       29  Mon Aug 13 02:30:39 2018
                7022592 blocks of size 1024. 5586932 blocks available
smb: \>
```

After suppressing the host deny directive, we'll have access again from any host. In the example we used an IP address but we could have typed a name.

Another interesting parameter is valid users. This is a list of users, groups, or both that can log in to the share. If we use group names, we'll prepend the name with the @ character. Going back to the Docs share, if we want only the users Isabel and Rosalia to have permission to access the share, we'd add the corresponding line to the share definition in the /etc/samba/smb.conf file.

```
[Docs]
comment = Public documents
path = /shared_docs
public = yes
writable = yes
valid users = Isabel, Rosalia
```

From now on, the user Antonio won't be able to access the share.

```
[root@alpha ~]# smbclient //hotel.linuxaholics.com/Docs -U Antonio
Enter SAMBA\Antonio's password:
tree connect failed: NT_STATUS_ACCESS_DENIED
```

On the contrary, Isabel and Rosalia will be able to access the share successfully.

```
[root@alpha ~]# smbclient //hotel.linuxaholics.com/Docs -U Isabel
Enter SAMBA\Isabel's password:
Try "help" to get a list of possible commands.
smb: \> ls
  .                             D        0  Mon Aug 13 02:29:30 2018
  ..                            DR       0  Mon Aug 13 09:27:15 2018
  example.txt                   N       24  Sun Aug 12 10:38:49 2018
  english.txt                   A       33  Mon Aug 13 02:30:18 2018
  español.txt                   A       29  Mon Aug 13 02:30:39 2018

          7022592 blocks of size 1024. 5586972 blocks available
smb: \>
```

The [Doc] share has been created with the option `writable`, so every valid user can write to the share. If we want to grant some users read-only permission, we can use the `read list` parameter. For instance, we'll add the user Antonio to the list of valid users but we'll include it in the `read list`, too.

```
[Docs]
comment = Public documents
path = /shared_docs
public = yes
writable = yes
valid users = Isabel, Rosalia, Antonio
read list = Antonio
```

After restarting the service, the user Antonio will be able to access the share, but will not be able to upload any file. Even though the share is generally writable, the `read list` overrides this option for the specified user(s).

```
[root@alpha ~]# smbclient //hotel.linuxaholics.com/Docs -U Antonio
Enter SAMBA\Antonio's password:
Try "help" to get a list of possible commands.
smb: \> put somefile.txt
NT_STATUS_ACCESS_DENIED opening remote file \somefile.txt
```

As expected, the other users included in the valid users list can upload files without a problem.

```
[root@alpha ~]# smbclient //hotel.linuxaholics.com/Docs -U Rosalia
Enter SAMBA\Rosalia's password:
Try "help" to get a list of possible commands.
smb: \> put somefile.txt
putting file somefile.txt as \somefile.txt (1,0 kb/s) (average 1,0 kb/s)
```

A similar directive to read list is write list. As the name implies, it grants write access to the users included on the list, overriding the generic permissions. For example, if we make the [Docs] share not writable but include a write list, those users included on that list will be able to write to the share.

# Summary

File sharing is one of the most important roles of a server in a local network. In this chapter we have seen how to make a folder read-only or writable for certain users, groups, or both. We also outlined the main steps required to perform a migration. We also learned to limit access to the special share IPC$ and we saw several configuration parameters that apply to shares.

# CHAPTER 11

# Linux File System and Share and Service Permissions

A Samba server working as a file server relies on the underlying Linux file system permissions to work properly. We'll see how Linux permissions work and how they interact with Samba permissions. In this chapter, we'll cover the following concepts:

- Knowledge of file and directory permission control.

- Understanding how Samba interacts with Linux file system permissions and ACLs.

- Using the Samba Virtual File System (VFS) to store Windows ACLs.

We will also be introduced to the following terms and utilities: smb.conf, **chmod**, **chown**, create mask, directory mask, force create mode, force directory mode, **smbcacls**, **getfacl**, **setfacl**, vfs_acl_xattr, vfs_acl_tdb, and vfs objects.

## File and Directory Permission Control

We are all familiar with the Linux file system permissions model. Basically, every file or directory has three sets of permissions associated with it: the owner's permissions (user), the group permissions (group), and the rest (other). For example, if a local user creates a new file, these will be the default permissions:

```
[avazquez@bravo ~]$ touch example.txt
[avazquez@bravo ~]$ ls -l example.txt
-rw-rw-r--. 1 avazquez avazquez 0 Jun 29 23:31 example.txt
```

© Antonio Vazquez 2019
A. Vazquez, *Practical LPIC-3 300*, https://doi.org/10.1007/978-1-4842-4473-9_11

If we ever need to change these permissions, we can do so with the **chmod** command. The syntax is very simple. First, we specify whether we want to modify the permissions for the owner (-u), group (-g), other (-o), or all of them (-a). Then we indicate whether we are granting (+) or revoking (-) the permission, and finally we specify the permission itself: read (r), write (w), or execute (x).

For example, if we want to grant other users the permission to write to the file, this is what we'd need to type:

```
[avazquez@bravo ~]$ chmod o+w example.txt
[avazquez@bravo ~]$ ls -l example.txt
-rw-rw-rw-. 1 avazquez avazquez 0 Jun 29 23:31 example.txt
```

If later we want to revoke this permission, we can do it with **chmod**, too.

```
[avazquez@bravo ~]$ chmod o-w example.txt
[avazquez@bravo ~]$ ls -l example.txt
-rw-rw-r--. 1 avazquez avazquez 0 Jun 29 23:31 example.txt
```

There is also an alternative syntax, in which rather than using the flags -u, -g, -o, and so on, we specify the binary representation of the permissions assigned to each one of these three groups.

By default, each type of permission is assigned the following value: r = 4, w = 2, and x = 1. In our example, the binary representation of the permissions associated with the example.txt file will be 664, as the owner has read (4) plus write (2) permissions, the group has also read (4) plus write (2) permissions, and other users have only read (4) permissions.

We can check this point with the **stat** command, which shows us the file permissions in both formats, as well as other interesting information.

```
[avazquez@bravo ~]$ stat example.txt
  File: âexample.txtâ
  Size: 0            Blocks: 0         IO Block: 4096    regular empty file
Device: fd01h/64769d  Inode: 34311523  Links: 1
Access: (0664/-rw-rw-r--)  Uid: ( 1003/avazquez)   Gid: ( 1003/avazquez)
```

Therefore, if we want to give only read access to the group, we can again execute **chmod** like this:

```
[avazquez@bravo ~]$ chmod 644 example.txt
[avazquez@bravo ~]$ ls -l example.txt
-rw-r--r--. 1 avazquez avazquez 0 Jun 29 23:31 example.txt
```

Remember that when we created the example.txt file the default set of permissions assigned to it was 664. This is because when we create a new file in CentOS, the permissions initially assigned are 666 minus the umask value. The umask value has the default value of 002 and thus the permissions assigned to the new file were 664.

The umask value can also be modified if we want to change the default permissions assigned to newly created files.

```
[avazquez@bravo ~]$ umask
0002
[avazquez@bravo ~]$ umask 022
[avazquez@bravo ~]$ umask
0022
```

Now, after creating a new file the default permissions assigned to it will be 644; that is, owner (read/write), group (read), and other (read).

```
[avazquez@bravo ~]$ touch example2.txt
[avazquez@bravo ~]$ ls -l example2.txt
-rw-r--r--. 1 avazquez avazquez 0 Jun 30 21:01 example2.txt
[avazquez@bravo ~]$
```

The umask value is similar in concept to other parameters used in Samba that we'll see later, such as `create mask` and `directory mask`.

After creating a file or a directory, we can change its owner, as long as we have the appropriate permissions. By default, only the root user can do this.

```
[root@bravo avazquez]# chown root example2.txt
[root@bravo avazquez]# ls -l example2.txt
-rw-r--r--. 1 root avazquez 0 Jun 30 21:01 example2.txt
```

As we have seen so far, traditional permissions in Linux are limited to three different groups: the owner user, the owner group, and the rest of the users. It is not possible to assign specific permissions to single users and groups. To fill this gap, modern Linux file systems use access lists. Access lists give us a finer level of control over the permissions. Right after creating a file we can get its associated access list with the **getfacl** command.

```
[root@bravo avazquez]# getfacl example.txt
# file: example.txt
# owner: avazquez
# group: avazquez
user::rw-
group::r--
other::r--
```

At first, the access list only has three entries, one for each classical set of permissions: owner, group, and other. However, by using the **setfacl** command we can grant permissions to any existing user or group. Let's look at an example:

```
[root@bravo avazquez]# setfacl -m u:rrey:rw example.txt
[root@bravo avazquez]# getfacl example.txt
# file: example.txt
# owner: avazquez
# group: avazquez
user::rw-
user:rrey:rw-
group::r--
mask::rw-
other::r--
```

We're saying that we want to modify (-m) the access list associated with the example1.txt file, by granting the user (-u) rrey read and write (rw) permissions.

# Linux File System Permissions and Samba

Obviously, as Samba executes on top of the Linux file system, it relies on Linux file system permissions to work properly. For instance, if we want a file to be executable from Samba it will need to be executable at the file system level. Once we take into account the previous statement, we can proceed to fine tune the Samba permissions by editing the smb.conf file.

If we want to modify the default permissions a file has when it is created from Samba, we'll need to modify the create mask parameter (or its synonym create mode). To see how this parameter works, we'll start by having a look at the permissions assigned by default to a new Samba file. We connect from a Samba client (either Windows or Linux) to the shared_docs share we created in a previous chapter and we create a new file (Figure 11-1).

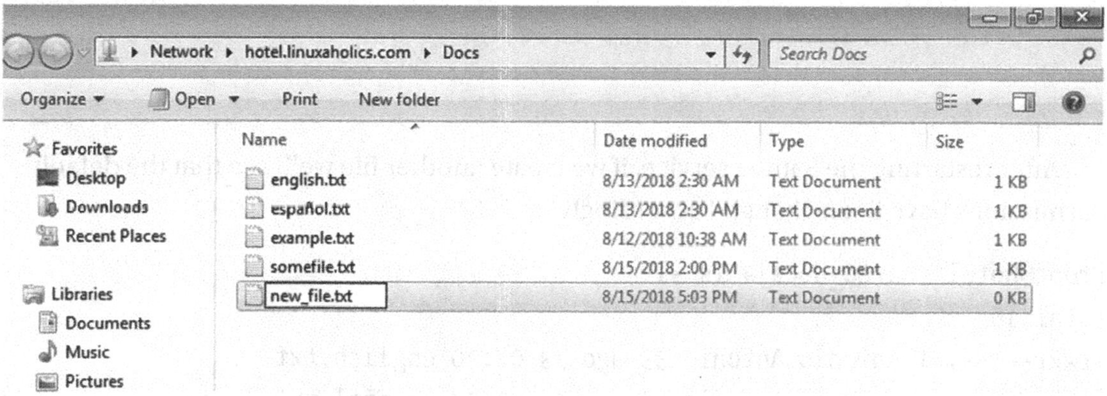

***Figure 11-1.***  *Creating a new file*

If we check the file permissions this is what we'll see:

```
[root@hotel shared_docs]# ls -l
total 16
-rwxr--r--. 1 Antonio Antonio 33 ago 13 02:30 english.txt
-rwxr--r--. 1 Antonio Antonio 29 ago 13 02:30 español.txt
-rw-r--r--. 1 root    root    24 ago 12 10:38 example.txt
-rwxr--r--. 1 Antonio Antonio  0 ago 15 17:03 new_file.txt
-rwxr--r--. 1 Rosalia Rosalia  4 ago 15 13:59 somefile.txt
```

The set of permisions is 744(rwxr--r--), which is the default value for the create mask parameter. We'll change that value into something different. We open the smb.conf file and add a new line to the share definition.

•

•

•

```
[Docs]
comment = Public documents
path = /shared_docs
public = yes
writable = yes
create mask = 0644
```

•

•

•

After restarting the Samba service, if we create another file we'll see that the default permissions have been changed accordingly.

```
[root@hotel shared_docs]# ls -l
total 16
-rwxr--r--. 1 Antonio Antonio 33 ago 13 02:30 english.txt
-rwxr--r--. 1 Antonio Antonio 29 ago 13 02:30 español.txt
-rw-r--r--. 1 root    root    24 ago 12 10:38 example.txt
-rw-r--r--. 1 Antonio Antonio  0 ago 15 19:26 new_file2.txt
-rwxr--r--. 1 Antonio Antonio  0 ago 15 17:03 new_file.txt
-rwxr--r--. 1 Rosalia Rosalia  4 ago 15 13:59 somefile.txt
```

However, if we try to apply a create mask such as in the following example, we'll see an unexpected result.

•

•

•

```
[Docs]
comment = Public documents
path = /shared_docs
public = yes
writable = yes
```

```
create mask = 0775
.

.

.

[root@hotel shared_docs]# ls -l
total 16
-rwxr--r--. 1 Antonio Antonio 33 ago 13 02:30 english.txt
-rwxr--r--. 1 Antonio Antonio 29 ago 13 02:30 español.txt
-rw-r--r--. 1 root    root    24 ago 12 10:38 example.txt
-rw-r--r--. 1 Antonio Antonio  0 ago 15 19:26 new_file2.txt
-rwxr--r--. 1 Antonio Antonio  0 ago 15 21:06 new_file3.txt
-rwxr--r--. 1 Antonio Antonio  0 ago 15 17:03 new_file.txt
-rwxr--r--. 1 Rosalia Rosalia  4 ago 15 13:59 somefile.txt
```

As we can see, the new file has the associated permissions rwxrw-r-- (764) instead of the value we had specified (775). The execute bit has been subtracted from the specified mode, so the final result was 775 – 011 = 764. This behavior has to do with Linux and Unix permissions and the value of the umask applied to newly created files.

If we really need to activate the execute bits for group and other, we'll need to use another parameter, force create mode. We'll comment out the create mask line and add a new one with the force create mode parameter.

```
[Docs]
comment = Public documents
path = /shared_docs
public = yes
writable = yes
#create mask = 0775
force create mode = 0775
```

If we create another file from our Samba client, we'll see that now the permissions assigned are exactly what we expected.

```
[root@hotel shared_docs]# ls -l
total 16
-rwxr--r--. 1 Antonio Antonio 33 ago 13 02:30 english.txt
-rwxr--r--. 1 Antonio Antonio 29 ago 13 02:30 español.txt
```

```
-rw-r--r--. 1 root     root     24 ago 12 10:38 example.txt
-rw-r--r--. 1 Antonio Antonio  0 ago 15 19:26 new_file2.txt
-rwxr--r--. 1 Antonio Antonio  0 ago 15 21:06 new_file3.txt
-rwxrwxr-x. 1 Antonio Antonio  0 ago 15 21:22 new_file4.txt
-rwxr--r--. 1 Antonio Antonio  0 ago 15 17:03 new_file.txt
-rwxr--r--. 1 Rosalia Rosalia   4 ago 15 13:59 somefile.txt
```

In the previous examples we have seen how to change the default permissions of any newly created file. The same principle applies to directories, but the parameters differ.

# Creating a New Directory in Samba

We can control the default permissions of a newly created directory in a similar way to what we did with files. First we can create a subdirectory inside the [Docs] share (Figure 11-2).

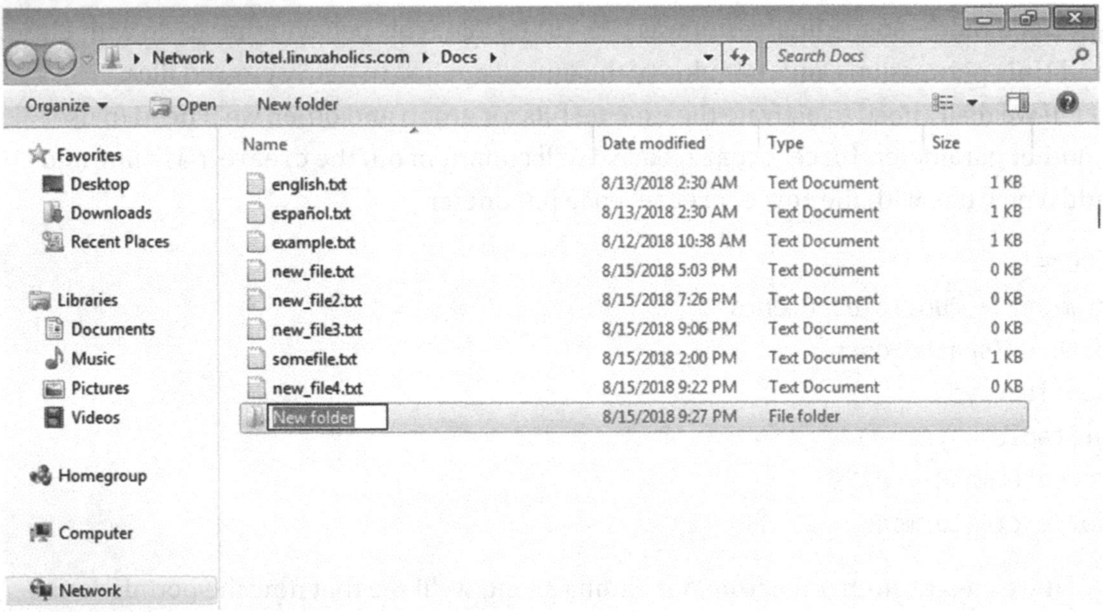

***Figure 11-2.*** *Creating a new directory or folder*

If we examine the permissions assigned to the new folder, we'll see that it has 755 permissions.

```
drwxr-xr-x. 2 Antonio Antonio  6 ago 15 21:27 New folder
```

We can assign new default permissions with the directory mask option. If we want any new subdirectory to have the 744 permissions, we'll have to add the line directory mask = 0744 to the [Docs] share definition in smb.conf.

```
[Docs]
comment = Public documents
path = /shared_docs
public = yes
writable = yes
#create mask = 0775
force create mode = 0775
directory mask = 0744
```

After creating a new subdirectory we'll see that the permissions associated are 744, as expected.

```
[root@hotel shared_docs]# ls -l
.
.
.
drwxr-xr-x. 2 Antonio Antonio  6 ago 15 21:27 New folder
drwxr--r--. 2 Antonio Antonio  6 ago 15 21:40 New folder (2)
.
.
.
```

The default behavior of Linux when applying the default permissions to new directories is far less restrictive than when dealing with new files, so it is quite possible that directory mask is the only parameter you'll ever need when defining new default permissions for directories. In any case, if you need to make sure that the new default permissions are applied no matter what, there is also a force directory mode parameter that works exactly the same way as the force create mode parameter we've already seen.

# Samba VFS

The Samba VFS modules have become a very popular way to extend Samba functionality. To use them we need to include the parameter vfs objects in our configuration file.

In the /usr/lib64/samba/vfs directory we'll see the VFS modules available.

```
[root@hotel ~]# ls /usr/lib64/samba/vfs/
acl_tdb.so        crossrename.so      media_harmony.so   snapper.so
acl_xattr.so      default_quota.so    netatalk.so        streams_depot.so
aio_fork.so       dirsort.so          offline.so         streams_xattr.so
aio_linux.so      expand_msdfs.so     preopen.so         syncops.so
aio_pthread.so    extd_audit.so       readahead.so       time_audit.so
audit.so          fake_perms.so       readonly.so        unityed_media.so
btrfs.so          fileid.so           recycle.so         worm.so
cap.so            fruit.so            shadow_copy2.so     xattr_tdb.so
catia.so          full_audit.so       shadow_copy.so
commit.so         linux_xfs_sgid.so   shell_snap.so
```

Samba VFS extends the functionality of Samba in many useful ways. Some of the advantages of using VFS, which we'll explore in detail now, are implementing file auditing or storing Windows ACLs. In the official Samba documentation (https://www.samba.org/samba/docs/current/man-html) we can see some information about each VFS module and how to use it. We'll look at a couple of examples to better understand how they work.

# Auditing Samba Operations

Windows systems allow the sysadmin to audit certain events, such as creating and deleting files or folders, modifying permissions, and so on. We can implement the same functionality with VFS modules. To enable it we need to add the following line in /etc/samba/smb.conf under the [global] section.

```
vfs objects = audit
```

The audit information will be sent to syslog, but we need to specify the facility and priority with these two parameters:

```
audit:facility = FACILITY
audit:priority = PRIORITY
```

For instance, if we want the audit information to be sent to the local3 facility with an INFO level of detail, these are the lines we should include in /etc/samba/smb.conf:

```
[global]
vfs objects = audit
audit:facility = local3
audit:priority = info
```

Besides, we need to edit the /etc/rsyslog.conf file to specify the file to which we want to log the information.

.

.

.

```
# Log SAMBA audit information
local3.*                                                    /var/log/samba_audit.log
```

.

.

.

After editing the config files, we restart both services.

```
[root@hotel ~]# systemctl restart rsyslog
[root@hotel ~]# systemctl restart smb
```

To check that everything is working fine, we'll connect from another computer to get a file.

```
[root@alpha ldif]# smbclient //hotel.linuxaholics.com/Docs -U Antonio
Enter Antonio's password:
Domain=[MYGROUP] OS=[Unix] Server=[Samba 4.1.1]
```

```
smb: \> ls
  .                                    D        0  Mon Aug 13 19:58:33 2018
  ..                                   D        0  Mon Aug 13 18:11:23 2018
  example.txt                          N       24  Mon Aug 13 19:58:33 2018

           54864 blocks of size 131072. 47949 blocks available
smb: \> get example.txt
getting file \example.txt of size 24 as example.txt (4,7 KiloBytes/sec)
(average 4,7 KiloBytes/sec)
smb: \> quit
```

In the /var/log/samba_audit.log file we see the following information:

```
Aug 14 09:44:15 hotel smbd_audit[4765]: connect to service IPC$ by user
                                        Antonio
Aug 14 09:44:15 hotel smbd_audit[4765]: disconnected
Aug 14 09:44:15 hotel smbd_audit[4765]: connect to service Docs by user
                                        Antonio
Aug 14 09:44:16 hotel smbd_audit[4765]: opendir .
Aug 14 09:44:24 hotel smbd_audit[4765]: opendir .
Aug 14 09:44:35 hotel smbd_audit[4765]: open example.txt (fd 12)
Aug 14 09:44:35 hotel smbd_audit[4765]: close fd 12
Aug 14 09:49:36 hotel smbd_audit[4765]: disconnected
```

# Using Samba VFS to Store Windows ACLs

To support Windows ACLs, Samba should have been compiled with the HAVE_LIBACL option. This is usually the case when working with the Samba compiled binaries of the main distributions like CentOS, but we can check it anyway:

```
[root@hotel ~]# smbd -b | grep HAVE_LIBACL
   HAVE_LIBACL
```

To enable the the support of extended ACL in our Samba server we could use two different VFS modules: vfs_acl_xattr and vfs_acl_tdb. The first one stores the ACLs in the file extended attributes, whereas the second one keeps that information in the file_ntacls.tdb file.

In our case we'll use vfs_acl_xattr, so we start by loading that VFS module in smb.conf.

```
vfs objects = audit, acl_xattr
```

Add the following lines in /etc/samba/smb.conf under the [global] config:

```
map acl inherit = yes
store dos attributes = yes
```

However, if we're working with a Samba domain controller, these parameters are automatically set. To check the actual value of these two parameters we can use the **testparm** command.

```
[root@hotel ~]# testparm -sv | grep -E "(vfs objects|map acl inherit|store
dos attributes)"
Load smb config files from /etc/samba/smb.conf
rlimit_max: increasing rlimit_max (1024) to minimum Windows limit (16384)
Processing section "[homes]"
Processing section "[printers]"
Processing section "[Docs]"
Loaded services file OK.
Server role: ROLE_STANDALONE
    map acl inherit = No
    store dos attributes = No
    vfs objects = audit, acl_xattr
```

In our case, both parameters have the No value, so we need to edit the /etc/samba/smb.conf file to set them to yes. Finally, the file should contain these lines:

```
[global]
vfs objects = audit acl_xattr
audit:facility = local3
audit:priority = info
map acl inherit = yes
store dos attributes = yes
```

We restart the SMB service again and we check again the value of both parameters.

```
[root@hotel ~]# testparm -sv | grep -E "(vfs objects|map acl inherit|store
dos attributes)"
Load smb config files from /etc/samba/smb.conf
rlimit_max: increasing rlimit_max (1024) to minimum Windows limit (16384)
Processing section "[homes]"
Processing section "[printers]"
Processing section "[Docs]"
Loaded services file OK.
Server role: ROLE_STANDALONE
        map acl inherit = Yes
        store dos attributes = Yes
        vfs objects = audit, acl_xattr
[root@hotel ~]#
```

To configure share permissions, the user must have the **SeDiskOperatorPrivilege** permission set. We can check which users have this privilege with the **net rpc** command.

```
[root@hotel ~]# net rpc rights list privileges SeDiskOperatorPrivilege -U
Antonio
Enter Antonio's password:
SeDiskOperatorPrivilege:
  BUILTIN\Administrators
```

As we can see, only the built-in group Administrators has the required privileges, so we need to grant user Antonio the required privileges as well.

```
[root@hotel ~]# net rpc rights grant "Antonio" SeDiskOperatorPrivilege -U
"Antonio"
Enter Antonio's password:
Failed to grant privileges for Antonio (NT_STATUS_ACCESS_DENIED)
```

We cannot use an ordinary user to grant those privileges, though; we need to use an admin user.

When installing Samba as a stand-alone server, we don't have any administrative accounts defined by default, but we can assign this role to any existing Samba user by adding the admin users parameters to the config file, under the [global] section.

```
.
.
.
admin users = Antonio
.
.
.
```

After restarting the SMB service we'll be able to grant the needed privileges.

```
[root@hotel ~]# net rpc rights grant "Antonio" SeDiskOperatorPrivilege -U
"Antonio"
Enter Antonio's password:
Successfully granted rights.

[root@hotel ~]# net rpc rights list privileges SeDiskOperatorPrivilege -U
Antonio
Enter Antonio's password:
SeDiskOperatorPrivilege:
  BUILTIN\Administrators
  HOTEL\Antonio
```

To see an example of how to store Windows ACLs, we'll create another share.

```
[root@hotel ~]# mkdir /Demo
[root@hotel ~]# chown Antonio /Demo
[root@hotel ~]# chmod 700 /Demo/
```

We'll then define the share in /etc/samba/smb.conf.

```
[Demo]
path = /Demo
writable = yes
public = yes
```

We also change the SELinux context.

```
[root@hotel ~]# chcon -t samba_share_t /Demo/
[root@hotel ~]# semanage fcontext -a -t samba_share_t "/Demo(/.*)?"
```

If we connect from a Windows workstation with the Samba administrator user (Figure 11-3), we can assign the share permissions as we'd do in a Windows server. We can see the process in Figures 11-4 through 11-6. To do it we'll have to authenticate with the credentials of the admin user we just set up in /etc/samba/smb.conf, in our case the user Antonio.

*Figure 11-3.* *Accessing the Samba server from a Windows workstation*

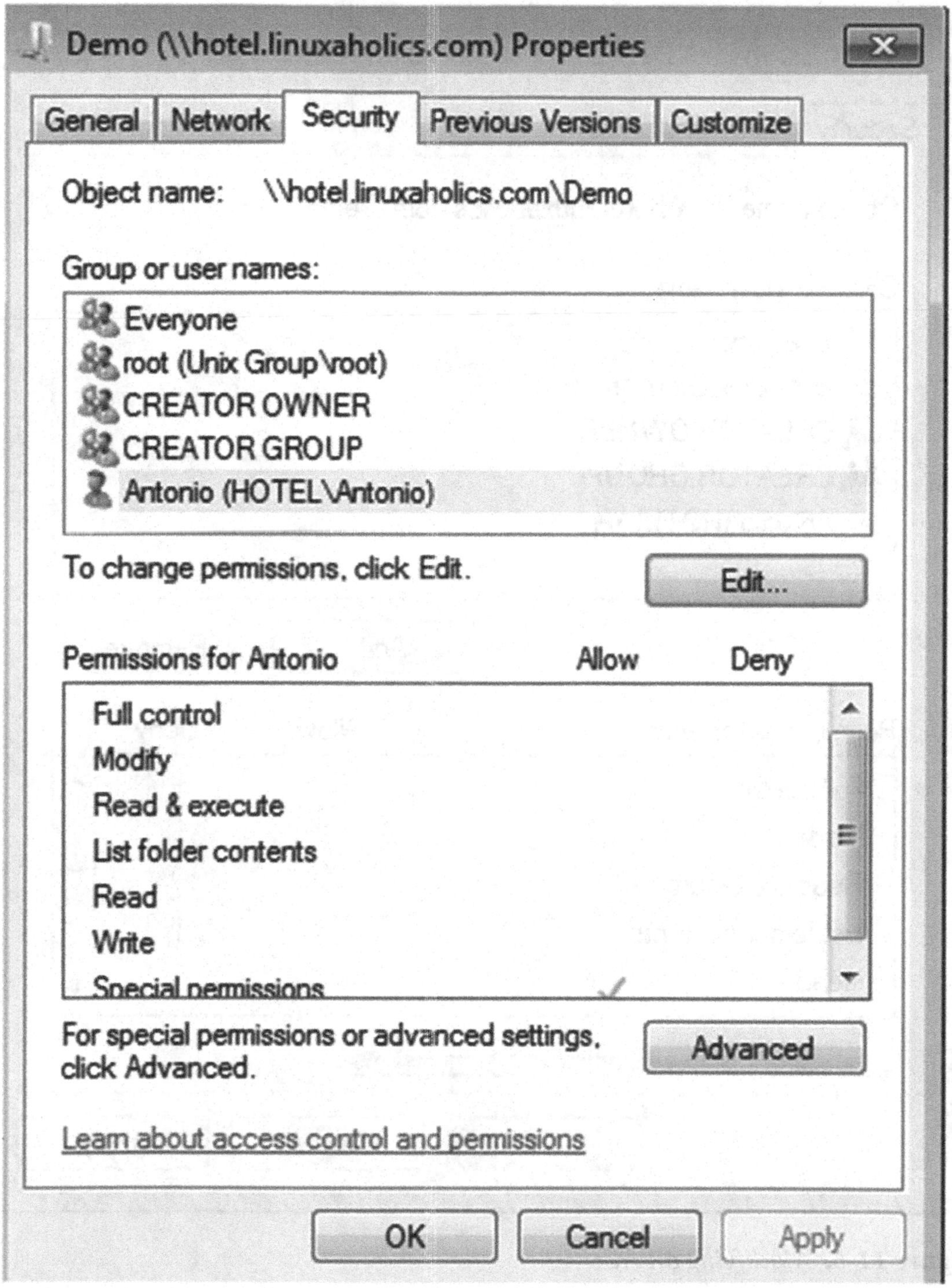

**Figure 11-4.** *Listing the ACLs in the folder*

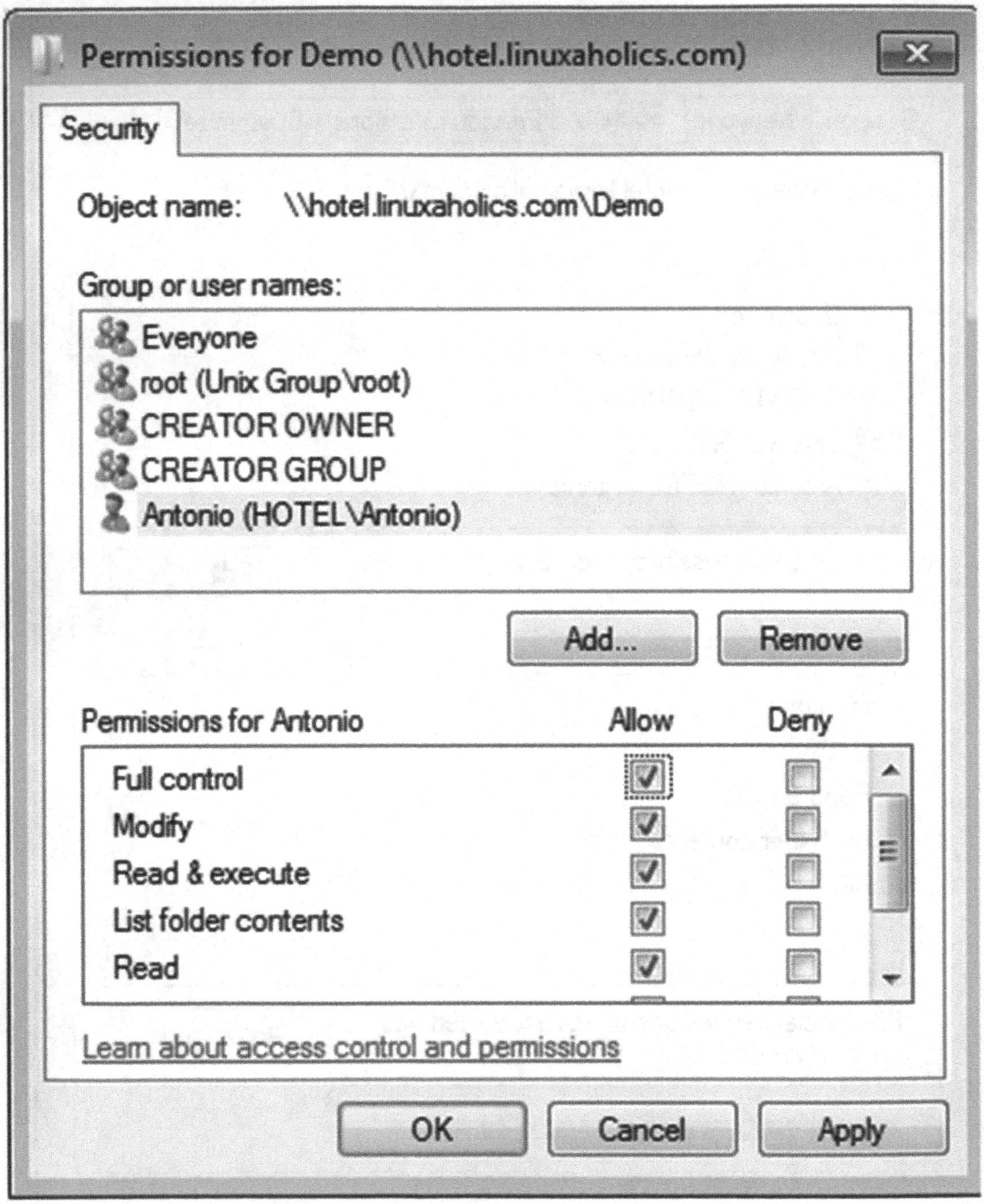


***Figure 11-5.*** *Modifying an ACL*

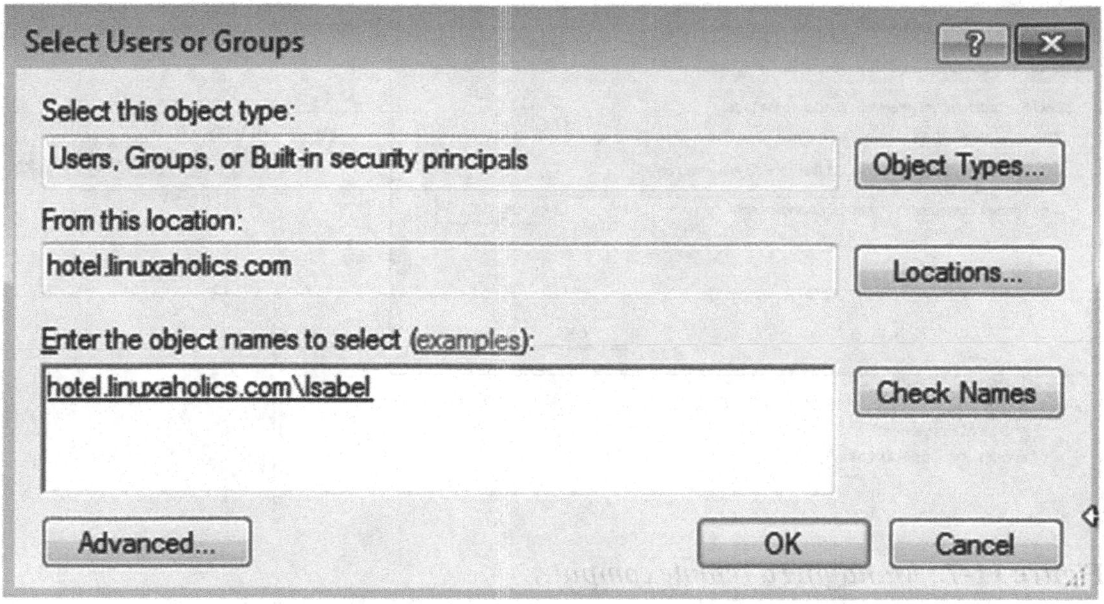

**Figure 11-6.** *Adding a new ACL*

We can also modify the share permissions. To do so we open the Computer Management console and select Connect to another computer (Figure 11-7). We'll connect to our Samba server with the appropriate credentials. Then go to System tools ➤ Shared Folders ➤ Shares (Figure 11-8) and select the Demo share. We can see its properties and the share permissions (Figures 11-9 and 11-10).

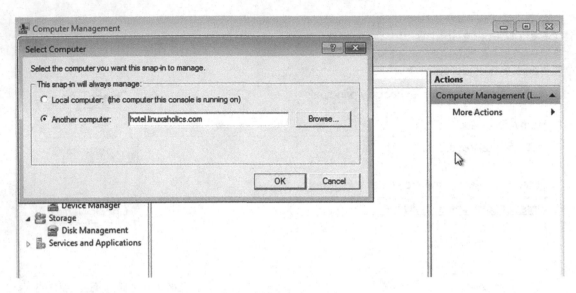

**Figure 11-7.** *Managing a remote computer*

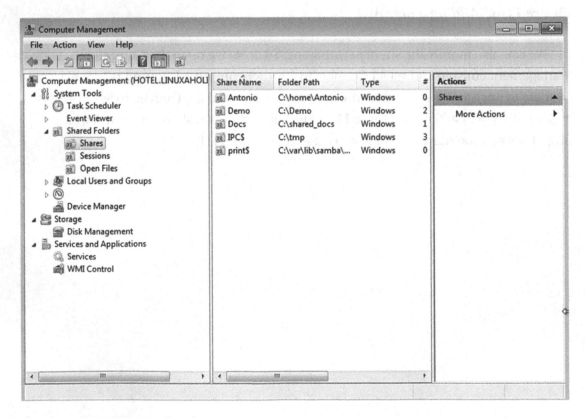

**Figure 11-8.** *Listing the shares*

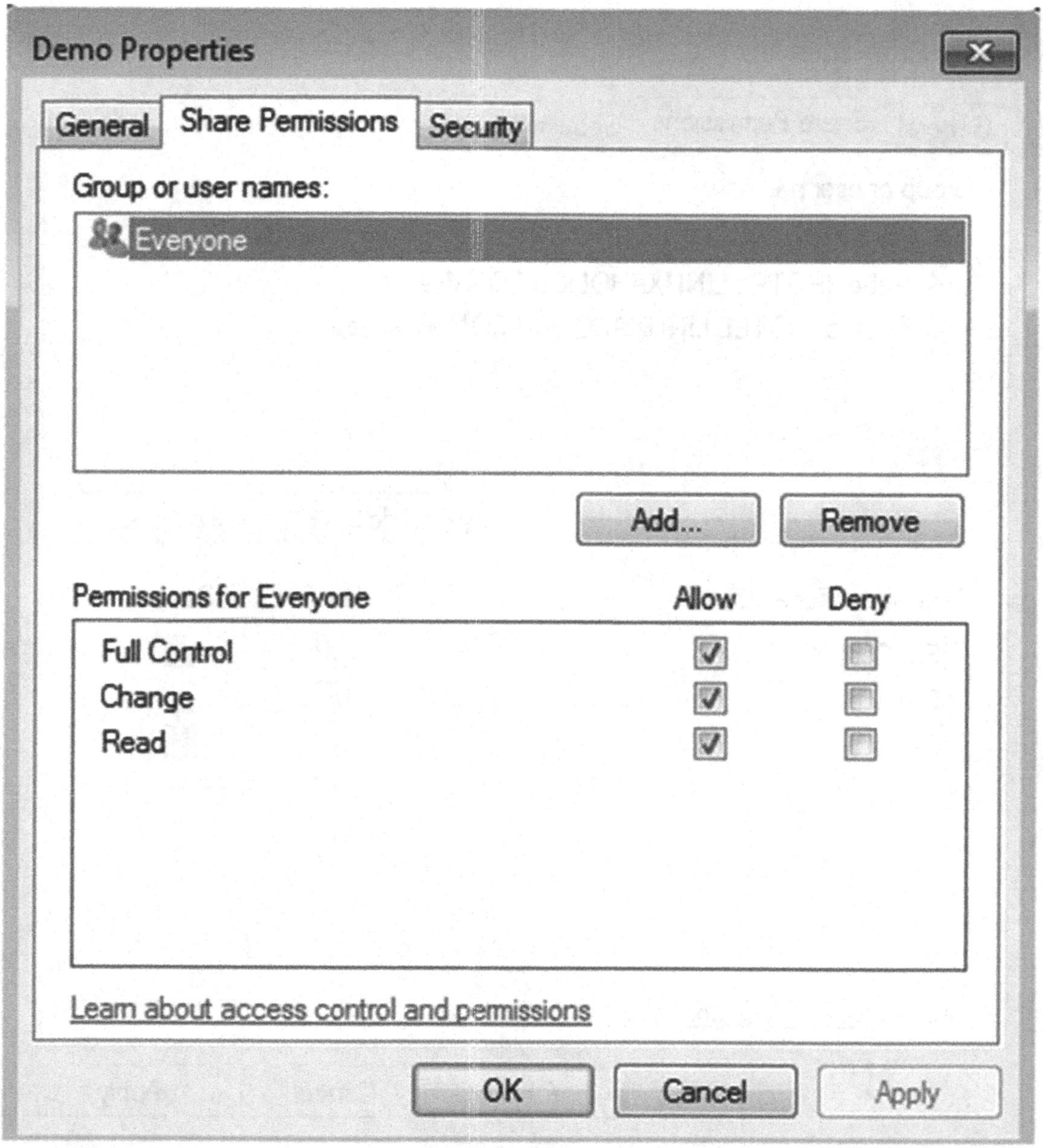


***Figure 11-9.*** *Listing the default share permissions*

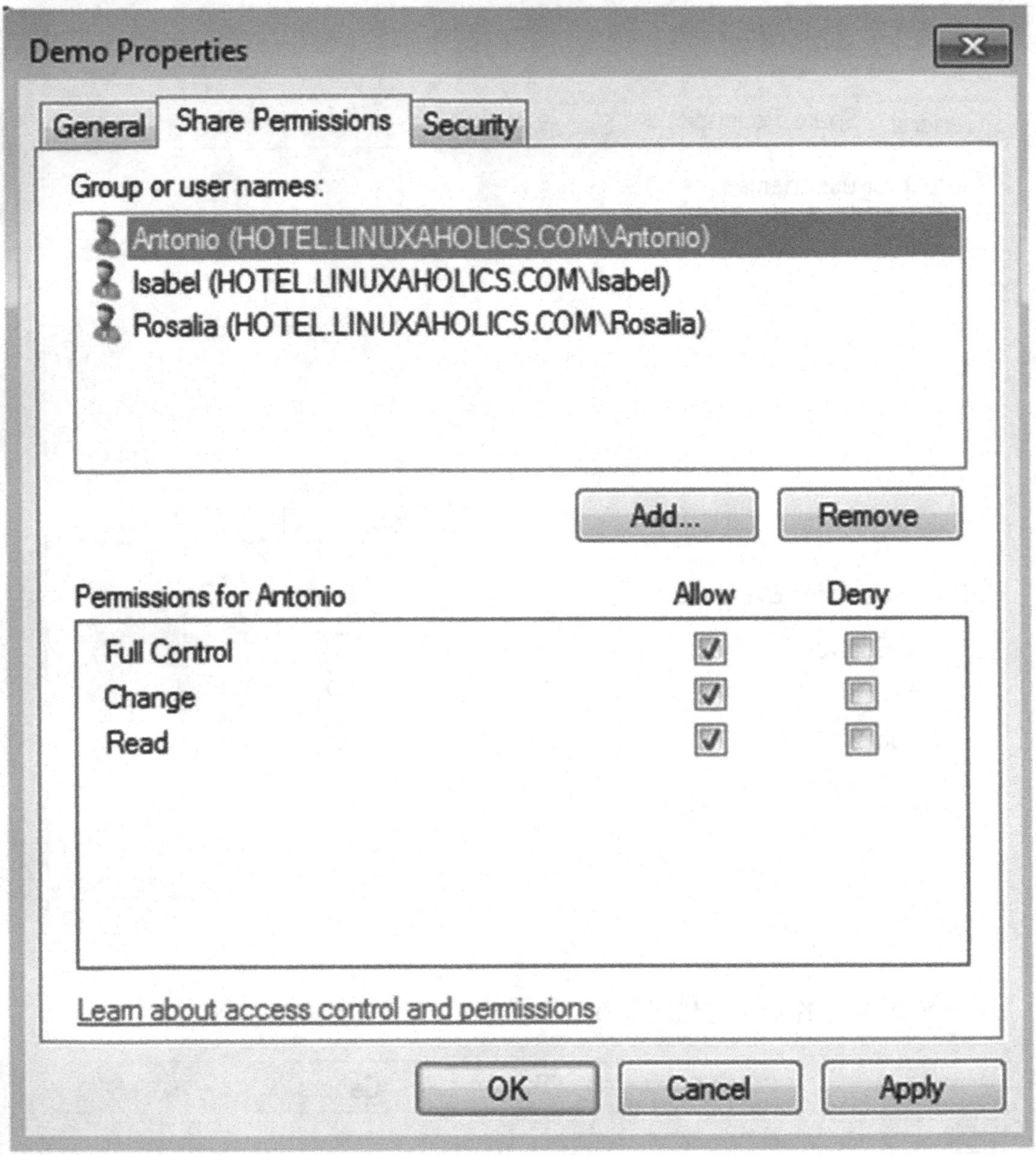

*Figure 11-10.  Customizing the share permissions*

We can also check the ACLs from the Samba server itself with the **getfacl** command.

```
[root@hotel ~]# getfacl /Demo/
getfacl: Removing leading '/' from absolute path names
# file: Demo/
```

```
# owner: Antonio
# group: root
user::rwx
user:Antonio:rwx
user:Isabel:r-x
group::---
group:root:---
mask::rwx
other::---
default:user::rwx
default:user:Antonio:rwx
default:user:Isabel:r-x
default:group::r-x
default:group:root:r-x
default:mask::rwx
default:other::r-x
```

We can also check this same ACL from a different computer with the **smbcacls** command.

```
[root@alpha ~]# smbcacls //hotel.linuxaholics.com/Docs example.txt -U
Antonio%antonio
REVISION:1
CONTROL:SR|DP
OWNER:HOTEL\root
GROUP:Unix Group\root
ACL:HOTEL\root:ALLOWED/0x0/RWDPO
ACL:Unix Group\root:ALLOWED/0x0/R
ACL:Everyone:ALLOWED/0x0/R
```

# Summary

In this chapter we have seen how permissions in a Linux system work, and their implications when working with Samba. We studied how to make a share read-only or writable by certain users or groups. We also used a VFS module to store Windows ACLs so that they could be used in Samba.

# CHAPTER 12

# Print Services

Apart from file services, many Windows computers work as print servers in their network, offering print services to every client computer in the domain or workgroup. In this chapter we'll cover the following concepts:

- Creating and configuring printer sharing.

- Configuring integration between Samba and CUPS.

- Managing Windows print drivers and configuring downloading of print drivers.

- Configuring [print$].

- Understanding security concerns with printer sharing.

- Uploading printer drivers for Point and Print driver installation using the Add Print Driver Wizard in Windows.

We will also learn about the following terms and utilities: smb.conf, [print$], CUPS, cupsd.conf, /var/spool/samba/, **smbspool**, **rpcclient**, and **net**.

## Printing in Linux

In Linux the de facto standard printing system is CUPS. CUPS includes several components: a scheduler and spooler that receives the print jobs, a series of filters that convert the print jobs to a format the printer will understand, and a back end that sends the resulting data to the destination printer.

Every Linux system can have its own cupsd service to manage a series of printers, or it can connect to a cupsd service running on a different server. We'll start by installing CUPS locally on our server.

```
[root@hotel ~]# yum install cups
```

© Antonio Vazquez 2019

A. Vazquez, *Practical LPIC-3 300*, https://doi.org/10.1007/978-1-4842-4473-9_12

We enable the service and start it.

```
[root@hotel ~]# systemctl enable cups
[root@hotel ~]# systemctl start cups
```

We also should install foomatic, which will provide us with access to a plethora of printer drivers.

```
[root@hotel ~]# yum install foomatic
```

In addition, we could also install the gutenprint package, which contains additional drivers.

```
[root@hotel ~]# yum install gutenprint
```

CUPS allows the use of many tools to create, delete, and manage printers. For that purpose, we can use graphical front ends as well as the older system-v or BSD console tools used before.

Let's suppose we have a network printer with the IP address 192.168.1.41 that uses the JetDirect protocol to receive print jobs from clients. We can use **lpadmin** to connect to this printer. If we execute it without parameters, we get the following info:

```
[root@hotel ~]# lpadmin
Usage:

    lpadmin [-h server] -d destination
    lpadmin [-h server] -x destination
    lpadmin [-h server] -p printer [-c add-class] [-i interface] [-m model]
                        [-r remove-class] [-v device] [-D description]
                        [-P ppd-file] [-o name=value]
                        [-u allow:user,user] [-u deny:user,user]
```

To create a printer, we need the FQDN or address of the print server (in this case the printer itself), the local name we'll assign to the printer queue in CUPS, and the driver (the .ppd file).

Depending on the way the printer is connected to the network, the URL of the printer will vary. For example, if the printer is directly attached to the network, we could type something like this:

```
[root@hotel ~]# lpadmin -p printer_Canon -v socket://192.168.1.41
```

Instead, if the printer wasn't connected directly to the network, but to another computer instead, and shared through lpd the command would be this:

```
[root@hotel ~]# lpadmin -p printer_Canon -v lpd://x-ray.linuxaholics.com/
Canon
```

If the printer is shared by a different CUPS server, this is what we would type:

```
[root@hotel ~]# lpadmin -p printer_Canon -v ipp://x-ray.linuxaholics.com/
printers/printer_Canon
```

In any case, right after installing the printer, it won't be ready to accept new jobs yet.

```
[root@hotel ~]# lpstat -a
printer_Canon not accepting requests since mar 14 ago 2018 16:46:02 CEST -
    reason unknown
```

To enable the printer and make sure that it accepts incoming jobs we also need to execute these two commands:

```
[root@hotel ~]# cupsaccept printer_canon
[root@hotel ~]# cupsenable printer_canon
```

We can check that the printer is now accepting jobs with the **lpstat** command.

```
[root@hotel ~]# lpstat -a
printer_Canon accepting requests since Wed 28 Dec 2016 06:36:11 PM CET
```

If we need more details about the printers currently installed on the system, we can use the -t parameter.

```
[root@hotel ~]# lpstat -a -t
printer_Canon accepting requests since mar 14 ago 2018 23:53:17 CEST
scheduler is running
no system default destination
device for printer_Canon: ipp://192.168.56.1/printers/printer_Canon
printer_Canon accepting requests since mar 14 ago 2018 23:53:17 CEST
printer printer_Canon is idle.  enabled since mar 14 ago 2018 23:53:17 CEST
```

After creating a printer the way we just did it, the system will not have a suitable driver associated with it, so we'll only be able to use it to print text, not images, fonts, and so on. Besides, as Linux uses the \n character as an end of line (EOL) character instead of \r\n, the file won't be printed properly. Let's see an example:

```
[root@hotel ~]# lpr -P printer_Canon /etc/passwd
```

Of course, we could create a program to translate the trailing \n characters to \r\n but it is much easier to use an appropriate driver. We can check the list of available drivers for the CUPS server with **lpinfo**. We'll search for a driver for the Canon LBP6650.

```
[root@hotel ~]# lpinfo -m |grep -i "Canon" |grep -i "LBP" | grep 3650
[root@hotel ~]#
```

Because it looks like there is no driver available for that printer, we'll choose a driver from a similar model.

```
[root@hotel ~]# lpinfo -m |grep -i "Canon" |grep -i "LBP" | grep 3
foomatic:Canon-LBP-4sx-ljet3.ppd Canon LBP-4sx Foomatic/ljet3
foomatic:Canon-LBP-310-lbp310.ppd Canon LBP-310 Foomatic/lbp310
foomatic:Canon-LBP-320_Pro-lbp320.ppd Canon LBP-320 Pro Foomatic/lbp320
foomatic:Canon-LBP-350-lbp320.ppd Canon LBP-350 Foomatic/lbp320
gutenprint.5.2://canon-lbp-430/expert Canon LBP-430 - CUPS+Gutenprint
v5.2.9
gutenprint.5.2://canon-lbp-430/simple Canon LBP-430 - CUPS+Gutenprint
v5.2.9 Simplified
foomatic:Canon-LBP-430-hpijs-pcl5e.ppd Canon LBP-430 Foomatic/hpijs-pcl5e
foomatic:Canon-LBP-430-lj4dith.ppd Canon LBP-430 Foomatic/lj4dith
foomatic:Canon-LBP-430-ljet3.ppd Canon LBP-430 Foomatic/ljet3
foomatic:Canon-LBP-430-ljet4.ppd Canon LBP-430 Foomatic/ljet4
gutenprint.5.2://canon-lbp-3360/expert Canon LBP-3360 - CUPS+Gutenprint
v5.2.9
gutenprint.5.2://canon-lbp-3360/simple Canon LBP-3360 - CUPS+Gutenprint
v5.2.9 Simplified
foomatic:Canon-LBP-3360-hpijs-pcl5e.ppd Canon LBP-3360 Foomatic/hpijs-pcl5e
foomatic:Canon-LBP-3360-lj4dith.ppd Canon LBP-3360 Foomatic/lj4dith
foomatic:Canon-LBP-3360-ljet4.ppd Canon LBP-3360 Foomatic/ljet4
foomatic:Canon-LBP-3360-ljet4d.ppd Canon LBP-3360 Foomatic/ljet4d
```

```
foomatic:Canon-LBP-3360-pxlmono.ppd Canon LBP-3360 Foomatic/pxlmono
foomatic:Canon-LBP-3460-pxlmono.ppd Canon LBP-3460 Foomatic/pxlmono
foomatic:Canon-LBP-5360-cljet5.ppd Canon LBP-5360 Foomatic/cljet5
```

We can see that we have many drivers to choose from, provided by gutenprint and foomatic. We'll install one from foomatic. First, we identify the driver.

```
[root@hotel ~]# foomatic-ppdfile list | grep Canon | grep LBP | grep 3360
"foomatic-ppdfile:Canon-LBP-3360-hpijs-pcl5e.ppd" en "Canon" "Canon LBP-
3360 Foomatic/hpijs-pcl5e (recommended)" "DRV:Dhpijs-pcl5e,R1,MO,Sv,TI,
X600,Y600,CO,t100,l100,g100,p100,s70;"
"foomatic-ppdfile:Canon-LBP-3360-pxlmono.ppd" en "Canon" "Canon LBP-3360
Foomatic/pxlmono" "DRV:Dpxlmono,RO,MO,TG;"
"foomatic-ppdfile:Canon-LBP-3360-lj4dith.ppd" en "Canon" "Canon LBP-3360
Foomatic/lj4dith" "DRV:Dlj4dith,RO,MO,TG;"
"foomatic-ppdfile:Canon-LBP-3360-ljet4.ppd" en "Canon" "Canon LBP-3360
Foomatic/ljet4" "DRV:Dljet4,RO,MO,Sv,TG,X600,Y600,CO,t90,l90,g60,p30,s90;"
"foomatic-ppdfile:Canon-LBP-3360-ljet4d.ppd" en "Canon" "Canon LBP-3360
Foomatic/ljet4d" "DRV:Dljet4d,RO,MO,TG;"
```

Next, then we generate the .ppd file for the driver we chose, in this example the first one.

```
[root@hotel ~]# foomatic-ppdfile cat "foomatic-ppdfile:Canon-LBP-3360-
hpijs-pcl5e.ppd" > CanonDriver.ppd
```

We can now add the driver to the printer with **lpadmin**.

```
[root@hotel ~]# lpadmin -p printer_Canon -P CanonDriver.ppd
```

Now if we try to print any file, the result will be much better. As we've just seen, installing a printer by using only command-line utilities can be tedious sometimes, so most Linux distributions have graphical front ends to ease the process. In CentOS we could have used **system-config-printer** (Figure 12-1). Clicking Add launches a wizard that will guide us in the process of adding a new printer (see Figures 12-2 through 12-6).

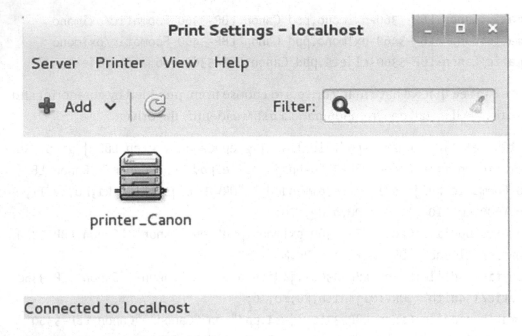

***Figure 12-1.*** *system-config-printer*

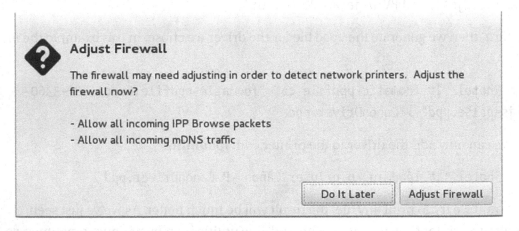

***Figure 12-2.*** *Remember to adjust the firewall*

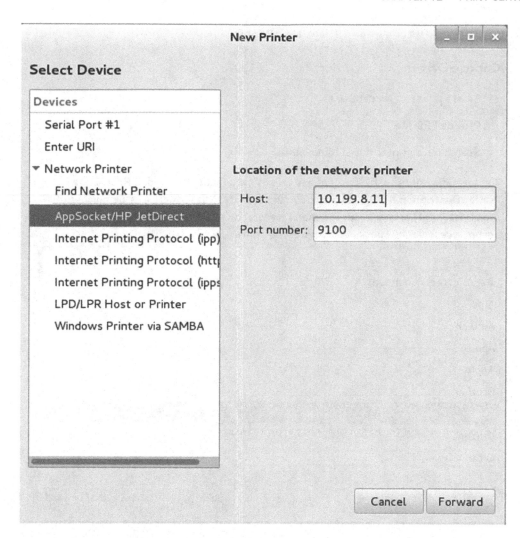

***Figure 12-3.*** *Selecting the device type*

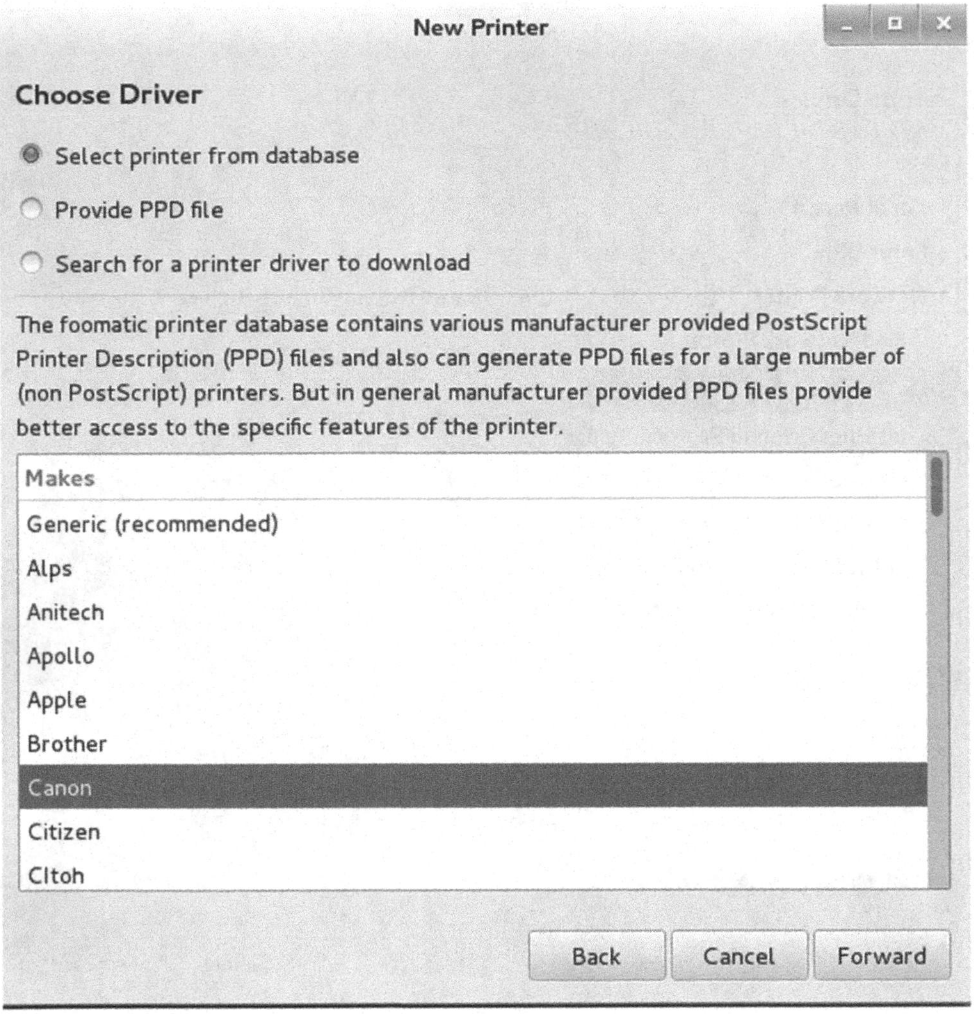


***Figure 12-4.*** *Adding the driver*

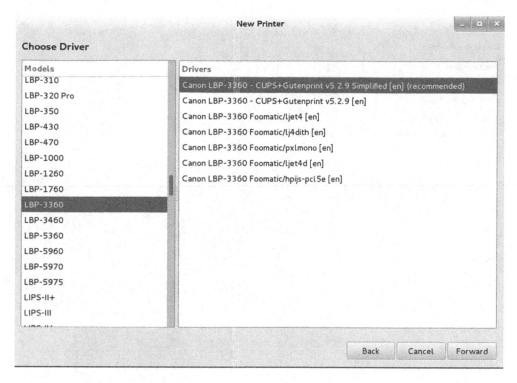

***Figure 12-5.*** *Adding the driver*

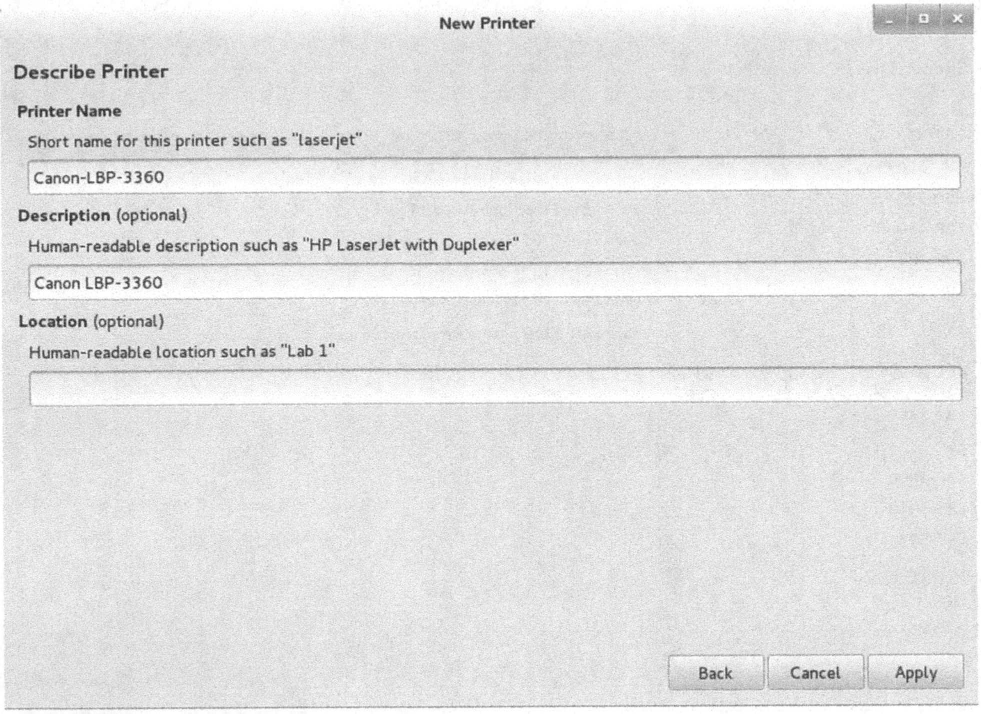

New Printer

**Describe Printer**

**Printer Name**

Short name for this printer such as "laserjet"

Canon-LBP-3360

**Description** (optional)

Human-readable description such as "HP LaserJet with Duplexer"

Canon LBP-3360

**Location** (optional)

Human-readable location such as "Lab 1"

Back    Cancel    Apply

***Figure 12-6.*** *Finishing the installation*

Another possibility is to access CUPS through the Web interface (Figure 12-7), which can be accessed by default on port 631.

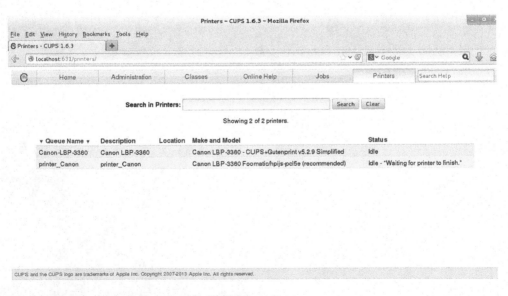

***Figure 12-7.*** *Accessing the CUPS Web interface*

On the Printers tab we can see and modify the existing printers, and on the Administration tab we can add new printers, manage print jobs, and so on.

A full description of CUPS is beyond the scope of this book, but at least now you know the basics to provide printing services in a Linux environment.

Before finishing this section, though, we'll take a quick look at the main configuration file of CUPS. This file is located at /etc/cups/cupsd.conf.

```
[root@openldap ~]# cat /etc/cups/cupsd.conf
MaxLogSize 0
#
# "$Id: cupsd.conf.in 7888 2008-08-29 21:16:56Z mike $"
#
# Sample configuration file for the CUPS scheduler. See "man cupsd.conf" for a
# complete description of this file.
#

# Log general information in error_log - change "warn" to "debug"
# for troubleshooting...
LogLevel warn

# Only listen for connections from the local machine.
Listen localhost:631
.
.
.
```

At the top of the file we can configure the LogLevel, as well as the port CUPS listens on. The syntax of this file is very similar to that of the /etc/httpd/httpd.conf file. We can limit access to administrative tasks to certain users, configure different ways to authenticate users, and so on.

# Printer Sharing

The easiest way to share a CUPS printer is by using the Web interface. We can do this from the Administration tab by selecting the Share printers connected to this system check box (Figure 12-8). By default, the printers will be shared with the clients from the local network; if we want to share them with clients from external networks, we'll have to select the Allow printing from the Internet check box.

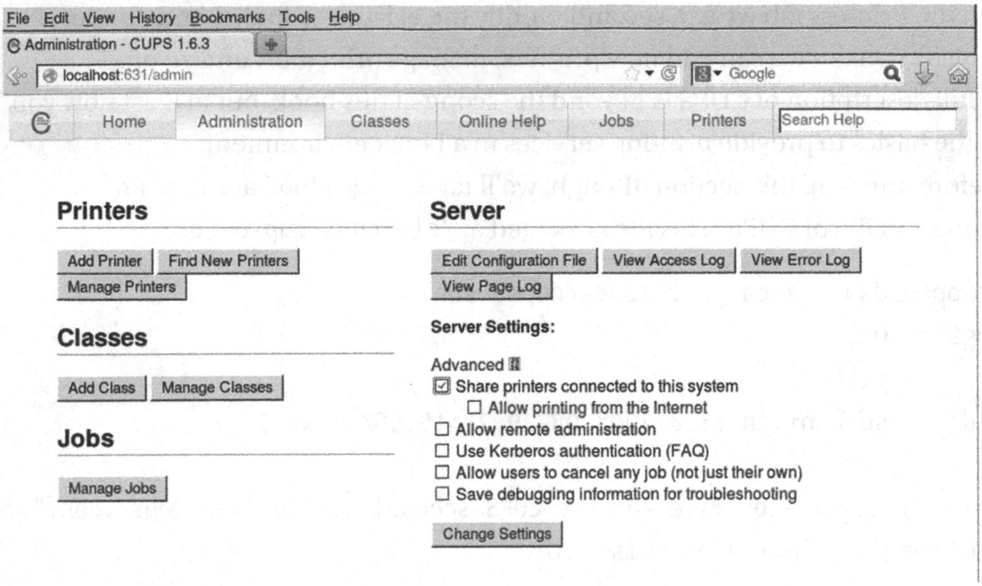

*Figure 12-8.*  *Sharing a printer*

However, we could also use the command-line utility **cupsctl** for this:

```
[root@hotel ~]# cupsctl –share-printers
```

Again, if we want the clients from external networks to connect to the shared printers, we must include the `--remote-any` option.

Now, if we execute **cupsctl** again without parameters we'll see that the system is sharing the printers (`_share_printers=1`).

```
[root@hotel ~]# cupsctl
_debug_logging=0
_remote_admin=0
_remote_any=0
_share_printers=1
_user_cancel_any=0
BrowseLocalProtocols=dnssd
DefaultAuthType=Basic
JobPrivateAccess=default
JobPrivateValues=default
MaxLogSize=0
```

```
SubscriptionPrivateAccess=default
SubscriptionPrivateValues=default
WebInterface=Yes
```

Whatever method we use, in the end the printers in our CUPS server will be accessible to the clients through the Internet Printing Protocol (IPP), so we'll need to configure the local firewall accordingly so that incoming connections to TCP port 631 aren't rejected.

```
[root@hotel ~]# firewall-cmd --permanent --add-service=ipp
success
[root@hotel ~]# firewall-cmd --reload
success
```

## Connecting to a Shared Printer from a Windows Client

To install the printer, we'll need to use the Add Printer Wizard (Figure 12-9). On the second screen, click The printer that I want isn't listed" (Figure 12-10). On the next screen, type the printer's URL (Figure 12-11).

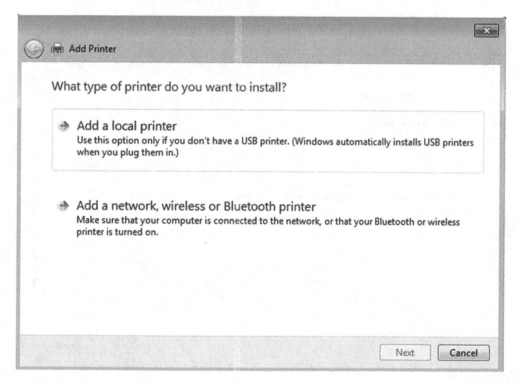

***Figure 12-9.*** *Adding a printer*

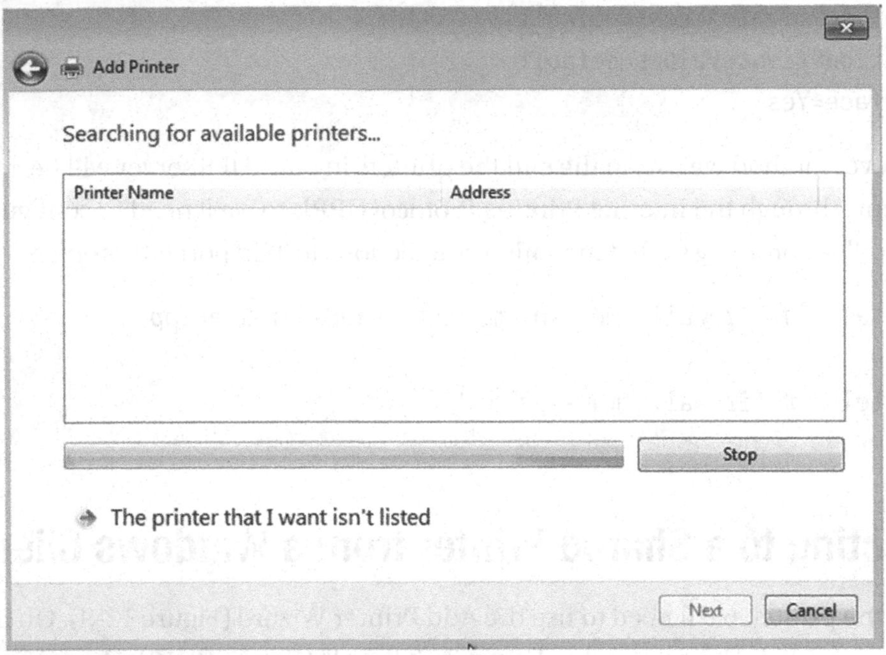

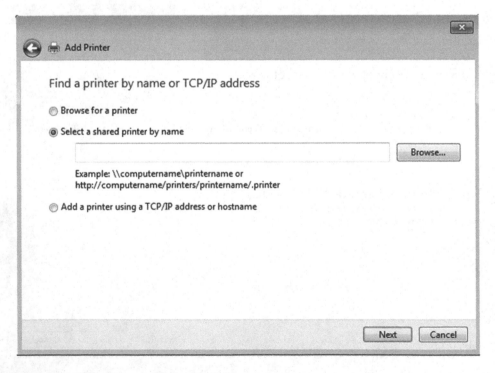

**Figure 12-10.** *The printer that I want isn't listed*

*Figure 12-11.* *Selecting a shared printer*

We select the driver from the list of those available (Figure 12-12) and, in a few seconds, we'll get a message saying that the printer was installed correctly (Figure 12-13). If we want to, we can print a test page to check that everything is working as expected (Figure 12-14).

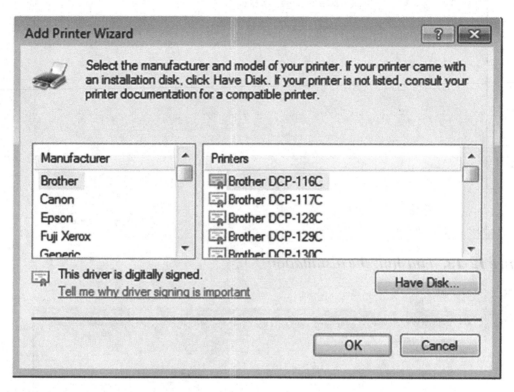

***Figure 12-12.*** *Selecting a driver*

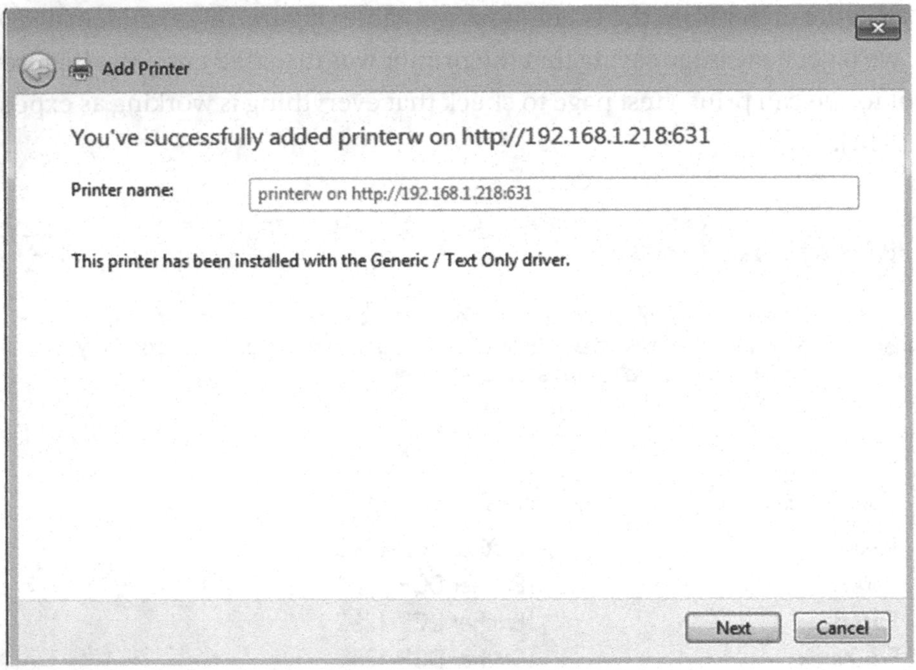

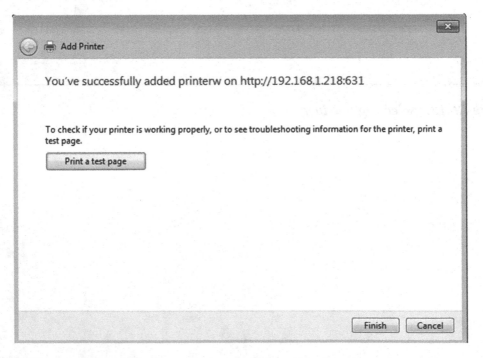

**Figure 12-13.**  *Finishing the installation*

**Figure 12-14.**  *Printing a test page*

# Connecting to a Shared Printer from a Mac Client

It is quite easy to connect to a shared CUPS printer from a Mac computer, after all CUPS was developed by Apple. To connect to the printer, we need to open System Preferences (Figure 12-15) and then open Printers & Scanners. When the new window opens, click + to add a new printer (Figure 12-16).

***Figure 12-15.*** *System Preferences*

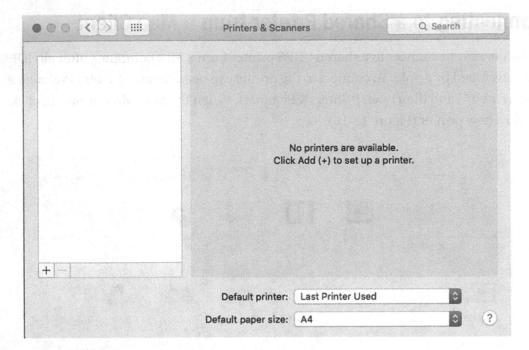

*Figure 12-16.* *Adding a printer*

Select the type of network printer (Figure 12-17) and type the address and the queue name. Click Add, and the new printer is available on our Mac computer (Figure 12-18).

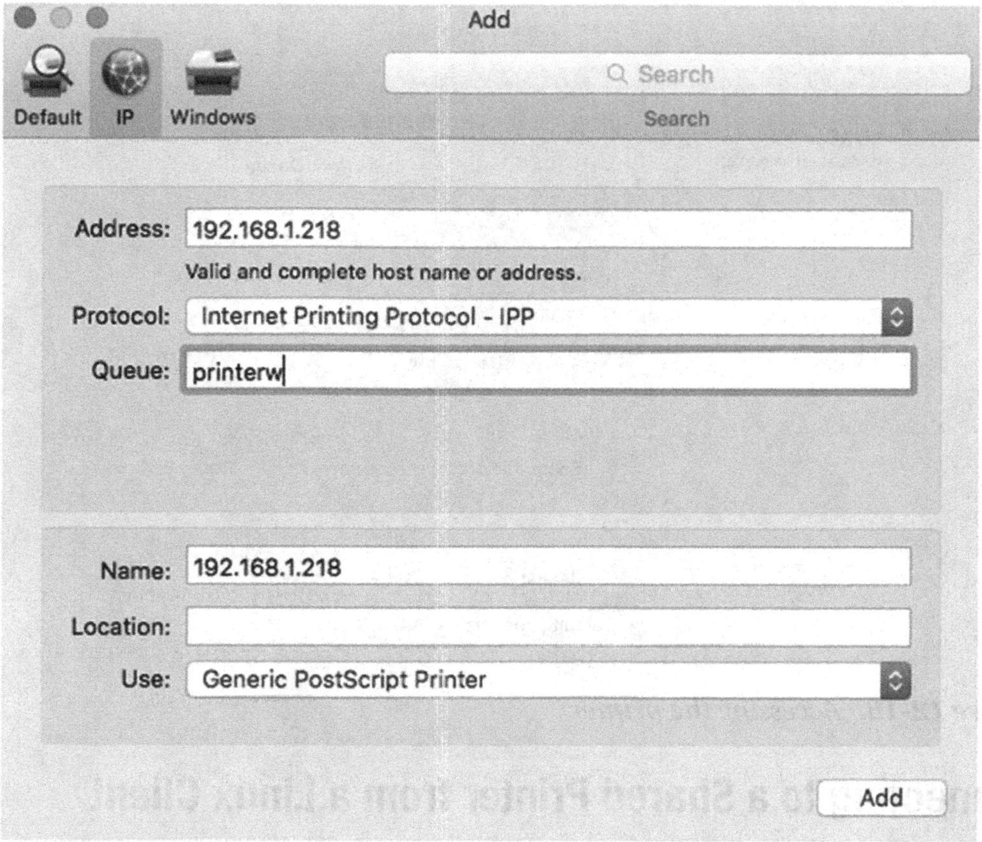

*Figure 12-17.*  *Selecting the shared network printer*

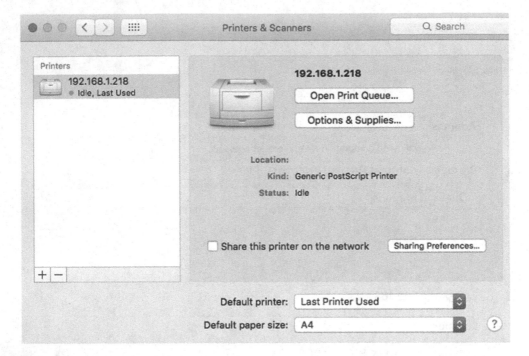

***Figure 12-18.*** *Accessing the printer*

## Connecting to a Shared Printer from a Linux Client

As we did previously from other OSs, we can also access the shared printers from a
Linux workstation using IPP. In CentOS, the procedure is very similar to what we did
when installed a network printer (Figure 12-3); in this case, however, we should choose
IPP and point to the computer acting as the CUPS server. If we're using another Linux
distribution, for instance Ubuntu, we should go to System Settings and select Printers
(Figure 12-19). Then click Add (Figure 12-20) and enter the printer's URI (Figure 12-21).

*Figure 12-19.* *System Settings*

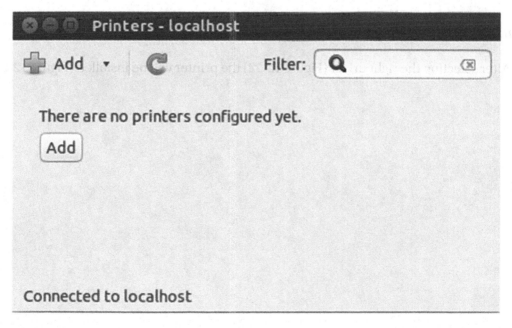

*Figure 12-20.* *Installing a printer*

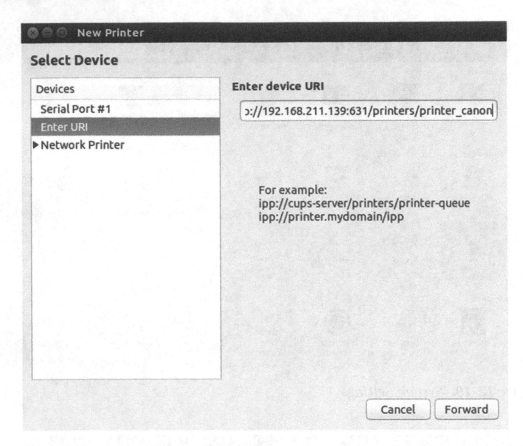

***Figure 12-21.*** *Selecting the printer*

After selecting the right driver (Figure 12-22) the printer will be installed (Figure 12-23).

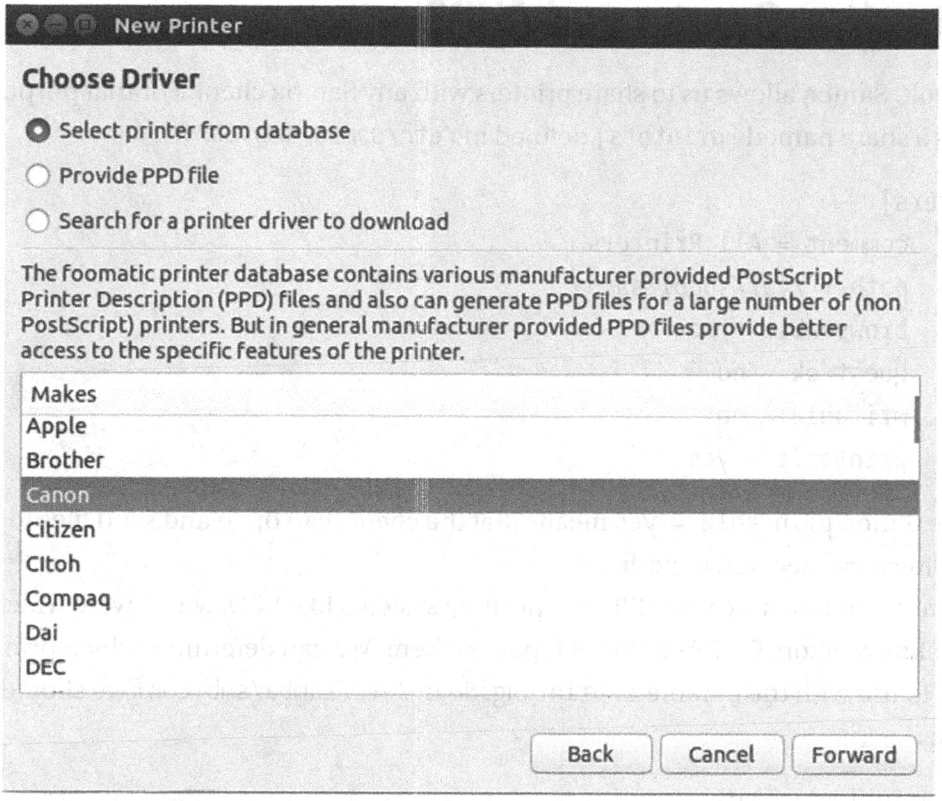

**Figure 12-22.** *Selecting a driver*

**Figure 12-23.** *Installed printer*

# Integrating Samba and CUPS

By default, Samba allows us to share printers with any Samba client. For that purpose, there is a share named [printers] defined in /etc/samba/smb.conf.

```
[printers]
        comment = All Printers
        path = /var/spool/samba
        browseable = no
        guest ok = no
        writable = no
        printable = yes
```

The option printable = yes means that the clients can open and send files to the spool directory specified in **path**.

Samba can integrate with different printing systems like LPD, which were widely used in Linux before CUPS gradually replaced them. We can determine which printing system to use with the parameter printing. So in /etc/samba/smb.conf we should add this line:

```
    printing = cups
```

However, this is the default value used if not otherwise specified, so we really don't need to include it here. We can check this by using the **testparm** command with the -v flag, so that it displays the default values in use.

```
[root@openldap ~]# testparm -sv | grep printing
Load smb config files from /etc/samba/smb.conf
rlimit_max: increasing rlimit_max (1024) to minimum Windows limit (16384)
Processing section "[homes]"
Processing section "[printers]"
Processing section "[Docs]"
Loaded services file OK.
Server role: ROLE_STANDALONE
        printing = cups
```

Depending on the value of the parameter load printers, the printers defined in CUPS may be shared automatically in Samba. We check the value.

```
[root@openldap ~]# testparm -sv | grep "load printers"
.
.
.
        load printers = Yes
```

In this case the printers are shared automatically and every Windows client will have access to them (Figure 12-24).

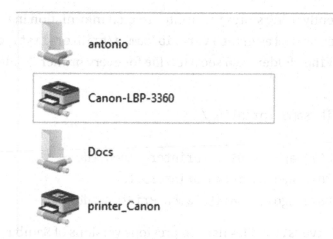

***Figure 12-24.***  *A Samba printer*

Apart from sharing all the printers installed on the server, we can also share individual printers by specifying their names in smb.conf.

We'll begin by commenting out the [printers] share, and we'll restart the service to make sure that the printers are no longer shared. If we prefer, we can use **smbcontrol** to reload only the printers' definitions.

```
[root@hotel ~]# smbcontrol smbd reload-printers
```

We check now that there are not shared printers and we add the following share to smb.conf.

```
[Samba_Printer]
      comment = Public printer
      path = /var/spool/samba
      guest ok = Yes
      printable = Yes
      printer name = printer_Canon
```

After restarting the service, we'll see that the printer can be accessed through the network.

The tdb back end we are currently using stores the printer-related information in the /var/lib/samba/printing/ folder, as well as in the /var/lib/samba/printer_list.tdb file. In the /var/lib/samba/printing/ folder we'll see a tdb file for every printer defined in Samba.

```
[root@hotel ~]# ls -l /var/lib/samba/printing/
total 84
-rw-------. 1 root Antonio 28672 ago 16 05:24 printer_Canon.tdb
-rw-------. 1 root root    28672 ago 13 19:40 printers.tdb
-rw-------. 1 root Antonio 28672 ago 16 06:15 Samba_Printer.tdb
```

The ntprinters.tdb and ntdrivers.tdb files used in previous versions of Samba are no longer used.

# smb.conf Printing-Related Options

Once we have our printer installed, there are a lot of parameters with values we can tweak in smb.conf to better suit our needs.

## CUPS-Related Options

We have seen the printing = CUPS, and the load printers = yes options that were used with their default values, meaning that Samba would use CUPS and would load the printers defined in the printcap file.

We have connected to the local CUPS server installed in the Samba server itself, but we could also connect with any other CUPS server with the `cups server` option. There is also a `cups connection timeout` parameter that specifies the number of seconds Samba will wait when trying to contact the CUPS server. This value is 30 seconds by default, but it could be adjusted according to our preferences. By default, the connection between CUPS and Samba is not encrypted, but it can be encrypted by specifying the `cups encrypt = yes` option.

## Spoolss

We can activate the `disable spoolss` parameter so that Samba will behave as a Samba 2.0 server. This change also disables the ability to upload drivers to a Samba server, something we will see in greater detail later. This parameter rarely should be used, and its default value is no. There is also an inverted equivalent parameter called `enable spoolss` that can be used exactly the same way.

## Customizing Printing Options

If we want to, we can provide the specific command we want to use when printing a job with the `print command` option. Let's look at an example.

We'll start by defining a new Samba printer. On this occasion we are not going to use a real printer, but a dummy text printer instead.

```
comment = Generic text printer
path = /var/spool/samba
guest ok = yes
printable = Yes
print command = echo Printing %s >> /tmp/print.log;
cp %s /tmp; rm %s
```

We have already learned about the first four parameters. In the fifth one we write a simple log and copy the job file to tmp. After that we delete the file from the spool. However, we should take into account one more thing. By default, our Samba server has the `printing = CUPS` option set. When this happens, the print jobs are managed by the CUPS API and any manually modified print command is ignored. To avoid this behavior, we'll define a new printing parameter only for our new Samba printer. The complete share definition will be this:

```
[Text_Printer]
        printing = BSD
        comment = Generic text printer
        path = /var/spool/samba
        guest ok = yes
        printable = Yes
        print command = echo Printing %s >> /tmp/print.log; cp %s /tmp
```

After reloading the Samba configuration, if we send a print job to the new printer we'll see the corresponding line in /tmp/print.log and the file copied to /tmp.

```
[root@hotel ~]# cat /tmp/print.log
Printing smbprn.ev7Bmh

[root@hotel ~]# ls /tmp/
ks-script-97bPGr   smbprn.ev7Bmh              systemd-private-wy5MyZ
print.log          systemd-private-RqlXf8   yum.log
```

Besides all these options defined in the global section we can also apply some other options to a single printer. For example, if we execute the **lpoptions** command we can see the default options of a given printer.

```
[root@hotel ~]# lpoptions -d printer_Canon -l
PageSize/Media Size: Letter Legal Executive Tabloid A3 *A4 A5 B5 EnvISOB5
Env10 EnvC5 EnvDL EnvMonarch
InputSlot/Media Source: *Default Upper Manual
Duplex/2-Sided Printing: *None DuplexNoTumble DuplexTumble
Option1/Duplexer: *False True
```

By using the cups options parameter at a share definition we can customize the default printing options for any given printer.

# Windows Printer Drivers

We've seen how easy is to share a printer through Samba. We can access the server from a Windows workstation and simply click on the shared printer. If we haven't previously installed the required driver, though, we'll get an error message (Figure 12-25).

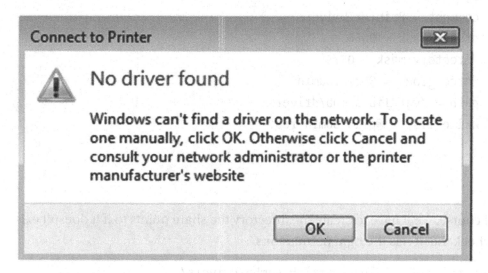

**Figure 12-25.** *Driver not found*

What happens when we connect from a Windows client to a shared Windows printer is that the client will try and download the needed drivers to install the new printer. We can mimic this same behavior in our Samba server with a few configuration changes.

According to the Samba Wiki (`http://wiki.samba.org`), Samba only supports the printer driver model version 3 supported in different Windows versions including Windows 2016. Version 4 drivers, however, are not fully supported. In addition, the driver should be uncompressed to be downloaded from the clients.

## Configure [print$]

Windows clients download the print drivers automatically from a share named `print$`. This behavior is hard-coded in every Windows box and it cannot be changed. Some of the more recent Samba versions have this share already defined by default, but if we don't have it, we'll need to create it manually on our Samba server.

In the smb.conf file we'll have to include the new share definition.

- 
- 
- 

```
[print$]
     comment = Printer Drivers
     create mask = 0664
     directory mask = 0775
     force group = @printadmin
     path = /var/lib/samba/drivers
     write list = @printadmin root
```

- 
- 
- 

Of course, we'll have to create the directory the share points to if it doesn't exist, and we'll check that it has the right permissions.

```
[root@hotel ~]# ls -ldZ /var/lib/samba/drivers/
drwxrwxr-x. root printadmin system_u:object_r:samba_var_t:s0 /var/lib/
samba/drivers/
```

Inside the path of the [print$] share we need to create a series of subfolders.

```
[root@india ~]# ls /var/lib/samba/drivers/
IA64  W32ALPHA  W32MIPS  W32PPC  W32X86  WIN40  x64
```

We copy the drivers for each OS in the corresponding folder. The driver should be uncompressed to be downloaded by the clients.

We'll see a bit more detail about the [print$] share later, when we learn about Point and Print.

# Printer Sharing Security

As with any device attached to a network, an incorrectly configured print server can also pose a security risk. Any user who has administrative rights on the print server could redirect print jobs to any destination, which could be a serious security breach.

Another problem arises when everybody is given permission to print. If this is the case, a malicious user could exhaust the paper or ink supplies of the printer by sending a large print job. They could even use the printer to print offensive material.

# Point and Print

We have seen that when a Windows client points to a Samba printer, the system asks for the location of the corresponding drivers. The administrator or the user can then manually select the driver(s) to install.

There is, however, a nice feature called Point and Print in Windows 2000 and later. This feature allows a user to create a connection to a remote printer without providing disks or other installation media. All the necessary files and information are downloaded from the print server automatically. This feature can also be implemented in Samba. Detailed instructions are available in the Samba wiki, but we'll outline the main points by seeing an example.

To properly set up Point and Print we need a domain, which we currently don't have. We'll assume that we have already installed a Samba 4 Active Directory domain controller (see the full details in Chapter 17).

Currently our domain controller is not a print server so, as we did previously on our stand-alone server, we would need to perform a series of actions in advance, such as installing CUPS, installing printers, and so on. This was covered in the previous section "Printing in Linux." Here we only focus on configuring Samba printing in our domain controller.

The first thing to do is to share the printer(s) in Samba. We could either create a [printers] share and share all the printers installed on the system or create a specific share for a single printer. In this example we'll use the dummy printer we created earlier in the section "Customizing Printer Options." This are the lines we should add to the configuration file, in this case /usr/local/samba/etc/smb.conf:

```
[Text_Printer]
        printing = BSD
        comment = Generic text printer
        path = /var/spool/samba
        guest ok = yes
        printable = Yes
        print command = echo Printing %s >> /tmp/print.log; cp %s /tmp
```

We also need to create the [print$] share to store the drivers, which currently doesn't exist. We'll add the following lines, too.

```
[print$]
        comment = Printer Drivers
        create mask = 0664
        directory mask = 0775
        force group = @printadmin
        path = /var/lib/samba/drivers
        write list = @printadmin root
```

We create the /var/lib/samba/drivers folder if it doesn't exist and we restart the service.

```
[root@mike ~]# /root/soft/samba-4.9.1/bin/smbcontrol smbd reload-config
[root@mike ~]# /root/soft/samba-4.9.1/bin/smbcontrol smbd reload-printers
```

To upload the drivers to the Samba server, we log in to a Windows workstation that is included in the domain as the admin user. Again, all the details about joining a workstation to the domain can be found in Chapter 17.

The user who will upload the drivers will need to have the SePrintOperatorPrivilege set. If this is not the case, we'll grant it now.

```
[root@mike bin]# /root/soft/samba-4.9.1/bin/net rpc rights list privileges
SePrintOperatorPrivilege -U "LINUXAHOLICS\administrator"
Enter LINUXAHOLICS\administrator's password:
SePrintOperatorPrivilege:
[root@mike bin]# /root/soft/samba-4.9.1/bin/net rpc rights grant
"LINUXAHOLICS\Administrator" SePrintOperatorPrivilege -U "LINUXAHOLICS\
Administrator"
Enter LINUXAHOLICS\Administrator's password:
Successfully granted rights.
[root@mike bin]# /root/soft/samba-4.9.1/bin/net rpc rights list privileges
SePrintOperatorPrivilege -U "LINUXAHOLICS\administrator"
Enter LINUXAHOLICS\administrator's password:
SePrintOperatorPrivilege:
  LINUXAHOLICS\Administrator
```

Once logged in, we launch the Print Management console (Figure 12-26).

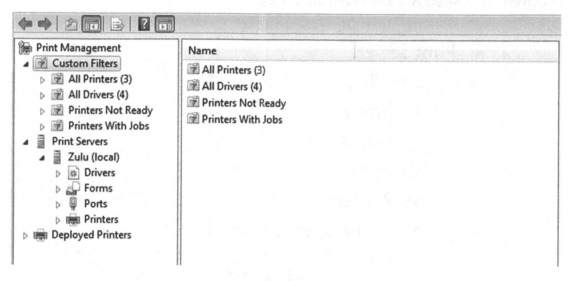

***Figure 12-26.*** *Print Management console*

By default, we can only manage the local print server at the workstation, so we need to add our Samba server as a remote print server (Figure 12-27).

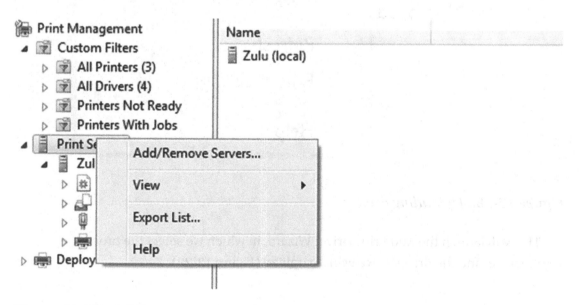

***Figure 12-27.*** *Adding a remote print server*

Now we're ready to upload drivers to the Samba server. Select mike.linuxaholics.com ➤ Drivers. Then select Add Driver (Figure 12-28).

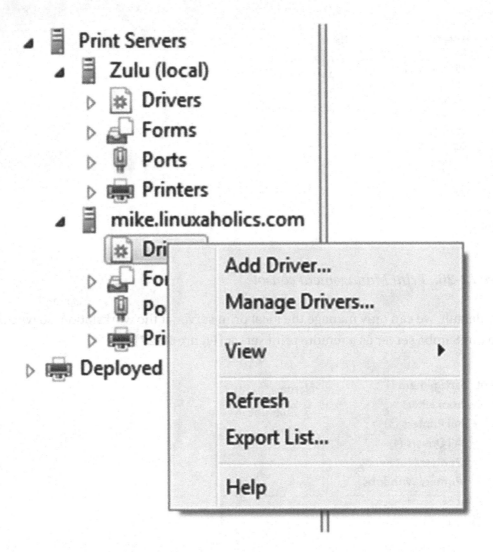

***Figure 12-28.*** *Uploading drivers*

This will launch the Add Print Driver Wizard, in which we select the processor architecture, and the driver(s) we want to upload (Figure 12-29).

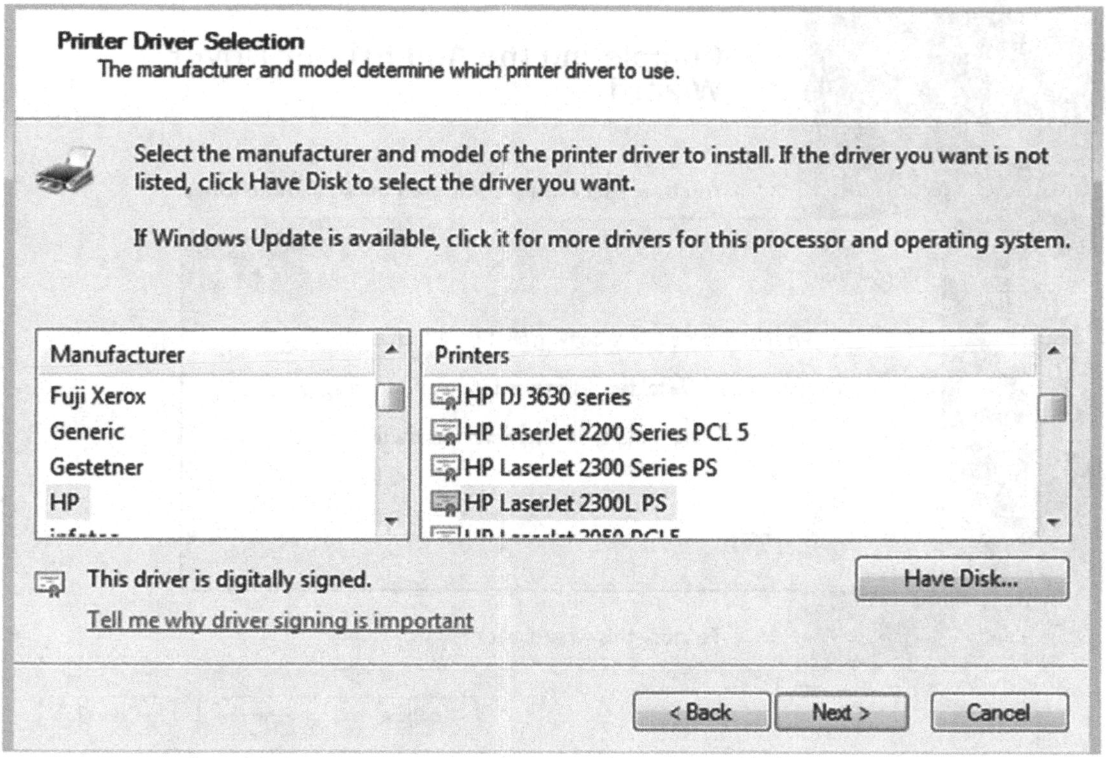

**Printer Driver Selection**
The manufacturer and model determine which printer driver to use.

Select the manufacturer and model of the printer driver to install. If the driver you want is not listed, click Have Disk to select the driver you want.

If Windows Update is available, click it for more drivers for this processor and operating system.

| Manufacturer | | Printers | |
|---|---|---|---|
| Fuji Xerox | | HP DJ 3630 series | |
| Generic | | HP LaserJet 2200 Series PCL 5 | |
| Gestetner | | HP LaserJet 2300 Series PS | |
| HP | | HP LaserJet 2300L PS | |

This driver is digitally signed.
Tell me why driver signing is important

Have Disk...

< Back     Next >     Cancel

*Figure 12-29.* *Selecting the printer driver*

After selecting the driver, the wizard will copy the files to the [print$] share in the Samba server. Unfortunately, though, we might get the error shown in Figure 12-30.

*Figure 12-30.* *Error copying the driver*

When we defined the [print$] share we restricted write access. We should allow the admin user the appropriate permissions to write to the [print$] share. However, as we still haven't seen how user and group mapping works and we are in a lab environment, we'll make the share writable for any user so that we can complete this proof of concept.

Of course, in a production environment we should grant write permissions only to those users who really need them, otherwise someone might upload drivers that could pose a serious threat to the whole network.

The modified share definition will be something like this:

```
[print$]
        comment = Printer Drivers
        create mask = 0664
        directory mask = 0775
        #force group = @printadmin
        path = /var/lib/samba/drivers
```

```
#write list = @printadmin root
writable = Yes
public = Yes
```

If we repeat the process after restarting the Samba service we'll see that now the
driver files are copied successfully (Figure 12-31).

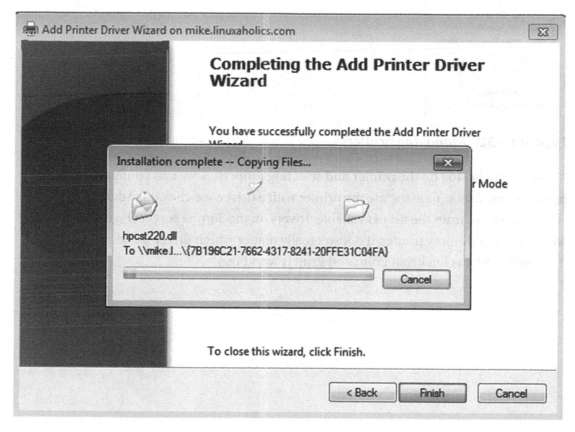

***Figure 12-31.***  *Uploading the driver*

The drivers have been uploaded, but now we need to associate the Samba printer
with the right driver. We do this in the Print Management console, too, by selecting
Printers (Figure 12-32).

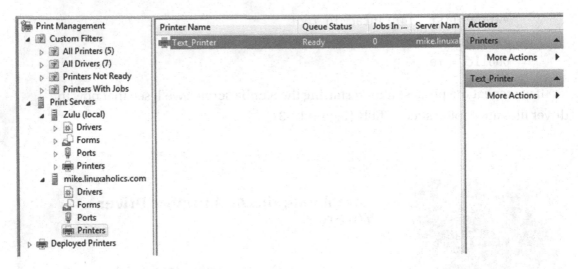

**Figure 12-32.** *Managing printers*

By right-clicking on the printer and selecting Properties we can configure many printer parameters. To associate the printer with a driver, we click the Advanced tab and select the driver from the list of available drivers on the Samba server (Figure 12-33). As we are using a dummy printer, it doesn't really matter which driver we select, as any of them will work to check that Point and Print is working.

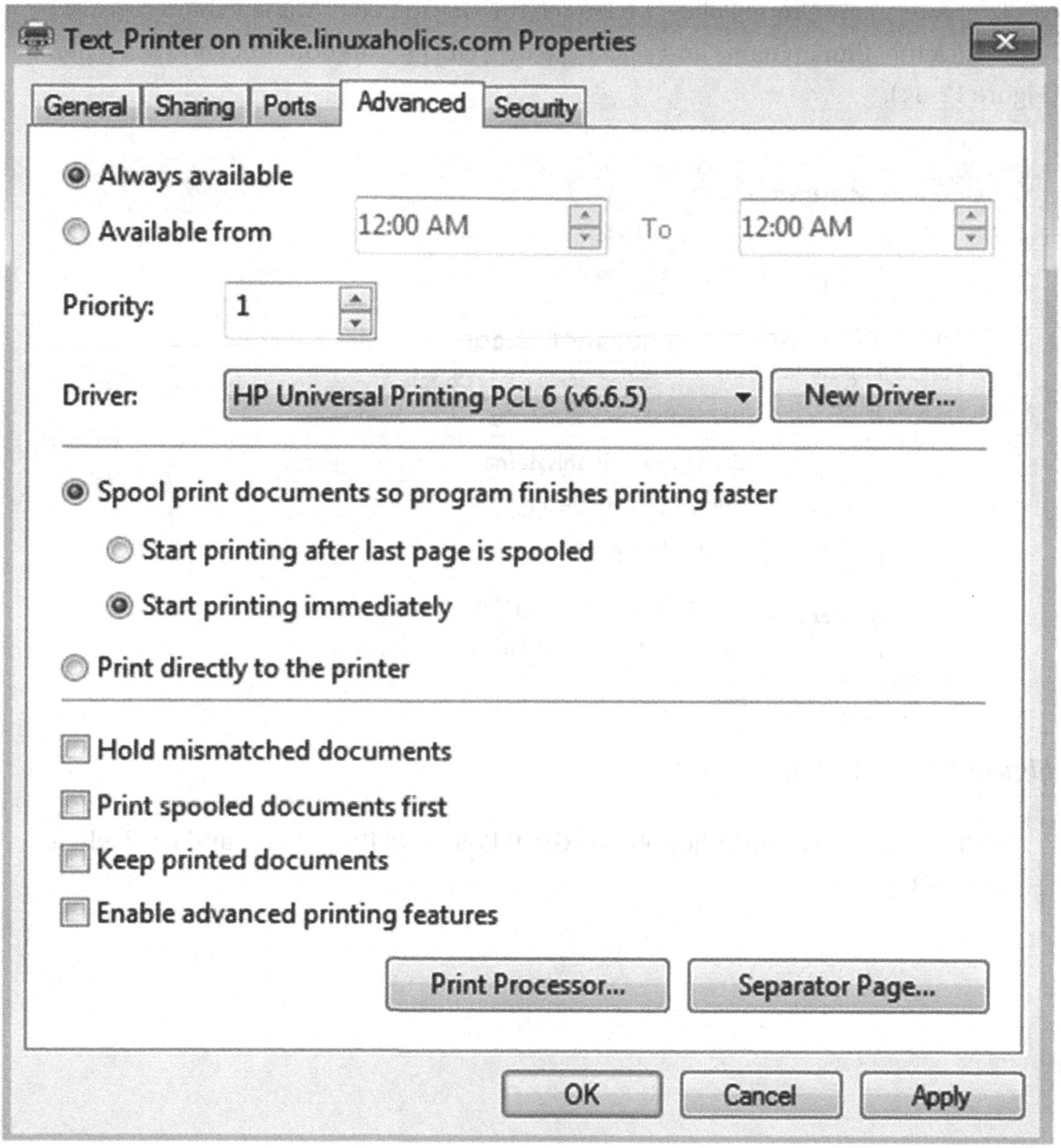

Text_Printer on mike.linuxaholics.com Properties                    ☒

| General | Sharing | Ports | Advanced | Security |

◉ Always available

○ Available from        12:00 AM    ▲▼   To   12:00 AM    ▲▼

Priority:        1      ▲▼

Driver:    HP Universal Printing PCL 6 (v6.6.5)    ▼        New Driver...

───────────────────────────────────────────────

◉ Spool print documents so program finishes printing faster

   ○ Start printing after last page is spooled

   ◉ Start printing immediately

○ Print directly to the printer

───────────────────────────────────────────────

☐ Hold mismatched documents

☐ Print spooled documents first

☐ Keep printed documents

☐ Enable advanced printing features

Print Processor...        Separator Page...

OK        Cancel        Apply

*Figure 12-33.*  *Printer Advanced Properties dialog box*

We already have associated the printer with its driver, so when a user clicks on the Samba printer, the driver will be automatically downloaded. It is possible, though, that the system warns the user about requiring elevated privileges. To avoid that, we'll create a new group policy that we'll customize.

To create a new Group Policy, we launch the Group Policy Management console. Right-click the domain name and select Create a GPO in this domain, and Link it here. (Figure 12-34).

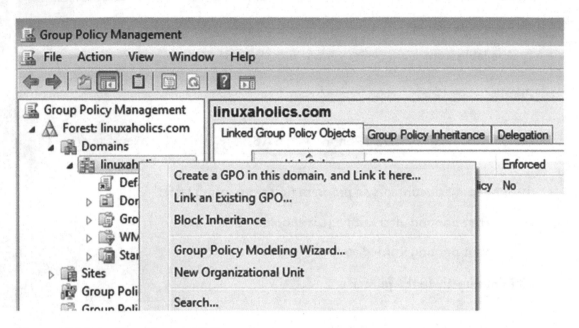

***Figure 12-34.*** *Creating a GPO*

We'll name our Group Policy object (GPO) Point and Print Policy and we'll edit it (Figure 12-35).

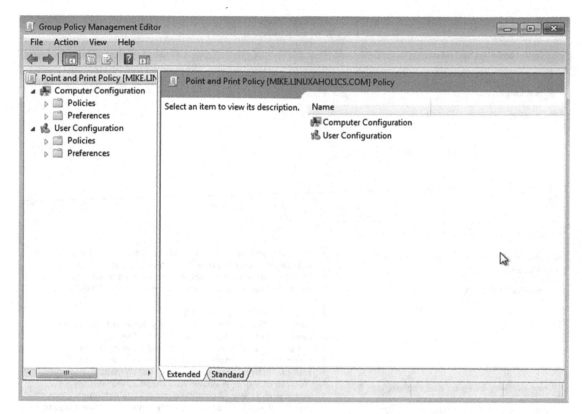

*Figure 12-35.  Editing the GPO*

Select Computer Configuration ➤ Policies ➤ Administrative templates ➤ Printers. We'll see several printer-related policies. Click Point and Print restrictions (Figure 12-36).

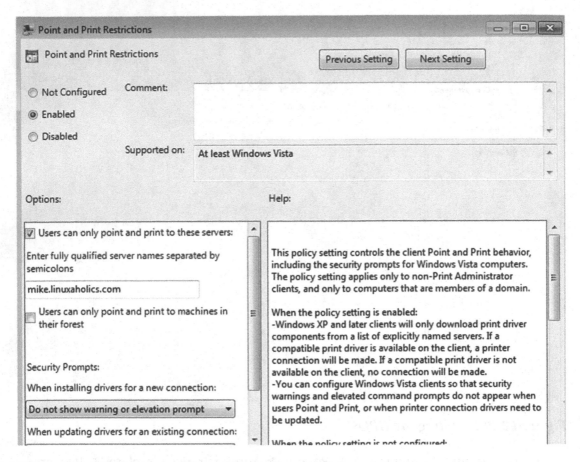

***Figure 12-36.*** *Point and Print Restrictions policy*

We enable the policy and select the "Users can only point and print to these servers: check box, and we enter the FQDN of our Samba server. Make sure that the option Do not show warning or elevation prompt is set when installing or updating drivers for a new connection.

After accepting the changes, we click on the policy Package Point and Print - Approved servers, we enable the policy, and we type the FQDN of our Samba server.

Now whenever a user clicks on the Samba server, the drivers will be automatically downloaded to their workstation and the printer will be ready to be used.

# Some Useful Command-Line Utilities

We have already seen many Samba client utilities, such as **smbclient**, **pdbedit**, and so on. On this occasion, we'll see two more utilities: **smbspool** and **rpcclient**.

# Smbspool

According to its man page, **smbspool** is used to send a print file to an SMB printer. The syntax of the command should be this:

```
smbspool {job} {user} {title} {copies} {options} [filename]
```

The command gets the Samba printer by querying an environmental variable, (DEVICE_URI), which should have one of these formats:

```
smb://server[:port]/printer
smb://workgroup/server[:port]/printer
smb://username:password@server[:port]/printer
smb://username:password@workgroup/server[:port]/printer
```

We'll create and export that variable.

```
[root@alpha ~]# export DEVICE_URI=smb://Antonio:antonio@192.168.56.102/
printer_Canon
```

Now we can execute **smbspool** with the required parameters. If we read the man page, we'll realize that many of these parameters (job, user, and options) are currently ignored; however, we must still provide dummy values for these parameters to keep the order. We'll execute this line.

```
[root@alpha ~]# smbspool 1 Antonio antonio 1 something test.txt
DEBUG: Connected with username/password...
```

The document will then be printed on the Samba printer.

# Rpcclient

This tool was developed to test MS-RPC functionality in Samba. It is very easy to execute and the only mandatory argument is the NetBIOS of the Samba server to which we are connecting. Nevertheless, if NetBIOS name resolution isn't working properly, we can force the utility to connect to a certain IP by using the -I parameter, in this case the NetBIOS server name is ignored. We can also specify the Samba user we'll be using to connect. In this example we used the user Antonio, which was given administrative privileges in a previous section.

```
[root@hotel ~]# rpcclient -I 127.0.0.1  -U Antonio hotel
Enter Antonio's password:
rpcclient $>
```

We can get some information about the server.

```
rpcclient $> srvinfo
        HOTEL             Wk Sv PrQ Unx NT SNT Samba Server Version 4.1.1
        platform_id    :      500
        os version     :      4.9
        server type    :      0x809a03
```

We can also list the network shares.

```
rpcclient $> netshareenum
netname: Docs
        remark:      Public documents
        path:        C:\shared_docs
        password:
netname: Demo
        remark:
        path:        C:\Demo
        password:
netname: Antonio
        remark:      Home Directories
        path:        C:\home\Antonio
        password:
```

As we can see, it uses C:\ to refer to the root Linux partition. We can request some more information about a network share.

```
rpcclient $> netsharegetinfo Demo
netname: Demo
      remark:
      path:        C:\Demo
      password:
      type:        0x0
      perms:       0
```

```
      max_uses: -1
      num_uses:  1
revision: 1
type: 0x8104: SEC_DESC_DACL_PRESENT SEC_DESC_DACL_AUTO_INHERIT_REQ SEC_
DESC_SELF_RELATIVE
DACL
      ACL       Num ACEs:       2      revision:       2
      ---
      ACE
            type: ACCESS ALLOWED (0) flags: 0x00
            Specific bits: 0x1bf
            Permissions: 0x1301bf: SYNCHRONIZE_ACCESS READ_CONTROL_ACCESS
            DELETE_ACCESS
            SID: S-1-5-21-793377898-1493187772-2337133042-1000

      ACE
            type: ACCESS ALLOWED (0) flags: 0x00
            Specific bits: 0x1bf
            Permissions: 0x1301bf: SYNCHRONIZE_ACCESS READ_CONTROL_ACCESS
            DELETE_ACCESS
            SID: S-1-5-21-793377898-1493187772-2337133042-1002
```

We can see the ACLs associated to the network share. To find out which user or group corresponds to an SID, we can use **rpcclient**, too.

```
rpcclient $> lookupsids S-1-5-21-793377898-1493187772-2337133042-1002
S-1-5-21-793377898-1493187772-2337133042-1002 HOTEL\avazquez (1)
rpcclient $> lookupsids S-1-5-21-793377898-1493187772-2337133042-1000
S-1-5-21-793377898-1493187772-2337133042-1000 HOTEL\Antonio (1)
```

We can obtain some detailed information about any user.

```
rpcclient $> queryuser antonio
      User Name   :      Antonio
      Full Name   :
      Home Drive  :      \\hotel\antonio
      Dir Drive   :
      Profile Path:      \\hotel\antonio\profile
```

```
    Logon Script:
    Description :
    Workstations:
    Comment    :
    Remote Dial :
    Logon Time              :        jue, 01 ene 1970 01:00:00 CET
    Logoff Time             :        mié, 06 feb 2036 16:06:39 CET
    Kickoff Time            :        mié, 06 feb 2036 16:06:39 CET
    Password last set Time  :        lun, 13 ago 2018 20:35:32 CEST
    Password can change Time :       lun, 13 ago 2018 20:35:32 CEST
    Password must change Time:       jue, 14 sep 30828 04:48:05 CEST
    unknown_2[0..31]...
    user_rid :        0x3e8
    group_rid:        0x201
    acb_info :        0x00000010
    fields_present: 0x00ffffff
    logon_divs:       168
    bad_password_count: 0x00000000
    logon_count: 0x00000000
    padding1[0..7]...
    logon_hrs[0..21]...
```

It is also possible to enumerate the Samba shared printers.

```
rpcclient $> enumprinters
    flags:[0x800000]
    name:[\\LSAENUMSID\printer_Canon]
    description:[\\LSAENUMSID\printer_Canon,,printer_Canon]
    comment:[printer_Canon]
```

There are many more useful subcommands that we can execute; to get a brief list of all of this we can type help at the rpcclient prompt.

```
rpcclient $> help
---------------              ----------------------
            FSRVP
fss_is_path_sup             Check whether a share supports shadow-copy requests
fss_get_sup_version         Get supported FSRVP version from server
.
.
.
```

# Summary

In this chapter we have seen the basics of printing in Linux using CUPS. We learned how to share printers from Linux in a heterogeneous network with Windows and Mac computers. Later we integrated Samba with CUPS to provide print services via Samba, and we saw some of the main printing-related options in smb.conf.

In addition, we also studied how to store Windows drivers on our Samba server so that they can be easily accessed and installed by the client workstations. Finally, we also explored a handful of useful command-line utilities.

## CHAPTER 13

# Managing User Accounts and Groups

Being able to effectively manage users and groups is a critical skill for every Samba admin. In addition, in Samba we need to associate Linux and Samba users and groups in the correct manner, so that our infrastructure works as expected. In this chapter we'll cover the following concepts:

- Managing user and group accounts.

- Understanding user and group mapping.

- Knowledge of user account management tools.

- Use of the smbpasswd program.

- Force ownership of file and directory objects.

We will also learn about the following terms and utilities: **pdbedit**, smb.conf, **samba-tool user** (with subcommands), **samba-tool group** (with subcommands), **smbpasswd**, /etc/passwd, /etc/group, force user, force group, and idmap.

## Managing User and Group Accounts

We have already seen in previous chapters how to use certain tools to manage user accounts, like **smbpasswd** or **pdbedit** (see Chapters 7 and 8). We also know that in any case, before we create a Samba user, we must have already an equivalent Linux user.

Every Linux system keeps a list of the local users in the /etc/passwd file, and a list of the local groups in the /etc/group file. When creating new users and groups the server admin will use commands like **useradd** or **groupadd** to create new users and groups, respectively. We'll now explore the use of **smbpasswd** and **pdbedit**.

© Antonio Vazquez 2019
A. Vazquez, *Practical LPIC-3 300*, https://doi.org/10.1007/978-1-4842-4473-9_13

# Smbpasswd

Throughout the book we have already used **smbpasswd** to create users, but it has many other uses. For instance, it can be executed without parameters by normal users to change their Samba passwords.

```
[avazquez@hotel ~]$ smbpasswd
Old SMB password:
New SMB password:
Retype new SMB password:
Password changed for user avazquez
```

The command works by connecting to the SMB service, so we must make sure that this one is running; otherwise, the command will fail.

```
[avazquez@hotel ~]$ smbpasswd
Old SMB password:
New SMB password:
Retype new SMB password:
Unable to connect to SMB server on machine 127.0.0.1. Error was :
NT_STATUS_CONNECTION_REFUSED.
```

In the preceding examples we launched the command on the Samba server itself, but it can also be executed on remote systems by providing the -r parameter. We can also specify the remote user whose password we want to change with the -U parameter.

```
[avazquez@alpha ~]$ smbpasswd -r 192.168.56.102 -U Antonio
Old SMB password:
New SMB password:
Retype new SMB password:
Password changed for user Antonio
```

If we don't include the -U parameter, the program will try to locate a Samba user with the same name as the logged on user on the client computer.

```
[avazquez@alpha ~]$ smbpasswd -r 192.168.56.102
Old SMB password:
New SMB password:
Retype new SMB password:
Password changed for user avazquez
```

We also executed **smbpasswd** before, as root, to create a Samba user after having created the corresponding Linux user:

```
[root@hotel ~]# smbpasswd -a jdoe
New SMB password:
Retype new SMB password:
Added user jdoe.
```

In addition to creating users, we can also disable them or delete them. For instance, if we want to disable the jdoe user we'll execute **smbpasswd** with the -d parameter.

```
[root@hotel ~]# smbpasswd -d jdoe
Disabled user jdoe.
```

After that, if jdoe tries to access any Samba resource he or she will receive a disabled account message.

```
[avazquez@alpha ~]$ smbclient  //192.168.56.102/Docs -U jdoe
WARNING: The "syslog" option is deprecated
Enter WORKGROUP\jdoe's password:
session setup failed: NT_STATUS_ACCOUNT_DISABLED
```

Of course, we can re-enable the account at any moment with the -e parameter.

```
[root@hotel ~]# smbpasswd -e jdoe
Enabled user jdoe.
```

If we no longer need to keep a certain user, we can delete it.

```
[root@hotel ~]# smbpasswd -x jdoe
Deleted user jdoe.
```

# Pdbedit

Another tool we have already used throughout the book is **pdbedit**. As opposed to what happened with **smbpasswd**, this tool can only be executed by root.

We have already used it to list the Samba users, but it can be used to retrieve much more information. For instance, we can list the users showing much more detail by passing the -v parameter.

```
[root@hotel ~]# pdbedit -L -v
---------------
Unix username:          Antonio
NT username:
Account Flags:          [U             ]
User SID:               S-1-5-21-793377898-1493187772-2337133042-1000
Primary Group SID:      S-1-5-21-793377898-1493187772-2337133042-513
Full Name:
Home Directory:         \\hotel\antonio
HomeDir Drive:
Logon Script:
Profile Path:           \\hotel\antonio\profile
Domain:                 HOTEL
Account desc:
Workstations:
Munged dial:
Logon time:             0
Logoff time:            mié, 06 feb 2036 16:06:39 CET
Kickoff time:           mié, 06 feb 2036 16:06:39 CET
Password last set:      mié, 15 ago 2018 03:03:09 CEST
Password can change:    mié, 15 ago 2018 03:03:09 CEST
Password must change: never
Last bad password    : 0
Bad password count   : 0
Logon hours          : FFFFFFFFFFFFFFFFFFFFFFFFFFFFFFFFFFFFFFFFFFFF
---------------
.
.
.
```

As we did previously with **smbpasswd**, we can add new users (as long as they already exist in Linux).

```
[root@hotel ~]# pdbedit -a -u jdoe
new password:
retype new password:
```

```
Unix username:         jdoe
NT username:
Account Flags:         [U          ]
User SID:              S-1-5-21-793377898-1493187772-2337133042-1004
Primary Group SID:     S-1-5-21-793377898-1493187772-2337133042-513
Full Name:
Home Directory:        \\hotel\jdoe
HomeDir Drive:
Logon Script:
Profile Path:          \\hotel\jdoe\profile
Domain:                HOTEL
Account desc:
Workstations:
Munged dial:
Logon time:            0
Logoff time:           mié, 06 feb 2036 16:06:39 CET
Kickoff time:          mié, 06 feb 2036 16:06:39 CET
Password last set:     mié, 15 ago 2018 17:13:48 CEST
Password can change:   mié, 15 ago 2018 17:13:48 CEST
Password must change:  never
Last bad password   : 0
Bad password count  : 0
Logon hours         : FFFFFFFFFFFFFFFFFFFFFFFFFFFFFFFFFFFFFFFFFFF
```

We can disable any user by passing the D account flag.

```
[root@hotel ~]# pdbedit -u jdoe -c "[D ]"
Unix username:         jdoe
NT username:
Account Flags:         [DU         ]
User SID:              S-1-5-21-793377898-1493187772-2337133042-1004
Primary Group SID:     S-1-5-21-793377898-1493187772-2337133042-513
Full Name:
Home Directory:        \\hotel\jdoe
HomeDir Drive:
Logon Script:
```

```
Profile Path:           \\hotel\jdoe\profile
Domain:                 HOTEL
Account desc:
Workstations:
Munged dial:
Logon time:             0
Logoff time:            mié, 06 feb 2036 16:06:39 CET
Kickoff time:           mié, 06 feb 2036 16:06:39 CET
Password last set:      mié, 15 ago 2018 17:13:48 CEST
Password can change:    mié, 15 ago 2018 17:13:48 CEST
Password must change:   never
Last bad password    : 0
Bad password count   : 0
Logon hours          : FFFFFFFFFFFFFFFFFFFFFFFFFFFFFFFFFFFFFFFFFF
```

As we can see, the account flags have changed from [ U ] to [DU ]. We could add more flags, for example, to make sure that the password does not expire.

```
[root@hotel ~]# pdbedit -u jdoe -c "[X ]"
Unix username:          jdoe
NT username:
Account Flags:          [UX         ]
```

We can also re-enable the account.

```
[root@hotel ~]# pdbedit -u jdoe -c "[ ]"
```

Alternatively, we can delete it.

```
[root@hotel ~]# pdbedit -x jdoe
```

# samba-tool

Both **smbpasswd** and **pdbedit** are used to manage local users, but if we want to manage Samba Active Directory users and groups, we'll need to use the **samba-tool** command. However, it is not included in the CentOS 7 Samba binaries. To use it we'll need to install the latest version of Samba from the the official Web page at https://www.samba.org/samba/download/.

To compile and install this Samba version, we'll need to install additional components such as the GCC compiler. The full details can be seen in Chapter 17 when installing a Samba 4 Active Directory domain controller. Once it is installed, we can use **samba-tool user** to list the existing users.

```
[root@mike ~]# /usr/local/samba/bin/samba-tool user list
Antonio
Administrator
krbtgt
Guest
```

We can create a new Active Directory user.

```
[root@mike ~]# /usr/local/samba/bin/samba-tool user create Jose
passwordJose123 --given-name=Jose --surname=Vazquez
User 'Jose' created successfully
```

We can manually edit the user we just created.

```
[root@mike ~]# /usr/local/samba/bin/samba-tool user edit Jose
```

In this case we see all the attributes of the user, and we can edit them manually as necessary.

```
dn: CN=Jose Vazquez,CN=Users,DC=linuxaholics,DC=com
objectClass: top
objectClass: person
objectClass: organizationalPerson
objectClass: user
cn: Jose Vazquez
sn: Vazquez
givenName: Jose
instanceType: 4
whenCreated: 20181017161440.0Z
whenChanged: 20181017161440.0Z
displayName: Jose Vazquez
.
.
.
```

We can also disable the user.

```
[root@mike ~]# /usr/local/samba/bin/samba-tool user disable Jose
```

A user can also be enabled.

```
[root@mike ~]# /usr/local/samba/bin/samba-tool user enable Jose
Enabled user 'Jose'
```

Of course, we can also delete the user.

```
[root@mike ~]# /usr/local/samba/bin/samba-tool user delete Jose
Deleted user Jose
```

Samba-tool can be also used to manage groups. For instance, we can list the existing groups in the domain.

```
[root@mike ~]# /usr/local/samba/bin/samba-tool group list
Allowed RODC Password Replication Group
Enterprise Read-Only Domain Controllers
Denied RODC Password Replication Group
Pre-Windows 2000 Compatible Access
Windows Authorization Access Group
.
.
.
```

We can list the members of a certain group.

```
[root@mike ~]# /usr/local/samba/bin/samba-tool group listmembers
"Administrators"
Enterprise Admins
Administrator
Domain Admins
```

It is also possible to add new members to the group.

```
[root@mike ~]# /usr/local/samba/bin/samba-tool group addmembers
"Administrators" Antonio
Added members to group Administrators
```

```
[root@mike ~]# /usr/local/samba/bin/samba-tool group listmembers
"Administrators"
Enterprise Admins
Administrator
Antonio
Domain Admins
```

We can also remove existing members from that same group.

```
[root@mike ~]# /usr/local/samba/bin/samba-tool group removemembers
"Administrators" Antonio
Removed members from group Administrators
[root@mike ~]# /usr/local/samba/bin/samba-tool group listmembers
"Administrators"
Enterprise Admins
Administrator
Domain Admins
```

We could add a new group.

```
[root@mike ~]# /usr/local/samba/bin/samba-tool group add "Permanent Staff"
Added group Permanent Staff
```

Any existing group can also be deleted.

```
[root@mike ~]# /usr/local/samba/bin/samba-tool group delete "Permanent Staff"
Deleted group Permanent Staff
```

# Understand User and Group Mapping

We have already created Samba users with **smbpasswd, pdbedit**, or both. In both cases, however, we should have created the corresponding Linux user first. That is, there is a mapping between the Linux user and the Samba user. By default, a stand-alone Samba server maps any Samba user with the corresponding Linux user of the same name. For instance, the Samba user avazquez is mapped to the Linux user avazquez. We can customize the mapping, though, by editing the /etc/samba/smb.conf file.

Before making any modifications, we can connect as avazquez to the [Docs] share.

```
[root@alpha ~]# smbclient //hotel.linuxaholics.com/Docs -U avazquez
Enter avazquez's password:
Domain=[MYGROUP] OS=[Unix] Server=[Samba 4.1.1]
smb: \>
```

If we execute the **smbstatus** command on the Samba server, we'll see that the user has been mapped to the Linux user avazquez as well.

```
[root@hotel ~]# smbstatus

Samba version 4.1.1
PID     Username        Group       Machine
-----------------------------------------------------------------
16868   avazquez        avazquez    192.168.56.101 (ipv4:192.168.56.101:34886)
.
.
.
```

If we want to map the Samba user avazquez to the Linux user Antonio we'll create a text file like this one:

```
[root@hotel ~]# cat /var/lib/samba/usersmap.txt
Antonio = avazquez
```

We add the username map option to the global section of the /etc/samba/smb.conf file.

```
.
.
.
username map = /var/lib/samba/usersmap.txt
.
.
.
```

After restarting the service, the user avazquez will be able to access the [Docs] share the same way as before.

```
[root@alpha ~]# smbclient //hotel.linuxaholics.com/Docs -U avazquez
Enter avazquez's password:
Domain=[MYGROUP] OS=[Unix] Server=[Samba 4.1.1]
smb: \>
```

In this case, however, the mapped Linux user is Antonio instead of avazquez.

```
[root@hotel ~]# smbstatus

Samba version 4.1.1
PID     Username    Group         Machine
-------------------------------------------------------------------
16885   Antonio     Antonio       192.168.56.101 (ipv4:192.168.56.101:34887)
.
.
.
```

Instead of the username map option, we could have used the similar username map script option, which points to the full path to a program or script that receives the invoking username as the input value and returns the Linux user it should be mapped to.

Another parameter related to user and group mappings is idmap. It is the mapping between Windows SIDs and Linux user and group IDs. In Chapter 8 we used this parameter when configuring the ldapsam back end. We included these two lines:

```
idmap backend = ldap:"ldap://alpha.linuxaholics.com"
idmap uid = 5000-50000
idmap gid = 5000-50000
```

These three lines mean that the range 5000–50000 will be reserved for the mapping of the UIDs and GIDs. The back end used in this case will be an LDAP server, but it could be also a TDB file, an Active Directory server, and so on. This syntax, however, is now deprecated and the following should be used:

```
idmap config * : backend = ldap:"ldap://alpha.linuxaholics.com"
idmap config * : range = 5000-50000
```

A special type of user mapping concerns the Guest user. Historically, Windows systems have included a special account called Guest to grant limited rights to any unknown user. In Samba this account is mapped by default to the Linux account nobody (guest account = nobody). It is possible to change this mapping by manually specifying a different user, although is not advisable to do so.

A related option is `map to guest`. Depending on the value of this parameter, Samba will behave differently:

- `Never`: In this case any login with an invalid password is rejected.

- `Bad User`: User logins with an incorrect password will be rejected, unless the username doesn't exist, in which case it will be mapped to the guest account.

- `Bad Password`: User logins with incorrect passwords are treated as guest logins. This can be confusing, as a user might not be aware of the incorrect password and will probably not understand why they cannot access resources they normally can.

- `Bad uid`: Only applicable when Samba is integrated in a domain.

In addition to map users, Samba also maps Linux and Unix group IDs to Windows SIDs. This can be done with the **net groupmap** command. We'll see many examples of this command in Chapter 15, when configuring Samba as a PDC.

# Forcing Ownership of File and Directory Objects

Usually when a user uploads a file to a share, this file is owned by that same user, and the same thing happens when creating new subfolders.

Currently we have defined the `[Docs]` share, which is publicly accessible but not writable.

```
[Docs]
comment = Public documents
path = /shared_docs
public = yes
writable = no
```

We must change the writable option to yes.

```
writable = yes
```

Next, we need to reload the service.

```
[root@hotel ~]# smbcontrol smbd reload-config
```

As we saw in Chapter 11, we also need the file system permissions to allow users to write to the shared folder.

```
[root@hotel ~]# ls -ld /shared_docs/
drwxr-xr-x. 2 root root 24 ago 13 19:58 /shared_docs/

[root@hotel ~]# chmod o+w /shared_docs/
[root@hotel ~]# ls -ld /shared_docs/
drwxr-xrwx. 2 root root 24 ago 13 19:58 /shared_docs/
```

Now any user can upload files to this share.

```
[root@alpha ~]# smbclient //hotel.linuxaholics.com/Docs -U Rosalia
Enter Rosalia's password:
Domain=[MYGROUP] OS=[Unix] Server=[Samba 4.1.1]
smb: \> put Rosalia_file.txt
putting file Rosalia_file.txt as \Rosalia_file.txt (0,6 kb/s) (average 0,6 kb/s)
smb: \>

[root@alpha ~]# smbclient //hotel.linuxaholics.com/Docs -U Isabel
Enter Isabel's password:
Domain=[MYGROUP] OS=[Unix] Server=[Samba 4.1.1]
smb: \> put Isabel_file.txt
putting file Isabel_file.txt as \Isabel_file.txt (0,4 kb/s) (average 0,4 kb/s)
smb: \>
```

As we can see, each file's owner is the user who actually uploaded it.

```
[root@hotel ~]# ls -l /shared_docs/
total 20
-rw-r--r--. 1 root     root     24 ago 13 19:58 example.txt
-rwxrwxr-x+ 1 Isabel   Isabel    4 ago 17 00:45 Isabel_file.txt
-rwxrwxr-x+ 1 Rosalia  Rosalia   4 ago 17 00:44 Rosalia_file.txt
```

Nevertheless, this default behavior can be changed by adding the parameter force user to the share definition. This should be more or less the complete definition.

```
[Docs]
comment = Public documents
path = /shared_docs
public = yes
writable = yes
force user = avazquez
```

After reloading the configuration, any file uploaded to this share will be owned by avazquez.

```
[root@alpha ~]# smbclient //hotel.linuxaholics.com/Docs -U Rosalia
Enter Rosalia's password:
Domain=[MYGROUP] OS=[Unix] Server=[Samba 4.1.1]
smb: \> put Rosalia_file2.txt
putting file Rosalia_file2.txt as \Rosalia_file2.txt (0,5 kb/s)
(average 0,5 kb/s)
smb: \>

[root@hotel ~]# ls -l /shared_docs/
total 28
-rw-r--r--. 1 root      root       24 ago 13 19:58 example.txt
-rwxrwxr-x+ 1 Isabel    Isabel      4 ago 17 00:45 Isabel_file.txt
-rwxrwxr-x+ 1 avazquez  avazquez    4 ago 17 02:37 Rosalia_file2.txt
-rwxrwxr-x+ 1 Rosalia   Rosalia     4 ago 17 00:44 Rosalia_file.txt
```

In addition to the owner, the default group of the uploaded file was also changed to the primary group of the user avazquez.

An option similar to force user is force group, which forces the default group for new files and folders. If we use both options in the share definition, the default group of the new file will be the one we specified with force group.

```
[Docs]
.
.
.
```

```
force user = avazquez
force group = users
```

If we repeat the test, we'll see that now the uploaded files belong to the user's group.

```
[root@alpha ~]# smbclient //hotel.linuxaholics.com/Docs -U Isabel
Enter Isabel's password:
Domain=[MYGROUP] OS=[Unix] Server=[Samba 4.1.1]
smb: \> put Isabel_file2.txt
putting file Isabel_file2.txt as \Isabel_file2.txt (0,5 kb/s) (average 0,5 kb/s)
smb: \>

[root@hotel ~]# ls -l /shared_docs/
total 36
-rw-r--r--. 1 root      root      24 ago 13 19:58 example.txt
-rwxrwxr-x+ 1 avazquez  users      4 ago 17 03:03 Isabel_file2.txt
-rwxrwxr-x+ 1 Isabel    Isabel     4 ago 17 00:45 Isabel_file.txt
-rwxrwxr-x+ 1 avazquez  avazquez   4 ago 17 02:37 Rosalia_file2.txt
-rwxrwxr-x+ 1 Rosalia   Rosalia    4 ago 17 00:44 Rosalia_file.txt
```

# Summary

In this chapter we learned how to manage local users in Samba by using **smbpasswd** and **pdbedit**. We also saw how to add and edit users in Active Directory with **samba-tool**.

Then, we studied user and group mapping in Samba and we learned how to force user and group ownership in Samba shares.

# CHAPTER 14

# Authentication, Authorization, and Winbind

We have already seen when talking about OpenLDAP that apart from authenticating against the local user database located at /etc/passwd, users could also authenticate against an OpenLDAP server. This has numerous advantages, as we can use a common centralized user repository, making user management much easier.

In this chapter we'll see how to authenticate users against a Samba or Windows server. We'll cover the following concepts:

- Setting up a local password database.

- Performing password synchronization.

- Knowledge of different passdb back ends.

- Converting between Samba passdb back ends.

- Integrating Samba with LDAP.

- Configuring Winbind service.

- Configuring PAM and NSS.

We will also see the following terms and utilities: smb.conf, **smbpasswd**, tdbsam, ldapsam, passdb back end, libnss_winbind, pam_winbind, **wbinfo**, **getent**, SID and foreign SID, /etc/passwd, and /etc/group.

© Antonio Vazquez 2019
A. Vazquez, *Practical LPIC-3 300*, https://doi.org/10.1007/978-1-4842-4473-9_14

# Setting Up a Local Password Database

The terms *authentication* and *authorization* are sometimes misunderstood, and so they need to be clarified. *Authentication* is the process of confirming the identity of a given user, whereas *authorization* is the assignment of rights to a certain user once they have been authenticated.

In Chapter 13, we saw many examples of how to use **smbpasswd** and **pdbedit** to create a local user database. For that reason we won't repeat that information here.

# Performing Password Synchronization

As we already know, when using local Samba accounts, we need to create both a Linux user account and a Samba user account. As maintaining different passwords for the same user can be cumbersome and prone to error, Samba offers the possibility to synchronize both passwords.

For this synchronization to work we need to add and modify a few parameters. The first of these parameters is `unix password sync`. Let's look at its default value.

```
[root@alpha ~]# testparm -sv | grep "unix password sync"
.

.

.

        unix password sync = No
```

We'll have to change its default value to yes. In addition, we should set the option `passwd program` to the full path of the program used to change the Linux password.

```
unix password sync = yes
passwd program = /usr/bin/passwd %u
```

Both options should be placed in the [Global] section.

Unfortunately, this option only works when the back end used is **smbpasswd**, the use of which is discouraged, as we'll see in the next section. Besides, it requires that the client use Lan Manager (LM) authentication, which is also not recommended for security reasons. For these reasons the actual use of this parameter is very limited.

# Knowledge of Different passdb Back Ends and Converting between Different Back Ends

Samba needs to store the passwords associated with each user somewhere, either in a database, an LDAP server, or somewhere else. The place where Samba stores this information is called the **passdb backend**. According to its man page, it can take three different values:

- **smbdpasswd**: This is the first back end used by Samba. It consists of a simple plain text file. At this moment it is still supported, but its use is discouraged, as some Samba features won't work with this back end.

- **tdbsam**: Widely used nowadays, it uses Trivial Database (tdb) files to store the information. This is the back end we've been using in most parts of this book.

- **ldapsam**: It uses an LDAP server as a back end. We already used this back end in Chapter 8.

Changing from a passdb back end to another is very easy; we only need to change the value of the parameter in smb.conf. Right now, this is the value set up in our configuration:

```
passdb backend = tdbsam
```

At any moment we can change it to **smbdpasswd**.

```
passdb backend = smbpasswd
```

The password file will be by default /var/lib/samba/private/smbpasswd, but we could use a different path if we wanted by adding the smb passwd file option.

After restarting the SMB service we'll see that we have no users defined, as we are using a completely different back end.

```
[root@hotel ~]# pdbedit -L
[root@hotel ~]#
```

If we list the users in the tdbsam back end, though, we'll see that no one is missing.

```
[root@hotel ~]# pdbedit -b tdbsam -L
Antonio:1001:
avazquez:1000:Antonio Vazquez
Rosalia:1003:
Isabel:1004:
```

We can add a user with **smbpasswd** the usual way.

```
[root@hotel ~]# useradd dummy
[root@hotel ~]# smbpasswd -a dummy
New SMB password:
Retype new SMB password:
Added user dummy.
```

The user will be added to the smbpasswd file.

```
[root@hotel ~]# cat /var/lib/samba/private/smbpasswd
dummy:1006:XXXXXXXXXXXXXXXXXXXXXXXXXXXXXXXXXX:BC62AC0F8EA9DD1AD703C8B4F0A968C
4:[U          ]:LCT-5B76A654:
```

In the file there is, at this moment, a single line that contains the username, the user ID, the Lanman Password hash, the NT Password hash, and the account flags. The part corresponding to the Lanman hash has no value stored because by default modern Samba distributions don't use it due to its security flaws.

To revert back to the use of the tdbsam back end we again edit the /etc/samba/smb. conf file.

```
passdb backend = tdbsam
```

# Winbind

The **winbind** service is part of the Samba suite. It enables a Linux server to become a full member in Windows domains and to use Windows users and group accounts in Linux. The installation in CentOS 7 is pretty straightforward. We start by installing the samba-winbind package.

```
[root@india ~]# yum install samba-winbind
```

Let's imagine we have a Windows Active Directory domain named `ventanas.local`, and a DNS server for that domain is located at the server `yankee.ventanas.local`, which also happens to be a Windows 2008 domain controller. To make our Linux server `india.linuxaholics.com` a full member of the `ventanas.local` domain we first need to change the DNS settings of the Linux machine so that it can locate the domain-related resources.

To make sure that our Linux server is resolving hostnames properly we can execute a simple query:

```
[root@india ~]# dig a +noall +answer yankee.ventanas.local
yankee.ventanas.local.      3600     IN      A      192.168.1.235
```

We are ready now to set up winbind. In CentOS 7 we can do it by executing the graphic utility **authconfig-gtk**, its n-curses equivalent **authconfig-tui,** or the command-line tool **authconfig**. For ease of use, we'll choose **authconfig-gtk**. Once launched, we must select Winbind in User Account Database, and ads as the security model because we are connecting to an Active Directory domain. We type the domain name, the ADS Realm, and the domain controller (Figure 14-1). On the Advanced Options tab, select the Create home directories on the first login check box, so that we can log in with any Active Directory user. Next, return to the Identity & Authentication tab and click Join Domain. Later we confirm that we want to save the changes (Figure 14-2).

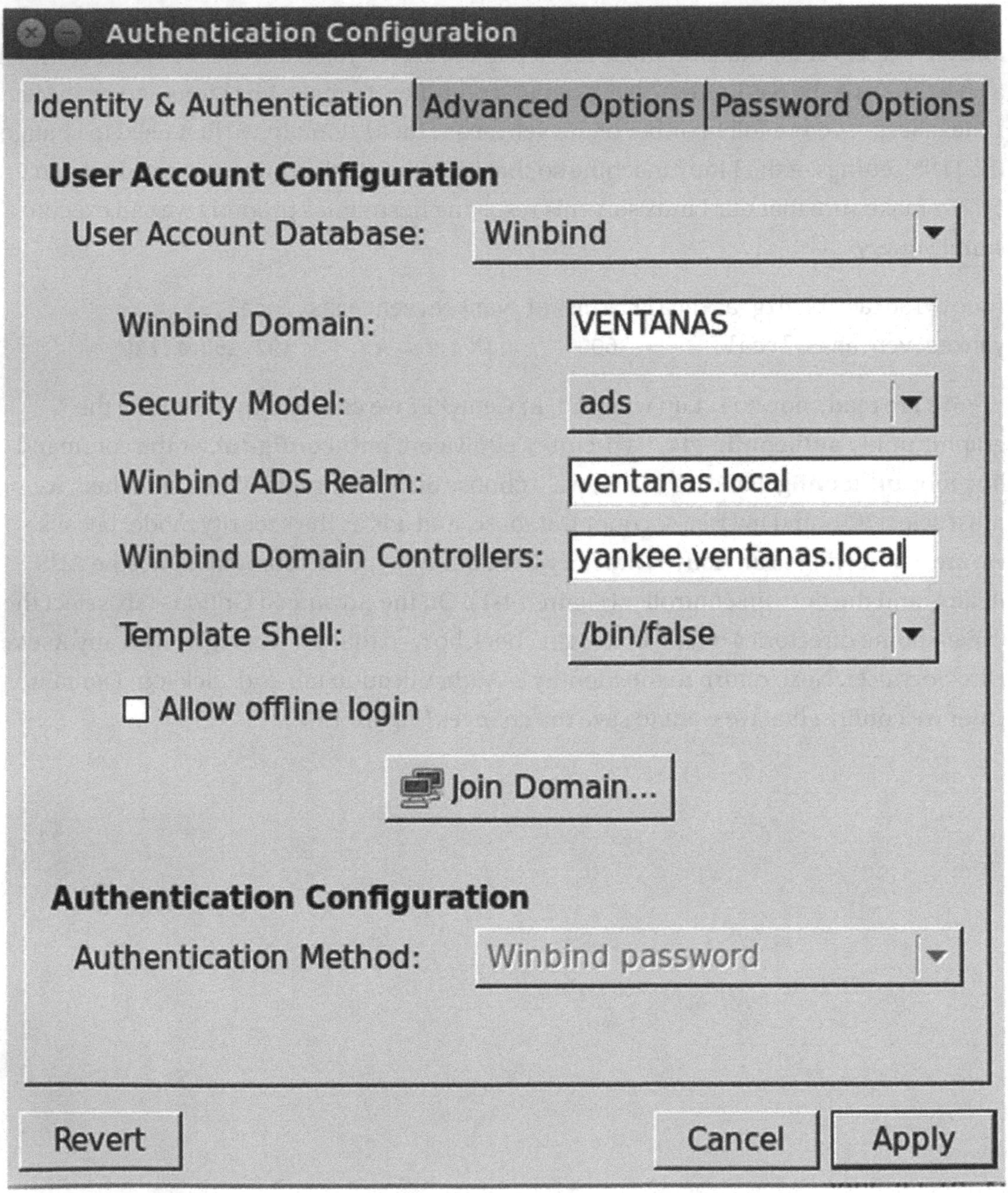

**Figure 14-1.** *Setting up Winbind*

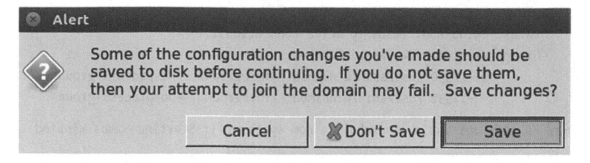

*Figure 14-2.* *Saving changes*

After a few seconds we'll be asked for the administrator password of the domain VENTANAS (Figure 14-3). Enter it, click OK, and close all open windows. The setup is now complete.

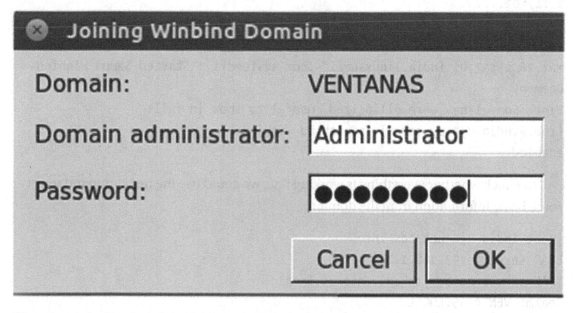

*Figure 14-3.* *Typing the administrative credentials*

Next, we make sure that the **winbind** service is enabled and running.

```
[root@india ~]# systemctl status winbind
● winbind.service - Samba Winbind Daemon
   Loaded: loaded (/usr/lib/systemd/system/winbind.service; enabled; vendor
   preset: disabled)
   Active: active (running) since dom 2017-03-26 15:17:01 CEST; 4min 22s ago
```

```
 Main PID: 12530 (winbindd)
   Status: "winbindd: ready to serve connections..."
   CGroup: /system.slice/winbind.service
           ├─12530 /usr/sbin/winbindd --foreground --no-process-group
           └─12532 /usr/sbin/winbindd --foreground --no-process-group

mar 26 15:17:01 india.linuxaholics.com systemd[1]: Starting Samba Winbind
Dae...
mar 26 15:17:01 india.linuxaholics.com winbindd[12530]: [2017/03/26
15:17:01....
mar 26 15:17:01 india.linuxaholics.com winbindd[12530]:   initialize_
winbindd...
mar 26 15:17:01 india.linuxaholics.com winbindd[12530]: [2017/03/26
15:17:01....
mar 26 15:17:01 india.linuxaholics.com winbindd[12530]:   STATUS=daemon
'winb...
mar 26 15:17:01 india.linuxaholics.com systemd[1]: Started Samba Winbind
Daemon.
Hint: Some lines were ellipsized, use -l to show in full.
[root@india ~]# systemctl is-enabled winbind
enabled
```

To check whether everything is working fine, we could use the **net** command to get some basic information from the domain.

```
[root@india ~]# net ads info
LDAP server: 192.168.1.235
LDAP server name: yankee.ventanas.local
Realm: VENTANAS.LOCAL
Bind Path: dc=VENTANAS,dc=LOCAL
LDAP port: 389
Server time: jue, 20 sep 2018 13:26:09 CEST
KDC server: 192.168.1.235
Server time offset: 46908080
Last machine account password change: dom, 26 mar 2017 15:16:05 CEST
```

To get more information about the domain we can use some client utilities included in the samba-winbind-clients package. We'll install that package if it is not already installed.

```
[root@india ~]# yum install -y samba-winbind-clients
.
.
.
```

We can list the existing users in the Active Directory.

```
[root@india ~]# wbinfo -u
VENTANAS\administrator
VENTANAS\guest
VENTANAS\krbtgt
```

We can also list the existing groups.

```
[root@india ~]# wbinfo -g
VENTANAS\domain computers
VENTANAS\domain controllers
VENTANAS\schema admins
VENTANAS\enterprise admins
VENTANAS\cert publishers
VENTANAS\domain admins
VENTANAS\domain users
VENTANAS\domain guests
VENTANAS\group policy creator owners
VENTANAS\ras and ias servers
VENTANAS\allowed rodc password replication group
VENTANAS\denied rodc password replication group
VENTANAS\read-only domain controllers
VENTANAS\enterprise read-only domain controllers
VENTANAS\dnsadmins
VENTANAS\dnsupdateproxy
```

If we create a new user on the DC, it will be inmediately listed in the Linux server.

```
[root@india ~]# wbinfo -u
VENTANAS\administrator
VENTANAS\guest
VENTANAS\krbtgt
VENTANAS\jose
```

As **winbind** is part of the Samba suite, it also uses the same configuration file (/etc/samba/smb.conf). For **winbind** to work properly, we need to change many parameters in the file, but luckily **authconfig** does the job for us. If we take a look at smb. conf we'll see the following section:

```
[global]
#--authconfig--start-line--

# Generated by authconfig on 2017/03/26 15:17:00
# DO NOT EDIT THIS SECTION (delimited by --start-line--/--end-line--)
# Any modification may be deleted or altered by authconfig in future

    workgroup = VENTANAS
    password server = yankee.ventanas.local
    realm = VENTANAS.LOCAL
    security = ads
    idmap config * : range = 16777216-33554431
    template shell = /bin/false
    kerberos method = secrets only
    winbind use default domain = false
    winbind offline logon = false

#--authconfig--end-line--
```

We see that the workgroup name has been changed to that of the Active Directory domain, and the same thing happened to the Kerberos realm. As our Active Directory domain only has a single DC, the option password server has been set to the name of the DC, so that all validations are performed by that server. Of course, becoming a member server implies that the security parameter has also been set to ads.

**Winbind** could use cached credentials to permit a user to log in when the DC is offline, but we decided not to use this option. If we want to use it in the future, we can change the value of the `winbind offline logon` from `false` to `true`, or we can execute **authconfig-gtk** and select the Allow offline login check box (Figure 14-1).

Another interesting option is `winbind use default domain`. In the next section we'll see how to log in to Linux by using an Active Directory account by specifying account name and Active Dirrectory domain name, separated by an @ sign. If we had configured winbind to use a default domain we could log in by specifying only the username. However, in certain cases this can cause confusion with local users and thus it is not recommended.

The `idmap configuration *` option tells winbind how to map Windows SIDs and Linux user and group IDs. In our case, the Active Directory users will be assigned IDs in the 16777216–33554431 range.

Finally, **authconfig** also includes the `kerberos method` option, which controls how Kerberos tickets are verified; `secrets only` is the default value used and is fine for our purposes.

Apart from listing the users we can get information about a certain user.

```
[root@india ~]# wbinfo -i jose@ventanas.local
VENTANAS.LOCAL\jose:*:16777216:16777216::/home/VENTANAS.LOCAL/jose:/bin/
false
```

Alternatively, we can get their SID.

```
[root@india ~]# wbinfo -n jose@ventanas.local
S-1-5-21-3621464426-1719048758-4169316838-1105 SID_USER (1)
```

# Configuring NSS and PAM

We studied NSS briefly when talking about OpenLDAP (Chapter 3). When Linux needs to locate a user, it looks at the `/etc/nsswitch.conf` file to know where to search. In this file we could find the following lines:

```
passwd:     files sss
shadow:     files sss
group:      files sss
```

This means that Linux will try to locate a certain username in the /etc/passwd and /etc/shadow files, and if it cannot find it there it will query the sssd service. Analogously when Linux needs to locate a group it will look it up in the /etc/group file.

After installing **winbind** and executing **authconfig** in the previous section, the system automatically changed those three lines in the /etc/nsswitch.conf file, which now looks like this.

```
[root@india ~]# cat /etc/nsswitch.conf
.

.

.

passwd:     files sss winbind
shadow:     files sss winbind
group:      files sss winbind
```

Now, after searching for a user in the local files and querying the ssd service, the system will also query the winbind service. So, for instance, if we try to log in as the user jose@ventanas.local on our Linux server, the system will find that user by querying the winbind service.

However, this is not enough to be able to log in to the system. It is necessary to authenticate the user through the use of a password or other method, check whether that user is authorized to log in to the system, and so on. All these tasks are accomplished by Pluggable Authentication Modules (PAM). We already saw a brief description of PAM when we studied OpenLDAP and an in-depth explanation is beyond the scope of this book, so we explain it only briefly.

When installing winbind, a new PAM module (**pam_winbind.so**) was installed, and we can see it in the /usr/lib64/security folder, with the rest of the PAM modules.

After executing **authconfig-gtk** the PAM configuration files were modified to grant access to Active Directory users. The PAM configuration files are located in the /etc/pam.d folder. There, we'll see many files. When a user tries to log in locally or through SSH the correspondent file determines what PAM modules are used to either grant or deny access.

For example, when the user jose@ventanas.local tries to log in through SSH these are the PAM modules used during the process.

```
[root@india ~]# cat /etc/pam.d/sshd
#%PAM-1.0
auth        required    pam_sepermit.so
auth        substack    password-auth
auth        include     postlogin
# Used with polkit to reauthorize users in remote sessions
-auth       optional    pam_reauthorize.so prepare
account     required    pam_nologin.so
account     include     password-auth
password    include     password-auth
# pam_selinux.so close should be the first session rule
session     required    pam_selinux.so close
session     required    pam_loginuid.so
# pam_selinux.so open should only be followed by sessions to be executed in
the user context
session     required    pam_selinux.so open env_params
session     required    pam_namespace.so
session     optional    pam_keyinit.so force revoke
session     include     password-auth
session     include     postlogin
# Used with polkit to reauthorize users in remote sessions
-session    optional    pam_reauthorize.so prepare
```

At first sight we don't see any reference to the PAM module pam_winbind.so, but if we take a look at the included file password-auth, we'll see several lines referring to pam_winbind.so.

```
[root@india ~]# grep pam_winbind.so /etc/pam.d/password-auth
auth        sufficient     pam_winbind.so use_first_pass
account     [default=bad success=ok user_unknown=ignore] pam_winbind.so
password    sufficient     pam_winbind.so use_authtok
session     optional       pam_winbind.so
```

To check that the setup is correct, we can try to log in as an Active Directory user.

```
[root@india ~]# su - jose@ventanas.local
Creating home directory for VENTANAS.LOCAL\jose.
Last login: dom mar 26 20:35:05 CEST 2017 on pts/0
```

As we can see, we were able to log in successfully.

# Summary

In this chapter we briefly reviewed the use of local user authentication, as well as the possibility of synchronizing Samba and Linux passwords. We also studied the different passdb back ends that Samba can use. In addition, we saw seen an interesting method to integrate Linux computers in a Windows network, the use of Winbind. This service, part of the Samba suite, allows us to use Active Directory users on our Linux servers.

# CHAPTER 15

# Samba as a PDC and BDC

Until now we have configured Samba as a stand-alone server, but Samba can also be configured to work in a domain, similar to what happens with a Windows server. Samba can act as a domain controller (DC) either in an NT-like domain or in an Active Directory domain. It can also integrate as a member server in both environments. In this chapter and the next one we'll see the different roles a Samba server can assume in an NT-like domain. We'll cover the following concepts in this chapter:

- Understanding and configuring domain membership and trust relationships.

- Creating and maintaining a PDC with Samba 3 and Samba 4.

- Creating and maintaining a BDC with Samba 3 and Samba 4.

- Adding computers to an existing domain.

- Configuring logon scripts.

- Configuring roaming profiles.

- Configuring system policies.

We will also learn about the following terms and utilities: `smb.conf`, security mode, server role, domain logons, domain master, logon script, logon path, `NTConfig.pol`, net, profiles, add machine script, and profile acls.

## Windows Domains

A Windows domain is a group of network resources such as users and computers that are organized according to a centralized security database, as opposed to workgroups, in which every computer holds its own security database. The server, or servers, on which this database is located are called domain controllers.

© Antonio Vazquez 2019
A. Vazquez, *Practical LPIC-3 300*, https://doi.org/10.1007/978-1-4842-4473-9_15

Formerly, in Windows NT, there could be two types of DCs: PDC and BDCs, the difference being that the PDC could modify and update the information in the database, whereas the BDC had a read-only copy of that same database.

## Trust Relationships

Given two domains DomainA and DomainB, if a user from DomainA wants to access resources from DomainB, that user will need to validate again, providing valid credentials in DomainB. However, there is a way to avoid this by establishing a trust relationship. If DomainB trusts DomainA, then users in DomainA can access resources in DomainB without having to authenticate again. These trust relationships are unidirectional, so DomainA won't trust DomainB unless we specifically create another trust relationship.

## Creating a Samba PDC

Since Samba 3, it is possible to set up a Samba server as a PDC. For that purpose, we need to modify a series of parameters in the /etc/samba/smb.conf file, assuming we have already installed the Samba server binaries.

First, we assign a name to the domain by editing the workgroup parameter.

```
workgroup = MY_SAMBA_DOMAIN
```

There are a series of additional changes needed to succesfully set up a PDC. We have to set the security parameter to user.

```
security = user
```

In turn, the **passdb backend** must be set to either tdbsam or ldapsam; for simplicity, we'll set it to tdbsam so that no additional configuration is required.

```
passdb backend = tdbsam
```

In every Windows domain there should be a domain master browser. As the Samba server will be the first server in the domain, we configure it as a domain master browser.

```
domain master = yes
```

For the Windows workstations to log in to the domain, we need to provide a network logon service. We'll have to activate this characteristic in /etc/samba/smb.conf with the domain logon parameter, and create a NETLOGON share. In the Samba version installed in CentOS 7 there is already a full definition of the [netlogon] share that we only need to uncomment.

```
        domain logons = yes
.
.
.
# Uncomment the following and create the netlogon directory for Domain
Logons:
        [netlogon]
        comment = Network Logon Service
        path = /var/lib/samba/netlogon
        guest ok = yes
        writable = no
        share modes = no
```

The path for the [netlogon] share might not exist; in that case we'll need to create it.

```
[root@juliet ~]# mkdir /var/lib/samba/netlogon
```

Finally, we also need to add a series of parameters regarding a few necessary scripts.

```
        logon script = %u.bat
;       logon path = \\%L\Profiles\%u
        # use an empty path to disable profile support:
        logon path =

        add user script = /usr/sbin/useradd "%u" -n -g users
        add group script = /usr/sbin/groupadd "%g"
        add machine script = /usr/sbin/useradd -n -c "Workstation (%u)" -M
        -d /nohome -s /bin/false "%u"
        delete user script = /usr/sbin/userdel "%u"
        delete user from group script = /usr/sbin/userdel "%u" "%g"
        delete group script = /usr/sbin/groupdel "%g"
```

Once we're done editing the file, we save it and restart the Samba service. After that, we check that our Samba server is acting as a PDC.

```
[root@juliet ~]# testparm
.
.
.
Server role: ROLE_DOMAIN_PDC
```

Nevertheless, to have a fully operational DC we still need to perform a few additional steps. First, we add a root user to Samba.

```
[root@juliet ~]# smbpasswd -a root
New SMB password:
Retype new SMB password:
Added user root.
```

When creating domain groups in Samba we need to map those groups to a preexisting Linux group, so we'll start by creating the corresponding Linux groups.

```
[root@juliet ~]# groupadd WinUsers
[root@juliet ~]# groupadd WinAdmins
[root@juliet ~]# groupadd WinGuests
[root@juliet ~]# groupadd WinBackupOperators
[root@juliet ~]# groupadd WinRestoreOperators
```

Once the Linux groups are created, we can map the domain groups with the **net** command.

```
[root@juliet ~]# net groupmap add ntgroup="Domain Admins"
unixgroup=WinAdmins rid=512 type=d
Successfully added group Domain Admins to the mapping db as a domain group
[root@juliet ~]# net groupmap add ntgroup="Domain Users" unixgroup=WinUsers
rid=513 type=d
Successfully added group Domain Users to the mapping db as a domain group
[root@juliet ~]# net groupmap add ntgroup="Domain Guests"
unixgroup=WinGuests rid=514 type=d
Successfully added group Domain Guests to the mapping db as a domain group
```

```
[root@juliet ~]# net groupmap add ntgroup="Domain Backup Operators"
unixgroup=WinBackupOperators rid=515 type=d
Successfully added group Domain Backup Operators to the mapping db as a
domain group
[root@juliet ~]# net groupmap add ntgroup="Domain Restore Operators"
unixgroup=WinRestoreOperators rid=516 type=d
Successfully added group Domain Restore Operators to the mapping db as a
domain group
```

To check that everything is right, we can list the existing groups.

```
[root@juliet ~]# net groupmap list
Domain Admins (S-1-5-21-2904745568-710709298-978122733-512) -> WinAdmins
Domain Users (S-1-5-21-2904745568-710709298-978122733-513) -> WinUsers
Domain Guests (S-1-5-21-2904745568-710709298-978122733-514) -> WinGuests
Domain Backup Operators (S-1-5-21-2904745568-710709298-978122733-515) ->
WinBackupOperators
Domain Restore Operators (S-1-5-21-2904745568-710709298-978122733-516) ->
WinRestoreOperators
```

After completing the mappings, we also need to grant the appropriate permissions to the different groups.

```
[root@juliet ~]# net rpc rights grant 'MY_SAMBA_DOMAIN\Domain Admins'
SeMachineAccountPrivilege
Enter root's password:
Successfully granted rights.
[root@juliet ~]# net rpc rights grant 'MY_SAMBA_DOMAIN\Domain Admins'
SePrintOperatorPrivilege
Enter root's password:
Successfully granted rights.
[root@juliet ~]# net rpc rights grant 'MY_SAMBA_DOMAIN\Domain Admins'
SeAddUsersPrivilege
Enter root's password:
Successfully granted rights.
[root@juliet ~]# net rpc rights grant 'MY_SAMBA_DOMAIN\Domain Admins'
SeRemoteShutdownPrivilege
```

```
Enter root's password:
Successfully granted rights.
[root@juliet ~]# net rpc rights grant 'MY_SAMBA_DOMAIN\Domain Admins'
SeDiskOperatorPrivilege
Enter root's password:
Successfully granted rights.
[root@juliet ~]# net rpc rights grant 'MY_SAMBA_DOMAIN\Domain Admins'
SeTakeOwnershipPrivilege
Enter root's password:
Successfully granted rights.

[root@juliet ~]# net rpc rights grant 'MY_SAMBA_DOMAIN\Domain Backup
Operators' SeBackupPrivilege
Enter root's password:
Successfully granted rights.
[root@juliet ~]# net rpc rights grant 'MY_SAMBA_DOMAIN\Domain Restore
Operators' SeRestorePrivilege
Enter root's password:
Successfully granted rights.
```

If we need to see a short description of each right, we can get it with the **net rpc rights list** subcommand.

```
[root@juliet ~]# net rpc rights list -U root
Enter root's password:
        SeMachineAccountPrivilege   Add machines to domain
        SeTakeOwnershipPrivilege   Take ownership of files or other objects
              SeBackupPrivilege   Back up files and directories
             SeRestorePrivilege   Restore files and directories
       SeRemoteShutdownPrivilege   Force shutdown from a remote system
         SePrintOperatorPrivilege   Manage printers
             SeAddUsersPrivilege   Add users and groups to the domain
          SeDiskOperatorPrivilege   Manage disk shares
            SeSecurityPrivilege   System security
```

Now we'll create a few domain users: a domain admin, a domain backup operator, and a domain restore operator.

```
[root@juliet ~]# useradd antonio
[root@juliet ~]# usermod -g WinAdmins -G WinUsers antonio
[root@juliet ~]# smbpasswd -a antonio
New SMB password:
Retype new SMB password:
Added user antonio.
[root@juliet ~]# useradd john
[root@juliet ~]# usermod -g WinBackupOperators -G WinUsers john
[root@juliet ~]# smbpasswd -a john
New SMB password:
Retype new SMB password:
Added user john.
[root@juliet ~]# useradd jane
[root@juliet ~]# usermod -g WinRestoreOperators -G WinUsers jane
[root@juliet ~]# smbpasswd -a jane
New SMB password:
Retype new SMB password:
Added user jane.
```

In addition, if we are using SELinux we should modify a couple of booleans to make sure that Samba can work effectively as a DC.

```
[root@juliet ~]# setsebool -P samba_domain_controller on
[root@juliet ~]# setsebool -P samba_run_unconfined on
```

# Add Computers to an Existing Domain

Once we have a working Samba PDC we can start adding workstations to it, but we need to take a few things into account before proceeding.

When we try to join a Windows workstation to a new Windows (or Samba) NT domain, the client will try to find the NetBIOS name associated with the domain. We will study NetBIOS and WINS in greater depth in an upcoming chapter, but for now we'll point out that we'll have to configure the Samba server as a WINS server in the TCP/IP properties of the workstation (Figure 15-1).

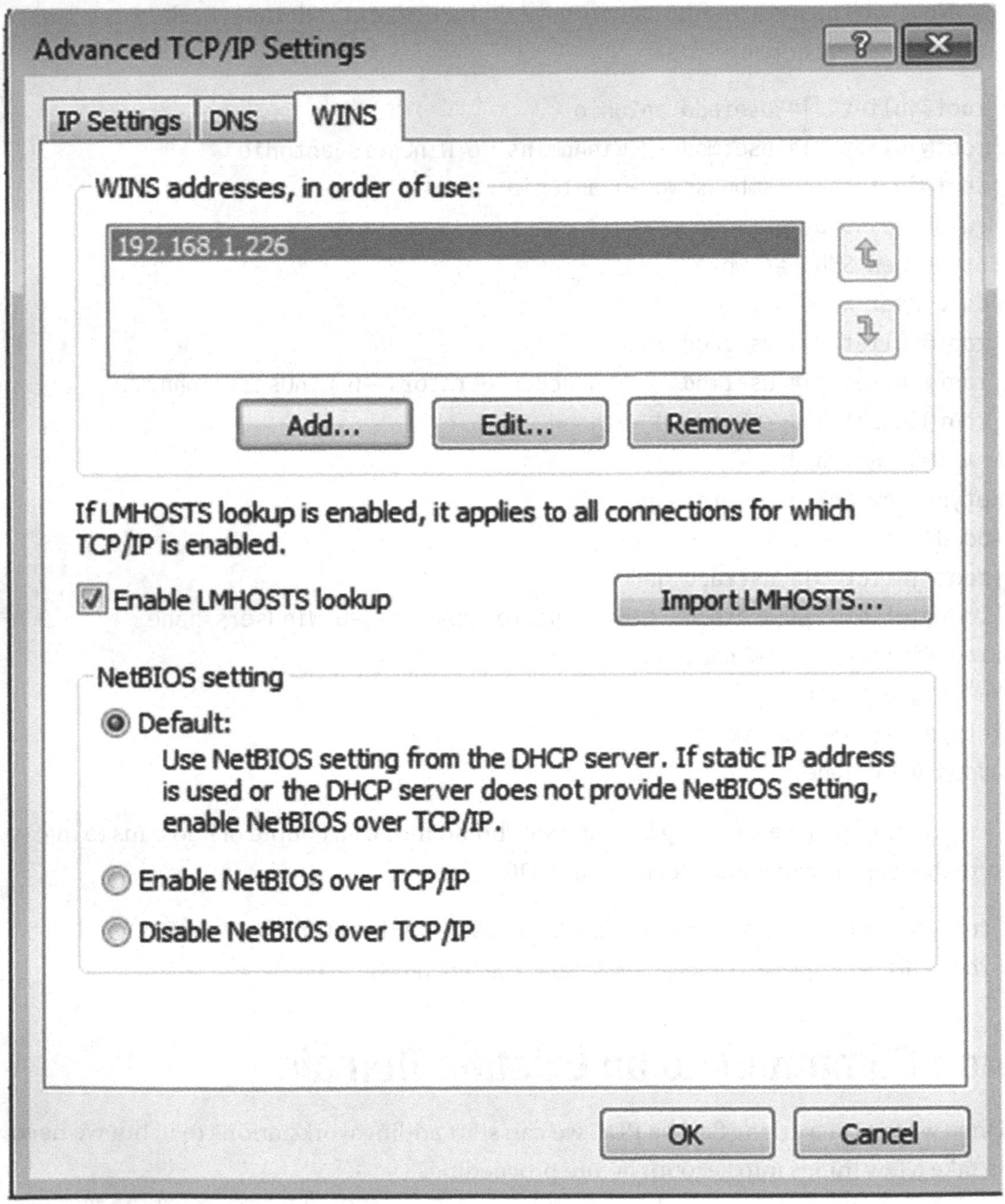


***Figure 15-1.*** *WINS server settings*

The Samba service in charge of answering any NetBIOS query is **nmb**, so if it's not started by default we will have to launch it.

```
[root@juliet ~]# systemctl enable nmb
Created symlink from /etc/systemd/system/multi-user.target.wants/nmb.
service to /usr/lib/systemd/system/nmb.service.
[root@juliet ~]# systemctl start nmb
```

In /etc/samba/smb.conf there are a few parameters that control the server behavior regarding the NetBIOS/WINS protocols. We'll include these two options in the configuration file.

```
.

.

.


        netbios name = JULIET
        wins support = yes

.

.

.
```

As the name implies, the netbios name parameter specifies the NetBIOS name of the server, and wins support = yes makes the Samba server work as a WINS server, too. For the changes to be effective, we need to restart the nmb service.

Apart from configuring the Samba server as a WINS server we need to open the corresponding ports in the firewall, so that when the workstations try to locate the PDC by the domain name, the WINS server answers with the right IP address.

```
[root@juliet ~]# firewall-cmd --add-port=137/udp
success
[root@juliet ~]# firewall-cmd --add-port=138/udp
success
[root@juliet ~]# firewall-cmd --add-port=139/udp
success
[root@juliet ~]# firewall-cmd --permanent --add-port=137/udp
success
```

```
[root@juliet ~]# firewall-cmd --permanent --add-port=138/udp
success
[root@juliet ~]# firewall-cmd --permanent --add-port=139/udp
success
```

To add a Windows workstation to a new domain in the System Properties dialog box (Figure 15-2), press Change. In the Computer Name/Domain Changes dialog box, enter the domain name and click OK (Figure 15-3). Then we authenticate as a user with administrative privileges (Figure 15-4) and wait for the process to finish.

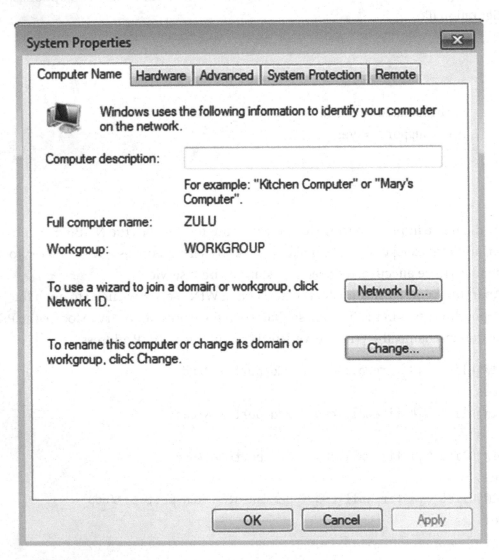

*Figure 15-2.* *System settings*

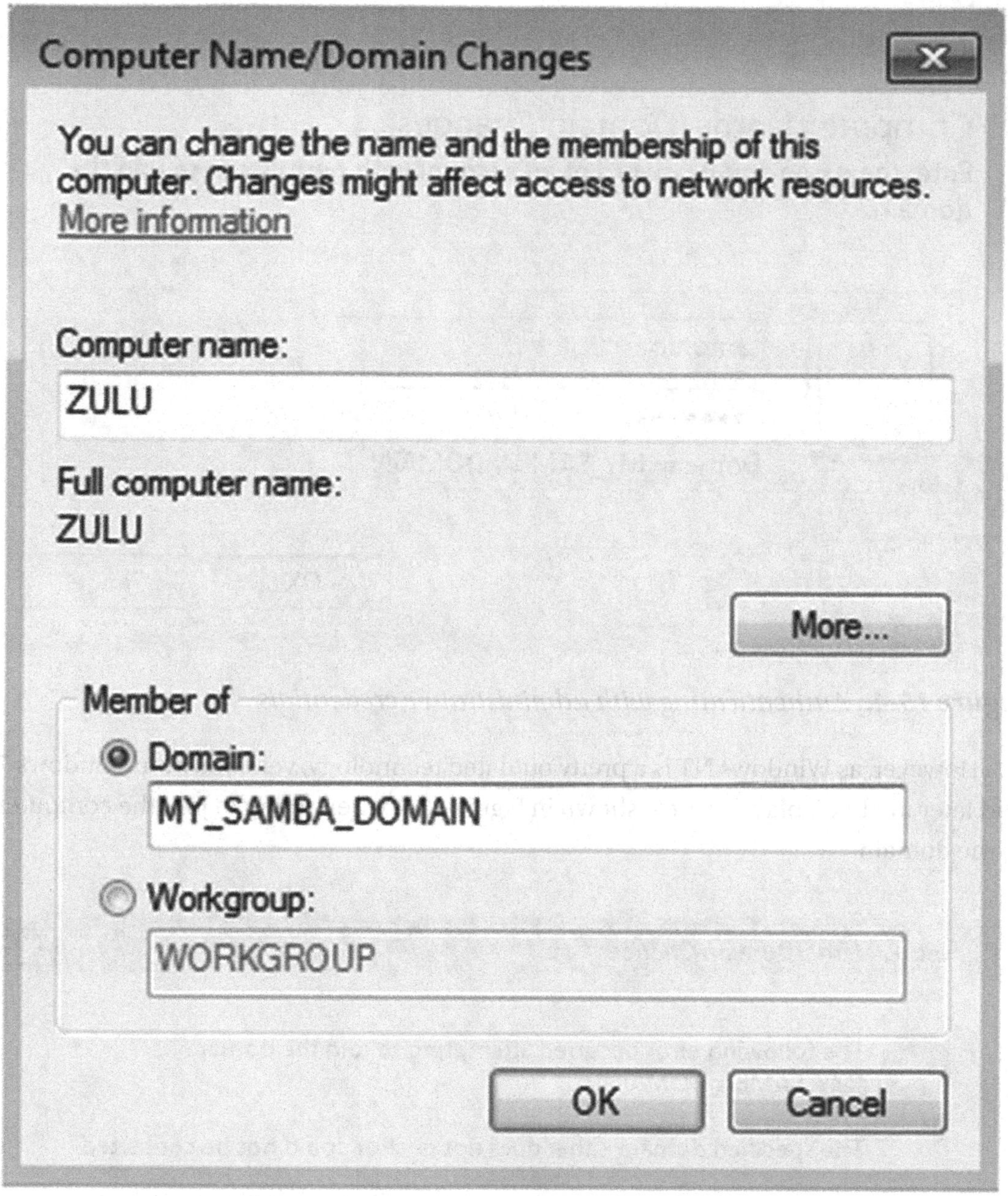


***Figure 15-3.*** *Adding the workstation to the domain*

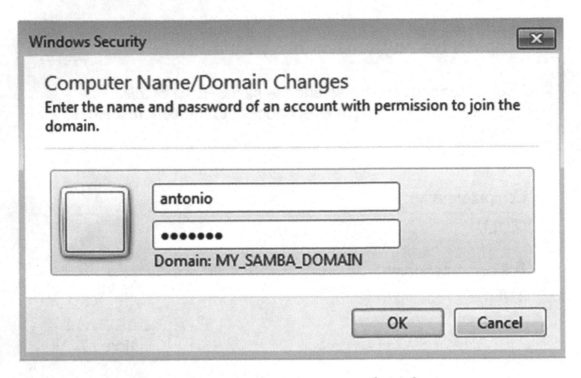

**Figure 15-4.** *Authenticating with administrative credentials*

However, as Windows NT is a pretty outdated technology, versions from Windows 7 and later might display the error shown in Figure 15-5 when trying to join the computer to the domain.

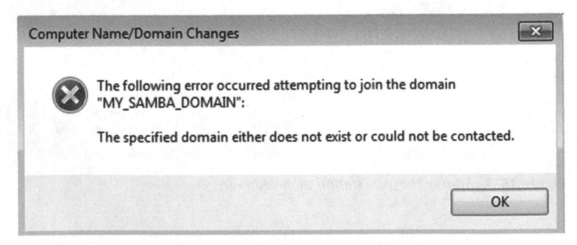

**Figure 15-5.** *Error when joining a Windows 7 to a Windows NT domain*

According to the Samba Wiki (https://wiki.samba.org/index.php/Required_ Settings_for_Samba_NT4_Domains), to enable the client to join a Samba NT 4 domain we need to edit the registry. We'll first create a file named fix_samba_7.reg with the following content:

```
Windows Registry Editor Version 5.00

[HKEY_LOCAL_MACHINE\System\CurrentControlSet\Services\LanManWorkstation\
Parameters]
"DomainCompatibilityMode"=dword:00000001
"DNSNameResolutionRequired"=dword:00000000
```

We log in using an account with administrative permissions and we import the content of the .reg file by double-clicking it. We accept the warning messages and restart the workstation so that the changes take effect and repeat the previous steps to add the computer to the Samba NT 4 domain. Now, though, we get another error (Figure 15-6).

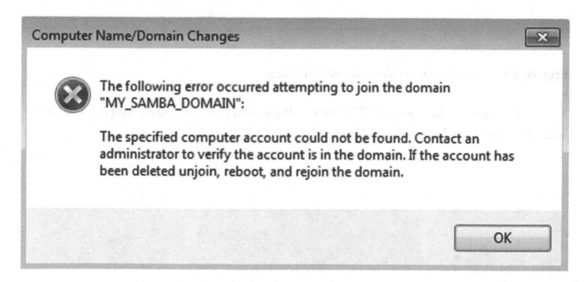

*Figure 15-6.*  *Unable to find the machine account*

We haven't explained it before, but when adding computers to a domain, every computer must have a machine account. Creating them in Samba is pretty easy. We basically need to add a user account with the NetBIOS name of the computer ending in $.

```
[root@juliet ~]# useradd -M -s /sbin/nologin ZULU$
[root@juliet ~]# smbpasswd -m -a ZULU$
Added user ZULU$.
```

Finally, we are informed that the Windows workstation is now part of our domain (Figure 15-7).

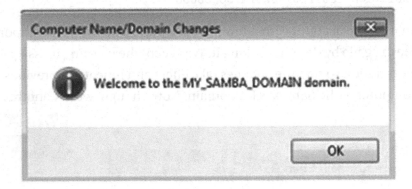

**Figure 15-7.** *Welcome to the domain message*

After restarting the client we'll be able to log in using any of the Samba NT 4 domain accounts we created previously (Figure 15-8).

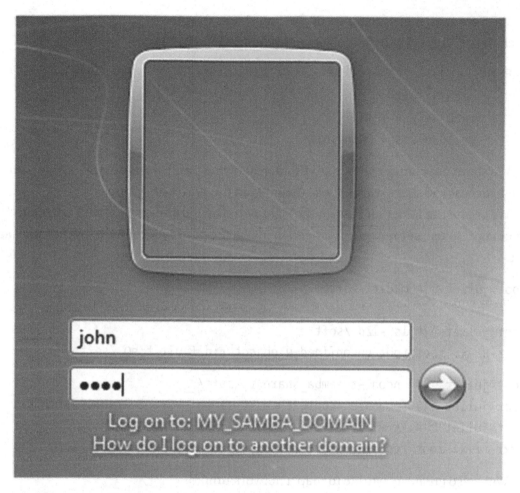

**Figure 15-8.** *Log on to our Samba domain*

# Configuring Logon Scripts

The admin can configure a logon script that will be executed whenever a user logs in. The script location will be set up in the `logon script` option and it will be a relative path to the `[netlogon]` share.

For example, let's assume that we want the user john to map a network unit to a certain network share. This share could be on any server of the domain. As currently we don't have any BDCs or member servers, we'll create the share in the PDC itself.

We have seen many examples of creating shares thus far, so we won't get into too much detail. The share definition should be something like this.

```
[Soft]
        path =/soft
        read only = Yes
        valid users = @WinUsers
```

We share the content of the /soft folder, allowing only read access. The only users able to access the share will be those included in the WinUsers group.

We create the folder and assign the right permissions and context with chcon and semanage. To use **semanage** we'll need to install the policycoreutils-python package first.

```
[root@juliet ~]# mkdir /soft


[root@juliet ~]# ls -lZd /soft
drwxr-xr-x. root root unconfined_u:object_r:default_t:s0 /soft

[root@juliet ~]# chcon -t samba_share_t /soft/
[root@juliet ~]# semanage fcontext -a -t samba_share_t "/soft(/.*)?"
[root@juliet ~]# ls -lZd /soft
drwxr-xr-x. root root unconfined_u:object_r:samba_share_t:s0 /soft
```

We'll also create a .bat file to map a network unit.

```
[root@juliet netlogon]# cat script.bat
net use y: \\juliet\Soft
```

Samba will execute any script file located in the path specified by two parameters. The path of the [netlogon] share will be the base path and the value set on the logon script option will be the relative path. In our case, we set the value of the logon script option to the name of the .bat file we'll use, script.bat.

```
[root@juliet ~]# cat /etc/samba/smb.conf
```
.
.
.

```
logon script = script.bat
.

.

.

[netlogon]
      comment = Network Logon Service
      path = /var/lib/samba/netlogon
.

.

.
```

We'll place the `.bat` file in the `/var/lib/samba/netlogon` folder. The next time a domain user logs in from a Windows workstation he or she will have a new network share mapped (Figure 15-9).

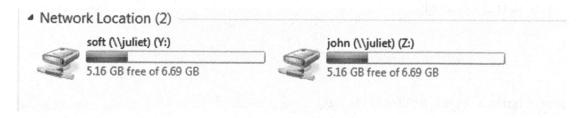

*Figure 15-9.*  *New network unit*

# Configuring Roaming Profiles

Users can customize their settings according to their preferences. All these customizations are stored in a series of files that are globally called the Windows profile. Usually when a user logs in from a workstation, the profile is stored locally in that same workstation. Any customizations made by the user will be saved in the profile so that they are available the next time the user logs in. However, if the user logs in from a different workstation, a new profile will be generated. Of course, that new profile won't have the customizations previously made by the user.

For users to have the same profile no matter which workstation they are logging in from, we can use roaming profiles. In this case the users' profiles are stored in a central repository instead of the local workstation.

To use roaming profiles in Samba we must set a value for the `logon path` option. Currently this option is idle, which means that roaming profiles are not used.

```
logon path =
```

We'll create a new network share to store the users' profiles, and we'll apply the right permissions and context to it.

```
[root@juliet ~]# mkdir /profiles
[root@juliet ~]# chmod o+t /profiles/
[root@juliet ~]# chown :WinUsers /profiles/
[root@juliet ~]# chmod g+w /profiles/
[root@juliet ~]# chcon -t samba_share_t /profiles/
[root@juliet ~]# semanage fcontext -a -t samba_share_t "/profiles(/.*)?"
```

In the configuration file we include the share definition and set the value of the `logon path` accordingly.

```
.
.
.
logon path = \\juliet\Profiles\%U
.
.
.
[Profiles]
        path =/profiles
        writable = Yes
        valid users = @WinUsers
.
.
.
```

From this moment on, when any user jane logs in, a new subfolder will be created in the [Profiles] share.

```
[root@juliet ~]# ls -l /profiles/
total 4
drwxrwx---+ 2 jane WinRestoreOperators 6 oct 16 09:13 jane.V2
```

The user, Jane in this case, can customize her desktop, change the background image, add direct links, and so on, and when she logs off, her profile will be stored on the server.

```
[root@juliet ~]# ls -l /profiles/jane.V2/
total 576
drwxrwxr-x+ 3 jane WinRestoreOperators     20 ago 17 08:55 AppData
drwxrwxr-x+ 2 jane WinRestoreOperators     43 ago 17 08:55 Contacts
drwxrwxr-x+ 2 jane WinRestoreOperators     75 ago 17 10:22 Desktop
drwxrwxr-x+ 2 jane WinRestoreOperators     24 ago 17 08:55 Documents
drwxrwxr-x+ 2 jane WinRestoreOperators     24 ago 17 08:55 Downloads
drwxrwxr-x+ 7 jane WinRestoreOperators   4096 ago 17 08:55 Favorites
drwxrwxr-x+ 2 jane WinRestoreOperators     85 ago 17 08:55 Links
drwxrwxr-x+ 2 jane WinRestoreOperators     24 ago 17 08:55 Music
-rwxrwx---+ 1 jane WinRestoreOperators 524288 ago 17 10:22 NTUSER.DAT
-rw-rwx---+ 1 jane WinRestoreOperators    250 oct 16 10:41 ntuser.ini
drwxrwxr-x+ 2 jane WinRestoreOperators     24 ago 17 08:55 Pictures
drwxrwxr-x+ 2 jane WinRestoreOperators     24 ago 17 08:55 Saved Games
drwxrwxr-x+ 2 jane WinRestoreOperators     85 ago 17 08:55 Searches
drwxrwxr-x+ 2 jane WinRestoreOperators     24 ago 17 08:55 Videos
```

# Implementing System Policies

The Windows NT Server editions used the program poledit.exe (Figure 15-10) to create policies that could be applied later to all of the users and computers in the domain, or to only a group of them. Unfortunately, Samba does not have a native tool to create system policies in an NT domain environment. We can create those policies in a Windows workstation running poledit.exe, though, and apply them later on the Samba server.

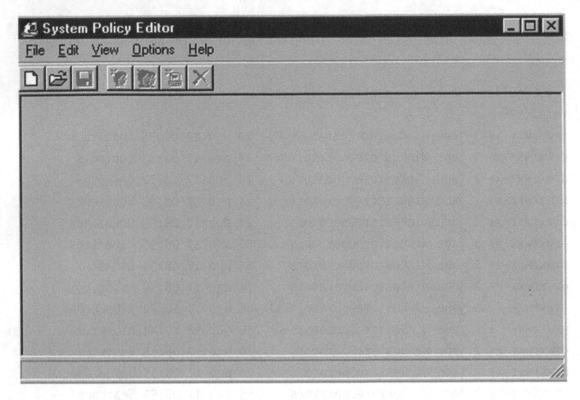

*Figure 15-10.*  *Policy Editor (poledit.exe)*

The Policy Editor allows us to customize settings about the computer, the user, or both (Figure 15-11). There are numerous options that can be adapted to our needs; for instance, we could edit the logon banner (Figure 15-12).

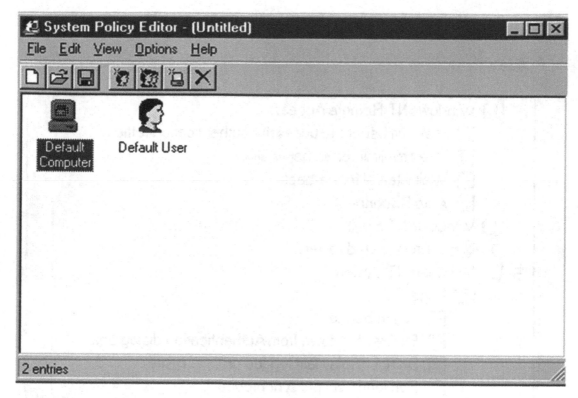

**Figure 15-11.**  *Computer and user settings*

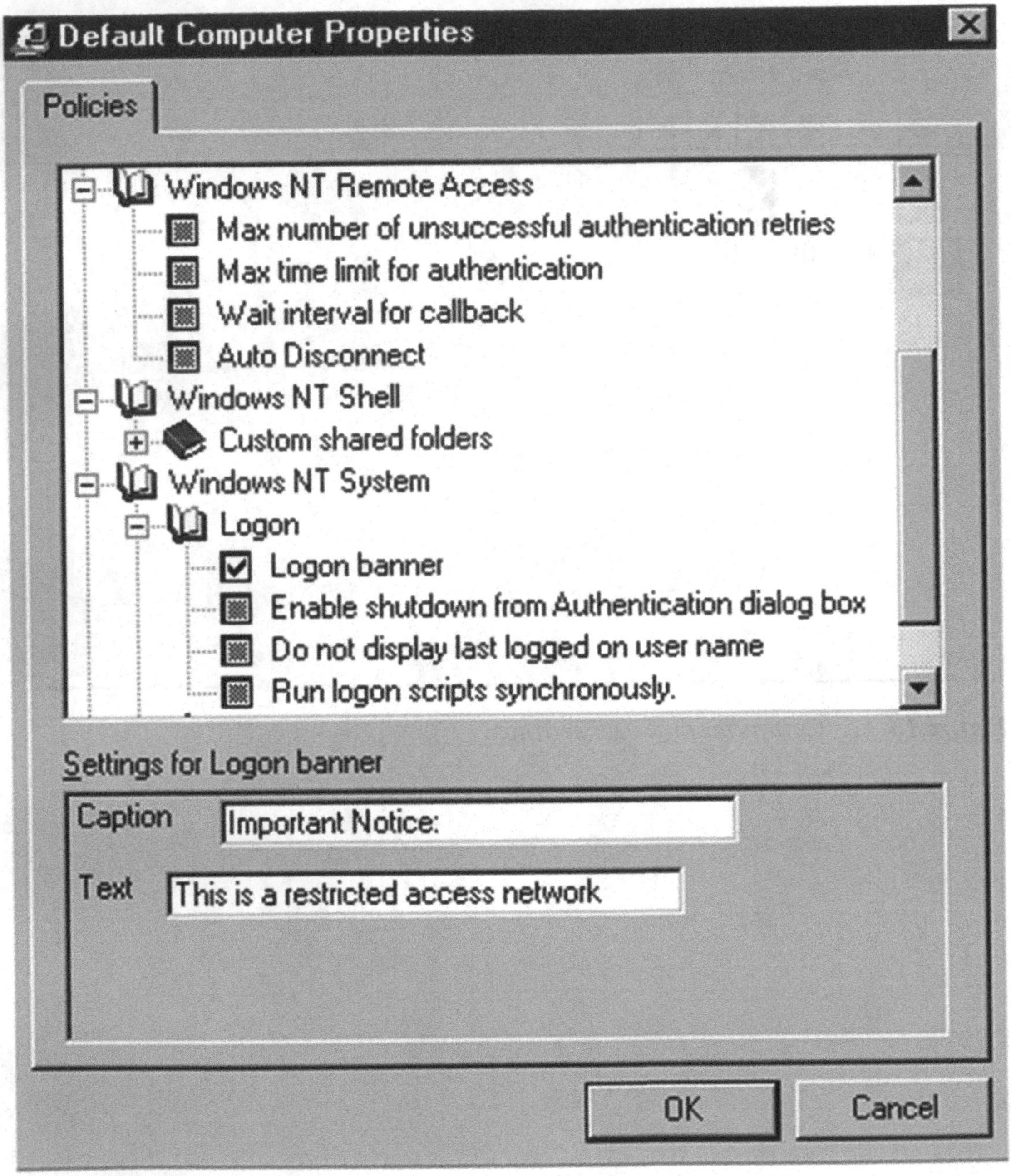


***Figure 15-12.*** *Customizing the settings*

Once we are done, we save the new policy with the name NTConfig.pol, then we copy that file to the [netlogon] share of the PDC and to the same location in any BDC we might have. We have to make sure that the file is readable by every user.

```
[root@juliet ~]# ls -lh /var/lib/samba/netlogon
total 12K
-rw-r--r--. 1 root root 8,0K abr 16 23:42 NTConfig.POL
-rwxr-xr-x. 1 root root   25 abr 15 18:34 script.bat
```

From now on, when any workstation in the domain is restarted, the new policy settings will be applied. Nevertheless, we must take into account that this will only work for workstations older than Windows 7, as the newer OSs use GPOs instead of NTConfig. pol files.

# Creating a Samba BDC

The way to install a Samba BDC doesn't differ much from the procedure we followed when installing a PDC. The users should be able to log in against the BDC, but the BDC should not be a master browser, as this function is performed by the PDC only. This means that we should set the following options in the /etc/samba/smb.conf file:

```
    domain master = no
    domain logons = yes
```

We also set the domain name.

```
    workgroup = MY_SAMBA_DOMAIN
```

Of course, the BDC will also need to have a [Netlogon] share, as the PDC. We therefore define this share in /etc/samba/smb.conf.

```
[netlogon]
        comment = Network Logon Service
        path = /var/lib/samba/netlogon
        guest ok = Yes
```

We need both servers, PDC and BDC, to have the same information about the accounts in the domain. With the back end currently in use in the PDC (tdbsam) this can be done simply by copying the `/var/lib/samba/private/passdb.tdb` file. If we also want the information related to group mappings or printers to be consistent, too, we'll have to copy the corresponding `.tdb` files, too, in this case `group_mapping.tdb` and `printers.tdb`. However, there are also `.tdb` files that should be unique to each server.

```
[root@kilo ~]# scp juliet.linuxaholics.com:/var/lib/samba/private/passdb.
tdb /var/lib/samba/private/passdb.tdb
```

```
[root@kilo ~]# pdbedit -L
root:0:root
john:4294967295:
ZULU$:4294967295:ZULU$
antonio:4294967295:
jane:4294967295:
```

To keep that information consistent in both PDC and BDC, we should create some sort of cron job to be executed periodically.

---

**Note**    This is not the optimal way to configure a BDC. The Samba official documentation says that copying `.tdb` files in this way is not recommended, as the files could be open and cause errors and inconsistencies when copied. Instead Samba recommends the use of ldapsam as a back end. This is obviously a better solution for a production environment, as the information is kept in an LDAP server and can be accessed by both the PDC and the BDC. However, for a lab environment like the one we are working with, copying the `.tdb` file is an acceptable solution as a proof of concept.

---

All DCs should store the same domain SID in the `/var/lib/samba/private/secrets.tdb` file. We can do this with the following **net** subcommand:

```
[root@kilo ~]# net rpc getsid
```

We might get this error, though:

```
Unable to find a suitable server for domain MY_SAMBA_DOMAIN
```

If that's the case, we'll edit the `smb.conf` file to configure our Samba server as a WINS client of the PDC server.

```
wins server = juliet.linuxaholics.com
```

Now the command should execute without any problems.

```
[root@kilo ~]# net rpc getsid
Storing SID S-1-5-21-852636792-403353388-521036446 for Domain MY_SAMBA_
DOMAIN in secrets.tdb
```

If we run **testparm** it will recognize the server as a BDC.

```
[root@kilo ~]# testparm
.

.

.

Server role: ROLE_DOMAIN_BDC
.

.

.

```

However, for our server to work as a BDC, we still need to modify a couple of SELinux booleans.

```
[root@kilo ~]# setsebool -P samba_domain_controller on
[root@kilo ~]# setsebool -P samba_run_unconfined on
```

To complete the configuration, we'll assign a NetBIOS name to our server and open the service in the firewall.

```
[root@kilo ~]# cat etc/samba/smb.conf
.

.

.


        netbios name = KILO_BDC
.

.

.

```

```
[root@kilo ~]# firewall-cmd --add-service=samba
success
[root@kilo ~]# firewall-cmd --permanent --add-service=samba
success
```

Now, if at some point the PDC is not available, the users will be able to log in to the domain by contacting the BDC instead (Figure 15-13).

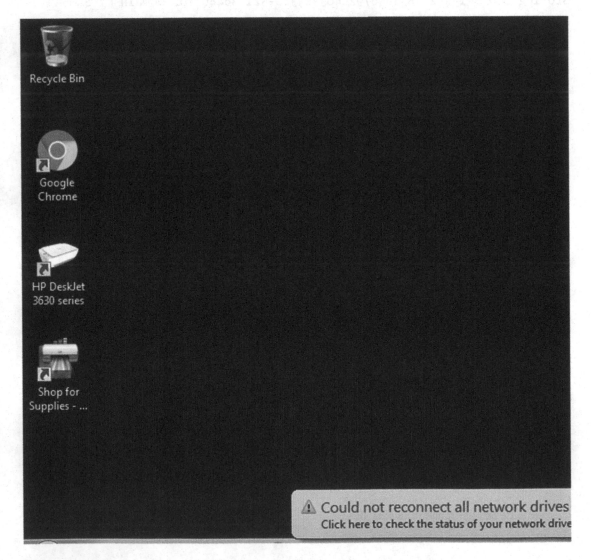

**Figure 15-13.** *Log in to the domain via the BDC server*

# Summary

In this chapter we have taken a leap forward, and configured a Samba domain, instead of a workgroup, for the first time. We reviewed some basic concepts regarding domains and we successfully set up our first DC. We added a workstation to the domain and we were able to automatically execute a script after the user logs in. We also saw a brief example of how to apply system policies. Finally, we added a BDC to provide some redundancy.

## CHAPTER 16

# Configuring Samba as a Domain Member Server in an Existing NT Domain

In Chapter 15 we configured a DC for the first time, creating our first domain. A Samba DC is in charge of authenticating the users of a domain. However, a Samba server can be part of a domain without acting as a DC. In this case, the server plays the role of a *member server*.

When a user tries to access the member server, this one delegates authentication to a DC. If the authentication is successful, the user will be able to access the the server resources, depending on the rights assigned to the user. In this chapter we'll cover the following concept:

- Joining Samba to an existing NT4 domain.

We will also explore following terms and utilities: `smb.conf`, server role, server security, and net command.

## Joining a Samba Server to an NT4 Domain

We already installed a PDC in the previous chapter; now we're about to add a member server to our newly created NT domain. We'll assume that the new member server has a fresh default Samba installation without any customizations before proceeding.

© Antonio Vazquez 2019

A. Vazquez, *Practical LPIC-3 300*, https://doi.org/10.1007/978-1-4842-4473-9_16

Any Samba server can be made a domain member. This has a series of advantages like having a centralized security, now the users will be able to authenticate against the domain Security Account Manager (SAM) database. This is also known as SSO.

As we saw in Chapter 15 when adding workstations to the domain, for a workstation (or server) to be a member of any given domain, a machine trust account is needed. This is a security measure used to prevent rogue servers or workstations from getting access to the domain. A Windows NT PDC stores all the machine trust accounts in the Windows registry; however, Samba uses a different approach.

Samba stores a domain security account in the passdb back end configured in the smb.conf file. In addition to this, a corresponding UNIX user account is required, which will be typically stored in /etc/passwd.

There are currently three ways to create machine trust accounts:

- Manual creation from the Linux command line.

- Using Windows NT Administrative Tools.

- As soon as a client joins a domain, a machine trust account is automatically created.

If we wanted to manually create a machine trust account for a workstation called foxtrot, this is what we'd do in the PDC.

```
[root@juliet ~]# useradd -g machines -d /dev/null -c "lima" -s /bin/false
lima$
useradd: group 'machines' does not exist
[root@juliet ~]# groupadd machines
[root@juliet ~]# useradd -g machines -d /dev/null -c "lima" -s /bin/false
lima$
useradd: warning: the home directory already exists.
Not copying any file from skel directory into it.
```

We make the account a member of the machines group (if we don't have a machines group, we have to create it), and we assign it a dummy home directory and no shell. We need to specify a name ending in $, otherwise it won't be recognized as a machine account.

After creating the Linux account, we create the associated Samba account with **smbpasswd**.

```
[root@juliet ~]# smbpasswd -a -m lima
Added user lima$.
```

Alternatively, we could use the newer **pdbedit** command.

```
[root@juliet ~]# pdbedit -a -m lima
Unix username:        lima$
NT username:
Account Flags:        [W          ]
User SID:             S-1-5-21-852636792-403353388-521036446-1005
Primary Group SID:    S-1-5-21-852636792-403353388-521036446-513
Full Name:            lima
Home Directory:       \\my_samba_pdc\lima_
HomeDir Drive:
Logon Script:         script.bat
Profile Path:         \\my_samba_pdc\Profiles\lima_
Domain:               MY_SAMBA_DOMAIN
Account desc:
Workstations:
Munged dial:
Logon time:           0
Logoff time:          mié, 06 feb 2036 10:06:39 EST
Kickoff time:         mié, 06 feb 2036 10:06:39 EST
Password last set:    mar, 16 oct 2018 17:45:30 EDT
Password can change:  mar, 16 oct 2018 17:45:30 EDT
Password must change: never
Last bad password   : 0
Bad password count  : 0
Logon hours         : FFFFFFFFFFFFFFFFFFFFFFFFFFFFFFFFFFFFFFFFFF
```

To join the new Samba server to an existing Samba NT domain we need to edit the /etc/samba/smb.conf file. We can do it manually, but it is much easier to use **winbind** instead. This component of the Samba suite was already studied in Chapter 14.

First of all, we need to install it.

```
[root@lima ~]# yum install samba-winbind
```

Then we launch **authconfig-gtk** (Figure 16-1).

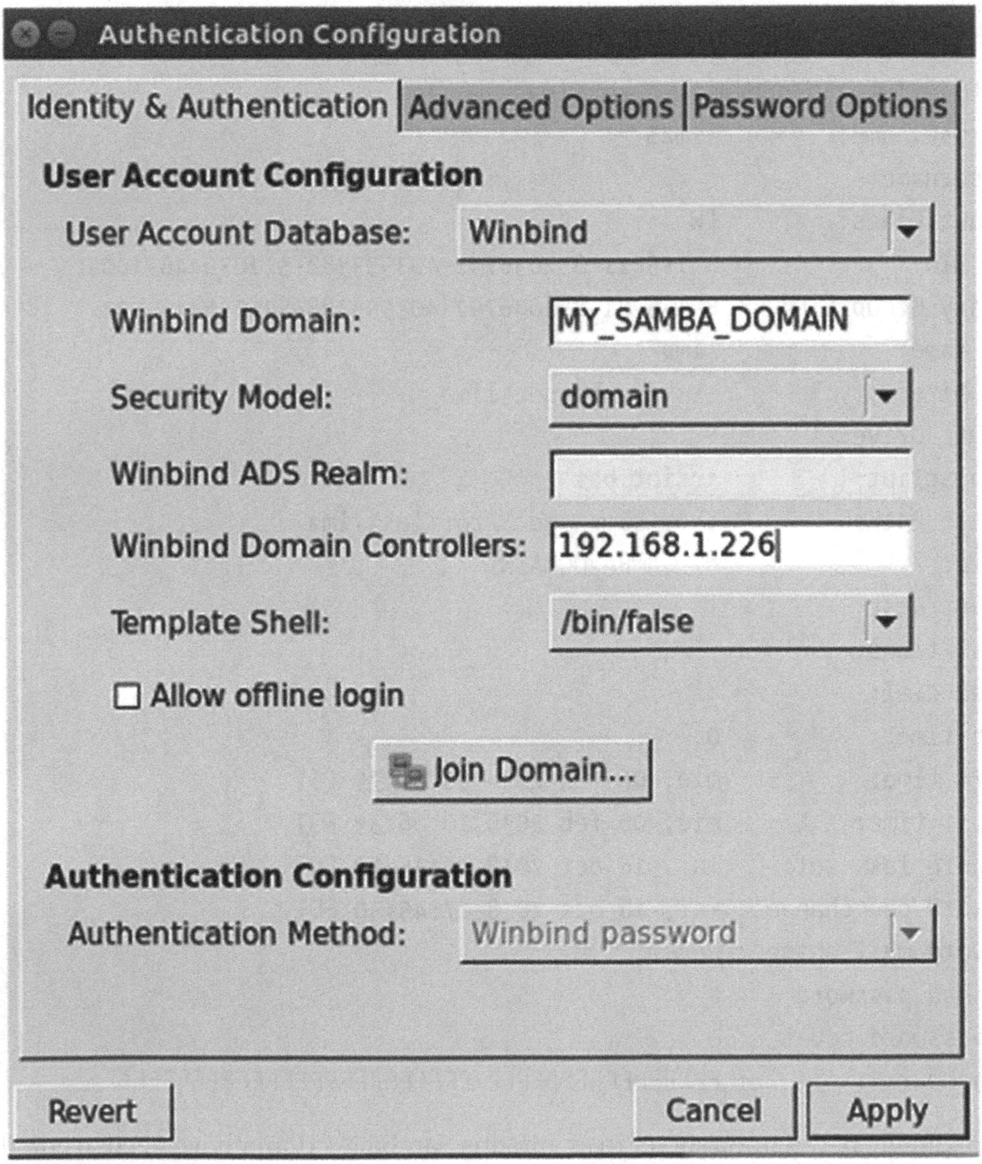

*Figure 16-1.* *Setting up Winbind*

We already saw the different parameters when we studied **winbind**. In this case as Security Model, we choose domain because we are working with a Samba NT domain. Click Join Domain button and enter the Samba root credentials we created when installing the PDC (Figure 16-2).

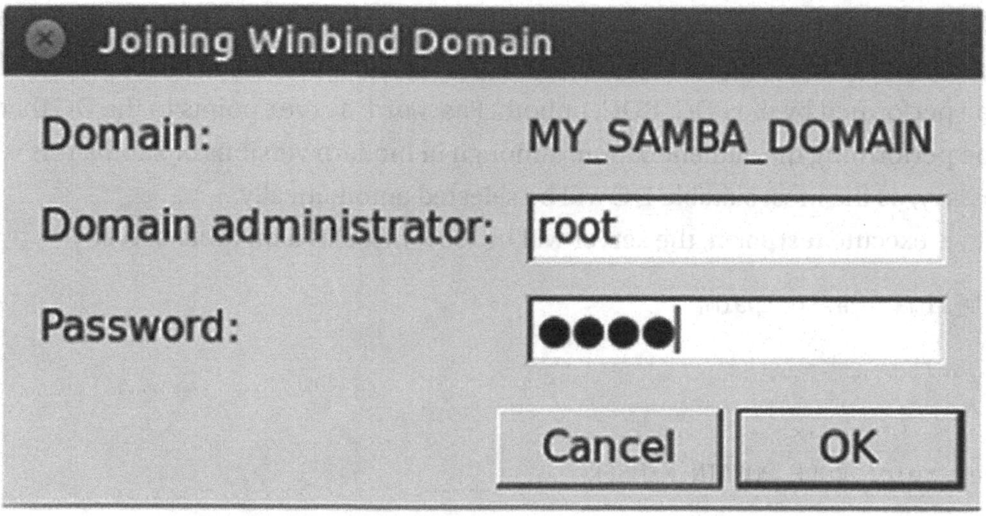

*Figure 16-2.* *Authenticating as root*

After a few seconds, our Samba server will have joined the domain. We apply the changes.

If we take a look at the /etc/samba/smb.conf file, we'll see the following lines added by winbind.

```
[global]
#--authconfig--start-line--

# Generated by authconfig on 2017/04/16 08:57:24
# DO NOT EDIT THIS SECTION (delimited by --start-line--/--end-line--)
# Any modification may be deleted or altered by authconfig in future

    workgroup = MY_SAMBA_DOMAIN
    password server = 192.168.1.226
    security = domain
    idmap config * : range = 16777216-33554431
    template shell = /bin/false
```

```
    kerberos method = secrets only
    winbind use default domain = false
    winbind offline logon = false
```

```
#--authconfig--end-line--
```

The name of the domain we are joining to is set in the `workgroup` option. `Security = domain` means that the server will be a member of the domain and the authentication will be performed by the PDC, BDC, or both. `Password server` points to the DC that will be performing the authentication, although in modern versions of Samba this is not necessary, as the most suitable DC will be selected automatically.

If we execute **testparm**, the server will be recognized as a member server.

```
[root@lima ~]# testparm
.

.

.
Server role: ROLE_DOMAIN_MEMBER
```

We can also execute **net** to check that the server successfully joined the domain.

```
[root@lima ~]# net rpc testjoin
Join to 'MY_SAMBA_DOMAIN' is OK
```

Another parameter we could change is the NetBIOS name.

```
    netbios name = LIMA_SERVER
```

Obviously, we will also need to allow access to the Samba services in the firewall.

```
[root@lima ~]# firewall-cmd --add-service=samba
success
[root@lima ~]# firewall-cmd --permanent --add-service=samba
success
```

Currently we haven't created any share in our server, but we could try to access any of the predefined shares from another computer by using a domain user. To do it, we can use the **smbclient** utility, included in the `samba-client` package.

```
[root@alpha ~]# smbclient //192.168.1.238/printers -U MY_SAMBA_DOMAIN\\jane
Enter MY_SAMBA_DOMAIN\jane's password:
Try "help" to get a list of possible commands.
smb: \>
```

As expected, we could access the shared resource authenticating with a domain user.

# Summary

In this brief chapter we completed what we had learned in Chapter 15 and installed a domain member server. We created the machine account and used Winbind, which made the necessary changes in the configuration file.

# CHAPTER 17

# Samba 4 as an AD Compatible Domain Controller

In Chapters 15 and 16, we configured a Samba domain for the first time, an NT-like Samba domain to be exact. Samba 3 and earlier versions could only implement NT-like domains, but not an Active Directory domain. All this changed when Samba 4 was released. Samba 4 can effectively work as an Active Directory DC, implementing all the necessary services. In this chapter we'll cover the following concepts:

- Setting up a new Active Directory domain using Samba.

- Adding a Samba DC to an existing Active Directory domain.

- Understanding and managing flexible single master operation (FSMO) roles.

- Verifying Active Directory replication.

- Configuring SYSVOL replication using rsync or robocopy.

- Configuring and testing Samba 4 as an Active Directory DC.

- Backing up and restoring an Active Directory DC.

- Understanding backup and recovery strategies for Active Directory DCs.

- Understanding the impact of virtualization on Active Directory DCs.

- Understanding and configuring Active Directory sites, including subnet assignments.

© Antonio Vazquez 2019
A. Vazquez, *Practical LPIC-3 300*, https://doi.org/10.1007/978-1-4842-4473-9_17

- Using smbclient to confirm Active Directory operation.

- Understanding how Samba integrates with Active Directory services: DNS, Kerberos, NTP, and LDAP.

We will also learn about following terms and utilities: `smb.conf`, server role, and **samba-tool** (with subcommands).

# Installing a Samba Active Directory Domain Controller

Creating an Active Directory DC implies that we need to have many different services (DNS, Kerberos, LDAP, etc.) working in perfect coordination. Luckily the Samba team has done a great job in easing this process, but it is not simple yet. We'll see now the detailed instructions to provision a Samba Active Directory DC.

## Preparing the System

According to the official Samba documentation, there are a few steps we must complete before installing an Active Directory domain controller in Samba.

We need a DNS domain for the Active Directory forest; in our case it will be `linuxaholics.com`. In addition, the server needs a static IP address.

We also have to make sure that the `/etc/resolv.conf` file is not updated by any process, so we'll stop and disable the NetworkManager service.

```
[root@mike ~]# systemctl stop NetworkManager
[root@mike ~]# systemctl disable NetworkManager
rm '/etc/systemd/system/multi-user.target.wants/NetworkManager.service'
rm '/etc/systemd/system/dbus-org.freedesktop.NetworkManager.service'
rm '/etc/systemd/system/dbus-org.freedesktop.nm-dispatcher.service'
```

We also have to make sure that none of the Samba services—that is **smbd**, **nmbd,** and **winbindd**—are enabled and running. If they are, we have to stop them now.

We check that the `/etc/hosts` file has the corresponding entries for the FQDN, as well as the short name of the future DC.

```
[root@mike ~]# cat /etc/hosts
127.0.0.1    localhost localhost.localdomain localhost4 localhost4.
             localdomain4
::1          localhost localhost.localdomain localhost6 localhost6.
             localdomain6
192.168.1.234       mike       mike.linuxaholics.com
```

# Getting and Installing the Software

So far, we have always installed the compiled versions of the software we needed
throughout this book. However, in this case we'll download the source code from
http://www.samba.org. To provision a new Samba Active Directory domain we'll need
to use commands that aren't included in the compiled versions included in the CentOS 7
repositories.

We uncompress and install the software the usual way.

```
[root@mike soft]# tar -xzvf samba-4.9.1.tar.gz
.
.
.
[root@mike soft]# cd samba-4.9.1
[root@mike samba-4.9.1]# ./configure
Checking for program gcc or cc          : not found
Checking for program icc                : not found
Checking for program ICL                : not found
Checking for program cc                 : not found
/root/soft/samba-4.9.1/lib/replace/../../buildtools/wafsamba/wscript:229:
error: could not configure a c compiler!
```

As we obviously need a compiler to compile the software, we install it and resume
the software installation.

```
[root@mike samba-4.9.1]# yum install -y gcc
.
.
.
```

```
[root@mike samba-4.9.1]# ./configure
•

•

•

Checking for program perl                                          : not found
/root/soft/samba-4.9.1/wscript:132: error: The program ['perl'] is required
```

This time the script complains because the Perl interpreter is not installed. We install it and launch the installation script again. We'll install the different software packages required as the script requests them. Another possibility to check if there are some missing packages would be to execute the configure script with the --enable-debug option and take a look at the config.log file generated.

```
[root@mike samba-4.9.1]# yum install -y perl
•

•

•

[root@mike samba-4.9.1]# ./configure
•

•

•

Checking for custom code                                          : Could not
find the python development headers
/root/soft/samba-4.9.1/wscript:140: error: the configuration failed (see
'/root/soft/samba-4.9.1/bin/config.log')
[root@mike samba-4.9.1]# yum install -y python-devel
•

•

•

[root@mike samba-4.9.1]# ./configure
•

•

•

Checking for lmdb >= 0.9.16 via header check                      : not found
Samba AD DC and --enable-selftest requires lmdb 0.9.16 or later
```

The package lmdb is not included in the standard repositories of CentOS, and we need to install the epel repository.

```
[root@mike samba-4.9.1]# yum install -y epel-release
.
.
.
[root@mike samba-4.9.1]# yum install -y lmdb-devel
.
.
.
[root@mike samba-4.9.1]# ./configure
.
.
.
Checking for jansson                                        : not found
/root/soft/samba-4.9.1/lib/audit_logging/wscript:24: error: Jansson
JSON support not found. Try installing libjansson-dev or jansson-devel.
Otherwise, use --without-json-audit to build without JSON support. JSON
support is required for the JSON formatted audit log feature and the AD DC
[root@mike samba-4.9.1]# yum install -y jansson-devel
.
.
.
[root@mike samba-4.9.1]# ./configure
.
.
.
Checking for gnutls >= 1.4.0 and broken versions            : not found
/root/soft/samba-4.9.1/source4/lib/tls/wscript:51: error: Building the AD
DC requires GnuTLS (eg libgnutls-dev, gnutls-devel) for ldaps:// support
and for the BackupKey protocol
```

```
[root@mike samba-4.9.1]# yum install gnutls-devel
.

.

.

[root@mike samba-4.9.1]# ./configure
.

.

.

Checking for gpgme_new                                     : not found
/root/soft/samba-4.9.1/source4/dsdb/samdb/ldb_modules/wscript:40: error:
GPGME support not found. Try installing libgpgme11-dev or gpgme-devel and
python-gpgme. Otherwise, use --without-gpgme to build without GPGME support
or --without-ad-dc to build without the Samba AD DC. GPGME support is
required for the GPG encrypted password sync feature
[root@mike samba-4.9.1]# yum install gpgme-devel
.

.

.

[root@mike samba-4.9.1]# ./configure
.

.

.

Checking for header archive.h                                     : no
/root/soft/samba-4.9.1/source3/wscript:225: error: libarchive support
not found. Try installing libarchive-dev or libarchive-devel. Otherwise,
use --without-libarchive to build without libarchive support. libarchive
support is required for the smbclient tar-file mode
[root@mike samba-4.9.1]# yum install libarchive-devel
.

.

.

[root@mike samba-4.9.1]# ./configure
.

.

.
```

```
Checking for acl_get_fd                                          : not found
/root/soft/samba-4.7.0/source3/wscript:507: error: ACL support not found.
Try installing libacl1-dev or libacl-devel.  Otherwise, use --without-acl-
support to build without ACL support. ACL support is required to change
permissions from Windows clients.
[root@mike samba-4.9.1]# yum install libacl-devel
.

.

.

[root@mike samba-4.9.1]# ./configure
.

.

.

Checking whether ldap_set_rebind_proc takes 3 arguments          : ok
/root/soft/samba-4.7.0/source3/wscript:703: error: LDAP support not found.
Try installing libldap2-dev or openldap-devel. Otherwise, use --without-
ldap to build without LDAP support. LDAP support is required for the
LDAP passdb backend, LDAP idmap backends and ADS. ADS support improves
communication with Active Directory domain controllers.
[root@mike samba-4.9.1]# yum install openldap-devel
.

.

.

[root@mike samba-4.9.1]# ./configure
/root/soft/samba-4.7.0/source3/wscript:951: error: PAM support is enabled
but prerequisite libraries or headers not found. Use --without-pam to
disable PAM support.
[root@mike samba-4.9.1]# yum install pam-devel
.

.

.

[root@mike samba-4.9.1]# ./configure
.

.

.

'configure' finished successfully (39.405s)
```

Now that the configuration script finally finished successfully we can compile the actual binaries with **make**.

```
[root@mike samba-4.7.0]# make
.
.
.
Waf: Leaving directory `/root/soft/samba-4.9.1/bin'
'build' finished successfully (9m29.705s)
[root@mike samba-4.9.1]# make install
.
.
.
Waf: Leaving directory `/root/soft/samba-4.9.1/bin'
'install' finished successfully (2m51.259s)
```

# Provisioning a Samba Active Directory

Provisioning consists of setting up all the infrastructure needed for a Samba Active Directory domain to run such as LDAP, Kerberos, and DNS servers. The easiest way to do it is by using the **samba-tool** command, which will now be located under /usr/local/ samba/bin/. With the **domain provision** subcommand we can provide the domain. There are many parameters available, and their descriptions can be viewed with --help. In this case we will use the --use-rfc2307 and --interactive parameters only. With the first one we make sure that POSIX attributes are stored in Active Directory, whereas the second one will ask the user for the necessary data to provision the domain, such as the domain name, the administrator password, and so on.

Throughout this chapter we'll work with just one Active Directory domain, but it is also possible to have several related domains with a shared administration. For instance, we could have a linuxaholics.com domain, a canada.linuxaholics.com domain, and a us.linuxaholics.com domain. In this case the three domains are part of the same *forest* and share a common administration.

The questions are self-explanatory, the only tricky one could be the administrator password, which requires compliance with some complex rules. In our exercise, we'll use the password Passw0rd, because if we choose an easier password we might get an error when provisioning the domain.

```
[root@mike ~]# /usr/local/samba/bin/samba-tool domain provision --use-
rfc2307 --interactive
Realm [LINUXAHOLICS.COM]:
Domain [LINUXAHOLICS]:
Server Role (dc, member, standalone) [dc]:
DNS backend (SAMBA_INTERNAL, BIND9_FLATFILE, BIND9_DLZ, NONE) [SAMBA_INTERNAL]:
DNS forwarder IP address (write 'none' to disable forwarding)
[192.168.1.1]: none
Administrator password:
Retype password:
Looking up IPv4 addresses
Looking up IPv6 addresses
No IPv6 address will be assigned
Setting up share.ldb
Setting up secrets.ldb
Setting up the registry
Setting up the privileges database
Setting up idmap db
Setting up SAM db
Setting up sam.ldb partitions and settings
Setting up sam.ldb rootDSE
Pre-loading the Samba 4 and AD schema
Adding DomainDN: DC=linuxaholics,DC=com
Adding configuration container
Setting up sam.ldb schema
Setting up sam.ldb configuration data
Setting up display specifiers
Modifying display specifiers and extended rights
Adding users container
Modifying users container
Adding computers container
Modifying computers container
Setting up sam.ldb data
Setting up well known security principals
Setting up sam.ldb users and groups
```

```
Setting up self join
Adding DNS accounts
Creating CN=MicrosoftDNS,CN=System,DC=linuxaholics,DC=com
Creating DomainDnsZones and ForestDnsZones partitions
Populating DomainDnsZones and ForestDnsZones partitions
Setting up sam.ldb rootDSE marking as synchronized
Fixing provision GUIDs
A Kerberos configuration suitable for Samba AD has been generated at /usr/
local/samba/private/krb5.conf
Merge the contents of this file with your system krb5.conf or replace it
with this one. Do not create a symlink!
Setting up fake yp server settings
Once the above files are installed, your Samba AD server will be ready to use
Server Role:          active directory domain controller
Hostname:             mike
NetBIOS Domain:       LINUXAHOLICS
DNS Domain:           linuxaholics.com
DOMAIN SID:           S-1-5-21-2526023654-1533215790-50031700
```

Now we can launch the Samba server. If you have followed the instructions in the previous section and compiled Samba, the binaries associated with each Samba service will be located at **/usr/local/samba/sbin**.

The appropriate way to work with the Samba services would be to create a target file associated with each one of the services so that they can be started every time the system restarts. For testing purposes, however, we can launch Samba manually.

```
[root@mike ~]# /usr/local/samba/sbin/samba
```

After launching the Samba service we can check that everything is working as expected. If we execute **testparm** we'll see that our server is recognized as an Active Directory DC.

```
[root@mike samba-4.7.11]# /usr/local/samba/bin/testparm
Load smb config files from /usr/local/samba/etc/smb.conf
.
.
.
Server role: ROLE_ACTIVE_DIRECTORY_DC
```

# Configuring NTP

If we want our Active Directory to work properly, synchronizing the time is mandatory. We install the NTP service with **yum** and we start and enable the service.

```
[root@mike ~]# yum -y install ntp
[root@mike ~]# systemctl start ntpd
[root@mike ~]# systemctl enable ntpd
Created symlink from /etc/systemd/system/multi-user.target.wants/ntpd.
service to /usr/lib/systemd/system/ntpd.service.
```

# Configuring Kerberos

When provisioning the domain, a Kerberos configuration file was created with the following content:

```
[root@mike ~]# cat /usr/local/samba/private/krb5.conf
[libdefaults]
     default_realm = LINUXAHOLICS.COM
     dns_lookup_realm = false
     dns_lookup_kdc = true
```

The way to install it is simply by copying it to the appropriate folder.

```
[root@mike ~]# cp /usr/local/samba/private/krb5.conf /etc/
```

# Checking the DNS

In an upcoming chapter we will see how Active Directory Name Resolution works in detail; however, we can perform an easy test here to check that the internal DNS server is working as expected.

```
[root@mike ~]# dig @localhost +noall +answer -t SRV _ldap._tcp.
linuxaholics.com
_ldap._tcp.linuxaholics.com. 900 IN    SRV    0 100 389 mike.linuxaholics.
com.
[root@mike ~]# dig @localhost +noall +answer -t SRV _kerberos._udp.
linuxaholics.com
```

```
_kerberos._udp.linuxaholics.com. 900 IN SRV   0 100 88 mike.linuxaholics.com.
[root@mike ~]# dig @localhost +noall +answer -t A mike.linuxaholics.com
mike.linuxaholics.com.        900 IN      A      192.168.1.234
```

For the clients to properly resolve the names, we'll have to edit the DNS settings accordingly.

## Checking Authentication with smbclient

To verify that the authentication is working correctly we can execute the following command and type the password we specified when provisioning the domain.

```
[root@mike ~]# smbclient //localhost/netlogon -U Administrator -c 'ls'
Enter SAMBA\Administrator's password:
  .                               D        0  Sun Oct 14 01:59:55 2018
  ..                              D        0  Sun Oct 14 01:59:59 2018

        7022592 blocks of size 1024. 4780864 blocks available
```

## Checking Kerberos

To check whether Kerberos is working as expected or not we can use the **kinit** command. This command is included in the krb5-workstation package.

```
[root@mike ~]# kinit administrator@linuxaholics.com
```

If we get this error message:

```
kinit: Cannot resolve servers for KDC in realm "linuxaholics.com" while
getting initial credentials
```

we might need to check our DNS settings, making sure that the Samba DNS server is queried first. This could be a valid example:

```
[root@mike ~]# cat /etc/resolv.conf
domain linuxaholics.com
nameserver 192.168.1.234
```

We have to pay close attention to the use of capital or lowercase letters, otherwise we might get the following error:

```
[root@mike ~]# kinit administrator@linuxaholics.com
Password for administrator@linuxaholics.com:
kinit: KDC reply did not match expectations while getting initial
credentials
```

In this case we typed the domain name in lowercase letters, but in the Kerberos configuration file it appears in capital letters. To get the expected result we have to type the domain in capital letters when invoking the **kinit** command.

```
[root@mike ~]# kinit administrator@LINUXAHOLICS.COM
Password for administrator@LINUXAHOLICS.COM:
Warning: Your password will expire in 27 days on dom 25 nov 2018 00:59:59 EST
```

Now we can check the Kerberos tickets.

```
[root@mike ~]# klist
Ticket cache: FILE:/tmp/krb5cc_0
Default principal: administrator@LINUXAHOLICS.COM

Valid starting     Expires            Service principal
29/10/18 00:31:04  29/10/18 10:31:04  krbtgt/LINUXAHOLICS.COM@LINUXAHOLICS.COM
        renew until 30/10/18 00:31:01
```

# Opening the Ports in the Firewall

So far we have checked that every needed service is actually working in the server, but for the clients to be able to access these services we need to open the corresponding ports in the firewall. By default the clients use DNS to locate the DC and the available service, so we need to allow incoming connections to UDP port 53 in our server.

```
[root@november ~]# firewall-cmd --add-service={dns,ldap,ldaps,kerberos}
success
[root@november ~]# firewall-cmd - permanent --add-service={dns,ldap,ldaps,
kerberos}
```

```
Success
[root@november ~]# firewall-cmd --add-port={389/udp,135/tcp,135/udp,138/
udp,138/tcp,137/tcp,137/udp,139/udp,139/tcp,445/tcp,445/udp,3268/udp,3268/
tcp,3269/tcp,3269/udp,49152/tcp}
Success
[root@november ~]# firewall-cmd --permanent --add-port={389/udp,135/
tcp,135/udp,138/udp,138/tcp,137/tcp,137/udp,139/udp,139/tcp,445/tcp,445/
udp,3268/udp,3268/tcp,3269/tcp,3269/udp,49152/tcp}
Success
```

# Managing the Domain with samba-tool

We have already provisioned the new Samba Active Directory domain with **samba-tool**. In addition, though, there are many more things that we can do with this versatile tool. For instance, we can list the current users.

```
[root@mike ~]# /usr/local/samba/bin/samba-tool user list
Administrator
Guest
krbtgt
```

We can also create an additional user.

```
[root@mike ~]# /usr/local/samba/bin/samba-tool user create Antonio P@ssw0rd
Antonio --given-name=Antonio --surname=Vazquez -UAdministrator%P@ssw0rd
User 'Antonio' created successfully
```

```
[root@mike ~]# /usr/local/samba/bin/samba-tool user list
Antonio
Administrator
Guest
krbtgt
```

We can list the existing groups in the domain.

```
[root@mike ~]# /usr/local/samba/bin/samba-tool group list
Replicator
```

Windows Authorization Access Group
Domain Guests
Users
Cryptographic Operators
DnsUpdateProxy
Account Operators
RAS and IAS Servers
Denied RODC Password Replication Group
Event Log Readers
Backup Operators
Remote Desktop Users
Performance Monitor Users
Certificate Service DCOM Access
IIS_IUSRS
Pre-Windows 2000 Compatible Access
Performance Log Users
Server Operators
Network Configuration Operators
Terminal Server License Servers
Print Operators
Group Policy Creator Owners
Domain Controllers
Guests
Read-only Domain Controllers
Domain Admins
Enterprise Read-only Domain Controllers
DnsAdmins
Allowed RODC Password Replication Group
Cert Publishers
Distributed COM Users
Schema Admins
Enterprise Admins
Domain Users
Administrators
Domain Computers

Incoming Forest Trust Builders

We can also add the user we just created to the Domain Admins group.

```
[root@mike ~]# /usr/local/samba/bin/samba-tool group addmembers "Domain
Admins" antonio
Added members to group Domain Admins
```

We can see what users are included in a given group.

```
[root@mike ~]# /usr/local/samba/bin/samba-tool group listmembers "Domain
Admins"
Antonio
Administrator
```

**Samba-tool** is also a useful tool for diagnostic purposes, as well as for getting some generic information. We can check that the internal database is okay.

```
[root@mike ~]# /usr/local/samba/bin/samba-tool dbcheck
Checking 271 objects
Checked 271 objects (0 errors)
```

We can also get some information about the domain.

```
[root@mike ~]# /usr/local/samba/bin/samba-tool domain info 192.168.1.234
Forest           : linuxaholics.com
Domain           : linuxaholics.com
Netbios domain   : LINUXAHOLICS
DC name          : mike.linuxaholics.com
DC netbios name  : MIKE
Server site      : Default-First-Site-Name
Client site      : Default-First-Site-Name
```

It is possible to query the internal DNS, too.

```
[root@mike ~]# /usr/local/samba/bin/samba-tool dns query localhost
linuxaholics.com mike ALL -U Administrator%Passw0rd
  Name=, Records=1, Children=0
    A: 192.168.1.234 (flags=f0, serial=1, ttl=900)
```

We can also list the GPOs in the domain.

```
[root@mike ~]# /usr/local/samba/bin/samba-tool gpo listall
GPO          : {6AC1786C-016F-11D2-945F-00C04FB984F9}
display name : Default Domain Controllers Policy
path         : \\linuxaholics.com\sysvol\linuxaholics.com\Policies\
               {6AC1786C-016F-11D2-945F-00C04FB984F9}
dn           : CN={6AC1786C-016F-11D2-945F-00C04FB984F9},CN=Policies,
               CN=System,DC=linuxaholics,DC=com
version      : 0
flags        : NONE

GPO          : {31B2F340-016D-11D2-945F-00C04FB984F9}
display name : Default Domain Policy
path         : \\linuxaholics.com\sysvol\linuxaholics.com\Policies\
               {31B2F340-016D-11D2-945F-00C04FB984F9}
dn           : CN={31B2F340-016D-11D2-945F-00C04FB984F9},CN=Policies,
               CN=System,DC=linuxaholics,DC=com
version      : 0
flags        : NONE
```

# Adding a Windows Workstation to the Active Directory Domain

Now that we have a working Active Directory, we can start adding workstations to it. As we mentioned earlier, the client queries the DNS by default to locate the required resources. For that reason, we must edit the DNS settings of the Windows workstation properly, making sure that the Samba internal DNS server we just created is queried first (Figure 17-1).

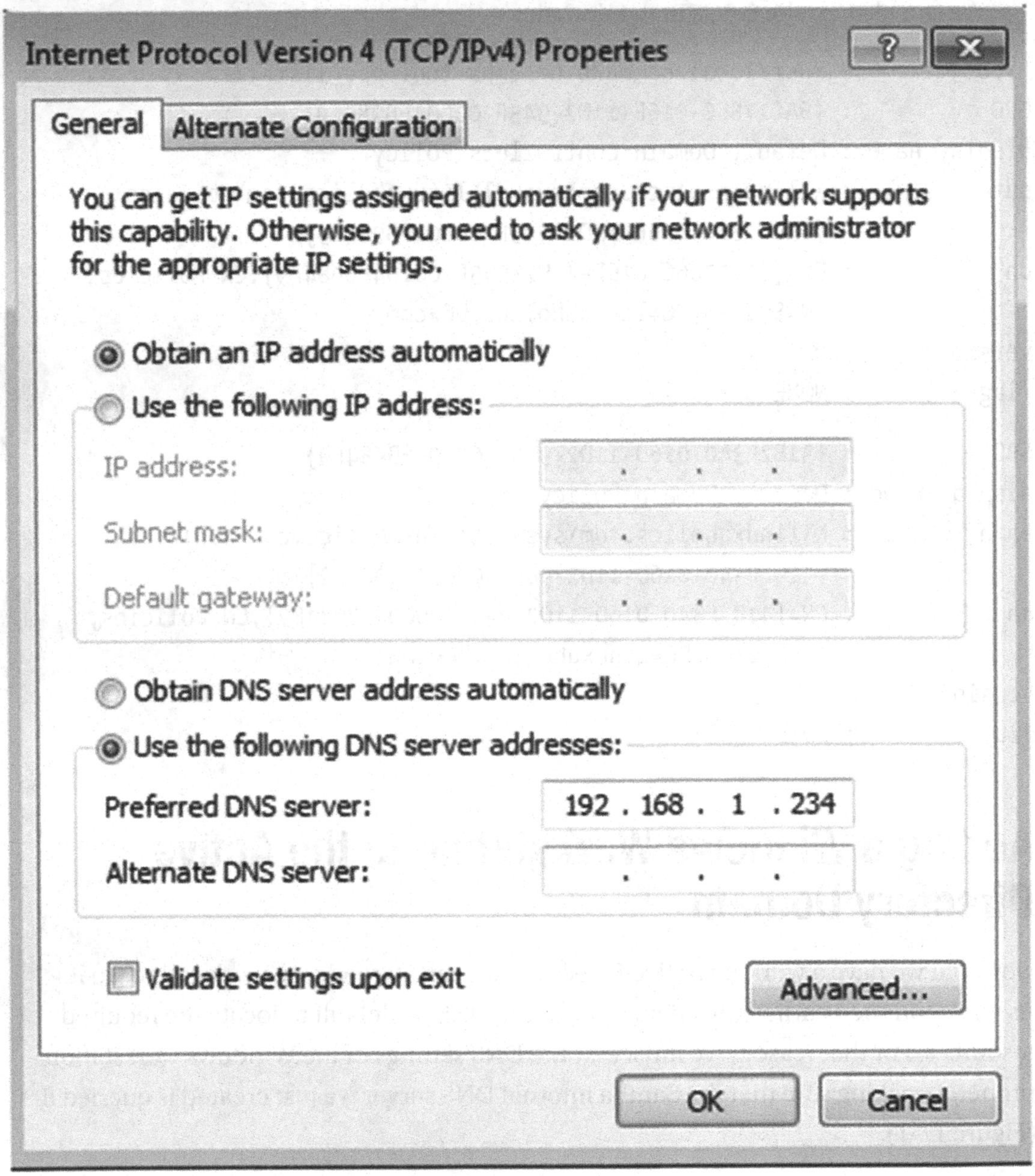


*Figure 17-1. DNS settings*

Next, we proceed to change the domain in the computer properties (Figure 17-2).

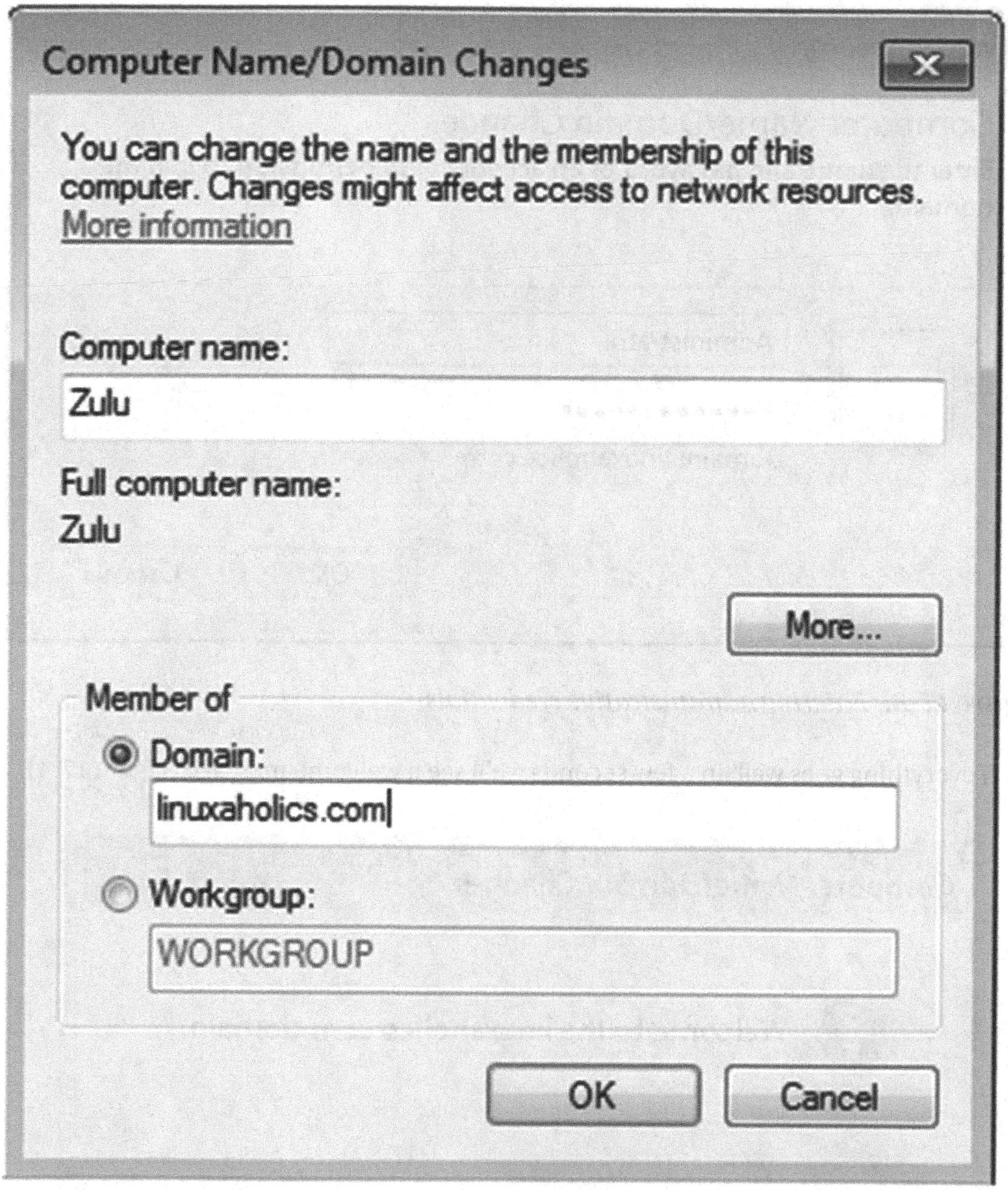

*Figure 17-2.* *Adding the workstation to a Samba Active Directory domain*

We'll need to provide administrative credentials to proceed (Figure 17-3).

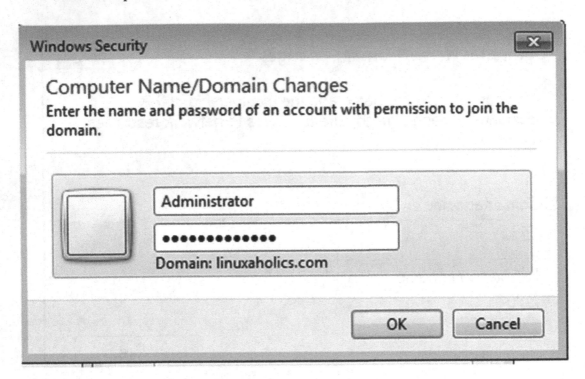

***Figure 17-3.*** *Entering administrative credentials*

If everything goes well, in a few seconds we'll see a welcome message (Figure 17-4).

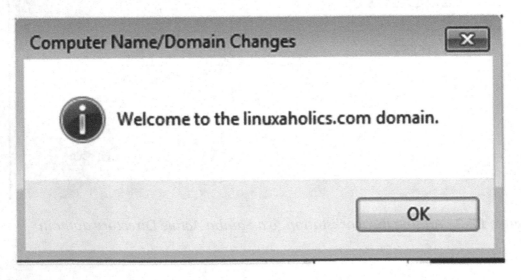

***Figure 17-4.*** *Welcome to the domain*

To complete the join, we'll need to restart the computer. After that we can log into the workstation as a domain user (Figure 17-5).

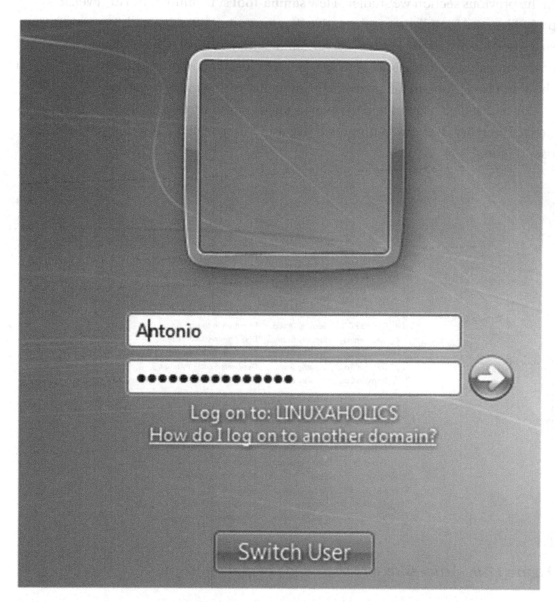

*Figure 17-5.* *Log in as a domain user*

# Installing Remote Server Administration Tools

In the previous section we studied a few **samba-tool** subcommands. However, it is probably more friendly to use the native Windows administrative tools instead. To do so we need to install the Remote Server Administration Tools (RSAT). These tools can be downloaded from the Microsoft web site. The installation procedure is very easy and shouldn't be a problem for anyone who is familiar with Windows systems.

Once installed, we can find these tools under Administrative tools. If we navigate to Active Directory Users and Computers (Figure 17-6) we can, for instance, create a new user (Figure 17-7).

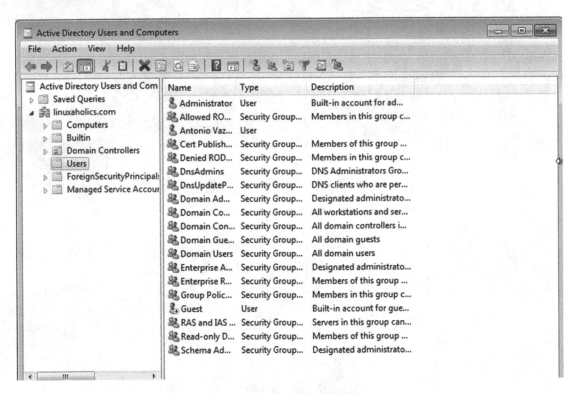

*Figure 17-6.* *Active Directory Users and Computers*

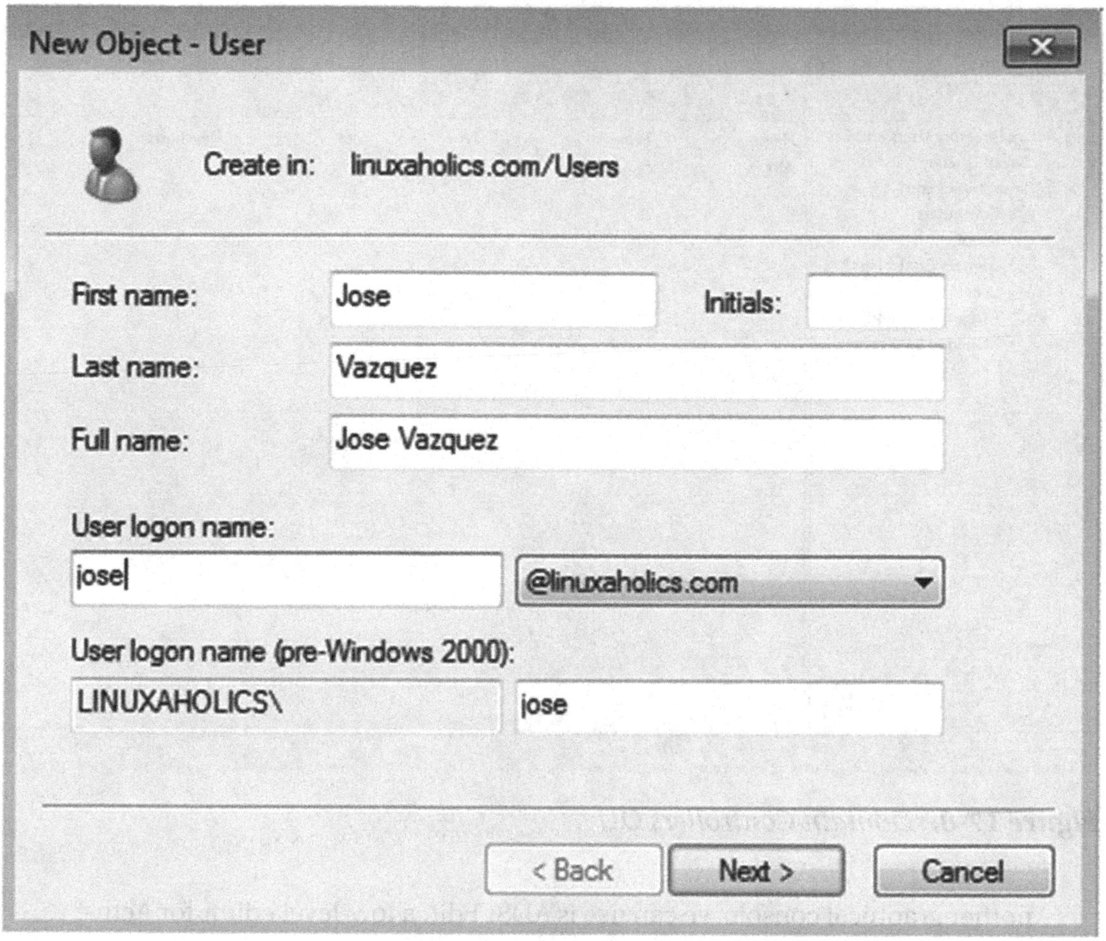

**Figure 17-7.** *Creating a new user*

We can also see the existing DCs in the network, under the Domain Controllers OU (Figure 17-8).

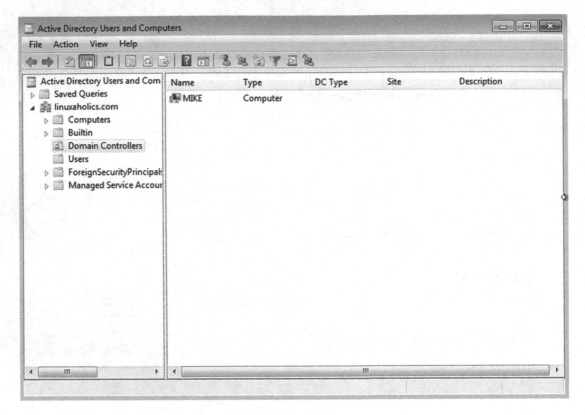

*Figure 17-8.*  *Domain Controllers OU*

Another graphical console we can use is ADSI Edit, a low-level editor for Active Directory. It is included in the Administrative tools we just installed. After executing, we connect to our DC and we'll see the different objects that are included in our domain (Figure 17-9).

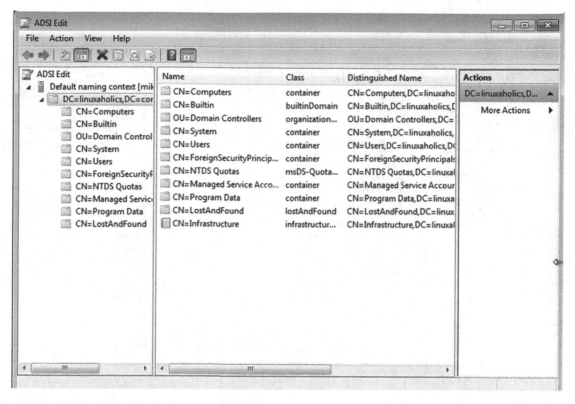

***Figure 17-9.*** *ADSI Edit*

If we select the entry CN=Users and then select Antonio Vazquez and right-click
Properties, we'll see the list of LDAP attributes associated with this object (Figure 17-10).

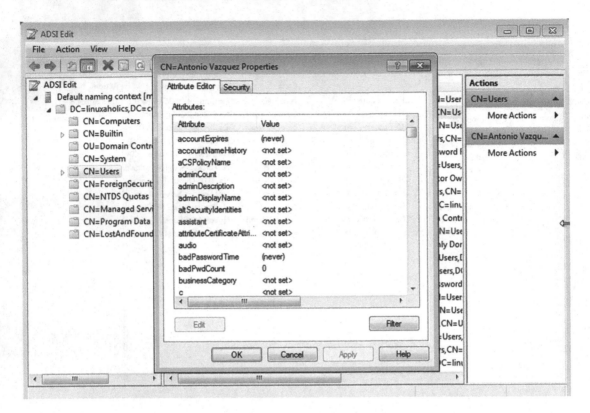

***Figure 17-10.*** *Listing the attributes*

By double-clicking any of the attributes on the list we can edit its value (Figure 17-11).

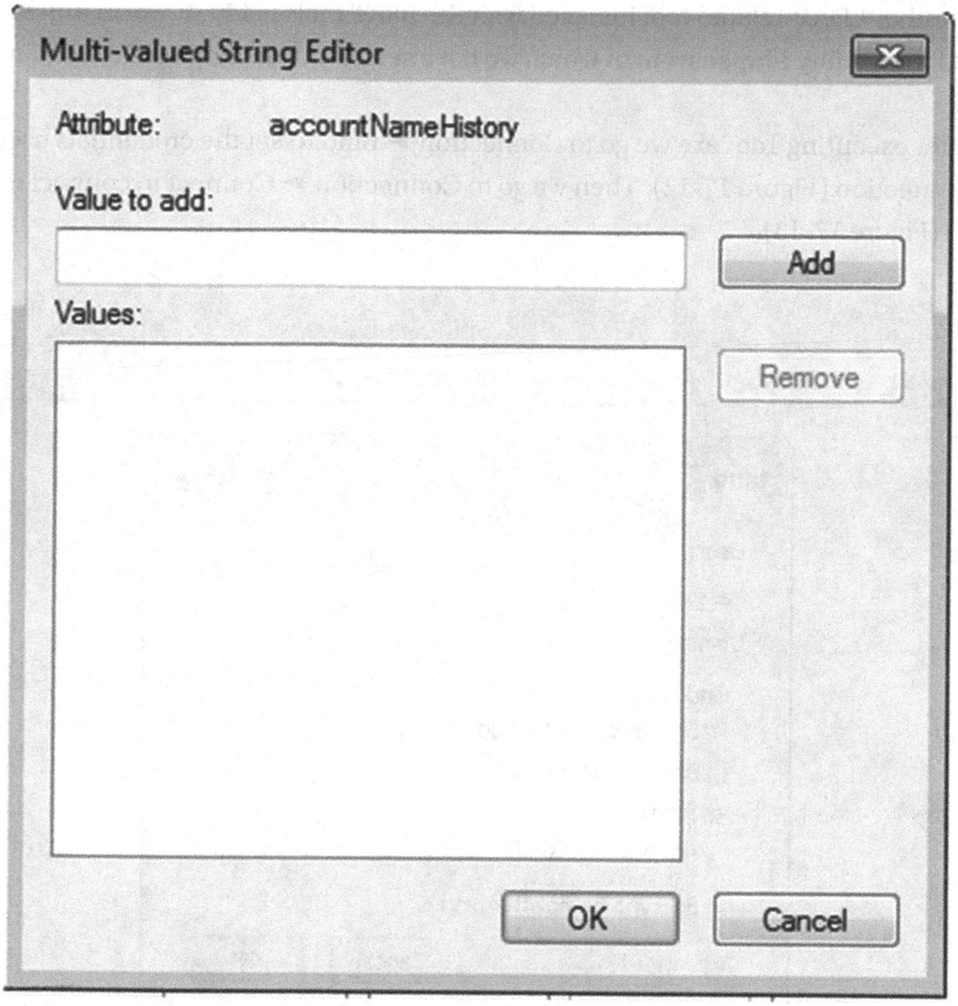

***Figure 17-11.*** *Editing an attribute*

Another LDAP-related tool installed with the RSAT tools is **ldp**. It works much like to the Linux utility **ldapsearch**, of which we have seen many examples throughout this book.

After executing `ldp.exe` we go to Connection ➤ Bind to set the credentials used for the connection (Figure 17-12). Then we go to Connection ➤ Connect to connect to a server (Figure 17-13).

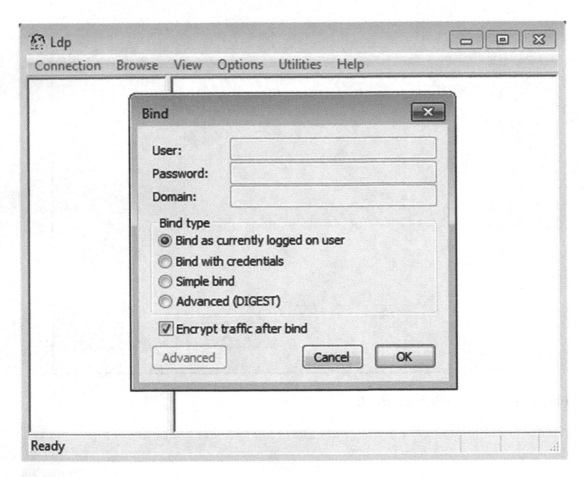

*Figure 17-12.*  *Binding credentials*

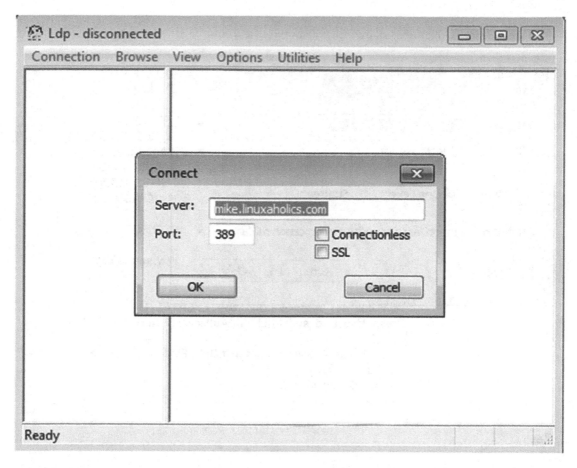

***Figure 17-13.*** *Connection parameters*

Once the connection is established, we can navigate to Browse ➤ Search to perform a search. We can customize parameters like the base DN, the scope, and so on (Figure 17-14).

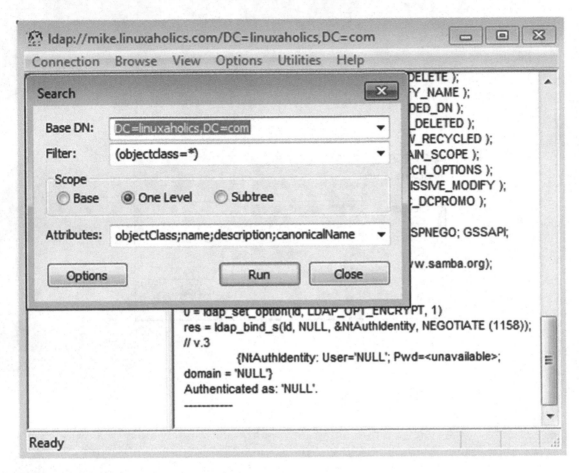

***Figure 17-14.*** *Searching in ldp*

In addition to these administrative tools, there are many more available. In addition, we can create and customize our own administrative console by running mmc.exe. Right after executing it, a blank administration console appears (Figure 17-15).

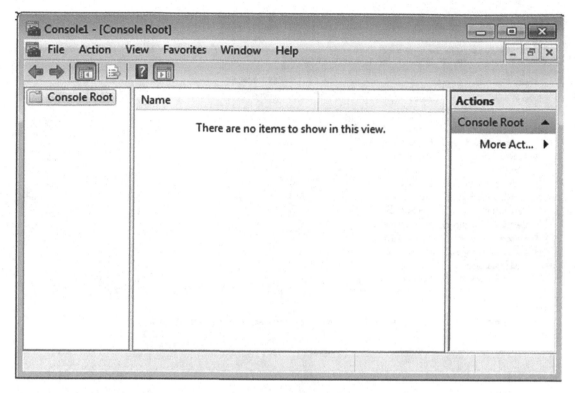

*Figure 17-15.  MMC*

Selecting File ➤ Add/Remove Snap In opens a new window with the list of snap-ins available (Figure 17-16).

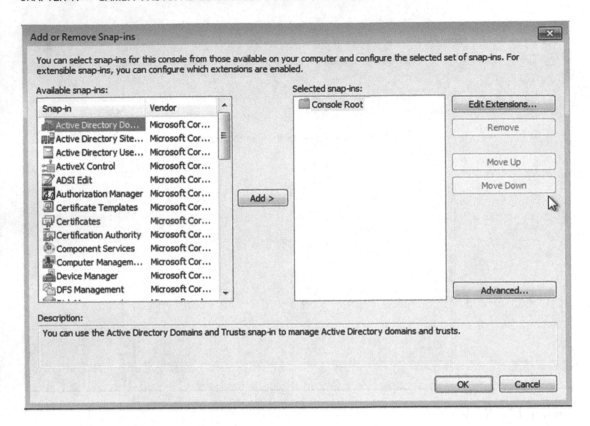

**Figure 17-16.** *Adding snap-ins*

After adding the desired snap-ins we can save our newly created console to be used later.

# Adding an Additional Domain Controller

A single DC is enough to have a working Active Directory forest, and such an infrastructure might be acceptable in a lab environment. However, in a production environment we should add at least a second DC for failover as well as for load balancing reasons.

We must be sure that every DC has the same date and time so we'll install ntp on the second DC, as we did previously on the first DC.

```
[root@november samba-4.7.11]# yum install -y ntp
```

Once we make sure that the time is synchronized, we'll install Samba. As we did in the first DC, we won't install the compiled binaries included in the official CentOS repositories, but we'll compile the source code downloaded from the Samba web site instead. The installation procedure is exactly the same as the one we followed when installing the first DC, so we won't repeat it here. As soon as the installation is finished, we'll use **samba-tool** to join the server to the existing domain as an additional DC.

```
[root@november samba-4.7.11]# /usr/local/samba/bin/samba-tool domain join
linuxaholics.com DC --server=mike.linuxaholics.com  -U Administrator
--password=Passw0rd
workgroup is LINUXAHOLICS
realm is linuxaholics.com
Adding CN=NOVEMBER,OU=Domain Controllers,DC=linuxaholics,DC=com
Adding CN=NOVEMBER,CN=Servers,CN=Default-First-Site-Name,CN=Sites,
CN=Configuration,DC=linuxaholics,DC=com
Adding CN=NTDS Settings,CN=NOVEMBER,CN=Servers,CN=Default-First-Site-Name,
CN=Sites,CN=Configuration,DC=linuxaholics,DC=com
Adding SPNs to CN=NOVEMBER,OU=Domain Controllers,DC=linuxaholics,DC=com
Setting account password for NOVEMBER$
Enabling account
Calling bare provision
Looking up IPv4 addresses
Looking up IPv6 addresses
No IPv6 address will be assigned
Setting up share.ldb
Setting up secrets.ldb
Setting up the registry
Setting up the privileges database
Setting up idmap db
Setting up SAM db
Setting up sam.ldb partitions and settings
Setting up sam.ldb rootDSE
Pre-loading the Samba 4 and AD schema
A Kerberos configuration suitable for Samba AD has been generated at /usr/
local/samba/private/krb5.conf
Provision OK for domain DN DC=linuxaholics,DC=com
```

```
Starting replication
Schema-DN[CN=Schema,CN=Configuration,DC=linuxaholics,DC=com]
objects[402/1550] linked_values[0/0]
Schema-DN[CN=Schema,CN=Configuration,DC=linuxaholics,DC=com]
objects[804/1550] linked_values[0/0]
Schema-DN[CN=Schema,CN=Configuration,DC=linuxaholics,DC=com]
objects[1206/1550] linked_values[0/0]
Schema-DN[CN=Schema,CN=Configuration,DC=linuxaholics,DC=com]
objects[1550/1550] linked_values[0/0]
Analyze and apply schema objects
Partition[CN=Configuration,DC=linuxaholics,DC=com] objects[402/1619]
linked_values[0/1]
Partition[CN=Configuration,DC=linuxaholics,DC=com] objects[804/1619]
linked_values[0/1]
Partition[CN=Configuration,DC=linuxaholics,DC=com] objects[1206/1619]
linked_values[0/1]
Partition[CN=Configuration,DC=linuxaholics,DC=com] objects[1608/1619]
linked_values[0/1]
Partition[CN=Configuration,DC=linuxaholics,DC=com] objects[1619/1619]
linked_values[30/30]
Replicating critical objects from the base DN of the domain
Partition[DC=linuxaholics,DC=com] objects[97/97] linked_values[24/24]
Partition[DC=linuxaholics,DC=com] objects[374/277] linked_values[24/24]
Done with always replicated NC (base, config, schema)
Replicating DC=DomainDnsZones,DC=linuxaholics,DC=com
Partition[DC=DomainDnsZones,DC=linuxaholics,DC=com] objects[41/41] linked_
values[0/0]
Replicating DC=ForestDnsZones,DC=linuxaholics,DC=com
Partition[DC=ForestDnsZones,DC=linuxaholics,DC=com] objects[18/18] linked_
values[0/0]
Exop on[CN=RID Manager$,CN=System,DC=linuxaholics,DC=com] objects[3]
linked_values[0]
Committing SAM database
Adding 1 remote DNS records for NOVEMBER.linuxaholics.com
Adding DNS A record NOVEMBER.linuxaholics.com for IPv4 IP: 192.168.1.235
```

Adding DNS CNAME record 604a4e5c-a897-45c9-b3ba-026b4d9c9b31._msdcs.
linuxaholics.com for NOVEMBER.linuxaholics.com
All other DNS records (like _ldap SRV records) will be created samba_
dnsupdate on first startup
Replicating new DNS records in DC=DomainDnsZones,DC=linuxaholics,DC=com
Partition[DC=DomainDnsZones,DC=linuxaholics,DC=com] objects[2/2] linked_
values[0/0]
Replicating new DNS records in DC=ForestDnsZones,DC=linuxaholics,DC=com
Partition[DC=ForestDnsZones,DC=linuxaholics,DC=com] objects[2/2] linked_
values[0/0]
Sending DsReplicaUpdateRefs for all the replicated partitions
Setting isSynchronized and dsServiceName
Setting up secrets database
Joined domain LINUXAHOLICS (SID S-1-5-21-2526023654-1533215790-50031700) as
a DC

If we open the Active Directory Users and Computers console in the Windows
workstation and we examine the content of the Domain Controllers OU, we'll see both
DCs (Figure 17-17).

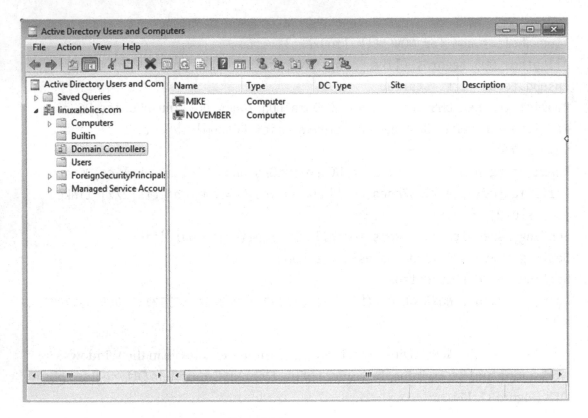

**Figure 17-17.**  *Domain Controllers OU*

Finally, if we want to demote a DC, we can do it with the **samba-tool domain demote** command.

# Active Directory Sites

The Active Directory domain we are working with has now two DCs, both of which reside in the same local subnet. This is not always the case, though; we might have an office in New York and another one in Los Angeles. In such a situation we would expect that the local area connection in both LANs would be fast and reliable, but the connection between both offices would probably be significantly slower.

For this kind of scenario, the use of different Active Directory sites is recommended. In the example just mentioned, we'd need to have two different sites, one for New York and one for Los Angeles. The communication between DCs on the same site would take place regularly without the need for the admin to configure anything, but the communication between both sites would be set up by the admin according to the particular needs of any case.

We could create a new site with the **samba-tool sites create** command.

```
[root@mike ~]# /usr/local/samba/bin/samba-tool sites create NYC
Site NYC created !
```

It is probably easier to do it with the Active Directory Sites and Services console, though, which is included with the RSAT tools we installed earlier. Once launched, it will show the NYC site we just created and the Default-First-Site-Name used by default if no site is created (Figure 17-18).

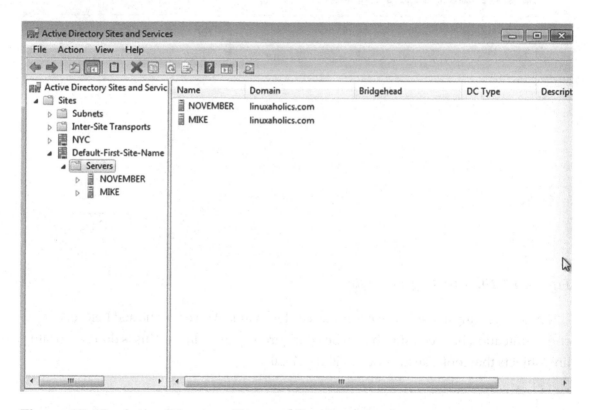

***Figure 17-18.*** *Active Directory Sites and Services console*

When selecting Sites we can right-click New Site to open a new window (Figure 17-19).

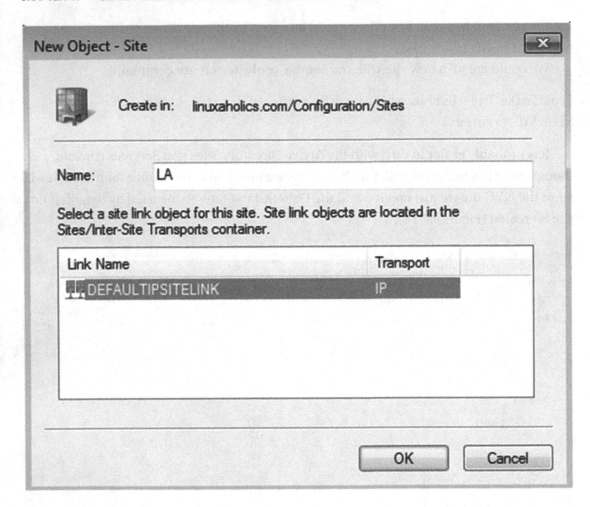

**Figure 17-19.** *Creating a new site*

When creating a new site, we must also select a link. As we mentioned before, the communication between sites has to be configured by the admin. This is done with site link objects that look like the one in Figure 17-20.

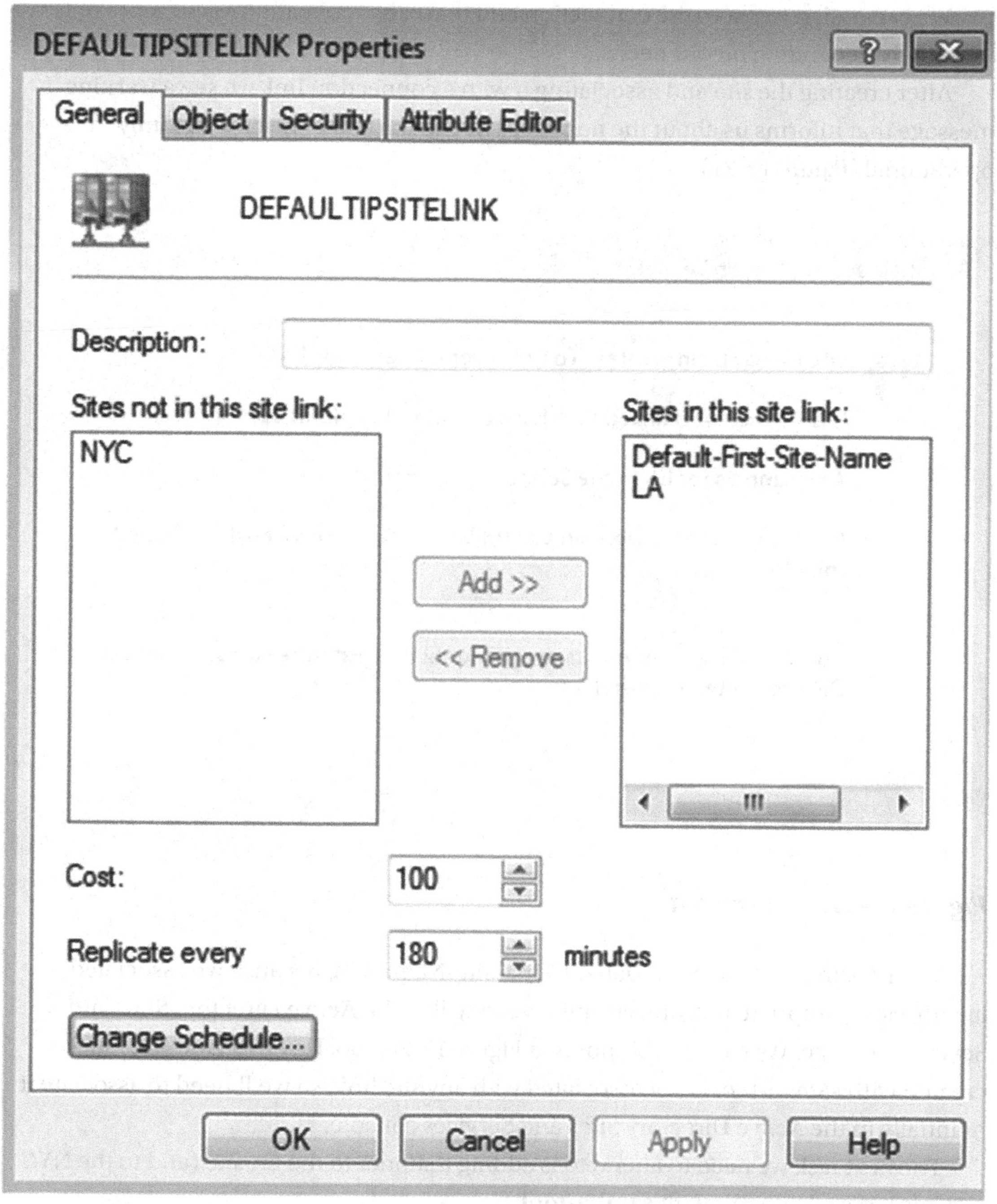


*Figure 17-20.* *Site link*

We can assign a cost to the connection and make the replication occur more or less frequently depending on our needs.

After creating the site and associating it with a connection link we see a warning message that informs us about the next steps needed to make the new site fully operational (Figure 17-21).

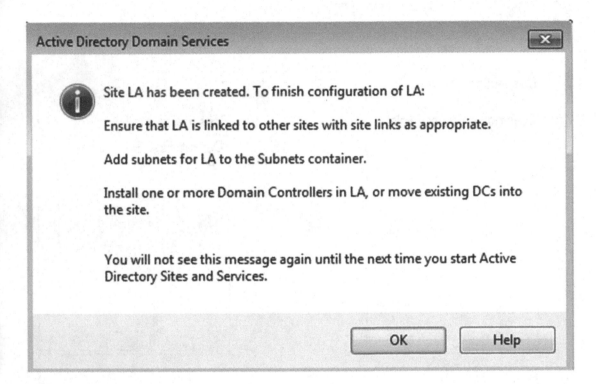

**Figure 17-21.** *Site created*

The LA site is linked to the Default-First-Site-Name site, because we associated it with the appropriate link object when creating it in the Active Directory Sites and Services console. We can see this point in Figure 17-20, too. However, the NYC site created with samba-tool is not associated with any site link, so we'll need to associate it manually in the Active Directory Sites and Services console.

The next task we need to attend to is adding a subnet to the LA site (and to the NYC site, too). We can do this with **samba-tool**.

```
[root@mike ~]# /usr/local/samba/bin/samba-tool sites subnet create
192.168.2.0/24 NYC
Subnet 192.168.2.0/24 created !
```

```
[root@mike ~]# /usr/local/samba/bin/samba-tool sites subnet create
192.168.3.0/24 LA
Subnet 192.168.3.0/24 created !
```

Right after creating the subnets, they are not associated with any site, so we'll use **samba-tool** again to associate them with their respective sites.

```
[root@mike ~]# /usr/local/samba/bin/samba-tool sites subnet set-site
192.168.2.0/24 NYC
Subnet 192.168.2.0/24 shifted to site NYC
[root@mike ~]# /usr/local/samba/bin/samba-tool sites subnet set-site
192.168.3.0/24 LA
Subnet 192.168.3.0/24 shifted to site LA
```

Now, when we install a new DC in LA or NYC with the right subnet assigned, it will be part of the new site. We could also move some of the existing servers in Default-First-Site-Name to the new sites, but we should be careful not to interrupt their connectivity.

# Understand and Manage FSMO Roles

Active Directory is a multimaster environment in which changes can be made in any DC. This has several advantages, as it is possible to load balance the operations performed when administering the domain. However, there is also a drawback. Over time, conflicts will appear, for instance when creating the same user in two different DCs. These conflicts can sometimes be difficult to resolve, and this is why some operations in Active Directory are performed in a single-master environment.

This can be achieved by assigning certain roles to one and only one DC. These roles are called FSMO roles, and they are as follows:

- PDC emulator.

- RID master.

- Schema master.

- Domain naming master.

- Infrastructure master.

- Domain DNS zone master.

- Forest DNS zone master.

## PDC Emulator

The PDC emulator provides time service. Password changes in the domain are replicated preferentially to this server. It processes account lockouts and the Group Policy Management console contacts this server by default. There is only one PDC emulator per domain.

## RID Master

The RID master makes sure that objects in the domain have unique identifiers. These unique identifiers are composed of two parts: a SID and a RID. The SID is the same for a single domain, but the RID is different for each object. The RID master assigns different ranges of RIDs to the DCs in the domain to make sure that these ranges do not overlap. There is one RID master per domain.

## Schema Master

One server is allowed to make changes in the schema, the Schema master. This server has to be online every time the schema is updated. There is one Schema master per forest.

## Domain Naming Master

This server is responsible for changes in the domain namespace at the forest level. For instance, when we provisioned the Active Directory domain we said that besides the `linuxaholics.com` domain we could have a `canada.linuxaholics.com` domain and a `us.linuxaholics.com` domain, which are part of the same forest. If we decide to add a `mexico.linuxaholics.com` domain, this change will be made in the domain naming master. There is one domain naming master per forest.

# Infrastructure Master

This server plays an important role whenever a trust relationship exists with a different domain. When this happens, users from a domain can be given access to resources in the other domain. It is also possible that a user in Domain A is made a member of a group in Domain B. In this case the identifier of the user should be updated by the infrastructure master.

We have seen the theory behind trust relationships before, but we haven't seen any examples yet. Later in the book when we study FreeIPA and integration with Active Directory we'll see an example of trust relationships. Even though in that case the trust relationship is between a Windows Active Directory Domain and a FreeIPA domain, it works pretty much like a trust relationship between two Active Directory domains. There is only one infrastructure master per domain.

# Domain DNS Zone Master

As we know, DNS is a critical part of every Active Directory infrastructure and it is deeply integrated with it. When new zones are added or deleted on the DNS servers that host the domain, the domain DNS zone master is responsible for coordinating the operation. There is only one domain DNS zone master server for a domain.

# Forest DNS Zone Master

This role is similar to the domain DNS zone master, but in this case it applies to the adding or deleting of records in the top-level DNS zone. There is one forest DNS zone master per forest.

# Global Catalog

The Global Catalog is not an FSMO role; in fact, we can have as many Global Catalog servers as DCs. A Global Catalog server stores partial copies of all the objects in the forest, so every time we need to locate an object in the forest we can get a quick answer by querying the Global Catalog server.

# Managing FSMOs in Samba

FSMO roles are managed in Samba with the **samba-tool fsmo** subcommand. We can get a list of the FSMOs assigned in the domain with the following command:

```
[root@mike ~]# /usr/local/samba/bin/samba-tool fsmo show
SchemaMasterRole owner: CN=NTDS Settings,CN=MIKE,CN=Servers,CN=Default-
First-Site-Name,CN=Sites,CN=Configuration,DC=linuxaholics,DC=com
InfrastructureMasterRole owner: CN=NTDS Settings,CN=MIKE,CN=Servers,
CN=Default-First-Site-Name,CN=Sites,CN=Configuration,DC=linuxaholics,DC=com
RidAllocationMasterRole owner: CN=NTDS Settings,CN=MIKE,CN=Servers,
CN=Default-First-Site-Name,CN=Sites,CN=Configuration,DC=linuxaholics,DC=com
PdcEmulationMasterRole owner: CN=NTDS Settings,CN=MIKE,CN=Servers,
CN=Default-First-Site-Name,CN=Sites,CN=Configuration,DC=linuxaholics,DC=com
DomainNamingMasterRole owner: CN=NTDS Settings,CN=MIKE,CN=Servers,
CN=Default-First-Site-Name,CN=Sites,CN=Configuration,DC=linuxaholics,DC=com
DomainDnsZonesMasterRole owner: CN=NTDS Settings,CN=MIKE,CN=Servers,
CN=Default-First-Site-Name,CN=Sites,CN=Configuration,DC=linuxaholics,DC=com
ForestDnsZonesMasterRole owner: CN=NTDS Settings,CN=MIKE,CN=Servers,
CN=Default-First-Site-Name,CN=Sites,CN=Configuration,DC=linuxaholics,DC=com
```

In this case all of the FSMO roles are assigned to the same server, but we can transfer one or more roles to a different server. For instance, we might want to transfer the infrastructure master role from mike.linuxaholics.com to november.linuxaholics. com. In that case, this is the command we should launch from the november. linuxaholics.com server:

```
[root@november ~]# /usr/local/samba/bin/samba-tool fsmo transfer
--role=infrastructure --username=Administrator --password=Passw0rd
```

The server november will try to connect to mike to transfer the FSMO role in an orderly fashion. There are situations, though, in which a server has suffered an unrecoverable error and can no longer be contacted. If this happens with a server holding one or many FSMO roles we wouldn't be able to transfer that role and we'd need to seize it instead with this command:

```
[root@november ~]# /usr/local/samba/bin/samba-tool fsmo seize
--role=infrastructure --username=Administrator --password=Passw0rd
```

# Verifying Active Directory Replication

The DCs in an Active Directory environment need to keep their information synchronized. We can check this point with the **samba-tool drs** subcommand. We could easily see the status of the replication with the following command:

```
[root@mike ~]# /usr/local/samba/bin/samba-tool drs showrepl
Default-First-Site-Name\MIKE
DSA Options: 0x00000001
DSA object GUID: c423727f-bd83-4512-bd85-487df0123444
DSA invocationId: 6cbe0bcd-9a32-4557-8557-a8312e825628

==== INBOUND NEIGHBORS ====


DC=DomainDnsZones,DC=linuxaholics,DC=com
        Default-First-Site-Name\NOVEMBER via RPC
                DSA object GUID: 604a4e5c-a897-45c9-b3ba-026b4d9c9b31
                Last attempt @ Sun Nov 11 15:14:45 2018 EST was successful
                0 consecutive failure(s).
                Last success @ Sun Nov 11 15:14:45 2018 EST

DC=linuxaholics,DC=com
        Default-First-Site-Name\NOVEMBER via RPC
                DSA object GUID: 604a4e5c-a897-45c9-b3ba-026b4d9c9b31
                Last attempt @ Sun Nov 11 15:14:45 2018 EST was successful
                0 consecutive failure(s).
                Last success @ Sun Nov 11 15:14:45 2018 EST

DC=ForestDnsZones,DC=linuxaholics,DC=com
        Default-First-Site-Name\NOVEMBER via RPC
                DSA object GUID: 604a4e5c-a897-45c9-b3ba-026b4d9c9b31
                Last attempt @ Sun Nov 11 15:14:45 2018 EST was successful
                0 consecutive failure(s).
                Last success @ Sun Nov 11 15:14:45 2018 EST
```

CN=Schema,CN=Configuration,DC=linuxaholics,DC=com
        Default-First-Site-Name\NOVEMBER via RPC
                DSA object GUID: 604a4e5c-a897-45c9-b3ba-026b4d9c9b31
                Last attempt @ Sun Nov 11 15:14:45 2018 EST was successful
                0 consecutive failure(s).
                Last success @ Sun Nov 11 15:14:45 2018 EST

CN=Configuration,DC=linuxaholics,DC=com
        Default-First-Site-Name\NOVEMBER via RPC
                DSA object GUID: 604a4e5c-a897-45c9-b3ba-026b4d9c9b31
                Last attempt @ Sun Nov 11 15:14:45 2018 EST was successful
                0 consecutive failure(s).
                Last success @ Sun Nov 11 15:14:45 2018 EST

==== OUTBOUND NEIGHBORS ====


DC=DomainDnsZones,DC=linuxaholics,DC=com
        Default-First-Site-Name\NOVEMBER via RPC
                DSA object GUID: 604a4e5c-a897-45c9-b3ba-026b4d9c9b31
                Last attempt @ NTTIME(0) was successful
                0 consecutive failure(s).
                Last success @ NTTIME(0)

DC=linuxaholics,DC=com
        Default-First-Site-Name\NOVEMBER via RPC
                DSA object GUID: 604a4e5c-a897-45c9-b3ba-026b4d9c9b31
                Last attempt @ NTTIME(0) was successful
                0 consecutive failure(s).
                Last success @ NTTIME(0)

DC=ForestDnsZones,DC=linuxaholics,DC=com
        Default-First-Site-Name\NOVEMBER via RPC
                DSA object GUID: 604a4e5c-a897-45c9-b3ba-026b4d9c9b31
                Last attempt @ NTTIME(0) was successful
                0 consecutive failure(s).
                Last success @ NTTIME(0)

```
CN=Schema,CN=Configuration,DC=linuxaholics,DC=com
      Default-First-Site-Name\NOVEMBER via RPC
            DSA object GUID: 604a4e5c-a897-45c9-b3ba-026b4d9c9b31
            Last attempt @ NTTIME(0) was successful
            0 consecutive failure(s).
            Last success @ NTTIME(0)

CN=Configuration,DC=linuxaholics,DC=com
      Default-First-Site-Name\NOVEMBER via RPC
            DSA object GUID: 604a4e5c-a897-45c9-b3ba-026b4d9c9b31
            Last attempt @ NTTIME(0) was successful
            0 consecutive failure(s).
            Last success @ NTTIME(0)

==== KCC CONNECTION OBJECTS ====

Connection --
      Connection name: 4ef6f109-55b0-4e97-b42c-c8c2834d4168
      Enabled        : TRUE
      Server DNS name : november.linuxaholics.com
      Server DN name  : CN=NTDS Settings,CN=NOVEMBER,CN=Servers,CN=Default-
                        First-Site-Name,CN=Sites,CN=Configuration,DC=linuxa
                        holics,DC=com
         TransportType: RPC
         options: 0x00000001
```

We see that in this case the replication has been successful.

# Configure SYSVOL Replication Using rsync or robocopy

Every Samba Active Directory DC, as well as their Windows equivalents, has a special share defined called SYSVOL.

```
[root@mike ~]# /usr/local/samba/bin/testparm -s
    .
    .
    .
```

```
[sysvol]
      path = /usr/local/samba/var/locks/sysvol
      read only = No
.

.

.
```

In this share we can find logon scripts and group policies.

```
[root@mike ~]# tree /usr/local/samba/var/locks/sysvol/
/usr/local/samba/var/locks/sysvol/
└── linuxaholics.com
    ├── Policies
    │   ├── {31B2F340-016D-11D2-945F-00C04FB984F9}
    │   │   ├── GPT.INI
    │   │   ├── MACHINE
    │   │   └── USER
    │   ├── {6987A430-D13C-4963-8EA9-EA5B56FB1010}
    │   │   ├── GPT.INI
    │   │   ├── Machine
    │   │   │   └── Registry.pol
    │   │   └── User
    │   └── {6AC1786C-016F-11D2-945F-00C04FB984F9}
    │       ├── GPT.INI
    │       ├── MACHINE
    │       └── USER
    └── scripts
```

Eventually we might end up having different contents in the SYSVOL shares of the different DCs; for instance, if we list the content of the SYSVOL share in the second DC we installed.

```
[root@november ~]# tree /usr/local/samba/var/locks/sysvol/
/usr/local/samba/var/locks/sysvol/
└── linuxaholics.com
    └── scripts
```

To solve this issue in Windows servers prior to Windows 2008, Microsoft used FRS replication. Since the release of Windows Server R2, however, this method has been largely replaced by DFS replication. Currently Samba does not support either method natively, so to keep the contents of the SYSVOL shares synchronized in the different DCs of the Active Directory domain we need to implement a workaround.

One of the recommended workarounds in the official Samba documentation is the use of **rsync**. This utility is usually not installed by default, so we'll have to install it first.

```
[root@mike ~]# yum install -y rsync
[root@november ~]# yum install -y rsync
```

The copy will be unidirectional; we'll choose as the master the server that has the PDC emulator FSMO role, which is mike.linuxaholics.com.

```
[root@mike ~]# /usr/local/samba/bin/samba-tool fsmo show | grep -i pdc
PdcEmulationMasterRole owner: CN=NTDS Settings,CN=MIKE,CN=Servers,CN=Defau
lt-First-Site-Name,CN=Sites,CN=Configuration,DC=linuxaholics,DC=com
```

In the PDC emulator we configure the **rsyncd** service by editing the /etc/rsyncd. conf file, so that in the end it looks like this:

```
[root@mike ~]# cat /etc/rsyncd.conf
# /etc/rsyncd: configuration file for rsync daemon mode

# See rsyncd.conf man page for more options.

[SysVol]
        path = /usr/local/samba/var/locks/sysvol/
        comment = Samba Sysvol Share
        uid = root
        gid = root
        read only = yes
        auth users = sysvol-replication
        secrets file = /usr/local/samba/etc/rsyncd.secret
```

The content of the file is almost self-explanatory: We set the path of the folder that will be synchronized, the user and group whose rights apply when performing the synchronization, and the authorized users to connect to the service (sysvol-replication). Finally, we specify a share secret that will be located in the /usr/local/samba/etc/

`rsyncd.secret` file. We create this file, we make it readable only by root, and add the following line:

```
sysvol-replication:VerySecretPassword
```

Now we enable and start the rsyncd service in the PDC emulator.

```
[root@mike ~]# systemctl enable rsyncd
ln -s '/usr/lib/systemd/system/rsyncd.service' '/etc/systemd/system/multi-
user.target.wants/rsyncd.service'
[root@mike ~]# systemctl start rsyncd
```

To allow for incoming connections to the service, we open the corresponding ports in the firewall.

```
[root@mike ~]# firewall-cmd --add-port=873/tcp
success
[root@mike ~]# firewall-cmd --permanent --add-port=873/tcp
success
```

On the other DC computer, `november.linuxaholics.com`, we create a file with the shared secret.

```
[root@november ~]# echo VerySecretPassword > /usr/local/samba/etc/rsync-
secret
[root@november ~]# chmod 600 /usr/local/samba/etc/rsync-secret
[root@november ~]# ls -l /usr/local/samba/etc/rsync-secret
-rw-------. 1 root root 19 oct 19 23:21 /usr/local/samba/etc/rsync-secret
```

We can test the synchronization with the `--dry-run` option; this way the command shows what files will be copied without actually copying them. Apart from this option we also choose to keep extended attributes, ACLs, and permissions; compress the files during the transfer; and delete those files on the destination server that don't exist on the source server. The full list of options can be seen in the man page of the utility.

```
[root@november ~]# rsync --dry-run -XAavz --delete-after --password-
file=/usr/local/samba/etc/rsync-secret rsync://sysvol-replication@mike.
linuxaholics.com/SysVol/ /usr/local/samba/var/locks/sysvol/
receiving file list ... done
./
```

```
linuxaholics.com/
linuxaholics.com/Policies/
linuxaholics.com/Policies/{31B2F340-016D-11D2-945F-00C04FB984F9}/
linuxaholics.com/Policies/{31B2F340-016D-11D2-945F-00C04FB984F9}/GPT.INI
linuxaholics.com/Policies/{31B2F340-016D-11D2-945F-00C04FB984F9}/MACHINE/
linuxaholics.com/Policies/{31B2F340-016D-11D2-945F-00C04FB984F9}/USER/
linuxaholics.com/Policies/{6987A430-D13C-4963-8EA9-EA5B56FB1010}/
linuxaholics.com/Policies/{6987A430-D13C-4963-8EA9-EA5B56FB1010}/GPT.INI
linuxaholics.com/Policies/{6987A430-D13C-4963-8EA9-EA5B56FB1010}/Machine/
linuxaholics.com/Policies/{6987A430-D13C-4963-8EA9-EA5B56FB1010}/Machine/
Registry.pol
linuxaholics.com/Policies/{6987A430-D13C-4963-8EA9-EA5B56FB1010}/User/
linuxaholics.com/Policies/{6AC1786C-016F-11D2-945F-00C04FB984F9}/
linuxaholics.com/Policies/{6AC1786C-016F-11D2-945F-00C04FB984F9}/GPT.INI
linuxaholics.com/Policies/{6AC1786C-016F-11D2-945F-00C04FB984F9}/MACHINE/
linuxaholics.com/Policies/{6AC1786C-016F-11D2-945F-00C04FB984F9}/USER/
linuxaholics.com/scripts/

sent 121 bytes   received 4114 bytes   8470.00 bytes/sec
total size is 1696   speedup is 0.40 (DRY RUN)
```

Everything seems to be correct, so we can execute it without the --dry-run option. To make sure that the client periodically updates the content of the SYSVOL share we'll execute rsync via a cron job.

The cron service is usually installed and run by default on every Linux system, but we'll check this point.

```
[root@november ~]# systemctl status crond
crond.service - Command Scheduler
   Loaded: loaded (/usr/lib/systemd/system/crond.service; enabled)
   Active: active (running) since lun 2018-10-15 03:50:21 EDT; 4 days ago
 Main PID: 586 (crond)
   CGroup: /system.slice/crond.service
           └─586 /usr/sbin/crond -n

oct 15 03:50:21 localhost.localdomain systemd[1]: Started Command Scheduler.
```

```
oct 15 03:50:21 localhost.localdomain crond[586]: (CRON) INFO (RANDOM_DELAY
                                             w...
oct 15 03:50:22 localhost.localdomain crond[586]: (CRON) INFO (running with
                                             i...
Hint: Some lines were ellipsized, use -l to show in full.
```

As the service is running, we'll edit the crontab associated with the root user with the **crontab -e** command. We specify that we want to execute rsync every five minutes to copy the files. When we're done we can list the new crontab of the root user.

```
[root@november ~]# crontab -l
*/5 * * * *      rsync -XAavz --delete-after --password-file=/usr/local/
samba/etc/rsync-secret rsync://sysvol-replication@mike.linuxaholics.com/
SysVol/ /usr/local/samba/var/locks/sysvol/
```

After a few minutes, we'll see that the SYSVOL share content has been replicated successfully.

```
[root@november ~]# tree /usr/local/samba/var/locks/sysvol/
/usr/local/samba/var/locks/sysvol/
```

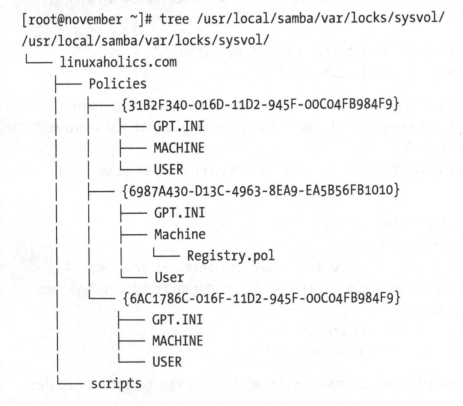

```
└── linuxaholics.com
    ├── Policies
    │   ├── {31B2F340-016D-11D2-945F-00C04FB984F9}
    │   │   ├── GPT.INI
    │   │   ├── MACHINE
    │   │   └── USER
    │   ├── {6987A430-D13C-4963-8EA9-EA5B56FB1010}
    │   │   ├── GPT.INI
    │   │   ├── Machine
    │   │   │   └── Registry.pol
    │   │   └── User
    │   └── {6AC1786C-016F-11D2-945F-00C04FB984F9}
    │       ├── GPT.INI
    │       ├── MACHINE
    │       └── USER
    └── scripts
```

An alternative to the use of **rsync** could be the use of **robocopy**. This is also a remote copy tool that is part of the Windows Resource Kit. Obviously in this case we'd need to perform the synchronization from a Windows workstation.

# Backing Up a Samba Active Directory Domain Controller

Since Samba 4.9, Samba includes a tool for backing up and restoring a DC. This tool is included in the samba-tool suite and it is very easy to use.

The command we need to use is **samba-tool domain backup**. Before making a backup of the Active Directory database, however, it is recommended that we check the state of the database with **samba-tool dbcheck** and fix any errors that might exist.

```
[root@mike ~]# /usr/local/samba/bin/samba-tool dbcheck
Checking 281 objects
Checked 281 objects (0 errors)
```

We'll create a local folder in which to store the backup .tar files.

```
[root@mike ~]# mkdir /AD_BACKUPS
```

We create the backup now by specifying the server to back up, the folder in which to keep the backup file, and the user to connect to the DC.

```
[root@mike ~]# /usr/local/samba/bin/samba-tool domain backup
online --server=mike.linuxaholics.com --targetdir=/AD_BACKUPS/
--username=Administrator
Password for [LINUXAHOLICS\Administrator]:
workgroup is LINUXAHOLICS
realm is linuxaholics.com
Calling bare provision
Looking up IPv4 addresses
Looking up IPv6 addresses
No IPv6 address will be assigned
Setting up share.ldb
Setting up secrets.ldb
Setting up the registry
```

Setting up the privileges database
Setting up idmap db
Setting up SAM db
Setting up sam.ldb partitions and settings
Setting up sam.ldb rootDSE
Pre-loading the Samba 4 and AD schema
Unable to determine the DomainSID, can not enforce uniqueness constraint on local domainSIDs

A Kerberos configuration suitable for Samba AD has been generated at /AD_BACKUPS/tmpFSOPCd/private/krb5.conf
Merge the contents of this file with your system krb5.conf or replace it with this one. Do not create a symlink!
Provision OK for domain DN DC=linuxaholics,DC=com
Starting replication
Using DS_BIND_GUID_W2K3
Schema-DN[CN=Schema,CN=Configuration,DC=linuxaholics,DC=com]
objects[402/1550] linked_values[0/0]
Schema-DN[CN=Schema,CN=Configuration,DC=linuxaholics,DC=com]
objects[804/1550] linked_values[0/0]
Schema-DN[CN=Schema,CN=Configuration,DC=linuxaholics,DC=com]
objects[1206/1550] linked_values[0/0]
Schema-DN[CN=Schema,CN=Configuration,DC=linuxaholics,DC=com]
objects[1550/1550] linked_values[0/0]
Analyze and apply schema objects
Partition[CN=Configuration,DC=linuxaholics,DC=com] objects[402/1620]
linked_values[0/1]
Partition[CN=Configuration,DC=linuxaholics,DC=com] objects[804/1620]
linked_values[0/1]
Partition[CN=Configuration,DC=linuxaholics,DC=com] objects[1206/1620]
linked_values[0/1]
Partition[CN=Configuration,DC=linuxaholics,DC=com] objects[1608/1620]
linked_values[0/1]
Partition[CN=Configuration,DC=linuxaholics,DC=com] objects[1620/1620]
linked_values[30/30]
Replicating critical objects from the base DN of the domain

```
Partition[DC=linuxaholics,DC=com] objects[97/97] linked_values[24/24]
Partition[DC=linuxaholics,DC=com] objects[378/281] linked_values[24/24]
Done with always replicated NC (base, config, schema)
Replicating DC=DomainDnsZones,DC=linuxaholics,DC=com
Partition[DC=DomainDnsZones,DC=linuxaholics,DC=com] objects[43/43] linked_
values[0/0]
Replicating DC=ForestDnsZones,DC=linuxaholics,DC=com
Partition[DC=ForestDnsZones,DC=linuxaholics,DC=com] objects[19/19] linked_
values[0/0]
Committing SAM database
Setting isSynchronized and dsServiceName
Cloned domain LINUXAHOLICS (SID S-1-5-21-2526023654-1533215790-50031700)
Creating backup file /AD_BACKUPS/samba-backup-linuxaholics.com-2018-11-
11T13-11-39.384643.tar.bz2...
```

In the /AD_BACKUP folder we now have a .tar file with the necessary information to restore the Active Directory database.

```
[root@mike ~]# ls /AD_BACKUPS/
samba-backup-linuxaholics.com-2018-11-11T13-11-39.384643.tar.bz2   tmp9JYCBq
```

# Restoring a Samba Active Directory Domain Controller

Restoring a Samba DC is as easy as backing it up. We just need to execute **samba-tool domain backup restore**. However, before restoring we must consider the best course of action.

If we have lost a DC, it is probably a better solution to purge all the entries that point to that DC and obtain from another DC the FSMO roles if needed. Later we would add DC to the domain to substitute for the one that we lost. On the other hand, if we have lost the last remaining DC, we would execute **samba-tool domain backup restore** to restore the domain. Later we would join the additional servers to the domain.

# Understand the Impact of Virtualization on Active Directory Domain Controllers

In recent years machine virtualization has become widely popular. Undoubtedly, this technology has made administrative tasks such as rollback operations much easier through the use of solutions like virtual machine snapshots, which allow us to revert a server to a known and working state.

However, there is also a drawback. Restoring a snapshot could have a negative impact in some cases. For example, when using cryptography, computers depend on a high level of entropy. Unfortunately, the entropy of the system is drastically reduced when restoring an online snapshot. Another service that could be affected when restoring a snapshot is the vector-clock synchronization, which could become corrupted.

To mitigate these problems, Microsoft has added a new feature to Windows Server 2018 and Windows Server 8 called virtual machine generation ID. This technology basically allows the server to realize that a time shift has occurred, so that the server can act accordingly. To see the full details, take a look at the white paper at `http://go.microsoft.com/fwlink/?LinkId=260709`.

# Summary

In this chapter we provisioned a Samba Active Directory domain with `samba-tool`. This tool automatically sets up all the components we need to have a fully operational Active Directory DC. We checked that all the needed services were running and we added a workstation to our brand new domain. Later, for redundancy, we added an additional DC to our domain. We checked that replication worked fine and learned what FSMO roles are and how to manage them in Samba. Finally, we performed a DC backup and studied what would be the best course of action to restore an Active Directory domain.

**CHAPTER 18**

# Configuring Samba as a Domain Member Server in an Existing Active Directory Domain

In Chapter 17 we saw how to install Samba 4 Active Directory DCs. Now we're focused on configuring Samba as a domain member in an Active Directory domain. This is similar to what we did in Chapter 16 when we installed a Samba 3 NT domain member. In this chapter we'll cover the following concepts:

- Joining Samba to an existing Active Directory domain.

- Ability to obtain a ticket-granting ticket (TGT) from a Key Distribution Center (KDC).

- Understanding DFS.

- Configuring DFS shares.

- Awareness of Samba clustering and Clustered Trivial Database (CTDB).

We will also learn about the following terms and utilities: `smb.conf`, server role, server security, **net** command, host msdfs, msdfs root, **kinit**, TGT, and REALM.

© Antonio Vazquez 2019

A. Vazquez, *Practical LPIC-3 300*, https://doi.org/10.1007/978-1-4842-4473-9_18

# Joining a Samba Server to an Existing Active Directory Domain

According to the Samba wiki, a Samba Active Directory domain member is a server that is part of the domain but does not provide domain services. As we did when we installed a Samba Active Directory DC, we'll start with a fresh CentOS 7 installation without any Samba software installed on it. We'll also stop the **NetworkManager** service so that it does not modify the /etc/resolv.conf file.

## Preparing the Server

The first thing we need to do is to change the DNS settings so that the Active Directory domain DNS server is queried first:

```
[root@oscar ~]# cat /etc/resolv.conf
search linuxaholics.com
nameserver 192.168.56.107
```

To make sure that our server can resolve hostnames, either through queries to the DNS server or to the internal /etc/hosts file, we can use the **getent** command.

```
[root@oscar ~]# getent hosts mike.linuxaholics.com
192.168.56.107  mike.linuxaholics.com
```

We also need to create a /etc/krb5.conf file. We can use the same file we used in the DC.

```
[root@oscar ~]# scp mike.linuxaholics.com:/etc/krb5.conf /etc/
root@mike.linuxaholics.com's password:
krb5.conf                                      100%   97     0.1KB/s   00:00
[root@oscar ~]# cat /etc/krb5.conf
[libdefaults]
      default_realm = LINUXAHOLICS.COM
      dns_lookup_realm = false
      dns_lookup_kdc = true
```

As domain members must have a synchronized time, we'll install the NTP service.

```
[root@oscar ~]# yum install -y ntp
.

.

.
[root@oscar ~]# systemctl enable ntpd
ln -s '/usr/lib/systemd/system/ntpd.service' '/etc/systemd/system/multi-user.target.wants/ntpd.service'
```

We make sure that we point to the same NTP server in all the computers of the domain. We can check this by having a look at the /etc/ntp.conf file. Next, we restart the service.

```
[root@oscar ~]# systemctl restart ntpd
```

Now, we should have the same time and date on both servers and we're ready to proceed with the next step.

## Installing Samba

Instead of using the CentOS 7 Samba binaries, we'll install the same version we used on the DC. Before that, though, we'll have to install the compilers, interpreters, and libraries needed.

```
[root@oscar ~]# yum install -y gcc perl python-devel gnutls-devel libacl-devel openldap-devel pam-devel
```

After uncompressing the .tar file with the Samba software we downloaded, we install it the usual way.

```
[root@oscar samba-4.9.1]# ./configure
.

.

.
[root@oscar samba-4.9.1]# make
.

.

.
[root@oscar samba-4.9.1]# make install
```

Now we need to edit the Samba configuration file located at `/usr/local/samba/etc/smb.conf`. If at any point we don't know what the current configuration file is, we can check it by invoking the Samba service with the `-b` parameter.

```
[root@oscar ~]# /usr/local/samba/sbin/smbd -b |grep CONFIGFILE
    CONFIGFILE: /usr/local/samba/etc/smb.conf
```

By default, the file does not exist yet, so we'll create it and add the following lines:

```
[global]
        security = ADS
        workgroup = LINUXAHOLICS
        realm = LINUXAHOLICS.COM

        log file = /var/log/samba/%m.log
        log level = 1
```

The first lines are self-explanatory: We type the names of the workgroup and the realm and we tell the server that is part of an Active Directory domain and thus all information concerning users and groups should be obtained from Active Directory. We also define a log file and assign it a level.

We already know that every user in a Linux system, whether it is a local user, an LDAP user, and so on, is assigned an ID by the system to uniquely identify it. Usually system users and groups are assigned IDs in the range from 0 to 999, and local users and groups are assigned IDs starting from 1000. With this in mind, it seems pretty reasonable to start assigning IDs to domain users and groups starting from 3000. We should also differentiate between the domain users and groups and the local built-in accounts existing on a member server, such as the local administrator, the local guest, and so on. These two groups must not overlap, so we assign the range 3000 to 7999 to domain built-in user and group accounts. The configuration line should be something like this:

```
        idmap config * : range = 3000-7999
```

We're not done yet, though; we also need to map the domain users and groups. To do so, we can use different back ends.

# The AD Back End

This ID mapping back end implements a read-only API to read user and group information from Active Directory. For this back end to work we need to add the following line in `smb.conf`:

```
idmap config LINUXAHOLICS : unix_nss_info
```

When adding this line we can specify two different modes:

```
idmap config LINUXAHOLICS : unix_nss_info = yes
idmap config LINUXAHOLICS : unix_nss_info = no
```

In the first case, the back end reads all the information available from Active Directory:

- Users: Account name, UID, login shell, home directory path, and primary group.

- Groups: Group name and GID.

In the second case, only a subset of the previous information is read:

- Users: Account name, UID, and primary group.

- Groups: Group name and GID.

The second mode (`unix_nss_info = no`) is the default.
Finally, these are the lines we'll add to the Samba configuration file.

```
idmap config LINUXAHOLICS:backend = ad
idmap config LINUXAHOLICS:schema_mode = rfc2307
idmap config LINUXAHOLICS:range = 3000-7999
```

We'll specify the shell and the home directory, too.

```
template shell = /bin/bash
template homedir = /home/%U
```

We'll also include the line mentioned previously:

```
idmap config LINUXAHOLICS:unix_nss_info = yes
```

491

# Joining a Domain with the net Command

We join the domain by executing **net** on the future member server.

```
[root@oscar ~]# /usr/local/samba/bin/net ads join -U Administrator%P@ssw0rd
Using short domain name -- LINUXAHOLICS
Joined 'OSCAR' to dns domain 'linuxaholics.com'
No DNS domain configured for oscar. Unable to perform DNS Update.
DNS update failed: NT_STATUS_INVALID_PARAMETER
```

If we get a DNS error, as we did in the previous command, we might need to edit the /etc/hosts file to add an entry for the FQDN.

```
127.0.0.1    localhost localhost.localdomain localhost4 localhost4.
localdomain4
::1          localhost localhost.localdomain localhost6 localhost6.
localdomain6
192.168.56.108    oscar.linuxaholics.com    oscar
192.168.56.107    mike.linuxaholics.com     mike
```

After repeating the **net ads join** command, we shouldn't get any more errors.

```
[root@oscar ~]# /usr/local/samba/bin/net ads join -U Administrator
Enter Administrator's password:
Using short domain name -- LINUXAHOLICS
Joined 'OSCAR' to dns domain 'linuxaholics.com'
```

We can easily check that the server is a member of the domain with the **testparm** command.

```
[root@oscar ~]# /usr/local/samba/bin/testparm
Load smb config files from /usr/local/samba/etc/smb.conf
rlimit_max: increasing rlimit_max (1024) to minimum Windows limit (16384)
Loaded services file OK.
Server role: ROLE_DOMAIN_MEMBER

Press enter to see a dump of your service definitions

# Global parameters
[global]
```

```
log file = /var/log/samba/%m.log
realm = LINUXAHOLICS.COM
security = ADS
template homedir = /home/%U
template shell = /bin/bash
workgroup = LINUXAHOLICS
idmap config linuxaholics:unix_nss_info = yes
idmap config linuxaholics:range = 10000 - 999999
idmap config linuxaholics:schema_mode = rfc2307
idmap config linuxaholics:backend = ad
idmap config * : range = 3000-7999
idmap config * : backend = tdb
```

Now that the server is part of the domain, we can list the domain users and groups with **wbinfo**.

```
[root@oscar ~]# /usr/local/samba/bin/wbinfo --domain-users
LINUXAHOLICS\antonio
LINUXAHOLICS\administrator
LINUXAHOLICS\krbtgt
LINUXAHOLICS\guest
[root@oscar ~]# /usr/local/samba/bin/wbinfo --domain-groups
LINUXAHOLICS\allowed rodc password replication group
LINUXAHOLICS\enterprise read-only domain controllers
LINUXAHOLICS\denied rodc password replication group
LINUXAHOLICS\read-only domain controllers
```

.

.

.

In addition, we can grant access to these users and groups in the shares defined in the member server.

# Getting a TGT from Kerberos

To get a TGT from Kerberos we can use the **kinit** command. This utility is included in the krb5-workstation package. After installing it with **yum** we can obtain a TGT with **kinit**:

```
[root@oscar ~]# kinit Administrator@LINUXAHOLICS.COM
Password for Administrator@LINUXAHOLICS.COM:
Warning: Your password will expire in 39 days on lun 26 nov 2018 20:26:19 EST
```

We can also list the ticket with **klist**.

```
[root@oscar ~]# klist
Ticket cache: FILE:/tmp/krb5cc_0
Default principal: Administrator@LINUXAHOLICS.COM

Valid starting     Expires            Service principal
18/10/18 02:55:19  18/10/18 12:55:19  krbtgt/LINUXAHOLICS.COM@LINUXAHOLICS.COM
    renew until 19/10/18 02:55:15
```

# DFS

DFS is a set of server and client services that allow an organization using Windows servers to organize many distributed SMB file shares into a single distributed file system. In Chapter 17 we briefly talked about DFS-R, when studying SYSVOL. DFS-R is generally viewed as a subfunction of DFS, even though both can be used independently. As we said in Chapter 17, DFS-R is not implemented in Samba, but DFS is, even though there are currently some limitations.

Currently we have in our domain two DCs: mike and november. We also have a member server, oscar. To see an example of DFS in Samba we'll begin by creating a share in mike. We create the /mnt/mike_share folder and add the following share definition to the /usr/local/samba/etc/smb.conf file.

```
[mike]
        path = /mnt/mike_share
        guest ok = Yes
```

In november we'll do something similar, as we create the corresponding folder and add this share definition to the /usr/local/samba/etc/smb.conf file.

```
[november]
        path = /mnt/november_share
        guest ok = Yes
```

We check that we can access both shares from oscar. If we can't, we'll need to check the firewall settings on both servers and allow incoming connections to Samba.

```
[root@oscar dfs]# /usr/local/samba/bin/smbclient -c "ls" //mike.
linuxaholics.com/mike -U Administrator%P@ssw0rd
  .                                 D        0   Sat Oct 20 02:24:45 2018
  ..                                D        0   Sat Oct 20 02:24:45 2018

        7022592 blocks of size 1024. 4900908 blocks available
[root@oscar dfs]# /usr/local/samba/bin/smbclient -c "ls" //november.
linuxaholics.com/november -U Administrator%P@ssw0rd
  .                                 D        0   Sat Oct 20 04:33:02 2018
  ..                                D        0   Sat Oct 20 04:33:02 2018

        7022592 blocks of size 1024. 5404156 blocks available
```

To implement DFS in our Samba member server, we'll include the following two lines in the configuration file, in the global section:

```
host msdfs = yes
vfs object = dfs_samba4
```

We will create a new folder for the DFS share and we'll also create a new share called DFS_test with the following definition:

```
[dfs_test]
    guest ok = Yes
    msdfs root = Yes
    path = /mnt/dfs
```

In addition, after creating the /mnt/dfs folder we'll create two symbolic links pointing to the shares in mike and november.

```
[root@oscar ~]# mkdir /mnt/dfs
[root@oscar ~]# cd /mnt/dfs/
[root@oscar dfs]# ln -s msdfs:mike.linuxaholics.com\\mike link1
[root@oscar dfs]# ln -s msdfs:november.linuxaholics.com\\november link2
[root@oscar dfs]# ls
link1  link2
```

We made every link to point to a target on a different machine, but we could also have made a link to point to two targets like this:

```
[root@oscar dfs]# ln -s msdfs:november.linuxaholics.com\\november,
mike.linuxaholics.com\\mike link2
```

This would be a way to provide high availability because link2 would be accessible even if one of the two targets fails.

Another way to provide high availability for Samba is through the use of CTDB. CTDB is a is a cluster implementation of the TDB database used by Samba. CTDB relies on a shared cluster files ystem to provide its services. There are many cluster file systems that can be used: RedHat GFS, Lustre, GlusterFS, OCFS2, and so on. Once the cluster file system is installed and operative, we can either install and configure CTDB from the official CentOS repositories or compile it after downloading the Samba source code from the official site.

---

**Note**   Configuring a cluster file system is beyond the scope of this book. It is something currently not included in the LPIC-3 300 objectives, but it is on the LPIC-3 304 exam. There are good books and resources on this subject like *Pro Linux High Availability Clustering* by Sander van Vugt (Apress, 2014).

---

The DFS share has been configured, and now we need to open the corresponding services in the firewall.

```
[root@oscar dfs]# firewall-cmd --add-service={samba,samba-client}
success
[root@oscar dfs]# firewall-cmd --permanent --add-service={samba,samba-client}
success
```

We restart the Samba service in oscar.linuxaholics.com, the Samba service located in /usr/local/samba/sbin, and we check that we can access the new DFS share from another computer.

```
[root@mike ~]# /usr/local/samba/bin/smbclient //oscar.linuxaholics.com/
dfs_test
Enter Administrator@LINUXAHOLICS.COM's password:
Anonymous login successful
Try "help" to get a list of possible commands.
smb: \> ls
  .                                   D        0  Sat Oct 20 04:02:24 2018
  ..                                  D        0  Thu Oct 18 05:35:01 2018
  link1                               D        0  Thu Oct 18 06:07:54 2018
  link2                               D        0  Sat Oct 20 04:02:24 2018

            7022592 blocks of size 1024. 5295956 blocks available
smb: \> cd link1
smb: \link1\> ls
  .                                   D        0  Sat Oct 20 02:24:45 2018
  ..                                  D        0  Sat Oct 20 02:24:45 2018

            7022592 blocks of size 1024. 4900916 blocks available
smb: \link1\> cd ..
smb: \> cd link2
smb: \link2\> ls
  .                                   D        0  Sat Oct 20 04:33:02 2018
  ..                                  D        0  Sat Oct 20 04:33:02 2018

            7022592 blocks of size 1024. 5404172 blocks available
```

We were able to access the DFS share as if it was at a single location, even though the targets were actually located in two different servers.

Unfortunately, Samba support of DFS is still far from perfect and we might get random access errors when trying to access an DFS resource. Hopefully these errors will be solved in newer versions of the Samba software.

# Summary

After configuring a couple of DCs, on this occasion we have successfully set up a member server. As we have done in other chapters of the book, we could have used Winbind, which is a very easy-to-use solution, but this time we've decided to manually modify the necessary parameters. Once the configuration was complete, we were able to list the users and obtain Kerberos tickets. We also learned about DFS and even set up DFS shares on a Samba server.

# CHAPTER 19

# NetBIOS and WINS

NetBIOS was the protocol originally used to communicate in Windows environments. Developed during the 1980s, this protocol is easy to implement and provides three different services: name service, datagram distribution service, and session service. The name server role is usually assumed by a Windows Internet Name Service (WINS) server. This WINS server is the Microsoft implementation of the NetBIOS name server service. In this chapter we'll cover the following concepts:

- Understanding WINS concepts.

- Understanding NetBIOS concepts.

- Understanding the role of a local master browser.

- Understanding the role of a domain master browser.

- Understanding the role of Samba as a WINS server.

- Understanding name resolution.

- Configuring Samba as a WINS server.

- Understanding NetBIOS browsing and browser elections.

- Understanding NetBIOS name types.

We will also learn about the following terms and utilities: `smb.conf`, **nmblookup**, **smbclient**, `name resolve order`, `lmhosts`, `wins support`, `wins server`, `wins proxy`, `dns proxy`, `domain master`, `os level`, and `preferred master`.

© Antonio Vazquez 2019
A. Vazquez, *Practical LPIC-3 300*, https://doi.org/10.1007/978-1-4842-4473-9_19

# NetBIOS

NetBIOS works at the session layer of the Open Systems Interconnection (OSI) model (see https://en.wikipedia.org/wiki/OSI_model). In the past it ran over IPX/SPX networks, but now it usually runs over TCP/IP. NetBIOS provides the following services:

- *Name service (NetBIOS-NS):* This works pretty much like the DNS service, allowing us to register and resolve names.

- *Datagram distribution service (NetBIOS-DGM):* This is used for connectionless communications.

- *Session service (NetBIOS-SSN):* This is used for connection-oriented communication.

## Name Service

For two computers to communicate through NetBIOS, either using datagrams or establishing a session, they need to register their NetBIOS names. NetBIOS names have a length of 16 octets, and the last octets usually designate the type of resource. When using NetBIOS over TCP, the name service runs on UDP port 137.

The service allows us to do the following:

- Add and register a NetBIOS name.

- Add and register a NetBIOS group name.

- Delete and unregister a NetBIOS name or group name.

- Look up a NetBIOS name in the network.

## Datagram Distribution Service

This is a connectionless service that runs on UDP port 138. It works by sending and receiving datagrams and broadcast datagrams.

## Session Service

This service runs on TCP port 139, and allows two computers to establish a reliable connection.

# NetBIOS Names

When using NetBIOS in a network, each computer can have a single NetBIOS name or multiple NetBIOS names associated. A NetBIOS name is supposed to be 16 characters long; in its implementation, however, Microsoft only uses 15, reserving the 16th character as a suffix.

From the Windows workstation we joined previously to the domain we can check the NetBIOS names of the computers in the same network.

```
C:\Users\john>net view
Server Name            Remark

---------------------------------------------------------

\\JULIET_SERVER        Samba 4.7.1
\\ZULU2
The command completed successfully.
```

In addition, to see all the NetBIOS names associated with a computer we can use the **nbtstat** command.

```
C:\Users\john>nbtstat -a juliet server

Local Area Connection:
Node IpAddress: [192.168.1.251] Scope Id: []

        NetBIOS Remote Machine Name Table

    Name               Type         Status
    ---------------------------------------------

    JULIET_SERVER  <00>  UNIQUE      Registered
    JULIET_SERVER  <03>  UNIQUE      Registered
    JULIET_SERVER  <20>  UNIQUE      Registered
    .._MSBROWSE_.<01>  GROUP         Registered
    MY_SAMBA_DOMAIN<00>  GROUP       Registered
    MY_SAMBA_DOMAIN<1B>  UNIQUE      Registered
    MY_SAMBA_DOMAIN<1C>  GROUP       Registered
    MY_SAMBA_DOMAIN<1D>  UNIQUE      Registered
    MY_SAMBA_DOMAIN<1E>  GROUP       Registered

    MAC Address = 00-00-00-00-00-00
```

According to the NetBIOS suffix used by the Microsoft NetBIOS implementation, we have several record types for unique as well as for group names.

These are the available record types for unique names:

- 00 Workstation Service

- 03 Windows Messenger Service

- 06 Remote Access Service

- 20 File Service

- 21 Remote Access Service

- 1B Domain Master Browser

- 1D Master Browser

These are the record types for group names:

- 00 Workstation Service

- 1C Domain Controllers

- 1E Browser Service Elections

As we can see, the computer JULIET_SERVER is a DC for MY_SAMBA_DOMAIN, as stated by the NetBIOS group name 20. It is also the master browser and domain master browser for the domain.

If we look at the NetBIOS associated with a workstation, we'll see that there are fewer of them.

```
C:\Users\john>nbtstat -a zulu2

Local Area Connection:
Node IpAddress: [192.168.1.251] Scope Id: []

        NetBIOS Remote Machine Name Table

    Name               Type         Status
    ---------------------------------------------
    ZULU2           <20>  UNIQUE     Registered
    ZULU2           <00>  UNIQUE     Registered
    MY_SAMBA_DOMAIN<00>  GROUP      Registered
```

```
MY_SAMBA_DOMAIN<1E>   GROUP            Registered

MAC Address = 08-00-27-EF-24-D4
```

Obviously in this case the workstation does not have the DC group name associated with it. We have seen in this example that the computer JULIET_SERVER, in addition to being a DC, also played the role of master browser and domain master browser. Let's explore what this means.

## Local Master Browser

The local master browser, or simply master browser, is a computer that keeps a list of every server, workstation, and service available in the network. This role is dynamically assigned to one of the computers in the network segment. However, we can influence this election process by tuning some parameters in the `smb.conf` file:

- `local master = yes`: By adding this line to the `smb.conf` file we tell our Samba server to try and become the local master browser in its network segment.

- `preferred local master = yes`: This will give the Samba server a higher preference when trying to become the master browser.

- `os level = 255`: The higher this value, the higher the chance to become the master browser. If we want to make sure that our Samba server wins every election, we can assign the value 255 to this parameter.

## Domain Master Browser

If the computers in our domain span across different subnets, to be able to browse every domain member we need to have in each subnet a domain master server. In the previous section we saw how to make our Samba server the local master browser in its network segment, simply by adding a few parameters to the `smb.conf` file. To make it a domain master browser, too, we just need to add a new line to the `smb.conf` file: `domain master = yes`.

# NetBIOS Names and Samba

We can look up NetBIOS names from a Linux computer similar to what we had done previously with Windows. To do this, we'll use the **nmblookup** tool, included in the `samba-client` software package. For example, we might want to know which computer is the local master browser by using the `-M` parameter.

```
[root@kilo ~]# nmblookup -M MY_SAMBA_DOMAIN
192.168.1.226 MY_SAMBA_DOMAIN<1d>
```

We can also query for the location of the DCs. In this case we need to specify the name of the domain and the appropriate suffix, `1c` in this case for DCs.

```
[root@kilo ~]# nmblookup 'MY_SAMBA_DOMAIN#1C'
192.168.1.226 MY_SAMBA_DOMAIN<1c>
```

If we want to query the computers that can work as workstations, we can do it in a similar way, using the suffix `00` instead.

```
[root@kilo ~]# nmblookup 'MY_SAMBA_DOMAIN#00'
192.168.1.251 MY_SAMBA_DOMAIN<00>
192.168.1.226 MY_SAMBA_DOMAIN<00>
```

We have seen that besides the **smbd** service, there is also an **nmbd** service that is in charge of the NetBIOS naming services. In the examples we've just seen, we performed the queries from the BDC computer, `kilo.linuxaholics.com`, but we didn't see any NetBIOS name associated with the BDC itself. This happened because we didn't start the **nmbd** service. If we start it and repeat the queries the result will be different.

```
[root@kilo ~]# systemctl start nmb
[root@kilo ~]# nmblookup 'MY_SAMBA_DOMAIN#1c'
192.168.1.236 MY_SAMBA_DOMAIN<1c>
192.168.1.226 MY_SAMBA_DOMAIN<1c>
```

Now **nmblookup** was able to locate two DCs, the PDC and the BDC. We can also resolve the NetBIOS names from an IP address.

```
[root@kilo ~]# nmblookup -A 192.168.1.236
Looking up status of 192.168.1.236
        KILO               <00> -        H <ACTIVE>
        KILO               <03> -        H <ACTIVE>
        KILO               <20> -        H <ACTIVE>
        MY_SAMBA_DOMAIN <00> - <GROUP> H <ACTIVE>
        MY_SAMBA_DOMAIN <1c> - <GROUP> H <ACTIVE>
        MY_SAMBA_DOMAIN <1e> - <GROUP> H <ACTIVE>

        MAC Address = 00-00-00-00-00-00
```

# NetBIOS Traffic

Let's now look at a practical example. We'll sniff the network traffic in the PDC server (juliet.linuxaholics.com).

```
[root@juliet ~]# tcpdump -w output.pcap
tcpdump: listening on enp0s3, link-type EN10MB (Ethernet), capture size
65535 bytes
```

Then we'll restart the workstation (zulu) and log in as a domain user. After that, we stop **tcpdump** and open the output file in Wireshark. One of the first NetBIOS datagrams will be similar to what we see in Figure 19-1.

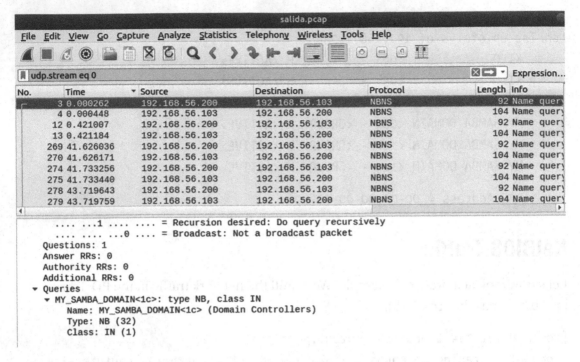

***Figure 19-1.*** *Searching for a domain controller*

The client queries the address of a DC (type 1c), for the domain MY_SAMBA_
DOMAIN. Right after that query, we can see the corresponding answer with the address
of a DC (Figure 19-2).

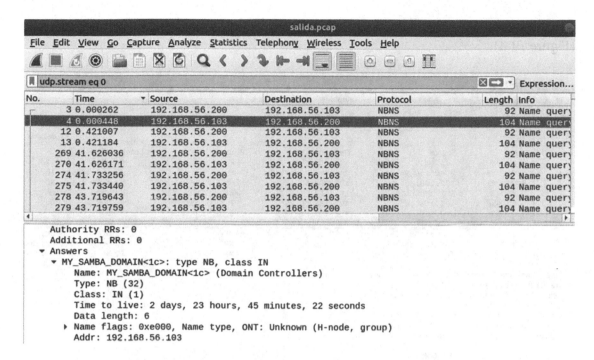

**Figure 19-2.** *Answering with the address of a domain controller*

Soon after that, we'll see a logon request from the workstation (Figure 19-3).

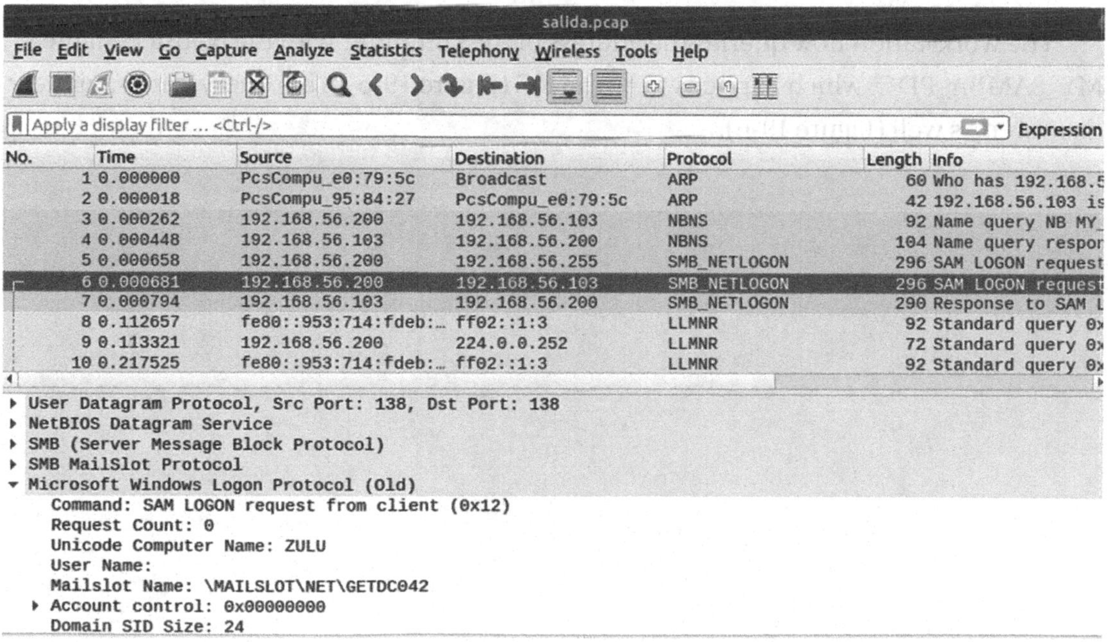

**Figure 19-3.** *Logon request*

This logon request will be answered promptly by the DC with its NetBIOS name (Figure 19-4).

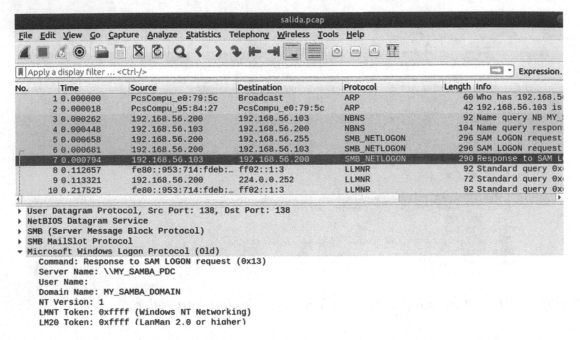

**Figure 19-4.** *Answering the logon request*

The workstation now queries the address of the computer with the NetBIOS name MY_SAMBA_PDC, which happens to be the DC (Figure 19-5). This query is immediately answered as well (Figure 19-6).

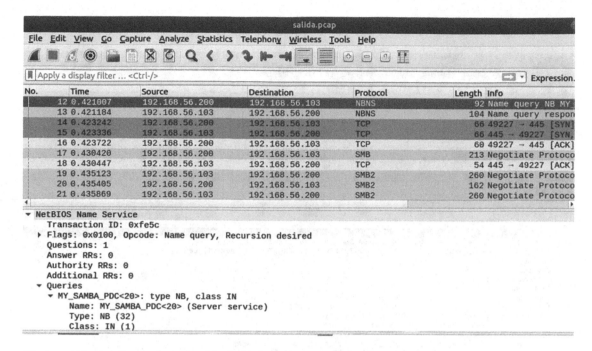

*Figure 19-5.* *Querying the NetBIOS name service again*

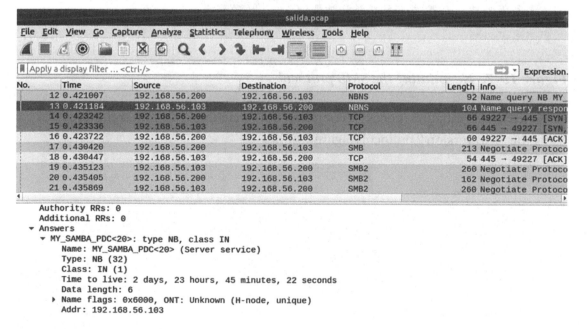

*Figure 19-6.* *NetBIOS response*

After that, workstation and server negotiate what protocol to use (Figure 19-7).

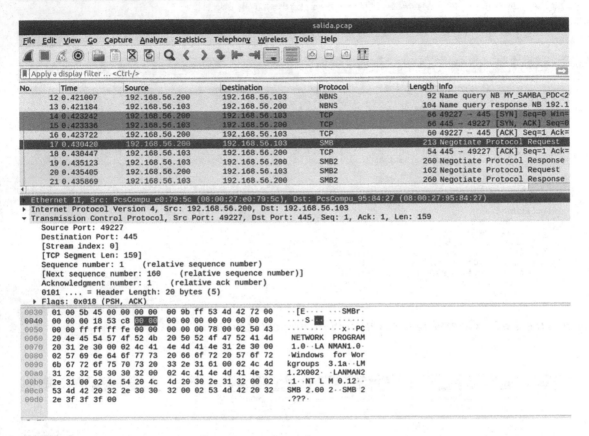

***Figure 19-7.***  *Negotiating the SMB protocol*

Once the negotiation process is complete, both machines begin to communicate using the SMB version 2 protocol (Figure 19-8).

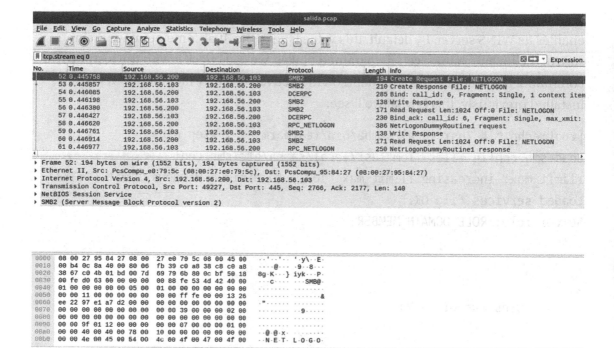

*Figure 19-8. Communicating through the SMB version 2 protocol*

# WINS

WINS was implemented by Microsoft as a name server for NetBIOS computer names. It is analogous to DNS, but it uses NetBIOS names instead of domain names.

As soon as a WINS client starts, it registers its NetBIOS name and IP address with the WINS server. In turn, when a WINS client launches a NetBIOS application it will query the WINS server about the destination NetBIOS name. If the WINS server finds the queried name it will respond with the corresponding IP address.

# Samba and WINS

In the /etc/samba/smb.conf file there are some parameters devoted to name resolution.

```
;       wins support = yes
;       wins server = w.x.y.z
;       wins proxy = yes
```

When we set the value of wins support to yes, the **nmbd** component of Samba enables its WINS server. By default, this value is set to no. If at some point we are not sure of the default value a certain parameter takes, we can check it with the **testparm -v** command. If we launch this command on the Active Directory member server we installed previously, this is what we'll see:

```
[root@echo ~]# /usr/local/samba/bin/testparm -v | grep wins
Load smb config files from /usr/local/samba/etc/smb.conf
rlimit_max: increasing rlimit_max (1024) to minimum Windows limit (16384)
Loaded services file OK.
Server role: ROLE_DOMAIN_MEMBER
.
.
.

        wins support = No

.
.
.
```

To make this server a WINS server we need to add the line wins support = Yes to the /usr/local/samba/etc/smb.conf file and reload the configuration with **smbcontrol**.

```
[root@echo ~]# /usr/local/samba/bin/smbcontrol smbd reload-config
[root@echo ~]# /usr/local/samba/bin/testparm -v | grep wins
Load smb config files from /usr/local/samba/etc/smb.conf
rlimit_max: increasing rlimit_max (1024) to minimum Windows limit (16384)
Loaded services file OK.
Server role: ROLE_DOMAIN_MEMBER
.
.
.

        wins support = Yes

.
.
.
```

For the WINS server to be queried over the network, we need to check that the corresponding ports in the firewall are open.

```
[root@juliet ~]# firewall-cmd --list-ports
137/udp 138/udp 445/tcp 8888/tcp 139/udp
```

On the computer that acts as the WINS client we need to include this line:

```
wins server = 192.168.56.103
```

Another two WINS-related options are wins proxy and dns proxy. The first one is used for the Samba server to listen to broadcast name queries and forward them to a WINS server. This could be useful if the WINS clients and the WINS server are on separate networks and broadcast traffic is not permitted. Today, however, this option is rarely used. The other option, dns proxy, means that the Samba server acting as a WINS server should treat any unresolved NetBIOS name as a DNS name and query the DNS server on behalf of the client.

We should also take into account the parameter name resolve order, which determines the order in which the client will resolve the NetBIOS name. By default, it has this value:

```
name resolve order = lmhosts, wins, host, bcast
```

This means that the computer will try to resolve the name first in the lmhost file, then it will query the WINS server. If it cannot resolve the name yet it will search the host file, and finally it will use a broadcast.

In the Samba WINS server there are two files where information related to NetBIOS names is stored. The first one is the file /var/lib/samba/wins.dat, which is a text file, the content of which can be easily seen.

```
[root@juliet ~]# cat /var/lib/samba/wins.dat
VERSION 1 0
"JULIET_SERVER#00" 1524267695 192.168.1.226 66R
"WORKGROUP#1e" 1524176448 0.0.0.0 e4R
"ZULU#00" 1524059778 192.168.1.250 64R
"JULIET#03" 1524189861 192.168.1.226 66R
"WORKGROUP#00" 1524176448 0.0.0.0 e4R
  .
  .
  .
```

The second one is /var/lib/samba/wins.tdb, a .tdb file that can be examined with **tdbdump**.

```
[root@juliet ~]# tdbdump /var/lib/samba/wins.tdb
{
key(65) = "MYGROUP\00\00\00\00\00\00\00\00\00\00\00\00\00\00\00\00\00\
00\00\00\00\00\00\00\00\00\00\00\00\00\00\00\00\00\00\00\00\00\00\00\00\
00\00\00\00\00\00\00\00\00\00\00\00\00\00\1E"
data(35) = "\E4\00\01\BF\19\CA[\8F\8A\C5[\0B\00\00\00\00\00\00\00\00\00\
00a\00\00\00\01\00\00\00\00\00\00\00"
}
.
.
.
```

We have already used **nmblookup** to query NetBIOS names, according to the order specified in the name resolve order parameter, but we can also force **nmblookup** to directly query the WINS server using the -U and -R parameters.

```
[root@kilo ~]# nmblookup -U JULIET_SERVER -R 'MY_SAMBA_DOMAIN#1C'
192.168.1.236 MY_SAMBA_DOMAIN<1c>
192.168.1.226 MY_SAMBA_DOMAIN<1c>
```

# Summary

In this chapter we have studied the NetBIOS protocol, which historically has played a dominant role in every Windows network. We have reviewed many concepts associated with this protocol and we implemented a Samba WINS server. For didactic purposes, we also saw a practical example of communication between a server and a workstation using NetBIOS.

**CHAPTER 20**

# Active Directory Name Resolution

In the previous chapter we studied NetBIOS, which historically has played a major role in Windows networks. With the release of Windows 2000, however, that started to change. From that moment on DNS started to gain importance; in fact, the latest versions of Windows don't even need NetBIOS to operate in a network.

When provisioning a Samba Active Directory domain, we can install an internal DNS server or use an existing Bind DNS server. In this chapter we'll cover the following concepts:

- Understanding and managing DNS for Samba 4 as an Active Directory DC.

- DNS forwarding with the internal DNS server of Samba 4.

We will also explore the following terms and utilities: **samba-tool dns** (with subcommands), `smb.conf`, `dns forwarder`, `/etc/resolv.conf`, **dig**, and **host**.

## DNS

As we said before, when Microsoft released Windows 2000, it also began to switch from NetBIOS to DNS to allow every computer in a domain to locate the required resources. When provisioning the Active Directory domain, we can choose whether to install an internal DNS server (as we did), or use a Bind DNS server instead.

If electing to use a Bind DNS server, we would have to choose in turn between using flat files or DLZ Bind. When using flat files, Bind stores the zone-related information in plain text files. These files can become very large in size and need to be loaded in RAM for Bind to work. On the other hand, DLZ Bind uses a database to store zone data.

© Antonio Vazquez 2019
A. Vazquez, *Practical LPIC-3 300*, https://doi.org/10.1007/978-1-4842-4473-9_20

Thus, Bind no longer needs to load all the zone information in RAM, as it will query the database to get the information it needs.

If we have a Windows workstation in the domain, we can manage the DNS server with the administrative tools provided by Microsoft. On the other hand, we can also manage the DNS in the Samba server itself by using **samba-tool dns**. For instance, we can list the zones:

```
[root@mike ~]# /usr/local/samba/bin/samba-tool dns zonelist
mike.linuxaholics.com -U Administrator
Password for [LINUXAHOLICS\Administrator]:
  2 zone(s) found

  pszZoneName     : linuxaholics.com
  Flags           : DNS_RPC_ZONE_DSINTEGRATED DNS_RPC_ZONE_UPDATE_SECURE
  ZoneType        : DNS_ZONE_TYPE_PRIMARY
  Version         : 50
  dwDpFlags       : DNS_DP_AUTOCREATED DNS_DP_DOMAIN_DEFAULT DNS_DP_ENLISTED
  pszDpFqdn       : DomainDnsZones.linuxaholics.com

  pszZoneName     : _msdcs.linuxaholics.com
  Flags           : DNS_RPC_ZONE_DSINTEGRATED DNS_RPC_ZONE_UPDATE_SECURE
  ZoneType        : DNS_ZONE_TYPE_PRIMARY
  Version         : 50
  dwDpFlags       : DNS_DP_AUTOCREATED DNS_DP_FOREST_DEFAULT DNS_DP_ENLISTED
  pszDpFqdn       : ForestDnsZones.linuxaholics.com
```

We can check the root hints, too.

```
[root@mike ~]# /usr/local/samba/bin/samba-tool dns roothints mike.
linuxaholics.com -U Administrator --password=Passw0rd
  Name=, Records=13, Children=0
    NS: h.root-servers.net. (flags=40000008, serial=0, ttl=0)
    NS: f.root-servers.net. (flags=40000008, serial=0, ttl=0)
    NS: b.root-servers.net. (flags=40000008, serial=0, ttl=0)
    NS: m.root-servers.net. (flags=40000008, serial=0, ttl=0)
    NS: l.root-servers.net. (flags=40000008, serial=0, ttl=0)
    NS: i.root-servers.net. (flags=40000008, serial=0, ttl=0)
```

```
  NS: e.root-servers.net. (flags=40000008, serial=0, ttl=0)
  NS: d.root-servers.net. (flags=40000008, serial=0, ttl=0)
  NS: k.root-servers.net. (flags=40000008, serial=0, ttl=0)
  NS: a.root-servers.net. (flags=40000008, serial=0, ttl=0)
  NS: g.root-servers.net. (flags=40000008, serial=0, ttl=0)
  NS: c.root-servers.net. (flags=40000008, serial=0, ttl=0)
  NS: j.root-servers.net. (flags=40000008, serial=0, ttl=0)
Name=h.root-servers.net., Records=1, Children=0
  A: 198.97.190.53 (flags=8, serial=0, ttl=0)
Name=f.root-servers.net., Records=1, Children=0
  A: 192.5.5.241 (flags=8, serial=0, ttl=0)
Name=b.root-servers.net., Records=1, Children=0
  A: 192.228.79.201 (flags=8, serial=0, ttl=0)
Name=m.root-servers.net., Records=1, Children=0
  A: 202.12.27.33 (flags=8, serial=0, ttl=0)
Name=l.root-servers.net., Records=1, Children=0
  A: 199.7.83.42 (flags=8, serial=0, ttl=0)
Name=i.root-servers.net., Records=1, Children=0
  A: 192.36.148.17 (flags=8, serial=0, ttl=0)
Name=e.root-servers.net., Records=1, Children=0
  A: 192.203.230.10 (flags=8, serial=0, ttl=0)
Name=d.root-servers.net., Records=1, Children=0
  A: 199.7.91.13 (flags=8, serial=0, ttl=0)
Name=k.root-servers.net., Records=1, Children=0
  A: 193.0.14.129 (flags=8, serial=0, ttl=0)
Name=a.root-servers.net., Records=1, Children=0
  A: 198.41.0.4 (flags=8, serial=0, ttl=0)
Name=g.root-servers.net., Records=1, Children=0
  A: 192.112.36.4 (flags=8, serial=0, ttl=0)
Name=c.root-servers.net., Records=1, Children=0
  A: 192.33.4.12 (flags=8, serial=0, ttl=0)
Name=j.root-servers.net., Records=1, Children=0
  A: 192.58.128.30 (flags=8, serial=0, ttl=0)
```

We can also query names.

```
[root@mike ~]# /usr/local/samba/bin/samba-tool dns query mike.linuxaholics.
com linuxaholics.com mike ALL -U Administrator --password=Passw0rd
  Name=, Records=1, Children=0
    A: 192.168.1.234 (flags=f0, serial=1, ttl=900)
[root@mike ~]# /usr/local/samba/bin/samba-tool dns query mike.linuxaholics.
com linuxaholics.com november ALL -U Administrator --password=Passw0rd
  Name=, Records=1, Children=0
    A: 192.168.1.235 (flags=f0, serial=2, ttl=900)
```

In addition, we can list all the records in a zone.

```
[root@mike ~]# /usr/local/samba/bin/samba-tool dns query --additional
mike.linuxaholics.com linuxaholics.com @ ALL -U Administrator
--password=Passw0rd
Specify either --authority or --root along with --additional.
Assuming --authority.
  Name=, Records=3, Children=0
    SOA: serial=2, refresh=900, retry=600, expire=86400, minttl=3600,
ns=mike.linuxaholics.com., email=hostmaster.linuxaholics.com.
(flags=600000f0, serial=2, ttl=3600)
    NS: mike.linuxaholics.com. (flags=600000f0, serial=1, ttl=900)
    A: 192.168.1.234 (flags=600000f0, serial=1, ttl=900)
  Name=_msdcs, Records=0, Children=0
  Name=_sites, Records=0, Children=1
  Name=_tcp, Records=0, Children=4
  Name=_udp, Records=0, Children=2
  Name=DomainDnsZones, Records=0, Children=2
  Name=ForestDnsZones, Records=0, Children=2
  Name=mike, Records=1, Children=0
    A: 192.168.1.234 (flags=f0, serial=1, ttl=900)
  Name=NOVEMBER, Records=1, Children=0
    A: 192.168.1.235 (flags=f0, serial=2, ttl=900)
```

```
Name=Zulu, Records=1, Children=0
  A: 192.168.1.131 (flags=f0, serial=110, ttl=1200)
Name=mike.linuxaholics.com., Records=1, Children=0
  A: 192.168.1.234 (flags=f0, serial=1, ttl=900)
```

We can display some information about the server itself.

```
[root@mike ~]# /usr/local/samba/bin/samba-tool dns serverinfo mike.
linuxaholics.com -U Administrator --password=Password
  dwVersion                    : 0xece0205
  fBootMethod                  : DNS_BOOT_METHOD_DIRECTORY
  fAdminConfigured             : FALSE
  fAllowUpdate                 : TRUE
  fDsAvailable                 : TRUE
  pszServerName                : MIKE.linuxaholics.com
  pszDsContainer               : CN=MicrosoftDNS,DC=DomainDnsZones,DC=linuxa
                                 holics,DC=com
  aipServerAddrs               : ['192.168.1.234']
  aipListenAddrs               : ['192.168.1.234']
  aipForwarders                : []
  dwLogLevel                   : 0
  dwDebugLevel                 : 0
  dwForwardTimeout             : 3
  dwRpcPrototol                : 0x5
  dwNameCheckFlag              : DNS_ALLOW_MULTIBYTE_NAMES
  cAddressAnswerLimit          : 0
  dwRecursionRetry             : 3
  dwRecursionTimeout           : 8
  dwMaxCacheTtl                : 86400
  dwDsPollingInterval          : 180
  dwScavengingInterval         : 168
  dwDefaultRefreshInterval     : 72
  dwDefaultNoRefreshInterval   : 72
  fAutoReverseZones            : FALSE
  fAutoCacheUpdate             : FALSE
  fRecurseAfterForwarding      : FALSE
```

```
fForwardDelegations         : TRUE
fNoRecursion                : FALSE
fSecureResponses            : FALSE
fRoundRobin                 : TRUE
fLocalNetPriority           : FALSE
fBindSecondaries            : FALSE
fWriteAuthorityNs           : FALSE
fStrictFileParsing          : FALSE
fLooseWildcarding           : FALSE
fDefaultAgingState          : FALSE
dwRpcStructureVersion       : 0x2
aipLogFilter                : []
pwszLogFilePath             : None
pszDomainName               : linuxaholics.com
pszForestName               : linuxaholics.com
pszDomainDirectoryPartition : DC=DomainDnsZones,DC=linuxaholics,DC=com
pszForestDirectoryPartition : DC=ForestDnsZones,DC=linuxaholics,DC=com
dwLocalNetPriorityNetMask   : 0xff
dwLastScavengeTime          : 0
dwEventLogLevel             : 4
dwLogFileMaxSize            : 0
dwDsForestVersion           : 4
dwDsDomainVersion           : 4
dwDsDsaVersion              : 4
fReadOnlyDC                 : FALSE
```

We can add a record with the **add** subcommand if we ever need to.

```
[root@mike ~]# /usr/local/samba/bin/samba-tool dns add mike.
linuxaholics.com linuxaholics.com dummy A 192.168.1.222 -U Administrator
--password=Passw0rd
Record added successfully
[root@mike ~]# /usr/local/samba/bin/samba-tool dns query mike.linuxaholics.
com linuxaholics.com dummy ALL -U Administrator --password=Passw0rd
  Name=, Records=1, Children=0
    A: 192.168.1.222 (flags=f0, serial=3, ttl=900)
```

If we have to delete a record, the process is almost identical, but using the **delete** subcommand instead.

```
[root@mike ~]# /usr/local/samba/bin/samba-tool dns delete mike.
linuxaholics.com linuxaholics.com dummy A 192.168.1.222 -U Administrator
--password=Passw0rd
Record deleted successfully
```

Of course, we can also query the internal DNS server with client utilities like **dig** or **host**. We'll use **dig** here.

```
[root@mike ~]# dig a @mike.linuxaholics.com mike.linuxaholics.com

; <<>> DiG 9.9.4-RedHat-9.9.4-61.el7_5.1 <<>> a @mike.linuxaholics.com
mike.linuxaholics.com
; (1 server found)
;; global options: +cmd
;; Got answer:
;; ->>HEADER<<- opcode: QUERY, status: NOERROR, id: 56401
;; flags: qr aa rd ad; QUERY: 1, ANSWER: 1, AUTHORITY: 1, ADDITIONAL: 0
;; WARNING: recursion requested but not available

;; QUESTION SECTION:
;mike.linuxaholics.com.            IN   A

;; ANSWER SECTION:
mike.linuxaholics.com.      900    IN   A     192.168.1.234

;; AUTHORITY SECTION:
linuxaholics.com.           3600   IN   SOA   mike.linuxaholics.com.
hostmaster.linuxaholics.com. 4 900 600 86400 3600

;; Query time: 0 msec
;; SERVER: 192.168.1.234#53(192.168.1.234)
;; WHEN: dom nov 11 09:25:35 EST 2018
;; MSG SIZE  rcvd: 102
```

With **host**, we can get that same information.

```
[root@mike ~]# host -t a mike.linuxaholics.com
mike.linuxaholics.com has address 192.168.1.234
```

# DNS Forwarding

When provisioning the domain, we decided to use the internal DNS server in Samba. This internal server was populated with all the records needed for the domain to function properly. However, this server has no knowledge about external records, so if we need to access resources on the Internet the Samba DNS server won't be able to provide the right answers to those queries.

To solve this problem we can use DNS forwarding; that is, when the internal DNS server cannot answer a query, it will forward that query to another server. When provisioning the domain with **samba-tool** we were given the choice to use a DNS forwarder.

```
[root@mike ~]# /usr/local/samba/bin/samba-tool domain provision --use-
rfc2307 –interactive
.
.
.
DNS forwarder IP address (write 'none' to disable forwarding)
[192.168.1.1]:  none
.
.
.
```

If we decided not to use it at first, however, we can easily set that option in smb.conf.

The option we need to include is dns forwarder. Right now, this parameter isn't set in our Samba Active Directory DC, so if we try to query any external record, such as www.apress.com, we won't find it.

```
[root@mike ~]# host www.apress.com mike.linuxaholics.com
Using domain server:
Name: mike.linuxaholics.com
Address: 192.168.1.234#53
Aliases:

Host www.apress.com not found: 3(NXDOMAIN)
```

To solve this, we edit the Samba configuration file, which in our case is located at /usr/local/samba/etc/smb.conf, and add the following line to the [global] section.

```
dns forwarder = 192.168.1.1
```

We'll use the IP address of the external DNS server to which we want the unsolved queries to be forwarded. After restarting the Samba service, we'll try to resolve the external name again.

```
[root@mike ~]# host www.apress.com mike.linuxaholics.com
Using domain server:
Name: mike.linuxaholics.com
Address: 192.168.1.234#53
Aliases:

www.apress.com is an alias for prod.springer.map.fastlylb.net.
prod.springer.map.fastlylb.net has address 151.101.132.250
```

## Summary

In this brief chapter we managed the internal DNS used by Samba, listing, adding, and deleting records. We also learned to forward queries that the internal DNS server could not resolve by itself.

# CHAPTER 21

# CIFS Integration

Throughout the book this far, we have seen briefly a few examples of CIFS integration in mixed environments. Here we'll go into more depth on its concepts and use. In this chapter we'll cover the following concepts:

- Understanding SMB/CIFS concepts.

- Accessing and mounting remote CIFS shares from a Linux client.

- Securely storing CIFS credentials.

- Understanding features and benefits of CIFS.

- Understanding permissions and file ownership of remote CIFS shares.

We will also learn about the following terms and utilities: SMB/CIFS, **mount**, **mount.cifs**, **smbclient**, **smbget**, **smbtar**, **smbtree**, **findsmb**, smb.conf, **smbcquotas**, and /etc/fstab.

## SMB/CIFS

SMB, also known sometimes as CIFS, is the protocol in charge of providing shared access to files and printers on Windows networks. To make things simpler we use both terms interchangeably. This service can run directly over TCP port 445, but it can also use the NetBIOS API.

## Accessing and Mounting Windows Shares from Linux

To access shares from a Linux computer we can use many utilities. In previous chapters we have already used **smbclient**, but there are many other options available.

© Antonio Vazquez 2019
A. Vazquez, *Practical LPIC-3 300*, https://doi.org/10.1007/978-1-4842-4473-9_21

# smbclient

The most frequently used tool to access Windows shares from a Linux workstation is probably **smbclient**. To list the available shares on a Windows server we would use the -L parameter.

```
[root@alpha ~]# smbclient -L //192.168.1.129 -U antonio
Enter SAMBA\antonio's password:

        Sharename       Type        Comment
        ---------       ----        -------
        ADMIN$          Disk        Remote Admin
        C$              Disk        Default share
        IPC$            IPC         Remote IPC
        public          Disk
Reconnecting with SMB1 for workgroup listing.
Connection to 192.168.1.129 failed (Error NT_STATUS_RESOURCE_NAME_NOT_FOUND)
Failed to connect with SMB1 -- no workgroup available
```

After we have the share list, we can connect to any of them.

```
[root@alpha ~]# smbclient //192.168.1.129/public -U antonio
Enter SAMBA\antonio's password:
Try "help" to get a list of possible commands.
smb: \>
```

Once connected, we can move into the share as if we were working with an FTP session.

```
[root@alpha ~]# smbclient //192.168.1.129/public -U antonio
Enter SAMBA\antonio's password:
Try "help" to get a list of possible commands.
smb: \> ls
  .                                   D        0  Sat Oct 13 23:19:59 2018
  ..                                  D        0  Sat Oct 13 23:19:59 2018
  2018feb.txt                         A        9  Sun Oct 14 06:16:53 2018
  2018jan.txt                         A        9  Sun Oct 14 06:16:46 2018

            6527487 blocks of size 4096. 3796380 blocks available
smb: \>
```

If we want to download the 2018jan.txt file we'll do so with the **get** command.

```
smb: \> get 2018jan.txt
getting file \2018jan.txt of size 9 as 2018jan.txt (0,3 KiloBytes/sec)
(average 0,3 KiloBytes/sec)
smb: \>
```

In a similar way, we can upload files from the Linux client to the Samba share with the **put** command, if we have the right permissions, of course. When we're done we can exit the session.

```
smb: \> exit
[root@alpha /]#
```

# smbget

An alternative way to download files from a Samba share is by using the **smbget** utility, which is quite similar to **wget**.

```
[root@alpha ~]# smbget smb://192.168.1.129/public/2018feb.txt -U antonio
Password for [antonio] connecting to //public/192.168.1.129:
Using workgroup SAMBA, user antonio
smb://192.168.1.129/public/2018feb.txt
Downloaded 9b in 5 seconds
```

# smbtar

Another useful client utility is **smbtar**, which allows us to download multiple files from a Samba share into a single file or tape.

```
[root@alpha ~]# smbtar -s 192.168.1.129 -x public -d . -t fichero.out -u
antonio -p antonio -v
server     is 192.168.1.129
share      is public\.
tar args   is
tape       is fichero.out
blocksize is
tar:1709 DUMP:t->to_process        = 1
```

```
tar:1710 DUMP:t->mode.operation    = TAR_CREATE
tar:1711 DUMP:t->mode.selection    = TAR_INCLUDE
tar:1712 DUMP:t->mode.blocksize    = 20
tar:1713 DUMP:t->mode.hidden       = 1
tar:1714 DUMP:t->mode.system       = 1
tar:1715 DUMP:t->mode.incremental  = 0
tar:1716 DUMP:t->mode.reset        = 0
tar:1717 DUMP:t->mode.dry          = 0
tar:1718 DUMP:t->mode.verbose      = 0
tar:1719 DUMP:t->total_size        = 0
tar:1720 DUMP:t->tar_path          = fichero.out
tar:1721 DUMP:t->path_list_size    = 0
tar:1727 DUMP:t->path_list @ (nil) (0 elem)
rlimit_max: increasing rlimit_max (1024) to minimum Windows limit (16384)
added interface enp0s3 ip=192.168.1.229 bcast=192.168.1.255
netmask=255.255.255.0
tar:316  tarmode is now full, system, hidden, noreset, quiet
tar:717  Total bytes received: 18
```

## smbtree

We could also use the **smbtree** utility, which shows every Samba server present in the network and its shares. However, it can be a bit tricky to set up at first. The program needs to be able to resolve NetBIOS names, otherwise it won't show any information. As we saw in Chapter 19 when talking about NetBIOS, the way to resolve NetBIOS names can be determined by the `name resolve order` option in the `smb.conf` file. As this configuration file is used by the server as well as by client processes, it is a good idea to use a new configuration file to be used exclusively by the clients. We'll copy the original `/etc/samba/smb.conf` file and name the new copy `smb_client.conf`.

In this `smb_client.conf` file, we'll include this line:

```
name resolve order = lmhosts, bcast
```

This way, when we execute **smbtree**, it will try to use the `lmhosts` file to resolve the names, so we need to create and edit that `lmhosts` file.

```
[root@alpha ~]# cat /etc/samba/lmhosts
#
# Sample Samba lmhosts file.
#
192.168.56.102    HOTEL#20
192.168.56.102    MYGROUP#1D
192.168.56.102    MYGROUP#1B
```

This way, when we execute the command again, it will show output similar to this:

```
[root@alpha ~]# smbtree -s smb_client.conf -U Antonio%antonio
MYGROUP
        \\HOTEL                          Samba Server Version 4.1.1
                \\HOTEL\Antonio          Home Directories
                \\HOTEL\IPC$             IPC Service (Samba Server Version
                                         4.1.1)
                \\HOTEL\Text_Printer     Generic text printer
                \\HOTEL\Samba_Printer    Public printer
                \\HOTEL\Demo
                \\HOTEL\Docs             Public documents
```

# smbfind

There is another tool that can show the machines in the network that respond to SMB queries: **smbfind**. It is really a Perl script that uses **nmblookup** and **smbclient** to get the needed information. This tool is not included in the CentOS 7 binary packages, but it is included in the Samba package we downloaded and installed when creating a Samba Active Directory DC.

```
[root@mike ~]# /usr/local/samba/bin/findsmb

                        *=DMB
                        +=LMB
IP ADDR         NETBIOS NAME    WORKGROUP/OS/VERSION
-------------------------------------------------------------------
192.168.56.102  HOTEL          +[      MYGROUP        ]
192.168.56.107  MIKE           [       LINUXAHOLICS   ]
```

# mount

It is also possible to mount a Samba shared folder locally with **mount** or **mount.cifs**.

```
[root@alpha ~]# mount -t cifs -o username=antonio,password=antonio
//192.168.1.129/public /mnt/public_docs/
[root@alpha ~]# mount.cifs -o username=antonio,password=antonio
//192.168.1.129/public /mnt/public_docs/
```

For the system to automatically mount the Samba/CIFS shares, we should add this line to the /etc/fstab file:

```
//192.168.1.129/public /mnt/public_docs/ cifs username=antonio,password=
antonio 0 0
```

# Securely Storing CIFS Credentials

We've seen that when mounting SMB/CIFS shares we can specify the username and the password as parameters of the **mount** command. However, it is more advisable to keep this information stored in a file instead of passing them in plain text as command parameters. We could create a file like this:

```
[root@alpha ~]# cat credentials.txt
username=antonio
password=antonio
```

Then we could use the --credentials parameter when executing the **mount** command.

```
[root@alpha ~]# mount -t cifs -o credentials=/root/credentials.txt
//192.168.1.129/public /mnt/public_docs/
```

Thus the line we included in /etc/fstab in the previous section could be replaced by this one:

```
//192.168.1.129/public /mnt/public_docs/ cifs credentials=/root/
credentials.txt 0 0
```

This way the username and password are no longer visible in plain text. Obviously, we should also give the appropriate permissions to the credentials.txt file, making sure that it is not world readable.

# Features and Benefits of CIFS

According to Microsoft, CIFS/SMB has a series of features that give it many benefits over other network protocols.

- *Integrity and concurrency:* CIFS allows concurrent access to the same file, while providing the needed locking mechanisms to prevent conflicts.

- *Optimization for slow links:* The CIFS protocol has been optimized over the years to work well even over slow links.

- *Security:* A CIFS server allows both anonymous as well as authenticated secure access to the resources.

- *Performance and stability*

- *Unicode file names*

# Permissions and Ownership of Remote File Shares

We can list the permissions of a remote Samba share with **smbcacls**.

```
[root@alpha ~]# smbcacls //192.168.1.129/public 2018jan.txt -U antonio
Enter SAMBA\antonio's password:
REVISION:1
CONTROL:SR|DI|DP
OWNER:Zulu\Antonio
GROUP:Zulu\None
ACL:Zulu\Antonio:ALLOWED/I/FULL
ACL:BUILTIN\Administrators:ALLOWED/I/FULL
ACL:NT AUTHORITY\SYSTEM:ALLOWED/I/FULL
```

We can see the permissions assigned as well as the owner. If we want to, we can add a new ACL.

```
[root@alpha ~]# smbcacls //192.168.1.129/public 2018jan.txt -U
antonio%antonio -a ACL:Jose:ALLOWED/O/READ
```

Now the user Jose will have read permissions to the 2018jan.txt file in the public share of the computer with IP address 192.168.1.129. We can check this by executing **smbcacls** again.

```
[root@alpha ~]# smbcacls //192.168.1.129/public 2018jan.txt -U
antonio%antonio
REVISION:1
CONTROL:SR|DP
OWNER:Zulu\Antonio
GROUP:Zulu\None
ACL:Zulu\Jose:ALLOWED/0x0/READ
ACL:Zulu\Antonio:ALLOWED/I/FULL
ACL:BUILTIN\Administrators:ALLOWED/I/FULL
ACL:NT AUTHORITY\SYSTEM:ALLOWED/I/FULL
```

The ACL for the user antonio is listed with a capital I because the permissions are inherited from the parent folder, as opposed to the permission we granted specifically to the user jose. We can check the permissions from a Windows workstation, too (Figure 21-1).

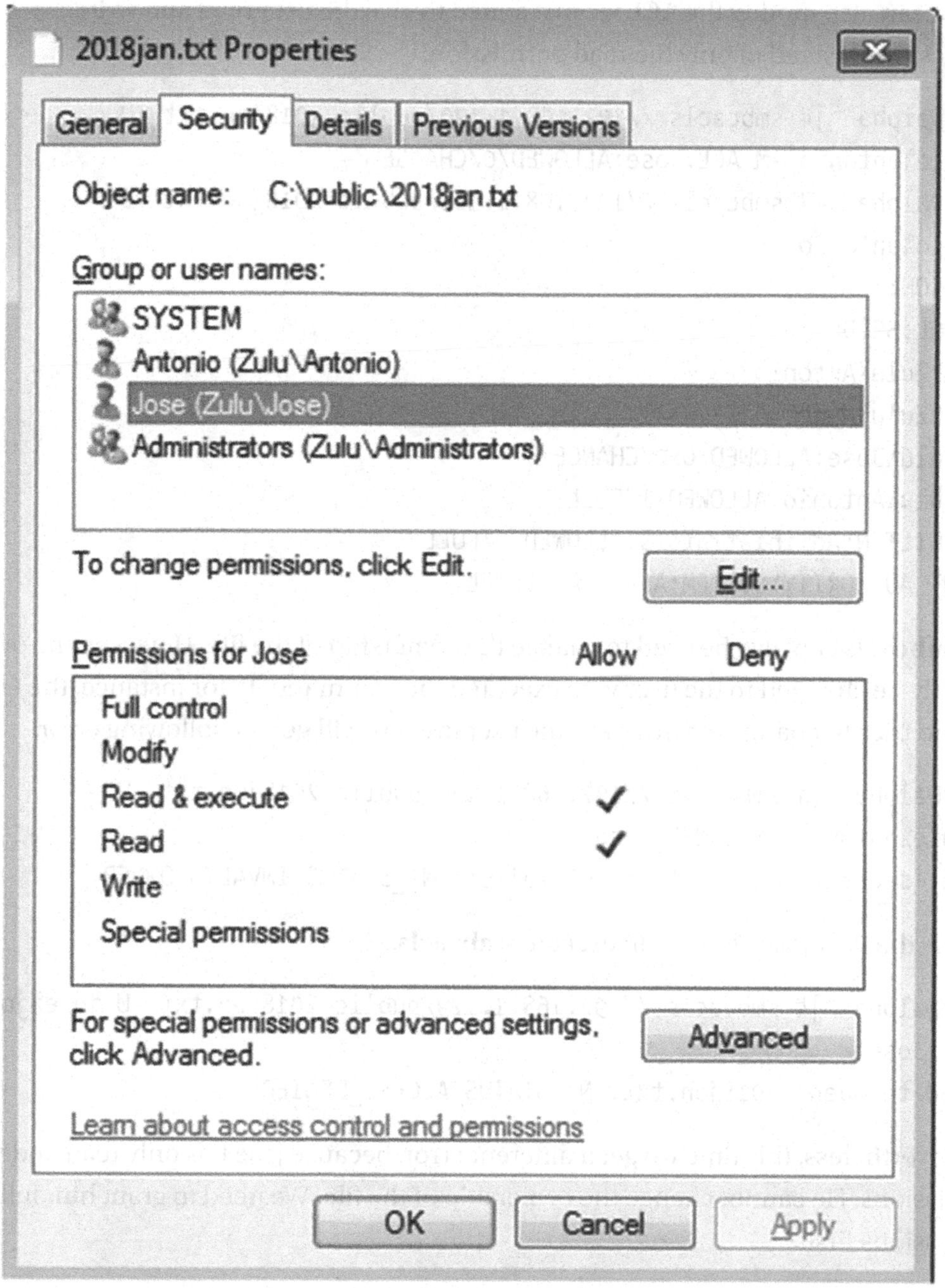

**Figure 21-1.** *Listing the ACLs*

We can also modify the ACL we just added to give the user read and write permissions instead of only the read permission.

```
[root@alpha ~]# smbcacls //192.168.1.129/public 2018jan.txt -U
antonio%antonio -M ACL:Jose:ALLOWED/0/CHANGE
[root@alpha ~]# smbcacls //192.168.1.129/public 2018jan.txt -U
antonio%antonio
REVISION:1
CONTROL:SR|DP
OWNER:Zulu\Antonio
GROUP:Zulu\None
ACL:Zulu\Jose:ALLOWED/0x0/CHANGE
ACL:Zulu\Antonio:ALLOWED/I/FULL
ACL:BUILTIN\Administrators:ALLOWED/I/FULL
ACL:NT AUTHORITY\SYSTEM:ALLOWED/I/FULL
```

**Smbcacls** can also be used to change the ownership of the file. However, the owner can only be changed to the user who executed the command. If, for instance, the user antonio tries to change the owner to the user jose, he will get the following error.

```
[root@alpha ~]# smbcacls //192.168.1.129/public 2018jan.txt -U
antonio%antonio -M OWNER:Jose
ERROR: security description set failed: NT_STATUS_INVALID_OWNER
```

It is the user jose who has to execute **smbcacls**.

```
[root@alpha ~]# smbcacls //192.168.1.129/public 2018jan.txt -U jose%jose -M
OWNER:Jose
Failed to open \2018jan.txt: NT_STATUS_ACCESS_DENIED
```

Nevertheless, this time we get a different error, because jose has only read and write permissions. He cannot change the ownership of the file. We need to grant him full permissions first.

```
[root@alpha ~]# smbcacls //192.168.1.129/public 2018jan.txt -U
antonio%antonio -M ACL:Jose:ALLOWED/0/FULL
```

Now jose can effectively take ownership of the file.

```
[root@alpha ~]# smbcacls //192.168.1.129/public 2018jan.txt -U jose%jose -M
OWNER:Jose
[root@alpha ~]# smbcacls //192.168.1.129/public 2018jan.txt -U jose%jose
REVISION:1
CONTROL:SR|DP
OWNER:Zulu\Jose
GROUP:Zulu\None
ACL:Zulu\Jose:ALLOWED/0x0/FULL
ACL:Zulu\Antonio:ALLOWED/I/FULL
ACL:BUILTIN\Administrators:ALLOWED/I/FULL
ACL:NT AUTHORITY\SYSTEM:ALLOWED/I/FULL
```

Finally, we can restore the ownership of the file and delete the ACL we created.

```
[root@alpha ~]# smbcacls //192.168.1.129/public 2018jan.txt -U
antonio%antonio -M OWNER:antonio
[root@alpha ~]# smbcacls //192.168.1.129/public 2018jan.txt -U
antonio%antonio -D ACL:Jose:ALLOWED/0x0/FULL
```

# Summary

In this chapter we have seen many ways to access a Windows share from a Linux workstation. Besides the well-known **smbclient** utility, we have seen many other less popular alternatives. We learned a bit more about the CIFS/SMB protocol and we saw how to store in a file with the appropriate permissions the credentials used to mount a remote share. Finally, we listed and changed the permissions and ownership of a remote share.

# CHAPTER 22

# Working with Windows Clients

In this last chapter about Samba, we'll focus on how to operate on a Samba server from a Windows client. We'll share Samba resources from Windows and we'll get familiar with some command-line utilities. In this chapter we'll cover the following concepts:

- Knowledge of Windows clients.

- Exploring browse lists and SMB clients from Windows.

- Sharing file and print resources from Windows.

- Use of the **smbclient** program.

- Use of the Windows **net** utility.

We will also explore the following terms and utilities: Windows **net** command, **smbclient**, and **rdesktop**.

## Windows Clients

Over time, as the Windows Server OS evolved, so did Windows clients. Since the early days of Windows 95/98 and Windows NT Workstation, clients could browse through the network. Initially the clients used NetBIOS, as we have already seen, but since the release of Windows 2000, DNS has been the preferred protocol used in Windows networks.

## Sharing Resources from a Windows Client

If we want to share a folder from a Windows client, the procedure is very easy. We right-click the folder and select Properties. In the Properties dialog box, click the Sharing tab (Figure 22-1). Next, click Share (Figure 22-2).

© Antonio Vazquez 2019

A. Vazquez, *Practical LPIC-3 300*, https://doi.org/10.1007/978-1-4842-4473-9_22

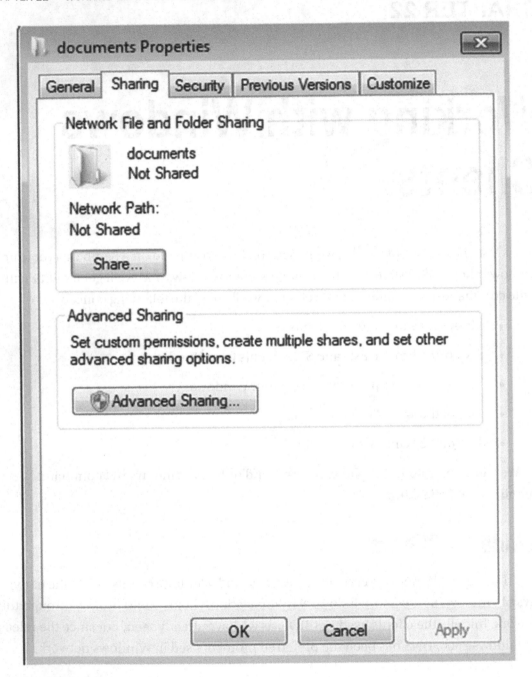

*Figure 22-1.* *Sharing a folder*

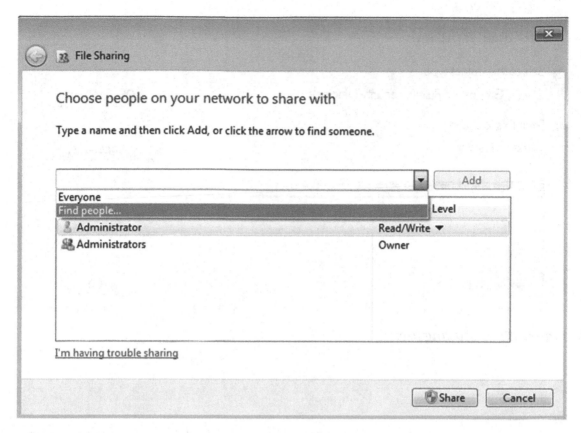

***Figure 22-2.***  *Searching for users*

When we select Find people, the Select Users or Groups dialog box opens (Figure 22-3). Here we can type the usernames we want to add to the shared resource. If we're not sure of a name we can click on Advanced to see a list of all the available users and groups (Figure 22-4).

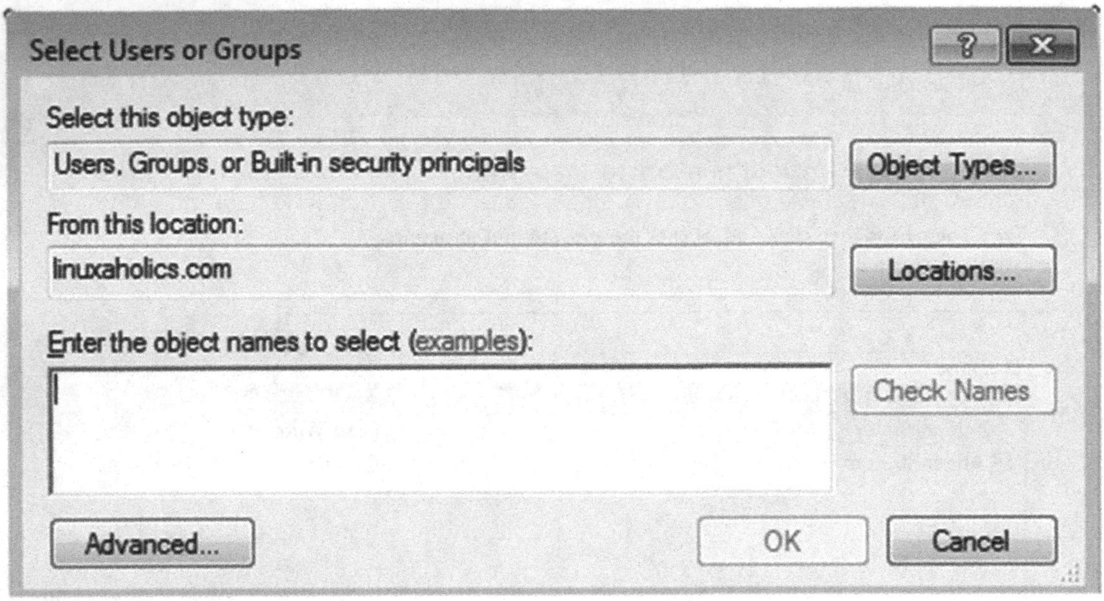


***Figure 22-3.*** *Adding users*

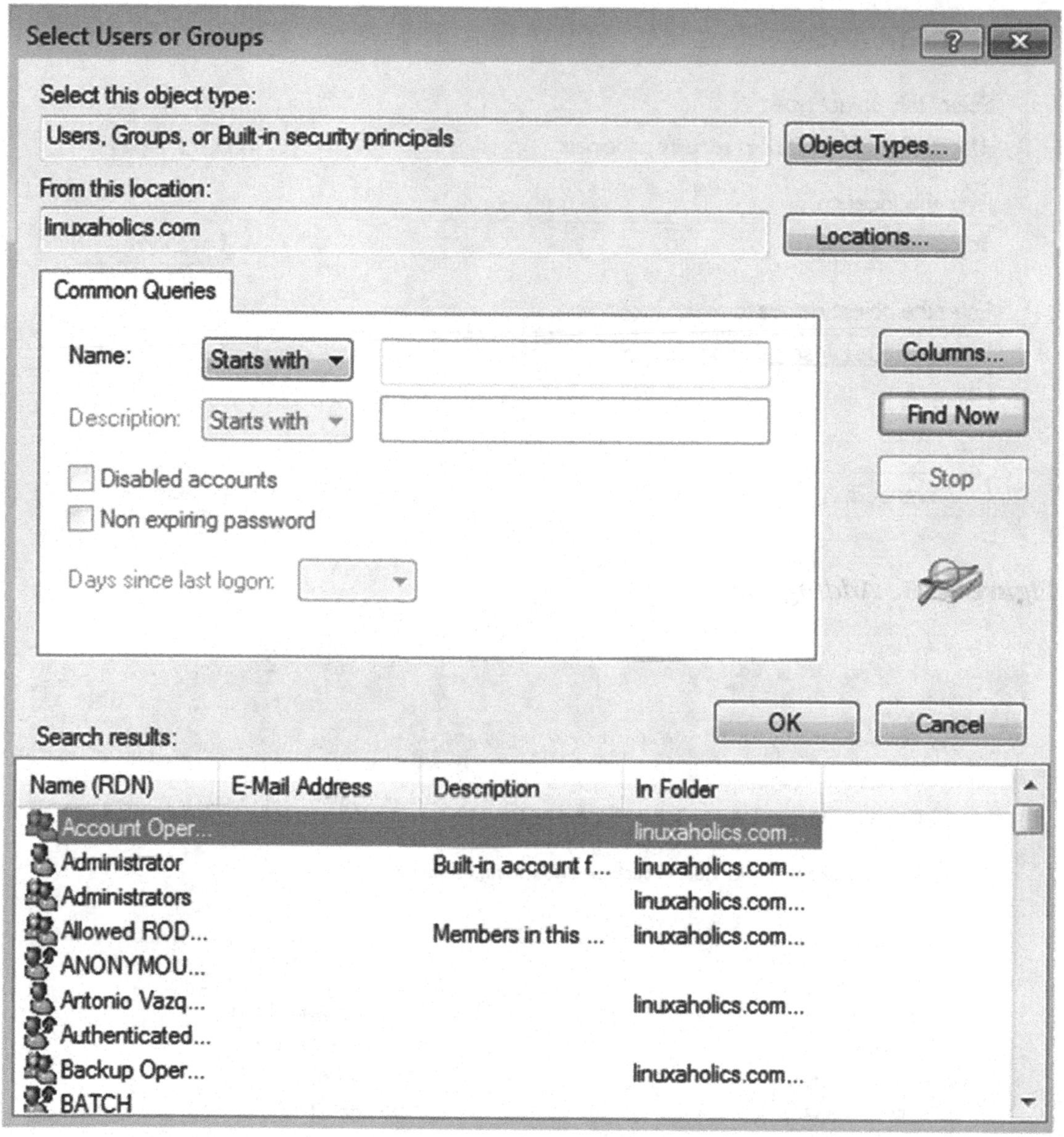

**Figure 22-4.** *Listing all users and groups*

We select the user we want to add (Figure 22-5) and give them read or read/write permissions (Figure 22-6). After you click Share button, the resource is officially shared (Figure 22-7).

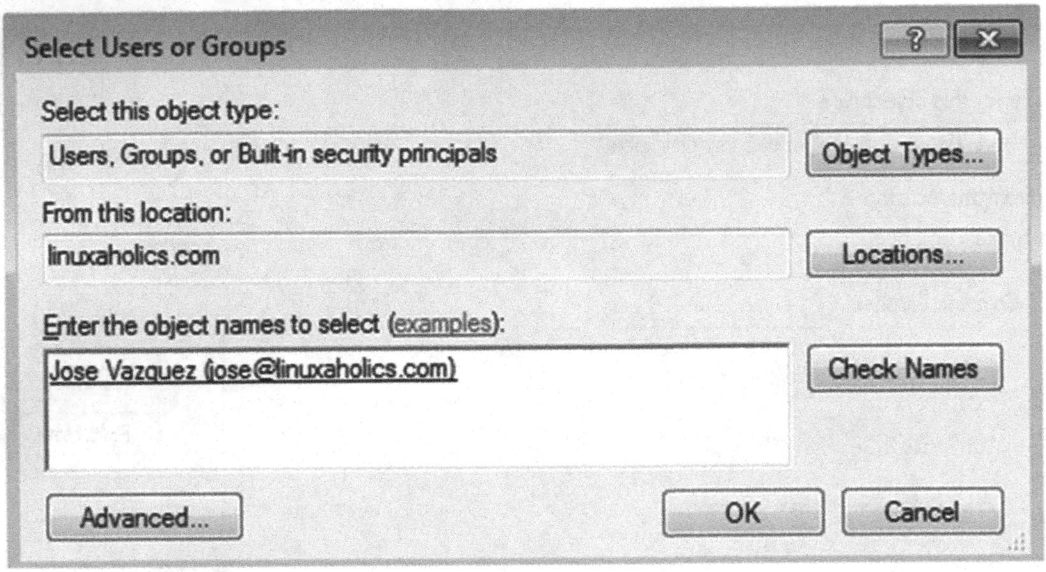

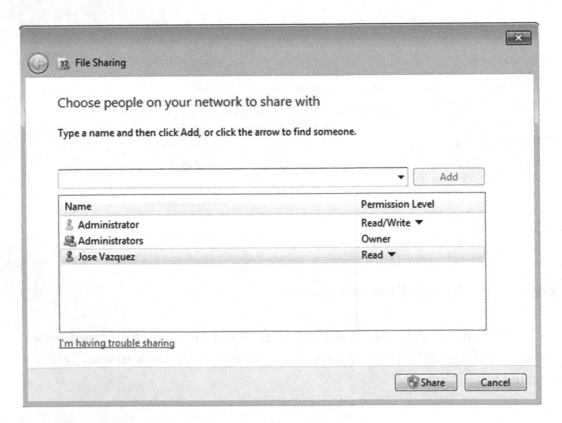

**Figure 22-5.** *Adding a user*

**Figure 22-6.** *Granting permission*

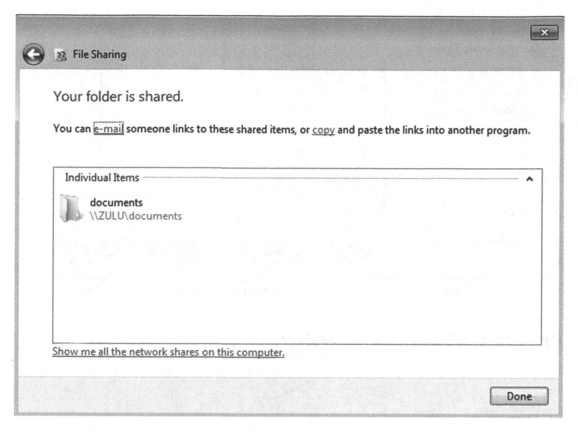

**Figure 22-7.** *Shared resource*

The procedure to share a printer is similar to that for sharing a folder. Double-click the printer we want to share (Figure 22-8). Then, on the Sharing tab, select the Share this printer check box and assign a name to the shared printer (Figure 22-9).

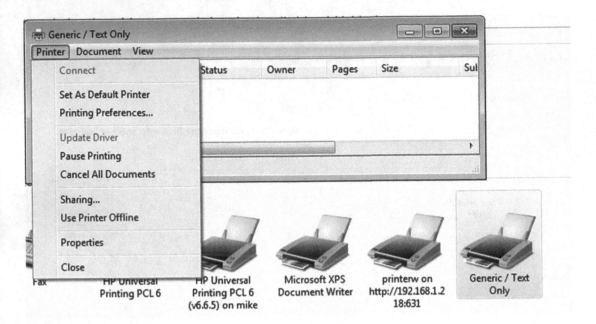

**Figure 22-8.** *Selecting the printer to share*

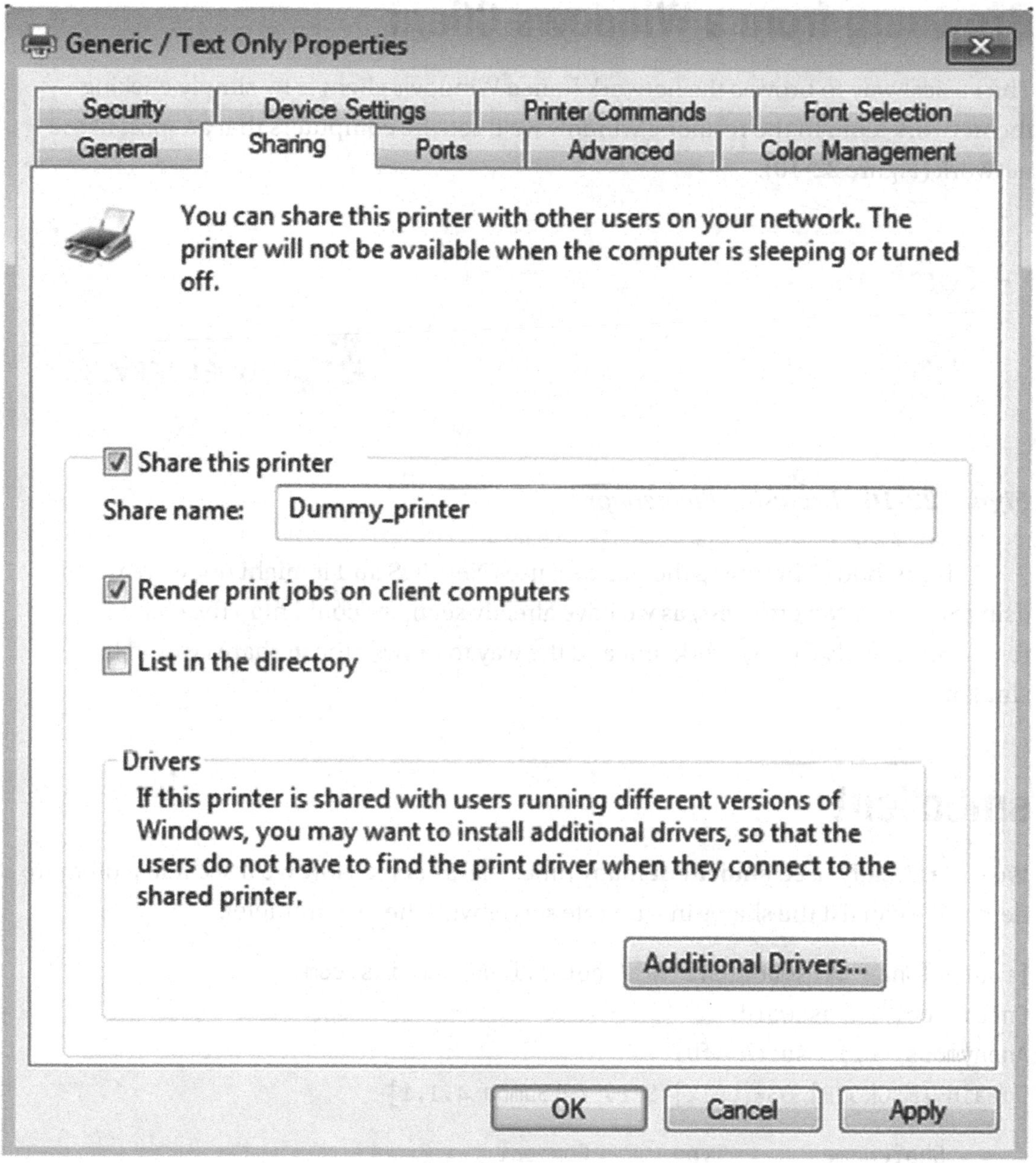

**Figure 22-9.** *Sharing the printer*

# Browsing from a Windows Client

The easiest way to browse the network from a Windows client is by simply clicking the network icon. In the resulting window we'll see the computers that are part of the network (Figure 22-10).

*Figure 22-10.*  *Browsing the network*

This method of browsing the network uses NetBIOS and it might not work when using Samba 4. Nevertheless, as we have already seen, we could map the shared resources directly to a network unit and the way to browse those shares would be very similar.

# smbclient

We have already used **smbclient** many times in this book. Now we'll see it in a bit more depth. We can list the shares in a remote server with the -L parameter.

```
[root@alpha ~]# smbclient -L //hotel.linuxaholics.com
Enter root's password:
Anonymous login successful
Domain=[MYGROUP] OS=[Unix] Server=[Samba 4.1.1]

        Sharename       Type        Comment
        ---------       ----        -------
        Docs            Disk        Public documents
        Demo            Disk
        Samba_Printer   Printer     Public printer
        Text_Printer    Printer     Generic text printer
        IPC$            IPC         IPC Service (Samba Server Version 4.1.1)
```

```
Anonymous login successful
Domain=[MYGROUP] OS=[Unix] Server=[Samba 4.1.1]

        Server                  Comment
        ---------               -------
        HOTEL                   Samba Server Version 4.1.1

        Workgroup               Master
        ---------               -------
        MYGROUP                 HOTEL
```

We're asked for the password of the root user, the Linux user who executed **smbclient**. As we didn't type any password, we logged in anonymously. We could have specified a different Samba user, though, by using the -U parameter.

```
[root@alpha ~]# smbclient -L //hotel.linuxaholics.com -U Antonio
Enter Antonio's password:
Domain=[MYGROUP] OS=[Unix] Server=[Samba 4.1.1]

        Sharename       Type    Comment
        ---------       ----    -------
        Docs            Disk    Public documents
        Demo            Disk
    .
    .
    .
```

If we want to, we can also specify the password by appending the % symbol and the actual password to the username.

```
[root@alpha ~]# smbclient -L //hotel.linuxaholics.com -U Antonio%antonio
Domain=[MYGROUP] OS=[Unix] Server=[Samba 4.1.1]

        Sharename       Type    Comment
        ---------       ----    -------
        Docs            Disk    Public documents
    .
    .
    .
```

# net utility

The **net** utility is one of the most useful for a Windows administrator. It can be used to list the local as well as the domain users:

```
C:\Users\Administrator>net user

User accounts for \\ZULU

-----------------------------------------------------------
Administrator              Antonio                  Guest
Jose
The command completed successfully.

C:\Users\Administrator>net user /domain
The request will be processed at a domain controller for domain
linuxaholics.com
.

User accounts for \\mike.linuxaholics.com

-------------------------------------------------------------------------
Administrator              Antonio                  Guest
jose                       krbtgt
The command completed successfully.
```

It can also be used to list the shared resources on the computer.

```
C:\Users\Administrator>net share

Share name    Resource                             Remark

-------------------------------------------------------------------------
C$            C:\                                  Default share
IPC$                                               Remote IPC
print$        C:\Windows\system32\spool\drivers
                                                   Printer Drivers

ADMIN$        C:\Windows                           Remote Admin
documents     C:\documents
Users         C:\Users
```

```
Dummy_printer
        LPT1:                           Spooled  Generic / Text Only
HP Universal Printing PCL 6
        LPT1:                           Spooled  HP Universal Printing PCL 6
The command completed successfully.
```

The command can also show some configuration data for the workstation on which the command is launched.

```
C:\Users\Administrator>net config workstation
Computer name                   \\ZULU
Full Computer name              Zulu.linuxaholics.com
User name                       Administrator

Workstation active on
        NetBT_Tcpip_{17F44087-3A81-4CD6-8287-4CA9F11F38C1} (080027EF24D4)

Software version                Windows 7 Professional

Workstation domain              LINUXAHOLICS
Workstation Domain DNS Name     linuxaholics.com
Logon domain                    LINUXAHOLICS

COM Open Timeout (sec)          0
COM Send Count (byte)           16
COM Send Timeout (msec)         250
The command completed successfully.
```

# rdesktop

**rdesktop** is not a Samba-related utility, but a remote administration tool. However, as it is included in the exam objectives, we include it here. Currently it is not part of the compiled binaries of the CentOS distribution, but it is included in desktop Linux distributions like Ubuntu. It can be launched from a graphical interface or executed from the command line.

```
antonio@antonio:~$ rdesktop 192.168.1.133
ERROR: 192.168.1.133: unable to connect
```

Before being able to connect, though, we must allow the remote administration on the Windows workstation. On the Remote tab of the System Properties dialog box, select the Allow connections from computers running any version of Remote Desktop option and click OK (Figure 22-11).

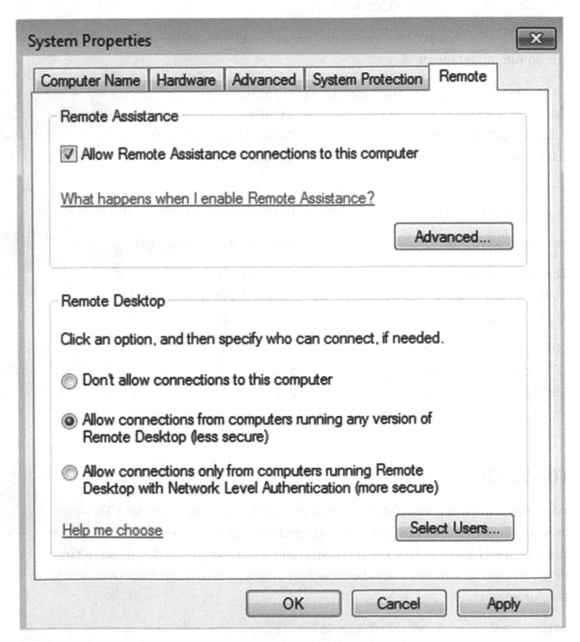

*Figure 22-11.*  *Allowing Remote Desktop connections*

Now we'll be able to connect to the Windows workstation from our Linux desktop
(Figure 22-12).

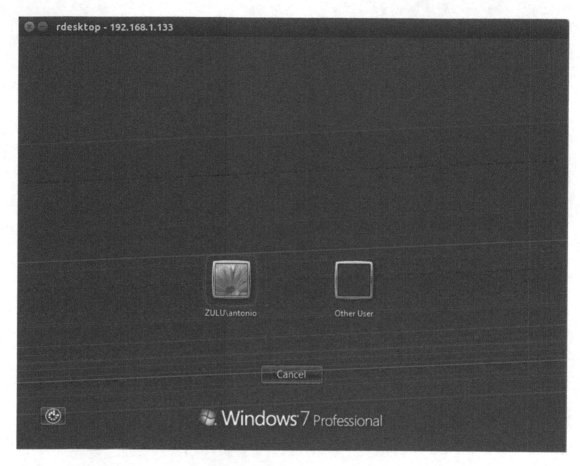

***Figure 22-12.***   *Connecting with rdesktop*

# Summary

In this final chapter on Samba, we have focused more in the side of the Windows client.
We learned how to share folders and printers and used some interesting command-line
utilities like **net**.

# PART III

# FreeIPA

**CHAPTER 23**

# Starting with FreeIPA

According to the official web page of the FreeIPA project:

> *FreeIPA is an integrated security information management solution combining Linux (Fedora), 389 Directory Server, MIT Kerberos, NTP, DNS, Dogtag (Certificate System). It consists of a web interface and command-line administration tools.*

> —https://www.freeipa.org/page/About

The definition mentions Fedora as the Linux part of the solution, but FreeIPA works perfectly well with related Linux distributions such as CentOS or RedHat.

## Structure and Components

As we said before, FreeIPA integrates many components into a complete identity management system. We'll take a look at each one of these components.

## 389 Directory Server

389 Director Server is an open source LDAP server implementation sponsored by Red Hat. Similar in many aspects to OpenLDAP, it supports advanced features such as multimaster replication, secure connections, and so on. It is, however, easier to manage. This LDAP directory is the place where the network elements—users, groups, computers, and so on—are stored.

© Antonio Vazquez 2019
A. Vazquez, *Practical LPIC-3 300*, https://doi.org/10.1007/978-1-4842-4473-9_23

# MIT Kerberos

MIT Kerberos is the component in charge of authenticating the users. We already have studied Kerberos and its free implementation from the Massachusetts Institute of Technology in Chapter 4. We studied how the protocol works and how it could be installed on CentOS 7. Then, we saw a few practical examples and we'll study a few more later in this chapter.

# Network Time Protocol

NTP is a protocol used to synchronize the time in a network. As we have already seen throughout the book, it is extremely important that every computer in the network has the same date and time.

# DNS

The DNS service provides a centralized naming system for network devices. This protocol has become a key component in most of today's network infrastructures, as it is used to locate network resources. FreeIPA uses Bind as the DNS server. A comprehensive study of Bind is beyond the scope of this book, but we'll see some practical examples in the upcoming chapters.

# DogTag Certificate System

Throughout the book we have already created a CA by using the command-line utility **openssl**. DogTag implements a CA and supports all the management operations needed during a certificate life cycle. FreeIPA uses DogTag together with Kerberos to authenticate users.

# Installing FreeIPA

Before installing FreeIPA, we need to make sure that the server can resolve its hostname. We can achieve this by editing the etc/hosts file.

```
[root@quebec ~]# cat /etc/hosts
127.0.0.1    localhost localhost.localdomain localhost4 localhost4.localdomain4
::1          localhost localhost.localdomain localhost6 localhost6.localdomain6
192.168.56.110       quebec.linuxaholics.com
```

Now we install the ipa-server package.

```
[root@quebec ~]# yum -y install ipa-server
```

The installation will take a while, as it needs to download and install many components. Once the installation is complete, we still need to configure the FreeIPA server with the **ipa-server-install** command.

```
[root@quebec ~]# ipa-server-install
```

```
The log file for this installation can be found in /var/log/ipaserver-
install.log
==========================================================================
This program will set up the IPA Server.

This includes:
  * Configure a stand-alone CA (dogtag) for certificate management
  * Configure the Network Time Daemon (ntpd)
  * Create and configure an instance of Directory Server
  * Create and configure a Kerberos Key Distribution Center (KDC)
  * Configure Apache (httpd)

To accept the default shown in brackets, press the Enter key.
```

As we can see, the installation program interactively asks the user about the different options. During the first stages of the installation process we'll be given the choice to configure an integrated DNS server.

```
Do you want to configure integrated DNS (BIND)? [no]: yes
```

However, if we haven't installed some additional packages, we'll get an error.

```
ipa.ipapython.install.cli.install_tool(Server): ERROR  Integrated DNS
requires 'ipa-server-dns' package
ipa.ipapython.install.cli.install_tool(Server): ERROR  The ipa-server-install
command failed. See /var/log/ipaserver-install.log for more information
```

To solve this issue, we'll install the `ipa-server-dns` package.

```
[root@quebec ~]# yum install -y ipa-server-dns
.
.
.
```

Now we can resume the FreeIPA server installation.

```
Do you want to configure integrated DNS (BIND)? [no]: yes

Existing BIND configuration detected, overwrite? [no]: yes
Enter the fully qualified domain name of the computer
on which you're setting up server software. Using the form
<hostname>.<domainname>
Example: master.example.com.

Server host name [quebec.linuxaholics.com]:

Warning: skipping DNS resolution of host quebec.linuxaholics.com
The domain name has been determined based on the host name.

Please confirm the domain name [linuxaholics.com]:

The kerberos protocol requires a Realm name to be defined.
This is typically the domain name converted to uppercase.

Please provide a realm name [LINUXAHOLICS.COM]:
```

After providing a realm name we need to provide a password for the directory manager.

```
Certain directory server operations require an administrative user.
This user is referred to as the Directory Manager and has full access
to the Directory for system management tasks and will be added to the
instance of directory server created for IPA.
The password must be at least 8 characters long.

Directory Manager password:
Password (confirm):
```

In addition to the Directory Manager, FreeIPA also uses an administrative user whose password we need to specify as well.

```
The IPA server requires an administrative user, named 'admin'.
This user is a regular system account used for IPA server administration.

IPA admin password:
Password (confirm):
```

The setup program will perform a DNS check now.

```
Checking DNS domain linuxaholics.com., please wait ...
ipa.ipapython.install.cli.install_tool(Server): ERROR    DNS zone
linuxaholics.com. already exists in DNS
ipa.ipapython.install.cli.install_tool(Server): ERROR    The ipa-server-
install command failed. See /var/log/ipaserver-install.log for more
information
```

As we can see, the installation failed because there is already an existing linuxaholics.com zone on the Internet. To circumvent this problem, we'll change the domain name to linuxaholics.local. We'll also edit the server hostname and the /etc/hosts file.

```
[root@quebec ~]# hostnamectl set-hostname quebec.linuxaholics.local
[root@quebec ~]# cat /etc/hosts
127.0.0.1    localhost localhost.localdomain localhost4 localhost4.
             localdomain4
::1          localhost localhost.localdomain localhost6 localhost6.
             localdomain6
192.168.1.243     quebec.linuxaholics.local
```

Then we can execute **ipa-server-install** again.

```
[root@quebec ~]# ipa-server-install
.
.
.
```

Do you want to configure DNS forwarders? [yes]:

.

.

.

Server host name [quebec.linuxaholics.local]:

Warning: skipping DNS resolution of host quebec.linuxaholics.local
The domain name has been determined based on the host name.

Please confirm the domain name [linuxaholics.local]:
The kerberos protocol requires a Realm name to be defined.
This is typically the domain name converted to uppercase.

Please provide a realm name [LINUXAHOLICS.LOCAL]:
Certain directory server operations require an administrative user.
This user is referred to as the Directory Manager and has full access
to the Directory for system management tasks and will be added to the
instance of directory server created for IPA.
The password must be at least 8 characters long.

Directory Manager password:
Password (confirm):

The IPA server requires an administrative user, named 'admin'.
This user is a regular system account used for IPA server administration.

IPA admin password:
Password (confirm):

Checking DNS domain linuxaholics.local., please wait ...
Do you want to configure DNS forwarders? [yes]:
Following DNS servers are configured in /etc/resolv.conf: 192.168.1.1
Do you want to configure these servers as DNS forwarders? [yes]:
All DNS servers from /etc/resolv.conf were added. You can enter additional
addresses now:
Enter an IP address for a DNS forwarder, or press Enter to skip:
Checking DNS forwarders, please wait ...
Do you want to search for missing reverse zones? [yes]:

The IPA Master Server will be configured with:
Hostname:        quebec.linuxaholics.local
IP address(es): 192.168.1.243
Domain name:     linuxaholics.local
Realm name:      LINUXAHOLICS.LOCAL

BIND DNS server will be configured to serve IPA domain with:
Forwarders:         192.168.1.1
Forward policy:     only
Reverse zone(s):  No reverse zone

Continue to configure the system with these values? [no]: yes


The following operations may take some minutes to complete.
Please wait until the prompt is returned.

Configuring NTP daemon (ntpd)
  .
  .
  .
Configuring directory server (dirsrv). Estimated time: 1 minute
  .
  .
  .
Configuring certificate server (pki-tomcatd). Estimated time: 3 minutes 30
seconds
  .
  .
  .
Configuring directory server (dirsrv). Estimated time: 10 seconds
  .
  .
  .
Configuring Kerberos KDC (krb5kdc). Estimated time: 30 seconds
  .
  .
  .

Configuring kadmin
- 
- 
- 

Configuring ipa_memcached
- 
- 
- 

Configuring ipa-otpd
- 
- 
- 

Configuring ipa-custodia
- 
- 
- 

Configuring the web interface (httpd). Estimated time: 1 minute
- 
- 
- 

Applying LDAP updates
Upgrading IPA:
- 
- 
- 

Configuring DNS (named)
- 
- 
- 

Configuring DNS key synchronization service (ipa-dnskeysyncd)
- 
- 
- 

Configuring client side components
Using existing certificate '/etc/ipa/ca.crt'.

Client hostname: quebec.linuxaholics.local
Realm: LINUXAHOLICS.LOCAL
DNS Domain: linuxaholics.local
IPA Server: quebec.linuxaholics.local
BaseDN: dc=linuxaholics,dc=local

.

.

.

Configured /etc/openldap/ldap.conf
Configured /etc/ssh/ssh_config
Configured /etc/ssh/sshd_config
Configuring linuxaholics.local as NIS domain.
Client configuration complete.

================================================================================
Setup complete

Next steps:
    1. You must make sure these network ports are open:
        TCP Ports:
            * 80, 443: HTTP/HTTPS
            * 389, 636: LDAP/LDAPS
            * 88, 464: kerberos
            * 53: bind
        UDP Ports:
            * 88, 464: kerberos
            * 53: bind
            * 123: ntp

    2. You can now obtain a kerberos ticket using the command:
    'kinit admin'
        This ticket will allow you to use the IPA tools (e.g., ipa
        user-add)
        and the web user interface.

Be sure to back up the CA certificates stored in /root/cacert.p12
These files are required to create replicas. The password for these
files is the Directory Manager password

Our server is ready, but we need to open a series of ports in the firewall so that the clients can connect.

```
[root@quebec ~]# firewall-cmd --permanent --add-service http
success
[root@quebec ~]# firewall-cmd --permanent --add-service https
success
[root@quebec ~]# firewall-cmd --permanent --add-service ldap
success
[root@quebec ~]# firewall-cmd --permanent --add-service ldaps
success
[root@quebec ~]# firewall-cmd --permanent --add-service kerberos
success
[root@quebec ~]# firewall-cmd --permanent --add-service kpasswd
success
[root@quebec ~]# firewall-cmd --permanent --add-service dns
success
[root@quebec ~]# firewall-cmd --permanent --add-service ntp
success
[root@quebec ~]# firewall-cmd --reload
success
```

# Basic Management

The easiest way to manage our newly installed FreeIPA server is by accessing the web interface. We just need to open a browser and point it to the FreeIPA server address, in our case quebec.linuxaholics.com. The first time we connect we might get a warning because currently we don't trust the server certificate (Figure 23-1).

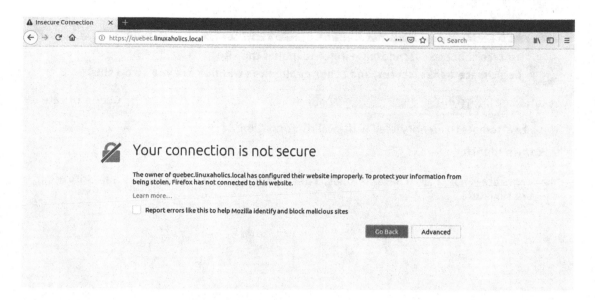

***Figure 23-1.*** *Trusting the server connection*

Click Advanced and confirm that we understand the risk and trust this connection (Figure 23-2).

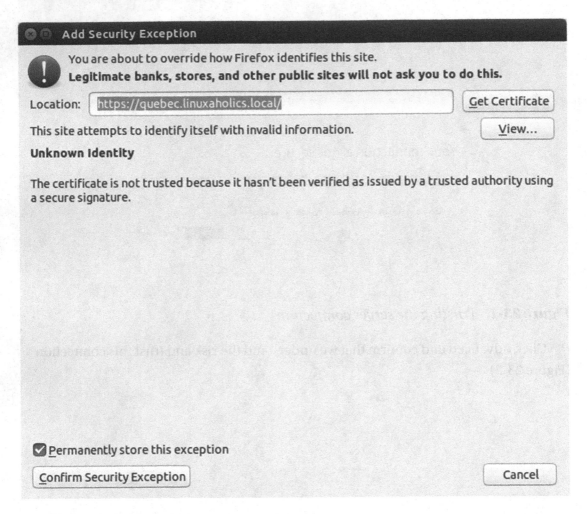

***Figure 23-2.*** *Adding a security exception*

Now we get to the login page (Figure 23-3).

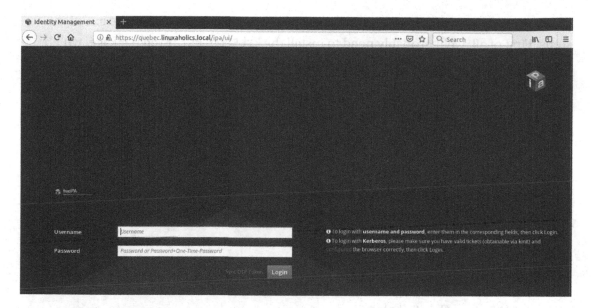

***Figure 23-3.*** *Accessing the web user interface*

We can log in with the username admin and the password we specified when configuring the FreeIPA server. First, though, we need to obtain a valid Kerberos ticket. If we work from the FreeIPA server itself, we can easily get a ticket by executing **kinit**, which is already installed and set up.

```
[root@quebec ~]# kinit admin
Password for admin@LINUXAHOLICS.LOCAL:
```

After obtaining a ticket we can get a list of the ticket(s) by running **klist**.

```
[root@quebec ~]# klist
Ticket cache: KEYRING:persistent:0:0
Default principal: admin@LINUXAHOLICS.LOCAL

Valid starting     Expires            Service principal
15/10/18 21:56:09  16/10/18 21:55:31  HTTP/quebec.linuxaholics.com@
LINUXAHOLICS.LOCAL
15/10/18 21:55:35  16/10/18 21:55:31  krbtgt/LINUXAHOLICS.LOCAL@
LINUXAHOLICS.LOCAL
```

However, if we work from another computer, we need to perform some additional steps. First of all, we'll probably need to install the krb5-workstation package, which includes useful commands such as **kinit** and **klist**.

```
[root@romeo ~]# yum -y install krb5-workstation
.
.
.
```

Then we need to configure Kerberos in the client. This is done by editing the /etc/ krb5.conf file. The file should be something like this:

```
[root@romeo ~]# cat /etc/krb5.conf
[logging]
 default = FILE:/var/log/krb5libs.log
 kdc = FILE:/var/log/krb5kdc.log
 admin_server = FILE:/var/log/kadmind.log

[libdefaults]
 default_realm = LINUXAHOLICS.LOCAL
 dns_lookup_realm = false
 dns_lookup_kdc = true
 rdns = false
 ticket_lifetime = 24h
 forwardable = yes
 default_ccache_name = KEYRING:persistent:%{uid}

[realms]
 LINUXAHOLICS.LOCAL = {
  kdc = quebec.linuxaholics.local:88
  master_kdc = quebec.linuxaholics.local:88
  admin_server = quebec.linuxaholics.local:749
  default_domain = linuxaholics.local
}

[domain_realm]
 .linuxaholics.local = LINUXAHOLICS.LOCAL
 linuxaholics.local = LINUXAHOLICS.LOCAL
```

Now we can request a ticket with **kinit**.

```
[root@romeo ~]# kinit admin
Password for admin@LINUXAHOLICS.LOCAL:
[root@romeo ~]# klist
Ticket cache: KEYRING:persistent:0:0
Default principal: admin@LINUXAHOLICS.LOCAL

Valid starting       Expires              Service principal
16/10/18 14:06:25   17/10/18 14:06:22   krbtgt/LINUXAHOLICS.LOCAL@
LINUXAHOLICS.LOCAL
```

If for some reason we want to discard the existing Kerberos ticket(s) associated with the user, we can run **kdestroy**.

```
[root@romeo ~]# kdestroy
[root@romeo ~]# klist
klist: No credentials cache found (ticket cache KEYRING:persistent:0:0)
```

To be able to later access the FreeIPA web interface, we'll request the ticket again.

```
[root@romeo ~]# kinit admin
Password for admin@LINUXAHOLICS.LOCAL:
[root@romeo ~]# klist
Ticket cache: KEYRING:persistent:0:0
Default principal: admin@LINUXAHOLICS.LOCAL

Valid starting       Expires              Service principal
17/10/18 13:11:46   18/10/18 13:11:43   krbtgt/LINUXAHOLICS.LOCAL@
LINUXAHOLICS.LOCAL
```

We already have a Kerberos ticket, but we also need to configure the browser to access the FreeIPA web interface. If we're using Firefox, on the login page we can click Configured and then Firefox configuration page (Figure 23-4). If we're using a different browser, we'll click on manual configuration page. The Firefox configuration page looks like the one shown in Figure 23-5, although there could be some minor differences depending on the exact versions of IPA and Firefox in use.

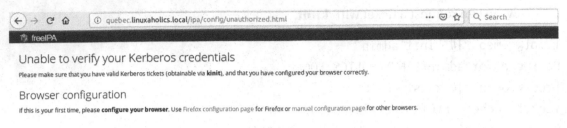

*Figure 23-4.* *Browser configuration page*

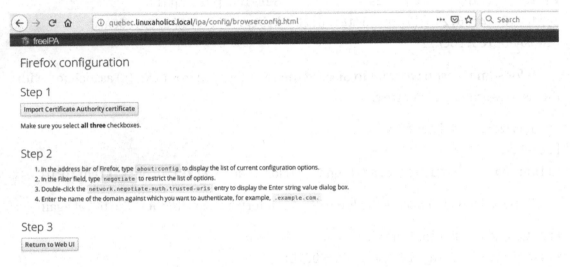

*Figure 23-5.* *Firefox configuration page*

Click Import Certificate Authority certificate and select all the check boxes to trust the CA (Figure 23-6).

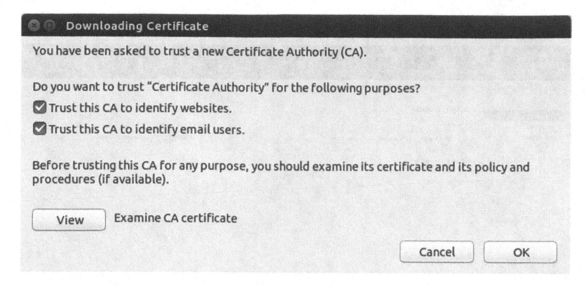

*Figure 23-6.*  *Trusting the new CA*

Then we follow the instructions in Step 2 and enter the name of our domain
(Figure 23-7).

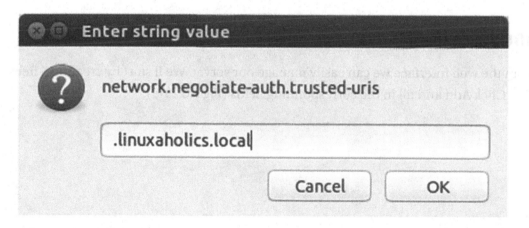

*Figure 23-7.*  *Adding our domain*

The browser is already configured. We check with **klist** that we have a valid
Kerberos ticket, and if we don't we run **kinit** again. Now we can access the web console
(Figure 23-8).

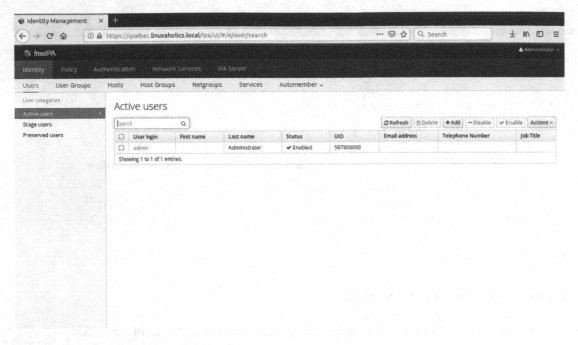

***Figure 23-8.*** *FreeIPA web interface*

# Adding a User

From the web interface we can easily manage our server. We'll start by creating a new user. Click Add and fill in the corresponding fields (Figure 23-9).

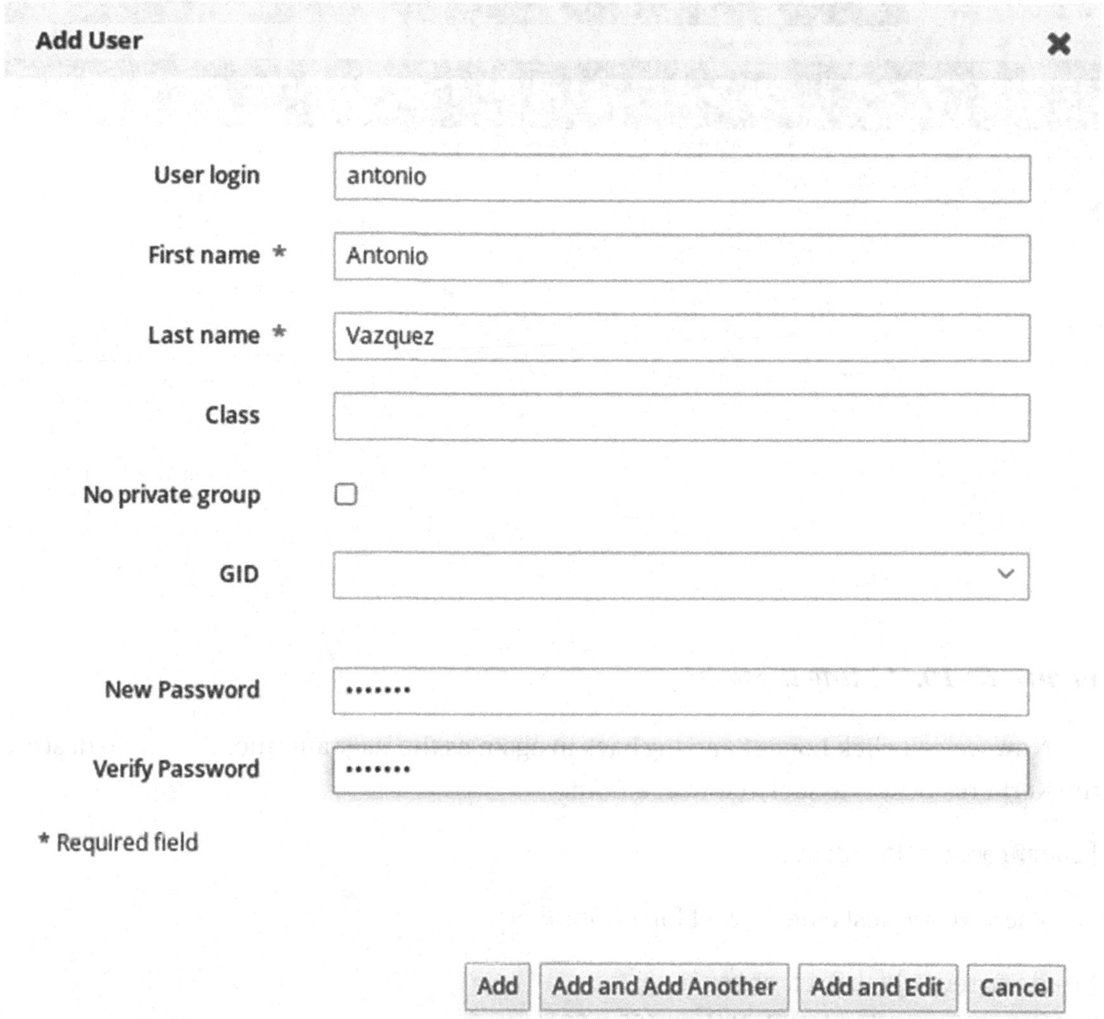

**Add User**                                                                                        ✖

| | |
|---|---|
| User login | antonio |
| First name  * | Antonio |
| Last name  * | Vazquez |
| Class | |
| No private group | ☐ |
| GID | ⌄ |
| New Password | •••••••• |
| Verify Password | •••••••• |

\* Required field

Add    Add and Add Another    Add and Edit    Cancel

***Figure 23-9.*** *Adding a user*

After clicking Add, we'll see that we now have two users: admin and antonio (Figure 23-10).

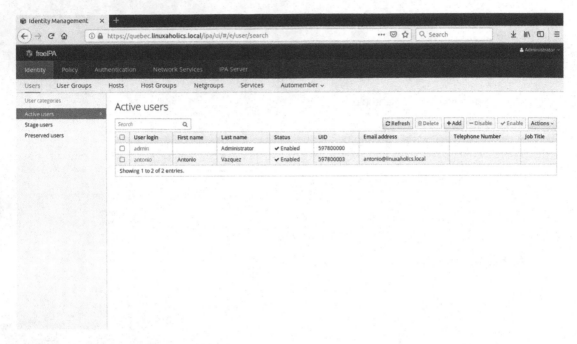

***Figure 23-10.*** *Listing the users*

Now we can click Logout and log back in again as the user antonio. First we'll destroy the Kerberos tickets associated with admin.

```
[root@romeo ~]# kdestroy
```

Then we request a new ticket for antonio.

```
[root@romeo ~]# kinit antonio
Password for antonio@LINUXAHOLICS.LOCAL:
Password expired.  You must change it now.
Enter new password:
Enter it again:
[root@romeo ~]# klist
Ticket cache: KEYRING:persistent:0:0
Default principal: antonio@LINUXAHOLICS.LOCAL
```

```
Valid starting      Expires            Service principal
16/10/18 23:03:34   17/10/18 23:03:34  krbtgt/LINUXAHOLICS.LOCAL@
LINUXAHOLICS.LOCAL
```

Now we can log in to the web interface as the user antonio (Figure 23-11).

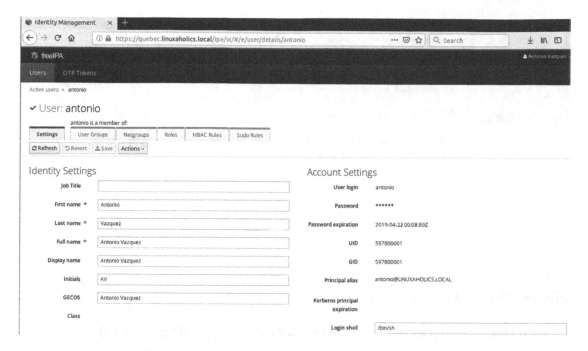

**Figure 23-11.**   *Logged in as a normal user*

In this case, however, the interface looks quite different, as a normal user does not have the permissions to perform administrative tasks.

# Deleting a User

If we want to delete a user, it is a very simple task. We log out and log back in as the admin user. We'll have to request a Kerberos ticket for the admin user as we have seen many times in this chapter. Right after logging in, we'll see the list of the current users. We select the user we want to delete and simply click Delete (Figure 23-12).

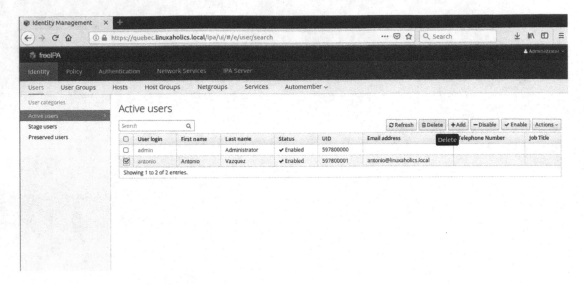

***Figure 23-12.***  *Deleting a user*

Confirm that we want to delete the user, and press Delete (Figure 23-13).

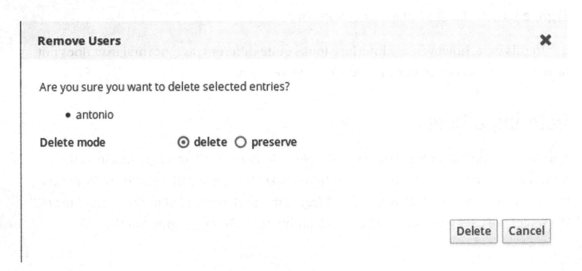

***Figure 23-13.***  *Confirming the delete operation*

The user has been successfully deleted.

# Summary

In this chapter we have seen a brief description of FreeIPA, a comprehensive identity management solution. Despite the fact that we need to install and integrate many different software components for FreeIPA to work correctly, the installation and configuration are very easy. After completing the setup, we got familiar with the web management console and added and deleted our first user.

# CHAPTER 24

# FreeIPA Replication: Adding Clients to the Domain

In the previous chapter we had our first contact with FreeIPA. We even performed the basic operations of adding and deleting users. In this chapter we'll add an additional server to work as a replica, and we'll add different computer clients to the domain. We'll cover the following concepts:

- Understanding replication topology and configuring FreeIPA replication.

- Joining clients to an existing FreeIPA domain.

- Awareness of ipa-backup.

We will also learn about the following terms and utilities: **ipa-server-install**, **ipa-replica-install**, **ipa-client-install**, and **ipactl**.

## FreeIPA Replicas

At the moment, we have a single FreeIPA server, `quebec.linuxaholics.local`, the one we installed in the previous chapter. In a production environment it would be mandatory to have at least one additional server, so that if one of the servers crashes, clients are still able to log in.

A replica server is essentially a copy of another server. When we studied OpenLDAP we saw how to replicate parts of the LDAP tree to another server. Fortunately, the process to replicate information in FreeIPA is much easier.

© Antonio Vazquez 2019
A. Vazquez, *Practical LPIC-3 300*, https://doi.org/10.1007/978-1-4842-4473-9_24

# Installing a FreeIPA Replica

As we did on the original server, we start by installing the ipa-server package on the future replica server.

```
[root@sierra ~]# yum -y install ipa-server
```

After installing the software, we make sure that we can successfully add the names of the original and replica servers. We edit the /etc/hosts file of the replica server accordingly.

```
[root@sierra ~]# cat /etc/hosts
127.0.0.1     localhost localhost.localdomain localhost4 localhost4.
              localdomain4
::1           localhost localhost.localdomain localhost6 localhost6.
              localdomain6
192.168.1.243       quebec.linuxaholics.local
192.168.1.245       sierra.linuxaholics.local
```

In addition, we need to keep time and date synchronized between the two servers and we need to change the DNS settings so that the server points to the FreeIPA server. To do that, we'll stop the NetworkManager service and edit /etc/resolv.conf so that the FreeIPA server is queried first.

```
[root@sierra ~]# systemctl stop NetworkManager
[root@sierra ~]# cat /etc/resolv.conf
nameserver 192.168.1.243
nameserver 192.168.1.1
```

We check that DNS resolution is working by using **dig** to query the name of the FreeIPA server.

```
[root@sierra ~]# dig a +noall +answer quebec.linuxaholics.local
quebec.linuxaholics.local. 1200      IN      A      192.168.1.243
```

We make sure that the firewall allows the incoming connections needed for the IPA server to work, like we did previously in the original server.

```
[root@sierra ~]# firewall-cmd --permanent --add-service http
success
[root@sierra ~]# firewall-cmd --permanent --add-service https
success
[root@sierra ~]# firewall-cmd --permanent --add-service ldap
success
[root@sierra ~]# firewall-cmd --permanent --add-service ldaps
success
[root@sierra ~]# firewall-cmd --permanent --add-service kerberos
success
[root@sierra ~]# firewall-cmd --permanent --add-service kpasswd
success
[root@sierra ~]# firewall-cmd --permanent --add-service dns
success
[root@sierra ~]# firewall-cmd --permanent --add-service ntp
success
[root@sierra ~]# firewall-cmd --reload
success
```

We will also install the additional package to use an integrated DNS server.

```
[root@sierra ~]# yum install -y ipa-server-dns
```

With previous versions of FreeIPA (3.x), we needed to create on the original server a replica configuration file that would be copied later to the future replica server. In the command we specified the name and IP address of the replica server.

```
[root@quebec ~]# ipa-replica-prepare --ip-address 192.168.1.244 sierra.
linuxaholics.local

Replica creation using 'ipa-replica-prepare' to generate replica file
is supported only in 0-level IPA domain.

The current IPA domain level is 1 and thus the replica must
be created by promoting an existing IPA client.
```

To set up a replica use the following procedure:
```
    1.) set up a client on the host using 'ipa-client-install'
    2.) promote the client to replica running 'ipa-replica-install'
        *without* replica file specified
```

'ipa-replica-prepare' is allowed only in domain level 0
The ipa-replica-prepare command failed.

We can see that this procedure doesn't work with our current FreeIPA version, as the command is only allowed in domain level 0. The domain level is a concept that indicates that the server is capable of certain operations. A FreeIPA server with a domain level 1 can do things like using the topology management plug-in. We'll see more information about topology later in this chapter.

At any point we can query our current domain level.

```
[root@quebec ~]# ipa domainlevel-get
-----------------------
Current domain level: 1
-----------------------
```

We'll follow the suggested procedure and set up the client on the future replica server. In the section "Joining Clients to the Domain" later in this chapter we'll see in greater detail how to install the FreeIPA client, so we won't go into much detail on the different options here.

```
[root@sierra ~]# ipa-client-install --domain=linuxaholics.local
--realm=LINUXAHOLICS.LOCAL
Discovery was successful!
Client hostname: sierra.linuxaholics.local
Realm: LINUXAHOLICS.LOCAL
DNS Domain: linuxaholics.local
IPA Server: quebec.linuxaholics.local
BaseDN: dc=linuxaholics,dc=local

Continue to configure the system with these values? [no]: YES
Synchronizing time with KDC...
Attempting to sync time using ntpd.  Will timeout after 15 seconds
Attempting to sync time using ntpd.  Will timeout after 15 seconds
```

Unable to sync time with NTP server, assuming the time is in sync. Please check that 123 UDP port is opened.
User authorized to enroll computers: admin
Password for admin@LINUXAHOLICS.LOCAL:
Successfully retrieved CA cert
    Subject:     CN=Certificate Authority,O=LINUXAHOLICS.LOCAL
    Issuer:      CN=Certificate Authority,O=LINUXAHOLICS.LOCAL
    Valid From:  Sun Apr 16 08:45:09 2017 UTC
    Valid Until: Thu Apr 16 08:45:09 2037 UTC

Enrolled in IPA realm LINUXAHOLICS.LOCAL
Created /etc/ipa/default.conf
New SSSD config will be created
Configured sudoers in /etc/nsswitch.conf
Configured /etc/sssd/sssd.conf
Configured /etc/krb5.conf for IPA realm LINUXAHOLICS.LOCAL
trying https://quebec.linuxaholics.local/ipa/json
Forwarding 'ping' to json server 'https://quebec.linuxaholics.local/ipa/json'
Forwarding 'ca_is_enabled' to json server 'https://quebec.linuxaholics.local/ipa/json'
Systemwide CA database updated.
Hostname (sierra.linuxaholics.local) does not have A/AAAA record.
Failed to update DNS records.
Missing A/AAAA record(s) for host sierra.linuxaholics.local: 192.168.1.245.
Incorrect reverse record(s):
192.168.1.245 is pointing to 192.168.1.245. instead of sierra.linuxaholics.local.
Adding SSH public key from /etc/ssh/ssh_host_rsa_key.pub
Adding SSH public key from /etc/ssh/ssh_host_ecdsa_key.pub
Adding SSH public key from /etc/ssh/ssh_host_ed25519_key.pub
Forwarding 'host_mod' to json server 'https://quebec.linuxaholics.local/ipa/json'
Could not update DNS SSHFP records.
SSSD enabled
Configured /etc/openldap/ldap.conf

```
NTP enabled
Configured /etc/ssh/ssh_config
Configured /etc/ssh/sshd_config
Configuring linuxaholics.local as NIS domain.
Client configuration complete.
```

Now we promote the client to replica.

```
[root@sierra ~]# ipa-replica-install --setup-ca --setup-dns --no-forwarders
Password for admin@LINUXAHOLICS.LOCAL:
ipa          : ERROR    Reverse DNS resolution of address 192.168.1.243
(quebec.linuxaholics.local) failed. Clients may not function properly.
Please check your DNS setup. (Note that this check queries IPA DNS directly
and ignores /etc/hosts.)
Continue? [no]:
```

We got an error. When we installed the first FreeIPA server, we didn't tell the program to create a reverse zone. Not having one might cause some problems with the clients, though. We'll create a reverse zone by accessing the the web management interface. We'll navigate to Network Services ➤ DNS (Figure 24-1).

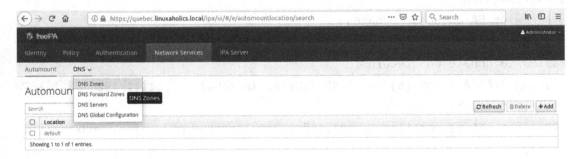

***Figure 24-1.*** *Managing DNS zones*

Click Add and fill in the data as shown in Figure 24-2.

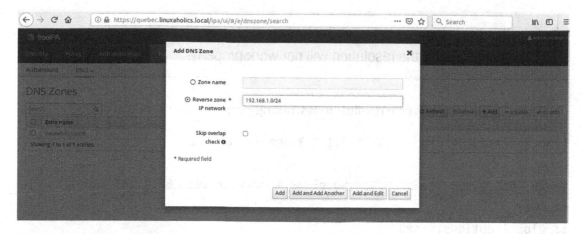

*Figure 24-2.*  *Adding a reverse zone*

After confirming, we see that the new zone has been added (Figure 24-3).

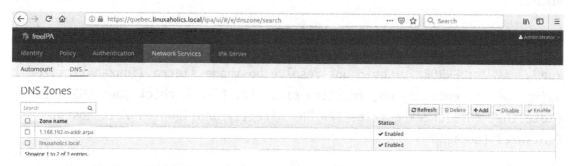

*Figure 24-3.*  *Listing the zones*

We already have created the reverse zone, but we still need to add a record for
quebec.linuxaholics.local. We can do it from the web interface or from the command
line. In this example we'll do it from the command line.

```
[root@quebec ~]# ipa dnsrecord-add 1.168.192.in-addr.arpa 243 --ptr-
hostname=quebec.linuxaholics.local.
  Record name: 243
  PTR record: quebec.linuxaholics.local.
```

> **Note**   It is important not to forget the trailing dot in quebec.linuxaholics.local. If we forget it the resolution will not work properly.

To make sure that reverse resolution is working properly, we execute a query with **dig**.

```
[root@sierra ~]# dig -x 192.168.1.243 +noall +answer

; <<>> DiG 9.9.4-RedHat-9.9.4-50.el7_3.1 <<>> -x 192.168.1.243 +noall
+answer
;; global options: +cmd
243.1.168.192.in-addr.arpa. 86400 IN    PTR     quebec.linuxaholics.local.
```

We launch the installation of the replica again, and this time we will get another error.

```
[root@sierra ~]# ipa-replica-install --setup-ca --setup-dns --no-forwarders
Password for admin@LINUXAHOLICS.LOCAL:
ipa           : ERROR    Could not resolve hostname sierra.linuxaholics.local
using DNS. Clients may not function properly. Please check your DNS setup.
(Note that this check queries IPA DNS directly and ignores /etc/hosts.)
Continue? [no]:
```

Similar to what we did previously, we'll add an A register for the host sierra.linuxaholics.local.

```
[root@quebec ~]# ipa dnsrecord-add linuxaholics.local sierra
-a-ip-address=192.168.1.245
```

We'll add the corresponding record for the reverse zone as well.

```
[root@quebec ~]# ipa dnsrecord-add 1.168.192.in-addr.arpa 245
--ptr-hostname=sierra.linuxaholics.local.
  Record name: 245
  PTR record: sierra.linuxaholics.local.
```

Now, we're ready to launch the replica installation again.

```
[root@sierra ~]# ipa-replica-install --setup-ca --setup-dns --no-forwarders
Password for admin@LINUXAHOLICS.LOCAL:
Run connection check to master
Connection check OK
Configuring NTP daemon (ntpd)
  .

  .

  .

Done configuring NTP daemon (ntpd).
Configuring directory server (dirsrv). Estimated time: 1 minute
  .

  .

  .

  [29/44]: setting up initial replication
Starting replication, please wait until this has completed.
Update in progress, 4 seconds elapsed
Update succeeded
  .

  .

  .

Done configuring directory server (dirsrv).
Configuring ipa-custodia
  .

  .

  .

Done configuring ipa-custodia.
Configuring Kerberos KDC (krb5kdc). Estimated time: 30 seconds
  .

  .

  .

Done configuring Kerberos KDC (krb5kdc).
Configuring kadmin
  [1/2]: starting kadmin
  [2/2]: configuring kadmin to start on boot
```

Done configuring kadmin.
Configuring ipa_memcached
  [1/2]: starting ipa_memcached
  [2/2]: configuring ipa_memcached to start on boot
Done configuring ipa_memcached.
Configuring the web interface (httpd). Estimated time: 1 minute
  .
  .
  .
Done configuring the web interface (httpd).
Applying LDAP updates
Upgrading IPA:
  .
  .
  .
Done.
Configuring ipa-otpd
  [1/2]: starting ipa-otpd
  [2/2]: configuring ipa-otpd to start on boot
Done configuring ipa-otpd.
Configuring certificate server (pki-tomcatd).
  .
  .
  .
Done configuring certificate server (pki-tomcatd).
Configuring DNS (named)
  .
  .
  .
Done configuring DNS (named).
Configuring DNS key synchronization service (ipa-dnskeysyncd)
  .
  .
  .

Done configuring DNS key synchronization service (ipa-dnskeysyncd).
Restarting ipa-dnskeysyncd
Restarting named
Updating DNS system records

Global DNS configuration in LDAP server is empty
You can use 'dnsconfig-mod' command to set global DNS options that
would override settings in local named.conf files

We can query the DNS server in the new replica to check that it has all the necessary records.

```
[root@sierra ~]# ipa dnsrecord-find
ipa: ERROR: did not receive Kerberos credentials
[root@sierra ~]# kinit admin
Password for admin@LINUXAHOLICS.LOCAL:
[root@sierra ~]# ipa dnsrecord-find
Zone name: linuxaholics.local
  Record name: @
  NS record: sierra.linuxaholics.local., quebec.linuxaholics.local.

  Record name: _kerberos
  TXT record: "LINUXAHOLICS.LOCAL"

  Record name: _kerberos._tcp
  SRV record: 0 100 88 sierra.linuxaholics.local., 0 100 88
          quebec.linuxaholics.local.

  Record name: _kerberos-master._tcp
  SRV record: 0 100 88 sierra.linuxaholics.local., 0 100 88
          quebec.linuxaholics.local.

  Record name: _kpasswd._tcp
  SRV record: 0 100 464 sierra.linuxaholics.local., 0 100 464
          quebec.linuxaholics.local.

  Record name: _ldap._tcp
  SRV record: 0 100 389 quebec.linuxaholics.local., 0 100 389
          sierra.linuxaholics.local.
```

Record name: _kerberos._udp
SRV record: 0 100 88 sierra.linuxaholics.local., 0 100 88
            quebec.linuxaholics.local.

Record name: _kerberos-master._udp
SRV record: 0 100 88 sierra.linuxaholics.local., 0 100 88
            quebec.linuxaholics.local.

Record name: _kpasswd._udp
SRV record: 0 100 464 sierra.linuxaholics.local., 0 100 464
            quebec.linuxaholics.local.

Record name: _ntp._udp
SRV record: 0 100 123 quebec.linuxaholics.local., 0 100 123
            sierra.linuxaholics.local.

Record name: ipa-ca
A record: 192.168.1.245, 192.168.1.243

Record name: quebec
A record: 192.168.1.243
SSHFP record: 3 2
CBB9F850E1D7C9E000526FF6427F8066F58CFEE83B0281EBE702F4C2
            4AFB4CA4, 1 2
            89034841F6231D048A1BD64C1A5EC40259FAD5DD6ECC6CA730195ABD
            F257BB58, 3 1 16AC1B380E35749DBEAACC21E3EC5B2C6F89A3CC, 1 1
            289D3D3E43C6E72BCAD87608276B5B7465F156D4, 4 2
            EEE860F01A6000563B837545609D83219B8EEF4564471A1E57790241
            9D11A297, 4 1 6324E43548204439642C9A434C27FD2DB8B170B6

Record name: sierra
A record: 192.168.1.245
------------------------------
Number of entries returned 13
------------------------------

# Replication Topology

The IPA server's data are stored in its LDAP server, in two different locations. The domain suffix, in our case dc=linuxaholics, dc=local contains all the domain-related data. In addition, those servers with a CA installed store data for certificate server components in the ca suffix.

We can list these two suffixes in any of our FreeIPA servers.

```
[root@quebec ~]# ipa topologysuffix-find
-----------------------------
2 topology suffixes matched
-----------------------------
  Suffix name: ca
  Managed LDAP suffix DN: o=ipaca

  Suffix name: domain
  Managed LDAP suffix DN: dc=linuxaholics,dc=local
-----------------------------
Number of entries returned 2
-----------------------------
```

The data stored in the IPA server will be replicated to other servers. The way this replication occurs is defined by replication agreements. These replication agreements need to be set for both suffixes. Agreements are represented by topology segments. By default, a topology segment represents two replication agreements, one for each direction, A to B and B to A.

We can also check whether the replication agreements in both suffixes are okay.

```
[root@quebec ~]# ipa topologysuffix-verify ca
=================================================
Replication topology of suffix "ca" is in order.
=================================================
[root@quebec ~]# ipa topologysuffix-verify domain
=====================================================
Replication topology of suffix "domain" is in order.
=====================================================
```

If at some point we need help with a command we can use the `--help` parameter; for instance, ipa `topologysuffix-show --help`.

To find out which servers are part of the replication segment we can execute the following command.

```
[root@quebec ~]# ipa topologysegment-find ca
-----------------
1 segment matched
-----------------
  Segment name: quebec.linuxaholics.local-to-sierra.linuxaholics.local
  Left node: quebec.linuxaholics.local
  Right node: sierra.linuxaholics.local
  Connectivity: both
----------------------------
Number of entries returned 1
----------------------------
[root@quebec ~]# ipa topologysegment-find domain
------------------
1 segment matched
------------------
  Segment name: quebec.linuxaholics.local-to-sierra.linuxaholics.local
  Left node: quebec.linuxaholics.local
  Right node: sierra.linuxaholics.local
  Connectivity: both
----------------------------
Number of entries returned 1
----------------------------
```

In our example, we only have two FreeIPA servers and they communicate with each other, but if we were working with tens or hundreds of servers, we would have to pay attention to our topology architecture. Much of what we studied in Chapter 5 is valid here as well.

We can have basically three different replication topologies:

- *Peer to peer:* In this case there is a string of servers A – B – C – D, and so on, and every one of them replicates the information with its neighbor (Figure 24-4).

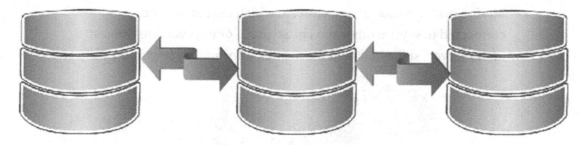

***Figure 24-4.*** *Peer to peer replication topology*

- *Star:* There is a central server that connects to all of the other servers to replicate the data (Figure 24-5).

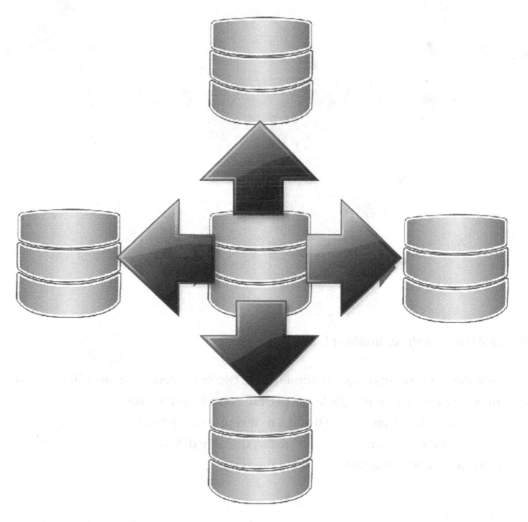

***Figure 24-5.*** *Star replication topology*

- *Mesh:* This is a mixed architecture, in which the servers are connected to several other servers, so that if one server fails the rest of the servers still can obtain the needed information (Figure 24-6).

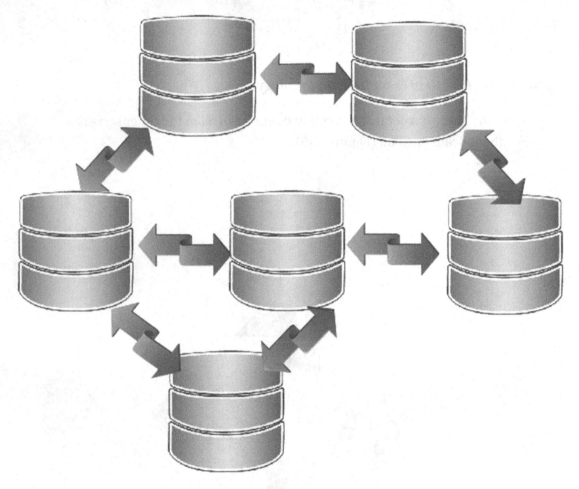

***Figure 24-6.*** *Mesh replication topology*

When designing a topology, we should have two considerations: avoiding a single point of failure and avoiding high levels of traffic on a single server.

To see a practical example, we'll add a new replica to our infrastructure. The procedure its the same as we have seen so far; the only difference is that when installing the client, we'll specify the name of one of the servers.

```
[root@romeo ~]# ipa-client-install --domain=linuxaholics.local
--realm=LINUXAHOLICS.LOCAL -server=quebec.linuxaholics.local
 .

 .

 .
```

Then, we'll promote the server to a replica server. Of course, we'll check that name resolution works as expected and add the corresponding direct and reverse records if needed.

```
[root@romeo ~]# ipa-replica-install --setup-ca --setup-dns -no-forwarders
 .

 .

 .
```

If we check the replication segments now, we'll see that we have two segments, one for each replica server.

```
[root@quebec ~]# ipa topologysegment-find ca
------------------
2 segments matched
------------------
  Segment name: quebec.linuxaholics.local-to-romeo.linuxaholics.local
  Left node: quebec.linuxaholics.local
  Right node: romeo.linuxaholics.local
  Connectivity: both

  Segment name: quebec.linuxaholics.local-to-sierra.linuxaholics.local
  Left node: quebec.linuxaholics.local
  Right node: sierra.linuxaholics.local
  Connectivity: both
----------------------------
Number of entries returned 2
----------------------------
```

```
[root@quebec ~]# ipa topologysegment-find domain
------------------
2 segments matched
------------------
  Segment name: quebec.linuxaholics.local-to-romeo.linuxaholics.local
  Left node: quebec.linuxaholics.local
  Right node: romeo.linuxaholics.local
  Connectivity: both

  Segment name: quebec.linuxaholics.local-to-sierra.linuxaholics.local
  Left node: quebec.linuxaholics.local
  Right node: sierra.linuxaholics.local
  Connectivity: both
----------------------------
Number of entries returned 2
----------------------------
```

The replication topology in this case is this:

sierra ↔ quebec ↔ romeo

We can see a graphical representation of the topology in the web management interface. Navigate to IPA Server ➤ Topology ➤ Topology Graph, and you will see an image similar to the one shown in Figure 24-7.

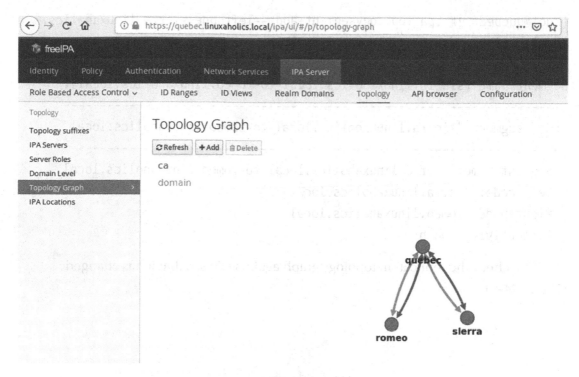

**Figure 24-7.** *Replication topology graph*

We could make `romeo` and `sierra` to replicate data to each other, so that we don't have a single point of failure in the server quebec.

```
[root@quebec ~]# ipa topologysegment-add --leftnode=sierra.linuxaholics.
local --rightnode=romeo.linuxaholics.local
Suffix name: ca
Segment name [sierra.linuxaholics.local-to-romeo.linuxaholics.local]:
-------------------------------------------------------------------
Added segment "sierra.linuxaholics.local-to-romeo.linuxaholics.local"
-------------------------------------------------------------------
  Segment name: sierra.linuxaholics.local-to-romeo.linuxaholics.local
  Left node: sierra.linuxaholics.local
  Right node: romeo.linuxaholics.local
  Connectivity: both
```

```
[root@quebec ~]# ipa topologysegment-add --leftnode=sierra.linuxaholics.
local --rightnode=romeo.linuxaholics.local
Suffix name: domain
Segment name [sierra.linuxaholics.local-to-romeo.linuxaholics.local]:
------------------------------------------------------------------
Added segment "sierra.linuxaholics.local-to-romeo.linuxaholics.local"
------------------------------------------------------------------
  Segment name: sierra.linuxaholics.local-to-romeo.linuxaholics.local
  Left node: sierra.linuxaholics.local
  Right node: romeo.linuxaholics.local
  Connectivity: both
```

If we check the replication topology graph again, we'll see that it has changed (Figure 24-8).

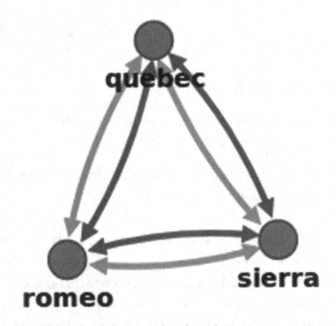

***Figure 24-8.*** *Replication topology graph after changes*

Just as we can add replication segments, we can also delete them. We're going to delete the replication segments we just added between sierra and romeo. If we don't know the name of a certain segment we can check it with **ipa topologysegment-find**.

```
[root@quebec ~]# ipa topologysegment-find
Suffix name: ca
-------------------
3 segments matched
-------------------
  Segment name: quebec.linuxaholics.local-to-romeo.linuxaholics.local
  Left node: quebec.linuxaholics.local
  Right node: romeo.linuxaholics.local
  Connectivity: both

  Segment name: quebec.linuxaholics.local-to-sierra.linuxaholics.local
  Left node: quebec.linuxaholics.local
  Right node: sierra.linuxaholics.local
  Connectivity: both

  Segment name: sierra.linuxaholics.local-to-romeo.linuxaholics.local
  Left node: sierra.linuxaholics.local
  Right node: romeo.linuxaholics.local
  Connectivity: both
----------------------------
Number of entries returned 3
----------------------------
```

To suppress the replication segment, we use the following command:

```
[root@quebec ~]# ipa topologysegment-del ca sierra.linuxaholics.local-to-
romeo.linuxaholics.local
------------------------------------------------------------------------
Deleted segment "sierra.linuxaholics.local-to-romeo.linuxaholics.local"
------------------------------------------------------------------------
[root@quebec ~]# ipa topologysegment-del domain sierra.linuxaholics.local-
to-romeo.linuxaholics.local
------------------------------------------------------------------------
Deleted segment "sierra.linuxaholics.local-to-romeo.linuxaholics.local"
------------------------------------------------------------------------
```

Finally, if we want to completely remove the replica at romeo we'll use the **ipa-replica-manage** command. If we remove the replica in quebec.linuxaholics.local, sierra and romeo won't be able to replicate information. The command itself will detect this situation and won't execute the action.

On the other hand, we could safely remove the replicas at sierra or romeo, as this will only affect them.

To remove replicas, we use the **ipa-replica-manage** command. We can also use this command to list all the replicas in the domain.

```
[root@romeo ~]# ipa-replica-manage list
sierra.linuxaholics.local: master
quebec.linuxaholics.local: master
romeo.linuxaholics.local: master
```

If we want to remove a replica, we have to use the command **ipa-replica-manage del replica_name**. However, this command cannot be executed on the replica server we're going to delete. If we try that, we get an error.

```
[root@romeo ~]# ipa-replica-manage del romeo.linuxaholics.local
Can't remove itself: romeo.linuxaholics.local
```

From the other server we can execute it without a problem.

```
[root@quebec ~]# ipa-replica-manage del romeo.linuxaholics.local
Updating DNS system records
ipa: ERROR: unable to resolve host name romeo.linuxaholics.local. to IP
address, ipa-ca DNS record will be incomplete
ipa: INFO: Skipping replication agreement deletion check for suffix 'domain'
ipa: INFO: Skipping replication agreement deletion check for suffix 'ca'
-----------------------------------------------
Deleted IPA server "romeo.linuxaholics.local"
-----------------------------------------------
```

# Joining Clients to the Domain

If we want to add a computer as a client to our FreeIPA domain, we'll need to make some advance preparations. We'll point the client computer to the internal DNS server used by FreeIPA, and we'll make sure that the date and time are synchronized.

Once all the preparations are complete, we only need to execute **ipa-client-install**. When doing so we can specify some data such as the domain name, the server name, and so on.

```
[root@papa ~]# ipa-client-install --domain=linuxaholics.local
--realm=LINUXAHOLICS.LOCAL --mkhomedir
```

In our case, we specified the domain and the realm name, and we also used the parameter mkhomedir, so that when users log in to the workstation for the first time the home directory will be created automatically.

```
Discovery was successful!
Client hostname: papa.linuxaholics.local
Realm: LINUXAHOLICS.LOCAL
DNS Domain: linuxaholics.local
IPA Server: quebec.linuxaholics.local
BaseDN: dc=linuxaholics,dc=local

Continue to configure the system with these values? [no]: yes
```

We confirm the data and resume the installation. As we'll see later, it is very important to have a synchronized time and date. Otherwise, the installation might fail.

```
Continue to configure the system with these values? [no]: yes
Synchronizing time with KDC...
Attempting to sync time using ntpd.  Will timeout after 15 seconds
Unable to sync time with NTP server, assuming the time is in sync. Please
check that 123 UDP port is opened.
```

Next, we have to provide the name and password of a user authorized to enroll computers. We'll use the admin user.

```
User authorized to enroll computers: admin
Password for admin@LINUXAHOLICS.LOCAL:
Successfully retrieved CA cert
    Subject:    CN=Certificate Authority,O=LINUXAHOLICS.LOCAL
    Issuer:     CN=Certificate Authority,O=LINUXAHOLICS.LOCAL
    Valid From: 2017-04-16 08:45:09
    Valid Until: 2037-04-16 08:45:09
```

```
Enrolled in IPA realm LINUXAHOLICS.LOCAL
Created /etc/ipa/default.conf
New SSSD config will be created
Configured sudoers in /etc/nsswitch.conf
Configured /etc/sssd/sssd.conf
Configured /etc/krb5.conf for IPA realm LINUXAHOLICS.LOCAL
trying https://quebec.linuxaholics.local/ipa/json
[try 1]: Forwarding 'schema' to json server 'https://quebec.linuxaholics.
local/ipa/json'
trying https://quebec.linuxaholics.local/ipa/session/json
[try 1]: Forwarding 'ping' to json server 'https://quebec.linuxaholics.
local/ipa/session/json'
[try 1]: Forwarding 'ca_is_enabled' to json server 'https://quebec.
linuxaholics.local/ipa/session/json'
Systemwide CA database updated.
Hostname (papa.linuxaholics.local) does not have A/AAAA record.
Missing reverse record(s) for address(es): 192.168.1.244.
Adding SSH public key from /etc/ssh/ssh_host_rsa_key.pub
Adding SSH public key from /etc/ssh/ssh_host_ecdsa_key.pub
Adding SSH public key from /etc/ssh/ssh_host_ed25519_key.pub
[try 1]: Forwarding 'host_mod' to json server 'https://quebec.linuxaholics.
local/ipa/session/json'
SSSD enabled
Configured /etc/openldap/ldap.conf
NTP enabled
Configured /etc/ssh/ssh_config
Configured /etc/ssh/sshd_config
Configuring linuxaholics.local as NIS domain.
Client configuration complete.
The ipa-client-install command was successful
```

At this point, the client computer is integrated into our FreeIPA domain. To check it, we can, for instance, log in to the client from a different workstation by using a FreeIPA user (admin in this case).

```
[root@alpha ~]# ssh admin@papa.linuxaholics.local
Password:
Last login: Fri Feb  1 21:44:09 2019 from papa.linuxaholics.local
[admin@papa ~]$
```

# Backing Up a FreeIPA Server

Included in the ipa-server package there is a useful command to back up our FreeIPA
server, **ipa-backup**. It is simple to us: Just running it without arguments will create a
backup in the /var/lib/ipa/backup folder.

```
[root@quebec ~]# ipa-backup
Preparing backup on quebec.linuxaholics.local
Stopping IPA services
Backing up ipaca in LINUXAHOLICS-LOCAL to LDIF
Backing up userRoot in LINUXAHOLICS-LOCAL to LDIF
Backing up LINUXAHOLICS-LOCAL
Backing up files
Backed up to /var/lib/ipa/backup/ipa-full-2019-02-02-02-54-49
Starting IPA service
The ipa-backup command was successful
```

The restore procedure is also quite easy. We need to use the **ipa-restore** command
and specify the location of the backup.

```
[root@quebec ~]# ipa-restore /var/lib/ipa/backup/ipa-
full-2019-02-02-02-54-49/
```

Then enter the password of the directory manager.

```
Directory Manager (existing master) password:
Preparing restore from /var/lib/ipa/backup/ipa-full-2019-02-02-02-54-49/ on
quebec.linuxaholics.local
Performing FULL restore from FULL backup
```

Next, simply confirm.

```
Restoring data will overwrite existing live data. Continue to restore?
[no]: yes
```

After a few minutes the restoration will be complete.

```
Each master will individually need to be re-initialized or
re-created from this one. The replication agreements on
masters running IPA 3.1 or earlier will need to be manually
re-enabled. See the man page for details.
Disabling all replication.
Unable to disable agreement on sierra.linuxaholics.local: [Errno -2] Name
or service not known
Stopping IPA services
Configuring certmonger to stop tracking system certificates for CA
Systemwide CA database updated.
Restoring files
Systemwide CA database updated.
Restoring from userRoot in LINUXAHOLICS-LOCAL
Restoring from ipaca in LINUXAHOLICS-LOCAL
Starting IPA services
Restarting SSSD
The ipa-restore command was successful
```

# Controlling an IPA Instance

An IPA server needs a lot of services running in an orderly manner: an HTTP server, a directory server, a Kerberos key distribution center, and so on. To see the state of all these services, as well as to stop or start them we can use **ipactl**.

```
[root@quebec ~]# ipactl -h
Usage: ipactl start|stop|restart|status
[root@quebec ~]# ipactl status
Directory Service: RUNNING
krb5kdc Service: RUNNING
kadmin Service: RUNNING
```

```
named Service: RUNNING
ipa_memcached Service: RUNNING
httpd Service: RUNNING
ipa-custodia Service: RUNNING
ntpd Service: RUNNING
pki-tomcatd Service: RUNNING
ipa-otpd Service: RUNNING
ipa-dnskeysyncd Service: RUNNING
ipa: INFO: The ipactl command was successful
```

# Summary

In this chapter we expanded the infrastructure we created in the previous chapter. We started by adding some replicas and then we changed the replication topology. We also added a client to the domain. Finally, we saw how easy it is to back up and restore a FreeIPA server. We used the **ipactl** command to control the IPA instance as well.

# CHAPTER 25

# FreeIPA Entity Management

In Chapter 24, we had our first contact with FreeIPA. We even performed the basic operations of adding and deleting users. Now we'll move on to more advanced topics. In this chapter we'll cover the following concepts:

- Managing user accounts and groups.

- Managing hosts, host groups, and services.

- Understanding the principle of IPA access control permissions, privileges, and roles.

- Understanding ID views.

- Awareness of sudo, autofs, SSH, SELinux, and NIS integration as well as host-based access control in FreeIPA.

- Awareness of the FreeIPA CA.

We will learn about the following terms and utilities: **ipa**, **ipa-user***, **ipa-stageuser***, **ipa-group***, **ipa-idview***, **ipa host***, and **ipa-advise**.

## Manage User Accounts and Groups

There are several ways to manage users in a FreeIPA server. We already saw very briefly how to create and delete users from the web interface, but we can also create users from the command line with the **ipa** command.

© Antonio Vazquez 2019
A. Vazquez, *Practical LPIC-3 300*, https://doi.org/10.1007/978-1-4842-4473-9_25

# The ipa User Subcommands

During the installation process of the FreeIPA server, numerous administrative commands and subcommands are installed as well. The command we'll be using most of the time is **ipa**. It would be more precise to say that it is a command suite, as there are a lot of subcommands associated with it. We can see the list of subcommands with ipa help topics.

```
[root@quebec ~]# ipa help topics
automember          Auto Membership Rule.
automount           Automount
ca                  Manage Certificate Authorities
caacl               Manage CA ACL rules.
cert                IPA certificate operations
certprofile         Manage Certificate Profiles
config              Server configuration
delegation          Group to Group Delegation
dns                 Domain Name System (DNS)
domainlevel         Raise the IPA Domain Level.
group               Groups of users
hbac                Host-based access control commands
hbactest            Simulate use of Host-based access controls
host                Hosts/Machines
hostgroup           Groups of hosts.
idrange             ID ranges
idviews             ID Views
krbtpolicy          Kerberos ticket policy
location            IPA locations
migration           Migration to IPA
misc                Misc plug-ins
netgroup            Netgroups
otp                 One time password commands
passwd              Set a user's password
permission          Permissions
ping                Ping the remote IPA server to ensure it is running.
privilege           Privileges
```

```
pwpolicy          Password policy
radiusproxy       RADIUS Proxy Servers
realmdomains      Realm domains
role              Roles
schema            API Schema
selfservice       Self-service Permissions
selinuxusermap    SELinux User Mapping
server            IPA servers
serverrole        IPA server roles
service           Services
servicedelegation Service Constrained Delegation
stageuser         Stageusers
sudo              commands for controlling sudo configuration
topology          Topology
trust             Cross-realm trusts
user              Users
vault             Vaults
```

To manage users, we'll type ipa user.

```
[root@quebec ~]# ipa user
Users

Manage user entries. All users are POSIX users.
.
.
.
EXAMPLES:

 Add a new user:
   ipa user-add --first=Tim --last=User --password tuser1

 Find all users whose entries include the string "Tim":
   ipa user-find Tim
.
.
.
```

```
Topic commands:
  user-add     Add a new user.
  user-del     Delete a user.
  user-disable Disable a user account.
  user-enable  Enable a user account.
  user-find    Search for users.
  user-mod     Modify a user.
  user-show    Display information about a user.
  user-status  Lockout status of a user account
  user-unlock  Unlock a user account

To get command help, use:
  ipa <command> --help
```

In the help message we can see the different subcommands we need to use to add users, modify users, disable users, and so on. For instance, if we want to add a new user, we'll type this:

```
[root@quebec ~]# ipa user-add antonio
ipa: ERROR: did not receive Kerberos credentials
```

If we don't have a valid Kerberos ticket, we'll request one.

```
[root@quebec ~]# kinit admin
Password for admin@LINUXAHOLICS.LOCAL:
[root@quebec ~]# ipa user-add antonio
First name: Antonio
Last name: Vazquez
--------------------
Added user "antonio"
--------------------
  User login: antonio
  First name: Antonio
  Last name: Vazquez
  Full name: Antonio Vazquez
  Display name: Antonio Vazquez
  Initials: AV
  Home directory: /home/antonio
```

```
GECOS: Antonio Vazquez
Login shell: /bin/sh
Principal name: antonio@LINUXAHOLICS.LOCAL
Principal alias: antonio@LINUXAHOLICS.LOCAL
Email address: antonio@linuxaholics.local
UID: 985600001
GID: 985600001
Password: False
Member of groups: ipausers
Kerberos keys available: False
```

By default, the newly created user has no password associated, but we can assign a new one with **ipa passwd**.

```
[root@quebec ~]# ipa passwd antonio
New Password:
Enter New Password again to verify:
--------------------------------------------------
Changed password for "antonio@LINUXAHOLICS.LOCAL"
--------------------------------------------------
```

From now on, we can locate the user with the **ipa user-find** command.

```
[root@quebec ~]# ipa user-find antonio
--------------
1 user matched
--------------
  User login: antonio
  First name: Antonio
  Last name: Vazquez
  Home directory: /home/antonio
  Login shell: /bin/sh
  Email address: antonio@linuxaholics.com
  UID: 1015200003
  GID: 1015200003
  Account disabled: False
  Password: True
```

```
  Kerberos keys available: True
-----------------------------
Number of entries returned 1
-----------------------------
```

The user data are stored in LDAP, and we could get that information by directly querying the LDAP server with the client tools like **ldapsearch**, similar to what we did when working with OpenLDAP.

```
[root@quebec ~]# ldapsearch -x "uid=antonio"
# extended LDIF
#
# LDAPv3
# base <dc=linuxaholics,dc=local> (default) with scope subtree
# filter: uid=antonio
# requesting: ALL
#

# antonio, users, compat, linuxaholics.local
dn: uid=antonio,cn=users,cn=compat,dc=linuxaholics,dc=local
objectClass: posixAccount
objectClass: top
gecos: Antonio Vazquez
cn: Antonio Vazquez
uidNumber: 1015200003
gidNumber: 1015200003
loginShell: /bin/sh
homeDirectory: /home/antonio
uid: antonio

# antonio, users, accounts, linuxaholics.local
dn: uid=antonio,cn=users,cn=accounts,dc=linuxaholics,dc=local
BMSU5VWEFIT0xJQ1MuQO9NAA==
     .
     .
     .
```

```
# search result
search: 2
result: 0 Success

# numResponses: 3
# numEntries: 2
```

In fact, it would be possible to add users by manually generating LDIF files and executing **ldapadd**. However, this is not the recommended way to add users, as it is prone to errors.

# The ipa stageuser Subcommands

In the previous section we added a user with the **ipa user-add** command. This user will be able to log in to the domain right after creation. However, many production environments require an advanced user management life cycle in which users can be in different states: staged, active, deleted, and so on.

The initial state would be the staged user. In this case the user account exists, but it might not have all of the properties. The user cannot authenticate. We create staged users with the **ipa stageuser-add** command.

```
[root@quebec ~]# ipa stageuser-add jose
First name: Jose
Last name: Vazquez
-----------------------
Added stage user "jose"
-----------------------
  User login: jose
  First name: Jose
  Last name: Vazquez
  Full name: Jose Vazquez
  Display name: Jose Vazquez
  Initials: JV
  Home directory: /home/jose
  GECOS: Jose Vazquez
  Login shell: /bin/sh
  Principal name: jose@LINUXAHOLICS.LOCAL
```

```
Principal alias: jose@LINUXAHOLICS.LOCAL
Email address: jose@linuxaholics.local
UID: -1
GID: -1
Password: False
Kerberos keys available: False
```

The user will be created in LDAP, but it won't be stored in the same location as the normal, active users (cn=users,cn=accounts,dc=linuxaholics,dc=local), but in cn=staged users,cn=accounts,cn=provisioning,dc=linuxaholics,dc=local. We can check this by executing a search in LDAP, but we'll need to launch the search with a user with the appropriate permissions, otherwise we won't see anything.

If we execute **ldapsearch** as an anonymous user the result will be similar to this:

```
[root@quebec ~]# ldapsearch -x -b "cn=staged users,cn=accounts,cn=provision
ing,dc=linuxaholics,dc=local"
# extended LDIF
#
# LDAPv3
# base <cn=staged users,cn=accounts,cn=provisioning,dc=linuxaholics,
  dc=local> with scope subtree
# filter: (objectclass=*)
# requesting: ALL
#

# staged users, accounts, provisioning, linuxaholics.local
dn: cn=staged users,cn=accounts,cn=provisioning,dc=linuxaholics,dc=local
objectClass: nsContainer
objectClass: top
cn: staged users

# search result
search: 2
result: 0 Success

# numResponses: 2
# numEntries: 1
```

However, if we execute the query again as the admin user, we'll see the staged user we just created.

```
[root@quebec ~]# ldapsearch -x -D "uid=admin,cn=users,cn=accounts,
dc=linuxaholics,dc=local" -w password3  -b "cn=staged users,cn=accounts,
cn=provisioning,dc=linuxaholics,dc=local"
# extended LDIF
#
# LDAPv3
# base <cn=staged users,cn=accounts,cn=provisioning,dc=linuxaholics,
  dc=local> with scope subtree
# filter: (objectclass=*)
# requesting: ALL
#

# staged users, accounts, provisioning, linuxaholics.local
dn: cn=staged users,cn=accounts,cn=provisioning,dc=linuxaholics,dc=local
objectClass: nsContainer
objectClass: top
cn: staged users

# jose, staged users, accounts, provisioning, linuxaholics.local
dn: uid=jose,cn=staged users,cn=accounts,cn=provisioning,dc=linuxaholics,
dc=lo
 cal
displayName: Jose Vazquez
uid: jose
krbCanonicalName: jose@LINUXAHOLICS.LOCAL
objectClass: ipaobject
objectClass: person
objectClass: top
objectClass: ipasshuser
objectClass: inetorgperson
objectClass: organizationalperson
objectClass: krbticketpolicyaux
objectClass: krbprincipalaux
objectClass: inetuser
```

```
objectClass: posixaccount
objectClass: ipaSshGroupOfPubKeys
loginShell: /bin/sh
description: __no_upg__
uidNumber: -1
initials: JV
gidNumber: -1
gecos: Jose Vazquez
sn: Vazquez
homeDirectory: /home/jose
mail: jose@linuxaholics.local
krbPrincipalName: jose@LINUXAHOLICS.LOCAL
givenName: Jose
cn: Jose Vazquez
ipaUniqueID: autogenerate

# search result
search: 2
result: 0 Success

# numResponses: 3
# numEntries: 2
```

To activate a staged user, we use the **ipa stageuser-activate** command.

```
[root@quebec ~]# ipa stageuser-activate jose
--------------------------
Stage user jose activated
--------------------------
  User login: jose
  First name: Jose
  Last name: Vazquez
  Home directory: /home/jose
  Login shell: /bin/sh
  Principal name: jose@LINUXAHOLICS.LOCAL
  Principal alias: jose@LINUXAHOLICS.LOCAL
  Email address: jose@linuxaholics.local
```

```
UID: 597800004
GID: 597800004
Password: False
Member of groups: ipausers
Kerberos keys available: False
```

From now on we can find the new user in the same location in which the user antonio is located, cn=users,cn=accounts,dc=linuxaholics,dc=local. The user will be completely operational as soon as we assign him a password.

```
[root@quebec ~]# ipa passwd jose
New Password:
Enter New Password again to verify:
-----------------------------------------------
Changed password for "jose@LINUXAHOLICS.LOCAL"
-----------------------------------------------
[root@quebec ~]# ldapsearch -x -b "cn=users,cn=accounts,dc=linuxaholics,
dc=local"
    .
    .
    .
dn: uid=admin,cn=users,cn=accounts,dc=linuxaholics,dc=local
    .
    .
    .
dn: uid=antonio,cn=users,cn=accounts,dc=linuxaholics,dc=local
displayName: Antonio Vazquez
uid: antonio
    .
    .
    .
dn: uid=jose,cn=users,cn=accounts,dc=linuxaholics,dc=local
displayName: Jose Vazquez
uid: jose
    .
    .
    .
```

```
search: 2
result: 0 Success

# numResponses: 5
# numEntries: 4
```

After some time, we might need to delete a user, which can be done from the web interface as well as with the **ipa user-del** command. However, maybe the user will be temporarily absent and we don't want to delete the account, but instead we want to deactivate it. In this situation we'd use the **ipa user-del** command with the --preserve option.

```
[root@quebec ~]# ipa user-del jose --preserve
-------------------
Deleted user "jose"
-------------------
```

If we execute a search on the LDAP tree we'll find the user in cn=deleted users, cn=accounts,cn=provisioning,dc=linuxaholics,dc=local.

```
[root@quebec ~]# ldapsearch -x -D "uid=admin,cn=users,cn=accounts,
dc=linuxaholics,dc=local" -w password3  -b "cn=deleted users,cn=accounts,
cn=provisioning,dc=linuxaholics,dc=local"
# extended LDIF
#
# LDAPv3
# base <cn=deleted users,cn=accounts,cn=provisioning,dc=linuxaholics,
  dc=local> with scope subtree
# filter: (objectclass=*)
# requesting: ALL
#

# deleted users, accounts, provisioning, linuxaholics.local
dn: cn=deleted users,cn=accounts,cn=provisioning,dc=linuxaholics,dc=local
objectClass: nsContainer
objectClass: top
cn: deleted users
```

```
# jose, deleted users, accounts, provisioning, linuxaholics.local
dn: uid=jose,cn=deleted users,cn=accounts,cn=provisioning,dc=linuxaholics,dc=
 local
krbPrincipalName: jose@LINUXAHOLICS.LOCAL
krbCanonicalName: jose@LINUXAHOLICS.LOCAL
uid: jose
krbExtraData:: AAIgIWJccm9vdC9hZG1pbkBMSU5VWEFIT0xJQ1MuTE9DQUwA
krbLoginFailedCount: 0
displayName: Jose Vazquez
objectClass: ipasshgroupofpubkeys
objectClass: ipaobject
objectClass: person
objectClass: top
objectClass: ipasshuser
objectClass: inetorgperson
objectClass: organizationalperson
objectClass: krbticketpolicyaux
objectClass: krbprincipalaux
objectClass: inetuser
objectClass: posixaccount
loginShell: /bin/sh
sn: Vazquez
gecos: Jose Vazquez
homeDirectory: /home/jose
mail: jose@linuxaholics.local
givenName: Jose
cn: Jose Vazquez
initials: JV
ipaUniqueID: 508a383c-2e65-11e9-b680-080027da8dc5
uidNumber: 597800004
gidNumber: 597800004

# search result
search: 2
result: 0 Success
```

```
# numResponses: 3
# numEntries: 2
```

As soon as the user needs to log in to the domain again, we can recover his account quickly.

```
[root@quebec ~]# ipa user-undel jose
------------------------------
Undeleted user account "jose"
------------------------------
```

# The ipa group Subcommands

In addition to users, we can also add, edit, and delete groups in our IPA server. By default, there are some groups defined that we can list with **ipa group-find**.

```
[root@quebec ~]# ipa group-find
----------------
4 groups matched
----------------
  Group name: admins
  Description: Account administrators group
  GID: 1015200000
  Member users: admin

  Group name: editors
  Description: Limited admins who can edit other users
  GID: 1015200002

  Group name: ipausers
  Description: Default group for all users
  Member users: antonio

  Group name: trust admins
  Description: Trusts administrators group
  Member users: admin
------------------------------
Number of entries returned 4
------------------------------
```

The user we just created is a member of the default group ipausers. Currently, the user is not a member of any other group.

If we want to, we can create a customized group with **ipa group-add**.

```
[root@quebec ~]# ipa group-add helpdesk
Description: HelpDesk members
----------------------
Added group "helpdesk"
----------------------
  Group name: helpdesk
  Description: HelpDesk members
  GID: 1015200004
```

To include users in the group we use the **ipa group-add-member** command.

```
[root@quebec ~]# ipa group-add-member helpdesk --users=antonio
  Group name: helpdesk
  Description: HelpDesk members
  GID: 1015200004
  Member users: antonio
-------------------------
Number of members added 1
-------------------------
```

We can also modify a given group.

```
[root@quebec ~]# ipa group-mod helpdesk --desc="HelpDesk staff"
-------------------------
Modified group "helpdesk"
-------------------------
  Group name: helpdesk
  Description: HelpDesk staff
  GID: 1015200004
  Member users: antonio
```

Apart from adding members to a group, we can remove them, too.

```
[root@quebec ~]# ipa group-remove-member helpdesk --users=antonio
  Group name: helpdesk
  Description: HelpDesk staff
  GID: 1015200004
  --------------------------
Number of members removed 1
  --------------------------
```

Finally, we can delete the group itself.

```
[root@quebec ~]# ipa group-del helpdesk
-------------------------
Deleted group "helpdesk"
-------------------------
```

# Managing Hosts, Host Groups, and Services

We have seen before how to manage users and groups in FreeIPA, but it is also of extreme importance to manage hosts, host groups, and services in an identity system such as FreeIPA.

## Managing Hosts

When provisioning a new FreeIPA domain, as well as when adding new servers and clients to the domain, new host entries are created in the directory. These host entries are used to establish relations with other hosts and services in the domain. We can list the hosts in the domain from the command line with the **ipa host-find** command.

```
[root@quebec ~]# ipa host-find
---------------
3 hosts matched
---------------
  Host name: papa.linuxaholics.local
  Principal name: host/papa.linuxaholics.local@LINUXAHOLICS.LOCAL
  Principal alias: host/papa.linuxaholics.local@LINUXAHOLICS.LOCAL
```

```
SSH public key fingerprint: 87:A2:4A:FA:F2:AC:65:B7:8D:78:80:37:
                            9B:59:26:99
                            (ssh-ed25519),
                            6F:FB:50:B6:52:1D:7C:A3:5A:78:97:DF:E3:D3
                            :D2:02
                            (ecdsa-sha2-nistp256),
                            E3:72:DD:A5:6E:62:86:26:EA:E8:FC:BB
                            :D6:99:56:23
                            (ssh-rsa)

Host name: quebec.linuxaholics.local
Principal name: host/quebec.linuxaholics.local@LINUXAHOLICS.LOCAL
Principal alias: host/quebec.linuxaholics.local@LINUXAHOLICS.LOCAL
SSH public key fingerprint: 87:A2:4A:FA:F2:AC:65:B7:8D:78:80:37:
                            9B:59:26:99
                            (ssh-ed25519),
                            6F:FB:50:B6:52:1D:7C:A3:5A:78:97:DF:E3:D3
                            :D2:02
                            (ecdsa-sha2-nistp256),
                            E3:72:DD:A5:6E:62:86:26:EA:E8:FC:BB
                            :D6:99:56:23
                            (ssh-rsa)

Host name: sierra.linuxaholics.local
Principal name: host/sierra.linuxaholics.local@LINUXAHOLICS.LOCAL
Principal alias: host/sierra.linuxaholics.local@LINUXAHOLICS.LOCAL
SSH public key fingerprint: 87:A2:4A:FA:F2:AC:65:B7:8D:78:80:37:
                            9B:59:26:99
                            (ssh-ed25519),
                            6F:FB:50:B6:52:1D:7C:A3:5A:78:97:DF:E3:D3
                            :D2:02
                            (ecdsa-sha2-nistp256),
                            E3:72:DD:A5:6E:62:86:26:EA:E8:FC:BB
                            :D6:99:56:23
                            (ssh-rsa)
```

```
--------------------------------
Number of entries returned 3
--------------------------------
```

We can also get the same information from the web interface (Figure 25-1).

***Figure 25-1.*** *Listing the hosts*

If we select a host, we'll obtain some more information (Figure 25-2).

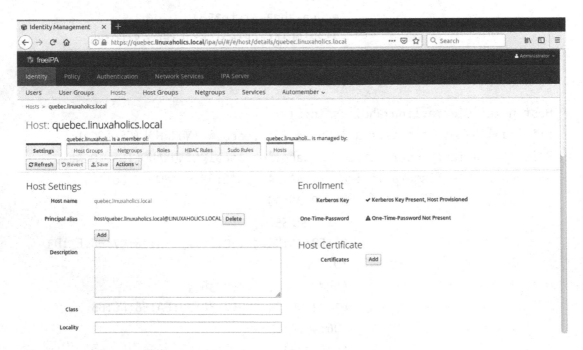

***Figure 25-2.*** *Host details*

In addition to automatically adding hosts when adding servers or workstations to the domain, we can also add them manually either via the web interface or the command-line utilities. Let's look at an example.

```
[root@quebec ~]# ipa host-add dummy.linuxaholics.local
ipa: ERROR: Host 'dummy.linuxaholics.local' does not have corresponding DNS
A/AAAA record
```

Because we need the corresponding DNS A record, we'll create it.

```
[root@quebec ~]# ipa dnsrecord-add linuxaholics.local dummy --a-ip-
address=192.168.1.254
  Record name: dummy
  A record: 192.168.1.254
```

Now we can try to add the host again.

```
[root@quebec ~]# ipa host-add dummy.linuxaholics.local
--------------------------------------
Added host "dummy.linuxaholics.local"
--------------------------------------
  Host name: dummy.linuxaholics.local
  Principal name: host/dummy.linuxaholics.local@LINUXAHOLICS.LOCAL
  Principal alias: host/dummy.linuxaholics.local@LINUXAHOLICS.LOCAL
  Password: False
  Keytab: False
  Managed by: dummy.linuxaholics.local
```

This time the host was successfully added. We can list it with **ipa host-find**.

```
[root@quebec ~]# ipa host-find
 .
 .

 .

  Host name: dummy.linuxaholics.local
  Principal name: host/dummy.linuxaholics.local@LINUXAHOLICS.LOCAL
  Principal alias: host/dummy.linuxaholics.local@LINUXAHOLICS.LOCAL

 .

 .

 .
```

As this host is just an example and does not exist, we'll delete it.

```
[root@quebec ~]# ipa host-del dummy.linuxaholics.local
-------------------------------------------
Deleted host "dummy.linuxaholics.local"
-------------------------------------------
```

We should also delete the DNS record we created for it.

```
[root@quebec ~]# ipa dnsrecord-del linuxaholics.local dummy --del-all
---------------------
Deleted record "dummy"
---------------------
```

# Managing Host Groups

Hosts can also be grouped into host groups, in which we find hosts with similar characteristics. We can see them in the web interface (Figure 25-3).

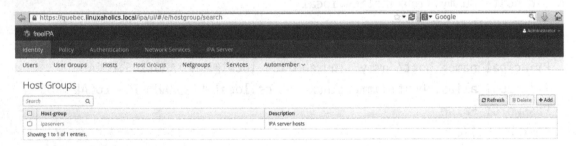

***Figure 25-3.***   *Host groups*

By selecting a host group, we can see its members (Figure 25-4).

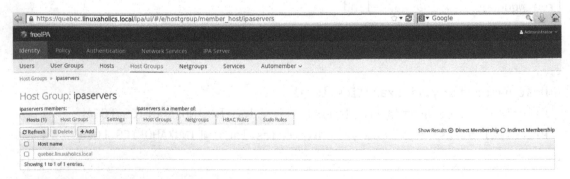

***Figure 25-4.***   *Host group members*

We can also obtain the same information with the command-line utilities.

```
[root@quebec ~]# ipa hostgroup-find
-------------------
1 hostgroup matched
-------------------
  Host-group: ipaservers
  Description: IPA server hosts
----------------------------
Number of entries returned 1
----------------------------
[root@quebec ~]# ipa hostgroup-show ipaservers
  Host-group: ipaservers
  Description: IPA server hosts
  Member hosts: quebec.linuxaholics.local
```

We are going to add a new host group to include web servers, which is very simple to do.

```
[root@quebec ~]# ipa hostgroup-add NFSServers --desc="Network File System
Servers"
----------------------------
Added hostgroup "nfsservers"
----------------------------
  Host-group: nfsservers
  Description: Network File System Servers
```

Now that we have created the host group, we need to add members to it.

```
[root@quebec ~]# ipa hostgroup-add-member nfsservers --hosts=sierra.
linuxaholics.local
  Host-group: nfsservers
  Description: Network File System Servers
  Member hosts: sierra.linuxaholics.local
-------------------------
Number of members added 1
-------------------------
```

# Managing Services

Right after installing the first FreeIPA server, there are many predefined services defined in the domain. We can list them with **ipa service-find**.

```
[root@quebec ~]# ipa service-find
-------------------
10 services matched
-------------------
  Principal name: ldap/quebec.linuxaholics.local@LINUXAHOLICS.LOCAL
  Principal alias: ldap/quebec.linuxaholics.local@LINUXAHOLICS.LOCAL
 .

 .

 .

  Principal name: DNS/quebec.linuxaholics.local@LINUXAHOLICS.LOCAL
  Principal alias: DNS/quebec.linuxaholics.local@LINUXAHOLICS.LOCAL
  Keytab: True

  Principal name: dogtag/sierra.linuxaholics.local@LINUXAHOLICS.LOCAL
  Principal alias: dogtag/sierra.linuxaholics.local@LINUXAHOLICS.LOCAL
  Keytab: True

  Principal name: HTTP/quebec.linuxaholics.local@LINUXAHOLICS.LOCAL
  Principal alias: HTTP/quebec.linuxaholics.local@LINUXAHOLICS.LOCAL
 .

 .

 .

  Principal name: dogtag/quebec.linuxaholics.local@LINUXAHOLICS.LOCAL
  Principal alias: dogtag/quebec.linuxaholics.local@LINUXAHOLICS.LOCAL
  Keytab: True

  Principal name: DNS/sierra.linuxaholics.local@LINUXAHOLICS.LOCAL
  Principal alias: DNS/sierra.linuxaholics.local@LINUXAHOLICS.LOCAL
  Keytab: True

  Principal name: ipa-dnskeysyncd/sierra.linuxaholics.local@LINUXAHOLICS.
  LOCAL
```

```
  Principal alias: ipa-dnskeysyncd/sierra.linuxaholics.local@LINUXAHOLICS.
                   LOCAL
  Keytab: True

  Principal name: ldap/sierra.linuxaholics.local@LINUXAHOLICS.LOCAL
  Principal alias: ldap/sierra.linuxaholics.local@LINUXAHOLICS.LOCAL
.
.
.

  Principal name: ipa-dnskeysyncd/quebec.linuxaholics.local@LINUXAHOLICS.
                   LOCAL
  Principal alias: ipa-dnskeysyncd/quebec.linuxaholics.local@LINUXAHOLICS.
                   LOCAL
  Keytab: True

  Principal name: HTTP/sierra.linuxaholics.local@LINUXAHOLICS.LOCAL
  Principal alias: HTTP/sierra.linuxaholics.local@LINUXAHOLICS.LOCAL
  Keytab: True
----------------------------
Number of entries returned 10
----------------------------
```

We can add additional services in the domain. For instance, we can add an NFS service that will be executed in `sierra.linuxaholics.local`. At this point we don't have a real NFS server installed in the domain (we'll install it later in Chapter 27), but we'll create the service in FreeIPA for didactic purposes.

To add the service from the command line we'll use the **ipa service-add command**. Of course, we could also use the web interface.

```
[root@quebec ~]# ipa service-add nfs/sierra.linuxaholics.local@
LINUXAHOLICS.LOCAL
----------------------------------------------------------------
Added service "nfs/sierra.linuxaholics.local@LINUXAHOLICS.LOCAL"
----------------------------------------------------------------
  Principal name: nfs/sierra.linuxaholics.local@LINUXAHOLICS.LOCAL
  Principal alias: nfs/sierra.linuxaholics.local@LINUXAHOLICS.LOCAL
  Managed by: sierra.linuxaholics.local
```

We can see the new service from the web interface, too, by navigating to Identity ➤ Services and selecting the name of the service we just created (Figure 25-5). There, we can edit its properties.

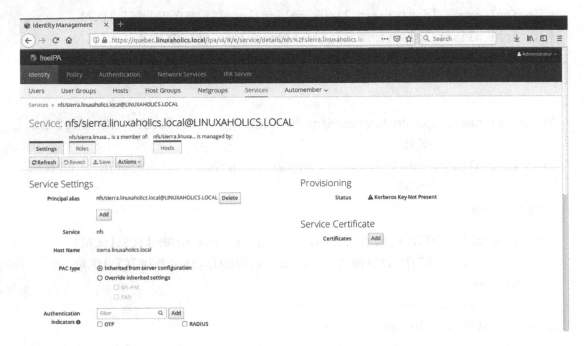

***Figure 25-5.*** *Editing the new service*

# Access Control: Privileges and Roles

Access control determines who can access certain resources and what they are allowed to do. FreeIPA divides access control rules into three types:

- *Self-service rules:* These rules define what users can perform on their own entry, allowing only editing attributes within the entry.

- *Delegation rules:* These rules allow certain users or groups to perform operations on specific attributes for other users or groups.

- *Role-based access control:* These are special access control groups that can be granted much more versatility to modify different entities in the domain.

# Self-Service Rules

As we mentioned before, self-service control rules define the operations that a given entity can perform on itself. By default, there are four self-service rules defined. We can see them with the **ipa selfservice-find** command or by accessing the web interface and navigating to IPA Server ➤ Role Based Access Control ➤ Self Service Permissions (Figure 25-6).

```
[root@quebec ~]# ipa selfservice-find
-----------------------
4 selfservices matched
-----------------------
  Self-service name: Self can write own password
  Permissions: write
  Attributes: userpassword, krbprincipalkey, sambalmpassword, sambantpassword

  Self-service name: Users can manage their own X.509 certificates
  Permissions: write
  Attributes: usercertificate

  Self-service name: User Self service
  Permissions: write
  Attributes: givenname, sn, cn, displayname, title, initials, loginshell,
              gecos, homephone, mobile, pager, facsimiletelephonenumber,
              telephonenumber, street, roomnumber, l, st, postalcode, manager,
              secretary, description, carlicense, labeleduri, inetuserhttpurl,
              seealso, employeetype, businesscategory, ou

  Self-service name: Users can manage their own SSH public keys
  Permissions: write
  Attributes: ipasshpubkey
----------------------------
Number of entries returned 4
----------------------------
```

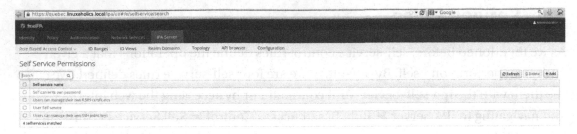

**Figure 25-6.** *Self-service rules*

By clicking one of the defined self-service permissions we can see a list of the attributes that are allowed to be changed (Figure 25-7). In that same window we can edit the list of attributes that can be changed by selecting them.

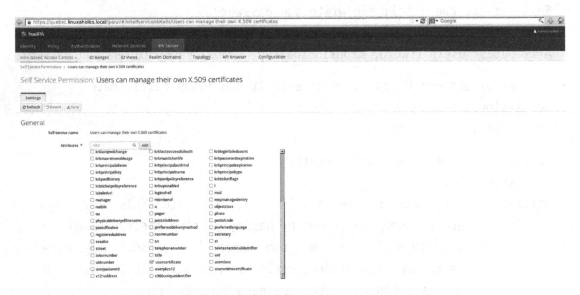

**Figure 25-7.** *Editing a self-service permission*

Again, we can obtain the same information from the command line.

```
[root@quebec ~]# ipa selfservice-show "Users can manage their own X.509
certificates"
  Self-service name: Users can manage their own X.509 certificates
  Permissions: write
  Attributes: usercertificate
```

To see an example, let's log in to the web interface as a normal user, edit the Last name field, and save the changes (Figure 25-8).

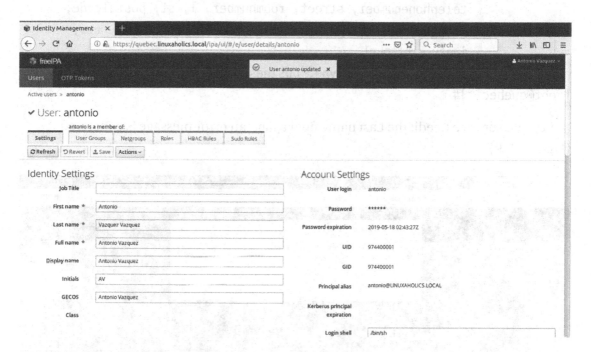

***Figure 25-8.***   *Editing the user properties by themselves*

After that, we'll modify the self-service permissions so that editing the Last name field is no longer supported. When doing so, it is important to specify the full list of attributes.

```
[root@quebec ~]# ipa selfservice-mod --permissions=write --attrs={givenname,
cn,displayname,title,initials,loginshell,gecos,homephone,mobile,pager,
facsimiletelephonenumber,telephonenumber,street,roomnumber,l,st,postalcode,
manager,secretary,description,carlicense,labeleduri,inetuserhttpurl,
seealso,employeetype,businesscategory,ou} "User self service"
-----------------------------------------
Modified selfservice "User self service"
-----------------------------------------
  Self-service name: User self service
  Permissions: write
```

```
Attributes: givenname, cn, displayname, title, initials, loginshell, gecos,
            homephone, mobile, pager, facsimiletelephonenumber,
            telephonenumber, street, roomnumber, l, st, postalcode,
            manager, secretary, description, carlicense, labeleduri,
            inetuserhttpurl,
            seealso, employeetype, businesscategory, ou
[root@quebec ~]#
```

If the user tries to edit the Last name field again, an error message is generated (Figure 25-9).

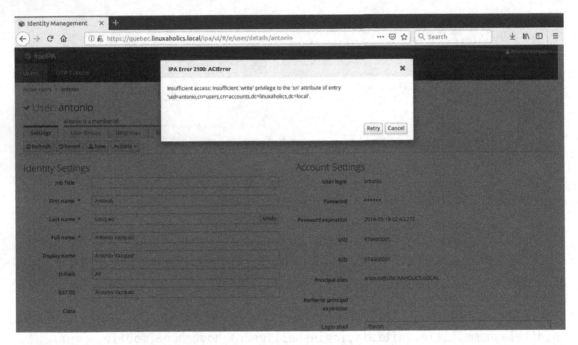

***Figure 25-9.*** *Trying to edit an attribute without permissions*

We'll again restore the original set of permissions and the user will be able to restore the original value of the Last name attribute.

```
[root@quebec ~]# ipa selfservice-mod --permissions=write --attrs={givenname,
sn,cn,displayname,title,initials,loginshell,gecos,homephone,mobile,pager,
facsimiletelephonenumber,telephonenumber,street,roomnumber,l,st,postalcode,
manager,secretary,description,carlicense,labeleduri,inetuserhttpurl,
seealso,employeetype,businesscategory,ou} "User self service"
```

```
------------------------------------------
Modified selfservice "User self service"
------------------------------------------
  Self-service name: User self service
  Permissions: write
  Attributes: givenname, sn, cn, displayname, title, initials, loginshell,
              gecos, homephone, mobile, pager, facsimiletelephonenumber,
              telephonenumber, street, roomnumber, l, st, postalcode,
              manager, secretary, description, carlicense, labeleduri,
              inetuserhttpurl, seealso, employeetype, businesscategory, ou
```

# Delegation Rules

This is similar to what we have seen in self-service rules, but in a delegation, a group is given permission to manage attributes from another group. We start by creating a group.

```
[root@quebec ~]# ipa group-add delegated_admins
--------------------------------
Added group "delegated_admins"
--------------------------------
  Group name: delegated_admins
  GID: 597800005
```

We also include the user antonio in that group.

```
[root@quebec ~]# ipa group-add-member delegated_admins --users=antonio
  Group name: delegated_admins
  GID: 597800005
  Member users: antonio
-------------------------
Number of members added 1
-------------------------
```

We can now create a delegation rule in the web interface. To do so, navigate to IPA Server ➤ Role Based Access Control and select Delegations. Click Add and fill in the form (Figure 25-10).

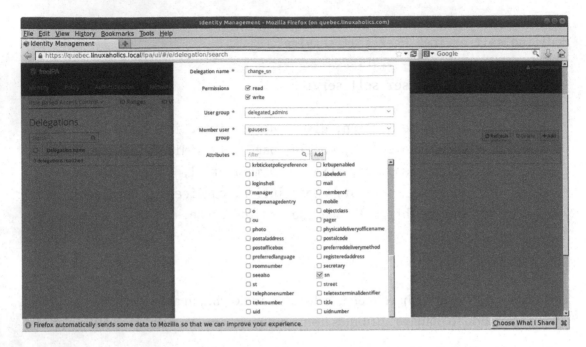

***Figure 25-10.*** *Creating a delegation rule*

We give a name to the rule, and specify whether we'll be giving read, write, or both permissions. In the User group field, select the name of the group that will be granted permission to edit attributes of users of the member user group. Finally, select the attributes that can be edited by selecting them. In our case, we'll give permissions to the users in the delegated_admins group to modify the Last name attribute (sn) of users in the ipausers group.

We could have done the same from a command line console by executing **ipa delegation-add**. Whatever method we choose, in the end we have created a new delegation.

```
[root@quebec ~]# ipa delegation-find
--------------------
1 delegation matched
--------------------
  Delegation name: change_sn
  Permissions: read, write
  Attributes: sn
  Member user group: ipausers
  User group: delegated_admins
```

```
--------------------------------
Number of entries returned 1
--------------------------------
```

If we log on now as the user Antonio, we'll be able to edit the Last name field for the user jose (Figure 25-11).

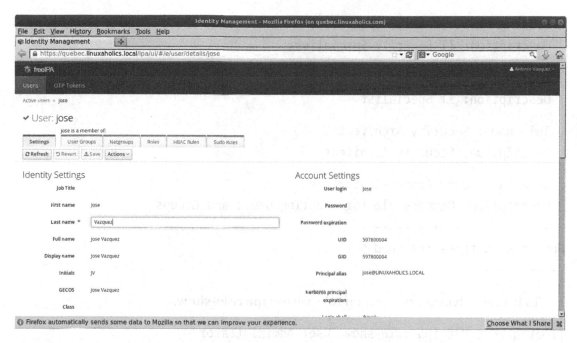

***Figure 25-11.*** *Editing attributes through delegation*

# Role-Based Access Control

Finally, we can use role-based access control, which is the most versatile way to customize permissions in the domain. To understand how it works we must differentiate its three components: roles, privileges, and permissions.

*Permissions* are the basic building blocks in this model. They specify read access, write access, or both, to a series of attributes. This is similar to what we just saw when talking about self-service and delegation rules.

Permissions are grouped into *privileges,* which in turn are grouped into *roles.* To see a practical example, we'll begin by listing the roles defined in the domain.

```
[root@quebec ~]# ipa role-find
---------------
5 roles matched
---------------
  Role name: helpdesk
  Description: Helpdesk

  Role name: IT Security Specialist
  Description: IT Security Specialist

  Role name: IT Specialist
  Description: IT Specialist

  Role name: Security Architect
  Description: Security Architect

  Role name: User Administrator
  Description: Responsible for creating Users and Groups
----------------------------
Number of entries returned 5
----------------------------
```

To list the privileges of a certain role, we use **ipa role-show**.

```
[root@quebec ~]# ipa role-show "User Administrator"
  Role name: User Administrator
  Description: Responsible for creating Users and Groups
  Privileges: User Administrators, Group Administrators, Stage User
              Administrators
```

In turn, we use **ipa privilege-show** to see the permissions assigned to a privilege.

```
[root@quebec ~]# ipa privilege-show "User Administrators"
  Privilege name: User Administrators
  Description: User Administrators
  Permissions: System: Add User to default group, System: Add Users, System:
               Change User password, System: Manage User Certificates, System:
               Manage User Principals, System: Manage User SSH Public Keys,
```

>           System: Modify Users, System: Read UPG Definition, System:
>           Read User Kerberos Login Attributes, System: Remove Users,
>           System: Unlock User
>   Granting privilege to roles: User Administrator

Finally, to see the definition of any permission we run **ipa permission-show**.

```
[root@quebec ~]# ipa permission-show "System: Modify Users"
  Permission name: System: Modify Users
  Granted rights: write
  Effective attributes: businesscategory, carlicense, cn, departmentnumber,
                        description, displayname, employeenumber,
                        employeetype, facsimiletelephonenumber, gecos,
                        givenname, homephone, inetuserhttpurl, initials,
                        l, labeleduri, loginshell, mail, manager,
                        mepmanagedentry, mobile, objectclass, ou, pager,
                        postalcode, preferredlanguage, roomnumber,
                        secretary, seealso, sn, st, street, telephonenumber,
                        title, userclass
  Default attributes: telephonenumber, cn, labeleduri, manager, street,
                      displayname, homephone, title, facsimiletelephonenumber,
                      loginshell, mail, employeenumber, employeetype,
                      description, businesscategory, preferredlanguage,
                      roomnumber, mepmanagedentry, carlicense, postalcode,
                      givenname, pager, seealso, departmentnumber,
                      objectclass, inetuserhttpurl, l, st, mobile, gecos,
                      sn, ou, secretary, userclass, initials
  Bind rule type: permission
  Subtree: cn=users,cn=accounts,dc=linuxaholics,dc=local
  Type: user
```

Permission flags: V2, MANAGED, SYSTEM
Granted to Privilege: User Administrators, Modify Users and Reset passwords
Indirect Member of roles: User Administrator, helpdesk

Again, we could obtain the same information from the web interface, by going to IPA
Server ➤ Role Based Access Control (Figures 25-12 through 25-15).

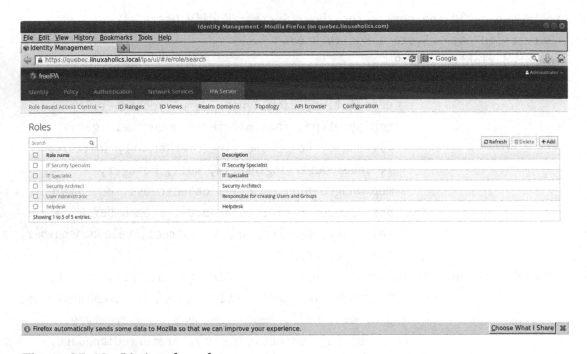

***Figure 25-12.***   *Listing the roles*

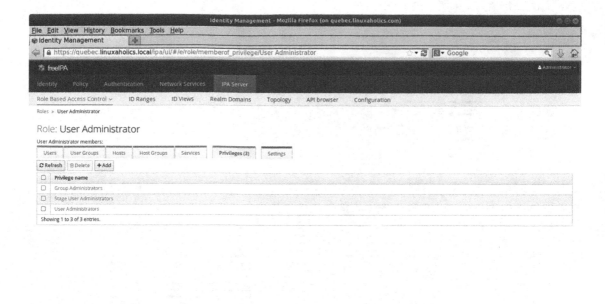

**Figure 25-13.**  *Listing the privileges associated with the User Administrator role*

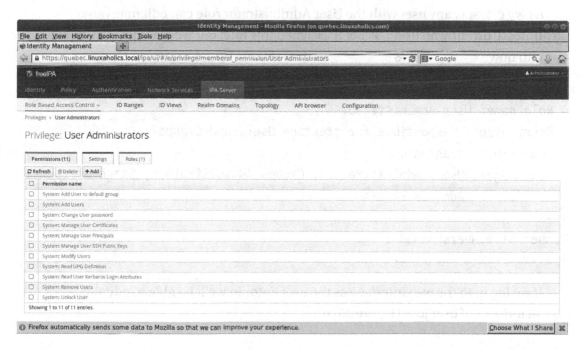

**Figure 25-14.**  *Listing the permissions associated with the User Administrators privilege*

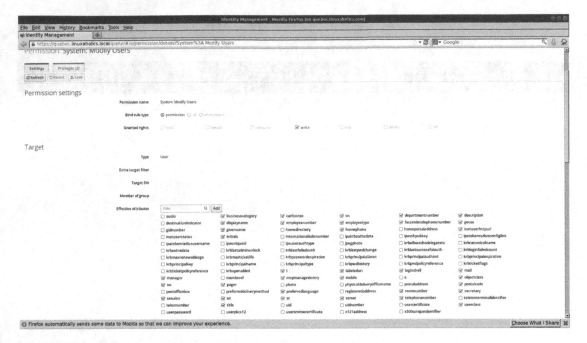

**Figure 25-15.**  *Viewing and editing the System:Modify Users permission*

As we can see, any user with the User Administrator role can edit many user attributes. Currently no user has been assigned this role, but we'll assign it to user antonio now.

```
[root@quebec ~]# ipa role-add-member "User Administrator" --users=antonio
  Role name: User Administrator
  Description: Responsible for creating Users and Groups
  Member users: antonio
  Privileges: Users Administrators, Groups Administrators, Stage Users
              Administrators
-------------------------
Number of members added 1
-------------------------
```

If we log in to the web interface as the user antonio we'll be able to edit the characteristics of user jose (Figure 25-16).

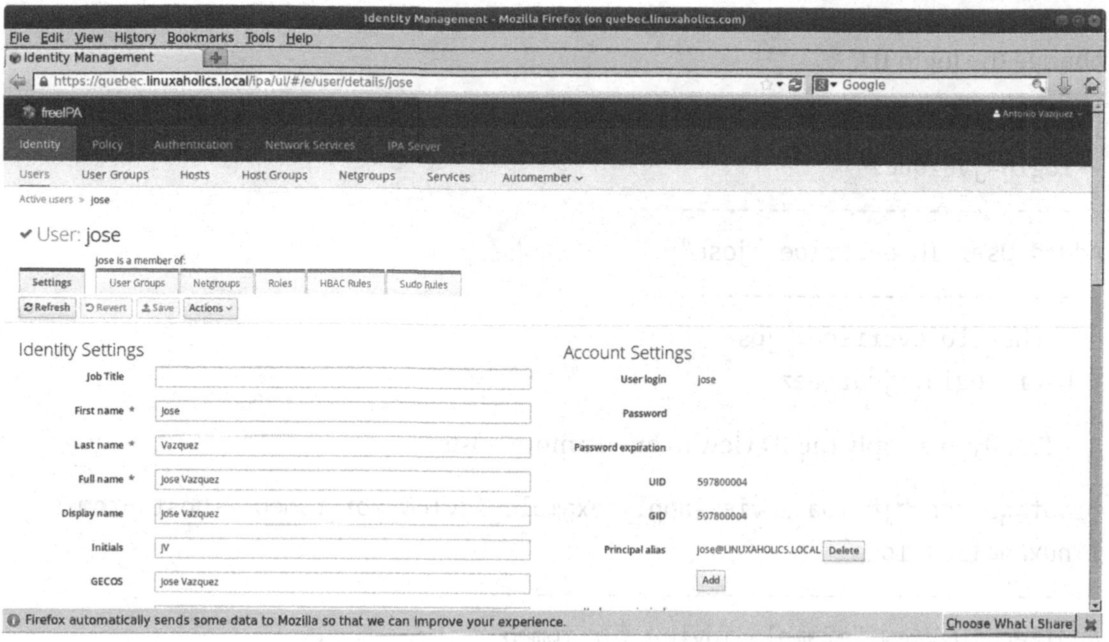

*Figure 25-16.*  *Editing a user*

Of course, in addition to using predefined roles, privileges, and permissions, we could also customize them, as well as add new ones. We can do it from the web interface or using the command-line tools **ipa role-mod**, **ipa role-add**, **ipa privilege-mod**, **ipa privilege-add**, **ida permission-mod,** and **ida permission-add**.

# ID Views

ID views are used to specify new values for user or group attributes, as well as to define on which host or hosts the new values will be applied. Let's look at an example. We begin by creating the view.

```
[root@quebec ~]# ipa idview-add example_idview_for_romeo
-------------------------------------------
Added ID View "example_idview_for_romeo"
-------------------------------------------
  ID View Name: example_idview_for_romeo
```

After creating the view, we specify the values that will be overridden, in our case we'll change the login ID.

```
[root@quebec ~]# ipa idoverrideuser-add example_idview_for_romeo jose
--login=jvazquez
-------------------------------
Added User ID override "jose"
-------------------------------
  Anchor to override: jose
  User login: jvazquez
```

Finally, we apply the ID view to one or more hosts.

```
[root@quebec ~]# ipa idview-apply example_idview_for_romeo --hosts=romeo.
linuxaholics.local
---------------------------------------------
Applied ID View "example_idview_for_romeo"
---------------------------------------------
  hosts: romeo.linuxaholics.local
-----------------------------------------------
Number of hosts the ID View was applied to: 1
-----------------------------------------------
```

Now, whenever the user jose logs on to romeo.linuxaholics.local, he will be assigned the login jvazquez.

To check this point, we'll restart the sssd service on the host(s) affected and try to log in to that same host.

```
[root@romeo ~]# systemctl restart sssd
[root@alpha ~]# ssh jose@romeo.linuxaholics.local
Password:
Last login: Wed Feb 20 03:57:51 2019 from gateway
Could not chdir to home directory /home/jose: No such file or directory
-sh-4.2$ id
uid=597800004(jvazquez) gid=597800004(jose) groups=597800004(jose) context=
unconfined_u:unconfined_r:unconfined_t:s0-s0:c0.c1023
-sh-4.2$
```

We could also check this without having to log in to the host, simply by using the **getent** command.

```
[root@romeo ~]# getent passwd jose
jvazquez:*:597800004:597800004:Jose Vazquez:/home/jose:/bin/sh
```

However, in other hosts where the ID view has not been applied, the login will not be changed.

```
[root@quebec ~]# getent passwd jose
jose:*:597800004:597800004:Jose Vazquez:/home/jose:/bin/sh
```

# Sudo, autofs, SSH, SELinux, and NIS Integration

FreeIPA client integrates with many Linux services, which can be centrally managed. Most of these services uses SSSD so they can use caching and be available offline.

Sudo is a program present in Linux as well as other Unix-like OSs that allows a user to run programs with the privileges of the root user. The local file /etc/sudoers determines which users can execute which programs as root. As the file is local, it only applies to the computer on which it is located.

With FreeIPA we can configure sudo centrally and the configuration will be applied to all the computers in the domain. By default, there are no sudo commands defined.

```
[root@quebec ~]# ipa sudocmd-find
-----------------------
0 Sudo Commands matched
-----------------------
----------------------------
Number of entries returned 0
----------------------------
```

We'll create a new sudo command, so that normal users can view log files. First, we check that, right now, standard users are not allowed to view log files like /var/log/messages.

```
-sh-4.2$ id
uid=597800003(antonio) gid=597800003(antonio) groups=597800003(antonio),
597800005(delegated_admins) context=unconfined_u:unconfined_r:unconfined_t:
s0-s0:c0.c1023
-sh-4.2$ tail /var/log/messages
tail: cannot open '/var/log/messages' for reading: Permission denied
```

After checking this point, we create the sudo command.

```
[root@quebec ~]# ipa sudocmd-add /usr/bin/tail
-----------------------------------
Added Sudo Command "/usr/bin/tail"
-----------------------------------
  Sudo Command: /usr/bin/tail
```

FreeIPA groups the sudo commands into command groups, so we create a new command group.

```
[root@quebec ~]# ipa sudocmdgroup-add view_log_files
------------------------------------------
Added Sudo Command Group "view_log_files"
------------------------------------------
  Sudo Command Group: view_log_files
```

We also include the sudo command we defined previously in the sudo command group.

```
[root@quebec ~]# ipa sudocmdgroup-add-member view_log_files --sudocmds=
/usr/bin/tail
  Sudo Command Group: view_log_files
  Member Sudo commands: /usr/bin/tail
-------------------------
Number of members added 1
-------------------------
```

Then, we create a sudo rule, which is the place where we associate the sudo commands or command groups with a certain user and one or more hosts.

```
[root@quebec ~]# ipa sudorule-add "log_files"
---------------------------
Added Sudo Rule "log_files"
---------------------------
  Rule name: log_files
  Enabled: TRUE
```

We add the sudo command group created earlier to the new rule.

```
[root@quebec ~]# ipa sudorule-add-allow-command log_files
--sudocmdgroups=view_log_files
  Rule name: log_files
  Enabled: TRUE
  Sudo Allow Command Groups: view_log_files
-------------------------
Number of members added 1
-------------------------
```

We also need to add the user we want to have run the sudo commands.

```
[root@quebec ~]# ipa sudorule-add-user log_files --users=antonio
  Rule name: log_files
  Enabled: TRUE
  Users: antonio
  Sudo Allow Command Groups: view_log_files
-------------------------
Number of members added 1
-------------------------
```

We specify the host on which the sudo rule will be applied.

```
[root@quebec ~]# ipa sudorule-add-host log_files --hosts=romeo.
linuxaholics.local
  Rule name: log_files
  Enabled: TRUE
  Users: antonio
  Hosts: romeo.linuxaholics.local
  Sudo Allow Command Groups: view_log_files
```

```
--------------------------
Number of members added 1
--------------------------
```

When executed, the sudo command will have the rights associated with a user, usually root. We define this behavior in the sudo rule.

```
[root@quebec ~]# ipa sudorule-add-runasuser log_files --users=root
  Rule name: log_files
  Enabled: TRUE
  Users: antonio
  Hosts: romeo.linuxaholics.local
  Sudo Allow Command Groups: view_log_files
  RunAs External User: root
--------------------------
Number of members added 1
--------------------------
```

The definition of the rule is now complete. We log in as the user antonio and we check that we can execute the sudo command on the host romeo.linuxaholics.local.

```
-sh-4.2$ sudo /usr/bin/tail /var/log/messages

We trust you have received the usual lecture from the local System
Administrator. It usually boils down to these three things:

    #1) Respect the privacy of others.
    #2) Think before you type.
    #3) With great power comes great responsibility.

[sudo] password for antonio:
Feb 20 05:20:01 romeo systemd: Starting Session 33 of user root.
Feb 20 05:22:48 romeo [sssd[krb5_child[3543]]]: Clock skew too great
Feb 20 05:22:48 romeo [sssd[krb5_child[3543]]]: Clock skew too great
Feb 20 05:22:48 romeo [sssd[krb5_child[3544]]]: Clock skew too great
Feb 20 05:22:48 romeo [sssd[krb5_child[3544]]]: Clock skew too great
Feb 20 05:22:49 romeo systemd: Created slice user-597800003.slice.
Feb 20 05:22:49 romeo systemd: Starting user-597800003.slice.
Feb 20 05:22:49 romeo systemd: Started Session 34 of user antonio.
```

```
Feb 20 05:22:49 romeo systemd-logind: New session 34 of user antonio.
Feb 20 05:22:49 romeo systemd: Starting Session 34 of user antonio.
-sh-4.2$
```

The command worked as expected. On the contrary, if we log in as the user jose, we won't be able to execute the command.

```
-sh-4.2$ sudo /usr/bin/tail /var/log/messages
```

```
We trust you have received the usual lecture from the local System
Administrator. It usually boils down to these three things:
```

```
    #1) Respect the privacy of others.
    #2) Think before you type.
    #3) With great power comes great responsibility.
```

```
[sudo] password for jvazquez:
jvazquez is not in the sudoers file.  This incident will be reported.
-sh-4.2$
```

In addition to sudo, another characteristic that is integrated in FreeIPA is automounting. When automounting is configured, the autofs service automatically mounts a file system as soon as it has to be accessed. This can be configured locally or it can be integrated in the FreeIPA domain. Automount is normally used with NFS shares, which are covered in Chapter 27.

SSH keys can also be easily integrated in FreeIPA. As we know, users can gain access to an SSH server by authenticating with a valid username and password, but it is also possible to authenticate with keys. To authenticate with keys, the user first needs to generate a key, and that key will then be copied to the server. We can associate the key with the host definition in FreeIPA.

When logged on as a normal user, we generate the keys.

```
-sh-4.2$ whoami
antonio
-sh-4.2$ ssh-keygen -t rsa
Generating public/private rsa key pair.
Enter file in which to save the key (/home/antonio/.ssh/id_rsa):
/tmp/antonio_id.rsa
Enter passphrase (empty for no passphrase):
```

```
Enter same passphrase again:
Your identification has been saved in /tmp/antonio_id.rsa.
Your public key has been saved in /tmp/antonio_id.rsa.pub.
The key fingerprint is:
83:ed:03:de:1a:df:f7:03:fb:cc:04:a9:74:3c:5c:05 antonio@sierra.
linuxaholics.local
The key's randomart image is:
+--[ RSA 2048]----+
|             E..|
|              . |
|             .  |
|     o  o o     |
|    o S . B     |
|   . + o o.o    |
|    o + . o.    |
|    + o  o+.    |
|    . . .. o=.  |
+----------------+
```

After executing the command, there will be two new files in the location we specified.

```
-sh-4.2$ ls /tmp/antonio_id.rsa*
/tmp/antonio_id.rsa   /tmp/antonio_id.rsa.pub
```

The public key will be contained in the .pub file. The content of this file will be something like this:

```
-sh-4.2$ cat /tmp/antonio_id.rsa.pub ssh-rsa
AAAAB3NzaC1yc2EAAAADAQABAAABAQCUKykQ3dlvmzCrK6npHvCcnRBXUx61r4Eum/EnMCf1dzs
Dfli+sdTmqWCcV1kq5Io5iz3wqziYpOnIwjWx/vGtLFgbRcepxLITqzxCNscrNQ/5gZWoyx+
TMndt9NRm7ndAqYgdoOCY3yNUWFUwfNsMaJNztXCGkAd5M5sJKpdOp+Hsp43D1DaO58jEpbXv
6XDC+LCPONbULL3cUZwXM5q4wKgy5z3UIKbye+5vuFTZeISiUh+TaDVVh1Mj3LwDvSFMmfvE3
PDvjmDwIcBzCoXdvOEX5qD18/o5JHDv46g3L/ajzbz1aG6pE46A3zTAwN2MFp/fOXdrfK9K/
WeALsKT antonio@sierra.linuxaholics.local
```

We'll have to include this value in the definition of the user in FreeIPA.

```
[root@sierra ~]# ipa user-mod antonio --sshpubkey="ssh-rsa AAAAB3NzaC1yc
2EAAAADAQABAAABAQCUKykQ3dlvmzCrK6npHvCcnRBXUx61r4Eum/EnMCf1dzsDfli+sdTmq
WCcV1kq5Io5iz3wqziYpOnIwjWx/vGtLFgbRcepxLITqzxCNscrNQ/5gZWoyx+TMndt9NRm
7ndAqYgdoOCY3yNUWFUwfNsMaJNztXCGkAd5M5sJKpdOp+Hsp43D1DaO58jEpbXv6XDC+
LCPONbULL3cUZwXM5q4wKgy5z3UIKbye+5vuFTZeISiUh+TaDVVh1Mj3LwDvSFMmfvE3PD
vjmDwIcBzCoXdvOEX5qD18/o5JHDv46g3L/ajzbz1aG6pE46A3zTAwN2MFp/fOXdrfK9K/
WeALsKT antonio@sierra.linuxaholics.local"
--------------------------
Modified user "antonio"
--------------------------
  User login: antonio
  First name: Antonio
  Last name: Vazquez
  Home directory: /home/antonio
  Login shell: /bin/sh
  Principal name: antonio@LINUXAHOLICS.LOCAL
  Principal alias: antonio@LINUXAHOLICS.LOCAL
  Email address: antonio@linuxaholics.local
  UID: 974400001
  GID: 974400001
  SSH public key: ssh-rsa
                  AAAAB3NzaC1yc2EAAAADAQABAAABAQCUKykQ3dlvmzCrK6npHvCcnR
                  BXUx61r4Eum/EnMCf1dzsDfli+sdTmqWCcV1kq5Io5iz3wqziYpOnI
                  wjWx/vGtLFgbRcepxLITqzxCNscrNQ/5gZWoyx+TMndt9NRm7ndAqY
                  gdoOCY3yNUWFUwfNsMaJNztXCGkAd5M5sJKpdOp+Hsp43D1DaO58jE
                  pbXv6XDC+LCPONbULL3cUZwXM5q4wKgy5z3UIKbye+5vuFTZeISiUh+
                  TaDVVh1Mj3LwDvSFMmfvE3PDvjmDwIcBzCoXdvOEX5qD18/o5JHDv4
                  6g3L/ajzbz1aG6pE46A3zTAwN2MFp/fOXdrfK9K/WeALsKT
                  antonio@sierra.linuxaholics.local
  SSH public key fingerprint: SHA256:soayP+TOQVbqS9mrDc/ttF7knxOHCsX1C7
                  f86q1SKWO
                  antonio@sierra.linuxaholics.local (ssh-rsa)
  Account disabled: False
  Password: True
```

```
  Member of groups: ipausers
  Kerberos keys available: True
[root@sierra ~]#
```

We also have the possibility to map SELinux users into FreeIPA users. First, we list the available SELinux users with **semanage**.

```
[root@quebec ~]# semanage user --list
```

| SELinux User | Labeling Prefix | MLS/ MCS Level | MLS/ MCS Range | SELinux Roles |
|---|---|---|---|---|
| guest_u | user | s0 | s0 | guest_r |
| root | user | s0 | s0-s0:c0.c1023 | staff_r sysadm_r system_r unconfined_r |
| staff_u | user | s0 | s0-s0:c0.c1023 | staff_r sysadm_r system_r unconfined_r |
| sysadm_u | user | s0 | s0-s0:c0.c1023 | sysadm_r |
| system_u | user | s0 | s0-s0:c0.c1023 | system_r unconfined_r |
| unconfined_u | user | s0 | s0-s0:c0.c1023 | system_r unconfined_r |
| user_u | user | s0 | s0 | user_r |
| xguest_u | user | s0 | s0 | xguest_r |

We add an SELinux user mapping with the **ipa selinuxusermap-add** command.

```
[root@sierra ~]# ipa selinuxusermap-add sample_SELinux_user_map
--selinuxuser=sysadm_u:s0-s0:c0.c1023
ipa: ERROR: SELinux user sysadm_u:s0-s0:c0.c1023 not found in ordering list
(in config)
```

In this case we received an error, because not all the SELinux users are included in the configuration of FreeIPA. We can see those already defined with the **ipa config-show** command.

```
[root@sierra ~]# ipa config-show | grep SELinux
  SELinux user map order: guest_u:s0$xguest_u:s0$user_u:s0$staff_u:s0-
  s0:c0.c1023$unconfined_u:s0-s0:c0.c1023
  Default SELinux user: unconfined_u:s0-s0:c0.c1023
```

We see that the SELinux user sysadm_u is not included by default in FreeIPA. We can also see that the default SELinux user that is used by FreeIPA is unconfined_u. In fact, if we log into `sierra.linuxaholics.local` as the user jose and run the **id** command, that's the SELinux context we'll see.

```
-sh-4.2$ id
uid=974400003(jose) gid=974400003(jose) groups=974400003(jose) context=
unconfined_u:unconfined_r:unconfined_t:s0-s0:c0.c1023
```

We could modify the FreeIPA configuration with the **ipa config-mod** command to include more SELinux users, but as we are only interested in a proof of concept we'll create the mapping with a SELinux user already defined.

```
[root@sierra ~]# ipa selinuxusermap-add sample_SELinux_user_map
--selinuxuser=user_u:s0
--------------------------------------------------
Added SELinux User Map "sample_SELinux_user_map"
--------------------------------------------------
  Rule name: sample_SELinux_user_map
  SELinux User: user_u:s0
  Enabled: TRUE
```

We add the host in which the map will be applied.

```
[root@sierra ~]# ipa selinuxusermap-add-host sample_SELinux_user_map
--hosts=sierra.linuxaholics.local
  Rule name: sample_SELinux_user_map
  SELinux User: user_u:s0
  Enabled: TRUE
  Users: jose
  Hosts: sierra.linuxaholics.local
-------------------------
Number of members added 1
-------------------------
```

We also add the user to which the SELinux map applies.

```
[root@sierra ~]# ipa selinuxusermap-add-user sample_SELinux_user_map
--users=jose
  Rule name: sample_SELinux_user_map
  SELinux User: user_u:s0
  Enabled: TRUE
  Users: jose
-------------------------
Number of members added 1
-------------------------
```

We restart the sssd service, and we log in to `sierra.linuxaholics.local`.

```
-sh-4.2$ id
uid=974400003(jose) gid=974400003(jose) groups=974400003(jose)
context=user_u:user_r:user_t:s0
```

We see that the SELinux context has been changed accordingly to the one that has been mapped.

```
[root@quebec ~]# su - jose
Last login: mié feb 20 12:58:25 CET 2019 on pts/0
su: warning: cannot change directory to /home/jose: No such file or
directory
-sh-4.2$ id
uid=597800004(jose) gid=597800004(jose) groups=597800004(jose) context=unco
nfined_u:unconfined_r:unconfined_t:s0-s0:c0.c1023
```

NIS was one of the first centralized management solutions for Unix-like OSs. Now, however, it has been largely replaced by other systems such as FreeIPA. To make this step easier, FreeIPA includes several features that help with migrating from NIS to FreeIPA.

To start, we'd have to use FreeIPA netgroups to integrate NIS entities. In addition, we should enable the NIS listener included whith the installation and the compatibility plug-ins.

```
[root@quebec ~]# ipa-nis-manage start
[root@quebec ~]# ipa-compat-manage status
```

Finally, we should start the port mapper service and restart the directory server.

```
[root@quebec ~]# systemctl start rpcbind
[root@quebec ~]# systemctl start dirsrv
```

# Host-Based Access Control

FreeIPA can grant or deny access to any user to any host. This is called Host-Based Access Control (HBAC). By default, there is an HBAC defined that allows every user to access any host.

```
[root@quebec ~]# ipa hbacrule-find
-------------------
1 HBAC rule matched
-------------------
  Rule name: allow_all
  User category: all
  Host category: all
  Service category: all
  Description: Allow all users to access any host from any host
  Enabled: TRUE
----------------------------
Number of entries returned 1
----------------------------
```

If we want to restrict access based on HBACs, however, we can create our own customized HBAC.

```
[root@quebec ~]# ipa hbacrule-add "Customized rule" -desc="Restricting
access"
---------------------------------
Added HBAC rule "Customized rule"
---------------------------------
  Rule name: Customized rule
  Description: Restricting access
  Enabled: TRUE
```

After creating the rule, we add some hosts and users to it.

```
[root@quebec ~]# ipa hbacrule-add-host "Customized rule" --hosts="romeo.
linuxaholics.local"
  Rule name: Customized rule
  Description: Restricting access
  Enabled: TRUE
  Hosts: romeo.linuxaholics.local
-------------------------
Number of members added 1
-------------------------
[root@quebec ~]# ipa hbacrule-add-user "Customized rule" --users=jose
  Rule name: Customized rule
  Description:  Restricting access
  Enabled: TRUE
  Users: jose
  Hosts: romeo.linuxaholics.local
-------------------------
Number of members added 1
-------------------------
```

In addition, we have to specify a service (or more) that will be affected by the HBAC rule.

```
[root@quebec ~]# ipa hbacrule-add-service "Customized rule" --hbacsvcs=sshd
  Rule name: Customized rule
  Description: Restricting access
  Enabled: TRUE
  Users: jose
  Hosts: romeo.linuxaholics.local
  Services: sshd
-------------------------
Number of members added 1
-------------------------
```

Right now, the rule would allow the user jose to access the sshd service on the host romeo.linuxaholics.local. To check this point, we can use a test tool provided by FreeIPA.

```
[root@quebec ~]# ipa hbactest --user=jose --host=romeo.linuxaholics.local
--service=sshd --rules="Customized rule"
--------------------
Access granted: True
--------------------
  Matched rules: Customized rule
```

As expected, the user jose can access the service. We'll repeat the test next with the user antonio.

```
[root@quebec ~]# ipa hbactest --user=antonio --host=romeo.linuxaholics.
local --service=sshd --rules="Customized rule"
--------------------
Access granted: False
--------------------
  Not matched rules: Customized rule
```

In this case the result is what we expected, too, and the user is denied access.

Now that we've seen how to create HBAC rules, we can delete the one we created.

```
[root@quebec ~]# ipa hbacrule-del "Customized rule"
------------------------------------
Deleted HBAC rule "Customized rule"
------------------------------------
```

# FreeIPA CA

One of the components of FreeIPA is DogTag, which implements a fully functional CA. We can manage the CA either from the web interface or from the command line. Under normal circumstances we shouldn't be too concerned about managing the certificates, as FreeIPA will take care of it automatically. We can, however, perform some basic operations. For instance, we can list the existing CAs.

```
[root@quebec ~]# ipa ca-find
------------
1 CA matched
------------
```

```
  Name: ipa
  Description: IPA CA
  Authority ID: 37acc1fa-8eac-48de-82b0-1971d73772db
  Subject DN: CN=Certificate Authority,O=LINUXAHOLICS.LOCAL
  Issuer DN: CN=Certificate Authority,O=LINUXAHOLICS.LOCAL
----------------------------
Number of entries returned 1
----------------------------
```

We can also list the certificates issued.

```
[root@quebec ~]# ipa cert-find
----------------------
10 certificates matched
----------------------
  Issuing CA: ipa
  Subject: CN=Certificate Authority,O=LINUXAHOLICS.LOCAL
  Issuer: CN=Certificate Authority,O=LINUXAHOLICS.LOCAL
  Not Before: Sun Apr 16 02:57:21 2017 UTC
  Not After: Thu Apr 16 02:57:21 2037 UTC
  Serial number: 1
  Serial number (hex): 0x1
  Status: VALID
  Revoked: False

  Issuing CA: ipa
  Subject: CN=OCSP Subsystem,O=LINUXAHOLICS.LOCAL
  Issuer: CN=Certificate Authority,O=LINUXAHOLICS.LOCAL
  Not Before: Sun Apr 16 02:57:22 2017 UTC
  Not After: Sat Apr 06 02:57:22 2019 UTC
  Serial number: 2
  Serial number (hex): 0x2
  Status: VALID
  Revoked: False

  Issuing CA: ipa
  Subject: CN=quebec.linuxaholics.local,O=LINUXAHOLICS.LOCAL
```

```
Issuer: CN=Certificate Authority,O=LINUXAHOLICS.LOCAL
Not Before: Sun Apr 16 02:57:22 2017 UTC
Not After: Sat Apr 06 02:57:22 2019 UTC
Serial number: 3
Serial number (hex): 0x3
Status: VALID
Revoked: False
.
.
.
----------------------------------
Number of entries returned 10
----------------------------------
```

# Getting Help

An interesting tool we haven't seen so far is **ipa-advise**. As we already know, it is not always easy to configure the different hosts so that they integrate properly in the FreeIPA domain. Fortunately, sssd makes this much easier, but there are circumstances in which we might not be able to or do not want to use it. In these cases, we should modify NSS and PAM files manually. By running **ipa-advise**, we'll get detailed instructions to help us.

By executing it without parameters, we'll get this output:

```
[root@quebec ~]# ipa-advise
trying https://quebec.linuxaholics.local/ipa/session/json
[try 1]: Forwarding 'schema' to json server 'https://quebec.linuxaholics.
local/ipa/session/json'
----------------------------------------------------------------------
List of available advices
----------------------------------------------------------------------
    config-client-for-smart-card-auth    : Instructions for enabling Smart
                                           Card authentication on a single
                                           FreeIPA client. Configures Smart
                                           Card daemon, set the system-wide
```

|                              | trust store and configures SSSD to allow smart card logins to desktop |
| config-fedora-authconfig     | : Authconfig instructions for configuring Fedora 18/19 client with IPA server without use of SSSD. |
| config-freebsd-nss-pam-ldapd | : Instructions for configuring a FreeBSD system with nss-pam-ldapd. |

.
.
.

We see that there are many options available depending on the system(s) we want to configure. If we choose any of these options, we'll see detailed instructions.

```
[root@quebec ~]# ipa-advise config-generic-linux-nss-pam-ldapd
#!/bin/sh
# ----------------------------------------------------------------------
# Instructions for configuring a system with nss-pam-ldapd. This set of
# instructions is targeted for Linux systems that do not include the
# authconfig utility.
# ----------------------------------------------------------------------
trying https://quebec.linuxaholics.local/ipa/session/json
[try 1]: Forwarding 'compat_is_enabled/1' to json server 'https://quebec.
linuxaholics.local/ipa/session/json'
# Schema Compatibility plug-in has not been configured on this server. To
# configure it, run "ipa-adtrust-install --enable-compat"
# Install required packages using your system's package manager. E.g:
apt-get -y install curl openssl libnss-ldapd libpam-ldapd nslcd

# Please note that this script assumes /etc/openldap/cacerts as the
# default CA certificate location. If this value is different on your
# system the script needs to be modified accordingly.
```

```
# Download the CA certificate of the IPA server
mkdir -p -m 755 /etc/openldap/cacerts
curl http://quebec.linuxaholics.local/ipa/config/ca.crt -o /etc/openldap/
cacerts/ipa.crt
```

.

.

.

# Summary

In this chapter, we became familiar with user and group management, and we learned about the user life cycle. We also studied how to grant permissions to users to perform certain operations. We covered how to grant or deny access to certain services on certain hosts by creating the corresponding rules. We also saw how a series of services native to Linux such as sudo and SELinux can be integrated into FreeIPA. Finally, we learned a bit more about the internal CA used by FreeIPA and the command **ipa-advise**.

# CHAPTER 26

# FreeIPA AD Integration

Most large networks now include different technologies, so it is quite possible that we need to integrate Active Directory and FreeIPA. Fortunately, this is not as complicated as it might sound at first because FreeIPA includes many tools to help us achieve this integration. In this chapter we'll cover the following concepts:

- Understanding and setting up FreeIPA and Active Directory integration using Kerberos cross-realm trusts.

- Configuring ID ranges.

- Understanding and managing external non-POSIX groups in FreeIPA.

- Awareness of Microsoft Privilege Attribute Certificates and how they are handled by FreeIPA.

- Awareness of replication-based FreeIPA and Active Directory integration.

We will also learn about the following terms and utilities: **ipa-adtrust-install** and **ipa** (relevant **trust-***, **idrange-*** and **group-*** subcommands).

## Trust Relationships

We have seen in previous chapters that users in a Kerberos realm are given tickets to access resources in the same Kerberos realm. It is also possible, though, for a user in a Kerberos realm to access resources in a different Kerberos realm, as long as there is a trust relationship.

When this happens, users from Domain A can access resources in Domain B. Domain B is said to be the trusting domain, and Domain A will be the trusted domain (Figure 26-1).

© Antonio Vazquez 2019
A. Vazquez, *Practical LPIC-3 300*, https://doi.org/10.1007/978-1-4842-4473-9_26

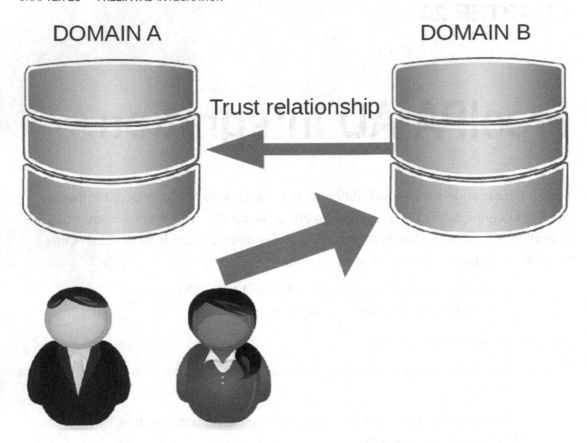

*Figure 26-1.* *Trust relationship*

Trust relationships can be unidirectional or bidirectional. For instance, in Figure 26-1, users in Domain A can access resources in Domain B, but users in Domain B cannot access resources in Domain A. In a bidirectional trust relationship, both domains trust each other and resources on any of the domains can be accessed by any user independent of the domain to which they belong.

Establishing a trust relationship between an Active Directory domain and a FreeIPA domain is the preferred way to integrate both systems.

## Cross-Realm Trusts

Now that we've seen the theory behind trust relationships, we'll look at how to actually implement them. As Active Directory servers use Kerberos, at least in theory, we can establish trust relationships between Linux and Windows domains, as well as between Linux domains.

---

**Note**   To this point we have been working with the latest version of FreeIPA available in the CentOS 7 repositories. This version has many improvements over the original version included with the CentOS 7.0 installation DVD. However, to successfully integrate FreeIPA with Active Directory, it is significantly easier to use the older version included with the CentOS 7.0 installation DVD. The topics we need to learn in this chapter work with this version as well.

---

At this moment we have a FreeIPA domain with its corresponding Kerberos realm, LINUXAHOLICS.LOCAL. As mentioned in the preceding note, in this chapter we'll work with the FreeIPA version included with the installation DVD.

To install the software versions included on the DVD instead of those in the official Internet repositories we need to make sure that we have the corresponding repository defined. Usually after installing CentOS 7 we should have a file named /etc/yum. repos.d/CentOS-Media.repo with the following content:

```
[c7-media]
name=CentOS-$releasever - Media
baseurl=file:///media/cdrom
gpgcheck=0
enabled=1
```

If the file doesn't exist, we'll have to create it. Then we create the /media/cdrom folder and we mount the CentOS 7.0 installation DVD.

From this moment on, whenever we want to install the software versions from the DVD we need to run **yum** by passing a couple of extra parameters. For instance, to install the FreeIPA server version included on the installation DVD, the full command would be this: yum --disablerepo=* --enablerepo=c7-media install -y ipa-server.

Therefore, we either have to uninstall the FreeIPA server and reinstall it from the DVD repository or reinstall the server from scratch and install **ipa-server** again from the installation DVD. Whichever method we choose, we'll end up with a FreeIPA server pretty much like the one we've used before, but without some advanced features like the use of DNSSEC.

To create a trust relationship, we need to create another Kerberos realm on another server. At first it might seem like enough to install a FreeIPA server on a different computer, `uniform.apress.local`. We'll use the version from the installation DVD, too, instead of that from the repositories.

```
[root@uniform ~]# yum -y install --disablerepo=* --enablerepo=c7-media ipa-
server
[root@uniform ~]# yum --disablerepo=* --enablerepo=c7-media -y install bind
[root@uniform ~]# yum --disablerepo=* --enablerepo=c7-media -y install
bind-dyndb-ldap
[root@uniform ~]# ipa-server-install
Server host name [uniform.apress.local]:

Warning: skipping DNS resolution of host uniform.apress.local
The domain name has been determined based on the host name.

Please confirm the domain name [apress.local]:

The kerberos protocol requires a Realm name to be defined.
This is typically the domain name converted to uppercase.

Please provide a realm name [APRESS.LOCAL]:
.
.
.
```

Of course, we would need to open all the necessary ports as we did when installing the other FreeIPA servers.

```
[root@uniform ~]# firewall-cmd --add-service={http,https,ldap,ldaps,
kerberos,kpasswd,dns}
success
[root@uniform ~]# firewall-cmd --permanent --add-service={http,https,ldap,
ldaps,kerberos,kpasswd,dns}
success
```

Before establishing the trust relationship, both FreeIPA and Kerberos servers should be able to resolve names in both domains. By default, their DNS settings point to themselves and they can only resolve names in their own domain. If their DNS settings do not currently point to themselves, we'll need to change those settings accordingly.

```
[root@quebec ~]# cat /etc/resolv.conf
search linuxaholics.local
nameserver 192.168.56.103
[root@quebec ~]# dig quebec.linuxaholics.local

.

.

.

;; ->>HEADER<<- opcode: QUERY, status: NOERROR, id: 35195

.

.

.

;; ANSWER SECTION:
quebec.linuxaholics.local. 1200        IN      A       192.168.1.243

.

.

.
```

When trying to resolve names in the newly created domain, it will return a SERVFAIL response.

```
[root@quebec ~]# dig uniform.apress.local

.

.

.

;; ->>HEADER<<- opcode: QUERY, status: SERVFAIL, id: 8119

.

.

.
```

To remediate this, we'll add the address of the new FreeIPA DNS server as a forwarder.

```
[root@quebec ~]# ipa dnsconfig-mod --forwarder=192.168.1.65
  Global forwarders: 192.168.1.65
```

Now, the server will be able to resolve names in both domains.

```
[root@quebec ~]# dig uniform.apress.local
.
.
.
;; ->>HEADER<<- opcode: QUERY, status: NOERROR, id: 9537
;; ANSWER SECTION:
uniform.apress.local.       1200      IN      A      192.168.1.65
.
.
.
```

In the new FreeIPA server, we'll do the same thing.

```
[root@uniform ~]# ipa dnsconfig-show
ipa: ERROR: did not receive Kerberos credentials
[root@uniform ~]# kinit admin
Password for admin@APRESS.LOCAL:
[root@uniform ~]# ipa dnsconfig-show
----------------------------------
Global DNS configuration is empty
----------------------------------
[root@uniform ~]# ipa dnsconfig-mod –forwarder=192.168.1.243
  Global forwarders: 192.168.1.243
[root@uniform ~]# dig quebec.linuxaholics.local
.
.
.
;; ->>HEADER<<- opcode: QUERY, status: NOERROR, id: 19693
.
.
.
;; ANSWER SECTION:
quebec.linuxaholics.local. 1200      IN      A      192.168.1.243
```

To make the Kerberos domain APRESS.LOCAL to trust the domain LINUXAHOLICS.LOCAL we need to add a new principal for krbtgt@LINUXAHOLICS.LOCAL in the APRESS.LOCAL realm.

```
[root@uniform ~]# kadmin.local
Authenticating as principal admin/admin@APRESS.LOCAL with password.
kadmin.local:  addprinc krbtgt/LINUXAHOLICS.LOCAL@APRESS.LOCAL
WARNING: no policy specified for krbtgt/LINUXAHOLICS.LOCAL@APRESS.LOCAL;
defaulting to no policy
Enter password for principal "krbtgt/LINUXAHOLICS.LOCAL@APRESS.LOCAL":
Re-enter password for principal "krbtgt/LINUXAHOLICS.LOCAL@APRESS.LOCAL":
add_principal: Invalid argument while creating "krbtgt/LINUXAHOLICS.LOCAL
@APRESS.LOCAL".
kadmin.local:
```

Unfortunately, the Kerberos installation included in FreeIPA has been tailored in such a way that it is almost impossible to create principals interacting directly with Kerberos. It encourages instead the use of the FreeIPA commands, which will interact with Kerberos in a proper way.

In a similar way we are expected to manage trust relationships using the **ipa** subcommands as well. Initially there will be no trust relationship defined.

```
[root@quebec ~]# ipa trust-find
----------------
0 trusts matched
----------------
----------------------------
Number of entries returned 0
----------------------------
```

We can add trust relationships with the **ipa trust-add** command, but we'll need to install some additional components first.

```
[root@quebec ~]# ipa trust-add APRESS.LOCAL
ipa: ERROR: Cannot perform join operation without Samba 4 support
installed. Make sure you have installed server-trust-ad sub-package of IPA
[root@quebec ~]# yum --disablerepo=* --enablerepo=c7-media -y install ipa-
server-trust-ad
```

```
[root@quebec ~]# ipa trust-add APRESS.LOCAL
ipa: ERROR: Cannot perform join operation without own domain configured.
Make sure you have run ipa-adtrust-install on the IPA server first
```

The **ipa-adtrust-install** command prepares the IPA server to establish trust relationships with an Active Directory domain. At the time of writing, these are the only trust relationships supported by FreeIPA. To establish a trust relationship with another Linux Kerberos realm, we'd need to do it manually. For now, then, we'll keep the new FreeIPA server installed in uniform.apress.local apart and we'll create a trust relationship with the Active Directory DC yankee.ventanas.local we used before when talking about Samba.

The recommended way to create an Active Directory trust relationship in FreeIPA is by executing **ipa-trust-add**. Before executing it, though, we need to run **ipa-adtrust-install**. Although both FreeIPA and Active Directory use Kerberos and theoretically integrating both should be relatively easy, that's not the case. Microsoft has added extensions to the standard protocol. One of those extensions is Microsoft Privilege Attribute Certificates (PAC), which we'll see in more detail in an upcoming section.

This command prepares the FreeIPA server by making the necessary changes and installing the software needed to support the trust relationship.

We'll install the ipa-server-trust-ad package, which contains the **ipa trust-add** command.

```
[root@quebec ~]# yum --disablerepo=* --enablerepo=c7-media provides ipa-
adtrust-install
Loaded plugins: fastestmirror
Loading mirror speeds from cached hostfile
ipa-server-trust-ad-3.3.3-28.el7.centos.x86_64 : Virtual package to install
     ...: packages required for Active Directory trusts
Repo      : c7-media
Matched from:
Filename  : /usr/sbin/ipa-adtrust-install
[root@quebec ~]# yum --disablerepo=* --enablerepo=c7-media install -y ipa-
server-trust-ad
```

We also need to make sure that both the FreeIPA server and the Windows DC resolve names in both domains. We'll begin by including the Windows DNS, which in this case is the DC itself, as a forwarder for the FreeIPA internal DNS server.

```
[root@quebec ~]# ipa dnsconfig-mod --forwarder=192.168.56.109
  Global forwarders: 192.168.56.109
```

Check that we can actually resolve the names.

```
[root@quebec ~]# dig yankee.ventanas.local
.
.
.
;; ->>HEADER<<- opcode: QUERY, status: NOERROR, id: 41163
;; ANSWER SECTION:
yankee.ventanas.local.      1200      IN      A      192.168.1.65
```

Of course, we need to do the same in the DC. We open the DNS console, right-click the Active Directory domain, and select Properties. On the Forwarders tab, add the FreeIPA server as a forwarder (Figure 26-2).

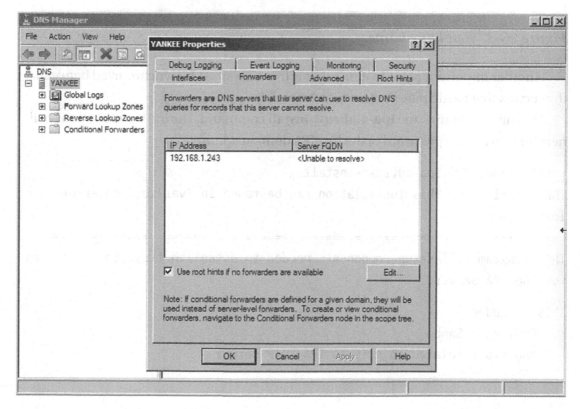

***Figure 26-2.*** *Configuring forwarders in Windows Server*

After configuring the forwarders, we check that the Windows server can resolve names in the FreeIPA domain (Figure 26-3).

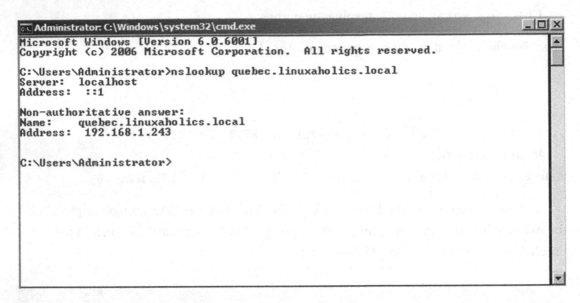

**Figure 26-3.** *Resolving names*

Another important point to remember is that time must be synchronized between the servers that participate in the trust relationship.

We can now launch the **ipa-addtrust-install** command. During the execution we'll need to provide the password of the FreeIPA domain admin user.

```
[root@quebec ~]# ipa-adtrust-install
The log file for this installation can be found in /var/log/ipaserver-
install.log
===========================================================================
This program will setup components needed to establish trust to AD domains
for the IPA Server.

This includes:
  * Configure Samba
  * Add trust related objects to IPA LDAP server
```

To accept the default shown in brackets, press the Enter key.

Do you want to enable support for trusted domains in Schema Compatibility plugin?
This will allow clients older than SSSD 1.9 and non-Linux clients to work with trusted users.

Enable trusted domains support in slapi-nis? [no]:

Configuring cross-realm trusts for IPA server requires password for user 'admin'.
This user is a regular system account used for IPA server administration.

admin password:

Enter the NetBIOS name for the IPA domain.
Only up to 15 uppercase ASCII letters and digits are allowed.
Example: EXAMPLE.

NetBIOS domain name [LINUXAHOLICS]:

WARNING: 4 existing users or groups do not have a SID identifier assigned. Installer can run a task to have ipa-sidgen Directory Server plugin generate the SID identifier for all these users. Please note, the in case of a high number of users and groups, the operation might lead to high replication traffic and performance degradation. Refer to ipa-adtrust-install(1) man page for details.

Do you want to run the ipa-sidgen task? [no]:

The following operations may take some minutes to complete.
Please wait until the prompt is returned.

Configuring CIFS
    [1/19]: stopping smbd
    [2/19]: creating samba domain object
    [3/19]: creating samba config registry
    [4/19]: writing samba config file
    [5/19]: adding cifs Kerberos principal

```
  [6/19]: check for cifs services defined on other replicas
  [7/19]: adding cifs principal to S4U2Proxy targets
  [8/19]: adding admin(group) SIDs
  [9/19]: adding RID bases
  [10/19]: updating Kerberos config
'dns_lookup_kdc' already set to 'true', nothing to do.
  [11/19]: activating CLDAP plugin
  [12/19]: activating sidgen plugin and task
  [13/19]: activating extdom plugin
  [14/19]: configuring smbd to start on boot
  [15/19]: adding special DNS service records
  [16/19]: restarting Directory Server to take MS PAC and LDAP plugins
            changes into account
  [17/19]: adding fallback group
  [18/19]: setting SELinux booleans
  [19/19]: starting CIFS services
Done configuring CIFS.


================================================================================

Setup complete

You must make sure these network ports are open:
     TCP Ports:
       * 138: netbios-dgm
       * 139: netbios-ssn
       * 445: microsoft-ds
     UDP Ports:
       * 138: netbios-dgm
       * 139: netbios-ssn
       * 389: (C)LDAP
       * 445: microsoft-ds

Additionally you have to make sure the IPA LDAP server is not reachable
by any domain controller in the Active Directory domain by closing down
the following ports for these servers:
     TCP Ports:
       * 389, 636: LDAP/LDAPS
```

You may want to choose to REJECT the network packets instead of DROPing them to avoid timeouts on the AD domain controllers.

============================================================================

As we can see, the command automatically performed a series of operations to prepare the server for the trust relationship, such as installilng some Samba components or customizing the Kerberos configuration. However, we still need to perform some additional steps manually. First, we open the necessary ports in the firewall.

```
[root@quebec ~]# firewall-cmd --add-service=samba
success
[root@quebec ~]# firewall-cmd --permanent --add-service=samba
success
[root@quebec ~]# firewall-cmd --add-service=samba-client
success
[root@quebec ~]# firewall-cmd --permanent --add-service=samba-client
success
```

As instructed by the installation program, we'll include rules in the firewall to prevent the DC from querying the LDAP server included in FreeIPA.

```
[root@quebec ~]# firewall-cmd --list-rich-rules
[root@quebec ~]# firewall-cmd --add-rich-rule='rule family="ipv4" source
address="192.168.1.235" service name="ldap" reject'
success
[root@quebec ~]# firewall-cmd --permanent --add-rich-rule='rule
family="ipv4" source address="192.168.1.235" service name="ldap" reject'
success
[root@quebec ~]# firewall-cmd --add-rich-rule='rule family="ipv4" source
address="192.168.1.235" service name="ldaps" reject'
success
[root@quebec ~]# firewall-cmd --permanent --add-rich-rule='rule
family="ipv4" source address="192.168.1.235" service name="ldaps" reject'
success
```

```
[root@quebec ~]# firewall-cmd --list-rich-rules
rule family="ipv4" source address="192.168.1.235" service name="ldaps" reject
rule family="ipv4" source address="192.168.1.235" service name="ldap" reject
```

We proceed now to create the trust relationship between the FreeIPA and the Windows domains. We need to specify the name of the Active Directory domain, a user with administrator privileges, and the corresponding password.

```
[root@quebec ~]# ipa trust-add VENTANAS.LOCAL --admin=Administrator
--password
Active directory domain administrator's password:
---------------------------------------------------------
Added Active Directory trust for realm "ventanas.local"
---------------------------------------------------------
  Realm name: ventanas.local
  Domain NetBIOS name: VENTANAS
  Domain Security Identifier: S-1-5-21-1754085188-4219036064-3012244413
  SID blacklist incoming: S-1-0, S-1-1, S-1-2, S-1-3, S-1-5-1, S-1-5-2,
                          S-1-5-3, S-1-5-4, S-1-5-5, S-1-5-6, S-1-5-7,
                          S-1-5-8, S-1-5-9, S-1-5-10, S-1-5-11, S-1-5-12,
                          S-1-5-13, S-1-5-14, S-1-5-15, S-1-5-16, S-1-5-17,
                          S-1-5-18, S-1-5-19, S-1-5-20
  SID blacklist outgoing: S-1-0, S-1-1, S-1-2, S-1-3, S-1-5-1, S-1-5-2,
                          S-1-5-3, S-1-5-4, S-1-5-5, S-1-5-6, S-1-5-7,
                          S-1-5-8, S-1-5-9, S-1-5-10, S-1-5-11, S-1-5-12,
                          S-1-5-13, S-1-5-14, S-1-5-15, S-1-5-16, S-1-5-17,
                          S-1-5-18, S-1-5-19, S-1-5-20
  Trust direction: Two-way trust
  Trust type: Active Directory domain
  Trust status: Established and verified
[root@quebec ~]#
```

If we list the Kerberos principals, we'll see that two new principals have been created, krbtgt/VENTANAS.LOCAL@LINUXAHOLICS.LOCAL and krbtgt/LINUXAHOLICS.LOCAL@ VENTANAS.LOCAL, as we have created a two-way trust relationship.

```
[root@quebec ~]# kadmin.local
Authenticating as principal admin/admin@LINUXAHOLICS.LOCAL with password.
kadmin.local:  listprincs
admin@LINUXAHOLICS.LOCAL
K/M@LINUXAHOLICS.LOCAL
krbtgt/LINUXAHOLICS.LOCAL@LINUXAHOLICS.LOCAL
kadmin/quebec.linuxaholics.local@LINUXAHOLICS.LOCAL
kadmin/admin@LINUXAHOLICS.LOCAL
kadmin/changepw@LINUXAHOLICS.LOCAL
ldap/quebec.linuxaholics.local@LINUXAHOLICS.LOCAL
host/quebec.linuxaholics.local@LINUXAHOLICS.LOCAL
HTTP/quebec.linuxaholics.local@LINUXAHOLICS.LOCAL
DNS/quebec.linuxaholics.local@LINUXAHOLICS.LOCAL
cifs/quebec.linuxaholics.local@LINUXAHOLICS.LOCAL
krbtgt/VENTANAS.LOCAL@LINUXAHOLICS.LOCAL
krbtgt/LINUXAHOLICS.LOCAL@VENTANAS.LOCAL
kadmin.local:
```

Despite having created the trust relationship, we are not done yet. We need to create external groups to include users or groups from the trusted domain. In our case, we'll create an external group for the domain admins from VENTANAS.LOCAL.

```
[root@quebec ~]# ipa group-add --desc='VENTANAS.LOCAL admins external map'
ad_admins_external --external
---------------------------------
Added group "ad_admins_external"
---------------------------------
  Group name: ad_admins_external
  Description: VENTANAS.LOCAL admins external map
```

We also have to create another group to include the external group we just created, so that users from the external group can access the FreeIPA domain.

```
[root@quebec ~]# ipa group-add --desc='VENTANAS.LOCAL admins' ad_admins
-----------------------
Added group "ad_admins"
-----------------------
  Group name: ad_admins
  Description: VENTANAS.LOCAL admins
  GID: 347800004
```

We include the users from the Active Directory domain in the external group.

```
[root@quebec ~]# ipa group-add-member ad_admins_external --external
"VENTANAS\Domain Admins"
[member user]:
[member group]:
  Group name: ad_admins_external
  Description: VENTANAS.LOCAL admins external map
  External member: S-1-5-21-1754085188-4219036064-3012244413-512
-------------------------
Number of members added 1
-------------------------
```

We also include the external group in the ad_admins group.

```
[root@quebec ~]# ipa group-add-member ad_admins --groups ad_admins_external
  Group name: ad_admins
  Description: VENTANAS.LOCAL admins
  GID: 347800004
  Member groups: ad_admins_external
-------------------------
Number of members added 1
-------------------------
```

We could get the following error when trying to include users from the Active Directory domain in the external group.

```
[root@quebec ~]# ipa group-add-member ad_admins_external --external
"VENTANAS\Domain Admins"
[member user]:
[member group]:
  Group name: ad_admins_external
  Description: VENTANAS.LOCAL admins external map
  Failed members:
    member user:
    member group: VENTANAS\Domain Admins: trusted domain object not found
-------------------------
Number of members added 0
-------------------------
```

This means that despite the fact that a cross-forest trust relationship has been established, it is not actually working. We should make sure that DNS name resolution is working fine in both the FreeIPA server and the DC, the necessary ports are open for communication, and we are working with the same time zone and date configuration. To better troubleshoot this issue, we could even stop the firewall temporarily on both servers.

A useful command we could launch when troubleshooting the cross-realm trust relationship is **ipa trust-fetch-domains**, used to refresh the list of domains associated with the trust. If the trust relationship is not working properly, we would get a message like this:

```
[root@quebec ~]# ipa trust-fetch-domains VENTANAS.LOCAL
ipa: ERROR: AD domain controller complains about communication sequence. It
may mean unsynchronized time on both sides, for example
```

We can also check the status of the trust from the DC. In this case we open Active Directory Domains and Trusts, select ventanas.local, right-click Properties, and click the Trusts tab (Figure 26-4).

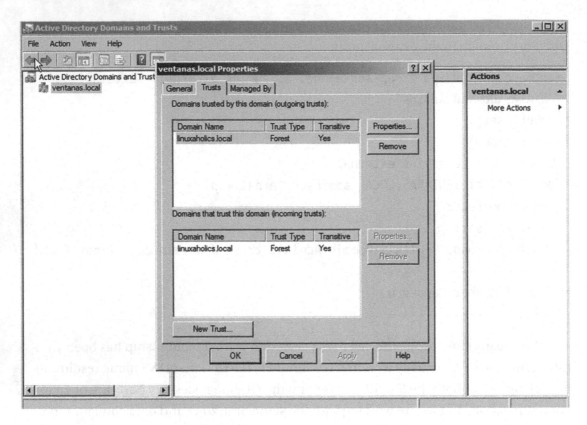

***Figure 26-4.*** *Domains and trusts*

When you select the trusted or trusting domain and click Properties, a new
Properties dialog box opens (Figure 26-5).

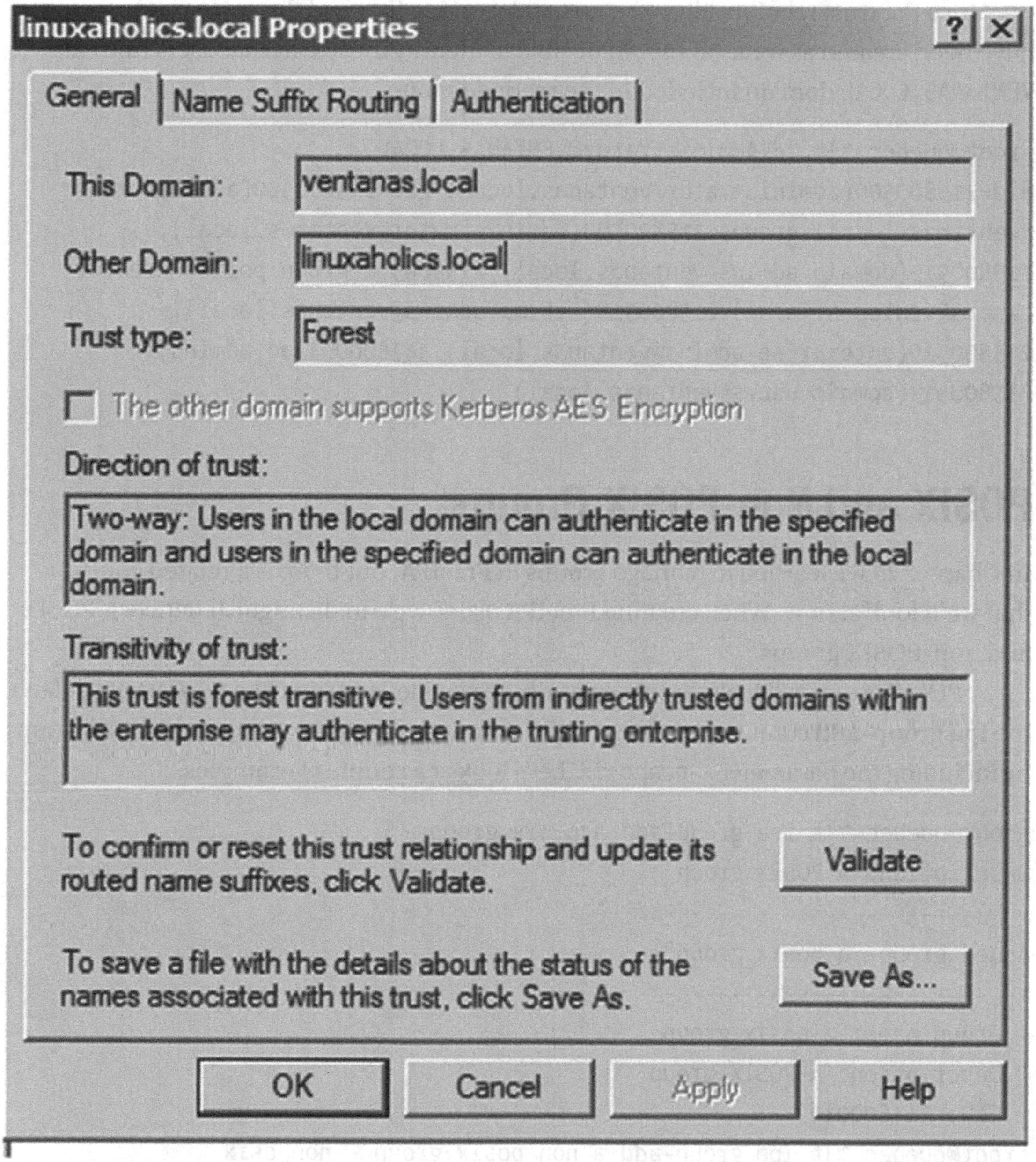

**Figure 26-5.** *Validating the trust*

Click Validate to check that everything is working; otherwise we'll get an informative error message.

Once the trust relationship is created and working fine and the appropriate groups have been created as well, we should be able to identify those external users from the VENTANAS.LOCAL domain included in the mapped group.

```
[root@quebec ~]# id Administrator@VENTANAS.LOCAL
uid=215800500(administrator@ventanas.local) gid=215800500(administrator
@ventanas.local) groups=215800500(administrator@ventanas.local),
215800512(domain admins@ventanas.local),215800520(group policy creator
owners@ventanas.local),215800518(schema admins@ventanas.local),
215800519(enterprise admins@ventanas.local),347800004(ad_admins),
215800513(domain users@ventanas.local)
```

# POSIX and Non-POSIX Groups

In Chapter 25 we learned to manage groups in FreeIPA, but there is a related concept that we'll look at now. When creating FreeIPA users, we can distinguish between POSIX and non-POSIX groups.

A POSIX group will include certain attributes needed in Linux like the GID. By default, the **ipa group-add** command creates POSIX groups, but we can create non-POSIX groups by including the parameter --nonposix. Let's look at a couple of examples.

```
[root@quebec ~]# ipa group-add a_posix_group
Description: A POSIX group
---------------------------
Added group "a_posix_group"
---------------------------
  Group name: a_posix_group
  Description: A POSIX group
  GID: 314600010
[root@quebec ~]# ipa group-add a_non_posix_group --nonposix
Description: A non-POSIX group
------------------------------
Added group "a_non_posix_group"
------------------------------
  Group name: a_non_posix_group
  Description: A non-POSIX group
```

When creating a POSIX group, this group will be assigned a GID, whereas a non-POSIX group won't be assigned any GID. We can list all the attributes associated with a group with the --all parameter.

```
[root@quebec ~]# ipa group-show a_posix_group --all
  dn: cn=a_posix_group,cn=groups,cn=accounts,dc=linuxaholics,dc=local
  Group name: a_posix_group
  Description: A POSIX group
  GID: 314600010
  ipantsecurityidentifier: S-1-5-21-331470152-946816622-3168006843-1010
  ipauniqueid: 08a4e4fa-3f6c-11e9-8a4f-08002731b753
  objectclass: top, groupofnames, nestedgroup, ipausergroup, ipaobject,
               posixgroup, ipantgroupattrs
[root@quebec ~]# ipa group-show a_non_posix_group --all
  dn: cn=a_non_posix_group,cn=groups,cn=accounts,dc=linuxaholics,dc=local
  Group name: a_non_posix_group
  Description: A non-POSIX group
  ipauniqueid: 27cd01a0-3f6c-11e9-8bf5-08002731b753
  objectclass: top, groupofnames, nestedgroup, ipausergroup, ipaobject
```

As we can see, apart from having a GID attribute, a POSIX group is also a member of the objectclass posixgroup. On the other hand, a non-POSIX group is not.

Most of the time we should use POSIX groups, but there are certain cases, like groups that interact with Active Directory or Samba users, that must be non-POSIX groups. This is the case of the ad_admins_external group we created a moment ago. This group wasn't created with the --nonposix parameter, but as we specified the –external option, FreeIPA recognizes that it must be created as a non-POSIX group.

```
[root@quebec ~]# ipa group-show ad_admins_external --all
  dn: cn=ad_admins_external,cn=groups,cn=accounts,dc=linuxaholics,dc=local
  Group name: ad_admins_external
  Description: VENTANAS.LOCAL admins external map
  Member of groups: ad_admins
  External member: admins. del dominio@ventanas.local
  ipauniqueid: dc482d08-3f0d-11e9-80ac-08002731b753
  objectclass: top, groupofnames, nestedgroup, ipausergroup, ipaobject,
               ipaexternalgroup
```

# Managing ID Ranges

In an Active Directory trust relationship, the FreeIPA server will need a way to map POSIX IDs to SIDs and back. This is done with the use of ID ranges that will be assigned to the local domain and to the trusted domains. Once an Active Directory trust relationship has been established, we can list the automatically created ID ranges with the **ipa idrange-find** command.

```
[root@quebec ~]# ipa idrange-find
-----------------
2 ranges matched
-----------------
  Range name: LINUXAHOLICS.LOCAL_id_range
  First Posix ID of the range: 347800000
  Number of IDs in the range: 200000
  First RID of the corresponding RID range: 1000
  First RID of the secondary RID range: 100000000
  Range type: local domain range

  Range name: VENTANAS.LOCAL_id_range
  First Posix ID of the range: 215800000
  Number of IDs in the range: 200000
  First RID of the corresponding RID range: 0
  Domain SID of the trusted domain: S-1-5-21-1754085188-4219036064-
                                    3012244413
  Range type: Active Directory domain range
----------------------------
Number of entries returned 2
----------------------------
```

By default, the local domain, LINUXAHOLICS.LOCAL, has been assigned IDs beginning from 347800000. We can assign 200,000 consecutive IDs before exhausting the ID range. If we check the ID associated with a user in the domain, we'll see values inside that range.

```
[root@quebec ~]# id antonio@linuxaholics.local
uid=347800008(antonio) gid=347800008(antonio) groups=347800008(antonio)
```

In turn, for the trusted domain, VENTANAS.LOCAL, the assigned ID range begins from 1553200000. In this case we can also use 200,000 consecutive IDs. We can also check this point with the **id** command.

```
[root@quebec ~]# id Administrator@VENTANAS.LOCAL
uid=215800500(administrator@ventanas.local) gid=215800500(administrator
@ventanas.local) groups=215800500(administrator@ventanas.local),
215800512(domain admins@ventanas.local),215800520(group policy creator
owners@ventanas.local),215800518(schema admins@ventanas.local),
215800519(enterprise admins@ventanas.local),347800004(ad_admins),
215800513(domain users@ventanas.local)
```

In our case the ID ranges were created automatically when establishing the trust relationship, but under certain circumstances we might need to create the ID ranges ourselves. This could happen, for example, if the ID range is exhausted or if the trusted domain trusts a third domain. We saw in Figure 26-1 that Domain B trusts Domain A. It could happen, too, that Domain C trusts Domain B (Figure 26-6). In that case we have a transitive trust relationship, and Domain C indirectly trusts Domain A, but we'd need to manually create an ID range.

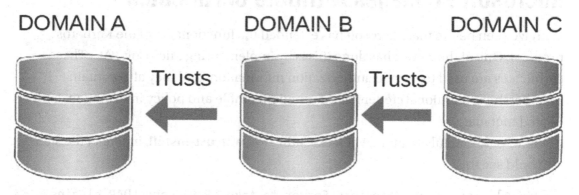

*Figure 26-6.* *A transitive trust relationship*

Whatever the reason, if we ever need to create a new ID range we can do it with the **ipa idrange-add** command. For example, suppose that we have exhausted the IDs for the local domain so we need to create a new range. We could do it by executing this command:

```
[root@quebec ~]# ipa idrange-add --base-id=414600000 --range-size=200000
--rid-base=120000000 --secondary-rid-base=1000000000 additional_range
--------------------------------
Added ID range "additional_range"
--------------------------------
  Range name: additional_range
  First Posix ID of the range: 414600000
  Number of IDs in the range: 200000
  First RID of the corresponding RID range: 120000000
  First RID of the secondary RID range: 1000000000
  Range type: local domain range
```

If we make a mistake when creating the ID range, we'll get an informative message like this one:

```
ipa: ERROR: Constraint violation: New primary rid range overlaps with
existing primary rid range.
```

# Microsoft Privileges Attribute Certificates

We have seen before that Microsoft has extended the functionality of the Kerberos protocol. One of the ways it has done this is by implementing Microsoft PAC. These certificates are used to encode authorization information, and they also contain memberships, additional credential information, profile and policy information, and related metadata.

If we paid careful attention when executing **ipa-adtrust-install**, in one of the steps we could see this:

```
[16/19]: restarting Directory Server to take MS PAC and LDAP plugins
changes into account
```

FreeIPA uses plug-ins as well as Samba components to interact with MS PAC. We could see an interactive example by executing the **net** command with the following set of parameters.

```
[root@quebec ~]# net ads kerberos pac dump --option='realm = LINUXAHOLICS.LOCAL'
--option='kerberos method = system keytab' -s /dev/null local_service=host/quebec.
linuxaholics.local@LINUXAHOLICS.LOCAL -U admin@LINUXAHOLICS.LOCAL
Enter admin@LINUXAHOLICS.LOCAL's password:
The Pac:      pac_data_ctr->pac_data: struct PAC_DATA
        num_buffers                  : 0x00000004 (4)
        version                      : 0x00000000 (0)
        buffers: ARRAY(4)
            buffers: struct PAC_BUFFER
                type                     : PAC_TYPE_LOGON_INFO (1)
                _ndr_size                : 0x000001b8 (440)
                info                     : *
                    info                 : union PAC_INFO(case 1)
                        logon_info: struct PAC_LOGON_INFO_CTR
                            info         : *
                                info: struct PAC_LOGON_INFO
                                    info3: struct netr_SamInfo3
                                        base: struct netr_SamBaseInfo
                                            logon_time           : NTTIME(0)
                                            logoff_time          : mié dic 31
                                                                   19:00:00 1969 EST
                                            kickoff_time         : mié dic 31
                                                                   19:00:00 1969 EST
                                            last_password_change : lun mar  4
                                                                   06:14:19 2019 EST
                                            allow_password_change : NTTIME(0)
                                            force_password_change : mié dic 31
                                                                   19:00:00 1969 EST
                                        account_name: struct lsa_String
                                            length               : 0x000a (10)
                                            size                 : 0x000a (10)
                                            string               : *
                                                string           : 'admin'
```

```
full_name: struct lsa_String
        length                : 0x001a (26)
        size                  : 0x001a (26)
        string                : *
            string            : 'Administrator'
logon_script: struct lsa_String
    length                    : 0x0000 (0)
    size                      : 0x0000 (0)
    string                    : *
        string                : "
profile_path: struct lsa_String
    length                    : 0x0000 (0)
    size                      : 0x0000 (0)
    string                    : *
        string                : "
home_directory: struct lsa_String
    length                    : 0x0000 (0)
    size                      : 0x0000 (0)
    string                    : *
        string                : "
home_drive: struct lsa_String
    length                    : 0x0000 (0)
    size                      : 0x0000 (0)
    string                    : *
        string                : "
logon_count                   : 0x0000 (0)
bad_password_count            : 0x0000 (0)
rid                           : 0x000001f4 (500)
primary_gid                   : 0x00000200 (512)
groups: struct samr_RidWithAttributeArray
    count                     : 0x00000000 (0)
    rids                      : *
        rids: ARRAY(0)
```

```
user_flags              : 0x00000000 (0)
           0: NETLOGON_GUEST
           0: NETLOGON_NOENCRYPTION
           0: NETLOGON_CACHED_ACCOUNT
           0: NETLOGON_USED_LM_PASSWORD
           0: NETLOGON_EXTRA_SIDS
           0: NETLOGON_SUBAUTH_SESSION_KEY
           0: NETLOGON_SERVER_TRUST_ACCOUNT
           0: NETLOGON_NTLMV2_ENABLED
           0: NETLOGON_RESOURCE_GROUPS
           0: NETLOGON_PROFILE_PATH_RETURNED
           0: NETLOGON_GRACE_LOGON
   key: struct netr_UserSessionKey
       key                     : 0000
```

.

.

.

# Replication-Based FreeIPA and Active Directory Integration

Another, but not the preferred, method to integrate FreeIPA and Active Directory is to replicate the information between both domains. In Chapter 24 we implemented replication among different FreeIPA servers. The process to share data between FreeIPA and Active Directory through replication is quite similar in principle.

To configure Active Directory and FreeIPA synchronization we first need to create an Active Directory user that will be used by FreeIPA when connecting to the domain, and this user should have the right permissions. As we are working in a lab environment, we'll use the Active Directory admin user to synchronize the information, but in a real production environment we should use a different user.

Download the FreeIPA CA certificate into the Windows server by navigating to the URL https://uniform.apress.local/ipa/config/ca.crt (Figure 26-7).

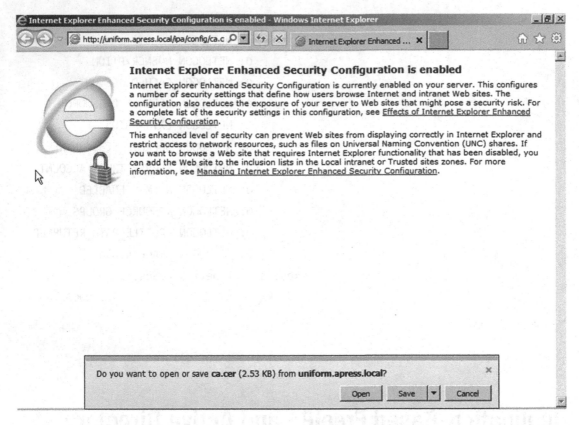

**Figure 26-7.** *Downloading the FreeIPA certificate*

Once downloaded, open its location in Windows Explorer, right-click the certificate, and select Install certificate. The Certificate Import Wizard will start (Figure 26-8).

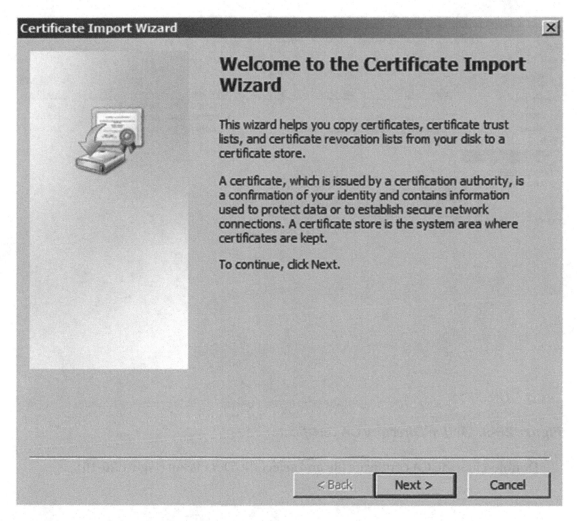

*Figure 26-8.* *Certificate Import Wizard*

Accept the default options and import the certificate. Next, we need to do the same thing on the FreeIPA server with the certificate from the Active Directory DC. To do so, we have to export the Active Directory CA certificate first. We might need to install Active Directory Certificate Services on the DC. After that, there should be a `C:\Windows\System32\certsrv\CertEnroll` folder where the CA certificate is located (Figure 26-9).

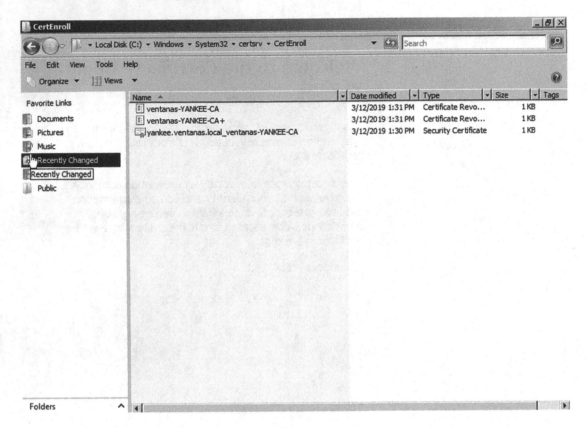

***Figure 26-9.*** *Active Directory CA certificate*

Double-click the CA certificate file and select the Details tab (Figure 26-10).

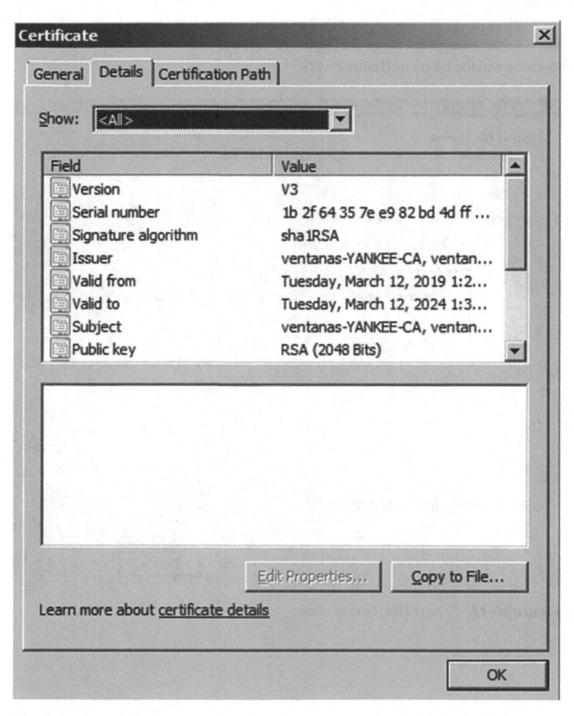

*Figure 26-10.* *Certificate details*

Click Copy to File to export the certificate. In the wizard we choose to export the file as a Base-64 encoded certificate (Figure 26-11) and specify the path where it will be exported and the file name (Figure 26-12).

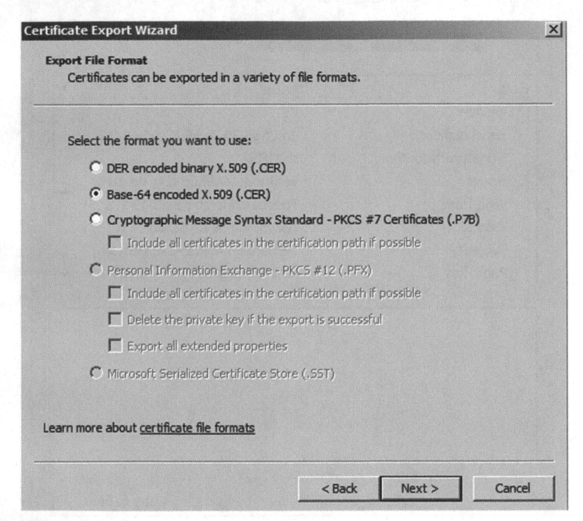

*Figure 26-11.  Export File Format page*

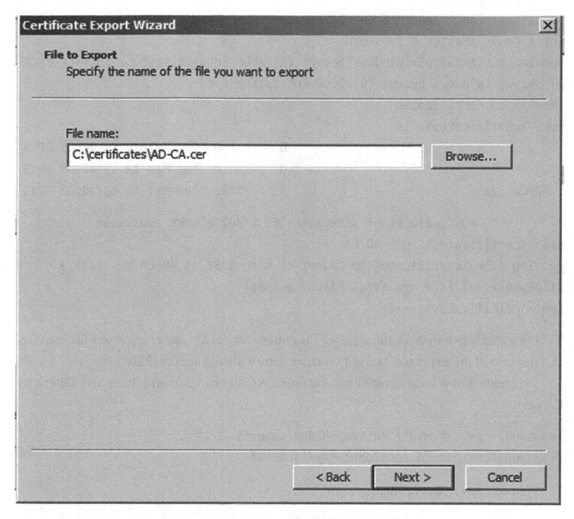

*Figure 26-12.*  *File to Export page*

We need to copy the exported certificate to the FreeIPA server using some of the Samba clients we've seen in the book so far.

```
[root@uniform ~]# smbclient //192.168.56.50/C$ -U Administrator
-bash: smbclient: command not found
[root@uniform ~]# yum --disablerepo=* --enablerepo=centos-media install -y
samba-client
[root@uniform ~]# smbclient //192.168.56.50/C$ -U Administrator
params.c:OpenConfFile() - Unable to open configuration file "/etc/samba/
smb.conf":
    No such file or directory
```

```
smbclient: Can't load /etc/samba/smb.conf - run testparm to debug it
Enter Administrator's password:
Domain=[VENTANAS] OS=[Windows Server (R) 2008 Enterprise 6002 Service Pack
2] Server=[Windows Server (R) 2008 Enterprise 6.0]
smb: \> cd certificates
smb: \certificates\> ls
  .                                   D        0   Tue Mar 12 13:42:08 2019
  ..                                  D        0   Tue Mar 12 13:42:08 2019
  AD-CA.cer                           A     1282   Tue Mar 12 13:42:08 2019

              40957 blocks of size 1048576. 23802 blocks available
smb: \certificates\> get AD-CA.cer
getting file \certificates\AD-CA.cer of size 1282 as AD-CA.cer (417,3
KiloBytes/sec) (average 417,3 KiloBytes/sec)
smb: \certificates\> exit
```

We initially get an error because we don't have an /etc/samba/smb.conf file, but we can download the exported Active Directory certificate file successfully.

We create a new location for both the FreeIPA CA certificate and the Active Directory CA certificate.

```
[root@uniform ~]# mkdir /etc/openldap/cacerts
[root@uniform ~]# cd /etc/openldap/cacerts/
```

We can copy both certificates there.

```
[root@uniform cacerts]# cp /root/AD-CA.cer .
[root@uniform cacerts]# wget http://uniform.apress.local/ipa/config/ca.crt
--2019-03-04 11:52:14--  http://uniform.apress.local/ipa/config/ca.crt
Resolving uniform.apress.local (uniform.apress.local)... 192.168.56.63
Connecting to uniform.apress.local (uniform.apress.
local)|192.168.56.63|:80... connected.
HTTP request sent, awaiting response... 200 OK
Length: 2592 (2,5K) [application/x-x509-ca-cert]
Saving to: 'ca.crt'

100%[====================================>] 2.592      --.-K/s    in 0s
```

```
2019-03-04 11:52:14 (335 MB/s) - 'ca.crt' saved [2592/2592]
[root@uniform cacerts]# ls
AD-CA.cer  ca.crt
```

For the LDAP client software to work, we need to rehash the certificates' path, as we saw when we studied OpenLDAP.

```
[root@uniform cacerts]# cacertdir_rehash /etc/openldap/cacerts/
[root@uniform cacerts]# ls
372b7ed9.0  AD-CA.cer  ca.crt  dbe7d6a1.0
```

Finally, we edit the file /etc/openldap/ldap.conf to include the following two lines:

```
TLS_CACERTDIR    /etc/openldap/cacerts
TLS_REQCERT      allow
```

If there is already a parameter that might cause conflict, such as TLS_CACERT or another TLS_CACERTDIR, we'll comment out those entries. In the end, the content of the file should be something like this:

```
[root@uniform ~]# cat /etc/openldap/ldap.conf
# File modified by ipa-client-install

# We do not want to break your existing configuration, hence:
#   URI, BASE, and TLS_CACERT have been added if they were not set.
#   In case any of them were set, a comment with trailing note
#   "# modified by IPA" has been inserted.
# To use IPA server with openLDAP tools, please comment out your
# existing configuration for these options and uncomment the
# corresponding lines generated by IPA.

#
# LDAP Defaults
#

# See ldap.conf(5) for details
# This file should be world readable but not world writable.

#BASE     dc=example,dc=com
#URI      ldap://ldap.example.com ldap://ldap-master.example.com:666
```

```
#SIZELIMIT      12
#TIMELIMIT      15
#DEREF          never

#TLS_CACERTDIR  /etc/openldap/certs
TLS_CACERTDIR   /etc/openldap/cacerts
TLS_REQCERT     allow

# Turning this off breaks GSSAPI used with krb5 when rdns = false
SASL_NOCANON        on
URI ldaps://uniform.apress.local
BASE dc=apress,dc=local
#TLS_CACERT /etc/ipa/ca.crt
```

Before we perform the data replication, we have to make sure that both servers have the same date and time and check that both can resolve DNS names from the FreeIPA as well as from the Active Directory domain. To do that we make the Active Directory DC a forwarder of the FreeIPA server.

```
[root@uniform ~]# ipa dnsconfig-mod --forwarder=192.168.56.50
  Global forwarders: 192.168.56.50
```

We do the same thing in the Active Directory DC by accessing the DNS console as we saw previously in this chapter when configuring the cross-realm trust relationship (Figure 26-2).

We can also perform a query against the Active Directory DC before replicating the data. To check that everything is working properly, we'll begin with a normal insecure LDAP connection.

```
[root@uniform ~]# ldapsearch -x -D "CN=Administrator,CN=Users,DC=ventanas,
DC=local" -b dc=ventanas,dc=local "(cn=Administrator)" -H ldaps://yankee.
ventanas.local -w P@ssw0rd
ldap_sasl_bind(SIMPLE): Can't contact LDAP server (-1)
[root@uniform ~]# ldapsearch -x -D "CN=Administrator,CN=Users,DC=ventanas
,DC=local" -b dc=ventanas,dc=local "(cn=Administrator)" -H ldap://yankee.
ventanas.local -w P@ssw0rd
.
.
.
```

```
# Administrator, Users, ventanas.local
dn: CN=Administrator,CN=Users,DC=ventanas,DC=local
objectClass: top
objectClass: person
objectClass: organizationalPerson
objectClass: user
cn: Administrator
description: Built-in account for administering the computer/domain
distinguishedName: CN=Administrator,CN=Users,DC=ventanas,DC=local
instanceType: 4
```

Next, we check that the secure connection also works.

```
[root@uniform ~]# ldapsearch -x -D "CN=Administrator,CN=Users,DC=ventanas,
DC=local" -b dc=ventanas,dc=local "(cn=Administrator)" -H ldaps://yankee.
ventanas.local -w P@ssw0rd
.
.
.
# Administrator, Users, ventanas.local
dn: CN=Administrator,CN=Users,DC=ventanas,DC=local
objectClass: top
objectClass: person
objectClass: organizationalPerson
objectClass: user
cn: Administrator
description: Built-in account for administering the computer/domain
distinguishedName: CN=Administrator,CN=Users,DC=ventanas,DC=local
instanceType: 4
```

We are ready to launch the replication, but first we need to destroy the Kerberos tickets that we might have associated.

```
[root@uniform cacerts]# kdestroy
[root@uniform cacerts]# klist
klist: No credentials cache found (ticket cache KEYRING:persistent:0:0)
```

We create the replica now with the **ipa-replica-manage** command. We specify that we are connecting to a Windows server (`--winsync`), as well as the user to connect to (`--binddn`) and their password (`--bindpw`). We also need to pass the location of the Active Directory CA certificate (`--cacert`) and the FQDN of the server we're connecting to (yankee.ventanas.local). When using the passsync Windows plug-in to synchronize passwords it is also necessary to specify the value of that password (`--passsync`). We are not using it, but we have to include the parameter as well.

```
[root@uniform ~]# ipa-replica-manage connect --winsync --binddn CN=Adminis
trator,CN=Users,DC=ventanas,DC=local --bindpw=P@ssw0rd --passsync=P@ssw0rd
--cacert=/etc/openldap/cacerts/AD-CA.cer yankee.ventanas.local -v
Directory Manager password:

Added CA certificate /etc/openldap/cacerts/AD-CA.cer to certificate
database for uniform.apress.local
ipa: INFO: AD Suffix is: DC=ventanas,DC=local
The user for the Windows PassSync service is uid=passsync,cn=sysaccounts,
cn=etc,dc=apress,dc=local
ipa: INFO: Added new sync agreement, waiting for it to become ready . . .
ipa: INFO: Replication Update in progress: FALSE: status: 0 Replica
acquired successfully: Incremental update started: start: 0: end: 0
ipa: INFO: Agreement is ready, starting replication . . .
Starting replication, please wait until this has completed.

Update succeeded

Connected 'uniform.apress.local' to 'yankee.ventanas.local'
```

The replica creation finished correctly, so at any point we can list the existing replicas.

```
[root@uniform ~]# ipa-replica-manage list
Directory Manager password:

yankee.ventanas.local: winsync
uniform.apress.local: master
```

Now, if we create a new Active Directory user, for example, John Windows, we'll see that user from the FreeIPA server as well.

```
[root@uniform ~]# ipa user-find
  .

  .

  .

  User login: jwindows
  First name: John
  Last name: Windows
  Home directory: /home/jwindows
  Login shell: /bin/sh
  UID: 643400005
  GID: 643400005
  Account disabled: False
  Password: False
  Kerberos keys available: False
```

# Summary

In this chapter we have seen how to successfully integrate FreeIPA and Active Directory. As the preferred method of integration, we established a trust relationship between both domains. We also looked at some alternative ways to integrate, however, such as replicating the information. We also learned a bit more about POSIX and non-POSIX groups and about ID ranges and how to create them manually when necessary. Finally, we studied some of the peculiarities of the Microsoft implementation of the Kerberos protocol, particularly the use of MS PAC.

# CHAPTER 27

# Network File System

NFS is a distributed file system originally developed by Sun. In this chapter, we'll cover the following concepts:

- Understanding major NFSv4 features.

- Configuring and managing an NFSv4 server and clients.

- Understanding and using the NFSv4 pseudo file system.

- Understanding and using NFSv4 ACLs.

- Using Kerberos for for NFSv4 authentication.

We will also learn about the following terms and utilities: **exportfs**, /etc/exports, /etc/idmapd.conf, **nfs4_editfacl**, **nfs4_getfacl**, **nfs4_setfacl**, **mount**, and /etc/fstab.

## NFS Main Characteristics

Sun initially released the NFS protocol in the late 1980s. As with many other protocols, it has undergone numerous updates.

It allows us to keep data at a central host to which the clients connect. The clients will connect to the central host by mounting the directories as if they were local. This host is very often used to store the home directories of the users at a central location from which they can be mounted either by modifying the /etc/fstab file or with automount.

In versions of the protocol older than NFSv4, when a client wants to mount a directory exported through NFS, it starts by contacting the **mountd** service in the server. This is done with an RPC call. Once the client has successfully mounted the directory, whenever it needs to access a file it will make a new RPC call. All this changed in version 4, which integrates support for those services. It is thus no longer necessary to have independent services for RPC and **mountd**.

Besides this, NFSv4 includes many improvements over its predecessors. It is a stateful protocol with better performance and more focus on security.

703

© Antonio Vazquez 2019
A. Vazquez, *Practical LPIC-3 300*, https://doi.org/10.1007/978-1-4842-4473-9_27

# Installing and Configuring NFS in CentOS 7

To install the NFS server, as well as the client, we need to install the nfs-utils package.

```
[root@tango ~]# yum install -y nfs-utils
```

After installing the package, we'll have a new file, /etc/exports. This file is empty by default and is used to specify the directories that will be exported through NFS. We'll create a new folder in our NFS server and add a new file to it.

```
[root@tango ~]# mkdir /NFS
[root@tango ~]# echo 123 > /NFS/file_one.txt
```

We edit the /etc/exports file accordingly.

```
[root@tango ~]# cat /etc/exports
/NFS        *(ro)
```

We say that we want to export the /NFS directory to everybody (*), with read-only permissions (ro).

We enable and start the **nfs-server** service:

```
[root@tango ~]# systemctl enable nfs-server
ln -s '/usr/lib/systemd/system/nfs-server.service' '/etc/systemd/system/
nfs.target.wants/nfs-server.service'
[root@tango ~]# systemctl start nfs-server
```

To effectively export the directories declared in the /etc/exports file, we need to execute the **exportfs** command. We export (-a) the directories and we want the command to be verbose (-v).

```
[root@tango ~]# exportfs -av
exporting *:/NFS
```

Besides, we need to open the corresponding port in the firewall, so that the client computers can connect to the NFS server.

```
[root@tango ~]# firewall-cmd --add-service=nfs
success
[root@tango ~]# firewall-cmd --permanent --add-service=nfs
success
```

On the client we'll create a local folder in which we will mount the NFS directory.

```
[root@romeo ~]# mkdir /mnt/nfs_client
```

Now we can manually mount the directory exported by the NFS server.

```
[root@romeo ~]# mount -t nfs4 tango.linuxaholics.local:/NFS /mnt/nfs_
client/
[root@romeo ~]# ls /mnt/nfs_client/
file_one.txt
```

With NFSv4 the mount worked as expected. Nevertheless, if we try to execute NFS client utilities like **showmount**, we'll get the following error.

```
[root@romeo ~]# showmount -e tango.linuxaholics.local
clnt_create: RPC: Port mapper failure - Unable to receive: errno 113 (No
route to host)
```

The command **showmount** can be used to show the directories exported by a certain NFS server. This command works like previous versions of NFS, using RPC calls. For this reason, if we want the client to be able to use this command, we need to permit incoming RPC calls in the firewall of the NFS server.

```
[root@tango ~]# firewall-cmd --add-service=rpc-bind
success
[root@tango ~]# firewall-cmd --permanent --add-service=rpc-bind
success
[root@romeo ~]# showmount -e tango.linuxaholics.local
rpc mount export: RPC: Unable to receive; errno = No route to host
```

We keep getting an error, because in addition to RPC, we also must allow incoming connections to the **mountd** service.

```
[root@tango ~]# firewall-cmd --add-service=mountd
success
[root@tango ~]# firewall-cmd --permanent --add-service=mountd
success
[root@romeo ~]# showmount -e tango.linuxaholics.local
Export list for tango.linuxaholics.local:
/NFS *
```

On this occasion the command worked properly.

We have seen before that we have read access to the files in the NFS directory.

```
[root@romeo ~]# cat /mnt/nfs_client/file_one.txt
123
```

However, if we try to write to it, we'll get an error.

```
[root@romeo ~]# echo 456 > /mnt/nfs_client/file_two.txt
-bash: /mnt/nfs_client/file_two.txt: Read-only file system
```

When we edited the /etc/exports file, we specified the read-only (ro) option, so clients can't write to the file system. If at some point we're not sure about the options that apply to a directory in NFS we can run **exportfs** with the -v parameter in the NFS server.

```
[root@tango ~]# exportfs -v
/NFS                <world>(ro,wdelay,root_squash,no_subtree_
                    check,sec=sys,ro,secure,root_squash,no_all_squash)
```

The most relevant option here is ro, which means read-only. We can also mention root_squash, which means that requests from the user with ID 0 will be mapped to the anonymous user. We'll edit the /etc/exports file again to export it with write permissions.

```
[root@tango ~]# cat /etc/exports
/NFS      *(rw)
```

We re-export (-r) the directories again.

```
[root@tango ~]# exportfs -rv
exporting *:/NFS
```

We also check that the export options have changed.

```
[root@tango ~]# exportfs -v
/NFS    <world>(rw,wdelay,root_squash,no_subtree_
        check,sec=sys,rw,secure,root_squash,no_all_squash)
```

We'll remount the directory on the client again.

```
[root@romeo ~]# mount -t nfs4 -o remount,rw tango.linuxaholics.local:/NFS
/mnt/nfs_client/
```

Next, we try to write to a new file.

```
[root@romeo ~]# echo 456 > /mnt/nfs_client/file_two.txt
-bash: /mnt/nfs_client/file_two.txt: Permission denied
```

This time we get a different error: Permission denied. This happens because we have exported the directory with the read/write option, but we didn't make sure that the folder has been given write permissions at the file system level.

```
[root@tango ~]# ls -ld /NFS/
drwxr-xr-x. 2 root root 25 feb 25 10:41 /NFS/
```

We'll give write permissions at the file system level with **chmod**.

```
[root@tango ~]# chmod a+rwx /NFS/
[root@tango ~]# ls -ld /NFS/
drwxrwxrwx. 2 root root 25 feb 25 10:41 /NFS/
```

Now at last, we can write a new file:

```
[root@romeo ~]# echo 456 > /mnt/nfs_client/file_two.txt
[root@romeo ~]# cat /mnt/nfs_client/file_two.txt
456
```

We have seen how to manually mount an NFS share, but it is usually more convenient to mount it automatically when the system boots. To do that, we'll edit the /etc/fstab file on the client computer.

```
[root@romeo ~]# cat /etc/fstab
/dev/mapper/centos-root /                            xfs      defaults     1 1
UUID=10511712-5a45-41a5-b3de-35ae8da587eb /boot  xfs      defaults     1 2
/dev/mapper/centos-swap swap                         swap     defaults     0 0
192.168.1.60:/NFS       /mnt/nfs_client              nfs      _netdev      0 0
```

The syntax of the file is easy to understand and we have already seen it when mounting Samba shares. We specify first the server and the remote directory, then the location of the local directory where the NFS directory will be mounted, the type of file system (which is NFS in this case), and a series of mount options. The mount options could be set to defaults, but as we'll be mounting a file system accessible through the network it is better to use the _netdev option. This means that the system will not try to mount the file system until networking is enabled. The last two fields are used by the old **dump** utility and by **fsck** and can be safely omitted or set to 0 in our case.

To test that everything is working fine we'll restart the client and check that the NFS directory has been mounted properly.

# NFSv4 Pseudo File System

NFSv4 servers create a pseudo file system to provide the clients with seamless access to exported folders. Here is an example.

Let's suppose we have the following directory tree on our NFS server:

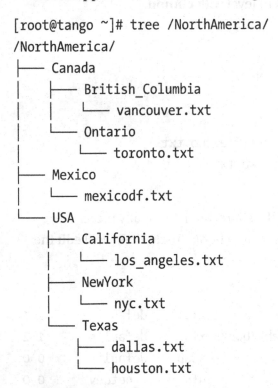

```
[root@tango ~]# tree /NorthAmerica/
/NorthAmerica/
├── Canada
│   ├── British_Columbia
│   │   └── vancouver.txt
│   └── Ontario
│       └── toronto.txt
├── Mexico
│   └── mexicodf.txt
└── USA
    ├── California
    │   └── los_angeles.txt
    ├── NewYork
    │   └── nyc.txt
    └── Texas
        ├── dallas.txt
        └── houston.txt
```

Assume that we want to share via NFS the content of the /NorthAmerica/Canada/Ontario/ and /NorthAmerica/USA/California/ folders. In that case we'd need to edit the /etc/exports file, so that it would look more or less like this:

```
[root@tango ~]# cat /etc/exports
/NFS          *(rw)
/NorthAmerica/Canada/Ontario/      *(rw)
/NorthAmerica/USA/California/       *(rw)
```

Of course, as we have included two new directories, we need to execute **exportfs** again to export the newly shared folders.

```
[root@tango ~]# exportfs -rv
exporting *:/NorthAmerica/USA/California
exporting *:/NorthAmerica/Canada/Ontario
exporting *:/NFS
```

With NFS versions older than version 4 we would need to create two different mount points: one for /NorthAmerica/Canada/Ontario/ and the other one for /NorthAmerica/ USA/California/. However, with NFSv4, we can mount the NFS directories by specifying only the root folder. The server will then create a pseudo file system that connects every exported directory. We'll see it in detail right now. First, we create a mount point.

```
[root@romeo ~]# mkdir /mnt/pseudo_fs
```

We then mount the NFS directories like this:

```
[root@romeo ~]# mount -t nfs4 192.168.1.60:/ /mnt/pseudo_fs/
```

If we browse the mount point, we'll see that a pseudo file system has been created to connect all the directories to which we have access.

```
[root@romeo ~]# tree /mnt/pseudo_fs/
/mnt/pseudo_fs/
├── NFS
│   ├── file_one.txt
│   └── file_two.txt
└── NorthAmerica
    ├── Canada
    │   └── Ontario
    │       └── toronto.txt
    └── USA
        └── California
            └── los_angeles.txt

6 directories, 4 files
```

As expected, we only have access to the folders we were allowed to explicitly on the server.

# NFSv4 ACLs

One of the features included with NFSv4 is the use of NFSv4 ACLs. To view and modify these ACLs we need to install the nfs4-acl-tools package on the client.

```
[root@romeo ~]# yum install -y nfs4-acl-tools
```

To better understand NFSv4 ACLs let's look at some examples:

```
[root@romeo ~]# nfs4_getfacl /mnt/nfs_client/
A::OWNER@:rwaDxtTcCy
A::GROUP@:rwaDxtcy
A::EVERYONE@:rwaDxtcy
```

The first character, A, means Allow; that is, the actions specified will be allowed, and whatever is not explicitly allowed will be denied. We could also use D in the ACL to deny certain permissions.

Next, we have the principal, and in our example there are three different principals: OWNER@, GROUP@, and EVERYONE@, that correspond with the owner of the file or folder, the group the owner belongs to, and the rest of the users.

Finally, we have the specific permissions allowed or denied by the ACL. These can be as follows:

- r: Read data (files) / list directory (directories).

- w: Write data (files) / create files (directories).

- a: Append data (files) / create subdirectories (directories).

- x: Execute (files) / change directory (directories).

- d: Delete file/directory.

- D: Remove files or subdirectories from a directory.

- t: Read attributes from the file/directory.

- T: Write attributes to the file/directory.

- n: Read named attributes from the file/directory.

- N: Write named attributes to the file/directory.

- c: Read the NFSv4 ACL from the file/directory.

- C: Write the NFSv4 ACL to the file/directory.

- o: Change ownership of the file/directory.

- y: Allows clients to use synchronous I/O with the server.

In addition to this long list of permissions, we can also use aliases, which are much easier to remember. These generic aliases are R (read), W (write), and X (execute). They will be translated to the appropriate set of permissions when used in an ACL. We'll see an example when we edit the NFSv4 ACLs.

Now that we've seen briefly what an NFSv4 ACL looks like, we'll edit it. First, we'll get the actual ACL.

```
[root@romeo ~]# nfs4_getfacl /mnt/nfs_client/file_one.txt
A::OWNER@:rwatTcCy
A::GROUP@:rtcy
A::EVERYONE@:rtcy
```

To edit the NFSv4 ACL we can use the **nfs4_setfacl** command. We specify that we want to add (-a) a new ACL entry that will be specified in the command line. The syntax of the command can be tricky so we'll use permissions alias and the ID associated with the principal. The ID associated with the principal can be obtained with the **getent passwd** command.

```
[root@romeo ~]# getent passwd antonio
antonio:*:1494400001:1494400001:Antonio Vazquez:/home/antonio:/bin/sh
```

We can launch the command now.

```
[root@romeo ~]# nfs4_setfacl -a A::1494400001:RW /mnt/nfs_client/file_one.txt
Failed setxattr operation: Operation not permitted
```

We get an error: Operation not permitted. This happens for the way the NFS protocol is working. When reading the default ACL, we have seen that the owner is the only one who can edit the ACL (C permission). We'll list the owners of the files in the NFS directory.

```
[root@romeo ~]# ls -l /mnt/nfs_client/
total 12
-rw-r--r--. 1 root       root       4 feb 25  2019 file_one.txt
-rw-rw-r--. 1 nfsnobody  nfsnobody  4 feb 25  2019 file_two.txt
```

The owner of file_one.txt happens to be root, but as the NFS directory was mounted with the root_squash option, everything that the user root in the client does in the NFS directory is mapped to the nfsnobody user. This is the reason we get an error.

---

**Note**   If we want to have more control over how users are mapped in NFSv4 we should take a look at the /etc/idmapd.conf file and its many options. Most of the time, however, it is unnecessary to make any modifications. This controls many aspects of how the users are mapped.

---

The second file, file_two.txt, was created when configuring write permissions. The user that was created was the root user from the client computer, but it was mapped to the nfsnobody user. In theory we should be able to edit the NFSv4 ACL of this second file without problems.

```
[root@romeo ~]# nfs4_setfacl -a A::1494400001:RW /mnt/nfs_client/file_two.txt
[root@romeo ~]# nfs4_getfacl /mnt/nfs_client/file_two.txt
A::OWNER@:rwatTcCy
A::1494400001:rwatcy
A::GROUP@:rtcy
A::EVERYONE@:rtcy
```

If we want to edit the ACL from the first file, we'll have to change the owner in the NFS server.

```
[root@tango ~]# ls -l /NFS/
total 12
-rw-r--r--. 1 root      root      4 feb 25 13:04 file_one.txt
-rw-rw-r--+ 1 nfsnobody nfsnobody 4 feb 25 13:05 file_two.txt
[root@tango ~]# chown nfsnobody:nfsnobody /NFS/file_one.txt
[root@tango ~]# ls -l /NFS/
total 12
-rw-r--r--. 1 nfsnobody nfsnobody 4 feb 25 13:04 file_one.txt
-rw-rw-r--+ 1 nfsnobody nfsnobody 4 feb 25 13:05 file_two.txt
[root@tango ~]#
```

Now we can edit the ACL associated to file_one.txt.

```
[root@romeo ~]# nfs4_setfacl -a A::1494400001:RW /mnt/nfs_client/file_one.txt
[root@romeo ~]# nfs4_getfacl /mnt/nfs_client/file_one.txt
A::OWNER@:rwatTcCy
A::1494400001:rwatcy
A::GROUP@:rtcy
A::EVERYONE@:rtcy
```

To see how versatile ACLs can be, we'll add a new one to deny write access to the user jose. First, we'll get the associated ID with **getent passwd**.

```
[root@romeo ~]# getent passwd jose
jose:*:1494400003:1494400003:Jose Vazquez:/home/jose:/bin/sh
```

We add the new ACL denying write access to jose.

```
[root@romeo ~]# nfs4_setfacl -a D::1494400003:w /mnt/nfs_client/file_one.txt
```

If we connect to the client computer as antonio and try to write to file_one.txt, we should not have any problems.

```
-sh-4.2$ whoami
antonio
-sh-4.2$ echo "Added by Antonio" >> /mnt/nfs_client/file_one.txt
-sh-4.2$ cat /mnt/nfs_client/file_one.txt
123
Added by Antonio
```

However, if jose tries to write, he won't be allowed to do it.

```
-sh-4.2$ whoami
jose
-sh-4.2$ echo "Added by Jose" >> /mnt/nfs_client/file_one.txt
-sh: /mnt/nfs_client/file_one.txt: Permission denied
```

So far, we have been editing NFSv4 ACLs with the **nfs4_setfacl** command, but we could also use **nfs4_editfacl**. This utility works by showing us our associated text editor, usually vi, with the content of the NFSv4 ACL.

```
[root@romeo ~]# nfs4_editfacl /mnt/nfs_client/file_one.txt
```

# Kerberized NFS

We have already seen how easy it is to configure an NFS server. The drawback, however, is that NFS configured by default is not a very secure protocol. In the /etc/fstab file we grant or deny access based on the hostname or IP address of the client computers. In our case we used the following line:

/NFS       *(rw)

We exported the directory to everybody (*), but we could also be more specific, giving read or write access to only a few computers, as in this example:

/NFS       romeo.linuxaholics.local(rw) sierra.linuxaholics.local(r)

In any case, this type of security based only on the host address is not desirable, especially when it is the only security measure. For this reason, the use of kerberized NFS is recommended whenever possible. This implies that Kerberos will be responsible to grant or deny access to the NFS server.

The NFS we've been using so far is not part of the FreeIPA domain, but for this example we should use Kerberos authentication for all the computers involved (server and client). This is definitely easier if both are part of the same FreeIPA domain, so we'll use our FreeIPA server quebec.linuxaholics.local as our new NFS server. We begin by adding the corresponding service.

```
[root@quebec ~]# ipa service-add nfs/quebec.linuxaholics.local
-----------------------------------------------------------------
Added service "nfs/quebec.linuxaholics.local@LINUXAHOLICS.LOCAL"
-----------------------------------------------------------------
  Principal name: nfs/quebec.linuxaholics.local@LINUXAHOLICS.LOCAL
  Principal alias: nfs/quebec.linuxaholics.local@LINUXAHOLICS.LOCAL
  Managed by: quebec.linuxaholics.local
```

Next, we add the corresponding key(s) to the keytab file. Users authenticate against Kerberos by using the **kinit** command to get their credentials. These credentials can later be seen with **klist**. The host, on the other hand, can also authenticate against Kerberos, but obviously they cannot use **kinit** interactively and they need a different approach. The solution is the use of keytab files.

The default keytab file for every server in the FreeIPA domain is located at /etc/
krb5.keytab. We use **kadmin.local** to add the needed key(s) for the NFS service.

```
[root@quebec ~]# kadmin.local
Authenticating as principal admin/admin@LINUXAHOLICS.LOCAL with password.
kadmin.local:  ktadd nfs/quebec.linuxaholics.local
Entry for principal nfs/quebec.linuxaholics.local with kvno 1, encryption
type aes256-cts-hmac-sha1-96 added to keytab FILE:/etc/krb5.keytab.
Entry for principal nfs/quebec.linuxaholics.local with kvno 1, encryption
type aes128-cts-hmac-sha1-96 added to keytab FILE:/etc/krb5.keytab.
Entry for principal nfs/quebec.linuxaholics.local with kvno 1, encryption
type des3-cbc-sha1 added to keytab FILE:/etc/krb5.keytab.
Entry for principal nfs/quebec.linuxaholics.local with kvno 1, encryption
type arcfour-hmac added to keytab FILE:/etc/krb5.keytab.
Entry for principal nfs/quebec.linuxaholics.local with kvno 1, encryption
type camellia128-cts-cmac added to keytab FILE:/etc/krb5.keytab.
Entry for principal nfs/quebec.linuxaholics.local with kvno 1, encryption
type camellia256-cts-cmac added to keytab FILE:/etc/krb5.keytab.
kadmin.local:  q
[root@quebec ~]#
```

We can list the keys included in a keytab file with **klist -k**:

```
[root@quebec ~]# klist -k /etc/krb5.keytab
.
.
.
   1 nfs/quebec.linuxaholics.local@LINUXAHOLICS.LOCAL
   1 nfs/quebec.linuxaholics.local@LINUXAHOLICS.LOCAL
   1 nfs/quebec.linuxaholics.local@LINUXAHOLICS.LOCAL
   1 nfs/quebec.linuxaholics.local@LINUXAHOLICS.LOCAL
   1 nfs/quebec.linuxaholics.local@LINUXAHOLICS.LOCAL
   1 nfs/quebec.linuxaholics.local@LINUXAHOLICS.LOCAL
```

We next install the nfs-utils package.

```
[root@quebec ~]# yum install -y nfs-utils
```

Now we create the directory we'll export through NFS.

```
[root@quebec ~]# mkdir /SECURE_NFS
[root@quebec ~]# touch /SECURE_NFS/kerberized.txt
```

As we created the folder and the file directly in the server, they both will be owned by root. This could cause problems when using NFSv4 ACLs, as we've already seen, so we'll change the owner to the nfsnobody user.

```
[root@quebec ~]# chown -R nfsnobody:nfsnobody /SECURE_NFS/
[root@quebec ~]# ls -l /SECURE_NFS/
total 0
-rw-r--r--. 1 nfsnobody nfsnobody 0 feb 21 18:49 kerberized.txt
```

When we first set up our NFS server we didn't change the default SELinux context, but because we now want to focus on security, we'll use a specific context for NFS directories. We'll use **semanage** to make sure that the directory has the right context when the system is rebooted and consequently relabeled.

```
[root@quebec ~]# semanage fcontext -a -t nfs_t "/SECURE_NFS(./*)?"
```

The context will be changed the next time the system is relabeled. To change it now we can manually perform a relabel with **restorecon** or change the present context with **chcon**.

```
[root@quebec ~]# restorecon -Rv /SECURE_NFS/
restorecon reset /SECURE_NFS context unconfined_u:object_r:default_t:s0→un
confined_u:object_r:nfs_t:s0
```

We edit the /etc/exports file to include the folder we just created, and we include the option sec=krb5 to use Kerberos authentication.

```
[root@quebec ~]# cat /etc/exports
/SECURE_NFS      *(ro,sec=krb5)
```

The parameter sec indicates different levels of security that will be used. There are many possible values:

- none: In this case no special security measure is applied.

- sys: This is the default value. It uses local UIDs and GIDs to authenticate users.

- krb5: This level uses Kerberos to authenticate users instead of performing local authentication.

- krb5i: Similar to krb5, this also adds integrity check.

- krb5p: Similar to krb5i, this also includes encryption.

We start the **nfs-server** and **nfs-server-secure** services.

```
[root@quebec ~]# systemctl start nfs-server
[root@quebec ~]# systemctl start nfs-secure-server
```

We then export the directories with **exportfs**.

```
[root@quebec ~]# exportfs -av
exporting *:/SECURE_NFS
```

We add the NFS service in the firewall.

```
[root@quebec ~]# firewall-cmd --add-service=nfs
success
[root@quebec ~]# firewall-cmd --permanent --add-service=nfs
success
```

On the client computer, we'll create the mount point and start the NFS service.

```
[root@romeo ~]# mkdir /mnt/secure_nfs
[root@romeo ~]# systemctl start nfs
```

Next, update the local keytab file and mount the directory.

```
[root@romeo ~]# ipa-getkeytab -s quebec.linuxaholics.local -p nfs/quebec.
linuxaholics.local -k /etc/krb5.keytab
Keytab successfully retrieved and stored in: /etc/krb5.keytab
[root@romeo ~]# mount -t nfs4 -o sec=krb5 quebec.linuxaholics.local:/
SECURE_NFS /mnt/secure_nfs/
[root@romeo ~]# ls /mnt/secure_nfs/
kerberized.txt
```

If we want the directory to be mounted automatically whenever the system boots up, we'll need to add the corresponding line in /etc/fstab.

```
quebec.linuxaholics.local:/NFS  /mnt/nfs_client  nfs  _netdev,sec=krb5  0 0
```

It is basically the same line we added at the beginning of the chapter, but we specify the option sec=krb5 and a different server.

# Summary

In this chapter we learned about the NFS protocol, one of the first protocols widely used to share files in Unix-like environments. We performed a basic configuration of the NFS server and successfully connected from the client. We explored some of the new features in NFSv4, such as the pseudo file system and the associated ACLs. Finally, we learned how to dramatically improve NFS security by integrating it with Kerberos.

# Index

## A

© Antonio Vazquez 2019
A. Vazquez, *Practical LPIC-3 300*, https://doi.org/10.1007/978-1-4842-4473-9

## T, U

## X, Y, Z

Printed in the United States
By Bookmasters